WOUNDED FEELINGS

Litigating Emotions in Quebec, 1870–1950

PATRONS OF THE SOCIETY

Blake, Cassels & Graydon LLP
Chernos, Flaherty, Svonkin LLP
Hull & Hull LLP
The Law Foundation of Ontario
McCarthy Tétrault LLP
Osler, Hoskin & Harcourt LLP
Paliare Roland Rosenberg Rothstein LLP
Pape Chaudhury LLP
Torys LLP
WeirFoulds LLP

The Osgoode Society is supported by a grant from
The Law Foundation of Ontario.

The Society also thanks The Law Society of Ontario
for its continuing support.

WOUNDED FEELINGS

Litigating Emotions in
Quebec, 1870–1950

ERIC H. REITER

Published for The Osgoode Society for Canadian Legal History by
University of Toronto Press
Toronto Buffalo London

© Osgoode Society for Canadian Legal History 2019
utorontopress.com
osgoodesociety.ca

ISBN 978-1-4875-0655-1

Publication cataloguing information is available from
Library and Archives Canada.

University of Toronto Press acknowledges the financial assistance to its
publishing program of the Canada Council for the Arts and the Ontario Arts
Council, an agency of the Government of Ontario.

   Canada Council   Conseil des Arts
                        for the Arts   du Canada

Funded by the   Financé par le
Government   gouvernement
of Canada   du Canada

Contents

ILLUSTRATIONS vii

FOREWORD ix

ACKNOWLEDGMENTS xi

Introduction 3

1 Feelings and the Law in Nineteenth-Century Quebec 29

2 Shame, Mortification, Disgrace, Dishonour 53

3 Family Dishonour 99

4 Bodily Intrusion 144

5 Betrayal 173

6 Grief and Mourning 220

7 Indignation, Anger, Fear 259

8 Conclusion: From Wounded Feelings to Violated Rights 295

ABBREVIATIONS 307

CASE CITATIONS 309

NOTES 315

BIBLIOGRAPHY 431

INDEX 469

Illustrations

0.1 Mary Sophia Grange and James Benning 4
1.1 François Dareau, *Traité des injures* 33
1.2 Maximilien Bibaud 43
2.1 Scenic Railway, Dominion Park 57
2.2 Slade residence, Lake St. Joseph 73
3.1 Rebecca Chiniquy Morin 103
3.2 "Les trois pendus" at the Eden Musée 112
3.3 Letter, Augustus Waterous Agnew to May Gober 134
4.1 Physician's attestation of plaintiff's virginity 153
4.2 Colbert O. Grothé 165
5.1 Marriage contract between François-Xavier Hébert and Rose de Lima Demers 188
5.2 Jean Gilot, Léonie Steile, and Elzéar Collin 216
6.1 Prescription by Dr. Herménégilde Jeannotte 223
7.1 Fred Johnson's tickets to *A Stranger in New York* 262
7.2 Imperial Theatre 273
7.3 Winifred Parsons and Olive Lundell 287
8.1 Justice Michel Mathieu 296

Foreword

THE OSGOODE SOCIETY
FOR CANADIAN LEGAL HISTORY

Professor Eric Reiter's *Wounded Feelings* is based on court cases involving what he terms "moral injury litigation" – defamation, separation of bed and board, compulsory medical examinations, breach of promise of marriage, and personality rights – all areas of "emotion" that lead to legal action. It integrates the legal history – how Quebec law, lawyers, and judges dealt with legal claims relating to the emotions – with how and why individuals brought such cases to the courts. The courts responded differently to different types of emotional injury, in the process requiring litigants to frame their stories in ways that reflected prevailing norms. As those norms changed, so too did the legal understanding of moral injury. This book takes on the very difficult task of extracting emotions from legal texts, and the detailed legal analysis is enriched throughout by analyses of the social, economic, and political contexts underlying individual litigation. The Osgoode Society is delighted to publish another book about the civil law, and one that breaks new ground for us by examining the emotional and the personal in the law books and the courtroom.

The purpose of the Osgoode Society for Canadian Legal History is to encourage research and writing in the history of Canadian law. The Society, which was incorporated in 1979 and is registered as a charity, was founded at the initiative of the Honourable R. Roy McMurtry and officials of the Law Society of Upper Canada. The Society seeks to stimulate the study of legal history in Canada by supporting researchers, collecting oral histories, and publishing volumes that contribute to legal-historical scholarship in Canada. This year's books bring the total published since 1981 to 109, in all fields of legal history – the courts, the judiciary, and the legal profession, as well as on the history of crime and punishment, women and law, law and economy, the legal treatment of ethnic minorities, and famous cases and significant trials in all areas of the law.

Current directors of the Osgoode Society for Canadian Legal History are Heidi Bohaker, Bevin Brooksbank, Shantona Chaudhury, David Chernos, Paul Davis, Linda Silver Dranoff, Timothy Hill, Ian Hull, Trisha Jackson, Mahmud Jamal, Virginia MacLean, Waleed Malick, Rachel McMillan, Roy McMurtry, Malcolm Mercer, Dana Peebles, Paul Reinhardt, Paul Schabas, Robert Sharpe, Jon Silver, Alex Smith, Lorne Sossin, Mary Stokes, Michael Tulloch, and John Wilkinson.

To find out more about the Osgoode Society for Canadian Legal History go to www.osgoodesociety.ca.

Robert J. Sharpe
President

Jim Phillips
Editor-in-Chief

Acknowledgments

Writing a book about emotions in the past raises some in the present as well, and now is my time to take stock of the feelings that come at the end of this long project: relief that it's finished, apprehension as it goes out into the world, but especially gratitude to all those whose help, friendship, and support made this possible.

I would like to start by offering thanks to four teachers who inspired me at various points along my academic path. Joe Goering, my doctoral supervisor at the University of Toronto, taught me to respect texts with a medievalist's care, and always to get the Latin right. Nicholas Kasirer, then law professor at McGill University and now justice of the Supreme Court of Canada, instilled in me by his example a fascination for the links between the civil law's past and its present. The late Rod Macdonald, who supervised my master's work in law, pushed me always to think outside the box. And Louise Otis, for whom I clerked at the Quebec Court of Appeal, taught me about law as practice and, most importantly, the meaning of justice.

Many colleagues and friends, at Concordia and elsewhere, offered encouragement and assistance large and small, from chance comments in hallways or at conferences that led me in fruitful directions, to longer conversations. My thanks to Ben Berger, Rachel Berger, Blake Brown, Lori Chambers, Don Fyson, Jane Harrison, Steven High, David Howes, Nora Jaffary, Erica Lehrer, Andrée Lévesque, Barbara Lorenzkowski, Jeff McNairn, Thierry Nootens, Alexandra Popovici, Mary Anne Poutanen,

Giorgio Resta, Ron Rudin, Carolyn Strange, Charlie Trainor, and Brian Young. Over the years I presented parts of this project at different venues in Montreal, Quebec City, Trois-Rivières, Drummondville, Ottawa, Toronto, Calgary, and Angers, France, and I thank all those audiences for their stimulating questions and comments. At the Osgoode Society, Jim Phillips supported the project from its early days, and in its late stages I benefited enormously from the careful reading and perceptive comments of Philip Girard and two anonymous readers. At the University of Toronto Press, Len Husband, Wayne Herrington, and Ian MacKenzie all helped bring the project smoothly to completion. Last, but certainly not least, Peter Gossage and Lyndsay Campbell each read large parts of the book and offered careful comments that helped me sharpen points and enrich the analysis. Needless to say, but say it I will, any shortcomings that remain should be laid nowhere but at my door.

Three excellent research assistants made valuable contributions at the beginning of this project. I sent Julie Perrone, Eric Fillion, and Etienne Stockland off to investigate the rather vague working questions I started with, and they each creatively identified useful avenues of inquiry and ferreted out many obscure sources. Julie deserves special thanks, as it was her careful search through all Quebec case reports that provided the core of the database of some seven hundred cases on which this project is based.

Some of the ideas in this book got tested in the classroom, and I thank my students at Concordia for being patient and engaged fellow travellers in legal history and emotions history, especially the members of my History of Emotions seminar in 2017 and the many students over the years in my course Law and Society in Canadian History.

On a practical level, research like this is impossible without the help of archivists, librarians, and others, and I acknowledge the assistance of the staff at Bibliothèque et Archives nationales du Québec, both the Vieux-Montréal and the Quebec City archival centres (particularly Yvan Carette at the latter, who went out of his way to make my brief visit there a great success), Concordia University Libraries, the Nahum Gelber Law Library at McGill University, the Houghton Library at Harvard University, and the McCord Museum (especially Hélène Samson for help with photographs in the Notman Collection). Alan Stein and Julie Korman at Stein & Stein in Montreal kindly checked their law firm's archives for records of the *Lundell* case in chapter 7 (alas, nothing survives). Larry Kredl generously shared a scan of the

Dominion Park postcard in chapter 2, part of his wonderful collection of Montreal postcards.

Even though my archival research was just a Métro ride away rather than in more exotic locales, I gratefully acknowledge essential research funding from the Fonds de recherche du Québec – société et culture (programme établissement de nouveaux professeurs-chercheurs), the Social Sciences and Humanities Research Council of Canada, and Concordia University's Faculty Research Development Program.

Though I never knew them personally, various jazz greats provided the soundtrack to which I wrote this book, and the rhythms of Duke Ellington, Horace Silver, Grant Green, Mose Allison, and others surely must have shaped my prose.

My final thanks express happiness and love, in contrast to the darker emotions in the stories told in this book. My parents, Ralph and Martha, and my brother Evan supported my scholarly activities from the beginning of their circuitous paths, despite frequent bemusement at the strange interests of the lone historian in a family of scientists. I'm sorry my father is no longer here to read this, but I'm delighted that my mother and brother will be able to.

Finally, thanks to Shannon, Alice, and Anna, for being my personal emotional community. When I started this project, my daughters Alice and Anna were pre-teens and would have preferred that I write a book more like Harry Potter than about obscure Quebec litigation from more than a century ago. They are now both scholars in their own right and heading out into the world to do great things. Shannon McSheffrey read countless drafts with her medievalist's eye, brought my sometimes weird theories down to earth, and shared with me more than thirty years now of love, friendship, and conversation. All three provided the emotions of real life, and I dedicate this book to them.

WOUNDED FEELINGS

Litigating Emotions in Quebec, 1870–1950

Introduction

In September 1869, a cause célèbre fascinated Montreal legal observers and the general public alike. Mary Sophia Grange sued wealthy auctioneer James Benning for the exorbitant sum of $40,000 for breaking off their engagement.[1] The couple had been engaged for about three months and at first all seemed fine, despite the significant age gap (she was twenty-four, he was forty-seven) and Benning's previous marriage having ended in divorce.[2] They had even visited the studio of William Notman, Montreal's premier society photographer, to have their portraits taken. When Benning heard rumours that his fiancée was in love with someone else, however, he changed his mind. He quickly sent her a letter calling off the wedding but expressing his wish that they might remain friends, and then hopped on a ship for England that same evening. The case was one of Quebec's earliest breach of promise actions after Confederation and had all the makings of a news sensation (or a Gilbert and Sullivan operetta): a sympathetic and attractive orphan as plaintiff, a rich and roguish divorced man as defendant, a ship's captain as alleged paramour, love letters read out in open court, and high-powered legal counsel on each side.[3] The lawyers wrangled over the morality of treating a betrothal like any other contract, but what the case really hinged on was whether there had been any damage. And for that, the focus was on Grange's injured feelings: did they exist in fact, should the law recognize them, and what if anything were they worth?

4 Wounded Feelings

Figure 0.1 "Miss Grange" (Mary Sophia) and James Benning, photographed by William Notman in April or May 1868, soon after their engagement. Mary Sophia's sister Sarah, two years her senior, was also photographed by Notman, and also identified only

as "Miss Grange." The proximity in time of the two photographs reproduced here suggests that this is Mary Sophia. McCord Museum, I-31283.1 and I-31523.1 respectively. Reproduced with permission.

Analysing those issues required the different participants in the case to move back and forth between different registers of discourse: subjective and objective, social and legal, narrative and normative. We cannot say for sure what Sophia Grange really felt. Her claim was an assertion of her emotions, but when turned (by others) into the dry lawyerly language of the declaration instituting her case, it became that she "hath been grievously wounded in her feelings, and hath, moreover, been greatly injured in her good name and reputation." In her testimony, which was limited to written answers to agreed-upon questions, since at the time parties could not give oral evidence in support of their own case, she simply repeated this formula.[4]

The others involved in the case were certainly not privy to her inner feelings, but all were ready to assess those feelings nonetheless, drawing on their own experiences of or assumptions about what a young woman who had just been jilted would have or must have or should have felt. The defence, of course, played down the claim. "The period of her engagement," Désiré Girouard argued to the jury, "was so short that she had hardly time to enjoy the satisfaction of having formed it; and scarcely anybody can believe that so short an interval was sufficient to stamp upon her heart such profound affection for the Defendant." He added, confidently asserting common knowledge, "In social life the quarrels of lovers are natural and ordinary events; they leave behind them no trace of material injury." Witnesses disagreed. Grange's guardian testified that after the break-up the formerly vivacious fiancée "was sick and looked downtrodden, she had no ambition, no spirit," while a long-time acquaintance said, "She looked like death. I thought she was going into consumption." Even one of the defence witnesses admitted that though there had been no material injury, "physically and morally" he was sure she suffered. Grange's lawyer, Bernard Devlin, brought in his own version of common sense and played up to the men in the jury how natural for a woman were the emotions involved: "I cannot open plaintiff's breast and tell what her inmost feelings were. I was not by her side when she received the insulting message of the 5th of June [breaking off the engagement]; but I can imagine the state of her feelings, and so can you, gentlemen." The public in the courtroom – a more female than usual crowd – agreed with Devlin and briefly applauded his summation.[5] A few days later, however, one "Hermione," writing in a Trois-Rivières newspaper, claimed to understand Grange's feelings while questioning her motives: "When the heart joins itself to a man worth $100,000, it is easy to understand that a break-up would cause a deep and quite bitter sorrow."[6]

As for the decision-makers, the jury put a value of $3,500 on Grange's wounded feelings. On appeal, the Court of Queen's Bench upheld both the verdict and the injured feelings Grange claimed. To do so, they had to balance legal rules with their own sense of the applicable social norms. In assessing an act such as Benning's, Justice William Badgley wrote, "The usages and customs and feelings of society come in to give them a definition, and hence modern life does not consider an act such as this reputable, it does not admit it to be allowable, but stigmatizes it as a wrong to be redressed." And righting that wrong required not just compensating the material outlays she had made in preparation of the wedding, but also redressing her "wounded feelings" as a result of the "social slander thrown over her by her promised husband's declaration of refusal."[7]

Wounded Feelings is a legal history of emotions in Quebec, a study of cases in which people sued others over their emotional injuries. I use the fluid idea of moral injury to explore the often uneasy interactions between emotional subjectivity and the rational world of the law. Cases like *Grange v. Benning* highlight the messy but revealing ways in which life and law intersected. Plaintiffs who blamed their dishonour or grief or betrayal on the wrongful actions of another took their stories to lawyers who shaped them into narratives that were compelling but at the same time met the requirements of legal categories. On the other side, the defence tried to fashion its own account of why the alleged feelings were overblown or unreasonable or otherwise not actionable. Judges, in the end, had to apply legal frameworks that were ever evolving, shaped as they were by judges' own understandings of the social norms that informed the rules. This back and forth between the subjective and the objective, between assertions of self-evident obviousness and counter-arguments of self-interested unreasonableness, provides a window into the cultural and social assumptions behind the law and at the same time sheds light on social understandings of emotions. In other words, this book is about the human dimension of law and the sometimes awkward fit between human stories of injury and the legal categories and recourses available at a given time and place. Hard cases may make bad law, as the adage goes, but for the historian they reveal points of fissure and slippage between a highly formalized legal system and society, as litigants, lawyers, and judges pushed at the edges of categories to try to accommodate unusual situations that did not quite fit.

The idea of moral injury was itself in tension, and how its contradictions manifested themselves and evolved is an important theme of this book. By the late nineteenth century, the general principle in Quebec civil law, as in its French counterpart, was that any injury caused by fault should be compensated. This applied to wounded feelings just as it did to a broken body or a diminished pocketbook, though exceptions applied and not all judges necessarily agreed in all cases. To be sure, in the case of emotional injury the principle caused a great deal of controversy and doctrinal headaches. How could emotional injury be evaluated? What proof could establish it? Should injuries that seemed subjective, open-ended, and, to be frank, feminine ("mere feelings") be treated the same as more defined and assessable material or physical harm? Imperfect though reparation of moral injury was, and though monetary damages tended to look more like a form of satisfaction or vindication than a *restitutio in integrum* (making whole again) when the injuries were emotional or aesthetic, most agreed that leaving such injuries unaddressed was worse than sacrificing some doctrinal coherence.[8]

Difficult or not, cases of wounded feelings regularly came before the Quebec courts and had to be argued, analysed, and assessed. Jilted lovers, bereaved spouses and parents, relatives outraged over the defamation of ancestors, men and women insulted in various ways before onlookers: in short a steady stream of individuals with complaints of dishonour or humiliation or shame or indignity brought their varied narratives before the law, demanding satisfaction. In working through the issues raised by cases like this, legal rules and social values converged. The rules provided an intellectual and institutional framework of terminology, categories, and precedents that shaped and limited how plaintiffs could tell their stories of emotional injury in court. The social values, for their part, provided a shorthand of norms – some shared, some contested – that gave social meaning to the rules and allowed a sort of informal judicial notice to operate, like the common knowledge the lawyers brought to bear in the case of Sophia Grange and James Benning. But as we will see in several of the cases in this book, while the goal was to evoke shared values, that consensus had boundaries defined by gender, class, race, and the individual backgrounds of particular judges. Litigating wounded feelings involved a back-and-forth between the obvious and the contentious, with formal rationality, practical morality, and affective subjectivity all vying for influence. Law was certainly a central part of Canada's liberal project.[9] But moral injury shows clearly how law also preserved older ways of thinking and feeling that privileged relationships, emotions, and social codes of honour, propriety, and virtue.

I develop two related arguments in this book. The main chapters are a series of studies of individual emotions as they were litigated in a variety of contexts. Together they comprise a social legal history of how feelings and sentiments were expressed, narrated, and legalized, shaped both by informal social codes and by the formal legal rules, practices, and institutions of the times. Law included an affective dimension alongside its culture of rational argument and analysis, and the legal system's rules – about fault and damage, about evidence, about repairing injury – were inflected by common-sense ideas about morality, proper (and gendered) expression of feelings, and correct interpersonal behaviour.[10] The fluidity of moral injury and its dependence on subjective ideas like honour and propriety and dignity meant that to establish it, litigants had to argue community norms, and to assess it judges had to establish the scope and content of those norms.[11] Much depended on what Paul Gerwirtz has called "narrative within a culture of argument": crafting compelling narratives to translate feeling into words and to describe situations in ways that served the argumentative purpose of making it obvious that wounded feelings must have happened.[12] Litigants could get compensation – could have their emotion validated by a court – if their story triggered an empathetic response from a judge.[13] Judges assessed the stories of the men and women and children before them according to shared social codes of honour, virtue, and propriety. In many cases, moral injury was accepted because it was self-evident to judges who occupied a shared social or cultural field with the plaintiff that a given act would cause that plaintiff some kind of harm. In some other cases, the injury was rejected because it was not self-evident or reasonable within the social world that the judge felt applied to the case. Sometimes judges were explicit about the discretionary nature of adjudicating wounded feelings, musing about what was a "proper" (read, "seemly") award in the circumstances. Usually, however, the application of social norms of prevailing morality was left implicit, leaving it to the historian to tease out the class, gender, and racial assumptions behind what was proper and correct that led judges to their self-evident and common-sense conclusions.

Alongside this is a second argument that traces legal changes in how Quebec judges and jurists conceptualized personhood and subjectivity over the time period we are considering. The arguments and judgments in cases of moral injury contributed to the development of the idea of subjective rights of personality within Quebec private law. The articulation of those rights – to honour, bodily integrity, liberty, name, privacy, and others – was a local manifestation of doctrinal developments in France and Germany in the later nineteenth century, though their roots went deep into the civilian tradition.[14] The changing ways in which feelings were translated into legal terms and dealt with by the courts illustrate the gradual development of the idea that individuals had certain inherent rights whose violation constituted a fault. In the nineteenth century, intangibles like feelings were described in various ways: as *biens* (akin to property), as interests, occasionally as rights. As we will see, however, the legal discussion of moral injury tended to stop at the question of what happened to the plaintiff, and in approaching that question the analysis focused more on evaluating, within the factual situation presented in the case, the defendant's duty not to injure another. Only rarely did judges consider whether something of the plaintiff's had been violated, and even more rarely whether that something might be a right. Where words like *violation* or *atteinte* were used, they applied more usually to socio-legal ideas like the plaintiff's feelings or reputation than to a more fully legalized idea of a right. The development of individuals as rights holders and the reclassification of feelings from vaguely articulated interests to subjective personality rights was a strong affirmation of liberal values within the law, and it resulted in a different view of the person within private law, one that borrowed from the citizenship rights and fundamental liberties of public law.[15] This was a long process, and the social meanings of moral injury reflected the persistence of what R.W. Sandwell has termed "a-liberal" values that characterized the family in particular, and other aspects of the individual within social relationships as well.[16] The stories behind the cases we will consider show the continuing vitality of older ways of imagining legal relations, but the gradual emergence and increasing traction of rights-based arguments within moral injury litigation shows that the liberal project within the private law had influence well beyond the more obvious areas of contract and commercial transactions.

Viewing issues like dishonour or bodily intrusion or discrimination as violated rights rather than wounded feelings led to a different analysis. Rights pushed aside (without removing entirely) the subjectivity and socially situated analysis evident in earlier cases, in favour of a more fully legalized, abstract concept. The empathy (or lack thereof) behind the situational analysis in earlier cases gave way to objectified legal questions about rights. Damage was still important and still required judges to assess social issues. But by the end of our period, judges were shifting from an almost unique focus on the factual question of assessing the individual's feelings against the expectations of social norms, towards the legal questions of the existence, delineation, and violation of rights. Emotions were still litigated in court, and human stories of wounded feelings were still told in support of those actions, but the legal analysis took on new shapes.

Feelings, Emotions, and Sentiments in Legal History

The legal history of emotions is a genre that requires some explanation. The history of emotions is a field with fairly deep roots, but it has come into its own only relatively recently.[17] It brings to the fore the long neglected affective side of history and so offers a counter or complement to pervasive presumptions of rationality in human motivation. Though emotions have a physiological and psychological side, and the relationship between science and humanities in this area has been the subject of much debate, historians have been especially interested in how individual expressions of emotion are influenced, and their meaning shaped, by social norms or codes. The descriptive question – what did individuals feel in the past? – is only a small part of the history of emotions. More interesting are broader questions about the dynamic links between individual feelings and society: What led individuals to feel (and to express their feelings) as they did? Why did people interpret their own or others' feelings in certain ways at certain times? How were norms of feeling defined and negotiated and contested in the past?

In contrast to the increasingly established history of emotions, the *legal* history of emotions is not yet even a field, though important studies by Natalie Zemon Davis, William Reddy, Daniel Lord Smail, and others that historicize emotions in law or use legal sources to get at historical emotions have begun to stake out its outlines.[18] The legal history of emotions obviously parallels the history of emotions generally, but the particular context of the judicial process creates for the historian special difficulties and unexpected riches alike. The adversarial argumentation that runs through the process of litigation and its documentary record is the most obvious difference, but important as well are the privileging of rationality within that process (though complemented by a heavy reliance on common-sense understandings of feelings), and the ways the process produced heavily mediated expressions of feelings (the product in particular of directed questioning by lawyers and judges, but more generally of translating vernacular ideas into the language of law).

The various ways that emotions come up in law has given rise to a growing field of "law and emotions" that explores the emotions that law variously provokes and requires.[19] Though like most "law and" scholarship this has been mostly contemporary in its focus, legal historians have begun pushing questions of law and the emotions back into the past, opening up sites for the development of a legal history of emotions. These include studies of emotions like anger, fear, pity, and despair raised among participants and observers to the legal process,[20] scholarship on feelings formally required by law, such as remorse in sentencing offenders,[21] and work on the rhetorical role of sentiment as a means of supplementing or replacing law's dominant rationality.[22]

My focus in this book is different. I look at emotions as legal objects, rather than as by-products of the legal process. Cases in which wounded feelings were the subject of litigation required plaintiffs to narrate their emotions, lawyers to translate them into legal terms, and judges to evaluate those stories and assess what emotional injuries were worth. A few key issues and questions from the history of emotions that will shape the analysis that follows deserve some brief discussion here; their implications will be worked out in the case studies throughout this book.

An obvious point to stress at the outset is that emotions themselves have histories. Over time, old emotions (honour is a good example) changed meanings or disappeared altogether, while new ones (such as anxiety) entered the lexicon of feelings, a process that Ute Frevert has termed the "lost and found" of emotions history.[23] Recovering the lost meanings of past emotions requires sensitivity both to the nuances of what individuals expressed to describe their feelings and to the unexpressed dynamics of situations that provoked emotional responses. Histories of emotions were also inflected by gender, class, and culture, each of which shaped in different ways the norms that defined what was proper in a particular time or place. Honour, for example, was originally associated with male elites before it became democratized, but debate persisted (as we will see in chapter 2) about whether lower social orders could have honour, and especially about whether honour could apply to women or was reserved to men only.[24] At the same time, assumptions about emotionality (or lack thereof) gleaned from the present can obscure the complexity of the past. William Ian Miller puts it well when he identifies the bias of "the upper-class sense" (among both historical elites and many present-day scholars) about who could feel and articulate which emotions. "The poor and the medieval, by this account, do not feel as much as do the sociologist and historian who study them; and although the poor and medieval may experience lust, rage, anger, hate, and joy, they are unlikely to experience angst, ennui, pity, embarrassment, and those aesthetic emotions that are elicited by the reading of good books."[25] Quebec judges often shared this mindset, as several of our examples will show.

Scholars have developed analytical frameworks to help understand the relationships between individual feelings and the social contexts in which those feelings were formed, expressed, and understood by various audiences. These concepts are key aspects of the historicization of feelings, and they provide researchers with powerful analytical tools to move beyond a relatively static descriptive view of feelings as individual emotional responses and towards a dynamic, historicized view of the confrontation between individual feelings and the social norms within which they were expressed and understood. In other words, these concepts allow us to move beyond the simple cataloguing of traces of past emotions towards an understanding of how the affective dimension of life shaped various kinds of interactions, both social and, for our purposes, legal.

The normative force of emotions is central to William Reddy's work. Individuals' statements about their emotions were not simply descriptive of an inner emotional reality, nor were they performative of that reality in a way analogous to the mutual "I do" statements that create a marriage. Rather, these "emotives," as he calls them, effectively created the emotion by naming it. Before a statement like "I am angry," the individual felt something, but the act of labelling turned that undifferentiated feeling into a specific emotion. As Reddy says, emotives "do things to the world": they "are themselves instruments for directly changing, building, hiding, intensifying emotions, instruments that may be more or less successful."[26] Emotives were not just individual expressions of inner feelings, however. They operated within politicized worlds of feeling, which he calls "emotional regimes," sets of agreed-upon or imposed norms that managed emotional expression. Those regimes – the sense of control conveyed by that word is important – facilitated social navigation (the title of one of his books is *The Navigation of Feeling*), but at the cost of a degree of emotional liberty. People felt things, of course, but their palette of feeling was limited by the society in which they lived, which discouraged certain forms of emotional expression while fostering others. Dominant modes of feeling were never all-powerful, but while it was possible to have recourse to what Reddy calls "emotional refuges" alongside dominant ways of feeling, those were marginalized and critiqued.

Reddy's emotives and the emotional regimes and refuges within which they functioned have obvious utility for understanding the normative world of the courts, and he has put his ideas to work in studies of court cases in post-revolutionary France that hinged on how inner feelings were linked rhetorically to broader social norms governing emotions within that society.[27] As we will see in the Quebec cases, the courts welcomed certain types of stories about emotional injury more than others, forcing litigants into categories and ways of telling their stories that reflected prevailing norms.

Related to Reddy's emotional regimes, but broader and to my mind more dynamic for historians, is medievalist Barbara Rosenwein's idea of emotional communities. She defines them as "groups – usually but not always social groups – that have their own particular values, modes of feeling, and ways to express those feelings."[28] Those communities had different "emotional styles," norms of feeling and expression of emotion, though because multiple emotional communities coexisted in the same time and place, those norms overlapped, influenced one another, and rejected influences. The communities varied in their vocabularies of emotion and in their ways of expressing feelings through speech, writing, gesture, dress, art, didactic literature, and so forth. Further, emotional communities were fluid, and their styles reflected the particular social and institutional contexts within which they operated. Rosenwein notes that "people move (and moved) continually from one such community to another – from taverns to law courts, say – adjusting their emotional displays and their judgments of weal and woe (with greater and lesser degrees of success) to these different environments."[29] This suggests an interesting idea, that people's emotional literacy led to their relative fluency in multiple emotional vocabularies specific to the different emotional communities in which they moved, and that those communities themselves had different ideas of what was appropriate.

In contrast to Reddy's political emotional regimes, emotional communities are a more sociological idea: they describe the emotional influences on individuals and how particular ways of feeling prevailed among certain groups at certain times. They also do more than describe: they provide a way to conceptualize the fluidity of people's emotional identity as they moved physically and intellectually from community to community, shaping their language, expression, and gesture in accordance with those movements. Emotional communities are thus a useful complement to the top-down emphasis of Reddy's emotional regimes, and they balance prescription and description by applying to the formation and development of emotional communities polyvalent and diffuse models of agency. They also, by focusing on the fine grain of a society's emotional life, bring forward the interface between individual and group at which the performance of emotion and the reception of that performance took place.

The emphasis on emotional norms in the work of both Reddy and Rosenwein helps in understanding and discussing the encounters about feelings that took place in the cases we will consider throughout this book. In reading the expression and evaluation of feelings in moral injury litigation, it quickly becomes apparent that much was grasped at an intuitive level rather than being expressed explicitly. Social norms of emotion, codes of proper behaviour, and assumptions about feelings, their causes, and their effects all played key roles in how individuals expressed feelings and how others interpreted those feelings. Those contexts changed and shifted in complex ways, which is an important theme of this book. The act of judging feelings had, like Reddy's emotional regimes, a top-down normative influence on how feelings were expressed and explained within the legal process and on which feelings were seen as legitimate for different litigants and in different contexts. At the same time, the ways in which litigants narrated and performed their feelings, bringing certain stories into court in certain ways, and shaping those stories as the legal process unfolded, parallels the organic development of Rosenwein's emotional communities. The cases we will consider reveal the confrontation – sometimes harmonious, sometimes conflictual – between different vernacular emotional communities and those centred on the courts and the legal system. Social norms, which varied both diachronically and synchronically, dictated how emotions were expressed, but also how they were interpreted, by lawyers translating them into legal terms, by judges assessing their effects, and by subsequent litigants, lawyers, and judges reviewing the jurisprudence to determine how to proceed in new cases.

Monique Scheer adds a third important dimension to understanding past emotions by stressing their embodied nature.[30] People expressed emotions in their bodies as well as in their words, and so to find past emotions the historian must go beyond words to consider how situations and actions simultaneously provoked affective responses and reflected the repertoire of emotional practices available in a given time and place. Furthermore, viewing emotions as embodied in actions allows the historian to move beyond a reactive view of individuals passively responding to emotional triggers. Instead, the individual's emotions – here Scheer echoes Reddy's idea of emotives – are communicative attempts that use prevailing conventions either in straightforward or subversive ways.[31]

As we will see, in many cases emotions were inscribed not just in words but in actions: the dishonour provoked by a physical affront, for example, or the shame and humiliation brought on by physical mistreatment by police, or the fear caused by forcible confinement. The emotions in those cases emerged not from (or not only from) what participants said, but from what they did, how they interacted with others (and how they were seen to interact with others), and how situations developed in space and time. Scheer notes that the historian must be sensitive to "traces of observable action" in the past, an idea that provides an important bridge between the first-person narratives that are the most obvious sources for emotions history and the much more numerous third-person accounts.[32] In the legal actions we will examine, individuals rarely narrated their emotions directly at any length. They did, however, carefully delineate situations, relationships, and in some cases movement of people through space, all of which provide evidence of emotionally charged situations that judges had to interpret to assess the wounded feelings being claimed.

Finally, all of these ideas – Reddy's emotives and emotional regimes, Rosenwein's emotional communities, Scheer's embodied emotions – foreground emotions as a kind of performance, a working out of feelings in relation to prevailing social norms and expectations, and a positioning of the individual within relationships and situations. This pushes aside the interesting but ultimately historically unknowable question of whether an individual's emotional expression was sincere or genuine or authentic. While this was of course a question of overarching importance for judges adjudicating emotional injury, more important for the historian looking at the socially situated nature of individual emotional expression are questions about interest and influence in how emotions were narrated or expressed. As Rosenwein notes, praise of genuine emotion or condemnation of feigned or insincere feeling is valuable because it reveals what the operative norms were and how those norms influenced emotional style or practice.[33] To cite just one example, the argued distinction between "genuine" emotion and "manipulative" or "inauthentic" sentiment, which as Jennifer Travis shows preoccupied male writers in the United States in the later nineteenth century, both described the gendered norms of emotional expression and authorized for men a distinctly masculine "emotional style."[34] Within the legal realm, the courts valued authenticity in an evidentiary sense, but operated according to an adversarial process that led strategically and inevitably towards emotional exaggeration and conventionalization, as we will see. Whether or not the plaintiffs in the cases really felt what they said they had experienced is beside the point. As Natalie Zemon Davis notes about reading the sources for early-modern French pardon requests, it is important "to let the 'fictional' aspects of these documents be the center of analysis. By 'fictional' I do not mean their feigned elements, but rather, using the other and broader senses of the root word *fingere*, their forming, shaping, and molding elements: the crafting of a narrative."[35] What matters, in other words, is how litigants tried to persuade the court what they had felt, how judges applied their own perspective to assess those emotional claims, and how the legal process and its substantive rules shaped the stories that were told to determine which emotions mattered and which did not.

Finding Emotions in the Legal Sources

Feelings are ephemeral, and their traces in written sources present important interpretive problems for a history of emotions, problems that are magnified in a legal history of emotions because of the nature of legal records. Litigation about wounded feelings produced case files preserved in judicial archives that contained various types of textual documents, all required by the legal process and each one shaped by procedural rules and the strategic choices of participants. These problems are well known to anyone who works with official documents, but they take on a different dimension when dealing with feelings. Case files, and more particularly legal case files, are rich but problematic sources.[36] They promise access to subjectivity within the archives and often preserve the voices of individual participants though depositions, affidavits, and other documents. But that subjectivity was filtered through the emotional, social, and legal contexts of the time, and so interpreting legal archival sources requires reconstructing multiple emotional communities – overlapping, reinforcing, conflicting – within which feelings-based litigation took place. Much depends on the language of the sources and its intermingling of the formulaic and the personal.

To what extent can juridical sources reveal something of the emotional norms within which emotional claims were made? Once an individual decided to initiate a case, its development and presentation, if not its substantive content, were to a large extent taken over by others who determined which documents were needed, what their specific content must be, and what norms of professional practice or legal requirements applied. Various filters worked to shape the documents and determine which would be included in a case file. The law of evidence, for one, determined certain things to be relevant, others irrelevant, and prevented certain testimony from being heard at all (such as spouses against each other). More fluidly, the exigencies and strategies of legal practice as they developed and were understood by lawyers at different times shaped how they presented their clients' stories in written submissions and in testimony. More unpredictable and implicit, though no less present, were judges' presumptions, assumptions, and, in some cases, blinders that affected how they heard and interpreted evidence and other submissions put before them. The fate of objections to particular questions or to whole lines of inquiry, for example, highlighted the working of judicial discretion. At times judges allowed objections on the basis of relevance (as opposed to more technical reasons like hearsay), the effect of which was to cut off what would have been valuable lines of inquiry for historians (though of course the judges were not there to serve the needs of future history writers). At other times judges allowed objected-to questioning to proceed under reservation, to the chagrin of the objecting party, but to the historian's relief.[37]

We will encounter a variety of documents in the cases discussed in this book, at various degrees of remove from the feelings at issue in the cases. These sources both entice and frustrate in their expression of emotion, though all suggest the outlines of the emotional norms in play. The declaration, for example, along with the writ summoning the defendant, initiated the action and alleged the basic facts of the case and the plaintiff's claimed emotional injury. Most of the cases we will consider framed the plaintiff's injury in similar terms: the defendant's actions, the declaration would state, affected me, the plaintiff, "in my honour, my reputation, my feelings, my person, and my *biens*" (*dans mon honneur, ma réputation, mes sentiments, ma personne et mes biens*), or variations thereof (we will consider the complex word *biens* in the next chapter). This was of course a formula, written by a lawyer to translate the plaintiff's vernacular explanation of the problem (about which we can only speculate) into a range of legally protected interests. That this was often about ticking legal boxes rather than articulating a legalized picture of what the plaintiff had experienced is evident in cases in which the claim included types of interference (with one's person, for example) that were hardly related to the case and that were not even mentioned subsequently. A case from the 1930s made this point in a comic way. The plaintiff was one of fourteen pharmacists suing another for a disparaging newspaper ad; he claimed the defendant's ad had caused him, "in his honour, in his person, and in his property, incalculable damage."[38] In cross-examination, the defendant's lawyer pressed the plaintiff on the formula:

> Q: In your person, your honour supposedly resides within your person? A. If you say so. Q. You're the witness, I'm asking you. A. I don't have an answer to give you about that. Q. Why are you asking for damages to your person, and more than that, why are you making a distinction between your person and your honour? You say that in your declaration – it's you who says that? A. You'd be better off arguing about that with Mr. Lanctot [plaintiff's lawyer], he's the one who wrote that.

* * *

> Q: I want to have an answer from you. Why have you demanded damages to your person? A. I didn't demand anything of the kind; I demanded $999 in exemplary damages, which includes all those things.[39]

The case was primarily commercial, so employing the formula as it was more usually used in personal defamation actions was perhaps ill-advised, but the distinction between the lawyer's articulation of the issues and the plaintiff's own understanding (basically "I was injured, and I want some money") is telling.

Statements like these were not just formulas, however, and in their variation they reveal something of the individual feelings behind the actions. In a 1912 alienation of affection case, for example, a love letter arrived in the plaintiff's household mail, which led him to accuse the defendant of having an illicit affair with his wife. His declaration departed from the usual wording to underscore the seriousness of his emotional wounds. The plaintiff, it alleged, "suffered and suffers and will forever suffer in the most intimate part of his being, that he was injured in his honour, his sensibility, his person, his heart, his family, and in his future."[40] Actions in alienation of affection like this one lent themselves to hyperbole, as we will see in chapter 5, but this wording suggests a characterization of the emotions involved that combined the plaintiff's vernacular recitation of heartache and violated intimacy and a creative lawyer's translation of that into a form that would work in court (and indeed the plaintiff was successful, but was awarded only a tenth of what he had asked for). As Brian Simpson put it, "Litigation entails a process of fitting – sometimes pushing and shoving – the messy and untidy business of life into artificial legal categories."[41] Emotions complicated that pushing and shoving still further.

Labels matter in emotions history: William Ian Miller calls emotion words "evaluative magnets" that shape responses to emotion by linking inner feelings to categories comprehensible to oneself and to others.[42] In the legal context, emotion words had the double task of expressing a factual situation (how the plaintiff felt) and linking that to a legal category a court might recognize. Like Reddy's emotives, the emotional labels in moral injury cases were rhetorical positions that both shaped the feelings being alleged and brought them into line with broader social norms about those feelings. For a plaintiff to state in a declaration "I was mortified" may or may not have reflected the plaintiff's actual feelings, but it certainly floated a claim about how he or she felt.

Documents like the declaration stating the case are obviously highly mediated. But even documents like witness depositions, a major source throughout this book, which transcribed individuals' testimony taken either outside the court or during the trial and so recorded the individual's words more directly than other documents in the judicial archive, still raise important issues for the legal history of emotions. At first blush such documents would appear to preserve the voices of people who otherwise tend to be silenced by history, such as the Black Montrealers who appear in chapter 7, or the butchers and domestic workers in chapter 5. The voices preserved, however, are careful constructions of the legal process: deponents spoke not as themselves, but as witnesses, playing a role in which they were asked certain questions (and were able to answer only what was asked), coached in what to say and what to avoid, and in short prepped for their part in the case.[43] Certainly witnesses were often asked formulaic questions couched in terms designed to elicit particular responses. But formula and feeling are not necessarily mutually exclusive. In the end, the words were the witnesses', and those words frequently suggested individual feelings (the plaintiff's words in particular) or reactions to and readings of others' feelings (the words of the other witnesses').[44] By narrating their feelings, plaintiffs were creating those feelings, not in an emotional sense – we assume they had felt something, though of course simulation or exaggeration were likely in some cases – but in a legal sense. The damage they were alleging, their wounded feelings, came out in the telling, which had to take certain forms, check off certain (legal) boxes, and be compelling to the decision-maker.

So to what extent do the legal archives with which we will be working contain the voices of real people? Witness depositions, at least, certainly record the words of real people, or at least a close approximation of their words as taken down by a stenographer and read back to the deponent for approval or correction. Other documents too reflect what the parties wanted them to contain, though more carefully filtered through the experience and strategizing of the lawyer. Still, as Natalie Zemon Davis points out about early-modern pardon requests, and her point is relevant to our subject as well, the production of legal documents tended to militate towards effacing the intermediary, since preserving the voice of the principal as far as possible would make a stronger case.[45] But the process also limited the extent to which feelings were discussed. While in a few types of case (alienation of affection actions in particular), plaintiffs were asked emotions questions ("how did you feel?"), in most cases feelings remained implicit. As we will see in chapter 1, unlike material loss, which had to be proved specifically, moral injury was dealt with generally, and so what mattered was to establish a plausible and compelling situation, a narrative that would make it self-evidently clear that anyone would have been affected as the plaintiff was alleging.

Given the mediated nature of legal sources, however, and given the reticence of the archive about the feelings being litigated, the historian ends up reading situations as well as words, piecing together the complex interrelations between what was felt, what was done, and what was said about both. This last aspect gets at the social expectations regarding emotions that shaped how they were litigated. Throughout the examples discussed in this book, we will see parties, lawyers, and judges grappling with individual, societal, and legal expectations regarding what people were supposed to feel and how they were supposed to express those feelings. Untangling those issues will be an important part of the case stories in the chapters that follow.

One final point is worth a brief mention. Emotions are fleeting, and the documents in the judicial archive preserve traces of moments in time. Even emotions that were strong enough to drive people to litigation could still soften with time, and people could and did move on and leave their emotions behind. In most cases evidence is lacking for a longer-term view of emotions and the relationships affected by them, but in some cases glimpses survive, which show people coping over time with their feelings and with the people who provoked those feelings in sometimes surprising ways.

Scope of This Book

Wounded Feelings develops these issues by a selection of case stories, each of which illustrates the confrontation of life and law through litigants' claims of different kinds of emotional injury and the narratives by which they presented those claims in court. The case stories are the sort of legal archaeology familiar in the common-law world but largely absent from the civil-law tradition, which tends to emphasize principle and doctrinal development more than the particularities of individual cases.[46] This book applies the insights of that approach to Quebec civil litigation, to explore how the concerns of individual litigants came into and influenced the world of law, and how the legal world in turn affected the experience of litigants as they sought redress for the wounded feelings they claimed.

The cases were chosen from a careful search of reported cases involving moral injury, admittedly the tip of a much larger litigation iceberg. Reported cases are of course an unrepresentative sample. They were selected for publication by editors not for their historical interest but for their importance to the legal profession, because they were novel judicial statements on a particular issue, authoritative rulings by an appellate court, or otherwise legally significant. By definition, then, these were exceptional affairs that stood out from the mass of cases that simply applied established principles of law. I was looking, however, to undertake not a quantitative study of moral injury actions, but an exploration that proceeded outward from individual stories. Since many of these hard cases challenged received wisdom and the established structures of the system, they forced litigants (and their lawyers) to work with often ill-fitting, contested, or wholly undeveloped conceptual categories. Tracing the reported cases back into the judicial archives allowed me to flesh out the legal side of the cases with their human dimension, which was either summarized or entirely stripped out of the case reports. As a consequence, these cases opened up more clearly than more routine affairs the struggle between people and the system, as litigants sought compelling ways to present their emotional injuries, and as professionals confronted the legal difficulties of bringing the endless diversity of human relationships within the limits of available legal categories.

The cases on which this book is based are almost exclusively private-law actions; the rich field of emotions engendered by criminal acts I leave to others. Private law, however, is particularly fertile ground for a legal history of emotions, since it reveals litigants contesting each other's feelings, while trying to formulate and validate their own, all based on competing social and legal understandings of affective situations. The main examples, some twenty presented in detail and a host of others discussed more briefly, are intended to be illustrative rather than representative.[47] They illustrate particular problems in feelings-based litigation, showing how at certain points in time litigants, lawyers, and the courts narrated, analysed, and adjudicated emotional injury. Though the arc of the analysis in the book as a whole follows a chronological trajectory from roughly 1870 to 1950, the individual cases highlight particular moments within that period, rather than tracing out a neat chronological development over time. The cases are also geographically illustrative rather than exhaustive: this is neither a focused study of one place nor a geographical survey of all of Quebec, and so while Montreal predominates (it was by far the busiest judicial district), I have brought in cases from Quebec City and rural areas as well.

My two intersecting themes come out in different parts. The overall argument about the changing legal understanding of moral injury is developed in chapters 1 and 8, which frame that development though two overviews, one from the beginning of our period, the other from the end. Chapter 1 canvasses key concepts and issues related to how Quebec judges and jurists understood and talked about moral injury circa 1870. It provides a starting point of reference for the language and conceptualization of intangible injury, the framework within which the cases to follow were analysed. Crucial are the gaps in that language, particularly the ways in which existing legal categories and terms failed to capture what plaintiffs were trying to narrate in their stories of wounded feelings. The basic building blocks of moral injury analysis at the time were four concepts. *Injure*, an old Roman law idea that was brought to Quebec via ancien-régime French law, meant insult, defamation, or more broadly most types of moral injury. *Biens* could mean property in a narrow sense, but its wider meaning embraced also any moral interests, the violation of which could give rise to moral injury.

Rights were part of the discussion, though early expressions of rights in private law were rather rare; much more common was the formulation "no right" (as in "the defendant had no right to …") that served to introduce the idea of fault. The final concept was the idea of damages and reparation of injury, and particularly the distinction between special damages, subject to strict rules of proof, and general damages, which applied to moral injury and for which proof was more narrative and situational. Together these ideas provided the basic framework of the legal language into which plaintiffs and defendants had to translate their stories for presentation within the courts. These ideas will be picked up again in the Conclusion in chapter 8.

The main part of the book explores in depth the legal history of specific emotions, focusing on their social aspects as brought before the courts in particular illustrative cases. Each chapter highlights one or more "negative" emotions – the feelings raised by injury to corresponding "positive" emotions. This is not to imply that the past was a pathological time of emotional misery, only that the nature of the legal process created what Darrin McMahan has called a "negativity bias" for emotions history.[48] The legal archives contain much about betrayal, little about love; much about shame and humiliation and mortification and dishonour, little about honour; much about grief, little about happiness. As we will see, careful attention to how negative emotions were narrated and analysed can reveal the positive emotions in their shadows, and indeed those shadowy and implicit positive emotions represented the social norms against which the negative feelings were evaluated and assessed. But the point remains that the courts were forums for discussing problems with emotions, and the topics considered here reflect that.

Chapters 2 and 3 look at aspects of wounded honour and related feelings like shame, mortification, and disgrace. Verbal defamation was central to the legal protection of honour, but my focus is on other forms of insult that brought out more clearly the emotions surrounding breaches of honour and propriety and how those emotions were inflected by gender, class, and culture. Two cases of respectable individuals, a man and a woman, each alleging mistreatment at the hands of perceived social inferiors allow for a close look at the gendered nature of honour and the emotional aspects of masculinity and femininity. Emotion was also a cultural idea, and the social codes judges used to evaluate emotion reflected the assumptions of the dominant culture. A family of Polish immigrants discovered this when police raided their baptism party to seize the liquor they were serving; the family's case against the town hinged on notions of disgrace and humiliation in the eyes of their community of newcomers to Quebec. A fourth case raised the collective side of honour: members of a rural community carried out a charivari on an unpopular and suspect neighbour to assert and restore the community's collective honour. The target sued the ringleaders to vindicate his own violated honour, bringing into confrontation individual and collective feelings of dishonour. All four of these cases hinged on contested ideas of respectability and socially expected comportment, which judges had to evaluate and apply.

The family was a specific site of honour and dishonour, in which individual and collective notions were in tension. Chapter 3 looks at four cases that each reveal different ways in which families sought to protect their collective reputational capital and the feelings provoked by its perceived loss. This took various forms: attacks on individuals' reputation through defamation of their relatives; defamation of the family collectively; insults to the memory of ancestors; and threats to the family's boundaries from unwanted associations with outsiders (such as a rash marriage against the wishes of parents). These cases, and the notion of family honour generally, also brought into relief the disjuncture between the liberal individualist framework of much of Quebec law and the relational and affective structure of the family. Cases like these challenged the integrity and completeness of liberal private law, and judges, at once required by their office to apply the law and formed by their own membership in family-based social structures, had to negotiate that tension in their rulings.

From dishonour we move in chapter 4 to a different aspect of mortification or shame: intrusion, or the feelings when one's body was invaded or handled without consent. The centrepiece of the chapter is the case of a young woman who was wrongly arrested as a prostitute and forced to undergo a legally mandated medical examination for venereal disease. She sued the City of Montreal for the distress this caused her, and the case involved a male judge conceptualizing the idea of violation of a woman's body, and then negotiating the difficulties in evaluating a rectification of that injury. The remainder of the chapter explores related issues, all of which come out of medical contexts: challenges to compulsory medical examinations, in particular those demanded for evidentiary purposes by insurance companies or other parties to litigation; cases of medical care done without or beyond consent, especially several involving women who claimed emotional injury after their ovaries were removed without prior consent; and the outrage experienced by family members whose deceased loved ones were subjected to autopsies without their consent. Like dishonour, the feelings surrounding bodily intrusion were heavily gendered, especially when women plaintiffs alleging those feelings confronted the male world of medical knowledge and its norms of expertise and best practices. The cases often strained judges' capacity to understand the injury alleged by the (mostly) female plaintiffs before them, leading to a shifting line between compensible injury and "mere feelings."

Love and affection gone wrong were a fertile source of litigation, and chapter 5 focuses on four cases of perceived betrayal: separation from bed and board within Montreal's Jewish community; breach of a promise of marriage between older rural residents; alienation of the affection of a hotel owner's wife; and an elderly man's attempt to revoke a gift made for his long-term care because of the recipient's ingratitude. Actions like these, particularly breach of promise and alienation of affection, tested the limits of the principle in the civil law that any damage, whether physical, material, or moral, could be compensated. The common law looked with suspicion on the "heart balm torts," and Quebec judges too were loath to award damages that served more to punish the defendant than to compensate the plaintiff. Add to that the gender politics of relationships and the difficulty, if not impossibility, of assessing expectations within intimate relationships, and cases like these became hotspots for the confrontation between social norms and legal rules.

Chapter 6 turns to the complex of emotions surrounding death, and how social practices at the end of life came to be legalized. The first part of the chapter looks at an anomaly: by the late nineteenth century, Quebec law barred close relatives from claiming damages for "solace for grief" (*solatium doloris*), an exception to the idea that all proved injury should be compensated. This anomaly (and the judicial resistance it sometimes provoked) came out clearly in a case of medical malpractice, in which the errors of a physician and a pharmacist in writing and filling a prescription resulted in the death by poison of a small child. The case reflected what to many judges, commentators, and certainly plaintiffs was an insupportable situation: bereaved families left with (at best) tiny material damages following the negligent deaths of their loved ones, while their emotional pain was pushed aside. That some judges sought workarounds for this seemingly heartless rule was an indication of the power of social norms within the law. Other aspects of end of life also led to litigation over the wounded feelings caused by vulnerability and the perceived loss of control of the process surrounding death. Examples are widows' disputes with their deceased husband's heirs over suitable provision for their mourning expenses, and especially litigation over who was to make the decision of where a deceased person should be buried. Driving all these cases were their undertones of questions about the legitimacy of affection and tensions over who was entitled to grieve.

The last emotions to be discussed, in chapter 7, are in some ways the most difficult to conceptualize: the complex feelings provoked by racial and religious discrimination, specifically indignation, anger, and fear. This serves as a transition within the book, since it begins to move the discussion from wounded feelings towards violated rights. Indignation and anger are explored through cases of refusal of service on racial grounds, and in particular a detailed look at the earliest such case in Quebec, in which a Black man sued a theatre for refusing to honour his tickets to the orchestra level. Several later examples contextualize this first case, and all together reveal individual emotional injury as well as how personal reactions gave rise to collective feelings and political action within the targeted community. The fear caused by the menace inherent in much discriminatory treatment is illustrated by a case involving two female Jehovah's Witness missionaries in Joliette, who were forced into a car by a hostile mob of men, driven for an hour to Montreal, and there abandoned on the steps of the women's prison with threats that they keep out of Joliette. As in some of the cases in the previous chapters, these cases mixed situational narratives outlining wounded feelings with hints that those feelings were linked to rights held by the plaintiffs and violated by the defendants.

Chapter 8 serves as a general conclusion by picking up the threads of chapter 1 to carry forward the legal story of how wounded feelings contributed to the development of private-law subjective rights of personality by the mid-twentieth century. It explores the shift, hinted at in various of the cases discussed in the other chapters, towards looking at moral injury as violated rights. This meant articulating the injury as a violation of some clearly defined, identifiable interest held by the plaintiff. The earlier cases tacitly assumed that something had been illicitly violated, without ever specifying what of the plaintiff's that something was. Beginning around the turn of the century in a few cases in specific areas of law, and then more definitively in the middle of the twentieth century, Quebec jurists and judges began to discuss what came to be called personality rights, that is subjective extrapatrimonial rights that stood for attributes of the personality like honour, bodily integrity, dignity, and privacy. Violation of those rights supported both the defendant's fault and the plaintiff's injury. Plaintiffs' stories of wounded feelings were still central to the analysis, indeed they still are in similar cases today, but the courts were beginning to treat intangible injuries differently than they had earlier, shifting the emphasis from reading social codes and assessing values like propriety and honour, to looking for the violation of particular objectively defined rights held by plaintiffs.

Notes on the Text

In transcribing archival documents and newspaper articles, I have silently corrected obvious errors, added punctuation and French accents according to today's usage, and regularized formatting. In archival citations, when pages of a document are numbered I cite those, but often only the front (recto) is numbered, not the back (verso). In those cases, I cite the side of the page by indicating r or v after the number.

All translations are my own, unless otherwise noted; the original is in the notes. In translating testimony, I have tried to capture the flavour rather than the literal wording. I have also retained contemporary usage of the universal male gender in the translations rather than adopting gender-neutral terminology.

1

Feelings and the Law in Nineteenth-Century Quebec

All the cases we will be examining dealt with aspects of what we might call the moral person, but nineteenth- and early twentieth-century jurists in Quebec would not have abstracted the issue in those terms. While the "law of persons" had been one of the constituent fields of the civil law from the time of Gaius's *Institutes* (along with the law of things and the law of actions), and while personhood issues such as status, capacity, domicile, and others came up frequently enough in the courts, thinking about such issues – as distinct from applying the rules to solve practical problems – left few traces in Quebec.[1] A rare few jurists like François Langelier, who had studied at Paris in the early 1860s and continued to follow the latest European ideas, might have paused to consider the implications of developments in the legal protection of personality coming out of Europe, such as Charles Aubry and Charles Rau's elaboration of the German Karl Salomo Zachariä's key idea of the patrimony, to be discussed below. But such reflections, had they been written down, would have been exceptional indeed. Quebec was slow to follow trends towards systematization evident in France and, later, the common-law world, where theorists were dividing the law into discretely articulated subfields of knowledge.[2]

The intellectual world of Quebec lawyers was shaped by various overlapping and interacting factors: legal education; the institutional framework of courts, bar, *notariat*, and law offices; newspaper coverage; legal libraries.[3] We will see examples of the influence of all of these in what follows. Particularly important in shaping the substance of Quebec law was the availability (or lack thereof) of books and periodicals to provide lawyers and judges with reported cases, with developments in Canada, the United States, Britain, and France, and with local or imported commentary.[4] Before private-law codification in 1866, and even for some decades thereafter, Quebec had little home-grown legal literature, and what was published tended to be oriented towards practice or elementary legal education.[5] Commentary, as distinct from exegesis, elucidation, or enumeration, was sparse. The cause and the result of this relative lack of domestic commentary was a vigorous circulation of foreign legal literature in Quebec, from France especially, but also from Great Britain and the United States.[6] In private law matters, French books were most obviously relevant, and until well into the twentieth century the Quebec courts regularly cited the classic resources of French law, such as Jean Domat's *Les loix civiles dans leur ordre naturel*, Jean-Baptiste Denisart's collections of French jurisprudence, Claude-Joseph de Ferrière's *Dictionnaire de droit et de pratique* and his commentary on the Custom of Paris, and the numerous commentaries on the French civil code.

This material transmission of ideas, through the books and periodicals that lawyers and judges owned, borrowed, read, and cited in court, was an important factor in the high degree of mixing of domestic and foreign ways of thinking about the structure and substance of the law, which contributed to the emergence of Quebec's distinctive legal culture.[7] Outside ideas brought a dynamism to the analysis of various legal topics, but also a degree of instability and unpredictability. This was especially true in the highly subjective area of emotional injury. While classificatory abstraction was little developed, lawyers and judges did employ a vocabulary of moral injury to articulate and understand the wounded feelings of the individuals undertaking the litigation. Especially after codification, the legal rules applicable on the one hand to civil liability, fault, and injury, and on the other to reparation and compensation, began slowly to attract conceptual articulation. Article 1053 of the *Civil Code of Lower Canada* (CCLC) in particular provided the foundation of most of the cases we will be discussing: "Every person capable of discerning right from wrong is responsible for the damages caused by his fault to another, whether by positive act, imprudence, neglect or want of skill." This article set out key ideas (drawn from its French model, and further back from its antecedents in Roman law) like responsibility, damage, fault, and right and wrong, concepts that, as we will see, provided basic vocabulary and grounded the analysis in individual cases.

What follows is a brief survey of a few key legal categories that in the nineteenth century provided the conceptual framework for the cases we will be examining. The purpose of this overview is to get a sense of the language in which judges and lawyers talked about these legal ideas at the beginning of our period. This will serve as a point of contrast and comparison for the discussion in chapter 8 on the development of the language of subjective private-law rights of personality by the mid-twentieth century. Because of the dearth of home-grown commentary, much of what follows is based on the French and English sources to which contemporary lawyers and judges turned to understand Quebec legal problems.

Injure

The overarching nineteenth-century term for the injury complained of in cases of wounded feelings was *injure*, which meant in a narrow technical sense defamation, but which regularly had the wider signification of any kind of moral injury. It represented, then, the basic legal characterization lawyers gave to the stories of emotional injury litigants brought forward, with their overtones of dishonour, outrage, mortification, humiliation, and shame.

Legally, *injure* was an ancient idea, closely based on the Roman idea of *iniuria*. While its earliest origins were in physical interferences with others, *iniuria* in Justinian's *Digest* protected free persons from any "deliberate anti-social attacks on their dignity."[8] It thus covered a wide range of non-fatal personal injuries, both physical and moral, extending to what today would be considered both civil and criminal liability, and principally the latter.[9] From its Roman origins, the idea of *injure* spread throughout the civil-law world and beyond, shaping responses to different kinds of moral injury.[10] In France, François Dareau's *Traité des injures dans l'ordre judiciaire* of 1775 was the most important discussion, and it remained the go-to citation for Quebec lawyers into the twentieth century. Superior Court Justice Michel Mathieu even began preparation of an updated Quebec edition of the work, though he never finished the project.[11] Dareau drew on earlier authors, particularly Domat, in defining *injure* as "whatever is said, whatever is written, whatever is done and even whatever is intentionally omitted to offend someone in his honour, in his person, or in his *biens*."[12] Dareau's definition suggests the usual complaint formula we examined in the Introduction (injury to one's honour, one's person, and one's *biens*), but it also ranges more widely than moral injury alone and could extend to physical and material injuries. However, as Dareau developed the definition, it is clear that honour and related ideas were paramount. The various meanings of *biens* will be the focus of the next section below; as to *injures* to the person, what Dareau had in mind were generally violations of the duties individuals owed to one another, such as seduction and other attacks on women's virtue, adultery and other breaches of spousal duties, violence by children towards their parents, failure of inferiors to give proper respect to superiors, and so on.[13] In other words, *injure* was less about physical interference with the person than the violation of social codes of honour and respect due within hierarchical relations, which gave seriously negative meaning to situations that were often otherwise of a trifling nature.[14] This status-based idea of *injure* continued to shape its application in Quebec, as the social norms that gave life to the concept were strongly influenced by ideas of proper relations between genders, classes, and races.

Alongside the broad understanding of the substance of *injure* was a continuing bifurcation in the nature and purpose of the *action d'injures* that addressed such affronts. As in Roman law, where the *actio iniuriarum* had a dual criminal and civil nature, its descendant French law too treated *injure* as both a public action giving rise to a criminal complaint and a private civil action leading either to damages or a right to a response rectifying the *injure* (a *réparation d'honneur*). The details need not concern us,[15] but this dual nature of the action reveals a tension in the different purposes of actions regarding *injures*. Were they about punishing the person responsible for the *injure*, or compensating the injured party? Were they to provide some measure of satisfaction or vindication to the plaintiff, or to attempt (as much as possible) to undo the effects of the *injure* and restore the victim to his or her previous state?

In Quebec, the starting point for understandings of *injure* was the old French law, brought to New France. Defamation in particular was viewed predominantly, though not exclusively, as a public matter.[16] As in Dareau, *injure* was treated mainly as a form of defamation, but defamation construed broadly to include not only words, songs, images, and the like, but also any action calculated to bring dishonour or shame to the target. Cases from the decades preceding our period show some of the substantive diversity of the *action d'injures*, alongside verbal

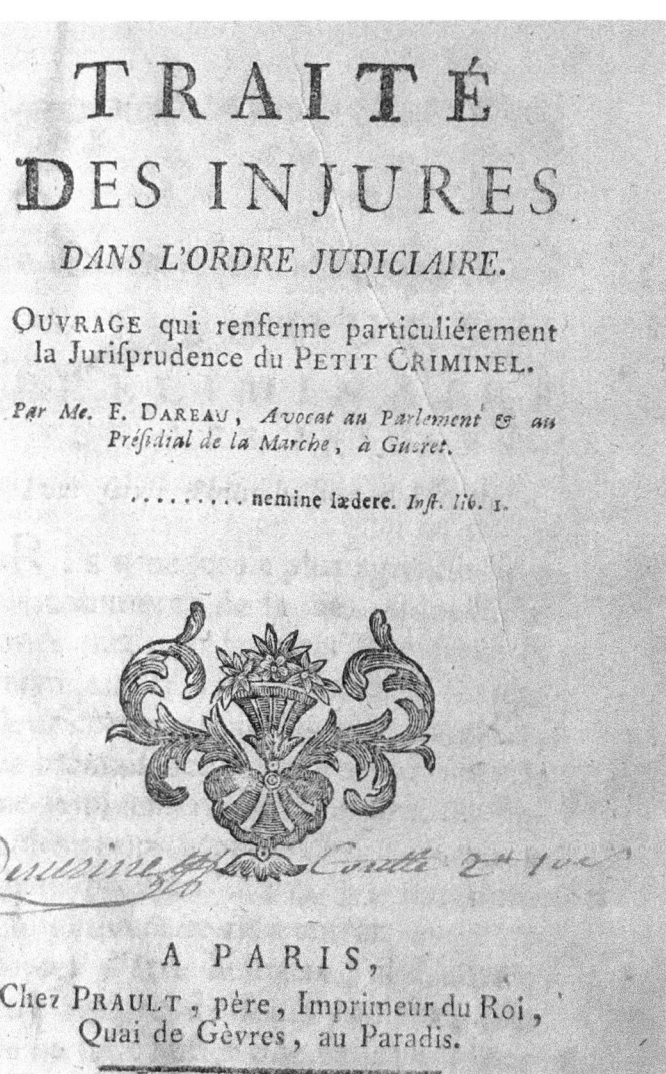

Figure 1.1 Title page of François Dareau, *Traité des injures dans l'ordre judiciaire* (Paris: Prault, père, 1777). Author's collection.

defamation itself: a physical assault on a churchwarden; a suit by a mother against the priest who performed the marriage of her underage daughter without parental consent; an action by a local notable for not being served communion first in his parish church.[17] The most interesting early Quebec discussion of *injure*, and one that fleshed out its meaning, came from Maximilien Bibaud, legal polemicist and founder of Quebec's first law school. In his *Commentaires sur les lois du Bas-Canada*, he defined *injure* as "injury to another or the voluntary violation of another's right. We say voluntary, according to the moral sense of *injure*; however, social law, which does not always consider intention, often gives the name *injure* to a purely material wrong, that is one caused without intent to injure."[18] This is interesting in various ways. Bibaud's emphasis on the intentional or voluntary nature of *injure* made clear the required element of malice – linking it to its roots in criminal liability – and so moved it away from civil liability, which recognized both intentional and unintentional infliction of injury (delict versus quasi-delict). His linking of *injure* to the violation of a right – as distinct from Dareau, who focused on violation of a duty – also moved the idea in a different direction. Bibaud's formulation was not new to him; it appeared, for example, in a treatise on confession by the Belgian priest Pierre Cocatrix, who wrote in 1830 that "the obligation to make right presupposes an *injure*, that is a voluntary violation of another's right."[19] Whether or not that was Bibaud's source, the link with moral theology is telling. Aside from being characteristic of Bibaud's natural-law approach to the law generally, it also linked *injure* with other threads in its long history. In English law, for example, certain kinds of defamation were until 1855 offences under ecclesiastical law and were pursued in the church courts.[20] In old French law too, secular understandings of *injure* drew from religious traditions of honour as a kind spiritual possession (or *bien*).[21] This mingling of the secular and the religious continued in Quebec: Brian Young's work on the Taschereau family of judges and ecclesiastical dignitaries shows the close intellectual and institutional relationship between secular and religious law.[22] Finally, Bibaud linked *injure* to a discussion of *biens*, that is, "everything that makes up man's faculties."[23] Different types of *injure* affected different *biens* of the victim and so required different kinds of reparation – a point we will address in the next section.

Under the CCLC, the courts drew on these earlier ideas in approaching cases of *injure*. Its criminal aspects came to be confined to relatively rarely used offences such as criminal libel, while the civil action did most of the work. Society had changed, and in the absence of explicit hierarchy based on social status as in ancien régime France, *injure* had to change with it. While in the early days in Quebec, seigneurial and other honorific rights (and their corresponding duties) could still ground an *action d'injures*,[24] by the 1870s the duties whose violation resulted in *injure* were no longer explicitly status-based (at least outside the family), but were rather duties based on the moral obligations between individuals established by social codes of behaviour (though these moral obligations were strongly inflected by ideas of social hierarchy nonetheless). *Injure* thus could refer to any attack on honour, however done: in essence, *injure* meant a wrong causing moral injury. Its use as a stand-in for emotional injury of various kinds was well established, and in this it contrasted with the common law, in which mental suffering was at the time not a compensible injury.[25]

Alongside this general use of *injure*, and drawing on it, were specific instances within the CCLC and the Code of Civil Procedure (CCP). In five main situations, *injure* – whatever that meant, since its precise meaning was the subject of controversy – could trigger certain legal consequences.[26] First, either spouse could demand separation from bed and board for "outrage, ill-usage or grievous insult / *excès, sévices et injures graves*."[27] Second, a donor could revoke a gift made *inter vivos* for the donee's ingratitude, defined among other things as "ill usage, crimes or grievous injuries / *sévices, délits majeurs ou injures graves*."[28] Third, a testament or legacy could be revoked for "grievous injury / *injure grave*" to the memory of the testator.[29] Fourth, one ground to demand civil imprisonment for debt (*contrainte par corps*) was a condemnation to damages for "personal wrongs / *injures personnelles*."[30] Finally, to further complicate matters, in damages actions resulting from "personal wrongs / *torts personnels*" (the word *injure* did not appear, but in practice the idea was similar), either party could request a jury trial, provided the amount in play was over a certain threshold (initially two hundred dollars).[31] These "wrongs" included the breach of promise in *Grange v. Benning*, as well as physical injuries or wrongful death, defamation, and other kinds of moral injury. Exercising the option often led to challenges, which hinged on the precise interpretation of "wrongs / *torts*."[32] The meaning of *injure* (and related ideas) in all these places resulted in considerable disagreement, exacerbated by the inconsistencies between the French and English versions, where the same term in one language gave rise to various equivalents in the other. This was more than just legalistic quibbling: *injure* had always been a term of varied meaning, and judges had to pin down its precise signification in dealing with cases under these articles. This resulted in some interesting discussion of the idea of *injure*, to which we will return in chapter 8, which helped somewhat to fill the gap left by the lack of Quebec commentary. It was also, of course, not strictly an academic issue. The scope of *injure* could determine whether or not a defendant could be threatened with imprisonment for failure to pay damages, whether or not damages awarded for *injure* could be seized by creditors (for example, whether or not they formed part of the community of property between spouses), and, in some cases, whether or not spouses could separate.

In all these contexts, the courts worked to distinguish *injure* from injury broadly construed (*préjudice*). That it was distinct from material injury (*préjudice réel*) was clear enough. The question was what sorts of physical and moral prejudice it included. *Injures personnelles*, for example, as used in relation to imprisonment for debt, was by the 1880s coming to be defined following Dareau's formula, which focused on the meaning of the act (or failure to act) that caused the damage. So according to Justice Michel Mathieu, physical injuries caused by a runaway horse, since they did not touch the honour or reputation of the plaintiff, did not count as "personal wrongs" and the defendant could not be imprisoned for failure to pay.[33] *Injures graves*, whatever their English translation, shone a different light on the idea. Given that *injure* was a reputational injury, assessing the effects of its severity was left to the discretion of the judge. This meant, as we will see throughout this book, consideration of the public face of subjective, highly personal injuries. In France, as William Reddy has noted, *injures graves* in the context of spousal separation from bed and board related to the public aspect of honour; the gravity lay in exposing to public view something that should remain private.[34] In Quebec, similar considerations went into judging what conduct crossed that line. To cite just one example, a wife sued for separation from her husband who, she alleged, failed to fulfil his conjugal duties and "was guilty of masturbation, his passion being for persons of his own sex."[35] The husband countered with a demurrer (a motion to dismiss the case for lack of legal basis) that none of her allegations constituted grounds for separation. The case centred on the meaning of "*injures graves*." In the end, the judge followed the French author Charles Demolombe in looking for "outrageous" words, writings, or deeds "by which one of the spouses attacks the honour and the esteem of the other, and shows towards him or her sentiments of hatred, loathing, or contempt."[36] The denial of marital relations, he found, rose to this level, since it was evidence of the husband's contempt for his wife. The husband's "shameful passion," however, did not constitute an *injure grave*, since it "could attack only his own personal honour, and could only destroy or affect the esteem that he might enjoy." It might have been different, the judge remarked, had he practised his passions in front of his wife, since "that revolting insult to her modesty and her morals would be an *injure grave* that would show his feelings of contempt for his wife."[37] *Injure* – whether *grave* or not – lay in the public effects of the personally experienced feelings, not the feelings themselves.

Finally, before leaving *injure*, a brief return is warranted to the questions posed earlier about the nature of the *action d'injures*. Throughout its early history the action was balanced between punishment and compensation. In Quebec, which abandoned criminal proceedings in *injure* in favour of the civil courts, the action quickly became simply a claim for damages. Damages came in various kinds, as we will see later in this chapter, but for now, the issue was whether *injures* were like other kinds of civil liability, which fell under article 1053 CCLC, or whether they grounded a special action governed by its own rules. This was an arcane question, to be sure, and the judges who raised it – Justice François Langelier foremost – were being self-consciously pedantic in insisting on the distinction. Still, the issue was important, as it involved what the *action d'injures* was supposed to accomplish legally in the face of the social wrong of insult.

For most lawyers and judges in Quebec, the *action d'injures* and the action in damages under article 1053 CCLC were indistinguishable. While France treated different sorts of honour-based wrongs in different ways – defamation proper was a criminal offence, while *injure* mixed criminal and civil aspects – in Quebec private law there was only an action in damages, which distinguished only the kinds of damages that could be sought (as we will see below). Justice Siméon Pagnuelo of the Superior Court expressed the prevailing opinion in 1893: "All our actions come down to the criminal prosecution for written libel and the action in damages. The latter is governed by the rules of common law [*droit commun*] alone."[38] For some, or at least for one, however, this fuzziness was unacceptable on a conceptual as well as practical level. This objection – it was hardly a debate – went nowhere at the time, but raised issues that would remain important in the decades to come.

Justice François Langelier of the Superior Court objected vociferously and at length on several occasions to the blurring of the action in damages and the *action d'injures*. Langelier, who taught at the Université Laval during his entire career, and who had studied for two years in Paris in the 1860s, was more academically minded than most judges of the time. He first raised the issue in a complex interdiction case in 1900.[39] A woman sued her son-in-law for having wrongly interdicted her for insanity, and claimed $25 in pecuniary losses plus $975 for injury to her honour and reputation. Her husband had already himself been interdicted. Could she, as a married woman, undertake this action herself? To further complicate matters, while the trial was underway, the woman died, and the case was continued by her two brothers. What was the nature of the moral injury claim in the case?

For Langelier, this all came down to the distinction between the action in damages and the *action d'injures*, and the separate natures of the two. An action in damages was compensatory, he argued, to put the victim back into the state she had been in before. The *action d'injures*, by contrast, had since Roman law been punitive rather than compensatory. Its purpose was "a kind of fine imposed to punish the guilty party, and given to the victim of the *injure* as a kind of *solatium*."[40] Old French law maintained this distinction (Langelier cited Dareau on this), and this applied as well in Quebec before codification. The effects of the distinction were that the cause of the action in damages was a material loss that for those in community of property became part of the community, since it gave rise to a sum of money. The cause of the *action d'injures*, on the other hand, affected only the victim's self-respect and the consideration she enjoyed; in itself it brought no material loss. In the present case, then, the plaintiff had no right to institute an action herself for the $25 material loss, since that right belonged only to her husband as head of the matrimonial community of property. The $975 claim, however, belonged to her alone, and so she could bring action herself on that score (and since the action had already been commenced before her death, her heirs could continue it, even if they would have had no right themselves to institute an action had she not begun one before her death). Langelier awarded the plaintiffs $200. The Court of Queen's Bench disagreed and overturned his carefully crafted, professorial reasoning, basing their decision principally on a recent judgment of the Supreme Court of Canada that rejected a married woman's right to act alone in matters of "personal wrongs."[41]

Langelier refused to leave the matter there. Beginning in 1905, and while still a judge, he published a six-volume treatise based on the lectures he had been giving at the Université Laval since 1872.[42] He took the opportunity to continue (away from the bench) his advocacy for a distinct *action d'injures*. In discussing damages, Langelier dismissed "French authors" who lumped both material and moral damages together and so confounded the action in damages and the *action d'injures*. Repeating what he had said in the overruled 1900 judgment, he argued that moral damages were "so-called damages" (*les prétendus dommages*); in fact, they were a kind of fine or punishment. The *action d'injures* was completely different from the action in damages in article 1053 CCLC. It was instead, he argued, a relic of the old law, never explicitly repealed by the transitional provision in article 2613 CCLC, and so still available. The appeals court's decision in the earlier case, and the Supreme Court decision on which it rested, were clearly in error, he wrote, as the result of the confounding of the two different kinds of actions and their effects. Though he grudgingly admitted this was not the law of the land, since the higher courts had spoken, he maintained that properly speaking a married woman could sue on her own for *injures*, while such an action was also intransmissible to one's heirs.[43]

Langelier's insistence on the distinction, despite its lack of traction among Quebec jurists and judges, foreshadowed some of the twentieth-century developments surrounding *injure* and personality that we will trace in chapter 8.[44] For Langelier, the question pointed to the division between the person and the person's attributes on the one side, and the person's things on the other. The effects of an *injure*, and the *action d'injures*, were closely connected to personal attributes of the person – his or her reputation, honour, and so on – and so were to be treated as such. Such a distinction would have had significant effects: personal attributes would not be part of the community in the case of a married woman, for example, nor would they be transmissible to heirs should the victim die before instituting an action. They would be, in other words, extrapatrimonial, though this terminology would not appear until much later. By contrast, damages – which for Langelier meant *dommages réels* – would be property, or *biens*, and so would be within the patrimony. A married woman's real damages would fall into the community, and in all cases such damages would be transmissible along with the rest of one's property.

Langelier's use of the term *biens* here was somewhat restrictive: certainly not all of his contemporaries would have agreed. This was a key term in nineteenth-century discussions of moral injury, and we turn now to consider some of its nuances.

Biens

Injure in the later nineteenth century was the juridical description of the act complained of and its effects. If we now move further into the legal characterization of moral injury, to consider on a more abstract level the interest that was being injured, we have even less domestic thinking on which to rely than was the case regarding *injure*. In Quebec especially, where the needs of practice so totally dominated legal writing and publishing in the nineteenth century, reflection on the substantive framework behind *injure* was absent, at least after some intriguing remarks by Maximilien Bibaud in the early 1860s. The issue here is legal categorization, and the meanings that derive from where something is put and how it is interpreted within the structure of the law. The common-law world was starting to explore classification anew in the second half of the nineteenth century, and early treatise writers were developing the outlines of a substantive law of torts, a law of contracts, and so forth.[45] In the civil-law tradition, the Institutional framework, derived from Gaius via Justinian's *Institutes*, provided the basic categories for civil codes and doctrinal treatises alike, so systematic thinking was much more developed.[46] What was new during the nineteenth century was work on conceptual challenges to the received structure of the civil law. One such new direction was particularly important in the development and understanding of moral injury: the idea of *biens* and the patrimony.[47]

The patrimony was an old Roman idea that was rethought and given new work to do in the first half of the nineteenth century by its most influential theorists, the German Karl Salomo Zachariä and his French disciples Charles Aubry and Charles Rau.[48] Conceived as the legal universality of all one's *biens* – a word whose multiple meanings make translation difficult, as we will see in a moment – the patrimony provided the conceptual glue between the foundational areas of the civil law: persons, things, and obligations. As the zone of possession and ownership, the patrimony defines what one has rather than what one is – having (*avoir*) rather than being (*être*), as Alain Sériaux puts it.[49] At the same time, it provided a structure within which to understand the legal relations between the personality and the exterior things of the world.⁵⁰ For understanding the moral interests of the person, this frontier of the patrimony, where *avoir* meets *être*, is most important, and the idea of *biens* was located squarely at that point of juncture.

The patrimony is the sum of all of a person's *biens*. The word *biens* was used in the early nineteenth century in distinction to *choses*: as most authors explained it, *choses* was the genre, *biens* the species.⁵¹ More specifically, however, *biens* were things that offered some utility, some increase in one's well-being. This meant of course one's material well-being, but more too: *biens* could also be those things whose utility served to increase one's moral well-being or happiness. As Aubry and Rau put it, utility was "broader than *price* or *monetary value*; it includes whatever can contribute to man's moral or material well-being, and as a consequence it includes advantages not appreciable in money."⁵² As examples, they gave those benefits deriving from familial relations and went so far as to suggest that persons themselves could constitute *biens*. Part of this wider understanding of *biens* were what they termed "inner *biens*" (*biens innés*), or those things "that merge with the existence of the person who has rights to exercise over them" such as the body, liberty, and honour.⁵³ Since the patrimony contained all one's *biens*, the attributes of the person represented by *biens innés* were no exception, and so the purely moral interests of the person were part of the patrimony.⁵⁴ Not all agreed, however, and the disagreement focused on whether attributes of the personality could themselves be within the patrimony, or whether they entered the patrimony only when converted into material terms via a damages award following their violation.⁵⁵ By their third edition, published in 1856, Aubry and Rau backed off, and their patrimony took on a more exclusively materialist orientation, as the universality of *biens* of material utility.⁵⁶ In their fourth edition, published starting in 1869 (and the last one they supervised), they withdrew the *biens innés* from the patrimony altogether. Even though in "pure theory" the patrimony contained all kinds of *biens*, the way the French code set up the law, they argued, the *biens innés* were excluded.⁵⁷

This excursus into the arcana of the patrimony in France raises a crucial point for our purposes. Even if the broad understanding of *biens* – and *biens innés* in particular – was a matter of "pure theory" only, and even if in the end the materialist view of the patrimony largely won out, the debates did raise the existence of an alternative notion of *biens* that preserved pre-liberal nuances, not defined strictly by market-driven concerns. Earlier authors, for example, used the language of *biens* to describe spiritual or moral interests within the law, a usage that drew on the Latin root of the word, *bona*, and before that on Aristotelian ideas, to associate the term with all potential sources of well-being, beyond strictly monetary ones. Honour, for example, was a kind of spiritual *bien*.[58] The debates thus touched not just the parameters of property, but also how attributes of the human personality – whether called interests, rights, or *biens* – were to be brought into the purview of the law. Eventually, as we will see in chapter 8, those attributes of the person were moved to a different category, the realm of the extrapatrimonial, and were theorized not as *biens* but as personality rights. For now, however, it is enough to emphasize that the moral aspects of the personality were part of the discussion, and that they were, as Nicholas Kasirer puts it, "not property in the conventional sense."[59]

If we turn from France to Quebec, those multiple meanings were evident in the earliest discussion of the idea of *biens*, from Maximilien Bibaud's *Commentaires*, based on his lectures from his law school in the early 1860s. In analysing article 88 of the Custom of Paris, Bibaud drew a definition of *biens* almost word-for-word from Claude de Ferrière's dictionary of juridical terminology, a definition itself based closely on Ulpian from Justinian's *Digest*. *Biens* (or *bona* in the original Latin) were "all kinds of possessions," and generally whatever "makes men happy." This was the *locus classicus* for discussions of *biens* and appeared in most French commentators. Bibaud diverged from his source, however, in an added final sentence: "Whatever brings us some utility or pleasure is thus properly called a *bien*."[60] This addition, which seems to be Bibaud's own, points to an exceptionally broad understanding of the moral side of *biens*. While Ferrière ended his definition with an observation that things not in commerce were not properly called *biens*, a restrictive view, Bibaud's reference to utility put him in line with later French commentators like Aubry and Rau. (Bibaud's *Commentaires* contain no citations to sources, so it is not clear whether he was familiar with Aubry and Rau.) Adding "or some pleasure" (*ou quelque plaisir*) to the mix, however, went further than most French commentators in underscoring the moral side of utility.

Bibaud returned to the idea of *biens* later in his lectures, during his discussion of criminal law. The juxtaposition is interesting. While *biens* were of course central to property law, the broad understanding – moral and material – in Bibaud's definition linked *biens* with the concerns of criminal law, as we saw above in our analysis of *injure*. German theorists were coming to define crime as an unauthorized interference with a *Rechtsgut* – in effect, a *bien*[61] – an idea analogous to Dareau's conception

Figure 1.2 Maximilien Bibaud, photographed by William Notman in 1862. McCord Museum, I-2573.1. Reproduced with permission.

of *injure*. Bibaud's discussion – unique in Quebec legal writing – left those deeper connections unexplored, but he did elaborate a taxonomy of *biens* that made clear the moral as well as material sides of the idea.[62] *Biens* were of four kinds: of the soul, of the body, of the reputation, and of the fortune. The last were one's material possessions, in other words one's patrimony. The first three, however, were the individual's moral attributes. The "natural *biens* of the soul" (*les biens naturels de l'âme*), for example, which were distinguished from the supernatural *biens* of the soul, the domain of theology, made up one's nature, such as one's intelligence and memory. The *biens* of the reputation, for their part, comprised one's honour and respect, the outward signs of one's inner virtues. Bibaud drew here not on the major French commentators we examined above, but rather on moral theologians and jurists within the natural-law tradition, with the idea of interior and exterior "goods" going back to Aristotle.[63]

Bibaud's view of *biens*, imbued as it was with a strong moral dimension drawn from Catholic theology, reflected a side of Quebec law that Murray Greenwood called "higher morality."[64] In the face of strong liberal individualism and materialism, some in Quebec urged restraint. Jurists like Bibaud, Édouard Lefebvre de Bellefeuille, and later Léo Pelland argued for a kind of Catholic ultramontanist jurisprudence that would reject changes like the abolition of lesion (that is, excessively one-sided dealing) between adults as a ground for the nullity of contracts[65] and any liberalization of the laws on marriage and family.[66] Defining *biens* more broadly than material interests alone brought that same morality into the realm of legal personhood, creating a humanistic alternative to the materialism evident in virtually all other areas of the law. Within the legalization of the person and the personality, for some the broad view of *biens* made it clear that moral and material interests were not the same thing.

As with most legal issues, Quebec judges and jurists seem to have been content to read about this issue without themselves engaging directly with it. For most, a situation either gave rise to damages or not, depending on the proof, whatever the nature of the interest that had been harmed. Occasionally we get glimpses of thinking about the nature of personality in cases focused mainly on other issues. In an 1862 case, for example, the question was whether damages for *injure* could be seized or not. Justice James Smith accepted the defendant's argument that such damages were by their nature not seizable. Since they were "so fully connected to the person," they remained distinct from the mass of *biens* in the patrimony.⁶⁷ In another case, from 1882, Justice Louis-Bonaventure Caron dismissed a fiancée's action in breach of promise to marry because "what she has lost or missed having is not in commerce, and so resists any evaluation." There could thus be no legal action to enforce or remedy it.⁶⁸ François Langelier's distinction between the action in damages and the *action d'injures*, discussed in the previous section, reflected the same reluctance to mix the material and the moral.⁶⁹ The language of *biens*, while imperfect, provided a way to speak of moral interests such as honour in a materialist system. In practical terms, whether those interests were treated as protected interests in themselves or simply as factual situations giving rise to damages which then entered the patrimony mattered little.

Before leaving *biens*, it is worth noting that in the nineteenth century, the language of *biens* and property more generally was linked with moral values beyond as well as within legal thinking. In popular language, emotions and affective ties were often discussed as a kind of property. In nineteenth-century Boston, for example, John Corrigan has shown that the language of contract and exchange was prominent in emotional contexts, particularly the family: "As an object, as a commodity that had value and that could be traded for other commodities (including an expression of emotion from others), emotion was always in play, being given and taken in a host of domestic situations."⁷⁰ As we will see in chapter 3, in Quebec too the family's reputation and its collective honour were seen as a sort of literal social capital, as goods that the family "possessed" as a treasure (or patrimony) held and enjoyed by all members.

"Right" and "No Right"

What of rights? Today, in both public law and private law, rights do a lot of the conceptual work that *injure* did in the past; this is one of the arguments of this book. If we go back to the nineteenth century, however, we find the word *right* being used with a different, narrower meaning than it would come to acquire over the course of the twentieth century. But though it was never the dominant way in which wounded feelings were characterized legally until more recently, the language of rights sometimes entered the analysis, even in the nineteenth century. We will develop this subject further in chapter 8, but it is worth introducing here a particular usage of rights language found in moral injury cases, the negative expression that one or the other party, usually the defendant, had "no right" to do something.[71] This conception of rights – as absence rather than presence – was one of the principal ways in which fault was discussed, focusing on what the defendant had or did not have, rather than on what the plaintiff had.

Most of the cases we will examine in this book, and particularly those from the nineteenth century, articulated rights in negative rather than positive terms. In a case from the late 1870s, for example, a physician seeking to collect an unpaid account read aloud in open court his bill to the patient, which contained the information that the treatment had been for "a *blennorrhoea*, vulgarly called 'hot piss.'"[72] The patient sued the physician for publicizing his gonorrhoea, and the case came down to "right" versus "no right." The physician claimed, and the trial judge accepted, that he was simply following the law, which gave him the "right" to name as specifically as possible the treatment giving rise to the unpaid bill. The patient, on the other hand, argued that the physician "had no right to prepare his bill giving the name of a venereal disease."[73] The Court of Queen's Bench ultimately sided with the patient, and held (in language that suggested what would later come to be called abuse of right) that "a physician does not have the right to publish in a bill for professional services the nature of the illness for which he is claiming payment, when such publication is of a nature to injure or insult his debtor."[74] Terminology was fluid at the time; though this matter was phrased in rights terms, it could as easily have been formulated in terms of the physician's legal *duty* to draft the bill as exactly as possible. But the main allegations in this case – and there were many other cases employing similar language – emphasized the absence of rights more than their presence. The focus was not on something the plaintiff had that had been violated (in this case, some substantive right to privacy or confidentiality or honour), but rather on the absence of a right on the defendant's side that would have made an illicit act licit.[75]

An important reason for this focus on the defendant's absent right rather than the plaintiff's present right was the way fault was defined at the time. Fault, along with some damage and a causal link between the two, was an essential element for certain kinds of civil liability, particularly under article 1053 CCLC (and its analogue, article 1382 of the French code). Fault was defined as an illicit act or omission, and because of this, one committed no fault for doing what one had a right to do.[76] There were exceptions, notably the new idea of the abusive exercise of one's right that was developing in property law in the later nineteenth century,[77] but the general principle was that something sanctioned by law could not be illicit. So while plaintiffs seldom alleged substantive rights behind their claims, defendants frequently asserted "I have a right" to negate their fault and to counter the plaintiff's argument that they had "no right" to do what they did. In defamation cases, for example, defendants characterized fair comment on politicians as the exercise of a right,[78] while the owners of theatres and other public establishments used rights like free use of one's property to justify refusing to serve visible minorities.[79]

Beyond the requirements of proving fault, however, the absence of positive rights in late nineteenth-century legal discourse about moral injury is interesting. Some French theorists – aligned with Kant and other German thinkers – were developing the idea of subjective rights in the private law. Alphonse Boistel, for example, in an 1899 treatise on legal philosophy, discussed the "innate rights of man" (*droits innés de l'homme*), drawing on earlier works like that of the German Heinrich Ahrens, writing in 1838: "These rights are called *innate* or *absolute*, and among them are included the right of everyone to life, liberty, dignity, honour, etc."[80] In Quebec, however, what discussion there was of substantive (as opposed to procedural) rights was confined mainly to the realm of public law and discussions of British liberty, similar to what Richard Risk and Robert Vipond observed for Upper Canada.[81] In moral injury cases, however, the plaintiff's interest was usually left unstated, undefined, and implicit. In a case from the 1880s, for example, a lawyer ducked into Montreal's swank St. Lawrence Hall hotel to use the washroom; a security guard suspected he had thrown paper on the floor and bodily dragged him out to the street. Both parties framed their arguments in rights terms – the lawyer claimed a right to be in a public space, the proprietor a right to expel an unruly guest. In discussing the real point at issue, however, that is the *injure* of humiliating a respectable lawyer by rough treatment, the language was not of rights but rather of a "dishonouring humiliation."[82] While it was clear that the plaintiff was alleging wrongful conduct on the defendant's part, he was not arguing that he had a "right" not to be expelled, and still less that he had some kind of "right" to honour or bodily integrity that the guard's treatment of him had violated. Rights language to capture that sort of moral prejudice would develop only during the twentieth century. In the nineteenth century, the plaintiff's interest in situations of that kind, abstract and intangible, was not just unstated, it was also largely unconceptualized. Moreover, even on the other side of the ledger, "no right" in cases of wounded feelings seems to have been thought of as much in emotional as in legal terms: "defendant had no right" often stood for "how dare you do that!" rather than "you have no legal justification for what you did."

Damages

Finally, the substantive issues we have just examined led to the question of reparation of the injury. The idea behind damages in extracontractual matters was to provide a monetary reparation for the loss the plaintiff had suffered through the defendant's fault, in other words to restore the plaintiff as nearly as possible to the same condition as before the injury. This could only ever be an approximation, however: an "Ersatz" as German law puts it.[83] In extracontractual liability, the difficulty of this act of translation, whether for material or moral injuries, hardly needs to be pointed out. It led both to judicial reluctance to award compensation for certain kinds of injury – "mere feelings" especially – as well as to considerable uncertainty among lawyers and litigants about what sorts of damages and in what amount they could claim. In the case of damages for moral injury, this raised thorny and controverted questions about how intangible injury could (or even whether it should) be turned into money, the relative roles in Quebec law of compensation and punishment for injurious behaviour, and the proper terminology for different kinds of damages.[84]

Cases of wounded feelings often included a material injury alongside the emotional one, and so they included a claim for material as well as moral damages. Grieving parents claimed funerary expenses for their accidentally killed child; a jilted fiancée sought recompense for her trousseau purchases; a Polish family whose baptismal party was broken up by police lost their investment in the beer that was confiscated. Such material loss lent itself readily to tabulation, and the courts accepted and assessed evidence of direct monetary loss. But in most cases of wounded feelings, any material injury was only a minor part of the claim, or even absent entirely. By contrast, general damages claims for moral injury could be huge: in the cases just mentioned, the bereaved parents, the abandoned fiancée, and the Polish family all alleged significant moral injuries that dwarfed their monetary losses. Indeed, that was often the point strategically for plaintiffs, as Alecia Simmonds shows for breach of promise to marry cases in Australia.[85] To reject the moral damage claim because of its subjectivity or impossibility to evaluate, as was done regarding claims for grief in certain wrongful death cases, as we will see in chapter 6, would leave plaintiffs with ludicrously small compensation – or none at all – for their proved injuries. Outside of the exception for grief, claims for general damages for emotional injury hinged on what we might call a narrative rather than actuarial basis. Certain specifics had to be established, depending on the case, to ground fault and injury, but the bulk of the plaintiff's efforts were spent in establishing the outlines of a situation that would make the resulting claimed injury undeniable to a judge.[86] This explains why direct questions along the lines of "how did you feel?" were rare, even after plaintiffs were allowed to testify on their own behalf starting in 1897. Such self-serving, abstract, and entirely subjective testimony added little; much more powerful was an objective case that drew on shared social norms and attitudes and that established that the plaintiff must have felt humiliated or mortified or otherwise aggrieved.

As this suggests, the sense of outrage in moral injury cases ("how dare you do that!") was both a great strength of those cases and a difficult problem that complicated their evaluation. Subjectivity and passion inevitably entered into the plaintiff's calculations – this helps explain the often ridiculously inflated claims – but the evaluation of injury was supposed to be a dispassionate balancing of the loss suffered, the degree of fault, and, in some cases, the situation and means of the parties. But how much was honour or marital prospects or even a life worth? Such abstractions had no agreed-upon value – indeed, it was something of a trope to assert that one's honour was so precious as to be of incalculable value. Plaintiffs in Quebec frequently echoed this in their claims, employing formulas such as this one, from a 1904 defamation case: "By these attacks on the innocence and fidelity of his fiancée, the plaintiff suffers in his feelings, his honour, his person, and his *biens* damage that no monetary compensation can make right, and that to avoid costs he will nonetheless reduce them to two hundred dollars."[87] Incalculable perhaps, but a calculation had to be made.

Unlike in France, where *injure* was treated mainly as a species of criminal offence, in Quebec it was a civil matter, and so supposedly compensatory rather than punitive. Article 1053 CCLC, the basis of civil liability, stated that one "is responsible for the damage caused by his fault to another," while article 1073 CCLC further specified that damages due the creditor "are in general the amount of the loss that he has sustained and of the profit of which he has been deprived." Here too, however, moral injury blurred an apparently clear rule. The law of damages in Quebec was a mixture, based mainly on French compensatory principles, but with certain elements foreign to French law – especially vindictive or exemplary damages – drawn from English common law.[88] Since moral injury could not be scientifically assessed, its evaluation naturally drifted towards a punitive rather than compensatory orientation. This was reflected in the terminology. As the Court of Queen's Bench put it in a celebrated 1896 case in which the lieutenant-governor of Quebec claimed defamation by a newspaper, "This damage, whether one calls it 'real' or 'exemplary,' 'general' or 'special,' 'vindictive,' 'penalty,' or 'fine,' 'punishment' or 'chastisement,' must always represent a reparation for the wrong caused to another."[89] In other words, the issue was not what damages were called, but rather what they were called upon to do – to repair the wrong caused to another. The court's confident brushing aside of complexity in that case, however, did not answer the basic question of whether repairing that wrong was to be done via compensation for the loss suffered by the plaintiff, or by some form of punishment for the wrong committed by the defendant.

Terminology for damages for moral injury was fluid and led to controversy over the question of compensation versus punishment.[90] The usual term for these damages was *exemplary* or *vindictive*, both of which underscored their symbolic role in the face of the impossibility of precise compensation. But some judges also used terms like *punitive* or *penal* and thus moved the issue from symbolism into clear chastisement, normally the role of the criminal courts.[91] Since precise compensation was impossible – indeed, the terms used often served simply as synonyms for general damages in cases without provable material loss – the calculation of damages was vague and subjective, and the amount was usually set so as to make a point. In an 1898 case from Sorel Circuit Court, for example, the plaintiff accused the defendant of telling anyone who would listen that the former had absconded with the latter's dog and kept it locked up all winter, a charge the defendant eventually admitted was groundless. The judge rejected any claim of special (material) damages, but nonetheless awarded the plaintiff ten dollars in "exemplary damages" for the "worry" (*ennui*) caused by the harassment.[92] At times awards were modest, expected to serve simply as a public affirmation of the plaintiff's injury. In an 1888 case, in which a father sued over allegations that his daughter had fornicated, the judge set damages at a relatively modest $20, since the plaintiff "seeks vindication and not money in this suit."[93] The symbolism could be literal as well, such as the twenty cents "exemplary damages" plus twenty cents costs awarded in a defamation case to a plaintiff who was found to have "grossly exaggerated" his claim.[94] In other cases the symbolism went in the opposite direction, with heavy penalties, sometimes with explicitly penal purpose, assessed against defendants whose actions bespoke malice or cruelty. In a case of defamation of ancestors that we will examine in chapter 3, for example, the Court of King's Bench reduced the trial judge's damages award from $3,000 to $200, since the latter sum was "a sufficient punishment for the fault committed by the respondent."[95] This terminological fluidity, if not the tension between compensation and sending a message, was cleared up only in the 1930s, when the Court of King's Bench ruled that although incorrect terminology would not defeat a claim, "moral damages" was the preferred name.[96]

An example from the early period will illustrate some of these issues.[97] On different occasions and in diverse contexts in 1877, James Reed, a physician of some twenty-seven years' experience, made various highly unfavourable remarks about fellow physician Reuben Levi, a recent McGill graduate, along the lines of "You are a murderer," "the most ignorant man in the profession," "mostly all his patients die after the first dose of medicine he gives them," and similar. The young physician sued for $10,000 damages. The trial judge awarded $1000 in "special and vindictive damages": "that the false and malicious accusations proffered against [the plaintiff] must have deeply wounded him, and must have caused him damage in the exercise of his profession, and in his pecuniary interests (*intérêts matériels*), is self evident."[98] The case went to the Supreme Court of Canada on various grounds, one of which was whether or not in cases of moral injury some special damage had to be proved. The Supreme Court accepted the plaintiff's argument that establishing general damage was enough, and in this case, the evidence was overwhelming. As Chief Justice William Johnstone Ritchie put it, "I do not know that in the whole course of my judicial experience I ever knew of a man who has been so persistently pursued by such slanderous, scandalous and malicious statements as was the appelant in this case."[99] In other words, establishing the self-evident nature of the claimed moral injury sufficed. Itemization was a fruitless endeavour in cases where, as Justice Télesphore Fournier pointed out, "however many heads, so many opinions," so precise evaluation was neither possible nor required.[100] Objectivity may have been the goal, but in practice subjectivity was ever present. As Justice Joseph-Guillaume Bossé of the Court of King's Bench admitted frankly in a 1908 defamation case, "The measure of these damages is not and cannot be fixed:

it must vary according to the fortune and position of the parties, their station, or their social influence, and also, it must be said, according to the balance in which each one of us weighs and evaluates the compensation to be granted and measures it in his own way, by applying it to the circumstances."[101]

This brief inquiry into some of the language surrounding moral injury in the later nineteenth century suggests a more general point that we will pursue throughout this book. If the cutting edge coming out of France (and Germany via France) employed new or newly redefined terminology like *patrimony, biens innés, moral damages*, and the like, Quebec jurists were still using older terms. As we saw, higher-level conceptual categories were largely absent: discussion hewed closely to the facts, and even legal characterizations of *injure* or *préjudice moral*, for example, drew on the vernacular language of sentiment, humiliation, honour, shame, and so forth. Codification of private law put Quebec law on a materialist footing, reflecting, as Codification Commission secretary Thomas McCord put it in 1866, "the tendency of the age ... to make Things subservient to Persons, and to bring immoveables as well as all other things under complete subjection to the will of man."[102] This vision, translated into positive law, was part of Canada's liberal project, but the practice of the law surrounding wounded feelings challenged the integrity of that materialist vision. Some aspects of moral injury – the necessity of quantifying any injury in monetary terms, for instance, or the individualistic process of "claiming" injuries – may have fit well into a nascent liberal paradigm. Other aspects, however – such as the relational nature of honour, or the class- and hierarchy-based social codes through which subjective injuries were narrated and evaluated, or most importantly for our purposes, the place of sentiments, feelings, and passions – fit less easily.[103] Alongside liberal values in law, like private ownership, freedom of contract, individual responsibility for one's actions, and the citizenship ideals of liberty and equality, were other values, in particular the affective concerns to which we now turn.

2

Shame, Mortification, Disgrace, Dishonour

Injury to one's reputation – *injure* – could result in a variety of feelings, depending on the circumstances of the situation and personal factors such as gender and social status. Plaintiffs claiming that they had been slandered or defamed or subjected to a physical affront with negative meaning used various words to express their reaction to the treatment: *shame, humiliation, mortification, dishonour, disgrace, outrage, embarrassment, horror*, and others. The precise nuances and distinctions between these feelings are difficult to separate and categorize, but all indicate an emotional state reacting to a perceived diminution of standing in the eyes of others. Turned around, these negative feelings suggest – and sometimes were expressed as – violations of positive personal assets. Those assets were various and interrelated: honour and reputation, of course, but also values like virtue and propriety. Honour and its relatives were seen as the most precious of one's *biens* – Belgian jurist François Laurent went further, calling them "the essence of our being."[1] Individuals described their reputation or honour or virtue as a kind of "treasure" that they worked diligently all their lives to build up, but it was particularly vulnerable to damage or loss in an instant, and once diminished was difficult or impossible to restore. The emotional effects of *injure* went beyond public diminution of one's standing or reputation, though that was a big part of it. The injury also included subjective feelings of offended sensibilities, such as when the way one was treated clashed with one's own assessment of one's status or self-worth. This mingling of the social and the personal – of one's performance of self and how others perceived that performance – was inflected by many factors, from ideas of masculinity and femininity to codes of behaviour linked to social standing, ethnicity, and race.[2]

This chapter will explore the feelings raised by words or actions perceived as affecting one's honour or propriety. The cases we will focus on are relatively unusual, at least as compared to more typical defamation actions such as when politicians sued newspapers. They serve, however, to bring into relief the emotional issues involved in injury to reputation. Two of the examples – a man's claim to have been dishonoured by physical treatment he received at the hands of a security guard, and a woman's claim to have been insulted by improper harassment by a railroad employee – indicate gendered distinctions between notions of honour and propriety, the former primarily male, the latter primarily female. Both notions were fluid, however, and applied to men and women, though with different nuances and different effects. Two further examples, involving a conflict over immigrants' customs regarding alcohol and a charivari in which a community expressed its disapproval of one of its members, bring in more explicitly the collective dimension of honour. They suggest how notions like honour and propriety extended beyond the individual, to become also an asset claimed and enforced collectively by a community. We begin with a hotel owner's bad day at the amusement park.

"Get Out, You Damned Sucker!": *Corbeil v. Dominion Park*

In 1906 Dominion Park was Montreal's newest and most popular summer attraction. Its grand opening on 2 June upped the ante considerably on its older and more staid competitor, Parc Sohmer.[3] Whereas Parc Sohmer had since its opening in 1889 focused more on refined activities like music and dancing (though with some vaudeville as well), the new park added thrilling mechanized rides like the Scenic Railway roller coaster and the Shoot the Chutes log flume and the scientific curiosity of live premature babies being cared for in sterile incubators, alongside more artistic pleasures like brass bands and vaudeville performers.[4] A day at the park – easily accessible by tramway, its advertisements said – was a chance to get away from the city and have some fun in a pleasant spot next to the river. An excursion to the park was also a way to see and be seen, and part of the experience was to perform one's respectability before an audience of one's peers (or hoped-for peers) – what Kathy Peiss has called the "public presentation of self."[5] Early postcards of Dominion Park show women promenading in elaborate hats and immaculate white dresses, men in suits and straw boaters.[6] The physical set-up of the park, with its long central boardwalk lined with benches, and an artificial lake around which one could stroll, facilitated this performance by ensuring that those moving through the park would always have an audience. And that audience was certainly large: on the park's first weekend, some ten thousand arrived on packed streetcars on Saturday, still a working day for most, and forty thousand on Sunday.[7]

Aside from being a pleasant recreational destination, the park was also a litigation magnet, not surprising given the inchoate state of amusement park safety at the time. During construction a building collapsed, injuring eighteen workers, at least one of whom sued for his injuries.[8] The roller coaster, its most thrilling and thus most dangerous ride, was the subject of unwanted publicity two months after opening, when an "aged gentleman" was thrown from the car during a descent and suffered serious injuries. The following year he successfully sued for almost $1700 in damages.[9] A major fire in 1907 caused an estimated $200,000 in damage to the park, though there were no injuries, while a larger 1919 fire killed at least seven.[10] The dense crowds also had their darker side: alongside the middle-class respectability of the promenaders, newspapers reported pickpockets and other shady operators at work in the park.[11]

This combination of performed and evaluated respectability lay behind an incident on 21 June 1906 at the ticket window to the Scenic Railway, the park's most popular attraction with up to ten thousand riders a day, and with wait times to match.[12] Wilfrid Corbeil was at the park that day with his friend and business associate Léon Couture. Corbeil was around forty-one years old and owned the Grand Hotel, located in the shadow of Montreal's courthouse.[13] Its dining room was a regular haunt of court workers and lawyers, which no doubt gave Corbeil some familiarity with the workings of the law, which might help to explain his actions in what followed. Corbeil also had more direct experience with the legal system: in 1894 he was charged with aiding the escape of a fugitive (he was acquitted), and in 1904 he was charged with liquor licence violations at his "Black Cat" saloon (he claimed he had been unaware of the actions of an employee).[14] Corbeil and Couture decided they wanted to ride the Scenic Railway, but hoped to avoid the ticket line, which extended halfway across the park. Couture spotted an acquaintance, Charles-Édouard Lamoureux, near the front of the line with his family, and handed him some money, asking him to buy them tickets. One can easily imagine what those behind Lamoureux thought of this; queue jumpers were a continual problem at that attraction, and so the park specially assigned a security guard to keep order at the ticket booth.[15] When Lamoureux got to the ticket window, he was evidently fed up with waiting in line. Unhappy with the speed at which nineteen-year-old ticket seller Sarah Caveny was serving the man in front of him, Lamoureux stuck his hand into the window with a dollar bill and demanded service, in the process knocking over Caveny's carefully arranged piles of change. She told him to keep his hands out of the wicket and threatened not to let him have any tickets, and he (depending on whose story one accepts) either politely said he wanted his tickets please, or berated Caveny in a loud voice. The incident attracted the attention of the guard, twenty-four-year old ex-soldier Theodore Lauezzari, who seems to have taken Lamoureux by the arm to lead him out of the line; Lamoureux stood his ground. Both sides agreed that the incident then calmed down, and Lamoureux and his family started towards the entrance to the roller coaster, with Corbeil and Couture in tow.

At this point Corbeil decided to get involved. Once again the stories diverged, this time sharply, but what seems clear is that Corbeil handed his card to Lamoureux, offering to be a witness in any legal action he might be considering. Lamoureux's wife, Marie Falardeau, said Corbeil announced Lauezzari's badge number, while Lauezzari said Corbeil threatened to get him fired, though Corbeil denied both of these allegations.[16] Corbeil's intervention had the effect (according to the constable) of reanimating Lamoureux, who "started the racket fresh again."[17] During the argument that followed, Corbeil seems to have touched Lauezzari on the arm several times, despite warnings that he should stop doing so and that he should stay out of the matter. Fed up, the constable turned on Corbeil and (according to Corbeil and his witnesses) smacked him on the head, shouted, "Get out, you damned sucker!" and then frog-marched him away from the line, knocking his hat off and dirtying his suit in the process. Lauezzari denied the remark and the crack on the head, but admitted he "shoved him along" about twenty feet at "a good step."[18] At this point, Lamoureux, Corbeil, and the rest

Figure 2.1 Ticket line at the Scenic Railway roller coaster, Dominion Park, Montreal, c. 1910. Collection of Larry Kredl, reproduced with permission.

of their party went to the park's management to complain, though according to defence witnesses the complaint centred on Lamoureux's ill treatment, not Corbeil's.[19] Two and a half weeks later Corbeil sued the Dominion Park Company for $500 in damages for the "profound humiliation" caused to "an honest and peaceful citizen" by Lauezzari's assault and insults, done with "the malicious intention to injure the plaintiff's reputation and to do him wrong and to disgrace him as a criminal in the eyes of his fellow citizens."[20]

As in other cases we will examine in this book, Corbeil's feelings and his strategy were closely aligned but still distinct. A large part of his strategy was to narrate the circumstances in a way that highlighted the insult and dishonour he claimed to have suffered, so as to make them appear self-evident to a judge. Though Corbeil's declaration employed the usual formula that he had been injured "in his honour, in his person, in his *biens* and his feelings," he made no claims for nor offered any evidence of material or physical injury.[21] The smack on the head and the dirty suit were not claimed as injuries in their own right, but were part of the circumstances to demonstrate purely moral prejudice: the implication given to onlookers – friends and strangers alike – that he was "a swindler, a thief, and an exploiter who allowed himself to attend performances without paying the price of admission."[22] As for the defence, its task was to create an equally self-evident counter-narrative of impolite and dishonourable behaviour (cutting in line, pestering the guard) to justify the actions of its employee. Each side also presented other, more formally legal arguments, in particular concerning the duties of a constable and whether Lauezzari had been justified in acting as he had, but the crucial points were the feelings-based arguments about Corbeil's wounded honour and whether in fact he was honourable at all.

At the hearing, eleven witnesses testified, including all the principals. Although the stories diverged in significant ways, all versions pointed to a clash in which different views of honour and proper behaviour confronted one another, exacerbated by class and linguistic differences. In Corbeil's eyes, the case was all about "insults" or dishonour towards respectable men: both himself and Lamoureux. He got involved in the first place, he testified, to stick up for Lamoureux whom Lauezzari had called a scoundrel or something similar: "I know Mr. Lamoureux a bit, he's a merchant tailor and his wife and two daughters were there; it was an insult."[23] Once his officious intervention turned Lauezzari's attention onto himself, the dishonour became personal: "Naturally everyone was looking at me, no one knew whether I was right or wrong; it was a great insult."[24] The insult ran throughout the testimony – Lamoureux's wife, Marie Falardeau, reported her husband's words as "You two saw it, you're witnesses that this policeman touched me; it's an insult."[25] Lauezzari's treatment of the two men jarred with their own self-images of respectability. In his factum for the Court of Review, Corbeil (or more accurately his lawyers, but the sentiments accord closely with his testimony) succinctly noted "that it is very humiliating for a respectable citizen to be pushed around by a constable in front of a large crowd.... No amount of money can indemnify such an affront."[26]

The insult, however, was not just Corbeil's personal sense that the security guard was not treating him as he should, it was that the way he was being treated was sending unfavourable messages to the various audiences watching: Lamoureux's family, Corbeil's friend Léon Couture, and the other patrons. All witnesses agreed that a lot of people were standing around watching: the park was busy that evening, and bored people standing in line were eager for diversion. While a day at the park was about performance, it was supposed to be performance on one's own terms: one wasn't supposed to be the entertainment. Here was a security guard, a social inferior, setting up respectable people as objects of suspicion or ridicule. Of course, the audience might have taken Corbeil's side, or it might have viewed his cutting into line as dishonourable. The only non-interested onlooker who testified did so for Corbeil, not the defence, so the reactions of the other onlookers remain unknown.[27] The audience's reaction was not, strictly speaking, the point, however. The unwanted attention from strangers was itself the key element of the insult and dishonour of the situation: it wasn't what any of them had bargained for when they headed to the park that evening. Marie Falardeau made explicit the sense of disconnect between the park as place of respectable amusement and the unwelcome scrutiny they had suffered: "That drew attention to Mr. Corbeil and the rest of us. When you go to a place like that and you're insulted as well, you can understand that all eyes were on us."[28]

The performances and perceptions alike were complicated by the linguistic differences that frequently affected situations like this in Montreal. I will explore more about the politics of language in this case below, in comparison with another similar affair in which the lines of social class and language aligned differently. On a more practical level, however, the sense of control over one's public persona could easily be shaken when one's audience spoke a different language and one could not be certain who that audience was or how they were reacting.

Several of the witnesses noted in their testimony that they had trouble following what was said in the other language. Ticket seller Sarah Caveny could not understand Lamoureux's remarks made in French to his family, but she assumed they were insulting her.[29] Both Lamoureux and Corbeil misunderstood Caveny's injunction to Lamoureux to keep his hands "out of the wicket," hearing instead "Keep your dirty hands in your pockets."[30] Corbeil's friend Couture heard Lauezzari say "God damn" but understood nothing else he said.[31] Lamoureux's wife and daughter understood none of the English at all and watched the situation as if it were a pantomime of sorts.[32] Though the depositions in the case file preserve only words on a page, the subtle politics of language and accent no doubt strongly contributed to the unfolding of events and how they were perceived.

Tangled up with Corbeil's self-image as an honourable businessman who did not deserve to be treated like a thief were issues of masculinity that complicated his reactions of dishonour and insult.[33] The initial confrontation between Lauezzari and Lamoureux was filled with male bluster. Lauezzari was a large ex-soldier, and Lamoureux himself was a big man. His reaction to the constable's order to leave the line was first to stand his ground stubbornly, but then, according to Couture's testimony, to challenge his challenger: "Let me at him, I can eat two or three like him for breakfast."[34] Corbeil, however, was a small man, and some sport was made of him during the hearing. Lorne McAllen, head cashier at the park, referred to him as "a little bit of a shaver" and "a little bit of a fellow," despite himself being scarcely larger, as the judge wryly pointed out.[35] Sarah Caveny too referred to Corbeil as "the little fellow."[36] Despite his size, his intervention was similar to Lamoureux's, at least at first: he resisted the constable's instructions and sought to take control of the situation himself. Lauezzari, however, confronted with a much smaller man who was pestering him and threatening to have him fired, reacted by asserting his physical dominance. When asked on cross-examination, "You were not going to stand and take lip from anybody?" Lauezzari's reply was, "I would not be a soldier if I did." He reported that when he "shoved him along," "it was very easy for me." Corbeil at first resisted, but by the end "he was very quiet and did not say a word."[37] This defeated, deflated reaction to being dragged around like a rag doll by a much larger man, all done before a staring audience, contributed to Corbeil's sense of insult. The humiliation of the scene was not lost on Falardeau: "For myself, I'd rather be punched than pushed around like that."[38]

Finally, this story of course had two sides, and alongside the aggressive and defensive performance of male honour were norms of propriety and manners. Corbeil clearly saw the situation as a malicious implication that he was a thief, trying to get in without paying. The defence, however, challenged his respectability by depicting the incident as involving a rude and intrusive patron intervening "in a noisy, objectionable and unwarranted manner" where he had no business.[39] From Lauezzari's perspective, the situation was about policing rude behaviour that would incommode other guests. Corbeil's handing money into the line so he would not have to wait at the back was something the constable had seen before: he even claimed he had seen Corbeil try to do it on past occasions and had told him to get in line.[40] More seriously, he took offence at how both Lamoureux and Corbeil treated the young woman selling tickets. He saw himself as chivalrously coming to Caveny's rescue, reacting when Lamoureux shouted at her and upbraiding him "that he should not shout and talk to a girl like that."[41] Caveny herself testified that Lamoureux had rushed her, called her names, swore at her, told her to shut her mouth, and generally spoke "roughly" to her. His failure to apologize for knocking over her money – as a respectable gentleman would have done – led her to threaten to withhold his tickets, since "I was a lady, and I did not think I was entitled to that treatment."[42] Lamoureux saw the situation differently, of course: he heard her tell him to keep his "dirty hands" out of her space, which he might have interpreted as implying that he was working class. He replied that his hands were just as clean as hers.[43]

After this rich testimony, with insults and emotional reactions on all sides, the judgments in the case were rather thin and legalistic. The judges left mostly unstated (though certainly not unobserved) the complex web of ideas about honour and propriety with which they had been presented. At trial, Justice John Sprott Archibald found in Corbeil's favour and awarded him $100 and costs. He delivered his judgment from the bench, an indication of the self-evident nature of the alleged injury. He stressed the duties of a constable and an employer's liability for the acts of its employees, and held that despite the constable's "duty of keeping order," he had "no right to lay his hands upon the Plaintiff." In escalating the situation so quickly, Lauezzari "appears to have been governed by anger at some remarks" of the plaintiff and did not follow proper procedure. Aside from repeating almost word-for-word Corbeil's declaration, the judge said nothing about the nature of the claimed injury or its proof.[44]

The company appealed to the Court of Review and tried valiantly to shift the analysis towards the question of damage. They argued that Corbeil had offered no proof of damage, and that as a result the damages awarded were excessive. On the subject of the incident itself, they argued that Corbeil had imposed himself into a discussion that did not concern him, had refused to stay out of it, and as a consequence had interfered with their constable's performance of his duties.[45] For his part, Corbeil addressed the issue of damage in words designed to appeal to the judges' common sense and their appreciation of shared social codes: "Would it not be a supreme degree of humiliation for the plaintiff to be dragged around like that when he had done absolutely nothing against order or good manners? What right does a constable have to drag a peaceful citizen around like that, without putting him under arrest?"[46] He offered the judges a handy psychological profile of Lauezzari as "a former English soldier used to very rigid discipline.... He is touchy and overly sensitive. He is arrogant."[47] As to evidence of damage, the circumstances of the case were self-evident, Corbeil argued, and in any case, as he reminded the Court of Review at some length, the sufficiency or not of evidence was up to the appreciation of the trial judge.[48] The review court agreed and affirmed the trial decision, though Justice Siméon Pagnuelo dissented, likely on the amount of damages. The majority took it as a given that injury would be caused by a constable who "satisfied his ruffled feelings by striking the plaintiff savagely on the head and handling him roughly and abusively addressing him."[49]

Varieties of Honour and Dishonour

Wilfrid Corbeil's successful case against the amusement park and its overzealous security guard brings forward certain key issues surrounding honour and dishonour. Though the incident was perhaps rather trivial in legal terms, it was clearly far from trivial for Corbeil, who claimed highly subjective injuries – feelings of humiliation and dishonour – resulting from his treatment that day. The judges for the most part agreed, but in coming to their decisions, they had to balance various understandings of honour and dishonour: Corbeil's, their own, and their evaluation of where Corbeil's claim stood in relation to collective and fluid social norms. This interplay between the personal and the social ran through all cases involving honour and dishonour, though in varied ways.

Clearly honour and law were distinct normative orders: that is obvious from the history of duelling (which was not in evidence in Quebec during our period) and the practice of charivari (which was, as we will see below). Just as clearly, the legal order asserted jurisdiction over parts of the world of honour, and primacy over the entirety of that world when its manifestations contravened written law. Translating honour-based values or norms into legal values or norms raised various problems, not least of which was negotiating between subjective and objective views of honour. From one perspective, honour and honourableness were highly subjective, and what would be perceived to dishonour one person may have had little effect on another. From another perspective, however, subjectivity was beside the point, since honour was also – perhaps principally – something whose existence only the judgment of others could determine.

Honour and its cognates – reputation, consideration, virtue, propriety, respectability – could be engaged in a great variety of situations, including words, images, implications of various kinds, and physical encounters like the stereotypical nobleman slapping a rival in the face with his glove. And if honour itself appeared in different guises and under different labels, that fluidity extended also to the articulation of its opposites: the feelings associated with the loss or violation of honour. Cases like *Corbeil* suggest the subtleties of terminology and the feelings behind it, as litigants, helped by their lawyers, used various words to describe their emotional injuries in situations that threatened their honour. Aside from the catch-all dishonour, parties asserted their shame, humiliation, embarrassment, mortification, and disgrace, synonyms to an extent, but each with slightly different valence and resonance in societies that were honour-conscious but ever-changingly so. In this section, we will draw out some issues surrounding the emotions attached to honour to provide context for the cases on which we will focus in the remainder of the chapter.

Honour is a slippery concept. Called by some obsolete or a "red herring" in the present-day West, in the nineteenth and early twentieth centuries it was a powerful notion, mentioned by name or by analogues in virtually every moral injury case.[50] Duels were fought over it (though by this period not in Quebec), it policed class boundaries, and it was a shorthand way to articulate both patriarchal norms and gender identity.[51] For centuries, honour had been the jealously guarded preserve of the nobility.[52] With the inevitable democratization of honour, claimed first by nobility-aping merchant elites, then by certain professionals, then by everyone else, came the democratization of dishonour and its blurring with the more universal emotions of shame or humiliation. If anyone could be honourable, then so too could anyone be dishonoured, at least unless they had already frittered away their honour through their own actions. The widening scope of the injury of dishonour strengthened the connection between honour and the law. Honour was certainly a legal idea – in Quebec, for instance, article 242 CCLC stipulated, "A child, whatever may be his age, owes honor and respect to his father and mother" – but a particularly fluid and hard to define legal idea. The difficulty was because honour was also, and more potently, a social idea that infused the legal process. The language of honour and dishonour allowed parties, lawyers, and judges alike to try to keep the framework of society in comprehensible alignment with its morality. Eva Circé-Côté, for example, addressing the women of Quebec in 1903, linked honour to general morality and saw both as social bulwarks against ever-encroaching capitalism and cupidity: "What will happen to our race, if we let the sentiment of honour atrophy among the younger generation? Woe if the holy fire comes to be extinguished! We the vestals set up to protect it will be buried alive in this flood of egoism that rises, ever rises, and threatens to overrun us."[53] Ideas like this made clear that honour was a kind of individual *bien* that one held, guarded, and transacted as part of one's social persona. Indeed, the language of property and treasure ran throughout discussions of honour and defamation in this period, as we saw above. But honour was at the same time something beyond the individual and the liberal individualism on which law came to focus during the nineteenth century. It was also a collective and relational interest that manifested in individuals. As an aspect of social morality, when subjectively perceived violations of that morality were brought to court, adjudicating those cases involved balancing an individual's feelings against the relevant social norms that both informed those feelings and provided the standards against which to judge them. In short, one's honour was an individual value, but it was always an individual value forged and affirmed in contact with the assessments of others.[54]

If we start briefly at the legal level, the law of honour and dishonour was a highly technical and quite fluid part of Quebec law. As we saw in chapter 1, *injure* was caught between the competing pulls of French and English traditions. In the early Quebec cases, judges, especially anglophone ones, could get considerably worked up about those distinctions and which set of rules applied to particular cases or to Quebec law generally. In 1866, for example, Justice William Badgley grappled with the notion of malice, stating confidently that "the jurisprudence of this Province has necessarily followed the English practice as in all respects the most fitting and convenient." Still, he continued by noting that both English and French authors agreed that it was the "legal signification" of malice (the speaker's intention) that applied, rather than its common usage (ill will).[55] Debates like this about tradition tied closely into a series of related technical questions, and nineteenth-century defamation cases went back and forth about defences such as privilege, private communications, provocation, and reconciliation between the parties. This fluidity included the place of feelings within this technical domain of law, and both traditions recognized (though English law had exceptions and particular evidentiary requirements) that certain remarks could on their own cause a compensable moral injury. By the early twentieth century many of the questions had been resolved, and Quebec defamation law settled into a hybrid of French and English traditions.[56]

Central to the analysis of honour was its dual nature, at once public and private. On a theoretical level, private litigation over honour blurred into wider public concerns, and the law of defamation was an early site in Quebec for discussion of certain civil liberties.[57] This moving between private and public law challenged the exclusivity of those developing conceptual categories, and for many judges, defamation actions, particularly but not exclusively those involving libel in the press, became quasi-constitutional cases. Here the English influence was particularly marked, as judges grounded their analysis in English constitutional principles like freedom of the press, ideas unknown to old French law, and this in turn shifted analysis from the plaintiff's injury to the defendant's attempts at justification.[58] A politician accused of Freemasonry or a trader called bankrupt or not credit-worthy had (once this was proved) obviously suffered an injury, even if putting a dollar value on that injury remained difficult. The thorny question, however, was the breadth of public interest in cases like this, since a line had to be drawn to determine when publication of damaging facts was justified and when it was not. In an 1889 case, for example, in which a voter circulated anticlerical remarks made by the defendant, who was a candidate in the provincial election, the Superior Court carefully balanced public rights of commentary against even a candidate's right to a degree of privacy, to find that the defendant had far exceeded his rights as a voter to comment on the merits of the candidates. The Court of Queen's Bench, however, unanimously allowed the appeal: the public's right – duty, even – to raise true points relevant to an election was unfettered, even when those points touched the candidate's private views or morality.[59] Not all judges would have gone so far, and when the words aimed at the public figure were untrue or doubtful – such as when a newspaper levelled allegations of illegal influence at Quebec Lieutenant Governor Auguste-Réal Angers – the courts were quick to allow the claims.[60] But in such cases, the attention was on the effects of the situation on the workings of the polity, rather than on the feelings of those involved. For private individuals, by contrast, the analysis of honour was more personal, as judges evaluated different variables to determine whether the individual had honour, how much effect the situation complained of had on that honour, and what was a reasonable way to repair whatever damage had been caused.

On a more individual level, honour was both a value plaintiffs sought to protect and a standard against which to judge both defendant and plaintiff. It could serve, in other words, as both shield and sword. Usually honour was something a plaintiff asserted and sought to vindicate – the concept served as an individual shield against attacks by others. In the 1880 case of the lawyer expelled from the hotel mentioned in chapter 1, the lawyer's response to being led out to the street was to assert, "I am a gentleman," a self-assessment the owner challenged, since (allegedly) it was said in a loud, disruptive voice and was followed with the statement that "he would be damned if he would pick up the paper" he was accused of throwing on the floor.[61] The plaintiff was thus asserting his professional and personal respectability in the face of treatment that called his honour into question. It worked, and he was awarded modest damages for having "suffered morally" as a result of "disgraceful treatment."[62] In some other cases, however, defendants or judges explicitly used honour as a sword rather than a shield, as a standard against which to measure plaintiff's conduct (and generally to find it wanting). In an 1897 case involving two rival candidates for the federal riding of L'Assomption, east of Montreal, the defendant allegedly said at a candidates' nomination meeting that the plaintiff had "sold himself as a candidate" in the previous federal election by accepting dubious sums of money. Justice John Joseph Curran found for the plaintiff, though he awarded only one per cent of the $10,000 damages sought. Despite the plaintiff's technically successful result, the judge upbraided him for seeming to care more about monetary damages than the vindication of his name, chastising him for having "neglected to do that which a man of sensitive honor would have done at once," namely immediately returning the money when he learned of its questionable provenance.[63] Intersecting senses of honour mingled and conflicted in this case: the plaintiff's own conception of his honour and the judge's standard of what an honourable man ought to do.

If we move beyond the legal side of the issue, the social values and norms surrounding honour often conflicted with the legal rules. Legally, some cases involving honour were more difficult than others, since the complaints of private individuals, women in particular, could seem (to male judges) to be "mere feelings" in ways that cases of defamed politicians or businessmen were not. But though some judges dismissed mere feelings, many more did not, because to do so would be to deny and subvert the social morality that honour represented. So the social continually intervened in the legal, and lawyers and judges had to negotiate the social codes of honour in addition to the legal rules. Lawyers invoked ideas of honourability and played up humiliation in an effort to convince judges of the defendant's reprehensibility and the plaintiff's suffering. Judges had to negotiate those codes themselves, trying to avoid simply applying their own notions of honour and dishonour. In some cases, however, this led judges to reject the strict applicability of the legal rules in favour of social norms. In an 1887 case, Justice Jonathan Wurtele found that news articles attacking the president of the Saint-Jean-Baptiste Society for alleged insults to Cardinal Taschereau, while true and so not in themselves libellous or defamatory, were nonetheless injurious to the plaintiff, and damages were warranted.[64]

This tension between defamation law and social propriety came out most clearly when press freedom was involved. Many judges took a dim view of an abstract and still unwritten constitutional principle, whatever its antiquity, when its application threatened values of decency and respectability. In the sensational libel case between Édouard-Charles Fabre, archbishop of Montreal, and the liberal *Canada Revue*, Justice Henri-Thomas Taschereau voiced the opinion of many of his fellow judges that "the press is an immense army that has already conquered the world." Though "it has its regular battalions, commanded by elite officers,... it also has its undisciplined hordes, the leaders of which are most often bandits, and the soldiers nothing but barbarians. Mind the latter's poisoned arrows! The state is seldom able to stop the excesses of these soldiers of fortune."[65] Some, of course, held the contrary position, such as Justice François Langelier, who argued strenuously in dissent in an 1899 appeal case that especially in the context of an election, any limits at all on vigorous public debate were a dangerous precedent.[66] But for most judges, when the press was simply feeding public appetite for scandal in an effort to sell more papers, public interest diminished to vanishing. Justice Charles Doherty made this point in 1903: "People who sacrifice the honor, the feelings and the reputations of others, in their endeavours to outstrip their rivals in the publication of sensational news, must be prepared to substantially indemnify the victims of their reckless haste to publish matter that to say the least, were as well unpublished."[67] Justice Doherty's reference to feelings makes clear the distinction: though legal rules meant something, social norms were important too.

Outside the public context, however, the moral aspects of *injure* came forward more clearly. In cases like Wilfrid Corbeil's, judges moved beyond the usual analysis of defences with an assessment of the plaintiff's injury, in effect shifting the analysis towards the social politics of honour and dishonour. While reputation and good name were central to all cases of defamation and *injure*, in political, professional, and commercial contexts the injury to reputation might best be described as more material than emotional. The politician, the businessman, the professional were not really complaining that their feelings were hurt (though the usual formula employed in their declarations might use that vocabulary), but rather that their reputation or honour had been materially attacked in such a way as to lose them votes or sales or the confidence of their clientele. Outside those contexts, by contrast, the main injury was more moral than material: individuals like Corbeil went to court because the insulting remarks or treatment caused them feelings of dishonour or humiliation or mortification. This was "material" injury in the sense that their *biens* had been diminished, but the *biens* were moral rather than material, linked more to self-image and social persona than to financial or political or professional prospects.

The distinction – with some overlap, to be sure – involved differing balances between the public and private injuries of defamation. One's honour always comprised public and private dimensions, what German criminal law theorist Moritz Liepmann termed "objectified" versus "subjectified" honour. The former was an individual's good reputation, created by and dependent on the assessment of others: what some French writers called *considération*. The latter, which some French authors called *honneur*, and which reflected Jean-Jacques Rousseau's idea of *amour propre*, was an individual's own perceived self-worth, shaped to an extent by others, but mainly a self-construction that might be at odds with one's public image.[68] This distinction moreover captures the two aspects of *injure* – the material and reputational injury in the eyes of others on the one side, and the emotional injury to one's self-worth on the other.

Judges had to make difficult assessments of both senses of honour, drawing on their knowledge of social norms as well as on their understanding or intuition of how individuals felt different kinds of insults. The difficulty judges had in assessing those feelings was really no different from the difficulty in assessing any type of abstract injury, or even from the difficulty in compensating material injury via equivalents. But the feminine overtones of concepts like "feeling" or "sentiment" made some judges reluctant. This meant that in most cases, "objectified" honour drove the analysis, even when what was objectified was the feelings that an individual claimed to experience. The community's role in defining and assessing honour, filtered through lawyers' and judges' views of common sense, was thus crucial, even if in most cases the emotional communities at issue varied and overlapped. In practice, when judges applied the various social norms surrounding honour and dishonour to the particular individuals standing in their courtrooms, the key variables were class and gender.

Class was a powerful determinant, as insults that would be seen as mortifying to someone of elevated social standing were expected to be borne by those less fortunately placed. In an 1874 case from the Circuit Court of St-Jean-sur-Richelieu, a maid who had served eight months in the defendant's employ without incident was one day asked (politely) to open her bag as she was leaving the house. The maid sued for the insult, but Judge Hubert-Wilfrid Chagnon dismissed her case, finding that a servant must bear a certain amount of "bruised feelings."[69] It would be an actionable insult to a servant if a master acted rudely or with violence or threats, but in this case a pleasant request to see the bag was perfectly acceptable. The master, in short, had behaved in a gentlemanly manner in keeping with his station, and a social inferior could have no complaint about that. *Injure* was not symmetrical, of course, and insults of the master by the servant were dealt with much more strictly than those going the other way. Inferiors were expected to handle a certain amount of suspicion and moderately insulting behaviour: their honour, such as it was, was less highly developed and so less susceptible to injury. Only when the behaviour complained of was truly excessive – when the social superior acted without honour – would an action succeed. A good illustration of these ideas comes from a long and bitter battle between two affluent and well-connected spouses over separation from bed and board and custody of their children.[70] The wife, Mary Stevenson, was the daughter of a wealthy Montreal merchant, while her husband, Maurice Day Baldwin, was a former Anglican minister, son of an Anglican bishop, and grandson of Robert Baldwin, one of Canada's fathers of responsible government. A key issue was the coarse language Baldwin habitually directed at his wife and children, and whether it rose to the level of "grievous insult," one of the grounds for legal separation. As one of the justices at the Court of King's Bench put it in awarding provisional custody of the children to the wife, "There is no excuse for the vulgar, improper and blasphemous epithets applied by respondent to his sons who are of an impressionable age. The respondent is a man of education and good parentage and is either a degenerate or perhaps, to take a more charitable view, his condition is the result of habitual use of intoxicating liquors."[71] Another judge, in a different part of the same case, put it differently, but the point was the same: "One must, in matters like this, consider the social position of the parties, their age, their habits, all the things that increase or lessen the gravity of the facts alleged. It is thus probable that a rude word would not be injurious if the parties lacked schooling or education."[72] Ordinary insults, in other words, were expected to be sloughed off, especially by people of lower social class, while those crossing the line to "grievous" or "considerable" were beyond anyone's tolerance. The line, however, shifted, depending on who was the target and who was the speaker.

Alongside and intersecting with class was gender, and it too was a crucial variable in how cases of honour were narrated, argued, and adjudicated. We saw this already in Wilfrid Corbeil's reactions to being manhandled by a large security guard. But few things called forth the chivalric impulses of elderly male judges more decisively than an attack on a woman's virtue. Judges were of course equally capable of being blinded by patriarchy and seeing women as schemers and connivers, especially in cases of sexual assault or seduction, but in situations where a woman's sexual reputation was unquestioned, judges were quick to construct around her elaborate codes of womanly virtue and respectability. Virtue intersected with class, however, and judges' chivalry was more readily directed towards socio-economically worthy women and girls. The following case, in many ways similar to Wilfrid Corbeil's, and from about the same time, was in important respects markedly different, since the protagonist was a wealthy woman. Her case brought assumptions of class into conversation with norms of propriety and respectable femininity, and it presents an instructive contrast to Corbeil's wounded masculinity.

No Proper Way to Treat a Lady: *Tudor v. Quebec & Lake St. John Railway*

Alongside attacks on honour and virtue, violations of norms of propriety were fertile ground for emotional injury. As with virtue, propriety was a heavily gendered notion, and one in which the gender dynamics intersected in complex ways with social standing. What was proper, what actions were perceived as improper, and how affronts affected different individuals all mapped onto social ideas about class, respectability, and normative femininity and masculinity. For women (and men, though the issues raised and the appropriate responses differed) of elevated social standing, improper treatment by perceived social inferiors could be particularly offensive, and result in an emotional response that might seem excessive in other circumstances. Judges and lawyers, themselves of elevated social standing, tended to read the social dynamics in certain situations through the eyes of the socially superior party. This turned fluid norms of propriety into more rigid standards that supported strong de facto legal presumptions, difficult for any defendant to rebut, but especially hard for those of lower social standing. Add to this social norms of chivalry towards women, and certain situations were strongly in the plaintiff's favour, so that their claims of emotional injury came to seem so self-evident as to brush aside the "mere feelings" obstacle. Such was the case in an apparently trivial, though strongly felt, situation on a train waiting to depart from Quebec City in 1908.[73]

On 30 July of that year, as Quebec City's tercentenary celebrations were winding down and the huge crowds were beginning to leave the city, Euphemia Tudor and her family were leaving town for their country home at Lake St. Joseph, a pleasant spot about an hour by train north of the city.[74] There were eight in the party – Euphemia, her two children, her mother, her sister-in-law, and three servants – as well as all their luggage. They arrived at the station more than twenty minutes early, both to beat the expected rush and because one of the children had injured her knee and needed to be carried. The train to Lake St. Joseph, on the Quebec & Lake St. John Railway, had two first-class cars, one nearly full, the other mostly empty. The family went into the empty car, only to be told by conductor Antoine Cantin that that car would be left behind since it was too empty to justify making the trip, and would they please shift to the other car. Tudor immediately went over his head, complaining to the stationmaster. Cantin's boss ordered him to keep both cars. The family settled into the empty car (which was beginning to fill up), and the train departed.

The actors in this developing drama presented a strong contrast. Tudor was a wealthy anglophone woman, about thirty-three years old, originally from Boston and only recently come to Quebec. Her husband, Edward Slade, was a prosperous electrical engineer, and when they were not summering at the chalet, the family lived in a fashionable part of town, on St. Louis Street near the Grande Allée. Tudor was clearly a decisive and strong personality. In 1919 she unsuccessfully sued the Pullman Company for allegedly causing her daughter to catch pneumonia when a conductor refused to close a ventilator in their compartment; Tudor eventually closed it herself.[75] A few years after that she obtained a parliamentary divorce from her husband on the grounds of adultery, and took up writing, publishing short stories in various magazines.[76]

Cantin was a working-class francophone man, about thirty-six years old. He lived not so far geographically from the Slade-Tudor home, but quite far removed socio-economically: on a decidedly less fashionable street near the Grey Nuns' residence. He had been employed by the railway for around fifteen years, but (as Tudor's lawyers uncovered) had been previously dismissed a few years earlier – something about negligence that caused a collision between two freight trains. Questions by Tudor's lawyers to the railway's assistant superintendent about whether Cantin had been drunk at the time were disallowed on objection, though as we will see the judge in Tudor's case might have picked up the hint.[77] These differences in gender, social standing, and language were important to the situation that unfolded on the train.

When Cantin came to the Tudor party to collect their tickets, a quarrel began. Tudor wanted to use one adult ticket to pay for her two half-price children; she claimed she always did this. Cantin (no doubt ill-inclined to agree with Tudor about anything by this time) objected. He testified later that he thought the older child looked too old for the reduced fare, but he seems not to have said anything at this point.[78] Tudor, rather peremptorily one imagines, told Cantin she would make inquiries about the ticket prices at Lake St. Joseph and if necessary would remit any extra money owed to the railway later. Cantin continued on his

Figure 2.2 "Mr. Slade's Residence" at Lake St. Joseph, Quebec, c. 1906, photographed by William Notman & Son. McCord Museum, VIEW-4108. Reproduced with permission.

rounds (grumbling, no doubt, but what could he say?). While he was gone, Tudor spoke with another man – a francophone stranger, and a "gentleman" – who was travelling with three small children. This man told her that he regularly used one adult ticket for all three children without any questions. When Cantin returned – by this time the train had progressed a few stops to Charlesbourg – Tudor resumed the discussion, reporting what the gentleman had told her. Cantin denied that there had been any such man on the train (the man had by this time disembarked). According to Tudor, "He said there was no such person on the train,... that I was not the Manager of the Road, and I would kindly mind my own business." She countered by invoking her honour: "I said: Do you mean to say that I am a liar? He said: Yes, I do; yes, I do – twice."[79] Cantin's version was similar, but diverged in important ways. To her accusation that he said she was lying, he replied (reporting the conversation as it had transpired in English), "No Madam, it would not be polite, I am only telling you that I don't believe – and I repeated it once more after the same thing."[80]

That was the verbal part of the incident, and on its face it would seem to be a trivial case. Cantin implied Tudor was lying, but only after Tudor had challenged him to draw that very conclusion. Had this been a case of defamation, it would have been difficult for Tudor to succeed. But Tudor's complaint was not about her reputation, but rather about the wounded feelings Cantin had caused her by his conduct during the whole situation of which the words were only a small part. Her experience on the train that day led her to sue the company for $100 in damages. The action was instituted in explicitly emotional terms: "The conduct of the said Conductor in the public car was of a nature to insult, vex, damage and mortify the plaintiff and actually did insult, vex, damage and mortify Plaintiff, and Plaintiff is entitled to be compensated therefor."[81]

A closer look at the incident as it developed provides a clearer idea of why Tudor felt so aggrieved that litigation was her only recourse. The situation was one that challenged the boundaries of propriety set and negotiated within a particular emotional community, which could give rise to the feelings of mortification, vexation, and insult alleged in the declaration. In assessing her situation, Tudor had to think about the limits of acceptable conduct of a train employee towards a lady in a first-class car, and more generally the acceptable treatment of a woman by a man. On the other side, and complicating the matter, was the acceptable conduct of a woman towards a social inferior.

Beyond the exchange of words, the principals' narratives in their testimony read something like a theatrical piece, with people moving through the train "set" to interact in various places with gestures and body language filled with meaning and that help clarify responses to the situation. As Tudor testified, she and Cantin had a series of verbal encounters, but body language was as important as the words spoken. During the first exchange on the train, Cantin – according to Tudor, but this was corroborated by other witnesses – positioned himself on the arm of the seat opposite her, and leaned in as he argued with her. He was slightly higher than she was, a mildly aggressive posture. Tudor said Cantin was speaking "in a very loud tone of voice, very roughly," Cantin said similar about Tudor, and both agreed that other passengers were looking in curiosity at the disturbance. Tudor's mother, watching, urged her daughter to leave the scene, saying "the man was crazy and I had better leave him alone."[82] Tudor's first reaction was to turn her head away from Cantin. He interpreted that as rudeness, but to her it was both a sign of her irritation and an indication of her mortification at the affront presented by Cantin's aggression towards her. It was a first attempt to preserve a proper distance from this man who was invading her space. When Cantin continued talking at her, she got up and moved to the back of the car, where she sat down, far from the rest of her party. But according to Cantin, it was Tudor who was behaving aggressively during this first altercation. He said he was calmly sitting on the armrest explaining himself, when she stood up – now she was higher than he was – and challenged him for calling her a liar. When she walked to the back of the car, however, he did not let the matter drop but followed her, saying, in English, "Madam, I listened to you, to all what you had to tell me, I listened to you and now if you are through I would like to explain you the reason why ... I wanted to drop the extra car at Quebec, and ... I think I should have the privilege of doing it." Tudor refused to listen, responding, according to Cantin, "Will you please go away."[83] She first turned her back to Cantin once again, and then she pushed past him in the aisle to return to her original seat. Here the situation ended, and Cantin resumed his duties.

Of course we cannot know for sure what Tudor or Cantin were feeling. We know only what they said they were doing and why they were doing it. Their testimony was also given more than two years after the incident, presenting further difficulties for reading the emotions involved. But the testimony about the drama on the train gives a sense of how the parties reacted to the situation, and the precise points at which each felt the other was crossing lines of propriety. For Tudor, the limit was reached when Cantin questioned her information about the tickets and then began lecturing her on politeness. From this point, Tudor's mortification – and anger, which she no doubt felt was righteous – grew, as a social inferior refused to leave her alone, and as a strange man pressed her even after she had indicated clearly she no longer wished to pursue the matter. Asked in rebuttal on what her grievance in the case rested, she answered, "On his having said what he did to me, on what he said and the manner in which he said it."[84] For Cantin, the boundary was breached earlier, likely already on the platform when Tudor questioned his management of the cars and went over his head to the stationmaster. He narrated a different story, unsurprisingly one in which he was the aggrieved party. From the start, Tudor had been peremptory with him, refusing to accept his explanation for why the car was being removed, and had threatened to report him to his superiors.

Tudor's feelings are not hard to understand, but labelling them is a challenge. Her complaint boils down to a violation of propriety, though she herself never used the word or any of its synonyms. Propriety comprised a complex set of norms, mixing gender, class, age, and context in varied and changing ways. Being able to read those norms was part of socialization, but that too depended in a circular way on the very norms one was being socialized to interpret. Behaviour shocking to the refined sensibilities of a woman like Tudor might have been tolerable to someone of a different social background. This could lead to conflict, as it did here, and this confrontation of norms – when the expected treatment or behaviour became the unexpected – was what provoked feelings strong enough to drive someone like Euphemia Tudor to court. In Tudor's case, she entered the car with certain expectations, drawn from her experience riding first class: of the proper treatment of passengers generally, of first-class passengers more particularly, of female first-class passengers more particularly still, and of herself most specifically. She clearly reacted negatively to Cantin's transgressions of her own gender-based expectations of how she should be treated. Though she said nothing directly about this, her American sister-in-law did. Asked whether Tudor had treated Cantin in a "ladylike" way, she replied, "Very. I should have been very much fiercer than she … I come from the States where they don't treat people like that."[85]

The dynamics of social class complicated this dispute over the request to move to the other first-class car, with its few remaining empty seats.

Tudor was bringing a party of eight onto the train; Cantin naturally enough interpreted this to mean that she wanted eight seats together. This would have made her request seem unreasonable, since although there were not eight seats together, there were smaller blocks of seats available in the crowded car. Tudor, however, wanted no such thing, as she testified on cross-examination: she "had not any intention of keeping our party together, because three of them were servants, and I do not care to sit with the servants."[86] Finally, although more could be said, propriety was also performed for and assessed by audiences, in this case the respectable travellers in the first-class car. Tudor's sense of mortification and transgression of the norms of polite behaviour would have been accentuated because her treatment by a lower-class railway employee became spectacle for curious onlookers, some of whom at least were judging her as well as him. One witness, an employee of the defendant who happened to have been on the train that day, found Tudor's behaviour insulting, particularly when she turned her back on Cantin. His judgment was that she "seemed to be in a bad mood."[87] Beyond being viewed and judged, she was also forced to initiate conversation with "a gentleman whom I did not know" to ask about his children's fares.[88]

Tudor's lawsuit was ample evidence that she felt norms of propriety had been transgressed. But Cantin also clearly believed norms had been violated – Tudor's refusal to listen to his explanation, coupled with her officious behaviour in questioning his management of the train, offended him. The railway, in its defence, presented a very different reading from Tudor's of the emotions and norms in the situation. It focused on manners, arguing that Cantin had acted throughout "with a great deal of courtesy and consideration," while Tudor treated their employee "impolitely." The railway thus challenged Tudor's monopoly on propriety, explicitly questioning her manners, but implicitly casting doubt on her adherence to proper gender norms. Her decisiveness during the incident – a sign of her perceived social superiority – was characterized by the defence as unwomanly behaviour. Women were not supposed to interfere in the management of complex systems like the Quebec & Lake St. John Railway, and she "only had herself to blame if she suffered problems on that occasion."[89] One of the defence witnesses, the assistant superintendent of the railway, testified that throughout the interaction Cantin had behaved in a "gentlemanly" manner – the choice of word is noteworthy – in response to a pushy and (the implication is clear) unladylike woman.[90] Similarly, another defence witness felt that Tudor "forgot herself, that is she went too far, she was not polite towards the conductor."[91]

Justice Charles Joseph McCorkill awarded Tudor the entire amount she demanded, $100 plus costs.[92] This was a modest demand in comparison to most similar cases, which in part explains why the judge did not reduce it. But the award is also evidence that the judge fully accepted Tudor's story and could himself see the injury she claimed to have suffered. The very fact that she had brought the action at all impressed him: he noted, rather oddly, "The plaintiff was not anxious for a law-suit[;] ladies do not like to go to court. She was annoyed and indignant at the manner in which she had been treated and insulted."[93] In emotions history terms, Tudor was part of the same emotional community and shared its norms, while Cantin was an outsider. The judge could relate to Tudor because he too (no doubt) travelled first class, and he expected deference from railroad employees in keeping with his elevated social status. He could have viewed the situation differently: as a hard-working man trying to keep an officious woman from interfering. But he did not. Inevitably, he preferred to see it as a working-class man importuning a respectable, privileged lady with what he characterized as "astonishing impertinence."[94] Cantin's conduct shocked and bewildered him; he could think of no explanation other than drunkenness: "In all my experience and I have travelled a good deal, I never saw or heard of more reprehensible and condemnable conduct on the part of a sober conductor towards a lady passenger, than Cantin's conduct towards Mrs. Slade. Had he been drunk one might have at least partially excused him on the ground that he did not know what he was doing or what he was saying. To do or say what he did deliberately and in his sober senses is unpardonable."[95]

He saw no rudeness or other impropriety on Tudor's part, at least nothing beyond justifiable frustration over the highly unseemly harassment of a respectable lady by a social inferior. His judgment was filled with the language of self-evidence, his conclusions presented as flowing inexorably from the situation on the train. He dismissed in its entirely the railway's argument that Tudor had been rude: "No person who has any self respect can be called a liar, or be told the speaker does not believe her, at any time." The insult was "all the more grievous" because it took place in public, before friends and strangers alike.[96] Summing up, he ticked off all the different factors contributing to the norms of propriety that governed the treatment of respectable ladies – sex, social position, audience, manners, and deference – and found that Cantin's conduct had violated them all.[97]

Euphemia Tudor's case compares in interesting ways with Wilfrid Corbeil's, and together they reveal how propriety was a fluid social norm whose violation could lead to various emotional responses. Both cases were everyday situations that got out of hand, so that boundaries of propriety were breached. For Corbeil, the physical manifestation of impropriety in his case meant dishonour and humiliation as his masculinity was ridiculed by the security guard. For Tudor, the impropriety was class- and gender-based, leading to her sense of mortification as the deference she expected as a woman of privilege was ignored by a pushy working-class man. Language was a factor in both situations, though in different ways. Corbeil's frustration and offence may have been due to a perceived social inferior's disrespecting him by addressing him dismissively in English, implicitly denying that a francophone could be respectable. In *Tudor* the linguistic markers were more typical of Quebec at the time – an affluent anglophone versus a working-class francophone – but Euphemia Tudor's assertion of privilege would similarly have irked Antoine Cantin by rejecting his French language. In both cases too, the locations of the incidents and the spectators looking on were crucial to the reactions of the principals. Both incidents took place in spaces that were charged with class-based respectability: the middle-class performativity of the amusement park, and the upper-class exclusivity of the first-class railway car. Corbeil, as a businessman, showed some concern for his public reputation and the danger that it might be diminished, though most of his reaction was about what his mistreatment meant for him personally. Tudor's case said nothing about specific effects of how she had been treated; she was confident in her social standing, and pursued the case not to protect or regain something personal that had been lost, but to reassert class boundaries and to register her personal disapproval that they had been ignored.

Alongside class and gender, and in many ways intersecting with them, was another source of honour-related injury: the ways of immigrants, when minority cultural practices came into conflict with majority social norms. This was a form of discrimination, of course, but it was also a confrontation of different attitudes in which the dismissal or ridicule of identity-based cultural practices led to particular emotional responses such as dishonour or shame or disgrace. An example comes from Quebec's experience with temperance and prohibition during the First World War years.

The Ways of Immigrants: *Rinkuk v. Ville St-Pierre*

In 1916, the village of Ville St-Pierre, also called St-Pierre aux Liens, just west of Montreal, was in the midst of a battle over alcohol, a front in the generalized war across the country. Temperance was a fraught issue in Quebec, where divisions over alcohol were particularly complex.[98] Ville St-Pierre's parish curate, Joseph-Placide Desrosiers, was a local temperance leader, head of the Société de tempérance de Saint-Pierre-aux-Liens and organizer and host of the first "Congrès de tempérance de Montréal (partie ouest)," held in the town in 1909.[99] In January 1911 the village held a plebiscite on whether to allow liquor licences; the anti-tavern faction carried the day.[100] Its larger neighbour, Lachine, was itself locked in temperance struggles, led there too by Father Desrosiers, and in October 1915 Lachine voted to move from strict licensing to complete prohibition.[101] During 1916, however, opposition to prohibition grew, and prohibition advocates like Father Desrosiers were confronted by others, such as MP for St. Hyacinthe Louis-Joseph Gauthier, a former temperance supporter, who at a public meeting in Lachine argued "that prohibition was an attack against the liberty of the person, and against justice."[102] During the summer of 1916, Ville St-Pierre's liquor by-laws again came under discussion, and while temperance activists never succeeded in drying out the town completely, Ville St-Pierre continued to prohibit the sale of alcohol and the issuance of new licences into the 1920s.[103]

By the early twentieth century, this area had come to be home to a growing immigrant community, attracted by work in the industries lining the nearby Lachine Canal.[104] The 1911 census of Ville St-Pierre showed a population mostly of French origin with a strong English minority, but with pockets of Eastern European immigrants along certain streets: Romanians, Bulgarians, Galicians, Poles, Bukovinians, Hungarians, Russians, and Austrians, in the categories of the census takers. Immigration conflicted with temperance, as immigrants in Quebec were among those most resistant to prohibition. Though French Canadians too were mostly opposed to temperance, their position was more divided, and the drinking customs of minorities could serve as a convenient pretext for nativist harassment by neighbours, the local police, or even other immigrant groups, particularly during the war when suspicions about immigrants, particularly those perceived to hail from enemy regions, ran high.[105]

In the midst of all this, Petro Rinkuk and his wife (she is never named in the case file or news coverage) held a celebration on 20 August 1916 to mark the baptism of their newborn child, an event that would end with a police raid, a trial (and acquittal) in police court on alcohol charges, and a civil suit against the town.[106] Petro worked as a labourer, shovelling coal for the local power company. He was from "Poland," which at the time could mean various parts of what are today Poland, Ukraine, and Belarus. The family lived in a modest apartment on the town's main street. Their guests – some sixty in all – spilled out of the packed apartment into the courtyard behind the house and the alleyway alongside. Alcohol flowed freely – Rinkuk testified that he had purchased four barrels of beer, two large and two small, as well as some whiskey – and there was a feast of meat, soup, cakes, and bread.[107] Polish christenings were a time of celebration for the community, which had expectations about showing relatives and friends a good time; indeed, the size of the gathering suggests the Rinkuks were trying to impress.[108] Rinkuk and his neighbours all testified that this was the accepted practice in "the old country," brought with them to Quebec.[109] But the liberal consumption of alcohol tended either to amuse or horrify outsiders, depending on their temperance leanings. Stories of such parties in North American Polish communities were a trope in the newspapers of the time, with moralizing reports of drunkenness and the inevitable fistfights. In 1909, for example, a Bridgeport, Connecticut, newspaper sarcastically rehearsed the usual stereotypes: "A christening among this element of the foreign population consists principally in the drinking of the health of the new arrival, of the mother, of the father, of all the uncles, aunts, cousins, and relatives by marriage and then of all the acquaintances on this side of the water and the other in turn. The more beer and vile liquor that is consumed, the more successful is the christening and, apparently, the brighter the prospects of the new arrival for success in later life."[110]

According to Rinkuk's witnesses, the celebration kicked off around four in the afternoon and began well, with people eating and drinking and generally enjoying themselves.[111] The Polish priest from Lachine who had performed the ceremony attended, at least until the party really got going.[112] Around six in the evening, however, the local police arrived, and here the stories diverged. The town's main witness was the recently installed chief of police, Emilien Leguerrier, who soon after these events successfully sued the town for unjustified dismissal after being accused of incompetence and insubordination.[113] According to Leguerrier, he had been called to the house because some men were fighting in the back courtyard, though Rinkuk claimed they were from a different house. He arrested the men, entered Rinkuk's house without a warrant or permission, and called for backups when he saw how many people were inside. He painted a wild picture, with drunken revellers and fights everywhere, and his decision to seize the liquor was made to prevent the situation from getting further out of control. As he was carting off the barrels and bottles, Rinkuk's wife intervened. According to Rinkuk, she tried to tell Leguerrier (in Polish) not to take the booze because they had paid a lot of money for it. Leguerrier saw things differently: Rinkuk's wife, he said, "was furious, she was like a tiger."[114] Another defence witness claimed the chief pulled his revolver at this point, threatening them if they did not get out of his way.[115] The appearance of the police was enough for most people, and the party broke up quickly. Though this ended the evening, Rinkuk's troubles continued, as Leguerrier had him summoned before the Recorder's Court on charges of possessing liquor for the purposes of sale. He was acquitted for lack of evidence that he had sold anything, though Recorder J.O. Lacroix made a point of stressing that he approved of the police's conduct in seizing the alcohol.[116] The beer was returned, but had by this time spoiled. Rinkuk sued the town for the lost beer as well as for "damage as to his feelings and general reputation amongst his co-religionists in and about Ville St. Pierre."[117]

The main legal issues were whether money had been collected and whether the police had reasonable grounds for entering the house and making the seizure. Much of the testimony focused on whether or not Rinkuk's wife had told the chief to wait before taking away the liquor until after a collection had been done ("une quête," a word the chief claimed to have heard, but Rinkuk denied knowing its meaning). But at root this was a cultural as much as a legal conflict, bringing into confrontation different linguistic and cultural communities, as the mention of "co-religionists" in Rinkuk's declaration makes clear. The plaintiff and most of his witnesses were recent Polish immigrants, the town's witnesses were francophone Quebeckers. All of the principals were Roman Catholics, but divided on linguistic lines into separate congregations. For his part, Rinkuk's lawyer, Isidore Popliger, was a young Romanian Jew with a recently minted McGill law degree, and was an active advocate within various immigrant communities.[118] The interpreter, Harry Hopmeyer, owned a grocery store next to the Rinkuks' apartment and was himself a Romanian Jew, evidently conversant enough in various Eastern European languages – as well as French and English – to mediate between the different parties.[119] The alliance-making is interesting, as Roman Catholic Eastern European "foreigners" used the services of better-connected Eastern European Jews – themselves "foreigners" – against the native French Roman Catholics of Ville St-Pierre.

Given the language differences, the testimony of the town's witnesses is hard to reconcile with the language realities of the scene at the party. Rinkuk's wife spoke neither English nor French, Rinkuk's own command of English was rudimentary, and the chief of police spoke no Polish. A local merchant, deputized on the spot by the police chief to help him enter the house, testified that Rinkuk and his Polish guests spoke broken English.[120] The chief himself testified that Rinkuk told him, "Leave my beer, leave me quest, me make money, give me after quest."[121] The language barrier is just one indication that this was at root a cultural as well as legal conflict. Rinkuk and his guests claimed simply to be following the usual practice in the Polish community, where a birth was an occasion for treating everyone else to a good time, regardless of expense. The police chief, the main voice on the defence side, refused to believe that a labourer who made $1.60 a day would serve up $25 to $30 worth of liquor without getting anything in return. He knew the practice well, he claimed, and in his experience a collection was always taken: "After they're drunk, they give their money."[122] Rinkuk's case was that the misunderstanding had caused him a particular kind of emotional injury, one linked to his customs, and comprehensible only within the context of the Polish community. This becomes clearer as we trace the ways in which his injury was articulated, by himself, his lawyer, his witnesses, and the judge.

The language dynamics in the courtroom were particularly striking, with an anglophone (though bilingual) judge, a mostly francophone defence, a Polish-speaking plaintiff represented by a Romanian Jew, and another Romanian Jew interpreting between Polish, English, and French. How conversant in Slavic dialects Hopmeyer was is unknown: was the recorded testimony a close translation of the original Polish, or was much of it an approximation done on the fly? An injury such as Rinkuk claimed was hard to articulate, let alone convince a judge about, and emotional nuance is particularly difficult to capture across languages. Certain acts – the entry of the police, the confiscation of the beer, the departure of the guests – stand in for deeper emotional injury in the testimony. The real issue for Rinkuk was the humiliation of having his party broken up and everybody sent home, frustrating his hopes of impressing his friends and neighbours as his culture demanded he do. A direct question about whether Rinkuk felt "very much hurt" when the police took the beer away was objected to as leading and so not answered. He did however manage to express something of the shame of being targeted in front of his friends at the party, though the judge seems to have played the situation for laughs:

BY THE COURT:
Q: How did it affect you by the Chief of Police coming in and your guests going away?
A: It gave me a headache.

BY PLAINTIFF'S COUNSEL:
Q: What was the cause of the headache?
A: I felt insulted at my guests going away.
...

Q: Now after this rather unceremonious departure of the guests (BY THE COURT: And the beer) what effect had your reputation or character after that amongst those people?
A: I was sick for two weeks after that on account of that affair.
...

BY THE COURT:
Q: What effect had this on your reputation amongst your co-nationals?

BY PLAINTIFF'S COUNSEL:
Q: What effect did this affair of the Chief of Police and the spoiling of the party and the taking away of the beer have as to your reputation amongst your people in the Town of St. Pierre?
A: All the people knew about it, and I had to explain continually that the beer was taken away for nothing.[123]

Rinkuk's answer mixed various effects: the insult of guests being forced to leave the party, physical illness (though likely the "headache" and being "sick for two weeks" was a way to underscore the strength of his emotional response), and social repercussions, as he was forced to explain the police intervention (and his subsequent acquittal) over and over.

Justice William Alexander Weir's flippant interjection about the confiscation of the beer notwithstanding, Rinkuk's headache and feeling of insult were not just in his mind. (And the judge's obvious sarcasm both proved and furthered the humiliation.) He had roles to play, that of proud father and generous host, and the police had humiliated him in front of everyone. Later in his testimony he noted that he tried to have another, smaller party afterwards, without any beer, but "only a few people came in, and all my previous guests did not want to come back."[124] One of his co-workers corroborated the change in mood once the police broke in. The guests "were sitting there and got kind of unsatisfied and left the house on account of the trouble."[125] Asked about the effects on the plaintiff's reputation of breaking up the party and seizing the beer, this witness testified, "Everyone looked at him and he was insulted and people said [it] did not turn out good, that the christening of the baby was not properly made."[126] For the defence, neither Polish customs nor Rinkuk's feelings had anything to do with it: this was simply a matter of public safety, general morality, and contravention of the town's liquor by-laws. Chief Leguerrier put it plainly: "Naturally, when a whole horde arrives, especially with people like that, when there are forty or fifty of them and they have lots of beer, lots of times at orgies like that I've seized the beer, there were already too many barrels of it, I took three prisoners, all three were drunk, it was to prevent orgies that I seized the beer."[127]

On the one side, a culturally mandated community celebration, the failure of which brought shame on the household. On the other side, a beer-soaked orgy among "those people," whose odd customs could not be tolerated in sober Ville St-Pierre. (The French word *orgie* could mean drunken revel, but the sexual connotation was present as well). Justice Weir seems to have shared some of the defence's prejudices about immigrants, and he ran the hearing in an unusually hands-on way, likely both because of the linguistic difficulties of the Polish plaintiff and witnesses, and because Rinkuk's lawyer was new to the bar. The judge was aggressively interventionist and did a large part of the examinations himself. His impatience frequently manifested itself, as in his questioning (through the interpreter) of Rinkuk's neighbour Katrina Hrecza:

BY THE COURT:
Q: What is your age?
A: I do not know.

BY THE COURT:
Q: Over twenty-one?
A: I do not know.

BY THE COURT:
Q: Over five years?
A: Yes, but I do not know my age.

BY THE COURT:
Q: Ask her if she knows she is over one year of age?
A: Yes.

BY THE COURT:
Q: Ask her if she is over two?
A: I think I am twenty-three or twenty-four. I do not want to say exactly because I do not know.[128]

The cultural gulf was obviously wide: it seems not to have occurred to Justice Weir that Hrecza's vagueness may have been due to a reluctance to give wrong answers after having sworn an oath on the Gospels to tell the truth.

Despite the unpromising hearing, Justice Weir found for the plaintiff and awarded him $150 in damages, $100 for the spoiled beer and $50 for his moral injury. Faced with the vague articulation of Rinkuk's reactions to the police raid, and working with the cultural explanation of the importance of baptismal celebrations in the Polish community, the judge characterized the injury as "disgrace."[129] This was a relatively unusual word in cases of this kind (*humiliation* was much more frequently used), and it appears neither in the plaintiff's declaration nor in any of the witness testimony. It does, however, capture the distinct nature of the reputational injury in this case, namely being cast in a light certain to bring one shame. That it was the judge who supplied the term is interesting and shows a degree of sensitivity on his part in reading the operative social norms within a particular cultural community, and the ways in which their violation would affect its members. The word *disgrace* did appear in other contexts, particularly in alienation of affection actions, which we will explore in detail in chapter 5. The disgrace in those cases, in which one's wife was lured away by another, was in the destruction of the husband's proper gender role, diminishing him in the eyes of the community by demonstrating his inability to keep his wife.¹³⁰ The injury was similar in *Rinkuk*, though in that case cultural and gender roles intermingled. Holding the christening party would have been the father's job – the mother had just given birth, after all – and throwing a big party regardless of expense provided him with a way to perform for all to see his masculine roles of father and provider. By raiding the house and dispersing the celebration, by preventing him from showing the expected largesse and hospitality to his friends and neighbours, the police challenged Rinkuk's standing as a father and as a man within the community. The defendant's actions, Justice Weir found, brought on Rinkuk the particular kind of humiliation that came from being made to fail to live up to the expectations of others.

The town appealed to the Court of Review, and each side's factum intensified their arguments. The town addressed the question of culture, but only by relying more strongly than before on the police chief's supposed experience with the cultural practices of Polish immigrants, that they habitually passed the hat during parties. Again, this pointed to a cultural grey area: if there was an expectation of passing the hat (which was never proved), the valence of that custom within the Polish community did not fit well with the licit options available (liquor was either provided for free legally, or it was sold illegally). More ominously, to establish reasonable grounds for the chief's actions, the town floated a new argument, that a short leash on immigrants was justified by the war: "Can one really blame Le Guerrier for wanting to prevent an orgy, when the law allows Austrians to be interned in concentration camps?"¹³¹ Rinkuk's lawyer followed Justice Weir's lead, and pushed the idea of disgrace further. He argued that though Rinkuk had been acquitted by the Recorder, he "felt the disgrace, having continually to make explanations to people as the fact of the seizure was known all over the town."¹³² He also articulated more explicitly the cultural differences between the Polish minority and the French majority: "'The christening was not well made' may cause a smile on Western faces, but to a Pole surrounded by and living only in and with his countrymen, it was a very real thing."¹³³ The Court of Review upheld the trial decision, without giving reasons.¹³⁴

Rinkuk's lawyer's reference to the widely divergent interpretations of the incident – trivial on one side, grievous on the other – underscores a key element of honour-based injury, present in all such cases, but particularly evident here. Social norms are always cultural, of course, but in this case the expectations of his own community put Rinkuk into a situation where the shutting down of his party caused him to feel shamed in the eyes of his friends and neighbours. Cultural expectations contributed both to Rinkuk's self-evaluation and to others' assessment of him. The Montreal papers could not resist commenting on Rinkuk's case when it came up and covered it with a mixture of amusement about the alcohol and disapproval of the heavy-handed policing. *Le Devoir* even sent a reporter to cover the hearing – rare for civil cases, except the juiciest among them – who began his article with a quick ethnography of Poles: "The Poles have the reputation of being good drinkers, and this reputation is not overrated if one judges by specific facts. What is nothing more than a simple apéritif for a Pole often looks to other people like a quantity sufficient to make the population of an entire city reel."[135] The cultural insensitivity of the police – echoed by the trial judge during the hearing – was certainly part of the injury, though no hint of the language of discrimination or inequality was voiced in the case (which at this early date is not surprising, though as we will see in chapter 7 it did arise in cases of discrimination against Blacks). That the judge in the end accepted this rationale of culturally based injury is interesting: despite his hectoring of the lawyer and condescending treatment of the plaintiff's witnesses, he accepted that Rinkuk had been injured by being shown up in front of friends whom he was trying to impress, and that this treatment jeopardized his standing within his community.

Petro Rinkuk's shame and disgrace were individual injuries that derived their meaning and their gravity from the collective, cultural context within which they arose and were talked about. Dishonour and humiliation could also be collectively experienced in certain situations, as a community itself perceived its honour to be challenged and its self-image to be threatened. Honour is a social concept, and this brings into confrontation an individual's self-assessment and a community's judgment of that individual. Such community standards were behind judges' evaluations of the situations complained of by those who alleged injury to their honour, but they operated for the most part extra-legally, as common-sense, intuitive applications of social codes. Sometimes, however, the tension between individual and collective views of honour and dishonour were the focus of the case, when individuals claimed to be the victims of organized public censure and humiliation. This was the case in the venerable tradition of charivari, in which nocturnal noisemaking, discordant music, derision, vandalism, demands for money, threats, and physical violence to persons and property served to police social codes against those whose aberrant behaviour the community saw as dishonouring. The few civil damages cases brought by charivari victims are interesting because they brought out clearly the contrast between social and legal notions of honour. In legal terms, the honour being invoked was the plaintiff's – the victim of the charivari. In social terms, the justification for the charivari (a social justification, since the means used were clearly illegal) was a collective notion of community honour, set up against the behaviour of the target.

Policing Community Honour: A Charivari in St. Léonard, 1891

Charivari was brought to New France in early days and took root both in rural and urban areas.[136] It involved groups within a community using ridicule or worse to sanction behaviour by individuals within the community. Traditional targets of charivari were ill-sorted marriages (typically older men marrying young women) and illicit sexual activity, but charivaris could also be politically or economically motivated.[137] For example, in 1890 in Côte-des-Neiges, where many of Montreal's tanneries were located, competition over a small brook that supplied water to the factories and that one family allegedly diverted for its own use gave rise to various lawsuits and two charivaris, in which insulting songs were sung and effigies of the head of the offending family and his adult unmarried daughter were hanged on a specially constructed gallows, then burned.[138] Like other forms of popular justice such as duels, charivaris operated outside formal legal institutions: as a British visitor put it in 1850, the charivari in Quebec was "intended to reach delinquents not amenable to the common process of law – offenders against propriety and the public sense of honour."[139] In some cases, however, the targets brought civil court actions in response to their treatment. In legal terms, these were damages actions, more specifically *actions d'injures*, in which the victims of the rough music, claiming to have been injured in their honour, sentiments, and *biens* – the usual formula – sued the charivari's ringleaders or whichever of the masked figures in the dark they could identify. The courts, seeking to squelch such community self-help, tended to take a strict line and usually voiced strong disapproval of the charivariers. The analysis of the action, however, and at times the result, was affected by the limitations of the law of defamation or *injure*, which focused on individual honour at the expense of its social aspects. To prove a violation of honour or reputation, the plaintiff had to establish that his or her standing or reputation in the community had suffered as a result of the defendant's words or deeds. In most defamation cases, the judge presumed that the plaintiff was honourable and so would naturally have suffered injury at being defamed. But in cases of charivari, that assumption was problematic, since the circumstances being alleged indicated in themselves that a portion of the plaintiff's community (and it could be a significant portion) judged that he or she lacked honour or virtue or a good name – hence the charivari. The charivari might have been mistaken or exaggerated or motivated by political, economic, or other scores to settle, as they often were, but it was a sure sign in social terms that the individual being ridiculed was seen to be on the wrong side of community values. Charivari cases thus provide interesting windows into community dynamics of belonging and exclusion, of relationship-based conflict, and of the politics of social standing. They reveal as well the tensions between individual and social perceptions of honour.

The exact parameters of the social conflict behind a litigated charivari are always obscure from the case files, especially at the remove of a century or more. Plaintiffs were not about to admit past transgressions that might have riled their neighbours; witnesses were reluctant to reveal anything at all, as the result of group solidarity and fear of reprisals; defendants knew that pleading justification would not get them very far (though usually that did not stop them from trying); and the legal process in general tended (indeed still tends) to zero in on the immediate narrow dispute, leaving aside as irrelevant the deeper conflict of which the dispute was a symptom. In the Côte-des-Neiges charivaris just mentioned, for instance, the case files are completely silent on why the main target's unmarried adult daughter was subjected to a separate charivari nine days later. Was she involved in redirecting the stream? Was she being singled out as a marriageable woman who had not yet married? Despite lengthy testimony, the file provides no clues. What is clear is that a general animosity toward the plaintiffs manifested in a collective attempt to humiliate them publicly. A similar situation prevailed in a charivari a year later, held over three nights in 1891 in a village just northeast of Montreal.

The word in the recently organized farming community of St. Léonard de Port Maurice was that Ovila Duquette was a bad apple.[140] (Whether he really was or not, the community's impressions are what concern us here.) Duquette was a saddler, aged about thirty-two, and lived in the village with his older wife (she was about thirty-nine). He was not a native of the area, having arrived perhaps ten years before from St. Eustache, some distance to the west and off the Island of Montreal.[141] His neighbours described him in unsavoury terms, as prone to drink and frequently engaged in suspicious behaviour.[142] Mayor Louis Sicard testified that he had received several informal verbal complaints about Duquette in recent years: once it was said that he was wandering around drunk and threatening to set fires, another time that he had gathered together a band of young men for drinking and thieving, and on a third occasion he was accused of being out on the road all night and up to no good.[143] His neighbours also described a litigious man, hardly unusual in a period before the courts had become priced out of the reach of ordinary people, but not a recipe for harmonious relations with one's peers. According to Louis Turcot, Duquette had bought some land from him but was unable to make the payments, so he and his wife had been working off the debt in Turcot's onion field. Nevertheless, Duquette sued Turcot for $8.39 he claimed as payment for the work the couple had done, and Turcot settled the case, saying, "I didn't want to go all the way to the end with him."[144] The local hotel keeper testified that on the day of the charivari, letters from Duquette's lawyer had arrived in the village, and the addressees gathered behind the hotel, where the letters (the import of which was never revealed in the case files) were read out to those who could not read for themselves and then discussed by the group.[145] The charivari was triggered by something more specific than Duquette's alleged litigiousness and general reputation, however.

On 12 July 1891 Duquette carried a large pot into his neighbour Turcot's potato field, going to pick raspberries, he later said. He claimed that on his way through the field he decided to see how Turcot's potatoes were growing and pulled up a couple of plants to check their progress, replanting them afterwards. A neighbour testified this was common practice – people often checked each other's crops to see how they were coming along and to make sure there was no rot, though this practice was presumably more usual among farmers than saddlers.[146] Turcot's mother, Catherine Martineau, was looking out from the house and saw Duquette go by on the road with his pot at eleven on Sunday morning; he gave her the raspberry explanation. She got suspicious when he entered the potato field, however, since no one cut through that field to get to the raspberries, they walked along the road. She confronted Duquette as he was on his knees pulling up some plants; he said he was just checking to see how big they were. At that point he left and Martineau went back to her business in the house. She saw him again later, this time with his pot covered with a piece of paper. When she went to check the potatoes, she found a twenty- to twenty-five-foot stretch where the potatoes had been pulled up and the rootless tops stuck back into the ground to hide the illicit harvest.[147] She told her son when he returned, and according to another witness Turcot summoned Duquette to come speak with him that evening, "for the love of potatoes." Duquette told Turcot he was just checking the progress of the crop.[148] Bazile Collerette testified that Duquette was bragging that afternoon that he had just feasted on "some good new potatoes."[149]

About a week later, on Monday, 20 July, the village was filled with gossip and activity. (The case file is silent on what went on in the interval.) People talked about the charivari that was going to happen that night, and various preparations were made, furtively but not overly so. This more-or-less open anticipation of the charivari seems to have been the usual practice – in Côte-des-Neiges, it was no secret that the effigies and scaffolds were being constructed the day of the charivari, and people popped into the carpenter's shop belonging to one of the defendants to check on their progress and contribute clothing for the effigies.[150] In St. Léonard, Sinaï Martineau (sixteen years old) and Joseph Collerette (fifteen) found an old horn and took it to the Duquettes' house (along with a harness Martineau wanted to get repaired) to fill it with water so it could be used as a noisemaker (apparently a moistened horn was more effective than a dry one for this purpose).[151] Some alleged that the Martineau boys were following Duquette's wife around the village that afternoon, banging on milk cans. Hotel keeper Alfred Deschamps denied this, but his denial suggested some of the pressures towards conformity surrounding a charivari: "If you don't want to get mixed up in something, you see nothing. When people say, 'There's going to be noise,' I stay peacefully at home."[152]

The charivariers gathered around ten o'clock that night on the property of Joseph Pesant dit Sans-Cartier, just across the main road from the Duquettes' residence. The charivari lasted somewhere between half an hour and an hour, with about thirty-five people participating or milling around, and more watching from nearby windows, balconies, and porches. The ringleaders were masked and hidden by the darkness as well. The duly moistened horn was blown, milk cans and iron frying pans were banged, and some participants mockingly shouted out insults while on their knees. Near the end, several shots were fired, terrifying Duquette's wife, already of a nervous disposition.[153] The charivari was repeated in more or less identical terms on Wednesday, two nights later, and once again on Sunday night, 26 July. It seems to have been the talk of the neighbourhood, though not everyone was impressed: Bazile Collerette dit Bourguignon was awakened by a gunshot on one of the nights, but said he rolled over and went back to sleep.[154] Witnesses testified that word of the charivari spread quickly: it was discussed in neighbouring villages and as far away as Montreal.[155]

Unlike some traditional charivaris – particularly those censuring matrimonial or sexual transgressions – the participants in this one made no demand for money to end the proceedings: E.P. Thompson has termed these "cruel" charivaris, and their purpose was to send a clear message, without holding out a possibility of reconciliation.[156] Duquette's business seems to have suffered following the charivari, forcing him to do more day work,[157] and one witness testified to having been threatened with a charivari himself if he continued doing business with Duquette.[158] Despite the charivari's pointed message and its economic effects on Duquette, this informal measure did not succeed in driving the offender away (if that was indeed its purpose). Within a few weeks each side was going to the formal institutions of the law against the other. In early August Turcot filed a complaint against Duquette at the Montreal Police Court over the stolen potatoes. At about this same time, in what might have been a tit-for-tat, Duquette had a lawyer begin civil proceedings against those he believed to be the charivari's ringleaders (or the parents of the ringleaders). On 11 August, after Duquette had finished selling some potatoes at Bonsecours Market in Montreal, Deputy Constable Lambert arrested him as he was leaving the market, a highly public place to make an arrest and one that caught the attention of at least two newspapers.[159] Duquette stood trial a few days later for the offence of "stealing growing plants"; he was acquitted after what was an unusually long hearing for the police court.[160]

In three separate civil actions, Duquette sued Louis Turcot for $500; Joseph Sans-Cartier for $400; and Joseph Pesant dit Sans-Cartier, Joseph Corbeil, Amable and Jean-Baptiste Martineau for $800 (joint and solidary), in each case claiming that they planned and carried out a charivari that caused injury to Duquette.[161] The charivari, Duquette claimed, had led to "calumnies spread in profusion" against him and was undertaken, he said in the Sans-Cartier action, "for the purpose of humiliating him, of injuring him in his honour, his feelings, and his *biens*."[162] In the other two actions, he dropped humiliation and claimed the charivari was held "for the purpose of ruining the Plaintiff."[163] Though the demands were presented in terms of real and exemplary damages, little proof of real injury was attempted, and Duquette's claims sank or swam on the question of moral injury alone. Duquette testified twice, once on his own behalf and once called by the defendant Turcot, but his testimony focused on the events of the charivari, not on the damage he claimed to have suffered.[164] Though the charivariers had called him a thief, Duquette's action was not a straight defamation claim but rather a broader claim of *injure*.

To support his claims, Duquette could not simply prove that a particular individual had called him a thief on a particular day before a particular audience. Rather, he had to prove the less precise complaint that in organizing the charivari the defendants had created and encouraged a situation whose general intent and outcome were injury to his previously good reputation. This was problematic, since to succeed he would have to establish his good repute within a community whose members had just demonstrated over three separate nights that they viewed him in a negative light. His main witness was his own father, who had been visiting from St. Eustache at the time of the charivari, and who unsurprisingly testified that before the charivari his son had earned an honest living as a saddler, but since then the whole parish had turned against him.[165] Frédéric Martineau (no relation to the defendant Martineau) testified that Duquette's reputation was good and that "he had always behaved honestly towards me."[166] Ovila Desautels, local blacksmith, similarly was vague about Duquette's general reputation, but testified that he continued to use Duquette's saddlery, even after the charivari.[167] Some of Duquette's other witnesses, however, could muster little more than lukewarm support. Delphine Constantineau, after claiming to have known Duquette for a long time, oddly testified that she knew nothing of his reputation.[168] Duquette's sister-in-law, Eliza Paquette, called in rebuttal to shore up that very point, testified about his reputation at slightly greater length, but in the end concluded only that "I never heard tell that he had done anything to anyone"; other witnesses were similarly cagey.[169] These were hardly ringing endorsements of Duquette's probity, couched as they were in such negative terms as "we have nothing to say against him."

Against this equivocal evidence was a near-unanimous litany of condemnation from the other side. The defence's argument was essentially that as a person without honour, Duquette had no reputation to lose, and so could not be defamed. This was a way of framing a justification argument without directly coming out and saying that the charivari – a form of self-help that judges would inevitably frown upon – was warranted in the circumstances. Mayor Louis Sicard denied the charivari could have hurt Duquette's reputation, since "the man was known to the public as being a man who was out on the road as often at night as day, a dangerous man."[170] Other witnesses agreed, citing Duquette's suspicious behaviour, his litigiousness, or simply vague impressions gleaned from rumour.[171] Bazile Collerette went about as far towards a positive assessment as any were willing to go: "I saw nothing; you hear a lot of things, but you can't judge a person without seeing."[172]

If we examine more closely the message of the charivari as revealed in the case files, we see a multifaceted critique of an outsider who had never been fully accepted into the community. The declarations in the three actions report the taunting words during the charivari as "my little Duquette, you're a thief, a potato thief; you need a few dollars to build your little cabin, you can go ask Vervais the hotel keeper for some."[173] Duquette's father recollected the taunts slightly differently: "Come on my little Duquette, come on and steal Mr. Louis Turcot's potatoes so your little father can eat and so you can sell a few to buy him some whisky."[174] Various grievances are evident or suggested: theft, drinking in the family, Duquette's outsider status. The reference to the "little cabin" and the lack of money for it may have referred to the land transaction with Turcot, and was certainly also a jibe at Duquette's lower socio-economic status. The accusation concerning Léon Vervais, an innkeeper in St. Laurent (to the west of St. Léonard), is harder to interpret. Duquette had apparently filed a complaint against Vervais for illegally selling liquor on Sundays, resulting in a fine against the innkeeper. Such accusations were a common way to settle scores and led at times to litigation.[175] Louis Turcot in his defence claimed that he had heard Duquette saying that he had made Vervais pay a fine, and a number of witnesses referred to it as one of the reasons for the charivari.[176] According to Duquette's father the incident with Vervais came out only on the second night of taunting, so the charivari may have broadened in its scope as new grievances against Duquette were aired.[177] If the accusation against Vervais was untrue, it would be another example of vexatious behaviour by the litigious Duquette, and the charivari would be a means of punishing a cranky outsider. If on the other hand the accusation was true, the charivari might be read instead as a cabal within the St. Léonard community seeing itself threatened, and taking action against a meddlesome whistle-blower. Charivaris were often linked to semi-organized groups of relatively powerful interests within the community: certainly the planning that went into any charivari gave the impression of a conspiracy. In St. Léonard (and the same is true of the Côte-des-Neiges charivari), prominent members of the community (the mayor, a justice of the peace, a hotel keeper) testified on the defendants' behalf, indicating something of the power dynamics that could lead to collective censure and exclusion of a particular individual.

Duquette's various actions resulted in a number of judgments spread over six months against the various defendants, with mixed results. Justice Charles-Ignace Gill awarded Duquette $25 against Pesant dit Sans-Cartier, who, he found, had encouraged the charivariers and been a willing participant (even though he withdrew early after being hit by a stone).[178] In the separate action against Sans-Cartier, Justice Michel Mathieu awarded Duquette $50, finding that the defendant had known of and tolerated the charivari taking place on his land.[179] Defendant Corbeil was condemned by Justice Gill to pay $12.50, since he encouraged and prolonged the charivari by his presence, he did nothing to stop it or reproach the participants, and he was there maliciously to enjoy Duquette's humiliation.[180] The other actions were unsuccessful.[181] All – the successful as well as the unsuccessful – were affirmed by the Court of Review, though the damages to which Pesant and Corbeil were condemned were modified to a joint and solidary award of $50 as had been demanded, rather than the individual awards made at first instance.[182]

None of the brief judgments were particularly probing in their analysis, which in itself is revealing of judicial attitudes towards injuries to honour. Despite Ovila Duquette's lame excuse for why he dug up the potatoes and the defence's evidence of his poor reputation, the judges clearly worked from the assumption that a charivari could never be justified and so must have caused injury to Duquette, regardless of the community's opinion of him. The *Montreal Daily Witness* made this explicit in its coverage, noting that some of the witnesses in the case, "old men, had declared that a charivari is justified when there is sufficient reason to hold it. This the Court could not countenance."[183] Brief judgments were thus sufficient to dispose of the matter. The judges' assumptions were made easier by their clear condemnation of the practice of charivari. Justice Gill noted that "this outdated usage of charivaris as well as the encouragement given to them by people's unhealthy curiosity, must be suppressed."[184] Newspapers reported that he went further in his remarks from the bench than he did in the filed judgments, condemning the dangers of the "ancient and barbarous custom of charivari" and referring to a recent charivari in Richelieu (of which he claimed personal knowledge) that had ended in murder.[185] The judges understood the purpose of the charivari: Justice Gill made clear that a charivari was intended "to bring public contempt on the plaintiff, to humiliate him and his family, and to cause him material injury by making him lose some of the clientele he had previously enjoyed in the exercise of his trade."[186] The gaiety and mirth of the nocturnal activities masked their purpose: the celebration by the community of the humiliation of one of its members. All charivaris were about power, however merry some might have seemed to participants (if not to targets), and as the St. Léonard charivari showed, humiliation was a potent weapon in an honour-conscious society to enforce conformity or drive someone away.

The situation in St. Léonard gave rise to two different kinds of normative responses, each seeking to vindicate honour. First was the informal charivari, in which certain self-appointed guardians of the community policed its collective honour. Second were the various formal court actions Duquette brought to vindicate his personal honour, injured, he claimed, by the accusations levied against him by the charivariers. The charivari clearly expressed the community's judgment, or at least the judgment of a vocal part of the community: Duquette was untrustworthy and a threat to community peace and harmony. The community was not necessarily an impartial judge, of course, and it may have been looking more to the material interests of certain segments within it than to some kind of collective and intangible honour. The judgment of the courts was in one sense clear: Duquette was awarded a sum, relatively modest compared to what he demanded but not trivial, for the injuries he had suffered to his honour, his sentiments, and his *biens*. In another sense, however, the work of the formal court of law was trickier and more nuanced, since in court the two aspects of honour, individual and collective, necessarily came together. The various courts involved in the different actions had to examine not just Duquette's subjective feelings that his tormentors had dishonoured him (and affected his business, of course), but also the community's assessment of those feelings. Many of the witnesses were asked by lawyers from both sides whether they thought Duquette's reputation had been damaged as a result of the public ridicule and accusations of the charivari. Predictably, the witnesses split on partisan lines: those for the plaintiff saw the charivari as having had a profound effect, while those for the defendants downplayed its seriousness. The judges wanted nothing to do with that sort of justification for lawlessness, and in rejecting it they were following a long history of formal legal responses to the practice of charivari.[187] But though the popular view of the charivari as a justified assertion of community honour failed to move the judges, it is telling that it nonetheless had a place in the courtroom. The question of Duquette's public reputation, and the evidence from the charivari itself that his reputation was bad, was raised in part to establish whether Duquette had suffered some loss. But it was also an assertion of the continuing relevance of the popular law of charivari, which depended on the assessment of the gap between Duquette's personal honour and that of the community.

3

Family Dishonour

While honour was most often litigated as a liberal, individual interest (and most often by men seeking redress for injuries to their public personas), social understandings of honour were broader, as was evident in the St. Léonard charivari. This collective dimension of honour tapped as well into older, pre- or non-liberal values surrounding family standing, family name, and the memory of ancestors.[1] As William Reddy has observed about early nineteenth-century France, honour itself was "a collective, familial state," with individual standing inextricably linked to family ties, and the family's reputation supported (or undermined) by the actions and individual reputations of its members.[2] Much of French family law, Reddy argues, and his point applies to Quebec as well, was implicitly (and sometimes explicitly) about the maintenance of collective honour. The male head of household's *puissance paternelle*, for example, defined his role as guardian of the family's honour, both within the home and, if necessary, before the courts. Similarly, the strict incapacities of married women, minors, and those under interdiction, while mainly about the preservation of patriarchy and the protection of the vulnerable, were also to prevent dangerous loose cannons from acting up within society at large to the detriment of the family.[3] Family honour was thus at once distinct from and tied to the personal honour of each individual making up the family: it was, as Bernard Beignier notes, and as contemporary jurists would have agreed, a solidarity or patrimony of honour, common to all members of the family.[4]

Family honour was constituted by a web of obligations adhering to relationships within the family: those owed between living family members, those owed by the living to their ancestors, and those owed by the living to the as-yet-unborn. Words or deeds that reflected badly on one family member, or on an ancestor, could affect the standing of the family as a whole, which in turn could ricochet back to injure indirectly those related to the initial victim. These broader aspects of honour were sometimes litigated, though such cases presented particular problems within the individualistic world of post-codification Quebec law. Whose injury counted in legal terms? How indirect, or how distant temporally, could an injury get before it was no longer legally relevant? And precisely how should a collective injury be understood? Though this kind of case was never numerous in Quebec, the social power of the idea of family honour was such that litigants in all sorts of cases frequently voiced concerns about the threat of collective dishonour. More directly, however, some litigants brought action specifically to avenge family honour in various ways. A good example involves the daughter of one of nineteenth-century Quebec's most controversial figures.

The Apostate's Daughter: *Chiniquy v. Bégin*

On 3 November 1911, several Montreal newspapers picked up a report from Worcester, Massachusetts, that Euphémie Allard, widow of Charles Chiniquy, had just died at age seventy-seven.[5] Chiniquy, who died in 1899, had for decades been a polarizing figure in Quebec and beyond.[6] Ordained a Roman Catholic priest in 1833, he made a name for himself as a temperance activist who drew huge crowds to his sermons, but from the beginning he had also been subject to accusations of insubordination and sexual misconduct. In the 1850s his bishop dealt with the controversy by sending Chiniquy off to Illinois, where he resumed his popular preaching and, perhaps inevitably, came again into conflict with the church hierarchy for refusing to submit to its discipline. The bishop of Chicago suspended him and, when Chiniquy continued to celebrate mass despite the suspension, excommunicated him in 1858. Chiniquy responded by formally and publicly breaking with the Roman Catholic Church and taking his followers with him. He was made a Presbyterian minister in 1860, married Allard in 1864, and spent the rest of his life preaching and publishing virulent polemics against the Catholic Church, both in Canada and in the United States.[7]

Allard's obituary in *La Patrie* described her as "the widow of the late *abbé* Charles Chiniquy" and briefly outlined Chiniquy's conflict with the Catholic Church.[8] The Catholic weekly *La Vérité* took issue with that wording, noting that strictly speaking it would have been more accurate to refer to him as "the ex-*abbé* Chiniquy," but that "here this apostate is known by the name *Chiniquy* full stop."[9] The more stridently ultramontanist weekly *La Croix* went still further, publishing on its front page a short piece entitled "We Call a Cat a Cat, and Chiniquy an Apostate."[10] The article, by one of the paper's editors, referred to Allard as the woman whom "the apostate Chiniquy took for a companion and dressed up with the title of spouse."[11] More provocatively, it stated that just as when referring to Chiniquy one should say "ex-*abbé*," when referring to Allard,

> the unfortunate person whom he wanted to join to his apostasy, one must do so in a manner that does not suggest that she was his wife. The apostate Chiniquy could no more contract a marriage than any other priest or religious bound by solemn vows.
>
> In consequence, Euphémie Allard was for Chiniquy nothing more than a concubine.[12]

The couple's daughter, Rebecca, took offence at what the article stated and implied about her parents, and sued Joseph Bégin, publisher of *La Croix*, for $10,000 damages.[13] Her declaration laid out a two-pronged argument.[14] First, the article had been published "for the purpose of insulting and in fact insults the memory of the father and mother of the plaintiff." Specifically, she objected to the word *concubine*, with its implications that her parents' union had been immoral. Second, the article cast doubt on the legitimacy of her own birth (in 1868, or four years after her parents' marriage), since it implied that her parents had been cohabiting outside of marriage, an insinuation "likely to expose the plaintiff to the execration and condemnation of the inhabitants of this province." Each of these insulting insinuations caused injury, but different injuries, and she alleged that the article "is likely to cause and causes the plaintiff a considerable wrong in injuring her in her honour, as well as in the honour of her father and mother, in her feelings and in her *biens*."[15] The case thus combined two different kinds of defamation. One was individual, like most defamation actions, and treated Chiniquy's reputation as a sort of *bien* she possessed individually; the imputation that she was a bastard injured her personally.

The other was familial, centred on the attack on her mother, and characterized her dead mother's reputation as something common to and shared by all members of the family, living and dead. Rebecca Chiniquy suffered injury from both: directly and personally because of the suggestion that her own birth was illegitimate, and indirectly as part of a family because of the allegation that her parents had lived together out of wedlock.

The defence approached the case as a typical defamation action, raising mainly the expected defences.[16] First, truth: in theological terms a priest could not marry, so Charles Chiniquy's union was invalid and Allard was quite literally, if not so politely, his concubine.[17] Second, public interest: since Chiniquy remained a public figure in Quebec, his purported marriage was a public act open to commentary. Bégin, as editor of a Catholic paper whose mission was to defend the faith, "had the right to criticize the man himself, his conduct, and his ideas."[18] Third, absence of malice: when he published the article Bégin had had no idea Charles Chiniquy had a daughter, so he could not have intended to injure her. (At the end of the trial, the day before judgment was rendered, the defence raised the question of whether Rebecca was actually Chiniquy's daughter, bringing forward affidavits from two surprise witnesses about the identity of Rebecca's alleged real father. Only one of the witnesses could be found to testify, and his testimony was contradicted by a witness who knew the Chiniquys in Illinois.[19]) Regarding Rebecca Chiniquy's alleged injuries, Bégin's lawyer for the most part ignored the question of family honour and focused almost entirely on the article's effect on Rebecca as an individual. Dispensing with the parents, the defence argued that any injury to Charles Chiniquy was entirely justified by his controversial career. Euphémie Allard was simply collateral damage of the justified attack on Chiniquy's non-canonical marriage, and "it is pure hypocrisy to get indignant and claim that we are attacking a wife."[20] Any injury to the memory of Rebecca Chiniquy's parents, in other words, was justified by the general defences of truth and public interest. Rebecca's own claimed injury was non-existent, since she was not even named in the article. The defence supported its arguments by English authorities, the common law being, as we will see below, much more restrictive regarding family honour than the civil law.[21]

Chiniquy, however, approached the matter differently. She was represented by Gonzalve Desaulniers, a poet, a former journalist, and a lawyer who frequently defended liberal interests against the Catholic

Figure 3.1 "Mrs. Morin," Rebecca Chiniquy Morin, photographed in 1891 by William Notman & Son. McCord Museum, II-94495.1. Reproduced with permission.

Church and was himself the frequent target of Catholic attacks.[22] His strategy in the case was less about establishing an injury to Rebecca as an individual, than on showing how the attack on the parents necessarily affected the daughter. He asked his client, in a formulaic way, whether she had suffered any injury to her honour, her feelings, or her *biens*. Her answer was similarly vague and pro forma: "It injured me a great deal, sir."[23] Later, called by the defendant, she admitted that after the article appeared, no one avoided her, no one showed her any scorn or contempt, indeed she noticed no differences at all in how her acquaintances reacted to her.[24] These would be curious answers if the case were about her only, though of course an allegation of illegitimacy was self-evidently injurious and needed no proof of effect. The testimony of some of the other witnesses made it clear that the case was not just about her personal injury, however. Chiniquy's husband, Joseph Morin, a Presbyterian minister and McGill French professor,[25] stated that his wife had been affected "very seriously, and I don't know if I am right to report this, but my wife has never received insults like those, which affected the whole family." Attacks on her father were to be expected, given his public persona, but "as for the rest of the family, I do not believe they had ever been attacked, and I do not believe that the question of his marriage had been raised." Among both Protestant and Catholic acquaintances, the insinuation of illegitimacy was seen as "very humiliating," such that "my wife was very profoundly injured to see an accusation like that attached to our family."[26]

The parties thus seemed to be litigating two different injuries: Chiniquy the attack on her family honour, and secondarily her own honour, Bégin the individual violation (which he denied), with only fleeting reference to the attacks on the dead. This was partly due to what the article said. Since it never mentioned Rebecca directly, and since Bégin testified that he never knew Rebecca existed (a point that was never contradicted), it would be hard to establish a traditional defamation action for an injury to Rebecca's reputation, at least as the law was understood at that time. (It is possible that the argument about family honour and the malicious attack on the parents was raised specifically to head off this point, since malice towards Rebecca would be difficult to establish if the defendant had indeed been ignorant of her existence.) Her rather desultory testimony on this issue – admitting that she had suffered nothing – indicates that this was not the main focus of her case. Rather, Chiniquy was looking beyond a strictly individual understanding of defamation, and beyond a view of the family as a collection of liberal individuals each with his or her own separate reputation. As her husband's testimony made clear, the family was a set of relationships, binding both living and dead, and it enjoyed a collective reputation, such that an attack on the reputation of one member would necessarily affect all the others.

The judges for the most part agreed with Chiniquy, but had some difficulty reconciling family honour with the exigencies of defamation law. At trial, Justice Robert Greenshields accepted as self-evident that the article was injurious to the memory of Chiniquy's parents and so required redress. Following two earlier Quebec cases, which we will consider below, he found the article actionable, not directly, as an attack on the memory of the Chiniquy parents, but because the words were "calculated, by reference to the dead, to injure, defame, humiliate and damage the living descendant."[27] As he remarked during the hearing in court, "You see, in this case you cannot impugn the character of the parents without directly injuring the offspring."[28] While he grudgingly agreed that Bégin had a right to critique the teachings of a public figure like Charles Chiniquy, "that does not involve the right of the defendant or his paper to besmirch, defame and vilify his memory by gratuitous statements, alleged to be facts, concerning his private life."[29] In the end, he straddled individual and collective honour: the article was "grossly defamatory, libellous to the memory of Charles Chiniquy and Euphémie Allard. In like manner, I declare it to be insulting, humiliating and damaging, in the extreme, to their daughter, the present plaintiff."[30] Bégin's duty, which he had neglected, was to determine before publishing whether "there were any to whom the memory of the deceased was dear, and who would suffer pain and anguish by reason of his uncalled for onslaught on their memory. Is it too much to say he should have well ascertained if any there were, who, by irresistible inference, would be branded as bastards?"[31] He awarded $3000 damages, a sum representing the gravity of the injury, Chiniquy's high social status as the wife of a professor, and Bégin's refusal to disavow the article in any way.[32]

The case descended into procedural wrangling over whether or not Chiniquy had been properly authorized by her husband to sue; the Court of Review overturned it on this ground, and sent it back for retrial.[33] It was eventually reheard by the Court of King's Bench on its merits, the justices all agreeing that there was a right of action and that there had been defamation.[34] The majority reduced the $3000 damages awarded at first instance to $200 but, despite the defendant's partial success on appeal, condemned him to costs, which added considerably to his financial burden (he estimated the costs would be more than $1000).[35] The highly subjective and personal nature of this kind of injury, however, led to markedly divergent opinions on the quantum of damages among the justices, reflecting how offensive each felt the affront had been. Chief Justice Horace Archambault, writing the majority opinion, recognized the intensely felt nature of Chiniquy's injury. "Her pain must have been immense," he wrote, when she saw the word *concubine* applied to her mother, "who had just been taken away from her affection, and whose ashes were not yet cold. Is there in the world any memory more sacred than that of the woman who gave us life, who cradled our infancy in her arms, and who played such a large part in our joys and sorrows?"[36] Still, he followed the general trend in cases of this kind towards suspicion of strictly moral injury. Since Chiniquy had alleged no material injury beyond including the formulaic "in her *biens*" in her declaration, any damages awarded would have a punitive rather than compensatory purpose, and so must reflect the degree of fault. In this case, the chief justice said, Bégin had crossed a line, but barely. Violent polemic was not prohibited, *injure* was, and even *injure* was less serious when it arose as part of a polemic than when it otherwise had no point. Furthermore, he noted, the defendant barely made a living, and a huge damages award would mean his ruin or prison, either of which was disproportionate to his fault.[37] Justice Alexander Cross signed on, but would have awarded Chiniquy much higher damages ($1000), given the "filthy affront" she had suffered.[38] Justice Norman Trenholme and Justice Henry Carroll each dissented: the former would have left the Superior Court's judgment alone, while the latter would have dismissed the action altogether for lack of the husband's authorization.[39]

Bégin had all along also been litigating the case in the court of public opinion, publishing a series of highly critical opinion pieces in *La Croix*. His largely clerical readership clearly found this mobilizing, as several sent money for Bégin's legal fees.[40] Bégin and others suggested that the entire case was nothing more than a campaign against the Catholic press – *La Vérité* and *Le Devoir*, in addition to his own paper – by Chiniquy's lawyer Desaulniers and his firm.[41] Still, at the end, despite being urged by at least one reader to take the case to the Supreme Court to make "the Chiniquyist sect" and its alleged Masonic backers pay to defend it,[42] Bégin contented himself with printing his lawyer's factums in their entirety and then moving on.[43] A year later he was sued by a politician whom he had branded a Freemason and was assessed $100 damages, a controversialist's cost of doing business.[44]

Family Honour: Social and Legal Meanings

Chiniquy points to the tension between social and legal views of family honour, a tension that cannot be resolved into two airtight categories. Plaintiffs like Rebecca Chiniquy brought into court a social understanding of affronts to their family, but an understanding already inflected by legal ideas and the demands of the legal process. Judges, for their part, when they turned to evaluate claimed injuries to family honour or the memory of ancestors, shared at least in part the social world of the litigants and took a common-sense view of what was proper alongside the legal framework (itself contested, as we will see) that their office required them to apply. One way to look at this tension is as revealing the opposing pulls of a liberal, individualist understanding of legal actors and pre-liberal yet no less powerful ideas of collective identity, lineage, and social status. Defendants like Joseph Bégin tended to argue that plaintiffs, as liberal individuals, suffered no damage from critique of their dead relatives and so had no right of action. (It is of course ironic to see a Catholic conservative adopt a liberal position like this, but necessity so demanded.) Plaintiffs like Rebecca Chiniquy voiced a different perspective: whether they had suffered personally was important, but not the only point, since an attack on dead relatives necessarily and self-evidently affected the family as a whole. At the same time, however, *Chiniquy* also reveals other valences of liberal and non-liberal ideas. Rebecca Chiniquy's case rested on an implicit argument that her father was free to leave the priesthood and determine for himself the life he wished to lead, whereas Bégin's position raised the sacramentality of Roman Catholic ordination, which transcended both individual choice and the state's power to recognize certain marriages. Family honour thus engaged in complex and sometimes contradictory ways with Canada's liberal order project.

Like the collective community honour that lurked around the edges of the charivari cases, family honour also challenged the analytical framework surrounding defamation, which in Quebec vacillated between English and French influences. In English law, the reputation was primarily an individual asset, and violations of family honour – specifically words directed at the dead with the intent of injuring the subject's family – were open to indictment for criminal libel, but not to a civil remedy.[45]

In other words, once outside the realm of injury to a living individual, the only recourse was punitive. The French *action d'injures*, by contrast, straddled punitive and compensatory responses. In its early forms the action was concerned mainly with punishing the offender, though damages had been available in certain cases. By the mid-nineteenth century, however, it was increasingly moving towards civil law.[46]

French writers, like their English contemporaries, also struggled to balance family members' visceral sense of outrage with the general principles that the law protected the living and that the dead had no legal personality. Joseph-Pierre Chassan articulated the dilemma: "Is it true that the law will in no way cover with its protection the cold dust of the tomb? The name that we leave behind us and that we bequeath to our children, to our relatives, to our friends, can it be insulted with impunity? In cases like this, are there no interests to guarantee, no hopes to protect, no community of memories, the veritable property of the family, that must be defended against the attacks of spitefulness?"[47]

However shocking it was to leave the dead exposed to attack, the law protected the living: the dead were "in another realm, where are happily unknown all the feelings of anger and vengeance that influence and possess us here below."[48] An action was possible, but only if the attack affected living relatives by ricochet. Chassan made that point quite literally: "The arrow directed against the father, in striking the stone of the tomb, can ricochet against the children and, by injuring their own reputation, can thus strike at their own interests."[49] Other writers agreed: family honour meant the honour of the living members of the family, even in such cases where the direct object of the attack was the memory of the dead.[50] Later in our period, some German scholars argued that the honour of the dead itself deserved direct protection, since it continued after death, even though the life was over.[51] Though this had little traction in France, there was at least rhetorical recognition of the existence of a common interest in cases like this, both in the use of the collective "family," and in the argument some jurists made that the deceased's honour and other similar interests passed not to the deceased's heirs, but rather to the family.[52] Not surprisingly, the parties in Quebec family honour cases selected their citations carefully according to what promised to get them their desired result. Plaintiffs sprinkled their arguments with references to Guyot and Sourdat, hoping to place their situations within the openings provided by French law, while defendants reached for Odgers and Starkie to argue for a complete bar against actions to protect family honour.

Judges were harder to predict. Individual judges might lean one way or the other, towards English or French ideas, but the general impression in family honour cases, as in other areas we are considering, was of judges deciding more on the basis of their reading of the social circumstances of the case than strictly applying either previous decisions or doctrinal positions. Apart from the technical question of whether an individual action could lie for a general insult, judges also had to determine when an injury had been proved and how serious that injury was. This required reading factors like social standing, since, as with individuals, family dishonour arose from being treated in a way not in keeping with the family's position among its peers.

Within this fluid doctrinal context, what did family honour mean? Or, put another way, what roles did family honour play in the Quebec legal world? On the basis of the cases brought forward, it meant various things – protecting the family name, avenging slights to the memory of one's ancestors, guarding the family unit against unwanted alliances – which we will consider in turn. Before reviewing these issues, however, it will be useful to begin by looking at some of the rhetorical uses of the idea of collective honour.

On a general level, plaintiffs in a variety of situations deployed violated family honour as an intensifier, something to allege in the hopes that it would resonate with the values of the judge hearing the case. This is not to say that attacks on relatives (whether alive or dead) did not deeply affect the individuals bringing suit. But showing that family honour and not just personal honour had been injured could allow plaintiffs to underscore the serious and self-evident nature of their injury, thereby (perhaps) moving it beyond the purely subjective level and into the realm of shared social codes regarding family relationships, family status, and family name.

In 1874, for example, one Théophile Leclerc, the male plaintiff in a defamation suit over accusations of his adultery, declined in his action to name the person with whom he was alleged to have committed adultery, stating only that it had been "a *certain person* whom the respondent [the defendant] has often indicated."[53] The defendant Gaspard Bizier demanded specifics, forcing Leclerc to divulge that his alleged partner in adultery was none other than Bizier's own daughter. "Little concerned with his family's honour," Leclerc argued, Bizier "turned his tongue into a *two-edged sword*, because at the same time as he injured the reputation of the appellant [Leclerc], he destroyed the honour of his daughter and sullied that of his own family."[54] Leclerc's dubious attempt to assume the moral high ground failed to sway the judges, and they allowed the defendant's motion to dismiss on the basis that Leclerc had admitted the truth of the alleged defamatory remarks.

In contrast to Leclerc's attempt to use family honour as a sword, the defendant in a 1926 case invoked it as a shield. A young widow's mother-in-law approached the local priest, Victor Lafontaine, for dirt on the man courting the widow, and the officious priest obliged with various (false) accusations, such as that he sold liquor without a licence. The marriage went ahead anyway, and the new husband sued the priest in defamation. In his defence, Lafontaine argued that he was only trying "to prevent this family and Mrs. Joyal [the fiancée] from being dishonoured by this alliance with the plaintiff." The priest's defences were unsuccessful, and the court awarded the defamed suitor $100 plus costs for revendication of his honour.[55]

Family honour also arose outside the context of defamation. A 1904 case involved a fist fight between the plaintiff and the defendant's son, which the former was winning until the defendant himself entered the fray, allegedly causing the plaintiff serious injuries. The defendant claimed he had been responding to provocation, since "the plaintiff insulted and defied the defendant's full-age son, the defendant himself, and his whole family, and it was following these provocations that the brawl began."[56] None of these cases is directly about family honour, but parties in each invoked the idea to bring into the debate its social resonance that (it was hoped) would be self-evident to a judge.

Family honour could also become a way to underscore the crossing of a line of propriety, which turned a remark or insinuation from something that an individual should perhaps shrug off into something intolerable. Attacking one's relatives – particularly one's deceased relatives – was seen as a cheap shot unless justified in some way (such as criticizing the reputation of a public figure, but even that justification was difficult to maintain when applied to the dead, who could no longer defend themselves). This was partly about politeness, but not entirely. Social standards surrounding proper debate and legitimate targets of commentary were crucial for evaluating cases like this. The line between justified (though harsh) criticism and unjustified attack was different for the dead than for the living, but was also different for a family than an individual. In *Chiniquy*, the paper's attack on Charles Chiniquy, public figure, was hardly discussed; Rebecca Chiniquy seemed to have recognized that she had to tolerate attacks on her deceased father. Attacks on her mother – a private figure, or at most a public figure by association – changed the circumstances, which then changed the interpretation of the injury alleged.

This rhetorically powerful argument arose more directly in various kinds of cases in which plaintiffs specifically alleged an injury to family honour, either by itself or in conjunction with other injuries. Although the collective honour of a family was rarely successfully protected via direct action, it was frequently protected indirectly when it could be individualized as affecting a particular living family member. This individualization, however, was more assumed than proved. The Quebec cases reveal three aspects of this issue, involving protection of the family name, vengeance of the memory of the dead, and protection of the family's self-identity against outsiders. Though all raised the issue of family honour, the different circumstances (both legal and social) brought out different nuances of the meanings of honour in the family context.

Defamation in Wax: *Decelles v. International Shows Ltd.*

On 23 January 1920, a triple hanging took place at Montreal's Bordeaux Prison of the three killers of St. Sulpice farmer Alcide Payette.[57] Within weeks of the execution, the Eden Musée, a wax museum on St. Lawrence Boulevard in Montreal, began exhibiting in its chamber of horrors wax effigies of the three condemned men, advertised by signs outside the museum proclaiming, "Today, the three hanged men."[58] Because of the timely interest, the museum added a ten-cent surcharge for the exhibit over the usual twenty-five-cent admission price.[59] The museum, modelled on identically named attractions in New York, Chicago, and elsewhere, opened in 1892 and featured a rotating display of tableaux alongside mummies and other curiosities. Catalogues of the Montreal museum present engravings and photographs of a mix of exhibits, from the historical – "Execution of Joan of Arc"; "Discovery of Canada 1534"; "Siege of Quebec" – to the sensational – "Opium Den"; "The St. Canute Murder"; "Gorilla Taking a Woman Away."[60] Its owners boasted that their purpose was not just to run a commercial enterprise, but "to organize in the metropolis of Canada an undertaking specially consecrated to fine arts and the glorious episodes of the history of the world." To achieve this mission, the museum's directors "have sought in the history, so full of remarkable incidents, subjects for the instruction and amusement of the public carefully excluding the vulgar or offensive."[61]

Figure 3.2 "Les trois pendus" at the Eden Musée, Montreal, photographed 4 April 1940 by Conrad Poirier. BAnQ-VM, P48, S1, P5192. Reproduced with permission of Bibliothèque et Archives nationales du Québec.

The tableau of the three hanged men showed the murderers in a prison cell, one wall of which was painted to depict the home of the murdered farmer. Also in the chock-full cell was a mock-up of the gallows, as well as a glass box that contained a piece of rope, purportedly from one of the nooses, and pipes belonging to the condemned men. The figures were identified by name on labels attached to their clothing, and plaques gave details of their crimes.[62] At the end of March, Ferdinand Lacoste, father of one of the executed murderers, brought criminal libel charges against the museum's manager, Édouard Mathurin, alleging that the exhibit reflected badly on his family and exposed them to "hatred and contempt."[63] Lacoste's lawyer, N.K. Laflamme, K.C., described the tableau as "a disgrace that the law could not allow," and the families of the other two condemned men considered similar charges.[64] Police immediately executed a warrant and removed the statue of Romeo Lacoste from the museum; the *Montreal Daily Star* reported that a bemused crowd watched the "weird procession" of four police officers carrying the head, torso, and limbs of the wax "corpse."[65] Mathurin's reaction was that the whole thing would be good advertising, leading Judge Seth Leet at the preliminary hearing at the Court of Sessions of the Peace to order the exhibit closed and sealed (though "sealed" simply meant draping a cloth over the remaining figures, which any curious visitor could easily lift to peek under).[66] By May charges against Mathurin had been dropped, and the museum's owner, International Shows Ltd., had been charged in his place.[67] At the preliminary inquiry of the owner, the company raised various arguments in its defence, in particular that presenting capital cases was in the public interest and had a salutary deterrent effect and, most interestingly for our purposes, that a charge of criminal libel was inapplicable to the circumstances of this case, since the charge was personal and so could be pressed only by the subject depicted (conveniently dead), not by his father.[68] Against this strong argument, based as it was on the nature of the criminal libel offence, Laflamme focused on family honour. The museum "had no right to coin cash on the shame of a name," he argued, and so the father "had a right to vindication for the exposure of his name." Though in no way responsible "for the sins of his son," the father "was entitled to the respect of his fellow citizens" and had suffered the "contempt of the community" from the exposure. He thus deserved redress before the criminal courts. Several newspapers agreed. The humorous weekly *Le Canard* judged the exhibit to be as shameful as a rumoured stage play being written about the recent notorious torture and death of the child

Aurore Gagnon by her stepmother, while *Le Nationaliste* condemned yellow journalists, municipal authorities, and anyone else who would make money from people's shameful "gawking."[69] Judge Leet took the case under deliberation, promising a decision the following week, though silence ensued until almost a year later, when charges against the company were quietly withdrawn.

Meanwhile, as the criminal libel proceedings were underway, one of the other families took a different (and more promising) tack and in April began a civil suit against International Shows Ltd. The plaintiff, Henri Decelles of Longueuil, was the husband of the sister of Patrick Lemay alias Delorme, another of the executed men. Though the case file has not survived, we can glean enough from the reported judgment and news articles to gain some further insights into the ways of family honour.[70]

Unlike *Chiniquy*, the context here was not journalism with its broad presumption of public interest, but a commercial establishment exhibiting a sensational subject to make money from public curiosity. The defendants' arguments about public interest and privilege were easily brushed aside by Justice Paul-Gédéon Martineau, whose brief judgment ruled (perhaps more easily than warranted) that a business could not be held to be in the public interest, and as a result did not enjoy the "privilege that the law grants, under certain conditions, to the historian, to the critic, etc."[71] Justice Martineau's comparators are telling – whatever the virtues of the Eden Musée, it remained a wax museum catering to thrills and was not, despite its own publicity materials, a place of legitimate historical education and "patriotic work."[72] At the same time, however, no direct defamation had occurred – the exhibit was a more or less faithful depiction of the three convicted and executed murderers, and aside from identifying the men by name, it made no other reference to their antecedents or families. The defence raised precisely that point: they argued that nothing in the exhibit indicated any relationship between the executed man and the plaintiff and his wife. The Decelles thus had to make a more general case, based on association via the family name and family relationships. They argued that their humiliation was caused by acquaintances who, knowing of the Decelles' connection to the executed man, specially made the trip across the St. Lawrence River from Longueuil to visit the exhibit in downtown Montreal. There seems to have been no allegation that their neighbours or friends reacted differently towards them afterwards, though some acquaintances did tell the Decelles that they had seen the exhibit. The mortification came rather from finding out or being reminded that their acquaintances knew of their shameful family connections and had partaken of the spectacle on offer at the Eden Musée.

Justice Martineau found for the plaintiffs, and awarded them $50, far less than the $5000 they had demanded. On the question of damage, always a sticky point in family honour cases, his conclusion was a fairly standard expression of ricochet damage, finding that the Decelles naturally would suffer from the defamation of the memory of their executed relative: "The said exposition constitutes an illegal defamation to the memory of the condemned man, which was legitimately likely to humiliate the plaintiff and his spouse when they learned that in the circle of their acquaintances whom they saw frequently there were some who, because of their relationship to Delorme, had recently visited this exposition."[73] Despite the unfavourable result, in the civil action at least, the Eden Musée at some point reopened the exhibit, and photographs survive from 1940 of "Les trois pendus" at the museum.[74] The clothing was different – the figures now wore prison stripes, while in 1920 news coverage stated that they had been dressed in the clothing worn when the crime was committed – and the figures were actually hanging from the gallows. If anything, the new configuration was even more potentially hurtful to the families than before. The museum may have calculated (or at least hoped) that the new clothing and the depiction of the men paying the ultimate penalty would have increased the public interest aspect of the exhibit by transmitting the clear lesson that crime did not pay.

The efforts of the Lacostes and Decelles to protect their family names against what they saw as defamatory association with unsavoury relatives were indicative of the most numerous type of family honour cases. Typically, a relative – usually a husband or father as head of household – sued for *injure* done to his wife, child, or another member of the family. Though the defamation was directed at the relative, the argument was that the effect of the *injure* touched the entire family collectively and so caused collective damage to the family's name, standing, or reputation that the head of the household had a direct interest in pursuing.

Almost any personal slander could be framed in that way, and frequently was, since almost any attacks on relatives reflected on the family as a whole. In an 1883 case from L'Assomption, a widow sued a churchwarden who at mass had physically forced her twenty-year-old son (still legally a minor until age twenty-one) to his feet and to his knees at appropriate moments during the service because the official objected to the young man's lack of devotion. The mother's argument was that "the insult ... rebounds onto the whole family." The action failed in part because the mother had not proved any injury to herself.[75] In an unreported case from 1885, the plaintiff sued for insinuations about the sexual propriety of his wife because they threatened "to humiliate and bring dishonour onto the plaintiff, his spouse, and his family."[76] In an 1888 case from Hull, a father successfully sued for damage to his own reputation caused by remarks that his daughter had been seen lying with a young man near some quarries. Justice Jonathan Wurtele rejected the defendant's argument (based on English law) that the father had no action for defamation of his daughter and relied on French authorities (Sourdat, Aubry and Rau, Laurent) to make clear that "the esteem and respect which are due to the good conduct of the father, mother and children are common to all, and a father's honor and reputation cannot but be hurt by a slanderous imputation against the character of his minor daughter."[77] In an 1896 case, a Montreal father was awarded damages against a woman who, during an altercation, said to his eighteen-year-old daughter "so go get felt up by your boyfriend on the stairs." The judge found those words (the version in the depositions in the case file was considerably more colourful than in the reported judgment just quoted) to be "of a nature to insult and humiliate not only her but her parents."[78] The nature of legal authority made such arguments of collective injury inevitable, since fathers had to pursue defamation of their minor children, and husbands had either to authorize or sue for their wives (unless separate as to property).[79] At the same time, socially the head of the household was seen to be responsible for the collective well-being of the family, and protecting the family name against attacks was both an individual and a collective necessity.

Cases like these clearly show collective family honour being felt (and argued), but they leave it ambiguous whether family honour was legally protected or not. In principle, an action for defamation affecting family honour could succeed only when there was ricochet damage to an individual member of the family – in the absence of demonstrable individual effects, there was no action for general damage to one's family name or reputation. In a 1912 case from Trois-Rivières, for example, the defendant wrote a defamatory letter questioning a woman's morality. Both her husband and her son sued. The husband sued conjointly with his spouse and claimed they had been "injured in their spousal feelings."[80] The son, however, although not mentioned in the letter, took a separate action "to avenge himself his mother's honour, outraged by this letter."[81] Justice François-Siméon Tourigny noted that "even if it is true that esteem and respect are the common patrimony of the family, we cannot simply admit that the dishonour of one of the members rebounds onto the others." The son's action was dismissed: he had not proved any injury personal to himself, and besides, allowing a simple family link to give a right of action would open the floodgates.[82]

Justice Tourigny's decision was not unusual, but was certainly at the restrictive end of the scale. Despite the nod to family honour as a "common patrimony," dishonour had to be personally felt: "Respect and honour are exclusive *biens* that every individual must defend, since he alone is the judge and has that responsibility."[83] One of the editors of the report added a brief note below the decision, taking issue with its implications: "As a result, do we not have to wonder whether insults to a father or a mother, even when they are alive, cannot do just as much harm, cannot injure the feelings just as sharply, do not call for just as much reparation, relief, healing, condemnation, as those to grandparents or ancestors, gone for half a century or more, whom one perhaps never saw nor knew?"[84] In other cases, however, judges took a less restrictive position and assumed that in certain circumstances there must have been ricochet damage, even in the absence of much or any proof beyond what social norms might dictate. Rebecca Chiniquy won her case not only because of undeniable individual injury, but also because of the judges' manifest distaste for the attack on her dead mother, which they were willing to assume must also have inevitably caused her injury. That position was easier to maintain in the case of dead relatives, as in *Chiniquy* and the cases we will consider in the next section. Judges were unwilling to allow clearly defamatory attacks to remain unavenged on the technicality that the dead had no legal personality: better to allow a living relative to step up on their behalf than to let defamers act with impunity. In the case of defamation of the living, however, unless one could show direct and personal impact, it was for the subject of the defamation to bring action. And in whatever situation, the further one moved from a clear individual injury to generalized effects on family honour, the harder the case was to make.

Eventually the idea of group libel – that defamation of a collectivity was actionable by any member of that collectivity – would be applied to some of these situations. This was a difficult argument to make in the family context, however. Group libel was first successfully argued by Quebec City's Jewish community against anti-Semitic speeches and calls for boycotts of Jewish businesses; it succeeded only because that community was small enough – at the time seventy-five families – that the judges were willing to see the attacks as necessarily aimed at particular Jews, rather than at Jews generally, and so to overlook the lack of a specific named target.[85] In the family context, judges remained resistant to similar arguments that downplayed the need for an individual victim and that urged liability for a collective injury. Still, in a 1946 case from Arthabaska, a judge made precisely that link. The defendant, believing that Charles-Édouard Raymond had been frequenting his wife, said in a loud voice before a crowd at the parish church door that the Raymonds were "womanizers, a stew and a gang of pigs and bastards"; he repeated the same words later in a shop. Charles-Édouard's brother Alcide sued. The defendant admitted making the statements, but argued that his intention was to refer only to two of the brothers, Charles-Édouard and Adélard, not to the plaintiff Alcide. The judge disagreed. Applying the Quebec City group libel case, he ruled that there was no doubt "that the insult was addressed to all the Raymonds," which was sufficient for liability. He awarded $50, to be reduced to $25 if the defendant made a public retraction of his statement at the church door.[86]

This long road to recognition of collective injury did not mean that previously family honour was nothing more than a collection of individual honours, linked by family relationships. The reluctance of judges to decide cases strictly on the technicalities of the rules suggests that collective honour was seen as something real. Put another way, the interest being attacked – family honour – was not in question; difficulties arose in dealing with the effects of those attacks. In the defamation cases we are considering here (and we will turn to other situations in the following sections), the plaintiffs argued and the judges for the most part accepted that something called family honour deserved protection against defamatory attacks. This had to be reconciled with defamation law's operative framework of liberal individualism, with its requirement of a personal injury. The idea of ricochet damage allowed judges to find a liberal individual subject in cases where family honour was at stake. At the same time, however, the low evidentiary burden applied to those ricochets allowed the same judges to ensure that the social norms of collective honour would prevail. This applied only in cases regarded as deserving, of course. In a 1929 Beauce case, a husband sued over alleged remarks that he and his wife kept a disorderly house, that his wife was "an actual whore" and regularly entertained men in her home.[87] The couple were twice acquitted of criminal charges brought by concerned townspeople for lack of evidence. The trial judge in the defamation case accepted the defendant's argument that his remarks were true and that the plaintiffs' moral character was common knowledge; he found the remarks to have had no effect on whatever honour the couple may have had and so dismissed the action. On appeal, however, the judges gave the benefit of the doubt to the plaintiffs, finding in the criminal acquittals evidence that their conduct had changed sufficiently to make the defendant's remarks no longer true and hence defamatory. They reversed and awarded nominal damages of $10, far less than the $1000 the plaintiffs had demanded. While judges were willing to treat the rules flexibly for deserving plaintiffs like Rebecca Chiniquy or the Decelles family, when those whose honour was questionable came before them, they would do no more than hold their noses and award the minimum.

The Memory of Ancestors: *Huot v. Noiseux*

The problem litigants in family defamation cases faced – consensus that an interest had been violated, but disagreement about whether any damage had been suffered – was magnified in cases where the defamatory words were directed at the memory of the dead. Did the dead possess post-mortem honour that living relatives could vindicate on their behalf? More particularly, since the dead had no feelings, could they suffer injury from defamatory words directed at them? In a liberal individualist sense, the answer to these questions was certainly no: the dead were outside the system. Since they were no longer liberal individuals, they could not bring action, and since they were dead they had no surviving interests that could be injured.[88] This interpretation, however logical it was within the assumptions of the legal system, was at odds with social attitudes. For family members – and as the *Chiniquy* case demonstrated, for most judges as well – it was self-evident that protection was needed against anyone who would wantonly defame those who could no longer protect themselves.

This was partly about propriety, as the attack on Rebecca Chiniquy's mother made clear. We see this in a variety of cases, but especially when women were involved, as was the case with the use of *concubine* in *Chiniquy*. It was also more than propriety, however. Even if in strict legal terms one's reputation ended with death, socially what one worked so hard to cultivate during life could not be left at the mercy of one's enemies after death. This idea found formal, if limited, expression in certain areas of law. The law of successions, for example, which existed to give legal force to the idea that death might not be the absolute end it appeared to be, permitted revocation of a legacy or an entire will if the heir did "grievous injury / *injure grave*" to the memory of the deceased testator.[89] This was the only example of the direct protection of memory in the code, and no examples of that specific situation seem to have been reported. The idea of protecting the memory of the dead did, however, give rise to damages actions, as family members sought to use the courts for posthumous protection of their relatives' honour.

The earliest reported case on family memory came from the Quebec City area in 1886.[90] A group of notables of the parish of Beaumont was discussing work needing to be done on the church, and whether it should be paid by the day or by the job. Joseph Turgeon pointed to the church floor, saying that it had been installed forty years earlier, the job given as a favour to a churchwarden who had been found short in his accounts. Turgeon said the work had been done badly – the failure to use tongue-and-groove meant that cold and unpleasant odours rose from the crypt below – and the shoddy work was because the churchwarden had been paid in advance. The churchwarden in question was Damase Roy's deceased father, Pierre, and this history was familiar to many in the parish. Roy sued, claiming among other things that Turgeon's words were spoken with the intention "not only to stain the memory of the said Pierre Roy but to attack the honour of the family to which the Plaintiff belongs and cause to rebound onto the latter … the shame imprinted onto the character of his father."[91]

Witnesses typically said little about the affective dimensions of the case. Led by the lawyers' questioning, they focused instead on whether such a remark should necessarily be seen as damaging to the deceased. The defendant's witnesses tried to downplay its effects, and the defence lawyers tried to limit damages by admitting that Pierre Roy had had a good reputation and that it had remained unsullied since his death.[92] The plaintiff's witnesses, unsurprisingly, questioned the propriety of such attacks on the dead; as Pierre Antoine Roy (no relation) put it, "Mr. Turgeon was wrong to wake up the dead like that."[93] The plaintiff himself testified briefly, called by the defence. The lawyers got him to admit that he and his brother had agreed to bring action if Turgeon did not retract his remarks; they were trying to create the impression that this was somehow cooked up. It may have been, but Roy's answer also underscored how honour connected the entire family: "It's all linked together, within the family."[94]

Justice Frederick Andrews had to determine not just whether the facts as presented gave rise to damages – he found that they did, but said little about it – but also whether Quebec law allowed actions to avenge insults to the memory of one's ancestors in the first place. Taking his cue from the plaintiff's arguments, he pushed aside English authorities (Hilliard and Odgers), who rejected any such action, and instead relied on a list of French authors (Guyot, Grellet-Dumazeau, Chassan, Sourdat).[95] He concluded that an action was available, and moreover that it could be brought by any heir of the deceased. But he found Roy's claim of $400 to be excessive and awarded only $10 and costs because, he said, "these sorts of action must not be encouraged."[96] Not a ringing endorsement of the protection of memory in Quebec law, perhaps, but enough to tip the balance towards the French understanding of post-mortem defamation and to open the door for others to raise the issue of collective honour.

Soon after the decision in *Roy v. Turgeon* was reported, a similar situation came before the courts. A more detailed look at that case will illustrate some of the ways in which the new legal opening intersected with social understandings of memory and family honour.[97]

By all accounts, the 1863 election for the United Canadas was hard fought in Rouville, east of Montreal, with partisans on both sides looking for any edge. More than twenty years later, during the 1886 federal election, elderly local politico Clovis Noiseux was chatting at the market in St. Césaire with all who would listen. He bemoaned the kinds of questionable practices that elections brought out, and in particular people voting at polls where they had no right. As an example, he brought up the old pre-Confederation election, recounting several examples of electoral fraud he had witnessed while serving at the polls for his candidate. He continued, moving on to a case he had only heard about: "I heard that Prudent Huot, the father, voted at St-Paul under the name of his son Prudent, and that he was allowed to do so by swearing an oath, and he did swear an oath."[98] One of those present, a friend of Prudent Huot – but Huot *fils*, not Huot *père* – reported to his friend what Noiseux had said, but got it a bit garbled, thinking it was the younger Huot who had been meant. Without looking into the matter, Huot consulted a lawyer and had him send Noiseux a letter, demanding $5000 compensation for defamation.[99] Noiseux spoke with Huot, explaining that he was not talking about him, but rather his father, who had been dead for more than a decade by that point, and that he was simply making a general point. Huot refused to accept the explanation. He rejected

Noiseux's charge that the threatened suit was just an attempt to get some money, stating instead (according to Noiseux) that he wanted a formal apology (*réparation d'honneur*).[100]

The action Huot instituted soon after was not for defamation of himself, but for defamation of his father's memory. He alleged Noiseux's remarks were made "with the intent to cause the plaintiff and his whole family pain and sorrow, and to do him wrong and cause him damage to his *biens*, his credit, and his reputation."[101] Noiseux, for his part, raised various defences. Aside from the truth of the remarks and his own lack of malice, he argued as well that his remarks were not of a nature that would affect the reputation of the rest of the family, and in any case "the sole interest of defending the outraged memory of his dead father does not suffice to give him a right of action against the defendant."[102] In other words, while Huot was arguing for the self-evident nature of the family's injury, Noiseux was questioning the legality of an action whose principal victim was no longer living.

The testimony of witnesses, including both the plaintiff and the defendant, sheds some light on how individuals within the community understood the idea of family honour. Huot was called by the defendant and was asked why he sued over the injury to his father's memory. His answer points to norms of propriety, while at the same time alluding to the role of his lawyer in framing the case: "It's because, when I saw that I have the same right to sue on my father's behalf, I sued on my father's behalf. That's what I did. I felt it wasn't very generous to attack my family and also my father, who has been dead these fifteen years."[103] Philippe Dupuis, Huot's son-in-law, testified that the whole family was clearly affected by Noiseux's remarks. Asked if for a few thousand dollars he could tolerate similar things being said about his own father, he responded, "No sir, for no amount; honour is too important to me for that." On cross-examination he was asked to specify what wrong Huot had suffered: "Oh dear, I tell you, that's a difficult question to answer; in my opinion, it's the same wrong as would be done to anyone who has a father who was, say, a forger." Pressed to specify what damage appreciable in monetary terms Huot might have suffered, his response was vague: "I can't swear that he did or didn't suffer any, I don't know about that at all."[104]

The question of whether or not there was damage posed something of a dilemma for Huot's witnesses, particularly for his relatives. If they answered there was no damage – that the deceased was a good man and their opinion of him was unaffected by the rumour – they would jeopardize the case. If on the other hand they answered there was damage – that their opinion of Huot *père* had been negatively affected – they were as good as admitting that their own family loyalty was so weak as to be influenced by idle village gossip. That was one reason why the questioning focused on the self-evidently harmful nature of Noiseux's remarks. Almost all witnesses were asked whether similar allegations about their own father would have affected them; the plaintiff's witnesses mostly admitted it would have, while the defendant's witnesses at best grudgingly conceded it might have.

That was also why the plaintiff's case focused on the feelings raised by the defamatory attack on his father, rather than on any effects it might have had on the family's reputation. Either might suffice in a defamation action, though purely emotional effects were harder to prove.[105] The witnesses distinguished between material and moral effects of the alleged defamation. One of Noiseux's main arguments was that there was no evidence Huot had suffered damage; this was only partly true. The lawyers, and the witnesses they had coached, clearly attempted to focus on the question of material injury. This is no surprise, since the system required special proof for material injury, as we will see in even starker terms when we consider grief in chapter 6. The evidence of material loss in this case was in fact virtually non-existent. Almost every witness, and all of the defence witnesses, began by testifying that the Huot family had suffered no discernible injury. They elaborated by noting that the remarks about Huot *père* had not affected the surviving Huots' business or livelihood in any way, and that the family generally enjoyed a good reputation in the community, whatever people said about the old patriarch's voting habits. Huot himself raised this point in his own deposition. While he could not point to any specific material effects on himself, he worried about his own sons, all of whom were in business where the taint of fraud might harm their prospects. In the end, he concluded, "I'm not able to say on my oath that it caused damage, but it brought up a lot of bad doubts."[106] Establishing some kind of material damage made things a lot easier in cases like this, and each side naturally focused first on that question.

When witnesses were pressed further, particularly the defence witnesses on cross-examination, we start to get a clearer understanding of what defamation of the dead meant in the community. Here Noiseux's argument about lack of evidence was contradicted, even by his own witnesses. The same witnesses who began by confidently asserting that the Huots' reputation was unaffected, backed off when asked whether there might not have been moral injuries associated with the remarks. Octave Sénécal was a typical example. On examination-in-chief by the defendant's lawyer, he first testified that the Huots had suffered no damage. When pushed on cross-examination, however, he was less emphatic, noting that the remarks about Huot's father "must have given him heartache, because no one likes to bring disgrace on oneself nor on one's relatives."[107] Other defence witnesses – with the exception of one or two obdurate individuals who refused to admit anything[108] – proceeded in a similar manner: initial denial of damage (that is, material loss), then on cross-examination admission of moral injury.[109] Nazaire Meunier, one of Huot's witnesses, admitted that the family had suffered no damage, but then went on to reflect on the nature of family honour and threats to it: "If my father had made a false oath I would probably be just as respectable as I am; but in dealing with others I would probably be less well regarded. It happens that a good child is born to dishonest parents. Because the matter is underway, the plaintiff's credit, honour, and reputation aren't diminished by the defendant's words, but if he had let the matter rest, that would have done something to him."[110] In other words, the allegation that Huot *père* had voted fraudulently could not but cause damage to the Huots, whether purely emotional – Octave Sénécal's "heartache" – or something more. Left unchallenged, the potential for injury would surely manifest in some way. The exception was Fortunat Huot, the plaintiff's brother, who claimed to have suffered no injury and denied that his father had either.[111] When the plaintiff was asked how two brothers could react so differently to words spoken against the same father, he responded with an affirmation of the subjective nature of honour and family reputation: "Not all hearts are the same, some are more sensitive than others. Some are able to endure insults and others aren't."[112]

At trial, Justice Michel Mathieu awarded Huot $50 damages, far less than the $5000 he had sought. The amount reflected the lack proof of special damage, as well as his finding that Noiseux had not acted maliciously. His dissatisfaction with Huot's exaggerated claim was evident in how he split the award of costs. Noiseux was responsible for costs up to the level of an action for $50, while Huot, despite his partial victory, was condemned to pay Noiseux the difference in costs between an action for $5000 and one for $50.[113] In coming to this conclusion, he had some interesting things to say about the newly minted action for protecting the honour of ancestors. To connect the honour of the father – no longer directly actionable – with that of the family, he resorted to property language. Like any other legacy, the father's honour was handed down to his children, "forming one of the most important parts of his children's patrimony." Any attack on the father's honour, then, gave to the children a right of action.[114] Calling honour a part of the patrimony – making it a *bien*, in other words – provided a legally recognized way of articulating the interest at stake in the case. Rather than leaving honour as something vaguely articulated, it became an interest with material value, whose violation could then be assessed. Moving from this interesting foundation, however, Justice Mathieu moved back to vaguely asserting that injury was self-evident. Rather than laboriously going through the testimony – much of which claimed that the remarks had no discernible effect on the Huot family's reputation – the judge simply asserted that there must be some injury: "Considering that any attack on the reputation of a dead man more or less affects the children."[115] His wording here – "more or less" – is a giveaway that he was assuming damage from his reading of social codes, typical for general damages, but not always so explicitly stated. As in the other family honour cases, because it was obvious in a social sense that an attack on a dead relative must somehow injure living relatives, particularly a son, nothing further was needed.

Both parties appealed, Huot over the reduced damages, Noiseux to dismiss the whole action. Noiseux's appeal, as well as his response to Huot's appeal, raised various grounds. Most prominently, he argued that neither Huot nor the family had suffered any injury.[116] Beyond that, however, he attacked the basis of Huot's action. The reputation of the dead, he argued, whether in its public or even its private aspects, belonged to history alone and so was subject only to the exigencies of good faith and truth.[117] In commenting on a matter of public interest, he was exercising a right "for a praiseworthy end" (the integrity of elections), which could not give rise to an action in defamation. He supported this point with Starkie on libel and slander.[118] Huot, for his part, sought to convince the judges of the significant emotional harm Noiseux's words had caused him and his family. The reduced damages were insufficient, he argued: "The Appellant's sorrow is amply proved, and moreover is easily understood.... From a moral point of view, the injury caused – the dishonour of a whole family – should have elicited an exemplary condemnation."[119] The appellate judges affirmed the result on the merits, accepting the trial judge's findings and in particular that the attack on the father's memory had ricocheted to affect the son. They changed only the penalty imposed on Huot via the costs; Noiseux's appeal they dismissed outright.[120]

Protecting the Boundaries of the Family

The family honour cases we have examined were all in a certain sense about control – control over the public image of the family in the face of threats from outsiders. Rebecca Chiniquy challenged the gratuitous insulting of her parents (and herself) against a newspaper claiming to speak in the public interest. Lacoste and Decelles were trying to shut down the wax exhibit in order to prevent their collective family identity and family name from being utterly overshadowed by and identified with the heinous acts of single members of those families. Prudent Huot pursued the perceived slights against the memory of his father in part because they threatened the integrity of his family's reputation for respectability and honesty within the community. Reputation was carefully constructed and cultivated, but it was of course always a balance between the individual's or the family's performed public image and society's assessment of that performance. Defamation threatened to usurp control over reputation by presenting to society a different, unauthorized view of the family, one that was untrue or unfair. But the verbal usurpations of control represented by defamation were only part of the story of the protection of reputation. In some cases, the unwanted associations that threatened the family's image were quite literally about control, as unwanted interlopers sought entry into the family circle, or as problematic insiders threatened to escape. This came out especially in cases involving contests over authority within the family, such as when parents objected to a proposed marriage alliance or when family members sought to interdict a member whose conduct was problematic. Situations such as these jeopardized the honour and public image of the family. As Thierry Nootens has shown for the nineteenth century, new relationships and marriage alliances served to project a family's collective reputation into the future, by expanding and developing the networks within which rank and honour were built and maintained.[121] Control over family members thus directly affected control over family honour, and this required continual vigilance by all family members over threats to the family's human and moral boundaries, its zone of familial identity.

Cases in which parents objected to their children's chosen marriage partners, or in which children sought court permission to marry despite their parents' objections, present interesting insights into the construction and maintenance of family honour.[122] Such cases often involved upper-class families concerned with what Patricia Seed, studying colonial Mexico, has called "honour as status," or the maintenance of social rank; this was the case in the example we will consider below.[123] But more modest families too had concerns about their collective public reputation, even if they less frequently brought their concerns before the courts. In legal terms such cases were framed around paternal authority (*la puissance paternelle*), a power closely aligned with broader social concerns. Pierre-Basile Mignault called it "the moralizing element of the family," and he saw it as the foundation of society as a whole.[124] One aspect of this moralizing mission of the father of the family was to safeguard his family's honour, name, and reputation, and a key part of that was the exercise of the parents' power to oppose the marriage of their minor children.

Drawing on old French law, article 119 CCLC stipulated that children under twenty-one required the consent of their father and mother (note, both parents) before contracting marriage. That this was really about the father's authority was made clear in the same article, which added the qualification that if the parents disagreed, the consent of the father alone sufficed. Further, the father also held the power to oppose a minor's marriage; the mother could exercise that power only if the father was absent, insane, stripped of his authority, or dead.[125] The parents' supervisory power was grounded explicitly in the notion of honour, specifically the honour that all children owed their father and mother.[126] Essentially, children were duty-bound (honour-bound) to consult their parents, a duty given some teeth via the parents' corresponding power to oppose their choice.

Marriage cases tended to focus on highly technical arguments – for example about dates (since the parents' action had to be instituted within six months of their knowledge of the marriage) and about the interaction of various provisions of the civil code.[127] But alongside the technicalities, the cases often also involved assertions of family honour, as the parents typically presented themselves as guardians of the family reputation, carefully constructed and maintained, but now jeopardized by an unwanted outsider seeking entry.

The rules in the CCLC, based on the French code, drew on a long tradition, both secular and ecclesiastic, against clandestine marriages and seduction.[128] Those rules were designed ostensibly to protect the interests of both the spouses and their parents. As Thomas Loranger put it in 1879, opposition to marriage was "a procedure of the highest utility.... [I]t safeguards the threatened honour of families and protects the good faith of the spouses themselves." Furthermore, he continued, opposition before the fact could prevent legal actions afterwards, the latter being a cure worse than the disease, since it meant preserving the marriage at the cost of shameful publicity of how it had been contracted.[129] Indeed, some of the litigation arising from the rules, as we will see below, involved assessing the relative strength of those various (and competing) interests. The minor spouses were to be protected from their own foolishness and lack of experience. As one author put it, "It is thus not about encroaching on the spouses' freedom but about protecting them against their own tendencies; it is really about giving them weapons against their own weakness."[130] As some maintained, however, this was a serious limitation on the liberty of the spouses and opened the door to others making decisions for them. The parents, however, were also recognized as having a personal stake in the matter because of the potential negative effects of an unwanted marriage on the family's interests. As Mignault wrote, since marriage involves the collective honour and prosperity of the family, it was too important to be left solely to the choice of the young couple when the parents were opposed.[131] Those family interests were both material and moral. Since ascendants were potentially obliged to support any children of the marriage, it was seen as natural that they should have a say in the matter. But beyond the material threat, honour was implicated as well. Parents whose children circumvented their authority were seen to suffer an actionable *injure* on a personal level,[132] but the injury was also seen to be broader, affecting the honour of the whole family.[133] The parents' action to annul such a marriage "has as a foundation the saving of the family's honour; it is so that they can maintain good order and enhance it by their good morals that they are permitted to act."[134]

Quebec judges echoed these different interpretations of the rules. In an 1895 case, a minor son (aged eighteen or nineteen) sought court authorization to marry after his father had refused his consent. The son ascribed the refusal to "pure malice and caprice," speculating that it might also have been due to his father's inaccurate idea of his son's salary; the father did not appear, so his reasons remained obscure.[135] The petitioner's mother, by contrast, had given her approval. Justice Charles Chamilly de Lorimier reaffirmed the father's role as guardian of the family. Except in the most exceptional of cases, he wrote, courts must not intervene in the exercise of paternal authority, a discretionary power that could not be abused, but that extended to a balancing of circumstances and consequences. In fact, he continued, the regime of paternal authority, including children's duty of respect to their parents, was of public order because it was crucial to the integrity of both families and society generally.[136] The son's motion for authorization was refused, the marriage did not go ahead, and in the 1901 census the son was still listed as a bachelor living (how happily one can only imagine) in his father's household in Montreal.

Alongside the marriage cases were situations in which family members' misbehaviour threatened family honour and led relatives to seek means of hiding or mitigating their shame. The treatment of illegitimate children and their mothers is a stark example, where the legal regime mirrored the social opprobrium of illicit sexual conduct.[137] In a 1902 Sherbrooke case, grandparents were found not to have an obligation to support an illegitimate grandchild. Justice François-Xavier Lemieux noted that such a child was "the product of illegitimate and disorderly relations," and as a result, although the father was required to support his offspring, the law "does not wish to inflict a chastisement on a whole family, which is not responsible for the fault of the father."[138] Mothers who had children outside marriage likewise could find themselves confronted by a legal regime designed to facilitate the protection of family honour at the expense of individual members.[139]

Similar fears were evident in cases of family members whose mental illness, habitual drunkenness, or prodigality led to interdiction proceedings, as Thierry Nootens has shown.[140] Prodigals could be interdicted when they "give reason to fear that they will dissipate the whole of their property"; a similar provision applied to those "of weak intellect."[141] Habitual drunkards (added to the CCLC in 1870) and narcotic users (added in 1895) could be interdicted if they "place[d their] family in trouble or distress."[142] The preamble of the legislation on habitual drunkards gave its rationale: that the drunkenness of heads of families and other adults had "heretofore, on many occasions, been the cause of ruin to their families, and of grievous injury as well to their relations as to their creditors." Though the material well-being of the family was foremost in legislators' minds, the moral threat was implied. Behind all these provisions was the idea – made more explicit in the language of "fear" employed – that this was in part to protect the family reputation and not just its material assets. The definition of habitual drunkard – "any person who, according to the common report of the neighborhood, has the reputation of being a drunkard"[143] – made it even clearer that the law was stepping in to provide protection against the shaming potential of such relatives. Many of the cases involving these provisions involved (among other reasons) a desire to ensure that the individual's conduct would be kept sufficiently in control to prevent behaviour that would reflect badly on the family. If opposition to marriage involved attempts to use paternal authority to prevent outsiders from entering the family, in interdiction cases authority was used to keep dishonourable behaviour from escaping the family circle and coming into public view. In an 1884 case, a lawyer's widow who "intoxicates herself in a degrading manner and wanders the streets of the City of Montreal half dressed" was held to be "a source of scandal for the public and of shame and disgrace for her family."[144] In cases like this, interdiction protected the individual, but at the same time served the collective purpose of limiting the potential reputational damage done by an uncontrollable relative. Justice François-Xavier Lemieux made this point clearly in a 1905 case, asserting that the interdiction of a drunkard served to keep him "from getting the family into trouble or difficulty, and from conducting his affairs to the prejudice of his family or his creditors and especially to keep him from ruining his health and cutting short his days."[145] At the same time, however, interdiction proceedings could also make public what had until then been diligently hidden behind closed doors, so it was potentially a double-edged tool.[146]

A detailed look at a cause célèbre will fill out this picture of threats to family honour, the means families used to prevent unfavourable associations, and the emotional reactions driving family conflicts. As ever in the family context, however, little is said and much needs to be inferred. The case involved the thorny question of the requirement in the CCLC that minors wishing to marry must first get their parents' consent.

The Cadet's Marriage: *Agnew v. Gober*

On 22 February 1905, Kathleen Agnew arrived in Kingston, Ontario, where her younger brother, Augustus Waterous Agnew, was a cadet at the Royal Military College.[147] This was no friendly sibling visit, however: Kathleen was on a serious mission. Word had somehow reached the Agnew home that Augustus had married Mary (or May) Gober the previous December and kept this news from his family.[148] Somehow the Toronto papers had already got hold of the juicy story of the cadet's marriage (the Montreal papers were slow to follow) – likely the news had broken a few days previously and was the talk of Kingston.[149] Augustus's father, William Agnew, was in France on business, but his wife, Emma Johnson Waterous, wasted no time in dispatching their daughter to retrieve the errant young man. Kathleen arrived in Kingston with news that their mother was gravely ill – most likely a ruse – and that Augustus had to return immediately to Montreal.[150] The siblings left the following day, with Augustus giving his wife assurances that he would return. That was the last she saw of him. Once back in Montreal, within a week his mother had packed him off to France to break the news to his father – a cable just would not do, she later testified – and he was promptly enrolled in an engineering course in Europe.[151] His parents pulled the necessary strings to secure his discharge from the college, which prevented his expulsion for violating the strict rules against married cadets.[152]

The couple had been married quietly in a Church of England ceremony (Gus was Anglican, while May was raised Presbyterian) at St. James Church in Kingston on 14 December 1904.[153] Augustus (or Gus as he signed a letter to his wife) was at the time twenty years old, the only son of a wealthy Montreal society family.[154] The Agnews lived on Dorchester Boulevard just west of downtown Montreal – a fashionable address – in a household that included two servants. William Agnew was an importer of silks and other fine cloths, which took him frequently on buying trips to Europe and elsewhere.[155] Their circle of acquaintances – as evidenced by those with whom they allegedly discussed the problem of their son's marriage – included the Anglican bishop of Montreal and prominent professionals in both Montreal and Kingston.[156] Sending Augustus to RMC was a way to open for him a career in the military or engineering. May was rather older than her young suitor: twenty-nine at the time of the wedding, though she seems to have put twenty-six on the marriage certificate. (The newspapers covering the case exaggerated the age gap to play up the May-September angle, with one article putting May's age at thirty-five to Augustus's eighteen.[157]) She was from Marietta, Georgia, near Atlanta, and was from a similarly privileged background. Her father, Newton Napoleon Gober, had been a physician and commanding officer in the Georgia Sharpshooters during the Civil War and was elected to the State House of Representatives in 1868, where he was instrumental in expelling from the legislature the ex-slaves elected to the Reconstruction government.[158] He continued as a prominent physician in Georgia after his political career. May was a top student and held a master of arts degree in English from Queen's University in Kingston, where she had won academic prizes. Since graduating in 1900 she had been owner and principal of the Kingston Ladies' College.[159] Her decisive and often feisty exchanges with the lawyers during her depositions in the cases ("I have answered that question"; "I did not say the things you are asking me") indicate a strong and confident personality,[160] and a bit of cheek was evidenced by her publishing, during the thick of the litigation, a piece of fiction drawing on her knowledge of cadet culture at RMC.[161] How May ended up studying in Canada is a mystery; her class at Queen's had some other foreign students (from New York and Vermont), but none except a few western Canadians from so far away.[162] Her father seems to have spent some time working as a physician in Montreal: the date is uncertain, but this may have been what brought her to Canada.[163] She later testified that she preferred living in Canada, but the hints of tensions with her father – she returned to Canada despite his opposition – perhaps get closer to the truth.[164]

May alleged that the couple had been engaged since April 1904.[165] The Atlanta papers reported (after the matter had blown up and become scandal fodder) that the wedding "was a quiet one owing to the ill health of the bride's father."[166] Dr. Gober seems indeed to have been ill, and perhaps he disapproved of the marriage, but a more immediate reason for keeping it quiet was the risk of expulsion Augustus ran.[167] According to Jessie McCann, May's friend in Kingston who seems to have been privy to the secret, the couple contented themselves with visits at Gober's home (a house she owned and from which she ran the school) whenever Augustus could get leave.[168] A fellow cadet testified that Augustus could not have spent the night at May's house; college rules were far too strict for that.[169] The marriage was consummated – Augustus grudgingly admitted that, after pointed questioning that took up a page and a half in the transcript – and May might have become pregnant: she later claimed that the stress of the conflict over the marriage caused her to miscarry.[170] Despite their best efforts at secrecy, on about 20 February word somehow leaked out. In a letter to May, Augustus was clearly attempting damage control:

> My Dearest May,
> I have written a long letter to Kathleen, and told her to break the news as gently as possible to mother, and to leave mother apply for my discharge immediately. I also wrote a letter to Peterson chief engineer of the Guelph and Goderich Railway, asking for a situation to be taken inside of a month. Keep up your spirits and work your side, and we will make things come out all right, I hope.
>   Good night.
>   Your own,
>   Gus[171]

Jessie McCann testified she was displeased that the marriage had become public, but Augustus, she continued, "faced it in a very manly way. He told me that he would have to face the matter like a man and that he had applied for a position."[172] On the same day as the letter to May, Augustus fired off the other letter he had mentioned, writing to a contact with the Guelph and Goderich Railway about a position as a rodman, stressing that his studies had given him a solid understanding of "the principles of levelling."[173]

However gently Kathleen broke the news to their mother, the result was far from an open-armed welcoming of a new daughter-in-law. In addition to the direct approach of separating the couple and spiriting Augustus out of the country, the Agnews moved quickly on the legal front. They retained the eminent Montreal firm of Greenshields, Greenshields, Macalister, and Languedoc, who instituted an action on 25 April 1905 to have the marriage annulled on the grounds that Augustus, a minor, had never obtained the required parental consent.[174] That initial action was discontinued on 9 June and replaced by an almost identical one the next day. The reason for this strategy is unclear. Augustus had turned twenty-one on 6 June, and while Quebec law did not explicitly bar an action in nullity by the parents when the child reached full age, that point was hardly sufficiently settled to rely on it. This would in fact be a key issue in the litigation that followed. A few months after initiating the action, the Agnews switched law firms, bringing in Geoffrion & Cusson, headed by star litigator Aimé Geoffrion, who retained the equally high-powered Eugène Lafleur, K.C., as counsel.[175] May went with another major firm, McMaster & Hickson, and they wasted no time countering the action with a series of preliminary exceptions. Battle was thus joined in the complex and arcane field of private international law to determine whether Augustus (and so May by marriage) was domiciled in Ontario or Quebec, and what effects that domicile might have on the Quebec requirement of parental consent for the marriage of a minor child.[176] A brief overview of the legal points will suffice to set up the discussion of family honour to follow.

The Agnews sought to annul their son's marriage on the ground that it had been performed without their consent. They argued the basics: Augustus had been a minor at the time of the marriage, but had never asked for nor received his parents' consent. Though he had since attained his majority, he remained domiciled in Montreal and so subject to Quebec law, which required parental consent for a minor's marriage. As a result, the union was irregular and invalid and should be

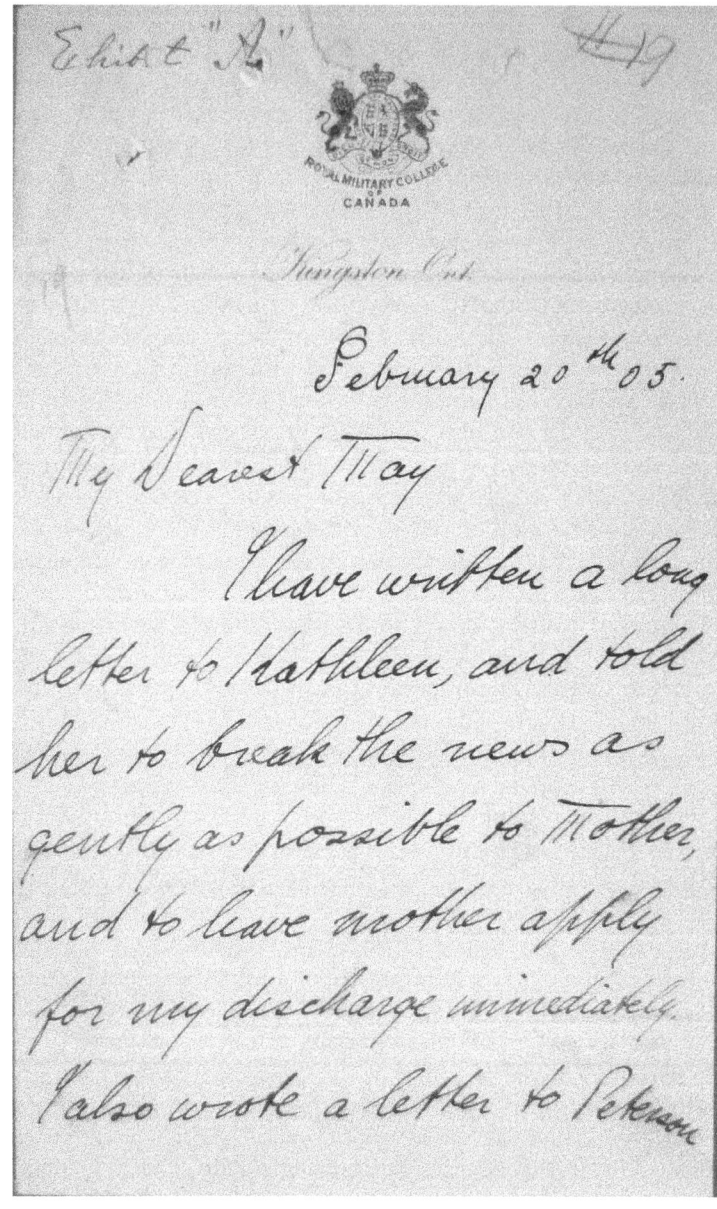

Figure 3.3 Letter from Augustus Agnew to May Gober, dated 20 February 1905, the day he left her. BAnQ-VM, *Agnew v. Gober*, Superior Court case

*chief engineer of the Guelph
and Goderick Railway,
asking for a situation to
be taken inside of 2 month.
Keep up your spirits and
work your side, and we
will make things come out
all right, I hope.
Good night.
Your own.
Gus.*

file (no. 801), Defendant's Exhibit A. Photograph by the author. Reproduced with permission of Bibliothèque et Archives nationales du Québec.

set aside.[177] The bailiff assigned to serve the writ on May could not find her: she had sold her house in Kingston and returned to Georgia at the time the first action was instituted, purportedly for her health.[178] The court granted permission to have her summoned by notice in Montreal newspapers, and small adds ran on consecutive days in the *Montreal Daily Herald* and *La Presse*.[179]

Gober's lawyers responded to the action in various ways. They began with two preliminary exceptions. First, they argued that the Quebec courts had no jurisdiction, since the couple were domiciled in Kingston. That was dismissed on 18 April 1906, and an appeal was abandoned for failure to post the required security (money would prove to be a problem for the otherwise independent May throughout the proceedings). Second, they argued that the Agnews' previous action, abandoned right after Augustus's birthday, constituted *lis pendens*, since it was substantially identical to the current action and had not properly been terminated. This too was dismissed, on 15 January 1907, and permission to appeal was rejected. Gober filed exceptions to both judgments.

With preliminaries out of the way (after a year and a half), the defence filed an inscription in law (a demurrer, that is, a motion to dismiss the action for lack of legal basis) and a plea on the merits. The inscription tried to exploit the earlier discontinued action by arguing that the parents' proceedings in nullity had been extinguished along with paternal authority once Augustus reached full age. They bolstered that with two alternative arguments: that consent was not essential to the validity of a marriage, but was simply a requirement of form, and that the law of the place where the marriage was celebrated should govern, not the law of domicile.[180] On 29 June 1907, Justice Charles Davidson accepted the principal argument (that the action was extinguished), allowed the demurrer, and dismissed the Agnews' case.[181] To allow the parents to nullify the marriage would be "repugnant to our institutions and laws, whether the right asserted is one of expiation for a scorned parental authority, or one for relief of the son from some injury he had done to himself during minority."[182] He did not specify what the parental consent requirement was for – protection of the parents' authority or protection of the minor from youthful mistakes – but his use of "scorned" in the passage just quoted, as well as elsewhere when he characterized Augustus's actions as "an affront,"[183] suggested that honour was involved, both the honour of the father holding paternal authority and the family honour of which the father was principal guardian. In Justice Davidson's reading of the case, however, the father's (and the family's) honour-based interest had to give way to higher principles of public order.

The parents appealed, and the Court of King's Bench overturned the decision on 22 May 1908, dismissing the inscription in law.[184] Issues of honour arose again, but in support of the opposite conclusion from Justice Davidson's. The two dissenting justices – the two anglophones on the bench – specified that parents' rights in such circumstances were there to protect the child and so were no longer necessary once the child reached the age of majority and paternal authority ended. Justice Norman Trenholme noted that allowing the parents to attack their now full-age child's marriage would effectively nullify article 324 CCLC, which stated that a person of full age was capable of exercising all civil rights, including the right to marry.[185] The majority disagreed, however, and developed a more expansive reading of the situation. Like Justice Davidson at first instance, they pointed to higher principles, but for them family honour was the higher principle before which others must give way. The case was not simply a matter of whether or not children should be protected against themselves, stated Chief Justice Henri-Thomas Taschereau. Rather, protecting children against their own weakness or lack of experience was necessary to further the higher purpose of protecting "the very honour of the whole family."[186] Even if the father's power ended for the future when the child came of age, it continued with respect to the past, and so the father retained "full interest, both personally and in the name of the family itself, to see to the annulment of the irregular marriage of his minor son." Once annulled, the now full-aged son could turn around and marry the same person the very next day and the father would have no recourse whatsoever. (At this point, the chief justice noted as an editorial aside that Augustus's silence indicated that he was not interested in that option.[187]) In other words, the law allowed the father only so much control over the family honour and no more. But within the constraints of paternal authority, parental control was in place for collective, and not just individual reasons.

The case on the merits went forward, with Gober's room to manoeuvre significantly limited by the interlocutory decisions. Her argument on the merits was two-pronged. First, Ontario law must apply, since the couple were domiciled in Kingston, and in Ontario spouses over the age of eighteen needed no parental consent. Second, even in Quebec law, the consent requirement was a matter of form and not capacity, and so was governed by the law of the place where the marriage was celebrated, not the domicile. She asked that the action be dismissed or, in the alternative, that she be declared to have been in good faith and be awarded alimony of $50 per month "during her natural lifetime."[188] Justice Paul-Gédéon Martineau dismissed those arguments on 23 February 1909 and declared the marriage annulled.[189] An appeal to the Court of Review was dismissed on 22 April 1910,[190] and that part of the affair came to a final close when Gober's petition for permission to appeal directly to the Judicial Committee of the Privy Council (*in forma pauperis*) – initially granted – was withdrawn in August 1911 by consent of the parties.[191]

In contrast to the Agnews, money was clearly an issue for Gober in this case, as the abandoned appeals suggest. The permission to appeal to the Privy Council as a pauper would have excused her only from fees due to the Privy Council office and any costs should she eventually lose; the rest of the tremendous expense of an overseas appeal remained, which doubtless influenced her decision to drop the matter.[192] In early 1907, in the thick of the litigation, May had moved back to Montreal, shifting from boarding house to boarding house ("I had to move about a good deal on account of not being comfortable"), and trying (in vain, apparently) to bring in some income by giving children piano lessons.[193] Her story preceded her. An employee at a Montreal music shop where she was inquiring about renting a piano testified that he knew who she was from coverage in the papers, and that his opinion was unfavourable: "From having heard something of her affair I really thought she was undesirable, and I made the terms prohibitive in a way, in other words I was riding for a fall, I did not want her business."[194] She had to make do with borrowed time on a rooming house piano. Later, in June 1909 in a sidebar to the main action that hinted at either desperation or vindictiveness, May petitioned for authorization to sue William Agnew for alimony. The argument was that Augustus had failed to provide for her since he abandoned her in February 1905, and he had no property that could be seized. Given that she was "now in want and in actual need of support and maintenance," and given William Agnew's affluence, she wished to pursue him for $50 per month for a period of twelve months. She was duly authorized by the court (though the marriage had been annulled four months earlier, by article 163 CCLC its civil effects continued as long as the spouses had been in good faith), but the case went no further.[195]

Meanwhile, alongside the Agnews' action in nullity of the marriage, May launched her own action in February 1907, claiming the astronomical sum of $53,000 in damages from William, Emma, and Kathleen Agnew for defamation and alienation of her husband's affection.[196] The Montreal legal community – and the press – gleefully looked forward to this case, which promised both juridical interest and (more to the point) scandalous behaviour among the rich. As the Ottawa *Citizen* reported under the headline "Big Sensation Society's Hit," "The amazing interest that attaches to [the action] here can scarcely be imagined. The cases in which a husband has brought action for the alienation of his wife's affection are rare here, or anywhere in Canada, but the reverse, as in the present case, is almost unknown."[197] According to her declaration, around this time May heard through her network of friends that the Agnews were saying alarming things about her. She was vague as to what was said, by whom, and when, but not its effects: the loss of Augustus's "love, affection, esteem and admiration" due to the conspiracy of the defendants to "poison the mind" of her husband.[198] In response to motions for particulars by the defendants, she elaborated. She alleged that they were accusing her of caring nothing for Augustus, but of having entrapped him for his money to deal with her own heavy debts. Furthermore, she claimed that they were saying she had been unfaithful to him, and that her pregnancy was the result: he could not have been responsible, they said, since the marriage had never been consummated. Statements like these "became matters of common rumour" in both Kingston and Montreal, spread through letters and oral conversation with a long list of people, including the Anglican bishops of Montreal and Kingston, various lawyers and physicians, a number of professors at RMC and their wives, the commanding officers at the college and their wives, and several of Augustus's fellow cadets. Moreover, she alleged, William Agnew had put notices in the Kingston papers disclaiming responsibility "for any debts contracted in his name or in the name of his son Augustus, without his written authority," notices that were understood to refer to her.[199] The defendants responded with the usual pleas: a general denial of having said anything, but even if they had, any such statements were true, were privileged, were already known to their audience, and caused the plaintiff no damage.[200]

In this case, even more than in the nullity action, the parties' expensive legal counsel earned their fees, and it became a continual – and slow-moving – blizzard of procedural documents and interlocutory judgments, some of which were appealed up the system. One indication of the procedural games was that in addition to making Gober file everything three times, once for each defendant, all three Agnews filed motions demanding security for costs, alleging that Gober should be treated as if she were not resident in Quebec. The motions were dismissed, but only after witnesses had been heard on the matter, and in any case the triplicate filing of all documents continued.[201] The case had still not come before the jury (Gober had opted for a jury trial, which the Agnews also challenged) by June 1910, when Gober reinscribed it for proof and hearing, but by this time little was being done by either side, and in March 1911 the case was struck from the roll, likely because Gober lacked funds to pursue it.[202]

So much for the legal framework of the various actions. To get at the Agnew family's feelings when confronted with an unchosen and unwanted new relation requires some reading between the lines and cutting through the lawyers' language in which the case was rendered. Augustus, William, and Emma all testified (Kathleen did not), but the focus of their testimony was always on establishing the newlyweds' domicile, not (at least not directly) on their reactions to the marriage or to May Gober.

The case files contain no specific allegations about why the Agnews objected to their son's marriage; the legal action needed no reason, just a ground of illegality. The bride's age and her apparently strained relations with her birth family were likely factors, especially since her social status was comparable to their own (though perceptions about fine gradations of status could be all-important in cases like these). It is also possible that there was a personal dislike, since May seems not to have been a complete stranger to the Agnews. Emma testified that she was "slightly" acquainted with May, since in the summer of 1904 – before the marriage – May had passed through Montreal on her way to visit friends in the country and stopped in at the Agnews.[203] Emma said nothing more about it, but May claimed that the visit had been made "on their invitation the summer before I was married."[204] If May had come to Montreal when her father was living there, it is possible that she and the Agnews moved in similar social circles and that she met them at that time. She did not elaborate on this point, but the hint was that the Agnews knew about the engagement. Whatever the reason for the Agnews' legal gambit – personal dislike, protecting their son and heir, or something else – its immediate purpose was to exclude this unwanted outsider from linkage to the family.

Hints of the family's feelings about May came out at various times, though they were heavily mediated by the lawyers and the requirements of the litigation. William Agnew, as gatekeeper of the family and its honour, was the only one asked about his attitude towards May, and he made clear his feelings about her as a potential member of the family. Asked whether he would receive May into his home as his son's wife, his reply was a curt, "No, emphatically."[205]

The alienation of affection case had a bit more scope to raise issues of attitudes and feelings (though still not a great deal, and once again it was coloured by the acrimony of that litigation). All three defendants, in their virtually identical pleas, agreed that Augustus had "never loved" May, and that she had enticed her youthful and inexperienced beau into marriage "by falsehoods, deceits, threats of suicide, scandal, and other similar threats; allegations that he had compromised her, ruined her financially and socially, appeals to his sense of honour, to his pity in view of her loneliness and infirmity."[206] Once he left Kingston and was back in Montreal, the pleas continued, he "had learned of her deceitfulness and of the means she had taken to entrap him into this marriage and had also come to know her real disposition, with the result that far from loving her, he hated her, and of his own accord declined to have anything more to do with her."[207] May filed a motion for particulars that forced them to elaborate:

> Plaintiff stated to Augustus W. Agnew that she loved him; that her father had cast her off on account of him; that if he did not marry her she would commit suicide publicly, leaving letters incriminating him; that he would be expelled from the military college, prosecuted, dishonoured and ruined, which should cause great grief to his parents, perhaps cause their death; that he had compromised her in the eyes of the public through his being too frequently with her, when it was generally at her request that he met her; that through her being thus compromised, she was ruined socially as well as financially, as she could not any more maintain her school, the building and furniture of which she had all paid; she was losing all her pupils. She appealed to his sense of honour by stating that it would not be honourable of him to refuse to marry her under such circumstances. All these statements, threats and appeals were false, deceitful, unsincere [sic] and unfounded.[208]

May of course ascribed any change in Augustus's feelings to the poisoning effects of his family.

The Agnews' fear of having their family exposed to public scrutiny was clear enough from the circumstances of the case. Faced with the alienation of affection action, their first instinct seems to have been to make it go away. The Ottawa *Evening Citizen* reported that the word in legal circles was "that a settlement would be effected outside of court and in that way all publicity could be avoided, but negotiations apparently fell through."[209] Publicity of course would have strengthened May's hand, but for the Agnews it no doubt contributed to their feelings that this was a shakedown in response to their opposition to the marriage. When *The Gazette* reported that May alleged "cruel and inhuman treatment" by the Agnews, the family immediately had their lawyers publish a firmly worded correction.[210]

Moreover, the threat to the family honour came not just from May the outsider, and the Agnews' actions recognized also the danger presented by Augustus himself. The solution to the parallel threat from inside the family was to close ranks, to make Augustus invisible by sending him to Europe and preventing all communication with May, and to try to erase the connection that his rogue behaviour had created. Augustus's role in all this was ambiguous. Depending on one's perspective, he either displayed a commendable degree of filial obedience or else a remarkable lack of backbone. The letter he wrote to May on 20 February 1905 suggested affection, but in taking his leave of her a few days later he seemed to hedge his bets. He gave her a story that he had been ordered by his commandants at RMC to return to Montreal to await his discharge and was not allowed to return to Kingston during that time. On cross-examination, he at first said that when his sister arrived to fetch him he was undecided about whether or not he would return to Kingston, and he told May "that I would see what my people said when I got home." Pressed, he admitted that he had told her that he would return.[211] Once back with his family, however, he seems to have accepted their story and acted accordingly. The arguments the Agnews' lawyers raised meshed closely with the view of the affair as involving a naive young man foolishly falling for the wiles of an older woman. They emphasized that the parental consent requirement was there to ensure that minors would not suffer for the rest of their lives for their youthful indiscretions. The idea was, they argued, that a minor would wise up at some point (with proper parental prodding) and regret the ill-advised marriage, and so should have a way to get out of the match.[212] May's lawyers for their part pointed out that that perspective hardly fit with the idea in Quebec law – bolstered by religious precept – that a marriage once established was dissolved only by death. They noted sarcastically that surely many spouses would all too happily avail themselves of such an escape clause were it available.[213]

But the view of parental consent as a form of sober second thought to protect wayward youth was powerful and carried the day in this case. William Agnew's role as family gatekeeper prevailed.

The threat repulsed, in 1913 the Agnews retired to the pleasant weather of Victoria, British Columbia, following a six-month transatlantic vacation, which took in Switzerland and Egypt.[214] Augustus, with newly minted engineering credentials, followed his family west around this time and worked for the Grand Trunk Railway and later on various sewer and waterworks projects in British Columbia. He enlisted in the Canadian Pioneers in 1915 as an engineer and served in France, building trenches, but was killed in battle at the Somme in 1916. Unsurprisingly, a long obituary in the *Transactions of the American Society of Civil Engineers* said nothing of his youthful annulled marriage.[215] May was still using "Gober Agnew" as her surname in 1912, the year her father died, when she appeared from time to time in the society column of the *Atlanta Constitution*, attending garden parties with friends.[216] Even as late as 1921, she listed herself as a widow under that name when she arrived (travelling first class) in New York from Antwerp on board *The Somme*.[217] Though our concern here has been the Agnews' family honour, May's honour and virtue were also at issue in the case. As we saw in chapter 2, the effects of reputational injury differed between men and women. Augustus could be spirited away with few apparent negative effects on his reputation. May, on the other hand, had it harder, and holding onto what she felt was her married name was a way to try to mitigate the effects of her rejection at the hands of the Agnews. She remarried twice, for the last time in her sixties, and died in 1953.[218]

4

Bodily Intrusion

Moral injury encompassed more than affronts to honour and reputation, and a fertile source of wounded feelings was physical interference with one's person. Such interference could of course be a symbolic proxy for dishonour and humiliation, as Wilfrid Corbeil found out that day at Dominion Park. A certain degree of physical contact was expected and to be tolerated: the legal idea *de minimis non curat lex* (the law does not concern itself with trifles) applied, but it was a flexible standard against which to judge complaints and was informed by social norms of propriety and honour, as well as by legal rules. In an 1890 defamation case, for example, an employee suspected of theft was subjected to a physical search of his person. Nothing was found, and the employee sued. Little was made of the search during proceedings: the plaintiff's main focus was not the physical intrusion per se, but the implication it carried that he was a thief.[1] In other cases, however, the physical interference itself produced the emotional reaction, rather than (or in addition to) its symbolic meaning as a form of insult. Those cases will be our focus here. The examples we will consider involved individuals subjected to unwanted, non-consensual physical treatment that affected them emotionally. This might arise in a great variety of situations, but medical encounters were particularly susceptible to feelings-based litigation, especially when norms of informed consent and professional practice were still in development. We will look at cases of forced medical examinations and non-consensual medical procedures in which individuals sued for unwanted interference with themselves, as well as cases in which relatives sued over non-authorized autopsies done on their loved ones.

Articulating the emotional injury in cases like these is difficult. Plaintiffs described or hinted at a wide variety of emotions, such as shock, horror, fear, apprehension, and outrage. These were the negative counterparts of a sense of what would eventually be described as bodily integrity and the decisional autonomy to grant or deny access to one's person. I will use the umbrella term *intrusion* to express the complex of feelings of powerlessness, outrage, even violation experienced when the body was manipulated and invaded without one's consent. To begin to explore the contours of this emotion, we start with one of the most powerful cases, from the end of our period.

The Virgin and the Police: *D. v. City of Montreal*

On Friday evening, 11 May 1945, three days after V-E Day, twenty-eight-year-old dressmaker Gabrielle D. was walking home from an evening concert at Collège Mont-St-Louis in Montreal.[2] The event, advertised as "Le Jardin du Bon parler français" and including dramas, sketches, and comedy, would certainly have been a more respectable evening than the entertainments of the famed Lili St-Cyr, "the fascinating blonde dancer," who performed later that night at the Gayety Theatre (also on the bill was a young Dean Martin).[3] As Gabrielle made her way south from Sherbrooke Street a bit after eleven that night, she reached the busy corner of St. Lawrence Boulevard and St. Catherine Street, where she noticed a crowd gathered to watch a disturbance. It turned out to be the police morality squad at work, arresting a young woman for intoxication and loitering. Rather than joining the gawkers, Gabrielle moved through the crowd to try to continue on her way home. The area was the centre of Montreal's notorious Red Light district, which for years had oscillated between the police turning a blind eye and suppressing the area's vices.[4] For about a year police had been cracking down harder than usual on prostitution there, in a concerted effort to protect the troops passing through Montreal from medical and moral threats.[5] A major campaign against venereal diseases had been launched in 1944, on the urging of federal authorities and the armed forces, and this resulted in much closer control over street prostitution, bawdy houses, rooming houses, dubious restaurants, and other vectors of sexually transmitted diseases.[6] In May 1945, 175 women and 13 men were arrested in Montreal for loitering and vagrancy, offences that effectively meant prostitution, part of a year that saw 2002 women and 151 men arrested on those charges.[7]

As Gabrielle pushed her way through the crowd, a plainclothes police officer grabbed her, slapped her face, and threw her to the ground. She thought she was being attacked by a "gangster"; a newspaper reported that she was hard of hearing, which would have exacerbated her feelings as she was dragged, bewildered, into a doorway where another young woman was already being held.[8] At this point she was told she was being arrested, and she could tell her story at the precinct. Gabrielle's story – that she was just coming home from a concert – was likely one the officers had heard before.[9] She was bundled into the patrol wagon with the other young woman, where the officer laughed at her for crying, mocked her as a "bitch" (*chienne*), and demanded to know at which brothel she worked. She was detained for "loitering at night and vagrancy," one of two arrests in the area that evening.[10] Her interrogation continued as it had begun in the patrol wagon: officers asked her how long she had been a working girl (she denied she was), and demanded "the name of the first man who debauched you" (she insisted she was a virgin).[11] She was held in jail overnight and fingerprints and mugshots were taken.

The next morning she was also subjected to a physical examination for venereal disease, mandated a few years before as a public health initiative. In an effort to control sexually transmitted diseases, in 1941 the Quebec legislature required "any person" (though in practice it meant women) arrested or imprisoned "for a sexual offence or as a prostitute, street-walker or vagrant" to be given a physical exam for venereal disease and, if found to be infected, to be confined for mandatory treatment.[12] Such laws had a long history, going back to the British *Contagious Diseases Acts* of 1864, versions of which were enacted in nineteenth-century Canada. Earlier similar legislation had been in force in Quebec as well.[13] During wartime especially, the urgency of such initiatives was particularly acute, and during both world wars highly restrictive federal and provincial legislation targeted women as threats to Canada's moral and military security.[14] During the debates on the 1941 bill in the Quebec Assembly, opposition leader Maurice Duplessis was sceptical about the provision requiring compulsory treatment of any infected patients found in hospitals, which he characterized as giving "dictatorial powers" to the director of the Department of Health. The similar provision subjecting prostitutes, streetwalkers, and vagrants to mandatory treatment, however, passed without comment.[15] Though such exams were mandated by law, they were open to abuse, evident in Gabrielle's case. As the judge in her civil action later pointed out, her conviction was for loitering, not one of the triggering offences listed in the statute.[16]

Lawyer Antonio Lamer (father of the future chief justice of Canada) outlined the procedure for the exam in a document written in 1944 for the Recorder's Court. Those detained under the applicable statutes and regulations would be held in the Recorder's cells without bail until the medical exam could be administered, ideally the morning after the arrest. The exam consisted of a blood sample drawn by a specially trained nurse and other unspecified samples taken by a physician; all samples were numbered and sent for analysis: the blood sample to the provincial hygiene office, the others to the municipal health office. The detention would continue (still without bail) until the results were received, usually within forty-eight hours. Even if the accused were acquitted in the interim, she would still be held until results were received and would be further detained for treatment if the results were positive.[17]

Though the specific details of Gabrielle's case are lacking, she would have been subjected to this or a similar procedure, including being moved from the jail to the Montreal women's prison, where a nurse and physician would have administered the blood test and physical exam to look for evidence of sexual activity and venereal disease.[18] Since the results of her exam were negative, her brother was allowed to post $25 bail at some point soon after her arrest. Four days later, on 15 May, she was tried before the Recorder's Court for loitering in contravention of a city by-law targeting those "strolling or loitering at night ... and who cannot satisfactorily account for [their] presence."[19] She was found guilty (in distinction to most of the other women tried on morals charges around the same time, who pleaded guilty), and was fined $5 and costs. In October, she instituted proceedings against the city for false arrest, claiming damages of $1966.50 for, among other things, her humiliation, injury to her reputation, and the physical and mental pain and suffering she had endured.[20]

The city's position was frankly untenable, and Justice Charles-Albert Duclos said as much. Aside from her treatment by the police and the questionable grounds for the exam, he also pointed out that the photographs and fingerprints were irregular, since only suspects of indictable offences were to be processed in that way, not those held on by-law infractions.[21] At the hearing, he urged the city to settle the matter and made clear that he would find in Gabrielle's favour if they did not. The city stuck by its story, however, maintaining that she had failed to identify herself and then had become violent, ripping the badge off one of the arresting officers and throwing it into the street.[22] The judge did not buy that at all, viewing the city's claims as a rationalization after the physical exam proved they had made a grave error. He gave no credence to the testimony of the city's witnesses, while Gabrielle's family members impressed him as a typical "honourable French Canadian family." Gabrielle herself, he found, was clearly "of outstanding moral character," as her priest attested.[23]

As he had signalled at the hearing, Justice Duclos found in Gabrielle's favour, awarding her $448 for material injury (six months' loss of earnings, medical expenses, drugs), plus "the very inadequate sum" of $500 for "her physical, moral and mental pain and suffering and for great injury to her reputation, character and humiliation."[24] Curiously, even though he was vocally outraged about how the young woman had been treated, both by the police and by the city's hardball tactics, and despite his admission that the amount he awarded was inadequate, he said in court that he was not awarding more in damages in order to discourage the city from appealing the decision – an odd and questionable departure from the compensatory principle of damages.[25] The judge also ordered that her whole police file, including photographs, negatives, fingerprints, and any copies, be surrendered to her.

Gabrielle D.'s successful action against the city was fuelled by overlapping emotions. That she was mortified by her treatment was clear. Her brother testified that when he bailed her out, "her left cheek was swollen, her stockings were torn and she was in a very nervous condition."[26] In court, even a year later, the trauma from the treatment she had received was still noticeable, prompting the judge to remark that "as she related her sad story in Court…, tears came to her eyes, her hands trembled and she had to stop on several occasions to regain her composure."[27] The feeling of intrusion and violation at the physical invasion she suffered was a significant part of the mix, though not all of it. Justice Duclos saw this clearly, and emphasized it in strong terms near the beginning of his judgment: "For a virgin to be branded and tried as a prostitute and to be compelled to submit to an examination of her sexual organs to ascertain if she was suffering from any venereal disease, is not only very humiliating but is almost equivalent to a rape on her maidenly modesty and there is no wonder that in consequence of this treatment she was a nervous wreck for some months after and could not sleep and could not work."[28] His equation of the VD exam with rape – a rape of her feelings, but the association was clear – was a powerful phrase, indeed beyond what many judges were willing to say in sexual assault cases of the day.[29]

Justice Duclos's distinction between the physical affront and the more generalized humiliation was telling as well. These were different sorts of feelings and led to different sorts of injury, evident in the distinction the judge made within the moral damages he awarded between "physical, moral and mental pain and suffering" and the "great injury to her reputation, character and humiliation." Initially, as the situation and Gabrielle's reactions to it developed, the humiliation and reputational injury predominated. She characterized her treatment by police at the scene as humiliating, since she, a respectable young woman, was associated with streetwalkers before an audience of amused gawkers. As she testified, when loaded into the wagon to go to the station, she was subjected by the officers accompanying her to "all kinds of abuse and humiliation, and treated as a vulgar prostitute."[30] The humiliation continued with the questioning at the station and eventually at her trial and conviction before the recorder. Alongside this, however, were different reactions, provoked by other aspects of her treatment and implied in her legal action, even if not expressed outright in the surviving sources. These were the feelings provoked by the ongoing and increasing bodily intrusions to which she was subjected: the rough hands during her arrest, the incarceration, the fingerprinting and photographing, and finally and most seriously the medical exam for what in French were pointedly called "shameful diseases" (*des maladies honteuses*). Such treatment would of course have been humiliating: it was intended only for prostitutes or the promiscuous, and the refusal to accept her assertions of her virtue would have aggravated the building humiliation. But more was involved too. Being driven to the women's prison, ordered to undress in front of strangers, forced to assume a vulnerable position on a table so a physician – possibly male, but regardless – could draw blood and examine her genitals, all that could only have provoked a complex of feelings of fear, embarrassment, shame, powerlessness, vulnerability, and outrage, emotions that contributed to and combined into the feeling of bodily intrusion upon which this chapter focuses.

Damages are only ever an imperfect reparation, particularly for moral injury. In Gabrielle's case, the different remedies that she demanded and that Justice Duclos granted worked simultaneously on the two aspects of the moral injury she had demonstrated. The destruction of the evidence of the illegal arrest – the mugshots and the fingerprints – was a way to redress the humiliation and injury to her reputation. The judgment and the news coverage would state publicly that she had been gravely wronged, but handing over the police file meant that even within police headquarters she would not be branded a prostitute. Beyond the attempt at rebuilding her anonymity, however, the violation could be redressed only by equivalence – the imperfect solution of a monetary payment for her suffering. Ironically, the latter reparation may have been the more effective in this case. While the photos and fingerprints may have been handed over, her name appears to this day in police morality squad reports from the time. And while the report of the judgment avoided naming her, giving the initial of her surname only, *Le Canada* trumpeted her victory by name in a bold headline, all except the *Montreal Daily Star* provided readers with her name and sometimes her full address, and newspapers as far as Calgary covered the story of her victory in court, by name.[31]

Gabrielle D.'s feelings of mingled humiliation and bodily intrusion illustrate the complex ways in which unwanted and unexpected physical treatment could provoke strong emotional responses that differed according to the circumstances. But as the Montreal police made clear in brutal fashion in that case, in certain situations the state had the power to invade one's body, and it occasionally went beyond its legal authority in the zealous pursuit of its objectives. Even when those powers were exercised properly, however, a legal justification did little to assuage the feelings such treatment could cause, and indeed the sense of powerlessness brought on by officially mandated bodily incursions would have aggravated them. Quebec's anti-venereal disease legislation was enacted for a specific public purpose – to protect the troops during wartime – but as Michaela Freund has shown for Vancouver's similar legislation, its targeting of prostitutes had collateral effects, identifying all women (but significantly not the men who sought sex for money) as disease vectors and so putting women's sexuality under universal suspicion.[32] Other legislation similarly authorized the state to act physically on the bodies of its citizens, with the operation of law substituting for consent. For those like Gabrielle D. who felt themselves unjustly forced within the ambit of the legislation, the feeling of intrusion or violation provoked by the invasion of one's person could give rise to legal action. The legal foundation for the interference made such cases difficult to win in the absence of clear abuse such as Gabrielle D. suffered, but the very institution of proceedings indicates something of the intensity of the emotions felt by the individuals in question.

The remainder of this chapter will build on Gabrielle's story to examine the feelings of intrusion occasioned by other kinds of non-consensual interference with the body, particularly conduct sanctioned by public or professional norms.

Stomach Pumps and Lumbar Punctures: Compulsory Medical Examinations

The human body was a legal object long before rights to bodily integrity were articulated, and in our period the state had broad power to interfere with individuals' bodies without their consent, as long as a judge felt sufficient justification existed. While most submitted, some of those non-consenting patients resisted. An extreme example was provoked by an early attempt by Montreal authorities to enforce the always-controversial idea of compulsory isolation and vaccination of smallpox sufferers.[33] During the 1885 epidemic in Montreal, many among the city's French-speaking populace, already on edge that autumn over the trial and impending execution of Louis Riel, saw programs of mandatory vaccination and the forced removal of the sick from their homes as yet another dangerous imposition by Protestant anglophones. Fear generated resistance, to the point that on 4 November 1885 labourer Elie Gagnon responded to the health inspectors sent to remove his sick children to the hospital by barricading his family in their apartment on Rolland Street, and then firing shots at the police whom mayor Honoré Beaugrand had sent to force the issue. The situation and its aftermath dominated press coverage for a time, but eventually the family was treated, and Louis Riel's execution and the attendant rioting in Montreal pushed the story out of news.[34] While the Gagnon family's violent reaction was extreme, other unwilling patients subjected to other forms of compulsory intervention went to court to challenge the sufficiency of the justification that claimed to authorize invasion of their person. Their responses to the bodily intrusions varied and were usually implied rather than articulated, but they suggest further aspects of the feelings evident in Gabrielle D.'s case.

Compulsory medical exams had long been part of many legal processes, aside from the VD exam in Gabrielle's case. Since the Middle Ages, women who "pleaded the belly," that is who claimed to be pregnant to avoid or delay execution, were to be examined by a jury of matrons (later replaced by a team of physicians).[35] In the early twentieth century, as Tamara Myers has shown, supposed female juvenile delinquents were subjected to various tests, in particular for virginity and sexually transmitted diseases. Though this was considered at the time a progressive approach to social reform, Myers notes that while young women were examined in physically invasive ways, suspected male delinquents were simply questioned about things like swearing and smoking.[36]

Even outside the context of publicly mandated exams linked to wrongdoing, people's bodies were of interest to the legal process, and that is our subject in this section. Physical examinations of individuals for evidentiary purposes were commonly practised in various situations, some mandated by law, others requested by an opposing party and performed on the order of a compliant judge. A spouse seeking annulment of a marriage on grounds of inability to consummate, for example, could ask the court to order an examination of the underperforming partner.[37] Added to whatever feelings the examination itself might provoke was the embarrassment of being publicly summoned to present oneself for testing. In a Montreal annulment case from the 1840s, the defendant husband's failure to appear resulted in the court ordering notices to be placed in newspapers summoning him by name to report to a certain physician on a particular date. Though the reason for the summons was left unstated, inferring it would not have been especially difficult.[38] While many of these court-ordered exams were minimally intrusive (physically, if not emotionally), often more invasive procedures were performed. Individual perceptions varied, however, and what some saw as minimal and easily tolerated could for others lead to litigation. The requested or performed physical exams tested the boundaries of modesty, virtue, and propriety, lines that were blurry in any case. In a fairly typical defamation case in 1899, for example, which centred on allegations of sexual impropriety against a young woman, the plaintiff was examined by a physician, whose letter attesting that "she seems to be a virgin" was added to the case file.[39] In contrast to Gabrielle D.'s forced exam, this woman's exam was voluntary, since the letter was filed by her lawyers as one of her exhibits. Perhaps "voluntary" is too strong, however: the exam with the subsequent public attestation of her physical integrity was clearly recommended by her (male) lawyer as strategically necessary, a quasi-voluntary invasion of her body, which she had little choice but to accept.

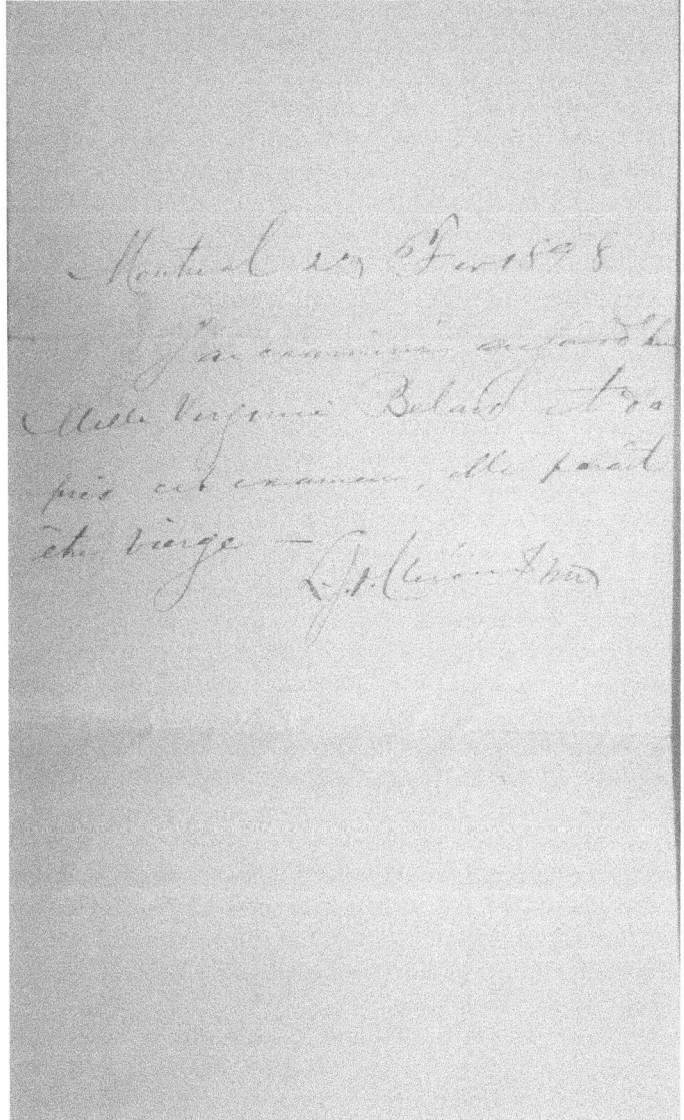

Figure 4.1 Note from physician L.J.O. Cléroux attesting to the plaintiff's virginity, dated 23 February 1898. BAnQ-VM, *Belair v. Chaussé*, Superior Court case file, Plaintiff's Exhibit A1. Photograph by the author. Reproduced with permission of Bibliothèque et Archives nationales du Québec.

Many such cases arose in the context of personal injury actions, in which the defendants' interest in knowing whether the plaintiff really suffered as grievously as alleged or was embellishing led them to ask the court to order the plaintiff to submit to a medical exam.[40] Unlike Gabrielle D.'s case, in which she sued the city for damages, these were interlocutory proceedings to challenge the exam itself, and so the thin record in the case files generally says nothing explicit about the plaintiffs' emotional reactions or even their reasons for challenging the procedure. But such manoeuvres by defendants clearly troubled plaintiffs, driving them to try to get the order quashed. On the one hand there was a legal danger: even if they were not embellishing, physicians might downplay the seriousness of their injury, putting an unfavourable expert opinion on the record. On the other hand, the procedures requested were always personally intrusive, and often extremely so. Behind the challenges one sees plaintiffs trying to assert something of the intrusion they were feeling as defendants used the authority of the court to force them into doctors' offices or hospitals.

The first such cases were reported in the 1890s, and for several years judges simply granted the motions with little or no recorded discussion, and plaintiffs duly complied.[41] Suddenly, in 1899 and for reasons now obscure, plaintiffs began to resist, and judges agreed that such motions were without formal legal basis, whether in statute or in the *droit commun*, aside from the general right of the parties to bring motions before the court. In two judgments in personal injury cases handed down the same day, Justice John Archibald dismissed motions for medical exams when the plaintiffs made it known that they had no intention of complying, since the court, he admitted, had no power whatever to enforce such orders.[42] Some judges continued to issue medical examination orders, and plaintiffs for the most part seem to have continued submitting,[43] though when they refused, the courts could do nothing outside the specific context of workplace injuries, where such exams were explicitly authorized by statute.[44]

A case in 1916 shifted the ground significantly in favour of plaintiffs. A father sued on behalf of his daughter, who had been struck and injured by one of the defendant's ice wagons.[45] The defendant moved for a medical exam, and the plaintiff contested, arguing lack of any legal basis. Given the pro-plaintiff results in the 1899 cases, the defendant proposed as a basis article 289 CCP, which provided that a party may ask the court to order "the opposite party to exhibit any object." The plaintiff, confident without arguing the point that the court would not find his living daughter's body to be an "object," countered that any judgment must be susceptible of execution.[46] Justice Farquhar Maclennan rejected the motion, quoting approvingly the reasoning of the United States Supreme Court that "no right is held more sacred, or is more carefully guarded by the common law, than the right of every individual to the possession and control of his own person, free from all restraint or interference of others, lest by clear and unquestionable authority of law." "To compel anyone," he continued, "and especially a woman, to lay bare the body, or to submit it to the touch of a stranger, without lawful authority, is an indignity, an assault and a trespass."[47] *Le Devoir* picked up on this quasi-theological language, proclaiming in a headline "The Person Is Sacred."[48] The motion was dismissed, since without explicit statutory authority, "the defendant has not the right asked for in this case."[49]

The Quebec legislature supplied the missing statutory basis in an amendment to the CCP in 1931, passed, one suspects, on lobbying from Quebec's growing insurance industry, which was behind many of the motions for medical exams.[50] It added a new provision (section 286*b*) to the rules regarding discovery, that in cases of "bodily injuries or from sickness," defendants could require the injured person to submit to a medical exam, with the defendant not required to plead until after the exam was complete.[51] This again reoriented the balance, now in favour of defendants, who were emboldened when it quickly became evident that despite lofty rhetoric of fundamental rights such as in Justice MacLennan's 1916 judgment, the courts would defer to the legislature. After a few years, however, the case reports again began to record examples of plaintiffs challenging the defendants' new right to invade their bodies seemingly with little justification. In 1936, a plaintiff objected to being ordered to undergo a lumbar puncture, arguing that the procedure was more like an operation than an examination. The judge issued the order anyway, placing full confidence in medical science: "In my opinion, these examinations do not constitute operations; they are simply observations following injections that offer no danger, that are made easy to bear, and that are necessary for the conclusions of modern medical science."[52]

A year later, another Superior Court judge allowed a defendant's motion on the basis that the new CCP provision gave defendants an absolute right. In that case, the plaintiff was initially willing to comply, but once the testing was underway balked at being subjected to a chemical analysis of his stool, a pumping of his stomach to analyse its contents, and an X-ray after ingestion of barium to evaluate his digestive tract. The defendant's physicians asserted that the additional procedures were medically necessary. The plaintiff argued that his own physicians had already administered the same tests, and he had found them "very painful" and had been so exhausted by them that he required several days of complete bed rest afterwards. On appeal, three of five justices at the Court of King's Bench deferred to medical opinion. The statute was clear, they said, in giving an absolute right to the defendant to demand the exam; the plaintiff could not object simply because he would feel a little tired.[53] The dissenting justices distinguished the stool analysis from the invasive procedures, but the majority saw all three tests as simply harmless daily hospital practice, and so the order stood.

The situation was developing fast, however. By 1941, the Court of King's Bench (including one member who had allowed the order to go ahead in the case just mentioned) was starting to question the necessity of tests defendants were demanding and was distinguishing between non-invasive and invasive procedures. In a case involving an insurance claim for invalidity caused by gastric problems, the defendant asked for and was granted an order requiring a battery of tests: X-rays, gastric analysis, stool examination, and others. While the exam was being administered, the defendant's physicians decided a blood test and a day of observation in hospital were needed too, but the plaintiff balked. The appeals court upheld the Superior Court's refusal to order the additional tests. Putting brakes on what was becoming carte blanche for defendants, the court held that section 286b must be interpreted literally and restrictively, since it was "a veritable constraint on human freedom."[54] The two dissenting justices dismissed the severity of a simple blood test, one of them going so far as to state that it was not up to a patient to dictate which tests were or were not medically necessary. But 1937's three-to-two majority deferring to the defendant's physicians had become 1941's three-to-two majority on the side of the patient's liberty to refuse.

As interlocutory proceedings, the scant record in these cases of compulsory medical exams says little about plaintiffs' reasons for objecting, whatever the arguments raised orally in court might have been. In some cases the objection seems to have simply been an unwillingness to do the defendant any favours, such as a 1901 case in which the plaintiff objected to baring his arm (mutilated and burned in the accident at issue) to the defendant before trial. The judge ordered him to do so, in a private room in the courthouse if the plaintiff so required.[55] In most of the cases, however, discerning the plaintiff's motivation requires little imagination, as defendants – often insurance companies or other corporate bodies – piled on test after test of a decidedly invasive nature. Despite the assurances of the defendants' physicians – in the early cases, judges accepted their opinions without question, while later on scrutiny became more substantial – plaintiffs knew that procedures like a stomach pump would cause discomfort, and in some cases (the lumbar puncture, for example) were far from risk-free, even if performed to the strictest professional standards. Plaintiffs' refusals to comply, though the reasons were unrecorded, reflected the sense of intrusion that non-consensual invasive medical procedures always occasioned. While the assurances of medical professionals were enough to assuage the doubts of most judges, for patients the inconvenience, the discomfort, even the fear of adverse effects were clearly decisive factors.

Hopes of Motherhood: *Parnell v. Springle*

Cases of medical care gone wrong reveal still more clearly the way perceived violations of bodily integrity could raise strong and varied feelings. These were damages claims brought by patients either for a botched procedure or, more interestingly, for unwanted bodily changes resulting from a procedure done on the physician's initiative and according to professional norms, but beyond what was consented.[56] The damage complained of was sometimes aesthetic (scarring or the like), sometimes functional (especially inability to have children), but in all cases involved the patient's subjective dissatisfaction with the outcome, to be measured against the court's objective assessment of that injury. Such cases tended to fail. The usual defences, such as medical necessity, life and death, impossibility of obtaining consent because the patient was unconscious when the need for the procedure was discovered, all rested on the strong foundation of best professional practices. Against this, claims of purely emotional damage – "mere feelings" – stood little chance. The difficulty was compounded because most of the plaintiffs bringing their feelings to court were women, suing for the emotional (and other) consequences of lost reproductive capacity or aesthetic prejudice. How could a patient complain of abstract psychic injury, the (male) medical and legal professionals argued, when the alternative was loss of life or permanent debilitating injury? Yet for the plaintiffs, the emotional pain was real, and their lawsuits reflected their belief that their unhappiness outweighed the medically preferred result.

Few early cases along these lines were reported, likely the result of slow development of the idea of informed consent, the legal basis on which these cases came to rest.[57] The earliest reported Quebec case, from 1899, illustrates the issues well.[58] Madge Parnell, a twenty-two-year-old unmarried stenographer, visited respected Montreal physician John Anderson Springle, complaining of "some derangement or affection of the womb." Springle examined her and recommended surgery, adding, she claimed, that the "operation would be but a slight one producing a very small wound which would soon be healed."[59] Parnell could not afford the private service Springle recommended, so he arranged to have the procedure done free of charge in one of the hospital's public wards by experienced surgeons.[60]

During the operation, the surgeons determined that Parnell's condition was much more serious than they had anticipated. Rather than an affliction of the uterus, it turned out that both sets of Fallopian tubes and ovaries were severely infected. With the patient unconscious on the operating table, the team quickly conferred and decided that the diseased organs should be removed immediately and entirely, or a generalized and likely fatal infection would ensue. The organs having been removed and the infection halted, Parnell recovered from the surgery. Upon learning of the result, however, she was less than grateful for the surgeons' quick action. She sued Springle for $1999, alleging that she had "lost her hopes of ever uniting herself to a suitable husband," and was also "for ever doomed to be bereft of the joys of maternity." Aside from the emotional effects, her new condition also deprived her of the chance of future material support from a husband and children.[61] Springle raised various arguments in his defence, among which was that because her organs were already irreparably damaged, she had suffered no injury on that score, "but, on the contrary, it was the means of continuing her life, and was absolutely necessary for the restoration of her health and life."[62]

Justice John Joseph Curran dismissed the action from the bench, even cutting off the defence partway through the presentation of its evidence ("most dramatically," according to the defence lawyer).[63] Since in the circumstances it had been impossible to obtain consent, and since a surgeon "is in duty bound to do everything necessary for the preservation of the life of his patient," the judge found Springle's actions to have been beyond reproach.[64] He made no mention of Parnell's claims of emotional damage: professional norms were clear, and life and health must trump all else.

Some indication of how such emotional injury was viewed, by professionals at least, is evident in a speech that Springle's lawyer, A.G. Brooke Claxton, gave to the Montreal Medico-Chirurgical Society soon after the judgment was handed down. For the benefit of an audience of medical men fearful of a flood of lawsuits by emotional women, Claxton made it clear that a patient who lived had nothing to complain about, and that this case and any others like it were simply patients "trumping up a case" and displaying "base ingratitude" towards the life-saving physician. Claxton had little sympathy for Parnell's reaction to her inability to have children: "Previous to the operation her condition was that of sterility, she could not have become pregnant, so this side of her house of cards was rudely thrown to the ground, her own experts would not back up these flimsy pretensions." His advice to the elite of Montreal's physicians? "In examining women, if possible, have a third party friendly to yourself present, so that, if the patient be hysterical, the third party will be able to state exactly what caused the hysteria."[65]

Both Justice Curran's decision and Claxton's less guarded comments afterwards reflected the state of the law in cases like this. Though Justice Curran cited nothing in his ruling, a recent English case on removal of ovaries without consent had quickly become well known in legal and medical circles. Like *Parnell*, *Beatty v. Cullingworth* had gone against the plaintiff, and doctors made much of the anxiety and trouble it had occasioned – anxiety and trouble for the defendant physician, of course, not the patient.[66] Jurists too saw a high degree of discretion as essential to the practice of medicine, and in rapidly developing situations in which obtaining consent was impossible, a physician following professional practice would normally be insulated from liability.[67]

As the twentieth century progressed, cases alleging non-consensual medical care began to appear in the reports more frequently. Surgery was becoming more common and more ambitious, professional standards were taking this greater confidence into account, and the consent requirement was becoming more explicitly defined. The influence of professionalization, however, increased the focus on physical outcomes and general health, further pushing to the side affective concerns. Several later cases involving women suing over the removal of their ovaries essentially sought to reopen the matter decided in *Parnell*, but similarly without success. In 1930, for example, a husband sued on his wife's behalf when a surgeon, operating for appendicitis, discovered that the twenty-year-old woman's ovaries were diseased, and removed them.[68] The plaintiffs did not contest the assessment of the condition of the organs or the need for their removal, but sought damages for the failure to obtain consent and for the moral prejudice suffered thereby, described as the frustration of their desire "to have children and raise a family, both for their consolation and to satisfy their need for affection."[69] Chief Justice François-Xavier Lemieux deferred without reservation to medical science: "It would be reckless for a court to interpose an opinion contrary to that of the physician concerning the operation, its urgency, and its necessity."[70] In dismissing the arguments about wounded feelings, he noted that such injuries could scarcely be assuaged by money anyway, and so "sometimes it is better not to expose or parade cases before the public."[71] Other cases went in a similar direction, for virtually identical reasons, such as a 1939 case in which diseased ovaries were removed, and the physician successfully argued the absence of injury since before the operation the woman had already been incapable of conceiving.[72]

In cases in which the patient's life was not on the line, however, courts were more receptive to arguments about the emotional effects of unwanted procedures. Without the possibility of loss of life or serious disability to support the physician's actions, taking into consideration the whole range of the prejudice caused was more possible. In a 1934 case, a young woman visited a dermatologist to have blemishes on her arms removed. The treatment performed, which allegedly included repeatedly burning the skin, failed to remove the spots and instead caused permanent scarring, which the plaintiff described as giving to her arms "a most ugly appearance." Justice Jean-Joseph Denis, in what seems to be the first reported case in which a Quebec physician was held to an informed consent requirement, found that the physician failed to inform the patient about the risks of the procedure. Since the plaintiff would never have consented to an aesthetic treatment that would make her condition worse, her lifelong moral prejudice warranted significant damages.[73]

The injury in cases like these was of course in large part the unwanted physical effects of the procedure, whether that was the surprise of waking up to a childless future, or removal of bandages to reveal permanent scarring. The injury went further, however, and also included an emotional aspect related to the lack of consent. The physician's judgment about the prognosis in such cases was not really in question – the plaintiffs in the 1930 case above made that point explicitly. But when a physician failed to inform the patient, that decision made without consulting the patient led to the feeling of intrusion that arose when the patient realized someone else had decided what to do with her body and had determined which result mattered and which alternative results did not. One can almost hear the patients: "I don't care if you saved my life, you had no business doing what you did to my body without my consent." As in the cases of Gabrielle D. and the plaintiffs forced to undergo unwanted medical exams, the feeling of powerlessness provoked when someone else used one's body without consent strongly influenced how that individual reacted to the situation. These cases were different from the disappointment or frustration or even anger over adverse results, such as when, despite the physician's best efforts, a condition was not corrected or cured. The surprise result of unanticipated procedures, even when a general consent had been given and even when the patient's life had been saved, turned a medically successful result into an emotional injury.

A noteworthy aspect of all of these cases of intrusion is how little protection plaintiffs had against interference with their body, at least until the civil code was amended in 1971 to guarantee the inviolability of the human person.[74] Gabrielle D. was compensated for her harrowing experience, but it was a general reparation of her injury, without a breakdown of its individual elements. Were her damages for the arrest and false conviction, or for the night in jail, or for the photographs, fingerprints, and genital exam? Probably all three – the general humiliation considered as a whole – but unlike material or physical injuries, which were itemized as specific damages, her moral injury was not. It was compensated (at least it was likely part of the judge's assessment), but without a clear label it became just one element among many added to general damages. In the case of the compulsory medical exams, the law clearly tipped against the individual subjected to the procedure. One had the right to refuse to submit, but to do so meant exposing oneself to a disadvantageous presumption, and so in practice most complied. Various factors operated against protection of bodily integrity, at least in cases where the procedures complained of had a colour of legality about them. Judges were quick to conclude "what's the harm?" about procedures, particularly when medical experts asserted the procedures were necessary. When a patient's life was in danger, judges saw that as an overriding interest, regardless of what the patient said later. But most importantly for our purposes, judges' scepticism about feelings-based injury – particularly when it was women feeling the injury – was on full display in many of these cases. Moral injury was always difficult to quantify, but in these cases it rarely reached the point of assessment, since mere feelings were no match for the weight of scientific opinion about medical necessity.

Unauthorized Autopsies: Between Propriety and Science

While the feeling I have called "intrusion" and its related emotions were most closely associated with interference with one's own body, in certain situations things done to another's body could provoke similar feelings in those close to the affected person. Autopsy of the body of a loved one in particular could be an unwelcome intrusion that imposed on the family processes over which they had neither choice nor control, whether the procedure was mandated by law, by medical practice, or by the needs of insurers or other third parties.[75] Families sometimes went to court to challenge decisions that forced them to stand by while the body of their deceased relative was taken from them and subjected to dissection and examination. In legal terms such actions were about consent, public good, and medical practice, like the cases we just examined. But to family members, they raised a complex of feelings, from the helplessness of their loss of control over their grief and mourning, to horror, revulsion, or general outrage at the undignified treatment of their loved ones. Legal and social norms mingled in these cases: as we will see, the language of rights often arose, as plaintiffs claimed rights to refuse autopsy and to determine the disposition of the body of their relative, but these were rights inflected by social practices about proper mourning and treatment of the dead.[76]

For their part, hospital authorities, the usual defendants in these cases, were in a difficult position, caught in a triangular pull among different interests. First, a long-standing legislative regime required autopsy of any death deemed by the coroner to have occurred "under such circumstances as require investigation."[77] In 1898 that was expanded to allow hospital superintendents to order autopsies on non-paying patients to determine the cause of death,[78] and still later to allow certain hospitals to perform autopsies when "desirable from a scientific point of view."[79] Second, professional standards required a high degree of certainty about the cause of death, and this was complemented by aspirations about furthering scientific knowledge, for which autopsies were seen to be invaluable. Already in 1859, the unclaimed body of any deceased non-paying hospital patient could be sent to local medical schools or teachers for dissection, and laws respecting anatomy continued to facilitate medical research and scientific inquiry.[80] Third, and in response to the preceding, the demands of propriety led to a consciousness of the difficulty of drawing a clear line between legitimate inquiry and unjustifiable mutilation of a corpse. These tensions were evident in a brief news report from 1890, in which a father complained to hospital authorities about an autopsy performed without his consent on his daughter, who had choked to death on a piece of meat. The physician, interviewed for the article, reported that since he was unsure of the cause of death, his duty was to ascertain it by autopsy. In the absence of any suspicion of foul play, however, he "was anxious to save the family the pain of a coroner's inquest and the elaborate post mortem examination which must follow." He assured readers that there had been "no mutilation of the body of any kind, and the course pursued was most necessary as much in the interests of the deceased's friends as of ourselves."[81]

For the public, propriety was paramount. Most outside the medical and law-enforcement communities – and some within them – saw autopsies, like the related issue of cremation, as mutilation of the body, plain and simple.[82] To some this was about the theological danger of jeopardized resurrection, to others it was simply distasteful, but in either case it was intolerable when it was imposed on one's own relatives. While the needs of crime investigation or establishing cause of death for insurance purposes might be grudgingly accepted, exploratory or scientific dissection was not. In 1935, for example, a bill in the Quebec legislature to expand non-consensual scientific autopsy to all hospital patients receiving public assistance raised considerable public resistance. Opponents of the proposal emphasized the cruelty of depriving relatives of the body of their loved one simply because they lacked means, a point vividly made by Pierre Bertrand, member for Saint-Sauveur, during the debates: "Just because they are poor, we take them away to the abattoir, to cut them up in the service of science. It's cruel. It's already hard to be on public assistance, within going to the abattoir after you die."[83] Despite passing third reading with a strong majority, the government withdrew the bill.[84] These legal and emotional tensions between families and authorities over non-consensual autopsies were evident in several cases over the course of the early twentieth century.[85] Such cases were never numerous but they were regularly covered in the newspapers, an indication that their subject matter fell right at the line of expected social norms of propriety.

The earliest reported Quebec case involved the remains of Colbert O. Grothé, a member of a prominent Montreal construction family but who himself had fallen on hard times.[86] In the months before his death from pneumonia in January 1905, Grothé had taken out a number of life insurance policies, transferring them to others to pay debts. After his death, one of the companies, North American Life, suspicious of the circumstances, began proceedings to annul the $5000 policy it had issued. To this end, the company sought and was granted an exhumation order, supported by the consent of Grothé's widow, to allow them to autopsy the body to determine whether Grothé had suffered from some pre-existing but undisclosed condition (tuberculosis or syphilis was suspected).[87] The body was duly dug up from the frozen February earth and transported to a hospital to thaw out. The problem was that the widow had been judicially separated from Grothé for several years and would in fact remarry a few weeks later. The company had also neglected to consult Grothé's four children and five siblings, who promptly went to court to argue that the exhumation was "a violation of the family's rights."[88] They got the order overturned for false representations and had the body reburied without the autopsy having been carried out.[89] Even without the evidence from a post-mortem, however, North American Life successfully had the policy cancelled, as a jury found that Grothé had untruthfully answered questions about his drinking habits and had failed to disclose several previous rejected insurance applications to other companies.[90]

While the challenge to the policy was working its way through the courts, Grothé's children, with one of his brothers serving as tutor to those not of full age, sued the company for the huge sum of $50,000 for emotional injuries caused by the alleged desecration of their deceased father's remains.[91] They argued – in tears before the judge and jury – that the company's allegations of false representations were a malicious attempt "to profane a tomb for a miserable financial question." No doubt the family was also upset at the company's tactics, which included hiring private detectives and suggesting that Grothé had had a healthy stand-in take the required medical exam in his place. Their declaration described in graphic detail the treatment of their father's corpse: taken from the tomb, it was stripped of its clothes, and "in a state of nudity the cadaver was stretched into the form of a semi-circle on the floor, near a furnace, to be thawed." This "desecration of the tomb of the said Colbert O. Grothé and indignity done to his mortal remains" caused the plaintiffs injury "in their affection for the memory of their dead father, in their respect for his mortal remains, in their

Figure 4.2 Colbert O. Grothé. From *La Patrie* (9 January 1905), p. 1. BAnQ JOU 669 CON. Reproduced with permission of Bibliothèque et Archives nationales du Québec.

feelings as children for a father whose mortal rest has been so shamefully disturbed, and in their outraged honour."[92]

The plaintiffs' framing of their case is interesting, mixing as it did individual and collective injury, in a manner similar to the family honour cases we considered in chapter 3. They asserted in their declaration that a relative's remains were "things sacred by their nature," while in the newspapers their lawyer (who also happened to be transferee of one of Grothé's insurance policies and the defendant and cross-plaintiff in the action to annul the policy) described the case as a revendication of "the right of the family to the inviolability of the cadaver of one of their own, who had the right to have his rest respected."[93] Whether this line of argument based on family members as guardians of family memory would have succeeded was never established, since on the morning of the hearing the case settled out of court for $500 and costs, on the strong urging of Justice John Joseph Curran.[94]

The legal framework of cases like this was very much up in the air at the time. The Grothé children's assertion that the exhumation and planned autopsy of their father caused them moral injury was perhaps self-evident in a social sense, but the legal foundation for such damages was still largely unexplored.[95] Some authorities viewed the cadaver as belonging to the family as a kind of property – the *Pandectes Belges* rather indelicately compared it to an owner's rights to the body of a dead animal[96] – whose mutilation could give rise to damages for moral injury. Others, however, following the common law tradition, rejected the property argument (as did the Grothé family with their "sacred things" characterization) while still recognizing the possibility of at least nominal damages.[97] This unsettled question of how to approach cases of unauthorized treatment of the dead in Quebec arose again a few years after the *Grothé* affair.

In June 1907, Charlotte Phillips's husband, James Cairns, died of cancer while at the Montreal General Hospital.[98] He had been there for several months, and his wife paid the bills as they came up (a relevant consideration, given the 1898 legislation allowing hospital authorities to order autopsies on patients whose treatment was publicly supported). Despite Phillips's instructions to the contrary, after Cairns's death the hospital performed an autopsy, leading her to sue for $5000 for physical and moral injuries, including "a moral depression that poisons her existence."[99] The hospital moved to dismiss the case on the grounds that Phillips had not established having inherited "any claim or right from said James Cairns to or in respect of his body after his decease," or any right of action against the hospital.[100] In other words – and this is an argument we saw in the family honour cases – any legally protected interest was personal to John Cairns, and had died with him.

Justice Charles Davidson's ruling on the motion was the first extended discussion of the law surrounding unauthorized autopsy in Quebec. He was clearly largely on his own in this area, searching high and low for guidance – Ontario, England, the United States, France, Belgium – but finding little beyond analogies. He began by acknowledging as "epigrammatic" that a dead body "does not represent property in the ordinary sense of the word," so that, for instance, "a great many years have passed since it was possible, in either England or France, to seize or retain a corpse for debt."[101] Quebec's statutory regime, however, which allowed cremation of those who expressed such a desire via testament and which permitted some dead bodies to be given to schools of anatomy, was "surely ... expressive of a right of property, in some sense of that widely comprehensive expression, tort or trespass," which could ground an action in damages.[102] Here he was fudging, as the common-law terminology makes clear, but he was hardly alone in such prevarication about the basis of these actions. Though he refused to specify whether liability was based in property, tort, or trespass, he decided, referring to American cases, that there must be liability, since there had been a violation of a personal right, whatever the specific nature of that right might be.[103] He was clear, however, in recognizing the emotional effects of an unauthorized autopsy as a form of moral injury. After noting that Quebec cases had awarded compensation for attacking the virtue of a minor daughter and for breach of promise to marry, he continued, "In as high a class, at the least, are the almost reverential feelings with which a family safeguards the body of its dead. Immunity as regards them all is itself a property. The control of a husband or wife over the remains of the other and their burial is paramount, provided normal relations of marriage existed at the time of death. Relatives come next in order of kinship.... Hence, if a right of action exists, the plaintiff has it."[104]

The interest in the body of a deceased relative, then, was a kind of *bien*, a sort of proprietary interest whose violation (whether that violation was seen as a trespass, a tort, or an *injure*) could give rise to an action in damages. (Though Justice Davidson did not use the language of *injure*, *Le Canada* did, noting that an unauthorized autopsy is "an act of *injure* against the remains of the deceased."[105]) The plaintiff's complaint thus disclosed a valid cause of action and the demurrer was dismissed, but the case seems never to have proceeded to a hearing on its merits.[106]

Litigation over unauthorized autopsies seems to have quieted following *Phillips*, at least as far as reported cases go. An exception was a 1919 case in which a father sued the Royal Victoria Hospital over an autopsy on his eight-year-old daughter for the ostensible reason that the cause of death was unknown but feared to be tuberculosis. The hospital argued, and Justice Thomas Fortin accepted, that certainty was necessary to assuage public fears, and moreover that the father had consented to the autopsy, though he had not fully understand what he was being asked. Furthermore, the only possible damage the plaintiff and his wife had suffered was to "have been hurt in their feelings and sentiments," so they had no claim against the hospital, since such moral damage was, the judge held, excluded in cases like this (for reasons we will explore in chapter 6). The action was dismissed.[107] In the 1930s, the issue arose again in the courts and legislature. The reasons for this resurgence of litigation require further study (did court actions inspire legislative action, or vice versa?), but the legal framework was clear. As Justice Joseph Archambault stated in one of the cases, based on *Phillips*, "there is no doubt" that a cadaver is "the property" of the spouse and family, who have a right of action for the "*injure*" or "*outrage*" caused by an autopsy without consent.[108] That case involved a widow who sued for $2500. Justice Archambault found no proof of material injury, despite allegations that the autopsy had gravely affected the widow's health. Any such effects, he found, were due to the death itself, rather than the autopsy. Though he found the plaintiff to be in good faith, he also saw no evidence of her alleged humiliation, and so awarded her only modest exemplary damages of $50 and costs.[109] The rhetorical framing of the cases reflected the public and political debates over autopsy referred to above. In a 1931 case, for example, the plaintiff sued a hospital for $17,500 following an unauthorized autopsy on her husband, who had died of a cerebral haemorrhage after an accident at work.[110] The damages included an accident insurance payout that she alleged had been refused because the autopsy ruled the death had been due to natural causes, as well as $10,000 in general damages. In describing the procedure, the wife's lawyer played up its grisly aspects: "She alleges that they cut the scalp from one temple to the other and then they removed the brain by sawing open the top of the skull. During the examination by the expert physicians, the skull supposedly slipped like the 'lid of a pot.' The internal organs were also removed and replaced by sawdust.... Embalming was rendered impossible and it was necessary to bury the deceased right away."[111]

Such detail was necessary to describe accurately what had been done to the body, but it served as well to provoke an emotional response in the judge who would hear the case. Against the hospital's argument of authorization (in this case, allegedly from the deceased's son), the plaintiff had to establish clearly the indignity to which the body was subjected, in language that would unambiguously and self-evidently establish the shock felt by relatives. In the end, the case settled just before the hearing was to take place.

Finally, in 1939 Auguste Ramaeckers, husband of Sarah Brouillette, died following prostate surgery in the Hôtel-Dieu Hospital, a Catholic institution.[112] Ramaeckers's will stated his desire to be cremated, and his widow informed the hospital of his wish. This sent up red flags for the hospital administration and the head surgeon, who was to fill out the death certificate. Though cremation was not exactly new in Quebec, it was still suspect, particularly among Catholics. A 1901 law permitted cremation only at Mount Royal Cemetery, and only for individuals entitled to be buried there (in practice mainly Protestants) who had expressed a testamentary wish for cremation, and excepting sudden or violent deaths unless the coroner granted permission. For Roman Catholics, however, cremation was religiously prohibited until the 1960s, though some like Ramaeckers chose it over burial.[113] After Ramaeckers's death, the hospital director asked Brouillette if she would consent to an autopsy, which she refused. Though news reports of debates over a bill to amend the charter of the Hôtel-Dieu Hospital mentioned that a clause was added requiring consent for autopsies, no such requirement was included in the statute that entered force in 1937, which allowed the hospital to "do vivisection, practise dissection and perform autopsy on a corpse" for educational purposes or to determine cause of death.[114] Despite Brouillette's refusal of permission, and unknown to her, the head surgeon approached the coroner, making cryptic comments about the death. He mentioned first that though the deceased was supposed to be buried, suddenly (he said) this had been changed to cremation. He went on to intimate ominously, as reported by the coroner, "Now, that person, we don't know what might have happened, there wasn't always someone from the hospital in the room, his wife was there." He concluded by suggesting that all those factors taken together "constitute for us a certain impression of strangeness."[115] The doctor's insinuations had the desired effect, and the coroner ordered an autopsy, which found that the deceased had died of natural causes. The hospital then released the body to the widow, and it was cremated soon after.

Already the day following her husband's death, when she found the body was no longer at the funeral home, Brouillette went to the newspapers to voice her irritation, complaining that her husband's body should never have been subjected to a useless autopsy.[116] She went on to sue the hospital for $999.99 in damages for injuries "to her person, her *biens*, for medical costs, her health."[117]

At trial in June 1941, Justice Alfred Forest applied the principles set out in *Ducharme* and the earlier cases.[118] The Quebec courts, he wrote, have "unanimously" upheld the principle that unauthorized autopsy "is a usurpation of personal rights likely to humiliate, to outrage, and to give rise to the sufferings that constitute the essential elements for civil redress." This "right," he explained, was the right of an individual to decide whether or not to subject his or her body to "mutilation," a right that passed to the spouse and other relatives in order of priority by degree of relation. By contrast, hospital officials and physicians "did not have the right" to order an autopsy based on suspicions about cremation, since that decision belonged to "the unlimited freedom of every person to decide and to order the cremation or not of his body after his death." Citing the story of Antigone and Creon, he made the point that if a general moral rule dictating respect for the dead was good enough for the ancient pagans, today no one should be allowed to violate "the right of the family, which gives to the memory of its dead all the veneration that a person holds with respect to someone who is dear to him." Given the outrage of the hospital's blatant violation of basic rules of humanity, Brouillette's emotional, psychological, and physical injuries were "undeniable," as all could "be linked directly to the emotions and the obsession with which she has been besieged since the mutilation of the body of her husband." The court awarded her $250 plus costs.[119]

The trial judge's recitation of the moral lessons of Greek antiquity left the majority of the Court of King's Bench unconvinced, and it overturned the result.[120] Ignoring entirely the question of Brouillette's claimed injuries and the issue of consent to autopsy, the majority focused exclusively on whether the doctor had reasonable grounds for referring the case to the coroner. Justice Errol McDougall ascribed to the physician the purest possible motives and found nothing more sinister in his actions than "professional zeal of an advanced order" to investigate the cause of death "as a matter of scientific curiosity." Having found that the doctor had good reason to wish to know more about the cause of death, there was no liability, and so no exploration of the questions of the rights of family members or the damage Brouillette claimed to have suffered.[121] Justice Antonin Galipeault's dissent took a very different approach from the majority. Brouillette's refusal to consent to the autopsy was "indisputably her right," he wrote, and in ignoring it, the doctor acted with utter disregard for the widow's interests and feelings. In cases like this, judges must be sensitive to "the sensibility, the feelings, the pain of living members of the family who have the custody, the administration, and even the ownership of the body of the deceased. It is for them to decide if the body should be kept whole or mutilated."[122] Justice Gregor Barclay agreed with Galipeault, but felt that the affair had caused Brouillette more damage than the $250 awarded at trial.[123]

The autopsy cases all show outraged (and angry) families seeking recognition of mistreatment of the body of their loved one and presenting wounded feelings of a largely self-evident nature, if one accepted generally prevailing norms of propriety towards the dead. Judges, however, walked a fine line between validating some of those feelings and upholding medical practice and public norms in the face of sentiment. The feelings in all the cases just described were similar, and not hard to imagine. The different outcomes depended on how the judges read the social norms involved, and how they balanced the workings of those norms against the public purpose of medical examination. In *Grothé*, with the defendant (a private corporation) looking for dirt on the deceased, the judge pushed for the parties to settle out of court, signalling that he would find for the plaintiff otherwise. In the later cases, the trial judges – best placed to see the emotional toll on the family – supported the plaintiffs, though they awarded less than the huge amounts demanded because they believed the good faith of the hospitals and physicians involved. In *Brouillette*, however, the appellate justices pushed aside emotional injury entirely in the face of the public good of medicine. Sentiments and propriety were up against powerful countervailing interests: the advance of medical knowledge, public welfare, law enforcement. But the plaintiffs' arguments about the unseemly intrusion into their grief were powerful as well. Moreover, sentiment in those cases was buttressed by the language of rights. Moving beyond feelings to assert violated rights was a way to strengthen the plaintiff's position, and at least some of the judges were receptive. The use of phrases like "personal rights" by Justice Davidson in *Phillips* and *"droits personnels"* by Justice Forest in *Brouillette* pointed to a developing broader usage of rights in the context of moral injury, an issue to which we will return in chapter 8.

5

Betrayal

The courts did not adjudicate affection, love, or friendship, but they did frequently deal with their opposites: scorn, contempt, neglect, and of course betrayal. These were relational emotions, provoked by the breakdown of bonds of affection, and they could lead to particular kinds of actions, such as separation from bed and board, alienation of affection, breach of promise to marry, even revocation of gifts made to family members or third parties acting in their stead. Plaintiffs in such actions had to prove that various forms of hostility or enmity existed between the parties: in legal terms, what the courts needed to see was evidence of ill-usage, grievous insult, ingratitude, and the like. Defendants typically responded either with their own version of grievance, or with a denial and an assertion that things were actually quite fine, and that affection and harmony in fact still reigned. A common thread running through actions like these was feelings of betrayal over the emotional side of a relationship that was supposed to exist but did not. The wife demanding separation, the husband seeking the return of his wife to the matrimonial home, the elderly parent trying to recover assets gifted to a neglectful child – all voiced regret over perceived ill-usage and the breakdown of the way they imagined relations should be.

In this chapter, we will look at the affective framework of these kinds of cases, both the emotional linkages of family life – affection, love, nurturing – and the feelings of betrayal when those bonds turned sour and broke down. One of the issues that came up was the way in which imagined family life collided – often brutally – with the realities of life together. The cases frequently depended on evidence of intimacy, or more accurately, on he said/she said, self-interested assertions of each party's impression of intimacy. That made some of these actions controversial to commentators and law reformers – in the common-law tradition, "heart balm torts" like alienation of affection or breach of promise to marry were regularly criticized and sometimes abolished outright.[1] In the civil-law tradition, debates were less absolute – after all, damage was damage, if it was proved – but situations like these still brought up difficult questions. My concern in this chapter is not with the futile question of which side's impression of domestic life was accurate, but rather with the impressions themselves. How did plaintiffs and defendants imagine their situation? What hopes or expectations did they bring to their relationship? And how did they express their feelings of having been betrayed or frustrated in those hopes or expectations? Alongside the views of the parties, judges too had expectations of what households and families of different configurations and social levels were supposed to look like. To measure the parties' expectations, judges used various yardsticks, but especially a combination of their own personal views and their understanding of social codes of propriety. The judges' metrics, however, were highly adaptable so as to account for the status and class of the parties, and were inflected also by standards of public policy translated into law, which themselves reflected views of status and class. We can start exploring these issues with a marriage gone sour among recent immigrants in Montreal's Jewish community.

Violins and Kimonos: *Weingart v. Jacobson*

Joseph Jacobson and Annie Weingart were married by Rabbi Jacob Colton of Congregation Shemerin Labeker (Shomrim Laboker) in Montreal on 8 April 1916.[2] Both were Jewish immigrants from what was then the Russian Empire, Joseph from Warsaw, Annie from Brest, and both had been married previously.[3] Joseph had come to Montreal about twenty-five years before. His first wife had died only about six weeks before his remarriage: a short interval, but thirty days was the minimum in Jewish law.[4] He was around forty years old, though when asked his age he guessed thirty-two or thirty-five, since "I was never told by my mother."[5] Annie was much younger, perhaps in her mid-twenties, and had arrived in the city only around six years before with her two young sons.[6] The marriage was arranged by a matchmaker. The resulting blended family was hardly a rarity, though the tensions inherent in such arrangements were a frequent source of litigation of various kinds, as Peter Gossage has shown for an earlier period.[7] Though Annie doubtless would have seen that Joseph was somewhat eccentric, he appeared to be a good catch – he was a self-described "professor of music" who taught young musicians violin, and he had various property holdings that brought in rents. The day before the wedding, the couple made a marriage contract before a notary. It stipulated they would be separate as to property, that Joseph would be responsible for household expenses, including the education of Annie's sons, and that there would be no dower. Further, "in consideration ... of the love and affection which the said future husband hath for and beareth towards his said future wife," Joseph gave as gifts to Annie all household furniture, several lots in Montreal, and rights to a $6000 hypothec on certain lots he had recently sold. The contract ended on a more ominous note, however: "It is specially covenanted that should any disputes arise between the said future consorts, which will lead to any action in a Court of Justice the donation abovementioned will become null and void."[8] Despite the hint of a controlling side to Joseph's personality, all seemed well at first as the family set up household in one of his properties on Colonial Avenue, in Montreal's Jewish neighbourhood.[9]

Just four months later, things had gone terribly wrong, and lawsuits were flying in all directions. Annie went to court on 17 August to get permission to institute proceedings. This was granted on 25 August, and on 1 September she filed for separation from bed and board, claiming ill-treatment, gross insults, assaults, threats of bodily harm, and failure to provide for her and her two sons. She also sought the property promised her in the marriage contract, and because she claimed that Joseph was continuing to collect rents on those properties, she sought various conservatory measures as well.[10] Joseph countered on 6 September with his own petition for separation, alleging adultery, that Annie had left the common domicile and refused to return, that she had assaulted him and threatened to poison him, and that in general life in common had become impossible due to "a great incompatibility of character." He also filed a conservatory seizure on more than $2000 in a bank account in Annie's name, which he claimed was really his money and which he feared she would withdraw. Finally, he sought to enforce the clause in the marriage contract that made all gifts conditional, arguing that Annie's separation action nullified the gifts.[11] Later in September, Joseph was sued in defamation by Louis Huberman, Annie's alleged paramour,[12] and as all those cases proceeded, a raft of motions and ancillary actions arose, bringing various third parties into the fray alongside the principals.[13]

Untangling exactly what had happened is impossible, since like all such cases of marital breakdown, everything depends on conflicting reports of the state of the couple's relationship and what went on behind the doors of the matrimonial home. Testimony does, however, provide an interesting (though problematic) view into the couple's private space: witnesses reported overheard conversations, glimpses into half-closed doors, and the like. Still, for our purposes, what actually happened is less important than how the parties themselves viewed their situation and described their emotional injuries. What follows is based mainly on the depositions in the different case files, focusing on matters on which the plaintiff's and defendant's witnesses agree.

The flashpoint of the breakdown seems to have been events surrounding Annie's trip to Joliette in July and August of 1916 to escape the summer heat in the city. The couple's neighbourhood was densely populated, and the streets and buildings quickly became airless and stifling in summer. She went off with her husband's blessing to spend a few weeks with her family on a farm her brother owned. Joseph seems to have sent her a small dog for company, and a bit of money, via his then friend, furrier Louis Huberman. While Annie was in Joliette, she wrote some letters back to her husband, giving him some news, some reminders about business matters back home, but mostly begging him to visit her. On 19 July she wrote, in Yiddish:

> To my dear husband we should be always happily together.
>   … I thank you very much for your kindness in sending me money and I would like that you should come and see me. Everyone is asking to me, why you do not come to see me. They suppose that you do not love me so come to see me for two hours so I will feel better, because I am very lonely and my heart aches very much to see you.… I have nothing more to write you remain happy, healthy and lucky.
>   From me,
>   Annie[14]

Shortly after this, she wrote again, repeating her unhappiness with his failure to visit:

> My dear husband live happily!
>   I have received your letter and I thank you very much for your letter and for everything that you sent me.… But I am very sorry that you did

not change your mind, and I was told from somebody that you would not change your mind and that you would not come to see me, so I ask you why and beg of you to come on Saturday.[15]

On 12 August the family decamped back to Montreal for the wedding of Annie's sister to Louis Citrin the following day. Joseph refused to go to the wedding, claiming not to have been invited. Annie went alone and returned home after midnight with Huberman in tow, insisting he should stay the night rather than walk the few blocks to his home at such a late hour. That Monday, 14 August, arguments over money flared up between Joseph and Annie. Joseph claimed Annie had taken $210 from his safe, while Annie accused Joseph of having drawn cheques on her own bank account, which a trip to the bank confirmed. By the end of the day, Annie had moved in with her newlywed sister, and Joseph had had the locks changed on the couple's home.

So much for what is reasonably well supported by the evidence presented in court by the two sides. At this point, however, we need to leave the relatively firm ground of the more public aspects of the case to explore the parties' emotional responses to events. Joseph testified at great length. His depositions, even if we recognize that they were shaped by the lawyers' questions, present a vivid picture of an eccentric and tormented (but also tormenting) spouse. Annie was called by Joseph to testify but was immediately ruled an incompetent witness; later in the trial she did testify briefly on her own behalf, in rebuttal.[16] Joseph's lawyer constantly undertook dubious lines of questioning and tried strategies doomed to failure like that one; the trial judge's frayed patience was clearly evident throughout the proceedings. The testimony of other witnesses – relatives, neighbours, business associates – must be used with more than the usual caution because of their obviously highly partisan positions. Still, it offers further hints of the emotional responses of the principals to the unfolding situation.

If we begin with Joseph, we get a story of increasing suspicion focused less on Annie herself than on Huberman and Annie's family – "that gang" as he termed them.[17] Joseph was clearly an odd character. His testimony was filled with fraught and over-the-top exclamations like, "Your Lordship, you can give me the electric chair, if she was present when I said it,"[18] and "I would not say, only once, but often, billions of times, I would swear to even that by black candles, by death, that I never said anything to her but compliments."[19] Annie's witnesses called Joseph "mad" and testified that his music pupils said he was "too crazy. We cannot get along with him."[20] His own physician, testifying on Joseph's behalf, described him as "a very very nervous man; even when he is well he is very eccentric," and as someone who "gets very angry at a very little thing."[21] While Annie was in Joliette, if not before, Joseph began developing strong suspicions about her relationship with Huberman.

Initially, Joseph seems to have encouraged Huberman, a former music student with whom he had been on friendly terms, to accompany his wife to the theatre when he was not able to himself. At some point, however, he began hearing things about them. Kolman Citrin, an in-law of Annie's but one of Joseph's witnesses, testified that he saw Huberman sitting on Annie's bed in Joliette, both of them not fully dressed. Citrin disapproved, and when he saw (he claimed) similar carryings-on back in Montreal, he told Joseph about it.[22] Another of Joseph's witnesses, his neighbour Agnes Hextes, claimed to have seen Annie at the window of the couple's house, laughing and beckoning Huberman with hand signals just after Joseph had left. She said she warned Joseph around that time that "you had better watch your wife a little better. She goes out with Mr. Huberman."[23] Joseph began complaining about Huberman around the neighbourhood, saying that he was taking his wife "to bad places" and having "illicit relations" with her. That resulted in a defamation suit by Huberman; Joseph failed to contest it and was condemned *ex parte* to $500 in damages, the decision handed down just before testimony began in the cases involving his wife.[24] Several of Joseph's witnesses reported a story about Huberman and Annie, each time in similar terms, which crystallized Joseph's fears about his wife and the younger man, younger than himself, but around Annie's age. Annie Stober, the wife of the landlord where Annie went to live after she left Joseph, testified for Joseph that Annie and Huberman spent a lot of time alone together in a room with the door closed, which Stober did not like. One morning, when Huberman was there, Annie "was undressed: just a kimono, she had a chemise on her when she came up for water from the kitchen."[25] Several of Joseph's other witnesses mentioned the kimono as well. Samuel Freifeld claimed to have called at Joseph's home one morning. Joseph was gone, but Annie answered the door in her kimono; the witness saw Huberman in the house as well, and both were in an "excited" state.[26] Philip Rothstein, asked by Joseph to intercede on his behalf after Annie had left, went to Annie's sister's house one evening, about nine o'clock. Annie answered the door barefoot in a kimono, but then went back inside and Huberman came to the door, barefoot and shirtless, and told Rothstein to "go to hell. He [Joseph] has no business to come around to her."[27] Huberman of course denied the kimono story as well as his own state of undress.[28]

The kimono stories were vague about timing: Freifeld placed the incident in the period before Annie went to Joliette, the others referred to the days following Annie's split from Joseph. All, however, linked it with the narrative of betrayal that Joseph developed. If we turn to Joseph's own testimony, he presented himself as an innocent and bewildered victim of events beyond his control. He saw changes as coming from outside to affect his life – particularly from those surrounding his young and (as he put it) impressionable wife. He steadfastly denied any quarrels with his wife and painted a uniformly (and unlikely) rosy picture of their cosy life together. The following exchange can stand for many others. Asked whether he had ever insulted Annie, he answered, "Well the insult was that she kissed me and I kissed her. I thought the world of her. To tell you the truth Your Lordship, I do not know what happened. There is something came to my house, and I do not know what happened. I am twenty-seven years in Montreal. And I never felt any such a trouble, the way I felt with her. I do not know what happened to me. Everybody is sorry for me. They do not know what is the matter."[29]

On the night of the wedding, when Annie returned with Huberman, Joseph said he felt "there is something funny going [on]."[30] He testified that his wife insisted that Huberman sleep upstairs, even though Joseph was going to sleep downstairs – not at her insistence, but by his own choice. His narration of events played up his own victimhood. He said at one point Annie came downstairs, kissed him, covered him with a quilt, and asked him why he didn't come upstairs. He refused, telling the judge, "Well Your Lordship, certainly I am not a fool. ... I dressed up and I walked out, because I felt disturbed, awfully bad. I could not say anything to her."[31]

His testimony about other aspects of the case continued this theme of betrayal, victimhood, and the intervention of others within his domestic life. In her declaration instituting her demand for separation, Annie necessarily made various allegations of ill-treatment by Joseph. He responded with denials, but his expected defence was inflected with emotional overtones of bewilderment and feelings of betrayal. Addressing an accusation that he had struck her and bloodied her face in a shop during an altercation over money, he responded, "I have been trying my best. I asked her to come home from the store, and she refused to go home. I said, Hannah, I have all the talk from you. I said, Hannah, please come home. Forget about everything. Because, I did not know that woman. I was married a few weeks with her."[32] Even after she had left, when she was living with her sister and brother-in-law, and her family were doing their best to keep the couple apart, he would have taken her back, he testified; he would even take her back now. He painted a forlorn picture of himself, futilely knocking at her brother-in-law's door in the hopes of convincing her to return. Eight days after she left, he saw her with Huberman, her brother, and others. He said to her, "Hannah, will you do me a favor, forget all about it ... look at the way I am suffering ... throw away all your bad company, come and be a good woman."[33] After she left, he saw her and Huberman arm-in-arm going to the movies – "They laugh at me, and made a fool of me, that is all."[34] He ended his deposition on the theme of betrayal and conspiracy, alleging that she and her family had taken everything of hers with them to Joliette, so that when she returned for the wedding, she could move out quickly and easily. His final evidence was, "She took everything I had. Six feather beds, and they took everything Your Lordship. This is as true as I am standing in front of you. They robbed me through and through from the house. That is all."[35] Clearly his testimony was self-serving, even delusional. At one point, he expressed the view that if his wife would only come home, everything would be all right: "If she will be home, we shall have a glass of champagne together, I hope so, we shall play a violin solo."[36]

Annie's view of the situation is harder to establish, since her testimony was so brief. Her first deposition began with a question from Joseph's lawyer about her first marriage, followed by an immediate ruling that she was incompetent to testify.[37] Later, testifying on her own behalf in rebuttal, she denied that anything untoward had happened with Huberman, whether in Joliette or Montreal. She admitted she had seen Huberman frequently, even gone with him to the theatre, but always either in the presence of her husband or with his encouragement and permission. A few of her answers provide brief glimpses into her reactions – hints only, because either she had been well coached to remain on her guard, or because language difficulties limited her ability to answer at greater length.[38] In denying Joseph's allegation that she had threatened him with a knife during an argument over the money taken from the safe, she hinted at his controlling nature: "Mr. Jacobson never left any two hundred and ten dollars lying around so loose as I could take it myself. Whenever he had to give me for dinner, he asked me, how much is this and that?"[39] Further along in her testimony, asked in cross-examination about her time in Joliette, she confirmed that Huberman had gone with the family, and added drily, "Mr. Jacobson sent him with me. I asked Mr. Jacobson to come with me, so Mr. Jacobson sent Mr. Huberman."[40] In her plea in response to Joseph's action, we have as clear a statement as any about her feelings towards her husband (though the wording is likely her lawyer's): life together had become impossible "owing to the hallucination, eccentricities and forms of insanity which the plaintiff is suffering from, and for which she is in no wise to blame."[41]

Some of Annie's witnesses provide further glimpses of relations between the couple: they describe a different picture than the happy home Joseph and his witnesses presented. Shopkeeper Israel Lake, for example, reported that soon after the couple were married, Joseph told him that he was tired of his wife and did not like her anymore. Asked by the judge to elaborate, Lake obliged: "He said that he did not like her, because he wanted to get a nice young lady for his use. ... He said, 'It is a very big size, and I have no taste for it; I want to get another young lady with a smaller size.'"[42] Lake further testified that Joseph had confided in him that he just had to get his property from her, then he would be off to California. "He was a professor, and he had lots of young ladies, and could get another young lady, he said."[43] Lake was one of those Joseph accused of actively subverting his relationship with his wife, to the point that Joseph seems to have employed a spy to peek into the back window of Lake's store when Annie was allegedly sitting on Lake's knee.[44] Annie's brother-in-law Louis Citrin, similarly hostile, according to Joseph, raised the issue of money, suggesting that married life for Joseph might have diverged from his expectations when his new wife arrived with two young boys. He asserted that the real reason for the break-up was that Joseph felt Annie was too free with money in comparison with his previous wife.[45] Some of Annie's other witnesses mentioned Joseph's antipathy to her children, a view with which Joseph himself concurred, calling the boys "very rough" and in need of education.[46] Huberman reported Joseph as saying about Annie herself that she "is not educated enough for me. Because he is a Professor of Music, and she cannot play music, that is why he don't want her."[47]

Finally, some of the witnesses reported hearsay evidence of Annie's own feelings about the relationship. Some of Joseph's witnesses claimed to have spoken with her and gotten a positive report of the newlyweds, especially soon after the wedding.[48] Other witnesses, however, on both sides, reported dissatisfaction. Huberman testified about Annie's feelings of neglect after Joseph had allegedly sent the two of them off together to the Midway Cinema. When they returned, Annie asked Joseph, "'Did I marry you, or did I marry Mr. Huberman?' … Then he commenced to insult her and use all kinds of language to her, and call her children bastards."[49] Samuel Freifeld reported that Annie told him that Joseph was "too old for me. I do not like him anymore."[50] And Max Crystal, testifying for Joseph, said that Annie told him that "she could not live with him, because he is crazy," though before this they seemed happy.[51]

The two main cases, the respective separation actions, were joined for hearing. Justice Farquhar Stuart Maclennan had little patience for the evasions, contradictions, and oddities of Joseph's witnesses, and dismissed his testimonial evidence in its entirety. Joseph's own testimony, he ruled, "shows that he is not a fit person to be the husband of any self-respecting woman, that he had no regard for the rights of his wife, and from his conduct in the witness box and the manner in which he gave his evidence, is not to be believed under oath." Joseph's treatment of Annie – the judge cited slaps, accusations of prostitution, threats, expulsion from the common home – was enough to ground Annie's allegations of outrage, ill-usage, and grievous insult. This was moreover aggravated by Joseph's parallel action in separation, which Maclennan held to be "an unjustified and unfounded attack upon her character which he endeavoured to support by evidence of witnesses wholly unworthy of belief." Maclennan granted Annie's petition for separation, awarding her alimony of $45 per month.[52] In dismissing Joseph's petition in the parallel action, he also declared illegal and null the clause in the marriage contract making all the donations conditional on Annie's never taking legal action against her husband. Such a clause, he ruled, was "contrary to good morals, to law and to public order" and "would have the effect of imposing upon defendant a position of absolute subjection and submission to ill treatment, outrage and grievous insult on the part of the plaintiff … and would deprive her of the liberty of exercising her civil rights against the plaintiff."[53]

Joseph appealed to the Court of Review, and Annie filed a motion soon after asking for speedy review and the appointment of a sequestrator, alleging that Joseph had paid nothing following the judgment and was continuing to collect rents from the property she had been awarded.[54] In Joseph's factum, he (through his lawyers) claimed that the situation "had practically ruined his financial condition" – he was unable to work, had been forced to carry on numerous concurrent and expensive legal actions, and whatever assets he still had were tied up in litigation. The sense of betrayal continued to animate his framing of his case. Before the problems, he and his wife "had lived as two turtle doves": he detailed how "he thought the world of his wife," how they walked arm-in-arm around town, and how they used to kiss one another and never quarrel. The problem, he asserted, was the intervention of "strangers" – Israel Lake and Annie's brother-in-law, Louis Citrin – who poisoned the couple's relationship. This, along with the actions of Huberman, who was "much more than a friend with Mrs. Jacobson," doomed his domestic happiness.[55] Annie, in her factums, stuck mainly to affirming the trial judge's conclusions – she was in the position of strength, after all – but did add insinuations about Joseph's relationship with his housekeeper, Minnie Walker, whose husband was absent and to whom Joseph, for inexplicable reasons, "magnanimously" gave a property worth $10,000 (though the insinuation was clearly about a sexual relationship, the property transfer may have been a ruse to prevent seizure of the assets in satisfaction of the various judgments).[56]

The Court of Review unanimously affirmed the illegality of the clause in the marriage contract; they split over the trial judge's evaluation of the evidence of improper relations between Annie and Huberman.[57] Chief Justice John Archibald for the majority framed his analysis in cultural terms, distinguishing between "us" and "them": "In the first place, it must be taken into consideration that we are dealing with a class of persons, many of whom have not long been used to our customs and our conventions, and particularly with regard to the association between men and women." He continued, "It would seem natural to come to the conclusion that a greater familiarity is practised among the class of people who are connected with this case than would be allowed under our usages." He moved from this to ascribe a similarly libertine character to Joseph himself, stating that although he knew things were going on, he "evidently did not consider them of any importance such as to justify him in forming any grave complaint against his wife's conduct." All in all, strange conclusions, given that Joseph had promptly begun separation proceedings against his wife, and that several witnesses had testified to being shocked by the behaviour of Annie and Huberman. While the trial judge had dismissed Joseph's evidence, the review court put great weight on the kimono story, though they read the evidence less than attentively, placing the incident in Joliette. In any case, the majority concluded that "we are in the presence of a number of people who have very low moral standing with regard to the association of men and women."[58] Justice Paul-Gédéon Martineau's dissent rested on a similar foundation. He would have overturned the decision, since the often odd testimony of the witnesses was due not to any inherent unreliability but rather to "the excitability with which immigrants from northern Europe give their testimony." He assessed blame differently than the trial judge. Rather than an unreasonable husband presenting dubious witnesses to uphold his attack on a blameless wife, Justice Martineau saw a gold-digging young woman who should not profit from a marriage of four months' duration. "It is not good," he wrote, "that certain women live in idleness."[59] In other words, though the majority and dissent differed over whether or not the trial judge's findings of fact should be upheld – and over which spouse was responsible for the break-up – they agreed that the actions of the parties in the case were to be ascribed to the questionable morality of foreigners. The trial decision was affirmed.

Joseph sought permission to take the case directly to the Supreme Court of Canada, but was denied on jurisdictional grounds, likely another example of dubious tactics recommended by his lawyer.[60] He also continued his attempts to stonewall Annie, conspiring with others to hide assets,[61] contesting various actions she tried to take to execute the judgments in her favour, and refusing his authorization for her to take further legal action, forcing her again to seek court permission.[62] Joseph similarly used various means to prevent Huberman from collecting on his default judgment for defamation, getting Minnie Walker to file oppositions to seizures of Joseph's property that was in her hands.[63] A year and half after judgment, Huberman's lawyer was in court getting the writ of seizure reissued.[64]

Even after the procedural wrangling had died down, the parties continued to be bound financially, as well as by their ongoing matrimonial bond (even had they obtained a religious divorce – doubtful, given Joseph's obstructionism – their marriage would have continued to have civil effect). In 1921, Annie was successfully sued by the Police Benevolent and Pension Society to recognize a hypothec on some property Joseph had granted her in the marriage contract.[65] She was also in court that year seeking permission from the court to exercise her legal rights, in the face of Joseph's continuing refusal to authorize her. This time she was seeking permission to sell her rights in the immovables that she held through the marriage contract. Justice Arthur-Aimé Bruneau, a specialist in matrimonial law who, around this time, published a treatise on impediments and other issues relating to marriage, read the terms of the marriage contract strictly and found that the sale would benefit Annie and more particularly her sons from the first marriage, something Joseph had clearly intended to prevent. He refused to authorize Annie for the sale.[66]

By this time, Annie seems to have been living in Outremont with her young sons, working as a dressmaker and using her first husband's surname (which would have been the boys' name).[67] Joseph appeared periodically in the news, still teaching music, and always depicted as an eccentric. In 1926 he testified in a fraud trial over a transaction in which he paid $2300 for some diamonds that turned out to be fake. He asked to be sworn on the New Testament, because "they stole from me on the Old Testament." After his testimony went on and on, the judge said, "If you are as great a musician as you are an orator, you must be an incomparable artiste," at which Joseph smiled.[68] He also continued his litigiousness, as attested by numerous legal notices in the newspapers.[69]

The differences between the judges in this case are interesting when considered in light of the parties' narratives we have examined. Where the trial judge saw Annie as a victim of her husband's inexcusable attack on her character, the review judges – both majority and dissent – saw her as an opportunist, looking to turn a brief marriage that went sour to her own advantage. At the Court of Review, Joseph's betrayal narrative resonated with the justices. While the majority paid the required lip service to deference to findings of fact by the trial judge, and in the end affirmed his decision, they did so while holding their noses. They had clearly been swayed by the allegations of sexual immorality in the case, building the kimono story into evidence of a kind of free love commune in Joliette. They did not let Joseph off the hook: he too, after all, was a foreigner of questionable morals, as his dubious relationship with his housekeeper showed. But the judges focused most of their disapproval on Annie's immorality and pushed aside Joseph's eccentricities, stinginess, hostility to her children, and controlling behaviour. The result was an odd review judgment. Annie won – she was granted separation, alimony, and substantial property – at the same time as she was condemned as the culpable party in the relationship. In the end, while both spouses felt betrayed by a marriage that did not go as either of them had planned, the process validated Joseph's and not Annie's feelings.

The disintegration of Joseph Jacobson and Annie Weingart's affective relationship gave rise to a variety of legal actions seeking to address the material and moral effects of the breakdown and the couple's continuing legal ties. Feelings of betrayal were present in all of them – the evident vindictiveness in the flood of litigation bears that out – but always in the background, as a motivation rather than the object of litigation. In certain other kinds of action, however, feelings of betrayal were the central element in the moral damages being sought. In what follows, three such actions will help expand on the themes introduced by the Weingart-Jacobson litigation. Two were traditional "heart balm" actions, breach of promise to marry and alienation of affection, which raised further issues about affective relationships and how the Quebec legal system dealt with them. The third, an action to revoke a gift because of the recipient's ingratitude, raised similar feelings of betrayal in a different legal context. While all three brought up interesting legal issues, our focus will mainly be on their emotional content.[70]

For Love or Money: *Demers v. Hébert*

On 28 March 1883, François-Xavier Hébert and Rose de Lima Demers met at the office of notary Clément Prosper Germain in St. Philippe, across the river from Montreal, to draw up a marriage contract in anticipation of their imminent wedding.[71] They had not yet formally fixed a date, but the couple had been seeing each other for some time, and the impending wedding was known and talked about in the community. The contract was the last formality before going to the altar within the next week or so. The couple were not youngsters – Rose was around thirty-five years old, while her fiancé was considerably older, around fifty.[72] Neither had been married previously. While both families were reasonably well off, Hébert was quite comfortable – as the notary put it, "according to the usual expression used in the country, he passed for rich."[73] Xavier, as he was known, would have been a catch, particularly for a thirty-five-year-old bride. Their courtship was a fairly low-key affair: they had begun seeing each other the winter before, and attended a wedding and a few parties together.[74] The couple had known one another for a long time, however, and were in fact distantly related, so nothing suggested that the visit to the notary would be anything more than a routine step before the wedding.

Rose's father, Pierre, accompanied his daughter to this important meeting. The extent to which the couple had discussed financial arrangements in advance is unclear. Both had provided the notary with a list of their assets and debts, since Germain was ready on the day with a draft contract reflecting the couple's wishes, including a six-page list of the couple's possessions (mostly Xavier's). The contract included various pre-printed boilerplate provisions, some modified by cancellations or additions, that specified things like community of property and the survivor's *préciput* of the bed linens (*lit garni*). In lieu of dower rights, duly cancelled on the form, Xavier had decided to grant his wife half of whatever gains they realized during the marriage as well as $200 yearly, should he predecease her, as long as she did not remarry and provided that the couple had no children.[75] Pierre Demers was less than thrilled with that arrangement. He may have suggested that his daughter would be better served by an outright grant of the land on which the future matrimonial home was situated (that was disputed), but in any event he certainly insisted she be given the usufruct of certain of Xavier's lands. According to the notary, Pierre laid it on thick – that a husband had nothing more precious in the world than his wife; that failing to grant her adequate rights, "it's not generous, it's flagrant, it's not fair, it's not nice"; that otherwise Xavier's heirs would lock her out of her own home on the very day of his funeral.[76] A usufruct on the husband's land with the matrimonial home to benefit a widow without children was normal in farming communities, the notary testified, to ensure that the widow would not be left without a place to live.[77] A provision to that effect was in fact pre-printed as article IX of the form contract the notary was using.

Bettina Bradbury, writing of an earlier period, notes that by the 1840s, among both Anglo and Canadien elites, rejection of dower, combined with annuities, lump-sum payments, or interest on a specific sum of money, was increasingly the choice in marriage contracts. Among Canadien crafts couples, by contrast, dower remained the majority choice in that earlier period, though annuities and the like were becoming more common. Among both groups, however, Bradbury notices a trend towards patriarchal control of the land and away from older customary ideas of the "proper portion of accumulated or inherited wealth that should be made available to a man's widow or children." By this slightly later period, replacing dower rights with annuities, life insurance, or other arrangements was becoming more the norm than the exception.[78] The relative value of the two offers, however, was less clear. On paper, the usufruct may have been worth more than what Xavier initially offered, though as several of Xavier's witnesses pointed out, it would require the widow to find ways to work the land to realize its

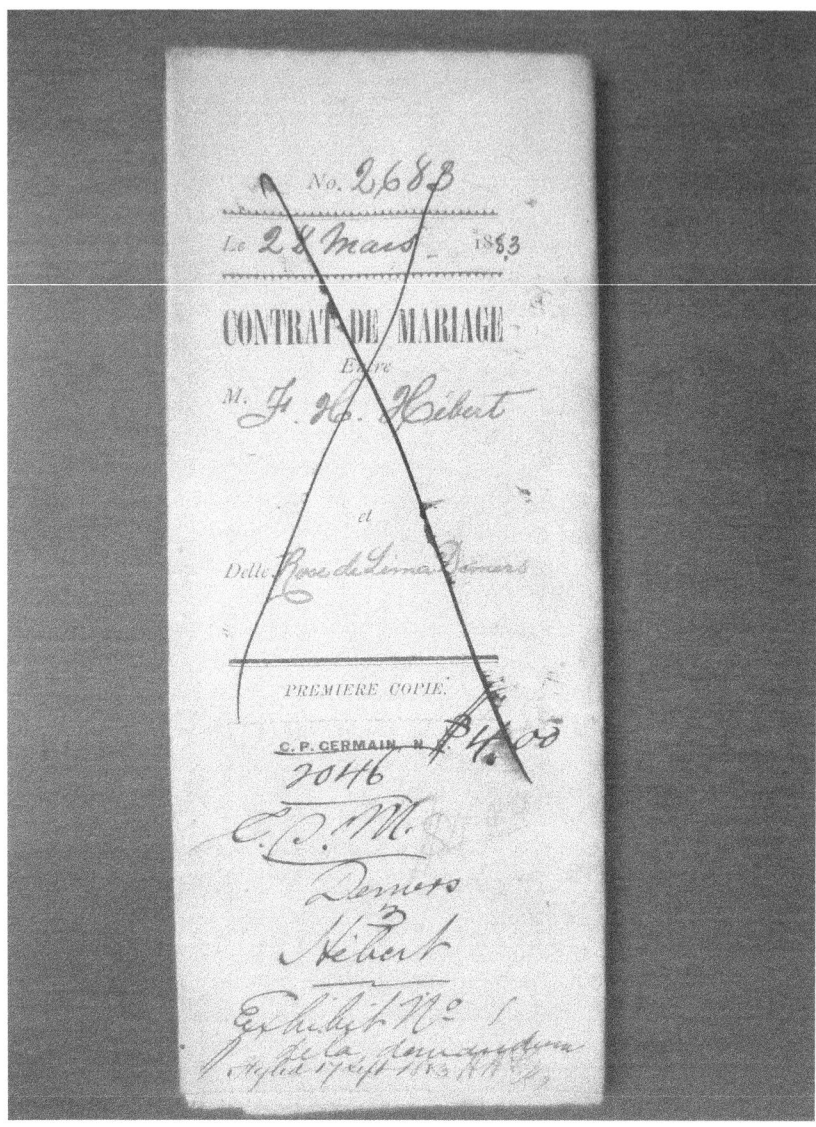

Figure 5.1 Copy of the marriage contract between François-Xavier Hébert and Rose de Lima Demers, dated 28 March 1883. BAnQ-VM, *Demers v. Hébert*, Superior Court case file, Plaintiff's Exhibit 1. Photograph by the author. Reproduced with permission of Bibliothèque et Archives nationales du Québec.

income, which might reduce the overall value of the gift. Still, they felt she would be better off with the land.[79]

Pierre Demers's complaints about the initial offer and insistence on the usufruct put Xavier in an awkward position. Little has been written on the negotiations surrounding marriage contracts (notarial registers contain finished acts, after all, not rejected drafts), but it is clear that while financial negotiations were a usual and accepted part of prenuptial preparations, they were not usually conducted in the notary's office on the very eve of the wedding.[80] They also always required delicacy and tact on both sides. Fiancés, especially well-off ones, and certainly ones in their fifties like Xavier, were presumed to have an overall plan for their assets, while the families of fiancées were understood to be seeking assurances that their daughters would not be condemned to a precarious existence should they become widows. But on both sides positions had to be argued within general norms of propriety. Too much zeal on either side in guarding one's own and one's family's interests could lead to the impression of stinginess (on his side) or grasping (on hers). Pierre Demers's vigorous advocacy of his daughter's interests may have crossed the line; Xavier's hesitance about handing over any of his land may have done likewise. The senior Demers's suggestion of stinginess – he claimed Xavier misinterpreted his actual remarks – seems to have hit home. Xavier, who comes across as not the most resolute of personalities, agreed to change the contract, and it was duly drawn up to provide his widow with a life interest in the piece of land including the matrimonial home. The contract was notarized, and away they went.

Once away from his fiancée and her father, doubts began to trouble Xavier almost immediately, and he suspected that his bride-to-be was more interested in his money than in him. He asked the notary what he thought, and Germain agreed that it looked like Rose was motivated by money: he sympathized that Xavier was in a difficult position.[81] Xavier turned next to his curé, George Laporte, complaining that the contract was made but he did not like its terms, since Rose seemed to be demanding too much. The priest counselled him to delay the wedding and to look into renegotiating the contract.[82] The parties contested the exact sequence of events that followed, as well as their meaning, but what transpired was a series of tentative but wary attempts on each side to salvage the relationship, under the cloud of the mutual doubts raised by the incident at the notary's office. The timeline of events is important for understanding the emotional responses of the parties, which we will consider shortly.[83]

A couple of days after the visit to the notary, Xavier came to the Demers home. They thought he wanted to fix the date of the wedding. Instead, he proposed putting off the wedding because he was unhappy with the arrangements they had settled on in the contract.[84] Rose claimed that he entered the home "brusquely, without greeting anyone," which Xavier denied.[85] About a week later, Rose wrote to a friend who knew Xavier, asking her to tell him that if he communicated with her (Xavier was illiterate), she would be pleased.[86] That seems to have provoked no further action on Xavier's part, and so on 21 June she had a lawyer send a letter to him, threatening legal action for the damages caused by his breach of promise.[87] Xavier seems to have responded with an assurance that if she was worried about the expenses she had laid out for her trousseau, he would reimburse those. Rose did not respond, and there the matter rested for some time.

On 17 August, the couple had an apparently chance encounter in Montreal.[88] Rose was walking down the street and spotted Xavier in a doorway. She walked by, pointedly ignoring him, but he tracked her down at the dock of the ferry *La Laprairie*. He asked if he could cross the river with her, saying that he had wanted to see her but feared a scene with her father. She refused his request, turned away from the four o'clock ferry, and hung out in town until the next one at six o'clock. In Laprairie, Xavier was waiting on the dock, and they spoke briefly. He asked if he could see her at her grandfather's or her sister's – neutral ground – but again she refused, since they lived near him and she feared people would talk.

That spurred Xavier into action again. Two days afterwards, on Sunday evening, he visited the Demers home, braving the presence of Rose's father and a couple of sisters. The visit lasted several hours, and the couple had a long discussion – Rose said it was mainly about this and that until the very end, when the issue of marriage came up.[89] Xavier renewed his offer, but Rose again refused, and the couple parted that evening without reconciling. Xavier's parting words, according to Rose, were, "Well, think about it, maybe in seven or eight days you'll come to feel differently and we'll be able to agree."[90] Rather than giving her time to think it over, however, the next day, 20 August, Xavier sent notary Germain back to the Demers home with a settlement offer of $45 for her troubles, accompanied by the warning that going to court would mean disgrace for them both.[91] Abandoning any reconciliation, he also charged Germain with asking Rose to return jewellery he had given her for the planned wedding (two wedding rings engraved with their names and a stickpin). Rose saw them as gifts and refused to return them, and referred Germain to her lawyers regarding the settlement offer.

Rose instituted the threatened action in breach of promise on 31 August 1883, alleging that Xavier's termination of their engagement had caused her moral and material injury in the amount of $500.[92] Her claim would have been almost entirely for moral injury: though Rose noted that she had spent approximately $100 on the trousseau, the items were still in her possession, and her conclusion prayed for compensation for moral prejudice only. The Demers family were anxious to keep the matter out of the newspapers, as no doubt was Xavier, and they had specifically instructed their lawyer to see to this.[93] Their worries were well founded, as breach of promise actions were a favourite source of Schadenfreude entertainment, providing, as Patrick Brode has suggested, moral lessons akin to charivari.[94] Despite their efforts, one Montreal newspaper did get wind of the action, apparently by a reporter's diligent perusal of the docket at the courthouse. The brief notice, which appeared in *Le Temps* on 3 September 1883 under the heading "$500 in Damages," gave the full names of the parties and suggested (erroneously) that the amount claimed represented Rose's expenditures on the trousseau.[95] Unlike most breach of promise cases, this one did not involve accusations of seduction or pregnancy, which no doubt tempered its salacious appeal.[96] As a result, however, it involved the parties' feelings much more directly, with each side arguing emotional mistreatment by the other. In other words, the case was about betrayal – betrayal of the affective investment each had made in the proposed marriage.[97]

The action in breach of promise had long been controversial, for various reasons.[98] Some, following Roman and early French law, had viewed the promise as a binding contract. Enforcement, however, such as specific performance to force the parties to marry to rectify the breach, ran afoul of the strictly voluntary nature of marriage in theology, canon law, and secular law alike. By the middle of the nineteenth century, most if not all commentators agreed that breach of promise was an extra-contractual matter, to be resolved via an action in damages. But even that raised moral issues, since it threatened to cast the shadow of lucre over what should have been a spiritual and affective union.[99] As Justice Louis-Bonaventure Caron put it in 1882, marriage was not simply an ordinary contract, assessable in money terms: "It is the union of two souls brought together by this intimate sentiment, spontaneous and so powerful that it is called love, or by another motivation, more modest, calmer, but no less respectable, the fondness that will later produce love."[100] Some also worried that the threat of heavy damages might force a reluctant fiancé(e) to marry unwillingly rather than walk away, thus again undermining the free consent essential to valid marriage. Concerns about liberty were especially strong in Quebec, where until the late 1960s a valid marriage ended only upon the death of one of the spouses.

These moral issues had arisen in some of the earlier cases in Quebec, particularly in *Grange v. Benning*, with which we began this book. The Court of Review in that case was categorical in rejecting the moral argument that the action in breach of promise was contrary to good morals because it restricted liberty of marriage: "As to the pretension that promises of marriage are contrary to good morals, such doctrine is preposterous, nay immoral in the highest degree, and would sap the very foundations of the social edifice."[101] A few years later, Thomas-Jean-Jacques Loranger confirmed that view in strong terms in his monumental (though never finished) commentary on the CCLC. To argue that a promise of marriage is immoral is "utterly false and contrary to the fundamental religious and civil principles of society. One might as well say that marriage itself is an illicit and immoral act, because it reduces even more than the promise does the freedom to contract with another during the life of the spouses."[102]

In addition to this moral controversy, in application the action for breach of promise to marry was heavily gendered and revealed strong social codes behind the legal doctrine.[103] Female plaintiffs were frequently suspected of using the action to cover their own fickleness, though that seems to have been less in evidence in Quebec than in common-law Canada, perhaps as the result of the long history of the action in French law.

On the other side, however, though the action was theoretically open to both sexes, courts recognized that an abandoned woman's future marriage prospects were much more decisively affected than a jilted man's and so tended to look askance at suits instituted by forsaken fiancés. In an 1873 case, Justice Henri-Elzéar Taschereau tore a strip off a male plaintiff who dared to bring an action against his former love: "There is a certain baseness in a young man dragging before the courts the woman whom he claimed to love enough to make the companion of the rest of his days. He who for a few dollars makes himself so contemptible shows clearly to the woman he courted how happy she should be and how much she should rejoice in having broken with him."[104] Men were expected to dust themselves off and get on with their lives and not go crying to court for redress. If the affront was particularly grave, however, a jilted fiancé's action might succeed. In an 1889 case, a young woman, egged on by her mother, was leading on two men at the same time. For Justice Louis Tellier, the unsuccessful candidate had clearly been publicly humiliated by the curious situation of banns being read out in church for the defendant with two different men. Even here, though, given prevailing gender attitudes, one wonders what the relative weighting of the stated grounds for damages was: the judge cited the public humiliation itself, the plaintiff's future difficulty in finding a suitable match, and the more respectably masculine ground of the negative effects of the public attention on the plaintiff's work.[105]

Rose's action fit into that evolving jurisprudence. By 1883, damages were seen to arise from prejudice caused by the fault of an unjustified breaking off of the engagement. The breach alone without more was not itself a fault; there had to be an element of malice, insult, or otherwise inexcusable behaviour, and that was up to the assessment of the court. The prejudice caused could be material or moral. Material damages were clear enough, as long as the expenses claimed were directly connected to preparing for the upcoming marriage, like expenditures on the trousseau. Moral damages posed more difficulties, as in all cases, since their assessment was effectively arbitrary. That could result in dismissal of cases where the evidence of fault was seen to be insufficient. In the 1882 case quoted above, for example, Justice Caron found no malice in the defendant's actions and further seemed to reject the dominant trend in the jurisprudence: "I am forced to respond to her that since what she has lost or missed having is not in commerce and is impossible to evaluate, and moreover that since the agreement she invokes is contrary to the liberty of marriage and consequently to public order, and so thereby null," her action must be dismissed.[106] General proof was necessarily indirect, and so the cases tended to be determined by judges' appreciation of what the parties must have felt.

The circumstances surrounding the end of Rose and Xavier's engagement were no exception. It would hardly have been surprising that the situation – Rose's apparent cupidity, Xavier's ham-fisted response – would have given rise to feelings of betrayal on both sides. The parties' initial filings staked out the emotional terrain. In her declaration, Rose alleged her injury in fairly generic terms: the breaking off of the engagement and the abandonment by Xavier "injured the plaintiff in her feelings and her affection, exposed her to ridicule and public laughter, and caused her a moral injury."[107] For his part, Xavier's defence was a bit more explicit about the emotional consequences of the situation. He alleged that the accusations by Demers *père* and *fille* that he was ungenerous were "hurtful and even insulting" to him, and that the whole incident "brought to the defendant's mind that his girlfriend did not have a lot of affection for him and that she probably only wanted to marry him out of self-interest."[108] For both sides, however, the testimony of the principals and other witnesses fleshed out the emotional aspects of the conflict and brought forward clearly the feelings involved.

Both Rose and Xavier testified at length, each called by the other, and their testimony gives revealing glimpses into some of the emotions surrounding the situation. Xavier's deposition focused on his reading of Rose's conduct during the meeting at the notary's. At first, he was categorical that she was clearly after his money, even going so far as to claim that she had admitted during the negotiations that she was refusing his offered annuity because "she wanted to make money."[109] Towards the end of his examination in chief, however, Xavier started to suggest that he might have misread the situation. In an exchange that strongly rings true, Xavier told of the meeting with Rose when he broke off the engagement. He told her he was doing so because he thought she didn't love him; she protested that she did love him a lot. The questioning continued:

> Q: Did it seem to hurt her when you said you didn't want to marry her?
> R: Yes sir.
> Q: Did she cry?
> R: No sir, she didn't cry.
> Q: Did she say that you would be the reason why she would be unhappy?
> R: Yes sir, she told me that.
> Q: Did she speak to you like someone who loved you?
> R: Yes sir. On that occasion, she spoke to me like someone who loved me.[110]

The absence of tears seems to have made a particular impression on the often obtuse Xavier – one can imagine Rose's stoic unhappiness presenting a powerful sense of injury, where tears might have instead given Xavier the impression she was being calculatedly theatrical. By August, when he renewed his offer, her refusal made clear that his conduct over the previous five months had made her mind up: "She said I had done too much to her."[111]

Some of the questions posed to Rose during her examination were suggestive about Xavier's reading of the situation. At several points the questions – denied – suggested there might have been talk among Rose's acquaintances of the age difference between them. Rose denied that she ever said to anyone that he was too old for her,[112] but there seems to have been some teasing on that score from one Édouard Pilotte, a nephew of Rose's grandfather. She denied that she had responded to Pilotte that she would never marry Xavier, and that it would be like marrying her father; she was not, she said, the sort of person who said whatever popped into her head.[113]

Rose's sense of betrayal was more evident, as was her understanding of what she could lose. While Xavier risked becoming known as a jilter, Rose would have been more keenly aware of the potential future impact of her situation on her chances of ever finding a mate. Xavier's betrayal was thus potentially the end of the line for her matrimonial chances, which helps explain her offers to reconcile, such as writing the letter to him in April and agreeing to meet him several times thereafter to talk things over. Still, she was self-assured enough to stand her ground and to express her feelings forcefully to Xavier. When he told her that he was afraid to return to her house for fear of her family, for example, she retorted, "I certainly believe he should have been a bit embarrassed after what he did."[114] She made those same feelings clear to notary Germain when he visited her with the settlement offer. She told him that she felt Xavier did not love her: if he did, he would at least have visited her instead of letting months go by without a word.[115]

Rose was clearly concerned about propriety, and what people in the community would think. Part of the betrayal was exposing her to the scrutiny and ridicule that would be the inevitable result of the breakup, particularly since the couple were of advanced age and matters had progressed so far. When Rose spotted Xavier in the doorway in Montreal, she walked right by without acknowledging him, since "one does not speak of one's business in the street."[116] Later, she refused his offer to meet at her grandfather's or her sister's, since they lived near Xavier and "everyone would be talking if I had been there; everyone would say that I went there to see him, and I didn't want that."[117] In relating Xavier's final offer in August, her testimony makes clear her sense of betrayal: "I said yes, I loved him; but after having done to me all the injustices he did, having caused me so much sorrow that whole time, I said that I had decided not to marry at that time." She rephrased slightly a moment later: "after all he did, after having insulted me."[118] She was certainly concerned with not letting Xavier off the hook too easily, but more than that, she was sensitive to appearing desperate in the eyes of local gossips. Her future prospects depended on her public reputation within her community, something Xavier's tardy change of mind had materially affected.

The testimony of the other witnesses put the principals' stories of betrayal into context. On Xavier's side, notary Germain confirmed Xavier's impression of Rose's feelings both during the drawing up of the contract and afterwards, testifying that "she didn't seem to regret it. I believed that she wanted to make money; that was my impression."[119] Xavier's curé expressed his opinion that he did not think Xavier was "a man who would take pleasure in causing trouble for someone else without reason, without grounds."[120]

Much of the testimony of course focused on Rose's injury and how the break-up had affected her. Predictably, the witnesses for plaintiff and defendant disagreed. Rose's father asserted that his daughter had suffered "very great sorrow" from being abandoned by her fiancé. The shame (*honte*) made her withdraw from her friends: she confined herself to the house for several months and even retreated to her room when visitors came, to avoid having to explain what had happened.[121] Several of Rose's witnesses affirmed it as self-evident that abandonment would particularly affect a young woman (despite their relatively advanced ages, Rose and even Xavier were consistently described by the witnesses as "young"). As neighbour Alexi Moquin testified, "A rumour that someone was about to marry and then was left by her fiancé, that would certainly keep others away.... That's likely to do a lot of damage to a young girl. That injures her reputation." Not for a thousand dollars would he want something similar to happen to his own daughter.[122] Another neighbour similarly testified that it was obvious other men would keep away.[123]

The defendant's witnesses took a more fluid – and less plausible, it must be said – view of the effects of broken promises to marry. Alexis Sers dit St. Jean, for example, recounted the story of his own daughter's engagement, broken off at an advanced stage, though before the marriage contract had been drawn up. (He carefully avoided specifying who had broken it off.) He painted a picture of happy and carefree youth, amicably freeing one another to look elsewhere. His daughter, he said, even made a joke of it: "Lose one, find ten others."[124] Eventually the young man married someone he had been seeing before, and after a brief but inconclusive courtship with the original fiancé's brother, the daughter ended up happily married to someone else. In the end his daughter suffered no distress and felt no shame in seeing her friends afterwards: "She was independent, you understand."[125] Another witness recounted a similar story in which his daughter broke off an engagement, and both she and the former fiancé went on to find other partners just as good. He confidently asserted that a broken promise would cause no injury, and he would not object if his own sons wanted to marry such a woman.[126] Notary Germain, however, when asked whether such a situation would injure his own daughter, avoided answering.[127] As David Desnoyers remarked about Rose, the situation would not affect her chances with other men, as she was "a girl of honour."[128] Pressed, however, a few of the defendant's witnesses grudgingly admitted that all was not equal between the genders. Several affirmed that if it were seen that Rose was only after Xavier's money, that would dramatically reduce her chances of finding another match.[129] Still, most would have agreed with Alexis Sers dit St. Jean that, even if there had briefly been some gossip, "it passed away like a leaf in the wind."[130]

Justice Michel Mathieu awarded Rose $250 damages, half of what she had demanded, for her material and moral prejudice.[131] He refused her claim for the benefits to which she would have been entitled under the marriage contract had the marriage gone ahead. Given how equivocal the evidence was, it would appear that Justice Mathieu simply assumed that the break-up could not have been without effect on Rose's reputation and future prospects. In any case, he provided little justification for the damages other than to assert that breaking off the marriage without a valid reason certainly caused Rose "a very real injury" and so damages were warranted.[132] Xavier's justification for the breach – Rose's lack of love – either left Mathieu unconvinced or else failed to rise to the level of a valid reason in the judge's assessment. All he said on that score was that the defendant should have taken steps to assure himself of his fiancée's devotion before letting things progress to such an advanced stage.[133] In this case, as in many breach of promise actions in this period, the judge had to rule on the idea of freedom of the will. Xavier's lawyer raised the issue when he argued that since marriage was for life, it was "in the interest of families and society" to recognize the parties' complete freedom to back out before irrevocably committing themselves.[134] Justice Mathieu was unconvinced. Instead, he stressed that breaking a promise of marriage was blameworthy in itself – absent some fundamental change to the parties – and so the breaching party should not be protected from answering for the material and moral consequences caused by his or her actions.[135]

Despite Rose's legitimate concerns about public ridicule, the newspapers not surprisingly covered the juicy story briefly in the days following the judgment, though their tone was relatively restrained.[136] In a plot twist perhaps not entirely unexpected, Xavier and Rose ended up together after all. Three and a half years later, they married in Montreal; Rose's father was one of the witnesses, and the couple received dispensation for a distant relationship (third or fourth degree of consanguinity). In the 1891 census for Laprairie, the couple had a one-year-old daughter named Marie Anne.[137] Rose died in March 1913, Xavier in November 1914. Betrayal was a powerful emotion, but clearly not necessarily fatal to relationships, even when litigated. Perhaps Rose found no other marriage prospects; perhaps she really was fond of Xavier, and her hard line was what it took to convince her irresolute fiancé. I have been unable to find a second marriage contract, so the material terms that led Xavier and Rose to marry, and that in the end satisfied her father, remain just as obscure as their emotions.

Betrayal was of course not limited to frustrated promises of hoped-for unions, but affected existing relationships as well. Separation from bed and board, for example, provided recourse for spouses whose mates betrayed their matrimonial duties. Love was specifically excluded from the legal evaluation of separation, however, since the spouses had no duty to love one another. As Justice John Sprott Archibald put it in dismissing a separation action in 1901, "Although it is exceedingly regrettable when the relation of affectionate harmony which ought to reign between husband and wife is lacking, yet something more than that is necessary to justify a judge in pronouncing a separation between them."[138] Love was, however, explicitly part of another available recourse for marital breakdown, the action in alienation of affection, in which a betrayed spouse could seek damages for lost love from an interfering outsider.

Seduction by the Abattoir: *Lebeau v. Plouffe*

Auguste Lebeau's hotel, in the very shadow of Montreal's Abattoirs de l'est, was where the butchers gathered, at least when they didn't walk an extra block to cheer on their favourites in the horse races at

Delorimier Park. By 1892 there were only one or two houses besides the hotel at that isolated northern end of Frontenac Street – the stockyard smell ensured growth would be slow. Lebeau's hotel was a draw, however, even if we assume he was no longer allowing illegal gambling on the premises, for which he had been fined ten dollars in police court in 1884.[139] Most days during the week, especially market days, its small bar was filled with groups of regulars, chatting, eating, drinking, and, for the inner circle, joking around with Lebeau's wife, Justine Leblanc, who tended bar. The couple had been married since 1871; Auguste was about forty-two years old, his wife a year younger. By all accounts Justine was a jovial woman – large, rather plain, but quick with the repartee and *badinage*.[140] Auguste seems to have owned a second hotel further north, at Sault-au-Récollet, and he often travelled between the two.[141]

By March 1892, the servants and the usual crowd at the hotel – everyone, it seems, except Auguste – started noticing that Joseph Plouffe, one of the butchers, had become the most regular of regulars. Plouffe was married and around thirty years old; his wife, Philomène, was six or seven years older. He lived nearby, and at first his visits came when the butchers were gathering, and he became known to both Auguste and Justine. Quickly, though, the hotel's three employees noticed that Plouffe was timing his visits for Auguste's absences, and that he and Justine would secrete themselves behind semi-closed doors, laughing and joking. By the summer, those visits had become an open secret among the butchers, who chuckled over it and began describing Auguste as a cuckold.[142] The situation placed the three employees in uncomfortable situations, especially Rose and Aurélie Raymond, two sisters who worked inside the hotel. Justine began asking the sisters to watch out for Auguste's return and to alert her when they saw him coming. At other times, Justine had Pierre Soette, the elderly hostler, bring messages to Plouffe at the abattoir. According to the sisters, each of whom testified at great length on Auguste's behalf, they began to come across the pair in compromising situations. Aurélie claimed she saw the two alone in a room on more than one occasion, Justine on Plouffe's lap, and each fondling the other.[143] Both sisters recounted an incident when Plouffe came to the house while Auguste was away, and Justine, in a nightgown, invited him upstairs. After about half an hour they came downstairs with "faces red as flame" and Plouffe had "a very curious appearance."[144] Just at that moment Auguste pulled up in the yard, prompting Justine to say to Aurélie, "There's Auguste, the Good Lord's luck that he didn't arrive earlier, or he would have surprised the two of us upstairs."[145]

That day, Auguste betrayed no anger on encountering Plouffe in his hotel, but he must have wondered at least. Around that time though he suspected something was up and began altering his schedule and taking to looping back home shortly after leaving. Despite his precautions, he never succeeded in catching the lovebirds in flagrante delicto. He tried to arrange outings with his wife, but she begged off, claiming illness, so she could remain behind and meet Plouffe.[146] Things came to a head in early August, when Auguste returned home, found Plouffe at the hotel, and saw his wife give a note to Aurélie Raymond (who was illiterate), which she then handed to Plouffe.[147] Plouffe came around a couple more times after that, but Justine told Soette to warn him no longer to visit. Justine then packed her things and moved to her mother's house. She would begin separation proceedings on 1 December, on the basis of ill treatment, and Auguste countered with his own action in separation on 24 December, alleging adultery.[148]

Before that, however, on 19 September, Auguste Lebeau sued Plouffe for $10,000 damages, needless to say an inflated sum.[149] As *La Minerve* later commented drily, "That is to say that he greatly appreciates his wife's love."[150] The emotional damage was everything in the case – there was some discussion of possible effects on the hotel's clientele, but no specific material injury was claimed. Auguste's declaration reflected that emotional basis (though as always we must remember that the wording came from the lawyer who drafted it). His main allegation was that Plouffe, "by improper temptations and indiscreet covetousness ... succeeded in making himself loved by the plaintiff's spouse." Further along, he framed the matter slightly differently: "That by his blameworthy attentions and his perverse familiarities, the defendant succeeded in seducing the plaintiff's spouse, the said Justine Leblanc." The effect of Plouffe's attentions, in the language of the declaration, was that "the plaintiff's wife declared that she loved the defendant and that no one would make her forget him."[151] Love and seduction – a common enough situation, but one whose legal basis was at this time in development.

Auguste's action was relatively new to Quebec law. Though the distinction was a fine one, he was not suing for adultery per se, but rather for seduction and the injury associated with Plouffe's activities with his wife. His declaration kept the nomenclature vague, unsurprising given the developing and controversial state of the law in this area. Interference between husband and wife – both sexual and non-sexual – could give rise to different actions under a variety of names in different jurisdictions, from adultery and seduction in France, to criminal conversation, loss of consortium, enticement, and harbouring in the common law. Beginning in the later nineteenth century, Quebec lawyers and judges drew on those varied sources to create a hybrid action, the terminological fluidity of which reflected the underlying uncertainty about what the action was for. Was it to punish illicit sexual activity? To compensate emotional injury? Or to protect the marriage bond? Elements of all of these were apparent in the cases.

In France, adultery was treated as a crime privately prosecuted by the husband. That approach was self-evident to Jean-François Fournel, writing in 1778, since the husband was the "born inspector of his wife's morals, in which he is the most interested party." To allow public prosecution would expose the privacy of the family to intolerable outside scrutiny.[152] The act of adultery was seen to be an attack on the husband, by the seducer but also by the wife herself, and the attack on the husband's interests justified the action. Considerable controversy, however, arose over the action's propriety and its legal basis, centred especially on the question of damages. On the one hand, some saw it as shameful to pursue a matter like this for the purpose of getting compensation: the vindication of a prosecution ought to have been enough, without putting a price on marriage and its affections. Eventually, by the mid-nineteenth century, most accepted the role of compensation in such matters, reasoning, as Auguste Sourdat put it in 1852, that one gives reparation to the aggrieved party "in money for want of being able to do better."[153] On the other hand, the lack of direct material loss in these cases made some commentators hesitate.[154] The moral effects of seduction – loss of affection, injury to honour – were clear enough, but not everyone agreed that they constituted a legally cognizable loss. The French courts, however, did not share the professors' doubts, and they regularly sided with aggrieved husbands.[155] The basis, as Fournel made clear, was the seducer's taking over "possession" of the wife from her husband, a usurpation from which moral injuries necessarily flowed. By withdrawing from the control of her husband and giving herself over to her seducer, the wife

> becomes the slave of one and the tyrant of the other. From that comes the wife's insubordination, her intractability, her resistance to her husband's projects, her firmness in combatting them. In such a situation, can one say that the husband truly possesses his wife? No, without a doubt. To possess a wife is not just to have the right to have her person at one's disposal ..., it is to occupy her heart, to be the object of her attentions, her fears, her

alarms; it is to direct her ideas, govern her mind, master her will. That is a husband's true possession, and it is precisely what the adulterer takes away from him.[156]

This basis in patriarchal property – the husband's control over his wife and her affection – meant that the action was starkly gendered. A wife could not complain of her husband's adultery, except as grounds for separation (and then a double standard applied, since she had to prove aggravated adultery). To hold otherwise "would be to furnish wives with the pretext for a multitude of scandalous claims."[157] And, as Fournel noted, however illogical that asymmetry might be, it was universally applied by the courts.[158]

In the common law, various forms of interference between husband and wife gave rise to different actions, most available only to husbands, some few open to wives as well.[159] If the interference was sexual, criminal conversation (also called seduction) was the civil action for adultery; for other forms of interference, actions in enticement (luring away a married woman) or harbouring (keeping a married woman from her husband) were possible. As in France, the conceptual origins of those actions were in interference with a husband's quasi-property rights in his wife's consortium, defined broadly as all that a wife brought to the marriage.[160]

Already in the eighteenth century, as is clear from Fournel and some common-law cases, and certainly over the course of the nineteenth century, the actions in marital interference came to emphasize more and more the moral effects of adultery or seduction on the husband (and later and more rarely, on the wife).[161] This was described in various ways – as violated honour, as humiliation, and so forth – but what was significant was the "alienation of affection" and its effects. The defendant's actions, then, were not an interference with some abstract property rights the husband had to his wife's companionship, but rather a poisoning of the emotional relationship that was supposed to be present between the spouses. This was related to Romantic ideas of sensibility; it was also a product of the increasing sophistication during the nineteenth century of the understanding of the role of the mind – in both its rational and affective aspects – in legal matters.[162] Feelings-based injury like this was still criticized – commentators in the common law, for example, came to disparage the frivolity of what they called the "heart balm" torts and saw them as leading to blackmail and other abuses[163] – but Quebec courts readily adopted the principle of alienation of affections, if not the exorbitant damages claimed by most plaintiffs.

The earliest cases, up to *Lebeau* and beyond, revealed lawyers and judges struggling with basic issues surrounding emotional prejudice. Though some earlier unreported cases raised similar issues, Quebec's first reported case of alienation of affection was from 1874.[164] In it, Justice Adolphe-Basile Routhier – French lyricist of "O Canada" – dismissed the action for want of proof, but along the way he established a framework within which later judges would work. He began, as judges often did when faced with moral injury, by noting the impossibility of evaluating any plaintiff's moral injury in monetary terms. As a point of principle, however, he suggested that difficulty in evaluating the injury should not be fatal to the case, and if such an action were satisfactorily proved, his solution would simply be to assume the effects of the injury and award the plaintiff the whole amount demanded.[165] A strong, even rash statement, considering that in this case the plaintiff had claimed $10,000; no doubt aggrieved husbands and their lawyers were gleefully anticipating future lawsuits. But Justice Routhier's strong stance reflected his distaste for marital infidelity – he noted (citing the Roman poet Ovid's exile for his adultery with the daughter of the emperor Augustus) that among all peoples and at all times, adultery was punished severely, whether by death, exile, whipping, or monetary damages.[166] Proof had to be to a high standard, but once proved, the defendant must bear the consequences. The legal basis of the action, according to the judge, was a husband's quasi-property interest in his wife. Like any property right, which could be asserted *erga omnes*, this one too was good against all the world, and so even if the wife were the pursuer, her accomplice should still be liable to the husband, since the married woman belongs not to herself, but to her husband. The injury, however, was emotional in nature: "What greater injury can one cause to a man than to ruin his domestic happiness, and take from him all the enjoyments of the conjugal life and the family?"[167] In this case, Justice Routhier put a positive (and somewhat naive) spin on the plaintiff's failure to prove his case, noting that the dismissal arrived "unfortunately or rather fortunately for the plaintiff, since his loss at trial returned to him the honour that he believed he had lost."[168] Apparently once the court spoke, everything would be rosy and harmonious again, and friends and neighbours would put aside suspicions and accept the court's judgment at face value.

Later cases developed certain legal points. Proof (of adultery in particular) could be by presumptions, since direct proof was difficult or impossible in most cases.[169] Reconciliation between the spouses would affect the amount of damages. (Later it would become a complete bar to the action, akin to a renunciation of the suit, since as one judge asserted in 1922, it was in the "true interest of society to facilitate reconciliation between spouses and to avoid a public scandal."[170]) Discomfort with purely affective injury remained, however. Some judges were willing to assume the husband had suffered a serious injury, given the circumstances. In an 1897 case, in which the defendant had lured the plaintiff's wife away to live with him in the United States, the judges resorted to some rhetorical legerdemain to affirm the plaintiff's "disgrace and humiliation": "Considering that although plaintiff hath not proved any precise amount of specific damage, yet the action of the defendant must have produced the most serious damage to the plaintiff."[171] Other judges, however, were less convinced of the morality of assessing matrimonial affection in monetary terms and echoed similar criticisms of "heart balm" actions as were heard elsewhere. In *Caron v. Guay*, from 1889, the trial judge awarded $500 to a husband who, after discovering his wife's affair with the defendant, kicked her out of their home and refused all reconciliation. The Court of Review clearly disapproved, but they could do nothing about it since only the plaintiff appealed, to get more damages. They affirmed the trial judgment, but refused to adopt the judge's reasons, using the occasion for a moral condemnation of the whole idea of alienation of affection. The action should really have been dismissed as against public order, they wrote, since the husband should have pardoned his unfaithful spouse instead of trying "to make a display of her dishonour in order to gain some money."[172]

Between those who would assume injury and those who felt such actions were immoral was considerable room within which to argue the specifics of individual cases. A key issue was the nature of affection, which set the action in alienation of affection apart from other cases involving betrayal and relationship breakdown like separation from bed and board or breach of promise. Since the emotional state – affection – was the direct focus of the action, plaintiffs could succeed only if they first established a baseline of amicable spousal relations before going on to show that the defendant's malicious interference had affected those relations by turning the wife's affections away from her husband. The actions relied, in other words, on a view of proper domesticity. Judges did not require proof of passionate romantic love, but something that could be characterized as "affection" had to be present, or the action would fail. In most cases, the court was willing to assume without elaborate proof that a married couple must be fond of one another, but circumstances could convince otherwise, as in the case of a marriage of convenience in 1948, in which the husband was looking for help with his invalid son, and the wife for support so she would no longer have to work outside the home.[173]

If we return to Auguste Lebeau's suit against his wife's seducer, we find these various threads running through the case. Most interesting is the way in which the couple's affection, and its alienation, were established in the testimony of the various witnesses. The testimony in the separation actions was taken in March and April 1893, while that for the action against Plouffe only in September. In what follows, I will focus on the latter, since it was directed towards alienation of affection, but will add details from the former where appropriate.

Auguste was called by the defence and testified relatively briefly; he said little about the nature or quality of his relationship with his wife, or about the specific effects of Plouffe's actions. This lack of direct testimony on emotions was not unusual, though it was perhaps more surprising in a case of this kind, which focused on the idea of affection. Auguste's reaction to the situation was rather odd – he seems to have been wilfully blind to what was going on, and then when he did find out about Justine's relationship with Plouffe, he was for whatever reason reluctant to confront his wife and never barred Plouffe from the hotel, though his hostler testified that he could tell Auguste was angry.[174] The couple continued to live together until Justine moved out: Auguste even told her not to go as she was moving out. Auguste explained his lack of reaction as "because I didn't want to cause a scandal."[175] Clearly he was concerned about his personal reputation and honour as a result of the situation, and those fears coloured his reactions. Asked why when Justine had left he made no efforts to try to get her to return, he said simply, "That was impossible for me."[176]

Justine's perspective is harder to ascertain, since the spousal bar prevented her from testifying.[177] Surely living near a slaughterhouse was less than ideal, and the attentions of a young butcher were likely a welcome diversion, coming as they did with gifts of tobacco, nuts, sweets, and a gold ring.[178] On the basis of testimony of other witnesses, she seems to have been infatuated with Plouffe, speaking of him to the employees as her "love" (*amoureux*) and "my boyfriend" (*mon cavalier*).[179] She seems also, not surprisingly, to have developed an aversion to her husband. According to Rose Raymond, when Auguste was getting ready to leave the house and not moving fast enough for Justine's liking, she would mutter things like, "Go already!" At one point, the same witness claimed, after Auguste had left, Justine said she hoped his horse would take fright and kill him, so that she would be rid of him.[180] According to Rose's sister Aurélie, Justine would laugh at her husband behind his back.[181] Auguste's suspicions, once awakened, led him to restrict her movements as much as possible, but that only intensified her desire to be away from him. As she was moving out, she told Rose Raymond that the reason was because "her husband held her back too much."[182]

Plouffe's defence was typical for actions of this kind.[183] He admitted that he was a frequent visitor to the hotel and that he may have joked around innocently with Justine like everyone else, but he denied anything untoward. He also suggested that an affair would be unlikely: he was thirty years old, while Justine was forty-five or fifty, and furthermore he was a married man, who had "at his own home all the domestic happiness he desired and that he never needed to have recourse to the plaintiff's spouse."[184] Finally, he argued also that whatever lack of affection had arisen between Auguste and Justine was not due to him but to troubles between the couple.

The case, then, came down to affection – who had it, who was looking for it, and where it was to be found. Though the witnesses' testimony ranged widely, it came back again and again to the question of the quality of the couple's relationship, before Plouffe's arrival and during his attentions towards Justine. The testimony of the main witnesses, the three employees, who all testified for Auguste, however "true" it might be about what happened that summer, is a good indication of the social codes against which the witnesses were judging the couple's affection. Aurélie Raymond, for example, gave a picture of the couple's relationship before Plouffe's arrival that outlined her view of respectable domesticity: they got on well, were happy, took carriage rides and walks together, never quarrelled, and seemed to respect each other.[185] Her sister agreed: the couple seemed "happy together" and "seemed to love each other."[186] Both painted a picture of contentment – an affectionate couple was one that was comfortable with each other, who went out together from time to time, who seemed happy. Little was said about physical affection between the couple. Auguste testified that they always slept in the same room, except occasionally in hot weather; they had never slept apart because of marital difficulties. Once the situation with Plouffe became known, however, Justine moved across the hall to the Raymond sisters' room.[187]

The contrast was striking as Justine and Plouffe became more intimate. Rose Raymond described the pair in terms similar to how she had described Auguste and Justine, though the lovers' affection was far more demonstrative than the quiet domesticity of the married couple: "When they were together, they had a lot of fun, and told all sorts of stories; they laughed a lot and you could see that they loved each other."[188] All three employees made it clear that they were uncomfortable with what they saw going on in the hotel. Soette, the hostler, avoided going near Justine and Plouffe when they were together; once he came upon them and was not happy about it: "I didn't like seeing things like that. If I had known that was going on, I wouldn't have walked by."[189] Outsiders too expressed disapproval, such as Justine's mother, who voiced her unhappiness about finding Plouffe with her daughter at the hotel in August.[190]

The effects on the marriage were clear – Auguste's case was well crafted to demonstrate that his wife's affections had been turned elsewhere. That established the success of the action. As for effects on Auguste himself, necessary to determine the amount of damages, some witnesses were asked whether the hotel lost clientele, but no one noticed any material change.[191] On the question of moral injury, however, witnesses on both sides agreed that the situation inevitably affected Auguste. Defence witness Napoléon Taillefer admitted on cross-examination that he would not want something similar to happen to him: "I would find that hard, that doesn't give you a good name."[192] On the other side, butcher Jules Leblanc agreed that the situation put Auguste into "a miserable and insulting situation," one "likely to bring trouble and to harm his reputation and his honour."[193] Some of the testimony in the separation action fills out this picture. Butcher Pierre Goyette, asked about the effects of the rumours on Auguste, said that it subjected him to ridicule, and that "any man" must consider it all a grave affront, though he admitted on cross-examination that he had been among those laughing at Auguste behind his back.[194] Another butcher mentioned that people were always talking about it, and when Auguste entered the room they would suddenly stop.[195]

The two aspects of the discussion, then, followed two of the threads of the action in alienation of affection. The question of the effects on the marriage reflected the view that what was lost was something a wife naturally owed her husband, what the common law called consortium. The issue of the impact on Auguste, by contrast, pointed in a different direction, towards the personal idea of masculine honour, its connection to competition with other men, and the public effects of its diminishment. Both of these sides of the case went into the final judgment.

That Plouffe would lose was probably a foregone conclusion: as Justice Routhier's decision in *Laferrière* had made clear in the 1870s, and other judgments in the interval had confirmed, the bar was not set very high for plaintiffs. The question was what the court would give Auguste, and how it would justify its decision. According to *La Minerve*, Justice Charles Joseph Doherty lectured the "Don Juan," Plouffe, during the hearing that "he was unwise to keep a treacherous love in his heart."[196] He accepted Auguste's version of events, finding that Plouffe had been "an assiduous and almost daily visitor of plaintiff's wife."[197] His conduct while at the hotel – in particular the "most compromising positions" in which Plouffe and Justine were repeatedly found – gave rise to presumptions that he "was there as the lover of plaintiff's wife." Justine became infatuated with him and as a result abandoned her husband, "expressing the greatest aversion for him." Though Justine was herself blameworthy, it was not her conduct but Plouffe's that mattered, and the judge found that Plouffe's "constituted a grave and serious outrage and wrong against plaintiff."

Though judges almost never awarded the huge sums plaintiffs demanded in cases like this, Justice Doherty had to come up with a number for a wrong that he described as "of the very gravest nature." In doing so, he faced a challenge, revealed by a draft judgment that unusually found its way into the case file. One paragraph of the draft contains, in its layers of crossed-out wording, a graphic outline of the judge's struggles with the proper basis of the alienation of affection action and with assigning blame for a situation to which all three parties contributed. He initially considered directing various barbs towards Auguste, chiding him for not reacting as a husband (that is, as a proper man) should. Each of these was crossed out as discretion prevailed and he settled on more neutral wording, but they are revealing about the judge's attitudes about proper masculine honour and sentiment. Auguste's own testimony, he initially wrote, showed him to be not "a person of very acute" or not "sensitive" or not "of any delicacy of feeling," or, most tellingly, not "one keenly alive to the dishonour brought upon him." In the final judgment, Justice Doherty settled on signalling as the main factors limiting damages the parties' class ("it would appear from the position and circumstances of the parties") and Auguste's slow reaction to the threat (which suggested condonation).[198]

But the deleted passages suggest other factors were in the front of the judge's mind. If Auguste did not care enough to take a man's expected steps to deal with peril to his domestic situation, if he was unconscious to his own honour or unwilling to vindicate it, was it the job of the courts to do so for him?

Justice Doherty awarded Auguste $500 as "fair and adequate" damages. Plouffe applied for review, seeking to have the case dismissed or at least the damages reduced. The Court of Review affirmed the result but agreed that the damages were excessive and reduced the award to $250.[199]

As the actions in alienation of affection and separation went forward, Auguste seems quickly to have fallen on hard times. By summer 1893 he was bankrupt and his hotel at Sault-au-Récollet was auctioned off, contents, buildings, and land. Among the principal creditors were his lawyers in his legal actions against Plouffe and his wife.[200] The separation actions took three years, with many of the same witnesses testifying, but eventually in 1895 Justine's action was dismissed, since, as Justice Charles Davidson ruled, Auguste "had so far as appears, always been a kind and well behaved husband," while Justine's relations with Pouffe were "a grievous insult and grievous attack upon her husband's honour and dignity." Ironically, though Auguste's separation was granted and Justine's dismissed, he was ordered to continue paying her the $12 per month in alimony that she had been provisionally granted at the start of her action.[201]

By 1901, according to the census and municipal directories, the couple were living apart. Auguste was back at his hotel on Frontenac Street, living with three employees (including Rose Raymond from the old days), a boarder, and his younger brother's four-year-old daughter.[202] Justine at that time had moved back in with her parents and an unmarried sister in the city of Montreal. Plouffe was still living near the abattoir with his wife. Eventually, though, late in life, Auguste and Justine appear to have reconciled. In the 1921 census, the initial enumeration recorded Auguste living alone as a lodger with a family named Latour near the site of his old hotel. On a supplemental enumeration, however, Auguste and Justine Lebeau, both in their seventies, were recorded as living together as husband and wife at the same address as Auguste alone on the original form.[203] The census, of course, says nothing about the quality of the relationship, but assuming that Justine in fact was living there, this does suggest that the alienation had not led to a permanent breach. Justine's life as an elderly woman on her own would have been precarious, and she may have preferred a form of reconciliation with her husband to the alternatives.

A different kind of case also raised issues of betrayal: the possibility of revoking a gift made inter vivos on the grounds of the recipient's ingratitude. In many cases those gifts were designed to set up long-term care of elderly people with relatives or others, creating a domestic situation that could lead to feelings of betrayal if it failed to meet expectations. Like the ways that witnesses and judges had to assess proper marital affection in the alienation of affection cases, revocation of gifts also required measuring relationships against norms of behaviour and accepted interaction. Individuals seldom fit those norms exactly and this made the meanings of ingratitude and betrayal particularly difficult to pin down.

Family Ties, Real and Simulated: *Collin v. Gilot* and Ingratitude

One of the legal roles of the family was to ensure the material support of its members. The husband was legally obliged to support his wife, parents their children, and children their aged parents. Those material obligations rested on emotional footings, or at least the presumption that such emotional ties existed: we saw, for example, Joseph Jacobson referring to his "love and affection" for his new wife in the marriage contract that handed over certain of his property to the bride. Even if those feelings were mere formulas or lip service, they spoke to cultural values of emotional attachment. One job of the law was to police those material obligations and ensure that the breakdown of actual emotional attachment would not lead to disregard of the material obligations resting on it.

One means of ensuring the maintenance of some degree of material comfort in an era before pensions and social insurance programs was for an aging individual to make a gift to another in exchange for a degree of security in old age. This formalized aspects of the gift economy that had long characterized both rural and urban Quebec, though which by the twentieth century was fading.[204] It had also long played a key role in inheritance strategies in Quebec.[205] Typically, the donor would transfer, via notarial act, cash, land, a house, or even everything they had in the world in exchange for room and board, clothing, medical care, and ultimately an appropriate burial. The provisions of the gift were necessarily highly specific. In a fairly typical case from 1900, for example, the donor gave a house worth $500 plus $200 in cash for commitments from the donee

> to board him for the rest of his life, with the donor in suitable rooms in the said house, with the right to come and go throughout the said house and the said property, to drive him, to let him eat at the common family table, to let him sleep in a room and bed suited to his condition and his means, to wash and mend and maintain his clothing properly, and finally to take good care of him and to procure for him all the consideration that his age, his means, and his condition require, and upon his death, to have him buried in the cemetery of the parish of St-Denis, with a $10 service.[206]

Long-term care, a decent standard of living, an appropriate burial: those were normally duties assumed by one's relatives – legal duties for immediate family, social duties (perhaps) for other relatives – and in most cases they were seen to without the need for court action. But some facing old age had no relatives, or had only relatives who were impoverished or estranged or otherwise unable or unwilling to see to the needs of their aging family member. In such situations, support and care could be bought, either from relatives not legally bound to support, or from strangers, via a mutually beneficial exchange.

The intimacy of such transactions made many uncomfortable, since they involved a material arrangement standing in for what were supposed to be familial duties. The discomfort was evident, for example, in the bar on such gifts between spouses. Claude-Joseph de Ferrière, commenting on the rationale behind that rule in the Custom of Paris, wrote that "it is not suitable for conjugal affection, which should mutually unite the hearts of the husband and wife, to become as it were venal and to be acquired or preserved by gifts."[207] Still, outside of the spousal relationship itself, such gifts allowed individuals to buy what they feared (or knew) was not otherwise available.

Quebec drew on a long tradition in the civil law whereby gifts, whether made between the living or in a will, were subject to revocation if the recipient acted in a way injurious to the donor. The most extreme case was attempting to take the life of the donor or testator, but other cases could trigger revocation as well. A testament or a particular legacy within it could be revoked for "grievous injury done to [the testator's] memory."[208] For gifts inter vivos, the grounds of revocation were broader. The donor could seek revocation of the gift on the grounds of the recipient's "ingratitude," defined in various ways, such as an attempt on the donor's life, refusal of maintenance, or if the recipient committed against the donor "ill usage, crimes or grievous injuries" (*sévices, délits majeurs ou injures graves*).[209]

This idea of "ingratitude" was a rare instance in which the CCLC required a particular emotional state in order to trigger legal effects, and the legal text brought feelings directly into the legal assessment of the relationships created by such gifts. The feelings surrounding this ingratitude requirement suggested the sense of betrayal with which we have been dealing. The gifts in question were reciprocal, not altruistic: the donor expected something in return, and the failure to deliver betrayed those expectations. Gifts were distinct from the regime of onerous contracts, which on paper at least the CCLC set up as a bastion of liberal free will that excluded sentiment and other affective concerns. Gifts, by contrast, remained governed at least partly by older notions of propriety, of acceptable treatment of others, even of affection. The feelings provoked by gifts gone wrong were compounded, because in most cases those gifts set up domestic relationships that inevitably came with certain affective expectations, however coldly mercenary they might have appeared on paper. Cases invoking ingratitude were never particularly numerous in the reports, but they were hardly rare: donors' expectations were usually high, the responsibilities the donee accepted could prove more onerous than anticipated, and in general what seemed like a good idea at the outset could easily become intolerable once it was underway.

The usual situation was a gift made to relatives, with court cases arising if the new burdens or changed personalities soured those family relationships. A mother sued her son for "the blackest ingratitude," alleging mistreatment, grave insults, and threats of physical violence, and successfully revoked a gift of land and cattle she had made to him.[210] A son lost a gift of various immovables from his parents for being "forgetful of the honour and respect that by law he owes to his father and mother," to the extent that he grabbed his father by the collar and threw him to the ground, threatened to break his parents' necks, called them pigs, and berated them with "shameful blasphemies."[211] In some cases, the complaint was that the terms of the agreement were not being upheld, making evaluation relatively easy. In others, judges had to use their discretion to determine what constituted ingratitude. The standard used in those cases – both by the parties in assessing their injuries, and by judges evaluating them – was that of normal family relationships, which of course posed the question of what those norms were. A mother-in-law complained in one case that her son-in-law did not treat her "as a good son ought to do." Her request to have a donation revoked was dismissed on technical grounds, but the judge agreed that the defendants treated the plaintiff with scorn and derision, and he urged the parties to reconcile.[212] In another case, also dismissed on technical grounds, a mother gifted movable and immovable property to her son, with the stipulation that he take care of his brother (unable to live on his own), giving him "the care and respect that he gave to his father and mother in the past." The brother sued for revocation, alleging that he was made to work like "a galley slave," was given little to eat, and was forced to sleep in a bed filled with bedbugs.[213]

More rarely, the gift was between non-relatives and involved a donor trying to create a simulacrum of family bonds when for whatever reason real family ties were absent. For some this meant seeking a place in a religious institution, the donation supplemented by the institution's charitable vocation.[214] For others, it meant reaching out to strangers with a mutually beneficial proposition: money now in exchange for future care. In such cases, the donor might frame the expected treatment in explicitly emotional terms, even though the transaction on its face was strictly material. In many of those cases it was the donor's rejection by relatives that led him or her to seek a stand-in, and so the donor–donee relationship was created with certain hopes evident in the language of the gift. In a 1905 case, the deed of gift stipulated that the recipient – who had been caregiver to the donor's deceased husband – would lodge and board the donor "as a good child would do for his own mother whom he loves and respects."[215] In that case, "love and respect" moved from being hopes to legal obligations, stipulated by notarial deed in exchange for a house in Ottawa. The frustration when those hopes were unrealized led to feelings of betrayal, exacerbated by fear born of vulnerability: having nowhere to live, nothing to eat, and no one to give one's body a proper burial.

As legal actions, cases of revocation were highly factually specific and discretionary, leading to many trial decisions being overturned on appeal, and numerous dissents at the appellate level. Judges had to be readers of relationships, negotiating the difficult terrain of frustrated expectations, exacerbated at times by personality differences, alcohol abuse, or other problems. Once inside the factual world of the case, things might go differently than plaintiffs expected. In a case from Kamouraska in 1913, two aunts sued their nephew for revocation of gifts made in exchange for an annuity of $150 in kind (food, clothing, medical bills, and so on), claiming ingratitude. The judge found that the ingratitude went the other way: despite fulfilling his obligations to the letter, and even paying more than the stipulated amount, the defendant's aunts were never satisfied and became increasingly demanding. After the nephew took out a notice in the newspaper renouncing responsibility for any debts his aunts might contract, the matter ended up in court.[216] In another case, a seventy-two-year-old indigent alcoholic woman with no relatives to whom she could turn gave $950 – all her assets – to the defendant in exchange for a promise of room and board. The judge described the woman in stark terms: "This woman's past is deplorable. She is a dipsomaniac who for a long time has engaged in illicit and clandestine traffic in alcoholic liquors." Given her past, the defendant made the promise subject to the resolutory condition of the donor's good behaviour, a condition that inevitably materialized quickly when the donor was arrested and jailed for illicit sale of alcohol (to finance her own drinking). The judge admitted that the donor's behaviour was such as would scandalize most respectable people, but the defendant too was hardly respectable. She lived apart from her husband, regularly received "dubious visits," and herself drank and illegally sold liquor. Given the circumstances, the donation was revoked.[217] Alongside the specifics of personalities, judges also applied their own ideas of class, culture, education, and the like to their assessment of the severity of mistreatment. In the 1905 case mentioned above, for example, the evidence showed insults going both ways. Insults directed at the plaintiff were minor, "given the circumstances and the condition of the parties." The defendant, however, suffered considerably more serious mistreatment at the hands of the plaintiff, described by the judge as "of a cantankerous and capricious character."[218] In another case, the Court of King's Bench made clear that a situation of drunkenness, blasphemy, and threats had to be assessed not by any absolute standard, but according to "social position, customs, education, and factors that could elude a judicial enquiry."[219]

A closer look at one of these cases will give a better sense of the emotional and relational dynamics behind them. The case took place in the later 1920s, when this sort of arrangement was perhaps becoming something of an anachronism, as more widespread insurance, annuities, and pensions took over. In July 1927, Elzéar Collin, seventy years old and unhappy in his current rental accommodations, visited a card reader named Léonie Steile to have his fortune told.[220] Collin mentioned that he was unhappy, and Steile (of course) confirmed that she saw his unhappiness in the cards. They continued chatting over two further meetings. Eventually it came out that Collin had some money, and Steile asked if Collin would like to live with her and her husband, a sculptor named Jean Gilot, at their home in Sault-au-Récollet (at the north edge of Montreal island).[221] Collin weighed the pros and cons, met Gilot, discussed terms, and soon they all went to notary Elisée Giguère to have the act of donation drawn up. By its terms, Collin would pay Gilot $2200 – all that he had – in exchange for a room in the Gilot home, meals at the same table and with the same food as the Gilots (unless Collin's medical condition required special food), medical care as required, an allowance of $66 every six months, and burial and payment of associated costs when the time came.[222]

Nothing in the record explains why Collin chose to finish his days living with strangers. At the time of his card reading, he was boarding for $8 a week at the house of a Madame Jasmin, opposite Steile's card-reading shop. Collin had at least two living children, a son and daughter, but as he said without elaborating, they "were not capable of taking care of me."[223] His son seems to have been getting married at the time; the younger Elzéar Collin visited his father at the Gilots only twice, on New Year's Day each year, and testified for the defence that his father seemed well treated.[224] Collin did in fact go to live with his daughter after the situation at the Gilots blew up, paying her $15 a month, so at least some relationship existed between them.[225] In any case, Collin seems to have initially preferred the flexibility of a paid arrangement to ensure his long-term care over whatever other options he had. He claimed that he told Steile during the negotiations that "when I stay somewhere, I like to pay, I pay my way, and I leave when it's not what I need."[226] This revealed a misunderstanding of what the donation he was negotiating meant for his freedom to act, but it also bespoke a fear of being locked into a relationship that did not meet his expectations.

Collin's independent streak might have been due to a difficult personality, though at this remove and given the limitations of the surviving evidence, it is impossible to tell. His own testimony, unsurprisingly, often drifted into narratives of victimization and martyrdom, as when in cross-examination he said that when he set up the arrangements, his requirements were simply "an allowance for milk, some milk and a little morsel of bread and a bit of porridge in the morning, that was my room and board."[227] Other witnesses hinted at tensions. Eva Beauregard, a domestic in the house while Collin lived there, testified that he was treated well, adding tellingly, "and even better than he deserved."

Figure 5.2 Jean Gilot, Léonie Steile, Pauline Gilot, and Elzéar Collin following an automobile accident. *La Presse* (12 April 1928), p. 3. BAnQ JOU 585 CON. Reproduced with permission of Bibliothèque et Archives nationales du Québec.

On cross-examination, she made a similarly cryptic and unexplained remark: "I have nothing against him, he was pardoned long ago."[228]

But alongside the grievances and independent posturing were hints of an old man, more or less alone, and seeking something in his final years. That he had two grown children distinguishes his case from the much more typical situation of donations to family members. On cross-examination about what had been promised during negotiations, Collin testified that he was convinced by Steile's promises of a large house with comfortable rooms and good food, and "that I would be better off than I ever was before in my life."[229] That rueful remark suggests the deal was more than a simple financial transaction. We know little of Collin's earlier life, though by this time he was unable to work, and according to Steile's testimony (which Collin denied) he had rheumatism and incontinence problems, and so needed help with personal hygiene.[230] Paying his way into the Gilot household would provide him both with a degree of independence and a standard of living that might have been better than whatever hardscrabble working life he had known before. Unfortunately, those expectations quickly came into confrontation and conflict with his personality and his sense of morality.

Once installed at the Gilot home in Sault-au-Récollet, Collin soon found that things did not at all meet his expectations. It started well enough: the Gilots purchased a cow to provide him with fresh milk (though Collin claimed they quickly sold it again), and he accompanied the family on road trips in their Essex automobile. On one of those trips, the party barely escaped death when the car was caught in flash flooding.[231] But certain aspects of life with the Gilots shocked the old man, revealing differences in culture and morality that he could not abide. He claimed that men and young women mixed far too freely in the house: "It wasn't nice, young girls sitting on boys' laps like that and putting their arms around their necks. I said to the oldest of them, 'Even if you girls were a bit older, it's not nice to act like that in public.'"[232] One man, he said, came to the house to have illicit relations with his niece in her room, near Collin's own. Another, one of the Gilots' employees, supposedly entertained various young women and lived in the house with a minor whom he had seduced out of a convent. Were the Gilots running a brothel, or simply a more libertine household than Collin was used to? Aside from those scandals, Collin also claimed that the Gilots insulted him verbally, refused to provide him with suitable food or drink, threatened him bodily, and condoned various assaults, verbal and physical, by others in the household.[233] The Gilots' narrative of events was of course considerably different from Collin's. All the defence witnesses – evidently well coached – parroted the line that Collin was treated "like a father." Jean Gilot testified that the old man was given pride of place at table, and in all things was treated "like the real father of the household."[234] His wife echoed that over and over again in her deposition: "At my house Mr. Collin was treated like the father. Every evening, the whole household, I told them, 'Treat him like a father.'"[235]

Faced with what he saw as a betrayal of the rosy life he had been promised, Collin sought to revoke the donation and recover the balance of his money. He claimed he had been seduced into making the deal by Steile's wiles, as she used "her secrets about the future" to take advantage of his age and ignorance to exploit him by "fraud and artifices."[236] The Gilots denied the allegations of immorality and abuse, and countered with the common argument in cases like this that the deal had in fact disadvantaged them, since Collin's upkeep cost them far more than anticipated.[237]

At trial, Justice Paul-Gédéon Martineau cancelled the gift, simply finding Collin more credible than the Gilots about the stories of immoral comings and goings in the house. He ordered Collin to reimburse the Gilots $684 for his board for the time he had lived with them, leaving a balance of $1516 to be returned to him, plus interest and costs. Gilot appealed, and the justices of the Court of King's Bench, like judges in other revocation cases, subjected the act of donation to a literal and technical reading. Justice Joseph-Mathias Tellier began by noting Collin's apparent sincerity, and that if his testimony about the nature of the Gilot household was true, "no honest person would consent to live in the defendant's home, knowing what went on there."[238] Nevertheless, not even such a state of affairs would give Collin the right to demand revocation of the gift, since immorality did not constitute the "grievous injuries" required by article 813 CCLC. Further, whatever acts of immorality may have been committed in the Gilot home, none were alleged, let alone proved, to have been committed by Gilot himself (the donee) against Collin, as the code required. Collin may have had an action to compel Gilot to fulfil his obligations under the donation – to provide him with a suitable home – but not an action in revocation of the gift. In dissent, Justice Victor Allard took a broader view of ingratitude: "For a respectable citizen of the plaintiff's age to be forced to live in a milieu where he is constantly witness to revolting and scandalous acts surely constitutes a grievous injury, an outrage to his person and a sign of contempt."[239] In fact, he continued, such a state of affairs would be even more injurious to Collin than verbal or physical assaults. By overturning the trial decision, he wrote, the majority would enrich Gilot by allowing him to keep the remainder of the money, while at the same time would force Collin to live "in a den of vice and corruption where he found it repellent to live."[240] The majority decision meant the donation stood, which left Collin to reconsider his options.

Collin took the broad hint offered by the Court of King's Bench. On 11 February 1930, less than a month after the appeal judgment was handed down, Collin was back in Superior Court, applying for permission to sue Gilot *in forma pauperis* for an alimentary allowance of $90 per month, a more impersonal and likely more stable means of long-term maintenance.[241] The action went ahead, delayed numerous times by continuances upon the urging of Justice Joseph Demers that the parties should settle. In the end that is what they did – a settlement out of court was reached on 18 June 1931 and homologated that day by Justice Demers.[242] The terms, like most such settlements, were not disclosed, so we do not know where Elzéar Collin lived out his days. Here the conflict apparently ended, though it was perhaps not unrelated that starting at this time Gilot was subject to numerous actions by creditors and saw repeated seizures and judicial sales of his household effects.[243]

Stories like that of Elzéar Collin are sad, even if we accept the court's interpretation that he was not the victim of sharp operators. Many such donations, and particularly those involving gifts to non-relatives, suggest a pathetic sense of desperation, as the donor had few options, limited resources, and not a lot of time. But as Bettina Bradbury observes, whether the decision was to live with family or to seek to avoid dependency by arranging a place with strangers, the individual was exercising a kind of autonomy.[244] The choice was a difficult and critical one before the social safety net of the welfare state, but it was still a choice. It might go well, and in most cases it did, but it could also go terribly wrong. The high stakes and the risk that one's gamble might not work out helps explain the evident sense of betrayal in those cases of elderly men and women seeking to salvage something from their final years.

6

Grief and Mourning

The death of a loved one affects those left behind both emotionally and materially. This hardly needs saying, but how those effects manifest in survivors is shaped by social and religious norms surrounding end of life and, when those norms are silent or ambiguous, by legal rules. In the nineteenth and twentieth centuries (as ever), grief and mourning were carefully culturally circumscribed processes, with prescribed duration, special clothing, and accepted and frowned-upon behaviours.[1] In the normal course of things families grieved and mourned as they saw fit, with the law at most providing a background framework, such as by providing public health rules about when and where bodies had to be buried. When the normal course broke down, however, because the death was caused by the act or omission of another, or because family members were in conflict over what should be done by whom, emotions could intensify and become antagonistic. At times like that, as everything became a matter of feeling, grieving individuals could find control slipping away. When the usual governing social norms or religious rules proved insufficient, some resorted to the courts.

In legal terms, grief and mourning posed various problems. First, whose grief counted? Certainly not everyone's, or at least not everyone's grief counted in the same way. The suspicion of the courts about "mere feelings" arose in this area as it did in others, but the difficulty in quantifying suffering from grief led to questions about moral injury claims for grief following fatal accidents. This was an important question, since courts heard a steady stream of such cases, as old and especially new technologies caused increasing numbers of sudden deaths that family members attributed to the fault of others. The stakes were high, and the emotional shock of the death of someone close could be intensified by the material effects of the loss. In our period, before widespread life insurance or workers' death benefits, but even after, the loss of a breadwinner or even a working-age child could mean destitution for survivors thrown onto the mercy of relatives or charitable institutions.[2] Material loss was one thing, but what about the emotional damage of a sudden death, often in horrific circumstances – a child run over by a streetcar and dragged to her death, or a husband whose legs were crushed in a workplace accident and survived a year in agony before succumbing?[3] Judges were not so heartless that they did not see the suffering, but should it be allowed as a legal claim? How could it be proved? And even if it could be proved, would it be possible to keep it within reasonable limits – to hold back the litigation flood?

A second issue was about control over the process of grieving and mourning. Families were fluid and complex entities, particularly in cases of remarriage with multiple wings of the family and sets of children from different unions all weighing in after the death of a member. Intractable conflicts could result over the proper amount to be paid a widow for her mourning expenses, and especially over the sometimes fraught issue of where to bury the deceased. Grief could sharpen positions in those fights, to the extent that the courts were called in to apply a combination of vague legal rules and judges' reading of social norms.

In none of these areas were the courts really determining who was allowed to grieve and how they were allowed to mourn; the courts had no such power. But the cases we will examine in this chapter, on fatal accidents, widows' "weeds" or mourning clothes, and place of burial, all involved the courts deciding whose grief would be validated in the public forum, and whose grief would remain a private matter. We begin with the confrontation of legal rules and the family tragedy of the negligent poisoning death of a small child.

A Fatal Error: *Couillard v. Jeannotte*

In summer 1889, Charles and Aline Couillard's two children, four-year-old Thomas and twenty-one-month-old Alexandre, were suffering from pneumonia.[4] The children were sickly at the best of times, and the parents had recently transferred their care from Alphonse Piché, the family doctor who had delivered the boys, to Herménégilde Jeannotte, a McGill-trained physician who had been in practice about fifteen years.⁵ Jeannotte recommended that the children be removed from Montreal during the July heat, and so while Charles remained in Montreal to work, Aline took them across the St. Lawrence River to nearby Chambly, where they lodged with relatives. The children had been taking quinine pills, but the younger boy had trouble swallowing them, so on Charles's request Jeannotte prescribed powder as an alternative, to be dissolved in a spoonful of water with some sugar and given every two hours. The doctor later claimed he told Charles explicitly to make sure the pharmacist knew it was the faster-working though medically identical *bisulphate* of quinine, rather than just sulphate.⁶ Through inattention, however, Jeannotte wrote bisulphate of "morphine" rather than "quinine" on the prescription itself, a fatal error, though not an uncommon one.⁷

Charles took the prescription to Richard J. Devins's pharmacy on Notre-Dame Street, where he was served by Lucien Bernard, who handled the retail trade. He told Bernard he was in a hurry, since the medicine needed to go to Chambly and the outbound train was leaving soon. Charles left the shop, promising to return shortly. Bernard noticed immediately upon setting to work that the prescription from the normally careful Dr. Jeannotte, with whom he frequently dealt, was odd. It read "Morphiae Bisulph. divid. in pulv. No. 40." *Sulphate* of morphine was a common drug; *bisulphate* of morphine, however, was a laboratory curiosity, unstable except at extremely low temperatures and under controlled conditions, and so not commercially used. The active ingredient (morphine) was the same in each; the only difference was the amount of acid bonded to the morphine, which allowed it to be absorbed by the body.⁸ Bernard knew nothing about the case or the patient, and interpreted the word *morphiae* – at the beginning of the prescription and written out in full – as indicating that Jeannotte wished to prescribe morphine. He proceeded to prepare the requested forty doses, of sulphate of morphine, and pack them up. He felt certain that the slip about the sulphate was a minor lapse and never thought to telephone Jeannotte for confirmation.

The medicine was in a box neatly wrapped in white paper and waiting for Charles when he returned twenty minutes later. Charles handed off the package to an acquaintance who took the train to Chambly each evening, with instructions for how to get it to his wife. It was duly delivered, and at seven that evening, 6 July, Aline was ready to give Alexandre his first dose.

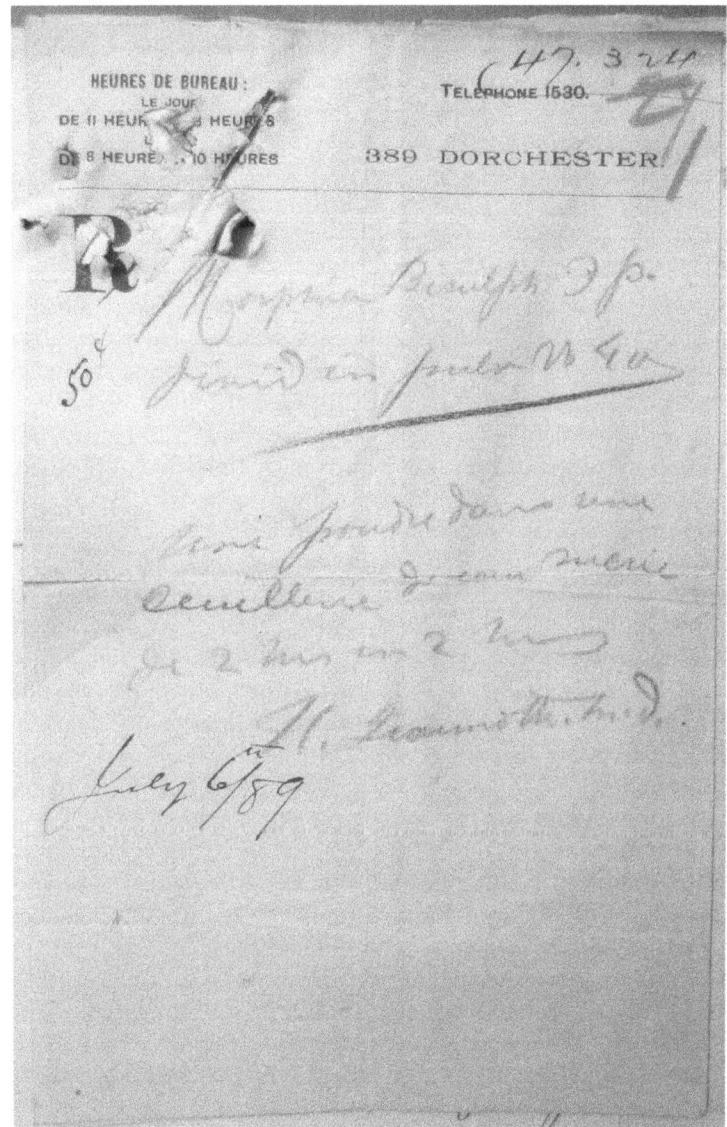

Figure 6.1 Prescription by Dr. Herménégilde Jeannotte for Charles Couillard's son, dated 6 July 1889, mistakenly ordering morphine instead of quinine. BAnQ-VM, *Couillard v. Jeannotte*, Superior Court case file, Plaintiff's Exhibit Z1. Photograph by the author. Reproduced with permission of Bibliothèque et Archives nationales du Québec.

Witnesses testified that the children were doing well in the country. Though hardly big strapping lads, they usually ate their meals in the dining room with the others, and that afternoon Aline and her cousin Henriette Lafrance (in whose home they were staying) had taken the boys for a stroll in the local cemetery. According to Lafrance, Aline felt Alexandre was doing better, though they were of course worried about the child's prognosis.[9]

Aline prepared the first dose as directed and administered it precisely at seven o'clock. Within half an hour the child was vomiting white fluid and was clearly in distress. Aline called Lafrance for help; when Henriette questioned the medicine, Aline assured her it was supposed to work like that.[10] At nine o'clock Aline gave Alexandre a second dose, and the child's condition worsened. Lafrance pleaded with her to stop, saying, "That medicine is going to kill your child," but Aline's faith in the physician's prescription was horrifyingly unshaken.[11] By the third dose at eleven o'clock, the child was comatose: he was listless, continued to vomit, and had spasms in his arms.[12] By around seven-thirty the next morning he was dead. Foam was coming from his mouth and nose, and his face and hands were covered in bluish-black spots, classic signs of morphine poisoning.[13]

Aline returned immediately to Montreal with the body, and she and Charles confronted Jeannotte, first Aline alone, and then both of them together. At the first meeting, three days after the death, Jeannotte claimed Aline threatened him with legal action. Asked how he responded, he said, "I answered no, that I owed her no damages for that, that she should sue me, that I was not responsible for that accident." The lawyer pressed him, asking whether he really said he would be happy to be sued. He answered, "I would be happy to be sued in that particular case to make it a test case, to know who was responsible in that case."[14] Written down like that, Jeannotte's testimony comes off as heartless, even flippant. Though he denied telling Aline that the whole affair would be good publicity for him, he did view the Couillards' loss as a useful test case that could serve his own interests. That may or may not accurately reflect what his attitude was when he spoke to Aline in July, or it may have been a defensive reaction to the plaintiff's lawyer's evident sarcasm (when Jeannotte denied that Aline had complained to him, the lawyer asked, "She congratulated you, I suppose?").[15] Jeannotte was unsurprisingly defensive about the mistake and its potential effects on his professional reputation. Even before the Couillards instituted their action, he had launched a libel action against the *Ottawa Daily Citizen* for an article that reported (without mentioning his name) that he had given the parents $1000 and the druggist $500 "to keep the affair secret."[16] Regardless, the doctor's report of the conversation, which stripped it of all feeling and emotion, seems implausible. Would a mother who had lost her child a few days before begin with legalized demands for reimbursement of the expenses she had incurred?

Charles Couillard brought action in September against both Jeannotte and the pharmacist Devins, alleging joint and solidary liability. He sued for $1500 in "damages both real and exemplary," a large amount, but surprisingly modest in comparison to many other wrongful death cases around this time.[17] The case was eagerly anticipated, less for the heartbreaking story of the child's death than for its impact on the developing field of professional liability.[18] Indeed, much of the coverage of the case as it developed featured strikingly insensitive back-and-forth sniping between physicians and pharmacists, which was inevitable, given the role of each in the mistakes causing the child's death.

Testimony was heard over seven days in June and October 1890 before Justice Louis-Amable Jetté, one of the more scholarly judges on the Superior Court at the time. The main legal issues were whether there was fault, whose fault it was, and whether there was solidarity between the two defendants. Justice Jetté had little difficulty in establishing liability. Writing *morphine* instead of *quinine* was "a gross error" on Jeannotte's part, and he assigned the lion's share of liability to the physician.[19] Devins, however, also committed a fault in filling the prescription, despite the shadow of doubt in the erroneous request for bisulphate of morphine. Since the two defendants' faults were distinct, there was no solidarity, and Justice Jetté apportioned liability at five-sixths for Jeannotte, one-sixth for Devins.

This was nothing particularly challenging, though it did contribute to the developing field of medical law. The difficult issue, and for our purposes the most interesting, came after liability was established and apportioned. For what injuries specifically could the Couillards claim, and how much? Alexandre's death brought on the Couillards various losses, from direct out-of-pocket expenses (the cost of transporting the body back to Montreal, the fees surrounding the funeral and burial), to indirect material losses (Alexandre's presumed future contributions to the household, even potentially his support of his parents in their old age), to emotional costs (grief, loss of the love and companionship of their child). These emotional injuries are what interest us. We will return to the Couillards and their case. First, a historical diversion is necessary.

Solace for the Grieving

Unbeknownst to the Couillards when they decided to sue, their grief would come up against the vexed question of how the courts in Quebec should deal with wrongful death. Their suit came precisely at a key moment in the doctrinal and judicial conflict over the concept of *solatium doloris* (solace for grief) – whether one could claim damages for the moral injury resulting from the death of a loved one.[20] For all concerned, the issue was in flux around 1890. For judges, the question of *solatium doloris* was a focal point in a legal identity crisis: should Quebec look to the English law of wrongful death (which the Supreme Court of Canada had endorsed in 1887), or to its traditional basis in French law?[21] For lawyers, both those representing bereaved plaintiffs and those representing defendants, it was a time of strategic uncertainty: how best to frame plaintiffs' feelings in legal language so as not to end up with a pittance despite the loss and grief they had suffered? How (on the other side) could a defendant neutralize a judge's natural sympathy in a case involving a mangled child or a destitute widow? And finally, for the bereaved families, it all must simply have seemed counter-intuitive, bewildering, even perverse: how could the unbearable pain they were feeling *not* count as a "loss" in legal terms?

The question of compensation for the wrongful death of a close family member was subject to a special provision of the CCLC. Alongside the general system of civil liability set out in article 1053, the legislature had added article 1056 when it enacted the code in 1866. To this day no one is quite sure how that article found its way into the code: it was absent from the codifiers' reports by which the draft civil code was first presented to the legislature, and it did not appear among the list of changes to the draft that were debated and ultimately authorized by the Assembly. But there it was, once the code was enacted and published, and all agreed that whatever its legislative history, it formed part of the law of the land.[22] The article dealt with deaths resulting from "offence/*délit*" and "quasi-offence/*quasi-délit*" as well as from duelling:

> In all cases where the person injured by the commission of an offence or a quasi-offence dies in consequence, without having obtained indemnity or satisfaction, his consort and his ascendant and descendant relations have

a right, but only within a year after his death, to recover from the person who committed the offence or quasi-offence, or his representatives, all damages occasioned by such death.

In the case of a duel, action may be brought in like manner not only against the immediate author of the death, but also against all those who took part in the duel, whether as seconds or as witnesses.

In all cases no more than one action can be brought in behalf of those who are entitled to the indemnity and the judgment determines the proportion of such indemnity which each is to receive. These actions are independent and do not prejudice the criminal proceedings to which the parties may be subject.

Though no record of debates exists, it seems clear that the provision was intended in part to prevent a flood of litigation. It gave one single action to the surviving spouse, the parents, and/or the children[23] of the deceased for "all damages," as long as the action was taken within a year of the death and no other form of satisfaction had been received (for example, an insurance payment or an out-of-court settlement).

Leaving aside the issue of duels, which seems never to have been raised in court, the interpretation of the article was particularly difficult because of Quebec's dual legal heritage. In private law, Quebec drew primarily on the French civil law, both in substance and in structure. The CCLC borrowed significantly from the French *Code civil*, both in its architecture and in individual provisions, many of which were virtually identical to their French models, though the French code had no provision similar to article 1056.[24] But even outside the text of the code, in the realm of the unwritten (but still in force) *droit commun*, as well as in the still more subtle influences on the reasoning processes of many Quebec judges, French ideas and ways of thinking dominated in the courts. That intellectual orientation was never unanimous, however. Some, but by no means all, anglophone judges (and even a few francophones) resisted – crafting judgments in the English style, reasoning from precedents rather than from principles, reaching by preference for English or if necessary American commentary to aid their analysis. Quebec law was never a pure civilian system, however, even in private law matters. Aside from anglophile judges, the courts ran according to English adversarial procedure, and the needs of commerce with the common-law world meant that in certain areas of the law English influence was pronounced. *Mixité* was thus far from the exception; we have already seen that this was true of the Quebec law of defamation.

Wrongful death fell into the middle of this tug of war of influences. The question was how to interpret the phrase "all damages" in article 1056.

As we saw in chapter 1, the rule in France had long been that any damage – whether material or moral – attributable to the defendant's fault could be claimed in a damages action. French authors were aware that moral injury could be vague and so subject to padding. That simply meant that the courts had to be vigilant in assessing damages and keep in mind that the purpose was compensation, not punishment. As a French court warned in 1872, "In the end, one cannot pay for the life of a father or of a husband, and his death must never become an object of speculation that might enrich his family."[25]

Across the Channel, things were more complex, and not in a good way: Frederick Pollock later called this "one of the least rational parts of our law."[26] The common-law rule had long been that no action could lie for wrongful death. The right of action was seen as personal, and so it died with the victim. Moreover, any private recourse was deemed to have been subsumed into the criminal action against the public wrong of homicide.[27] Industrialization and its growing toll of railway, steam engine, and factory accidents led to pressure to reform an apparently heartless rule that resulted in the anomaly of compensation being available for wounded victims, but nothing for the family of a fatality.[28] In 1846, the United Kingdom Parliament responded with *An Act for compensating the Families of Persons killed by Accidents*, but better known under the name of its sponsor as Lord Campbell's Act.[29] The act provided one single action per accident to a limited list of relatives (the victim's spouse, parents, or children) for death by wrongful act, provided that the action was undertaken within one year of the death. It also specified that in such actions, a jury could "give such Damages as they may think proportioned to the Injury resulting from such Death."[30]

The meaning of "such Damages" was the subject of an 1852 case brought by the widow of a rail passenger killed in a collision between two trains.[31] The jury awarded a sum for *solatium*, despite the presiding judge's having instructed them (in a rather vague and qualified way) that such damages were not permitted. On review, Justice Coleridge rejected that award: "The title of this Act may be some guide to its meaning: and it is 'An Act for compensating the families of persons killed;' not for solacing their wounded feelings."[32] If Parliament had intended the act to apply to *solatium*, something foreign to English law, it would have said so clearly. Allowing damages for "mental anguish" could lead to the ruin of defendants, which Parliament surely had not intended.[33]

In 1847, the legislature of the United Canadas imported a close parallel to Lord Campbell's Act, which differed most notably in broadening the class of persons who might bring the action to include the deceased's "personal representative, tutor or curator" as well as his or her heirs.[34] The colonial statute applied both to the former Upper Canada, where the English situation had prevailed and actions for wrongful death were barred, and to the former Lower Canada, where under the French regime of civil liability such actions were already possible. This caused some uncertainty in Canada East (Quebec). The purpose of the statute was clear enough for Canada West: it created an action where before there had been none. But was it to be understood as limiting the action that had always been available in Canada East? And if so, did it simply set up time limits and restrict who could bring suit, or did it also limit the types of damages that could be sought?

The matter of the statute's interpretation – including the question of *solatium doloris* – came up soon after the opening of the Grand Trunk Railway's Montreal to Toronto line. In November 1856, Thomas Wilson was struck and killed by the Kingston train while he was crossing the tracks near his farm at Coteau-du-Lac, to the west of Montreal.[35] Wilson's widow, Elizabeth Ravary, and children (there were twelve plaintiffs in all) sued the railway company for £10,000, comprising both material losses (Wilson's destroyed horse, wagon, and goods) and the moral injuries the family had sustained from the death of their husband and father. A jury found for the plaintiffs and awarded £319: £19 for the property loss, the remainder for the loss of Wilson's life. That was overturned on review, the main reason being that there had been no specific proof of the value of Wilson's life. Both Justice Charles Dewey Day and Justice Charles Mondelet rejected vindictive damages as part of Quebec law: only proved material loss could be compensated, and in this case there was no proof that the deceased had been a support (rather than a financial liability) to his family.[36] Justice James Smith, dissenting, accepted the premise that only proved loss could be compensated, but saw the mental suffering that necessarily followed loss of a husband or father as self-evident and requiring no special proof. In a case of wrongful death, he wrote, "the same rule would prevail as in other cases of damages, as, for instance, for seduction, where the mental suffering was the very thing which the damages were designed to compensate."[37] A new trial was ordered.

The plaintiffs appealed that order, and the Court of Queen's Bench overturned again and restored the jury verdict. The court split three to two on the issue of whether vindictive or emotional damages could be claimed, or whether compensation was for pecuniary losses only. The court's holding made it clear that *solatium doloris* was a valid claim: "Seeing that the damages which the party complaining is entitled to recover are not at common law confined to injuries of which a mere pecuniary estimate can be made, but comprehend a *solatium* to the widow and next of kin for their bereavement, *qui s'accorde au deuil des parents* [which corresponds to the relatives' grief], to be determined *à l'arbitrage du Juge* [by the judge's evaluation]."[38] If one tallies up the individual judges' reasons, however, a less confident picture emerges. Justice Thomas Aylwin, with whom Chief Justice Sir Louis-Hippolyte Lafontaine concurred, made a forceful case for damages for grief. Requiring proof of direct material loss opened the door to untenable arguments contrary to French and Lower Canadian law, such as "that the family of a dissipated or bankrupt father should receive nothing, while a large sum must be granted to the family of a man of different habits or position."[39] Aylwin's position clearly validated the grief Ravary and her children were suffering as a legally recognized injury: whether rich or poor, Wilson's death affected his family emotionally, and not just as a lost source of financial support. Dissenting, ad hoc Justice William Badgley, supported by Justice Jean-François-Joseph Duval, made it evident that only material loss could be proved, since such injuries "do not rest upon mere feelings, but upon the privation of some advantage." He followed that logic to its stark conclusion: "The death of a parent might in some cases be, in a pecuniary point of view, a blessing, when for instance he was dissipated, or so poor that it was necessary for his children to contribute to his support."[40] In other words, damages were not a lottery ticket: they compensated those who had suffered a loss, and were not intended to punish wrongdoers or to assuage "mere feelings." The final vote, Justice Jean-Casimir Bruneau (like Badgley serving ad hoc on the court for this case), failed to swing the reasoning one way or the other. He held simply that "it was plain that necessarily such a family must suffer loss from the death of a father by whose exertions they were maintained."[41] Though Bruneau voted with the majority – and so signed onto the "seeing that" quoted above that held *solatium* to be possible – his reasoning suggests rather that he followed the dissenting judges on what injuries could be compensated.[42]

That was where things stood when the CCLC was enacted in 1866 and article 1056 made its stealthy appearance. *Ravary* was the only reported judgment on wrongful death and *solatium doloris*, and while the holding of the Court of Queen's Bench in that case defined the issue, the strong dissents indicated that the matter was far from settled. Article 1056 hardly clarified things. It was not simply a direct copy of the British or Canadian Fatal Accidents acts. Aside from the addition of deaths by duel, it limited the action to the relatives themselves, excluding the deceased's heirs or representatives, which to some suggested that it created a new action for the relatives, rather than a continuation of the deceased's own action. Regarding grief and *solatium*, this in turn indicated (again, at least to some) that the legislature had intended the article to cover moral injury, since that would in many cases be the principal loss the relatives had suffered.

Two questions remained, then, as article 1056 went off into the lawyers' offices and courtrooms of Quebec. First, did it replace or work in concert with article 1053 for applicable cases? And second, what did "all damages" mean – all damages as would apply otherwise in Quebec, or all damages as the phrase would have been interpreted at the time of Lord Campbell's Act?

In the decades following *Ravary*, judges mainly followed the French model, interpreting article 1056 as operating alongside the general liability regime in article 1053, rather than treating relatives' wrongful death actions as an exception to the general rule. There were some outliers, but the general tendency was to allow claims for grief alongside the material losses occasioned by the death.[43] Indeed, many judges treated the issue as obvious and needing no particular justification. In a pair of cases arising from the collapse of a memorial arch erected in Place Jacques Cartier in Montreal to mark the arrival of Cardinal Taschereau to invest Édouard-Charles Fabre as archbishop of Montreal, Justice Michel Mathieu awarded damages for *solatium* in both cases, one under article 1056, the other under article 1053. In the first case, brought by the son of an elderly woman killed in the collapse, Justice Mathieu simply stated matter-of-factly that the plaintiffs were entitled to damages for their expenses and loss of their time, as well as for "consolation" for their mother's death.[44] In the second, in which the plaintiff was the deceased's son-in-law and the father of a girl injured in the accident (article 1056 applied to neither situation), Justice Mathieu justified moral damages by making it clear that the loss of "natural affection" was sufficient basis for damages for the loss of a loved one, whether or not material support was involved, "since in our legal system, one owes reparation for any injury one causes."[45]

This rough though not unchallenged consensus, based on opting for French over English traditions in *Ravary*, was not to last. The landscape changed in the 1880s, the result of another action under article 1056 involving a grieving widow and a railroad company. *Robinson v. Canadian Pacific Railway* was a decade-long legal odyssey from Agnes Robinson's husband's eventually fatal injury in the Canadian Pacific yards in August 1882, through two trials and trips up to the Supreme Court of Canada, to the final resolution of the case by the Judicial Committee of the Privy Council in July 1892.[46] Round one of the case, from the first trial in April 1885 to the first decision of the Supreme Court of Canada in June 1887, focused mainly on whether *solatium doloris* was a valid damages claim in Quebec. After a jury awarded the widow and her daughter $3000 damages, the bulk of that sum for their grief, majorities of the Court of Review and the Court of Queen's Bench both upheld the idea of damages for *solatium doloris*. As the Court of Queen's Bench made clear, "all damages" in article 1056 meant "all the descriptions of damages which such wife or children suffered, whether these damages were material or mental."[47]

The Supreme Court had other ideas. Unanimously, the justices declared themselves bound by the English precedents interpreting Lord Campbell's Act, leading to the conclusion that only material losses could factor into damages awarded. Chief Justice William Ritchie: "I think the damages must be estimated, not by the injured feelings of the plaintiff, but must rest on the privation of some advantage actually suffered or reasonably expected to be suffered from the homicide and to be compensated by a sum of money in lieu thereof."[48] Justice Henri-Elzéar Taschereau, for his part, found "no difference between the English law and ours on the subject." Even the old French authorities, he said, granted *solatium* only for damages resulting from crime. As a result, moral damages might be awarded "in cases where the party causing the death has acted with malice or committed a *délit*, but not when the death was caused by a *quasi-délit*," as here.[49] The court sent the case back to the Superior Court for a new trial.

Undeterred, and showing the stalwart common sense for which juries were both praised as bastions of British liberty and condemned as emotional loose cannons, the second jury awarded even larger damages, totalling $6500.[50] In this second round, given the Supreme Court's clear instructions, not a whisper was heard of *solatium doloris*, but it is hard to imagine that in the jurors' minds some of that large sum was not for the plaintiffs' grief. The company continued to press the issue and now brought in a new ground of appeal: prescription, since the victim had died more than year after the accident. The Court of Review and the Court of Queen's Bench rejected prescription as not pleaded, and though both courts made noises about excessive damages, they deferred to the jury's jurisdiction and upheld the award. The Supreme Court, however, clearly disturbed by what the high damages award might mean for Canada's railroad development if it stood as a precedent, grasped at a solidly technical ground and held that even if not pleaded, a court could take notice of prescription anyway.[51] They allowed the appeal and entered judgment for the company.

The case finally went to the Privy Council, with workers' groups undertaking subscription campaigns to assist the highly sympathetic plaintiff with the immense costs. The Lords cut through the technicalities and obstructionism and sided with the nearly unanimous Quebec courts to say enough was enough: "Their Lordships are not inclined to protract litigation already excessive.… [They] see no reason to suppose that any injustice will be done by their finally disposing of the case at this stage."[52] Rather than ordering a third trial, they restored the second jury verdict and awarded the widow costs at both the Supreme Court and the Privy Council.

What of *solatium doloris*? Here the normally thorough Judicial Committee left things vague – or perhaps that was by design? Though *solatium doloris* was no longer at issue – it had been decided by the Supreme Court in round one – it clearly still lurked around the edges of the question of damages. The Privy Council muddied the waters a bit, stating in an admirably circumspect and precise way, "In so far as they bear upon the present question, the terms of sect. 1056 appear to their Lordships to differ substantially from the provisions of Lord Campbell's Act and of the provincial statute of 1859."[53] A narrow reading of that remark would have their ruling apply only to the question of prescription; a broader one might see it as casting doubt on the exclusive reliance on English law to interpret article 1056. In the end, then, the Supreme Court had been overruled, but arguably not on the issue of damages for grief.

All these cases highlighted a crucial issue for many of the judges, even those who ended up supporting damages for *solatium doloris* in their rulings: allowing compensation for grief or other feelings could open the door to excessive windfalls, particularly when sentimental juries were involved. Even the French authorities, who supported moral damages in general, warned of that problem. But what was excessive? In the eyes of some, courts had to judge what was appropriate according to social codes of class and proper social standing; according to others, judges had to strike a balance between justice and the needs of commerce and industry. The Couillards pursued their own case against that backdrop.

Couillard v. Jeannotte Revisited

The Couillards brought their action right in the middle of Agnes Robinson's marathon through the Quebec, Canadian, and imperial legal systems. The lawyers on both sides would certainly have known where things stood with *Robinson*, and that the Supreme Court had in 1887 rejected any possibility of compensation for grief over the loss of a loved one. When the Couillards filed their action, however, the second trial in *Robinson* had resulted in even higher damages than the first trial, and that award had just been confirmed by the Court of Review. In June 1890, while Justice Jetté was hearing the Couillards' case, the Court of Queen's Bench dismissed the Canadian Pacific's appeal in *Robinson*, once again confirming the large $6500 damages award. The composition of those damages was not discussed – they were a lump sum of general damages, taken as proved by the jury and not challenged on appeal – so one could not say with any confidence that Quebec judges were disregarding the Supreme Court's rule against *solatium doloris*. But in the fall of 1889 and through 1890 it would have looked like a revolt was brewing in the Quebec courts against the imported English interpretation of "all damages" in article 1056, and that judges were trying to re-establish a broad reading of injury in line with the French authorities. In November 1889 Jeannotte's lawyers moved to dismiss the action, in part on the basis of lack of damage to the plaintiff, but this argument was rejected and the motion was dismissed.[54]

At trial, the Couillards' lawyers, like those in other wrongful death cases, refrained from asking direct questions about the parents' feelings.[55] Aline Couillard seems not to have testified at all, while Charles's deposition (called by the defendant Jeannotte) was mainly about the circumstances of filling the prescription and administering the medication.[56] Justice Louis Jetté, however, made it clear that he did not accept the new understanding of wrongful death damages and took aim at the Supreme Court in the strongest terms: "If someone murders your aged father, whom you are obliged to support, not only would you get no damages, but you would owe the killer thanks, since he relieved you of that burden. That is the consequence of the doctrine of the Supreme Court."[57] He went on to characterize this as "a barbaric principle that cannot be allowed" and rejected it in favour of the *Ravary* decision, which he identified as "the true doctrine."[58] He awarded Couillard $300 in damages, apportioned according to fault as $250 against Jeannotte, $50 against the pharmacist Devins.[59] He noted that although only $50 of material loss was proved, it was appropriate to add $250 "for exemplary damages and for penalty imposed on the defendants."[60]

Only the physician Jeannotte appealed; the pharmacist Devins was content to pay his damages and move on.[61] (A pharmacists' trade publication crowed that this justified "the belief of apothecaries that medical men are apt to be obstinate in defending their errors."[62]) The Court of Queen's Bench made short work of the issue of liability, unanimously affirming Justice Jetté's findings on liability and the share of each defendant.[63] Where they parted company was on the issue of moral injury. Justice Robert Hall, writing for the majority, rejected *solatium doloris* in the interests of establishing "a uniform jurisprudence upon this subject in the several provinces in the Dominion, and in Great Britain."[64] Interestingly, he left a small door open for cases where death was due to malice, echoing Justice Taschereau at the Supreme Court in *Robinson*: "We come to the conclusion that we cannot allow any recognition of pecuniary compensation for grief or mental suffering by the survivors, in the case of death resulting from accident, *délit* or *quasi-délit*, where no malice existed."[65] Justice Joseph-Guillaume Bossé dissented (he would have affirmed Justice Jetté's decision in all respects, including the possibility of damages for *solatium*[66]), but in the end the majority reduced the Couillards' damages to $50, or the amount that Devins had already paid. (Devins would have to pursue Jeannotte to collect five-sixths of that amount.) Ever concerned about windfalls, the court awarded Couillard his costs in the Superior Court, but pegged to the lowest class of action (rather than costs of the action as instituted, which sometimes happened), and made each party bear its own costs for the appeal.

If we turn to the Couillards' arguments, we get some glimpses of the difficult situation in which the bereaved found themselves following the Supreme Court's rejection of damages for grief in *Robinson*.[67] In the appeal factum, Charles and his lawyers tried to walk a fine line between asserting the family's injured subjective feelings and making a case that would acknowledge the increasingly clear legal limits on recovery for emotional distress. They began, as was only prudent, with a brief argument on their material losses, supporting their claim for maintenance of their child during the twenty-one months from his birth to his death, or $210 calculated at $10 per month.[68] Here the argument relied on viewing the child as an investment in their future, an investment that had been wasted and so must be compensated. For the bulk of their argument, however, they changed register from the material to the emotional, arguing that the moral injury they suffered must also be compensated.

In developing their arguments concerning moral injury, they valiantly, if in retrospect futilely, tried to validate sentiment against the prevailing materialist jurisprudence coming from the Supreme Court. They did this through several interrelated lines of argument, outlined in their factum. They began with an appeal to reason, hoping to give conservative judges a formalist basis on which to affirm moral damages. Was it not illogical, they argued, that the general prescription period for actions in damages arising from delict or quasi-delict was two years, but article 1056 prescribed its actions after one year only? The only explanation for this, they asserted, was that affection was the basis of the action, and "since sentiment is the greatest and most noble motive in human actions, there is no need for a long period of time for someone who suffered the death of his father or his child to decide whether to sue the person responsible." This was perhaps not the most compelling argument, given many judges' suspicions of "mere feelings," echoed in the Supreme Court's ruling in *Robinson*. But in for a penny, in for a pound, and the Couillards endeavoured to build up from this foundation by arguing that the company had tacitly admitted to causing them moral damage when they argued that the family had already been compensated by the happiness that their love for the child had brought them. "So you admit that you did me wrong in depriving me of that happiness which should have grown as my child advanced in age. Why do you deprive me of this happiness without any compensation?" They were attempting to reorient the debate in affective terms: what they were saying, in other words, was that by killing the Couillards' child "in such a cruel way," Jeannotte had thereby caused them losses. Material losses, yes, "but his grief, how will that be paid for?" Since the plaintiff was deprived of his son's love, and since "the memory of his death will continually break his heart," negligent doctors like Jeannotte must "know that if at times the earth hides their faults, at least when those faults are known, they will be severely punished by law."[69]

This was a crucial point in their argument and was nothing less than an attempt to turn back the clock to an earlier period, before the materialism of the new law of wrongful death. They were arguing for their happiness as a kind of *bien*, as something that they as parents possessed and whose loss was as actionable as the loss of any material object. This antique turn was further underscored by their linking of compensation and punishment, a move that recalled Sourdat (cited directly) and before him, Dareau on *injure*. Though the point was not made explicitly, the argument echoed the expansive view of the patrimony originally set out by Aubry and Rau, including the *biens innés*, as well as Maximilien Bibaud's view of *biens* as anything bringing happiness, whether tangible or intangible. Again, this was a hard argument to make, given that *biens* had by this time been solidified in strictly materialist terms by Aubry and Rau and others, as we saw in chapter 1.

The argument contained an awkward tension, though litigation frequently required arguing apparently contradictory positions simultaneously. On the one hand, they viewed their relationship with their child as an asset (to support the argument about material damages). On the other hand, they characterized the parent–child relationship as an emotional *bien* (to support the argument for moral damages). Both sides were evident in the testimony at trial, with the lawyers for both plaintiff and defendant trying to limit the issue to the child as asset, while the witnesses often strayed from the script and brought emotions in. Several witnesses were asked to evaluate the cost of raising a child, with the lawyers enjoining them each to leave aside the parents' affection for the child.[70] The witnesses – testifying for the plaintiffs, it should be noted – understandably had trouble separating the two. Dr. Norbert Fafard felt it was impossible to evaluate, and even when pressed to estimate how much it would cost to place a child with strangers, qualified his estimate (about $8 to $10 a month) by stating that the child would thereby lose the affection of its parents.[71] Similarly, Couillard's sister-in-law Clara Côté, under cross-examination, refused to give in to Jeannotte's lawyer, who tried to get her to admit that it was "no big deal" to lose a child of twenty months: "It's a big loss, because one always has hopes regarding a child."[72] On the other hand, the physician Jean-Baptiste Adolphe Lamarche got into the spirit of the assessment game. Though it was impossible to put a value on affection, he said, things were different in a small family than when "there are masses of them, ten, twelve." In the latter case, he argued, "the value would be less ... there is no doubt that it relieves the family when two or three leave. When a man earns fifty dollars a month and has eight children to raise, if he loses three or four, it seems to me that that's not a great loss, at least speaking in monetary terms. It could make the hearts of the father and mother bleed, but it seems to me that financially speaking they don't lose much." His testimony is a vivid example of Viviana Zelizer's point about the changing ways in which the value of children was expressed around this time.[73] Though he acknowledged the emotion of parenting, he saw materialist factors as overriding affective ones. And even so, he qualified his remark: "Regarding this evaluation, I would ask the court not to take me too seriously; I was just estimating things, and I'm not used to making that kind of calculation."[74]

Getting back to the Couillards' arguments, they pulled the various threads together by raising the old argument – heard already in *Ravary*, and voiced most recently by Justice Jetté in the trial decision of their case – of the immorality of treating human beings solely as assets with pecuniary value. The implication of that argument, of course, was that the Supreme Court's analysis of the law was profoundly out of touch with the values of Quebec society. *Biens* came in various kinds, they argued, distributed unequally within society. The rich and prominent had honour and gold upon which to base their happiness, "but for me who is poor, my happiness is the love of my children, my spouse, my father, my mother." The law gives an action to the rich when their gold is taken away, but it is different if this happiness – this *bien* – is taken away: "Far from recognizing my right to reparation, you would respond to me, 'Your child was dependant on you, so now your well-being has increased by the same amount.' Is that not profoundly immoral?"[75] The Couillards' arguments reveal them trying to bring the case – indeed the law – back onto a humanistic footing, against the common-law inspired materialism that the Supreme Court had recently authorized. That they failed suggests how profoundly things had changed.

For bereaved survivors, the refusal by the Court of Queen's Bench in *Couillard* to uphold even the minimal moral damages awarded the family at trial made it clear that the new order set out by the Supreme Court in *Robinson* was not to be ignored. Damages in wrongful death cases would henceforth be strictly limited to proved material losses and those claims for loss of future support that were direct and certain (yes if the deceased were a twenty-year-old son who had been giving most of his wages to his parents, no if the victim were a twenty-month-old child). Any demand for *solatium* for the moral injury suffered would be rejected outright. The legal exclusion of damages for grief was sufficiently notorious to be known outside the courts as well. After the Laurier Palace cinema fire in January 1927, for example, in which seventy-eight children were killed at a Sunday matinee, news coverage noted with some chagrin that the families of the victims "cannot count on very high damages," since the courts had determined that "they have no right to *solatium doloris*, to compensation for their moral pain."[76]

Not everyone accepted this reorientation of Quebec law from its traditional foundation in French civil law and its new alignment (in this area) with English law. Increasingly over the following decades, judges and commentators viewed the Supreme Court's ruling as an outside imposition on Quebec's civil-law tradition, one that clashed with the prevailing morality of Quebec law. Some judges criticized the rule from the bench, some worked to disguise damages for grief under a broadened reading of material injury, but since the Supreme Court had spoken the rule had to be applied.[77] As nativist sentiment grew within the Quebec legal community, *solatium doloris* became one of the focal points of the growing critique of the composition and jurisprudence of the Supreme Court, of Privy Council appeals, and of creeping common-law influence generally.[78] Critics frequently noted the irony: a law that had been intended to humanize the common law (by allowing a limited action where there had been none before) came to be seen in Quebec as itself inhuman for turning the deaths of fathers or children into material losses or gains. It was only in 1996, when the Supreme Court explicitly overruled *Robinson* in *Augustus v. Gosset*, that moral damages for grief again became a legitimate part of Quebec civil law.[79]

Alongside the grief attending the passing of a close relative, death also sometimes gave rise to conflicts between family members or with outsiders over the procedures and ceremonies surrounding end of life. Those conflicts fed into the turmoil of grief and related feelings and could lead to claims of emotional injury for which victims sought redress in the courts. Such injuries differed from grief itself: they touched feelings of loss of control, outrage, even anger, when others seemed to come between a person and his or her grief. In what follows, we will look at two such areas of conflict: disputes over a widow's right to mourning expenses, and intra-family disputes over who should decide where a body was to be buried. (The autopsy cases we discussed in chapter 4 are relevant to this discussion as well.) The cases touched more on public aspects surrounding loss of a loved one than on private grief, but at the same time they revealed ways in which law, social norms of propriety, and internal family dynamics all entered into and affected the highly emotionally charged period immediately following the death of a loved one.

Only What Was Suitable: Widows' Mourning Clothes

Grieving was both a private and a public process in Quebec in the nineteenth and twentieth centuries. For widows especially, strict rules governed the stages of mourning, its duration, proper behaviour during that period, and appropriate dress.[80] These were social and cultural codes, but aspects of them were also legalized and expressed as formal rights and duties. The elaborate legal regime surrounding the grieving process in ancien régime France had mostly fallen aside,[81] but mourning dress (known as *deuil* in French, more colourfully as "widow's weeds" in English) was still subject to express legal regulation, which led at times to litigation pitting a grieving widow against the executors of her deceased husband's estate, with family (and in many cases family from a previous marriage) in the background. This "right" of the widow thus became an interesting site of intra-familial conflict.[82]

Article 1368 CCLC granted a widow the right to an unspecified sum for mourning dress, to be charged to her late husband's estate:

> The mourning of the wife is chargeable to the heirs of her deceased husband.
>   The cost of such mourning is to be regulated according to the fortune of the husband.
>   It is due even to the wife who renounces the community.

The article set up a regime in which the courts – if the widow and heirs could not agree – would "regulate" the entitlement due to a particular widow. This gave judges considerable discretion: by law the mourning was to be proportional to the size of the husband's estate, but in practice that meant less a precise percentage than the assessment of what the judge felt was proper and fitting, given the parties' means and social position. The code made that explicit in article 2002, which, by making mourning and funeral expenses privileged claims, limited them to "only what is suitable to the station and means of the deceased."

In cases of disagreement, the litigation that sometimes ensued brought the widow's feelings of what she deserved and what she felt was proper up against the increasingly materialist ethos of the courts, abetted by executors and heirs whose resistance in many cases spoke to family conflicts. The right itself was not in doubt, and aside from situations of adultery, by which the widow forfeited her right,[83] the cases were not about whether mourning was owed, but rather how much. As we saw in the wrongful death cases, judges were strongly attuned to the potential for gold-digging by widows and sought, where possible, to limit mourning claims. How they did that reflects the social codes surrounding grief, codes that were partly shared, partly contested.

At a basic level, the duration of mourning was challenged on cultural grounds. Queen Victoria's almost forty-year mourning did much to reinforce the practice of public displays of mourning throughout the empire, and if ordinary widows' mourning was considerably shorter, the "official" duration for legal purposes had to be determined. Widows' claims for two years' mourning, for example, were presented in cultural terms. In a 1908 case, a widow claimed she should be reimbursed for wearing mourning for two years, since "in this province" that was the custom. In reducing her claim, Justice Arthur-Aimé Bruneau attempted to sort out the Quebec culture of mourning by reviewing, oddly, Roman law and old French customary law, both of which defined it as one year.[84] A widow could wear mourning as long as she liked, of course, but after one year she was financially on her own. The argument for a longer period was a long shot – most sources gave the mourning period as traditionally one year[85] – but the cultural argument is telling. Grief was personal, but in a legal sense that subjectivity was impossible to manage.

The amounts claimed were even more strongly contested and gave rise to allegations of unseemly behaviour by widows. Bettina Bradbury cites an unreported case from 1872 in which Justice Robert Mackay was faced with a remarried widow seeking mourning from the children of her first marriage. The judge "found both claims sound but noted in his private papers that 'to come now and ask for the mourning' smelled of 'indelicacy.'" The claim was reduced to $20 in punishment.[86] In assessing such claims, judges – aided by expert witnesses such as couturières[87] – went through submitted inventories of clothing either already purchased or planned, to determine what was necessary and what was "extravagant" or "superfluous." Below a certain threshold, judges were content to accept claims at face value, taking a kind of judicial notice of the self-evident nature of widows' modest needs for a special wardrobe to honour the memory of their dead husbands and to uphold society's expectations of their class. The aptly named Helen Fairgreave, for example, claimed only $25.35 in mourning expenses for herself and her children; despite the modest claim, the executors challenged including in it the children's mourning clothes, since neither article 1368 nor 2002 mentioned children. Justice Russell Thomas Stackhouse disagreed and, in the course of a discussion of mourning customs, framed with "as is well known," found it "unreasonable and unfair," even "inhuman" to exclude the children's needs. He went so far as to note that according to French authorities, mourning in France included not only the children but servants as well.[88] More substantial claims warranted closer scrutiny, as judges policed norms of class and propriety. Elodie Jodoin claimed $200, and though her husband's estate was worth between $12,000 and $15,000, the Court of Review reduced the sum awarded to $100, finding that since she had already been mourning her father when her husband died, and had to purchase only $85 of additional items, her full claim was excessive.[89] The widow of a poor farmer saw her claim of $500 characterized as "absolutely extravagant" and reduced to the $150 the defendant had offered, though Justice Wilfrid Mercier made clear that he would have limited her strictly to the $119.50 she had actually spent.[90]

Many of the litigated cases involved a second wife being challenged by the children of the deceased's first marriage, named as his heirs. The mourning expenses, along with dower rights, could be virtually all the widow received, and the estate, for reasons usually no longer evident, sought to fight even that. Second wife Rosa L'Heureux, who was expelled from the matrimonial home by her husband's executors immediately after the funeral and seems to have been excluded from the succession, which went to the children of the first marriage, was offered $200 mourning (against an estate valued at more than $40,000). The heirs further sought $57 of that amount, claiming it was compensation for a debt owed (the judge dismissed that claim).[91] In some cases, the widow's claims were used as evidence to question her motivation, as in *Mailloux*, in which Justice Bruneau suggested that in submitting a mourning claim of $165.24, despite her blacksmith husband's estate being worth only about $600, she was seeking to profit from the occasion. The judge elaborated: "The plaintiff had a small nest egg that she had amassed by her work from before the marriage. She thus personally had the means to purchase nice mourning dress. She seems to me to have taken advantage of the situation to refresh her wardrobe." He awarded her $75, a sum he judged "very liberal" and in keeping with the size of the deceased's estate.[92]

The family conflicts behind the cases reflect common enough tensions that surrounded inheritance generally and blended families in particular.[93] The results show judges seeking to strip a strongly subjective situation of its emotional and cultural overtones, to treat it as more or less strictly compensatory. The measure of that compensation, however, was in most cases not the widow's outlay – which would have reflected her subjective evaluation of how she wished to display her grief – but rather the judge's reading of class. As in the wrongful death cases, some judges only thinly disguised their opinion that mourning and other expenditures were frivolous luxuries to be minimized to "appropriate" levels in the interests of the heirs.[94] The result was a shift in the analysis from "right" to "propriety": the right created by article 1368 ensured that no virtuous widow (adulterers were excluded) would be left with nothing, but the terms of that article meant that in a highly emotionally charged atmosphere, widows were forced to justify that they were properly exercising their "right" to mourning expenses and not seeking to have their husband's estate fund overly sentimental or vain displays.

Certainly some of the plaintiffs were trying to get what they could from their husbands' estates, whether through a sense of their own financial vulnerability, the dictates of propriety, or a desire to get back at defendants who had sought to stymie their claims. But looked at from the other perspective, widows often found their already meagre financial allowances reduced further by defendants eager to maximize the estate for other heirs (or to punish a perceived interloping second wife) and by judges who tended to see non-essential expenditures not as culturally mandated honouring of the dead husband but as at best frivolous feminine indulgence and at worst as gold-digging.

Burying the Dead

Far more than mourning expenses, the question of who got to decide where to bury a body was an emotionally fraught issue.[95] Did the decision belong to the deceased? To the spouse and/or children? To the birth family? To the heirs? To church officials? In most cases the issue never arose, as the family, motivated by love, custom, or the pressures of decency, followed the deceased's wishes or, in the absence of any clear expression of choice, agreed among themselves on a suitable place and memorial. In some cases, however, the decision caused acrimonious litigation, as factions within the family – usually the marital versus the birth family, but not always – fought for control. Those family factions were likely also motivated by love, custom, and the pressures of decency, but at the same time by strong competitiveness, as plaintiff and defendant often went to great lengths to ensure that burial would be in their place and not the other's.

Though conflicts over burial could and did end up in court, Quebec's formal law was largely silent on the subject. The CCLC provided exhaustive rules on certain post-mortem issues, such as the order of successions, and it stipulated when a burial could take place (not before twenty-four hours after death), but it said nothing at all about who held the rights to determine where burial should take place. Other statutes governed cemeteries and interment, mainly from the perspective of public health, but also to prevent grave robbing and theft of cadavers, but they too stopped short of dictating what was generally seen as the family's personal decision.[96] Unlike France, where, by the early twentieth century, decades of court cases had resolved most of the main questions concerning burial rights (though not without disagreements),[97] Quebec saw few such cases during the nineteenth century. Those that were reported, and most notably the lengthy and notorious Guibord affair of 1869–74, dealt with religious authorities' refusal to bury a particular individual at all or in a particular place.[98] As legal matters, the early cases involved the writ of mandamus and not damages: the courts identified a "right of burial," but the effects of a contested burial on relatives were legally irrelevant.

With Quebec secular law largely silent on the respective rights of parents, spouses, and children, choice of burial was left primarily to the workings of religious laws and social norms of propriety. Christian teaching asserted that marriage created a new bond that superseded (but did not break) one's bonds to one's parents: "Wherefore a man shall leave father and mother, and shall cleave to his wife: and they shall be two in one flesh."[99] For Roman Catholics, canon law added some further stipulations. The 1917 *Code of Canon Law*, which reflected earlier church law on this point, made the choice of the deceased decisive. In the absence of express wishes, however, if a person had a family tomb, he or she was to be buried there, while a wife was to be buried in her husband's family tomb (her last husband if she had more than one).[100] While these religious rules provided some guidance, particularly for Catholics, they did not answer the question of what happened when surviving relatives could not agree, or took matters into their own hands and buried the body somewhere before opposition could be voiced.

Death tended to focus matters, and it put the various norms to the test. Burial was a zero-sum proposition: a dead body could rest in one place only (at least aside from the special case of the widely dispersed relics of Catholic saints), and that required a decision in the far from rare cases in which the deceased had been silent or unclear about his or her wishes. Disputes over burial made up a small but interesting set of cases among those involving the social and legal ramifications of the death of a loved one. And while they brought up numerous issues, our focus here and in the following section will be the question of the emotional injury of loss of control during a time of heightened emotion.

The newspapers reported some early cases of intra-family disputes about burial. In 1890, a young bride suffering from consumption moved from Montreal back to Terrebonne, north of the city, so that her mother could care for her. She died there and was buried in her family's plot, since her husband had judged it inopportune to oppose his in-laws at that time of grief. Later, after "every possible influence" with his in-laws had failed, he brought the matter to the courts and was granted an exhumation order, supported as the law required by the permission of the archbishop.[101] Though details about most such cases are lacking, the situations are suggestive of families seeking to manage grief (often in conflicting ways) by controlling the disposition of their loved ones' remains. The courts, for their part, sought to strip away the emotions from the conflicts before them. For most judges, the default position was that the courts were there to repair material injuries, and anything smacking of mere sentiment was beyond the court's mandate. A few brief examples will outline the issues for a more detailed look at a particularly rich case in the next section.

The first reported case of intra-family conflict over burial came in 1911, when John Driscoll died at the Montreal General Hospital, and his daughter and sisters battled over the burial of his body.[102] As was often the case, two burial plots were at issue: the family grave where the sisters wanted him buried, and John's own plot, purchased when his wife died, where the daughter sought to put him. The daughter, from whom the deceased had been at one time estranged, but who claimed they had reconciled, had the body quickly buried in the latter grave. The sisters, universal legatees of the deceased's will written just before his death, successfully applied to the courts to have the body exhumed and moved to the family plot. They then sued the funeral director who had worked with the daughter on the initial burial, claiming $152.40 in damages, $67.40 for their out-of-pocket expenses, the remainder for having "greatly affected the health of the Plaintiffs who are women of advanced age," because of "the worry of the proceedings."[103] Though much of the case remained at the level of legal rights, some of the testimony revealed the emotional stakes in a case like this (though of course we must remember that positions were carefully crafted for strategic purposes). Frances Driscoll, one of the deceased's sisters, in answering questions about the supposed health effects of her ordeal, said, "I have suffered grief, protracted and terrible, besides expenses I could not afford and such disappointment as not being [able] to fulfil my obligations as contained in my brother's will, to give him a suitable funeral, because his body was taken." There she was cut off by the defence's objection, rejecting anything but health effects as irrelevant, but her answer indicated both the emotional toll of dealing with a close relative's death, and the norms of propriety surrounding proper burial to which she felt bound. In the end, the trial judge awarded the sisters $100 as "nominal damages by reason of the violation of their rights." He dismissed the alleged health effects as unproved and said nothing about the claimed emotional injuries. Even that was overturned by a majority of the Court of Review, which rejected any fault on the part of the funeral director.[104] In a sad postscript to the case, the sisters, who had proceeded in their action *in forma pauperis*, saw their piano and other household effects seized and sold off to pay the costs.[105]

A later case, from 1931, similarly reveals the difficult fit between grief and other sentiments surrounding death and the law. In that case, the plaintiff's brother had been struck and killed by a streetcar in Westmount. The plaintiff sued the tramway company not for grief nor indeed for the wrongful death (since article 1056 CCLC excluded actions by collateral relations), but rather in unjust enrichment. He claimed that he had spent $1225 taking his brother's body to Pittsburgh "and there giving him a decent Christian burial," and he was trying to get the streetcar company to reimburse those expenses.[106] Assistant Chief Justice Robert Greenshields dismissed the case, since there was no legal reason for the brother to do what he did, only "a sense of duty or sentiment," and the latter could cause no legally recognizable injury.[107]

As in the cases of *solatium doloris*, judges in the burial cases were trying to set up lines between material loss and sentiment in an area (death and its surrounding rites and customs) in which the two blurred considerably. The ceremonies and observances surrounding burial of the dead were (and are) highly culturally and socially inflected, and cultural and social norms overlapped only partially with legal norms. Peter Stearns, in making observations about the United States that are applicable to Canada as well, has identified what he calls "a century of grief," in which "death became surrounded with high emotions."[108] Cases like those just outlined featured litigants coming to court with elevated emotional expectations, which judges were mostly reluctant to accommodate. A case from Quebec City involving a battle over burial between a widow and her in-laws illustrates these issues still more clearly.

Feelings and Rights: *Jinchereau v. Roy*

When Alphonse Roy, long-time Quebec City restaurateur, died on Tuesday evening, 11 March 1913, his widow Belzémire Jinchereau undertook funeral arrangements herself, since the couple had no surviving children.[109] She put notices in local papers, and that Friday the service was held at her parish church of St-Jean-Baptiste, following which the body was transported to the parish's Belmont cemetery in Sainte-Foy, west of town.[110] Jinchereau planned to have the body buried in nearby St-Charles cemetery, where the couple's only child, an infant daughter, had been buried years before. The ground was still frozen, so as was common practice, she had the body placed for the time being in the Belmont winter vault (*charnier*) to await spring thaw.[111] She had as yet no plot at St-Charles: her husband had been reluctant to plan for his demise and had died suddenly without ever having gotten around to making the necessary purchase.[112] Jinchereau seems to have made some inquiries about buying a plot, but the *fabrique* was not selling at that time. After the funeral, Alphonse Roy's family, including his sister Amaryllis and her husband, Octave Mercier, as well as a brother Alfred, who had travelled up from Worcester, Massachusetts, complimented Belzémire on her arrangements and agreed to pay for the service.[113]

In early May, Jinchereau approached her curé, Joseph-Damase Beaudoin, about having her husband's body moved to St-Charles and buried. To her shock, she learned that the body had already been removed from the *charnier* upon court order. She found out later that her husband's relatives had had the body interred in the family plot in St-Joseph-de-Lévis cemetery, across the St. Lawrence River.[114] She went home "almost unconscious" and confronted her in-laws, though what was said was unrecorded.[115] In October she began legal action, seeking an order for the relatives to surrender the body and have it reburied as originally planned at St-Charles, claiming also $400 damages for her suffering.[116]

How did things get to that point? As with any family conflict, the background and motivations are obscure to outsiders, more so when the only information comes from witness testimony and procedural documents, which tend to be self-serving. We must back up and interpret the sparse but suggestive hints about the deeper conflict scattered through the principals' testimony. The timeline is not always clear, but it is telling, and taking events in order gives a sense of the building tension and animosity between Jinchereau and her in-laws.

Alphonse and Belzémire had married in August 1895, when he was about forty-four and she about twenty-seven. This was likely his first marriage; it is unclear whether the same was true for her.[117] Alphonse was fairly well off. He had been running a restaurant on St. Augustin Street since 1886, and for a few years before that had had a restaurant on St. John Street.[118] Moreover, he had himself paid to have a stone fence built around his family's burial plot in St-Joseph cemetery.[119] He died intestate, without surviving children or parents, and so under Quebec law at that time his sister and brother became his heirs. Interestingly, the conflict over Alphonse Roy's remains took place on the eve of important changes to the legal status of widows. At the time of his death, the CCLC privileged blood over marriage and excluded the spouse from intestate succession if any descendant, ascendant, or collateral relatives survived. That would change in 1915, too late for Belzémire, and in any case the new legislation did not deal with the question of burial rights.[120]

Details about the estate were handled by Mercier and a notary, François-Xavier Couillard. Around the time of the funeral, certain of Belzémire's rights were discussed and settled in an apparently amicable fashion. She was entitled by marriage contract to $2000 in lieu of dower; they agreed on a mourning allowance of $250; and certain unspecified expenses were to be paid by the succession (likely the outlays she had made for the funeral).[121] According to the notary, her brother-in-law Alfred Roy said to her, "We'll give you everything you ask for,"[122] but unsurprisingly the meaning of those words was contested later. Jinchereau understood "everything" to include paying for a plot in St-Charles cemetery; the heirs had more minor expenses in mind.[123]

About ten days later, that more-or-less cooperative tone was thrown aside. According to Belzémire, Mercier and Couillard arrived in the restaurant bar (downstairs from her residence) "acting all high and mighty" and proclaiming "the house belongs to us."[124] At the same time, she said, they rooted around in her husband's clothing, asking where the rest of it was so they could take it away as assets of the succession; there was talk as well of a gold watch and an unspecified lease held by the deceased.[125] Belzémire was offended by their behaviour, something she brought up again and again during her testimony, to the point that the defence lawyer got testy: "Enough of that!"[126] The defendants painted a different picture, one of an abusive, drunken hellcat screaming at them for no reason and chasing them from the house. Couillard claimed he was afraid to have anything more to do with her, fearing physical assault: "I've never seen a woman as violent as that ... she seemed to me like she was drunk."[127] In support of that picture, they brought up an incident from early January 1914, in which Belzémire had been summoned before the Recorder's Court, charged by her landlord with disturbing the peace (that was after the heirs had reclaimed the restaurant/matrimonial home and she was living with her sister nearby).[128] She was fined $20, and her evasive testimony on the issue could not have helped her cause in the main action.

The characterization of Belzémire's behaviour and general bearing was important for the case. The defence depicted her as drunk, out of control, and violent, someone who could not fittingly be entrusted with her husband's burial. Belzémire, of course, disagreed. She admitted to taking the occasional drink, but never to excess, and she swore she was not drunk during the incident at the restaurant. She explained her hostility towards the defendants as due to her not having slept or eaten in days, and as having responded to rudeness with rudeness: "When they're polite, I receive them well, and when they're rude, I receive them likewise."[129] Moreover, Belzémire's father died two weeks after the incident at the restaurant; his being ill or fading might further help to explain her fragile emotional state.[130] In any case, the parties' versions of that key incident were fundamentally contradictory. She presented her reactions as emotional but justified in the circumstances. The defence argued they were irrational and excessive: notary Couillard professed surprise – he was being either disingenuous or strikingly insensitive – that she would have reacted badly to their innocent request for her husband's moveable property.[131]

The confrontation pointed to a deeper and probably prolonged family conflict, something evident in Belzémire's wariness towards Mercier. Certainly by the time of the testimony, after positions had hardened into demand and defence, the conflict had become highly personal. Belzémire interpreted the defendants' words and actions as indicating that they felt she was unworthy to have been Alphonse's wife, an emotional response that must be put into the context of her being about to lose her home and likely fearing that she was being written out of her husband's life entirely. That was hardly an unusual feeling for widows, whose position (especially when childless) was often precarious, but the behaviour of Belzémire's husband's heirs would have aggravated the usual apprehension.[132] The $2000 indemnity would have helped her situation as a widow, but the extent to which she had a support network on which she could rely is unclear. After her husband's death she lived with her unmarried sister, and she referred at one point to a brother-in-law, in whose plot her child had been buried.[133] The defence, by contrast, saw her as stonewalling their legitimate and legal rights as heirs, cooperating only when she stood to get something (like her *deuil*), and further as trying to tarnish the family image by burying her husband's body on the cheap in a common grave.[134] They probed her on her relationship with her husband: "A. ... I must have loved my husband, because I married him. Q. You always loved him? A. Certainly. Q. There was never any quarrelling between you? A. Like everyone else, some passing words, but never real fights."[135]

The animosity within the family towards Belzémire was evident in Mercier's testimony. After stating he was on good terms with the deceased, the most he could muster about Belzémire was "We had nothing against her."[136] Couillard too, while stressing that the principals had been on good terms with each other in the past, gave vague and somewhat terse answers that suggested relations had hardly been smooth.[137]

The argument at the restaurant over Alphonse's personal effects convinced the defendants that they should move the body, and at that point their animosity became manifest in their actions.[138] Their stated reasons for moving the body were so that Alphonse could be buried with his parents (which they felt was in conformity with his wishes, since he had paid to improve the plot), and also so that he would not be buried in a common grave.[139] Without informing Belzémire about what they were doing, they got the required permission from the archbishop and then filed an exhumation motion in Superior Court, asking to remove the body from the Belmont *charnier* to transfer it to the family plot in Lévis. By law anyone could present such a motion; to prevent unnecessary or unwanted exhumations, the motion was subject to the checks that it be accompanied by affidavits and, in the case of Roman Catholics, prior ecclesiastical authorization.[140] In the case of Alphonse's body those checks failed to operate as intended. The defendants presented their motion ex parte and made no mention that the deceased had a surviving spouse; Couillard seems to have advised the heirs that the scene at the restaurant showed that it was impossible to deal with

Belzémire, and his solution was to sidestep her completely.[141] Justice Charles-Édouard Dorion, with no reason to doubt the family's motives, granted the request on 16 April, and the body was duly moved and buried alongside the deceased's parents and sister.[142] Asked whether their actions were motivated by malice or a desire to get back at Belzémire, Mercier and Couillard retreated into legalism. Mercier saw nothing improper with going ahead with the transfer as they had, since the heirs had no legal obligation to inform the widow: "Q. You didn't think it would be at least decent to let her know? A. If it had been obligatory, that's right, but it was not obligatory."[143] Couillard's reason for not informing Belzémire was similar: "I didn't think I had to do so."[144] As to whether leaving her off the motion might not have indicated a degree of malice on the defendants' part, Couillard simply stated that he had "set out the facts honestly."[145] Asked whether he would have allowed the body to be buried at St-Charles if Belzémire had already procured a plot there, Mercier responded, "If she had that right, we would not have been able to prevent it."[146]

As this overview makes clear, the parties narrated their views of the family conflict using a variety of registers of discourse simultaneously, mingling appeals to emotion, to usage and propriety, and to legal rights and duties. If Belzémire's version leaned most heavily on emotion, and the defendants' version on legal positions, each combined different ways of framing the dispute. Before turning to consider how the courts dealt with the issues raised, it is worth pulling out the intertwined threads of feelings, propriety, and legal rights.

If we begin with emotion, the basis of Belzémire's claim in damages was the injury caused her by moving her husband's body. In her declaration, the defendants' actions were characterized as done with malice and the intent "to injure the plaintiff in her most dear and most intimate feelings."[147] Moreover, moving a body interfered with a widow's continuing relationship with her dead husband. It deprived her "of the consolation of easily being able to go to her husband's tomb and to care for it, as one has the honour to do for the dead who were dear to us," and it prevented a future reunion with him in the tomb.[148] She alleged no material loss in her declaration (indeed, the estate seems to have reimbursed all her out-of-pocket expenses from the funeral), but rather the emotional injury of anguish, intensified grief, and outright anger, as well as the harder to characterize interference with her rights, obligations, and powers that we will consider shortly. Still, in a reflection of the precarious position of many widows, her testimony mixed moral and pecuniary injury, indicating how closely linked emotional and material well-being were: "Q. The suffering you endured is worth at least $400.00? A. Certainly, and it all cost me lots of money. Q. I'm speaking of your suffering, the pain you had? A. Yes, and after all that, my health gave out."[149] She did not speak at any great length about her suffering (which, again, was not unusual in moral injury cases), but she did make it clear that she loved her husband. Naturally, therefore, the surreptitious move of his body caused her distress, coming as it did while her grief was still fresh, and intensified as it was by her in-laws' clear implication that she had not been a worthy wife.[150]

The defendants had to deny the injury and so could not concede that Belzémire might have had any justification for feeling misused or resentful. Their testimony, however, went beyond the strict needs of the litigation and evinced a high degree of obtuseness about a widow's suffering in the immediate aftermath of her husband's death. Octave Mercier, when asked whether he thought moving the husband's body without consulting or even notifying Belzémire might have caused her pain, responded, "No, I didn't think it would affect her much."[151] Couillard expressed surprise about being thrown out of the house when he and Mercier had asked "very politely, very gently" for Alphonse's clothes; he could imagine no other explanation for Belzémire's reaction than that she had been drunk.[152] Indeed, their testimony about Belzémire as drunk, ill-tempered, out of control, even indecent in her shouting and hostility created the image of a person whose feelings could be disregarded, as long as they were not supported by any formal legal rights. Belzémire's case depended on showing the judge that her claim of wounded feelings was reasonable. The defendants' case required convincing the judge that Belzémire's behaviour had forfeited any claims she might have had to participate in the decision about where to bury her husband's body.

The issue of the reasonableness of Belzémire's feelings linked closely with questions of proper behaviour, morality, and customs surrounding family relations. Which relationships counted, or which counted more: marriage or blood? That was a legal question, answered for the most part in favour of the latter by the CCLC (at least until the 1915 changes to successions law), but it was also – and for the parties perhaps more immediately – a question of propriety. Both sides made it clear that conduct had to be judged by social standards, and not just legal ones. The defendants, as in some of the family honour cases we considered in chapter 3, were claiming a power to police the family against unsuitable outsiders (or in this case, an insider whom they felt should be expelled). Belzémire did not fit in: she had shown herself to be "unapproachable" and "inflexible," someone acting against the interests of the family.[153] She, by contrast, was arguing that the power to decide where to bury belonged properly to the spouse, and that the law should conform to common usage. The burial decision thus became a focal point for a broader dispute over suitable relationships, proper behaviour, and acceptable treatment of family members.

Family was on both sides of the case, and the complex politics of burial brought it to the front. Henriette Jinchereau, Belzémire's sister, testified that the Jinchereau parents wanted everyone buried at St-Charles, and Alphonse and Belzémire's young child was already buried there alongside another sister; according to Belzémire the plot belonged to a brother-in-law.[154] On the other side, the defendants claimed to be representing the wishes of the Roy parents, who were already buried at St-Joseph along with the deceased's sister.[155] The usual practice was for a head of household to be buried in his parish, with his wife buried with him; this followed Roman Catholic canon law.[156] Individual situations made that custom fluid, the result, in part, of conflicting ideas about who belonged to a family, an issue brought to the fore by the ostensibly eternal decision of where a body was to rest. Henriette Jinchereau questioned the defendants' family argument by pointing out that the supposed "family plot" where the Roy parents were buried was actually owned by Mercier, an in-law, so "it's not a family plot."[157] The plaintiff herself doubted that upon her death she would be welcome among the Roy dead in the cemetery in Lévis, and given the state of matters by that point, her fears were no doubt well founded.[158]

Questions of family were influenced as well by views of the family's status and class and what sort of burial place was appropriate.[159] Each side accused the other of looking to save money on the burial. Belzémire's lawyer asked Mercier whether the decision to bury Alphonse with his parents was motivated less by reuniting the family than by saving the estate the expense of buying a plot at St-Charles.[160] The defence questioned Belzémire's statement that she was planning to acquire a plot; to them, the fact that she had not bought one, even by the time of the trial, was a sure sign that their brother would suffer the ignominious end of being laid to rest in a common grave (*une fosse commune*), the fate of those who could not afford a private plot.[161] Her failure to see to that most basic duty – a fitting burial for her husband – meant that she had shown herself to be unworthy by failing to live up to the conduct expected of a wife and widow. That argument echoed French law, where the widow's right to decide on funeral arrangements was generally established, unless it could be shown that she was unworthy.[162] It also reflected prevailing gender norms. As the defendants argued in their factum for the Court of Review, "The evidence establishes that the plaintiff is devoid of the intimate sense that reveals our conscience and our nature, since she showed signs of unworthy conduct, both from a moral point of view and from the point of view of the memory and pious attentions she owed to her husband."[163] Belzémire put things in a similar light, equating impropriety with malice: "Even if the defendants did not act with malice, … they certainly acted with a lack of understanding and with contempt for the most basic propriety and decorum, which certainly equates to malice."[164]

Finally, the case was not just about Belzémire's feelings at being treated as a stranger to her own husband and about conflicting views of what was a fitting burial for Alphonse. It was also suffused with the language of legal rights and obligations, and how they intersected with and inflected the emotional and social issues raised. That was mainly due to the lawyers' characterization of the case, but the parties picked up on it as well. Belzémire, in speaking about the decision of where to bury her husband, stated that Mercier "should not be involved; I was his wife, it seems to me that my husband ought to belong to me."[165] What belonged to her? Her husband's body? The power to decide the place of burial? The right to do so? She did not elaborate, but her answer expressed in informal terms the idea that a prerogative had been breached.[166] Octave Mercier was more explicit in using the language of rights, likely taking a cue from Couillard, who had seen to the liquidation of the succession and seems to have been the driving force behind the whole affair. When asked about the decision to move the body, Mercier's answer suggested that whatever the moral parameters of the situation, the existence of a legal right was enough for him: "Me, I don't want to make a fuss about this affair, I want it to be neat and clean, that we have the right to do that." Couillard, who seems to have suggested moving the body in the first place, had given him the assurance he was looking for: "We have the full right, from the moment His Grace signed with the judge, and it's you all who pay."[167]

The lawyers took those vague articulations of "rights" (somewhere between what was correct and what was legal) and turned them more explicitly into legal rights claims. In her declaration, Belzémire's lawyers asserted her "sovereign right ... to decide what to do with the body of her spouse and to choose the place of his burial."[168] The infringement of that right, they argued, in itself entitled her to damages, independent of the damages she was claiming for her suffering and the *injure* done to her.[169] The defence denied the existence of any such right, but at the same time asserted that their own rights, derived from their role as Alphonse's heirs, were predominant over any rights the plaintiff might claim.[170] (Later, at the Court of Review, they backtracked on that claim and argued that while ordinarily the widow had the pre-eminent claim, if she proved unworthy the right of other relatives should prevail.[171]) Their rights claim relied on the old idea that there could be no fault in the exercise of a right. Since they were simply exercising their legal rights (that is, the right of the heirs to seek authorization to move a body and determine where it was to be buried, in the absence of a clear expression by the deceased of his wishes), they had committed no fault and so could not be held liable for damages. In response, Belzémire's lawyers brought in the rather cutting-edge idea of abuse of rights, which had been developed in France in the later nineteenth century and was starting to make its way into Quebec law around this time.[172] The defendants, they argued, "exercised this right in an abusive way to prejudice the plaintiff's superior right."[173] That superior right was a widow's moral right to make decisions regarding her deceased spouse, regardless of the heirs' legal obligations. They developed their argument more fully in Belzémire's factum for the Court of Review, stressing the widow's right "to decide what to do with the body of her deceased husband and to choose the place of burial, to the exclusion of every other person."[174] Even if that right was nowhere expressed textually, it could be inferred from the moral foundations of the family and so was supported simultaneously by natural law, public order, custom, and proper sentiment. "This is an eminently respectable and absolutely universal sentiment, which demands that the union of the spouses be marked, up to the point of a common burial. This is a consolation for the survivor to know that when the call comes, he will go sleep the eternal sleep near the spouse taken away from his affection."[175] Such mingling of law, morality, and theology had a long history in Quebec, even if by the twentieth century it was seldom stated so expansively. It was a valiant attempt by Belzémire's lawyers to overcome the lack of a clear textual basis for their position, and at the same time to create a legal underpinning for the emotional and social aspects of her story. The rights she was asserting, then, were an amalgam of legal claims and norms of propriety. That characterization – as well as its theological rationale – worked to convince Justice Isidore Belleau at the Superior Court, at least up to a point.

In his judgment, Justice Belleau noted that he could not alone order the exhumation of the body (authorization by the ecclesiastical authorities was required also[176]), but he did rule that when the exhumation took place – and he expressed confidence that church officials would take into consideration the plaintiff's "primordial right ... sanctioned by this court" – it would be at the defendants' expense.[177] His decision focused instead on declaring the respective rights of the parties, and on finding that the rights of the widow trumped those of the heirs. As Belzémire's lawyers had argued, the issue was not strictly legal, but also moral, deriving "from a higher order of ideas, which takes its inspiration from the intimate relations created by nature, religion, and the law between the man and the woman united by bonds of marriage."[178] He went on to make it clear that though he was being called upon to juggle various balls – custom, religion, morality, law – this was a case where law must follow gut feelings confirmed by higher values: "It is repugnant to our intimate senses and to our Christian morals to declare that after death, no bond any longer connects those who so closely meshed their earthly existence, that they are henceforth to be strangers to each other and returned to their respective families."[179] Quebec was, after all, a "land where religious sentiment dominates, and where one can make the Christian note be heard."[180] In keeping with that sentiment, he quoted at length from Adam's words in Genesis, Christ's in the Gospel of Matthew, and Paul's in the letter to the Ephesians, all three to the effect that man and woman leave their parents to become one as husband and wife.[181] He also followed French authorities, and like them had no hesitation in declaring that the widow had a right to determine the resting place of her husband's body, even if he left vague the exact basis of that right.[182] It was, he said, a right that grew out of "feelings of family, respect for intimacy and affection, questions of morals, and custom."[183] The defendants, in complimenting Belzémire on the funeral service, could not then turn around and deny her right to make those arrangements.[184]

After recognizing Belzémire's right, however, he rejected her claim for damages entirely, finding she had suffered no injury. On a legal level, he refused to see the defendants' conduct in moving the body unilaterally and surreptitiously (at least from Belzémire's perspective) as motivated by bad faith or malice. Since they had gone both to the archbishop and the court and had obtained all the required orders, they were simply exercising a legal right they in good faith believed they had. He accepted without question notary Couillard's explanation for why they had failed to inform Belzémire, an explanation that must be considered disingenuous at best. Any sense that Belzémire's treatment – which Justice Belleau had just evaluated as contrary to secular, religious, and natural law – might have caused her some identifiable injury was absent. As in the other cases we have looked at in this chapter, judicial suspicion against "mere sentiment" was powerful, and since Belzémire's material outlays had been reimbursed, she had nothing further to claim.

The defendants appealed to the Court of Review, which unanimously affirmed the trial decision.[185] Five days before that, however, one final incident in the ongoing family conflict made it into the judicial archive. On 24 March 1914, Belzémire received a letter from the indefatigable notary Couillard, informing her that "the anniversary service" (note *the*, not *a* service) marking her husband's death would take place two days later, at the church of St-Joseph in Lévis. The letter was delivered late on the 24th for a service at eight in the morning on the 26th; its tone was suitably distant: "Madame: I have been tasked with telling you that the anniversary service for the late Mr. Alphonse Roy, your husband, will take place ..."[186] That sent Belzémire straight back to court to seek an emergency injunction to stop the service, arguing that since Justice Belleau had implicitly recognized that the rights regarding her husband's body belonged to her alone, that included rights to his memory, and her in-laws had no right to hold such a service. Should the service go ahead, she alleged further, she would suffer serious harm and irreparable damage. Justice François-Xavier Lemieux dismissed the motion on the grounds that the singing of an anniversary service could cause the petitioner "no real or moral injury."[187]

As a human drama, *Jinchereau* raised issues of proper conduct, feelings, and sensitivity within the context of antagonistic familial relations. As a legal drama, it revealed something of the transition taking place in our period, from an analysis focused on the result (the injury caused by the defendant's conduct) to one focused more, though of course never exclusively, on what in legal terms had been violated (the plaintiff's power or interest or, increasingly, right). *Jinchereau* was not a turning point: it was not the first case framing the issue of moral injury in terms of violated rights (we saw that already in some of the cases about honour), nor was it at all influential (it does not seem to have been cited in other reported cases). It does, however, suggest a new direction in the analysis of these cases, one that we will pursue in the next chapter, in the context of the injuries caused by discrimination.

7

Indignation, Anger, Fear

What emotions did discrimination provoke? The answer is complicated, since more clearly than most of the situations we have examined so far, discrimination raised a complex of emotions in its victims, some complementary, some contradictory. Those emotions varied according to the individual involved, the social and cultural context of the situation, and the time period. Psychologists who have studied contemporary discrimination and its emotions point to the overlapping nature of responses, but also to how reactions depend not just on the individual, but also on the situation and whether the discrimination was blatant or subtle. Anger tends to be the dominant emotion identified by victims, particularly when the discrimination is perceived as blatant or severe, and that anger often coexists with related emotions such as indignation, irritation, outrage, and frustration. But other, more subtle emotions arise as well, which point to less visible emotional states, such as the feeling of being disrespected or insulted, disappointment, sadness, and humiliation.[1] The contemporary literature also seeks to link the emotional states provoked by discrimination to responses or actions taken as a result. Much of the research focuses on trauma and the health effects of discrimination, but some points as well to an issue we will consider historically in this chapter: how individual feelings translate into action, particularly defiance of discriminatory behaviour or rules.[2]

Victims of historical discrimination, unlike participants in contemporary psychological studies, cannot, of course, be asked what they felt, and as we will see, at most they hinted obliquely at their reactions. Their responses to situations, however, can reveal much about their feelings if read with sensitivity to the slow development of legal terminology related to differential treatment of minorities. Today, discrimination-based prejudice is understood as arising from the violation of a right to equality or dignity, as one's equal humanity is questioned or denied through differential treatment. While it overstates the point to suggest that discrimination was an unthinkable argument in the early twentieth century[3] – as we will see, such arguments had some success, at least at the trial level – it was difficult to articulate the injury of discriminatory treatment. This was particularly true in a society that viewed hierarchies of various kinds (based on class, gender, education, or race) as natural and self-evident. The cases we will discuss in this chapter call the injury "humiliation" or "insult," which were the nearest commonly used legal equivalents to what I think were the emotions raised by the situations: indignation, anger, and fear. Compounding the problems with articulating the injury was the difficulty in winning such cases, since the claimed moral injury of discrimination came up against venerable and powerfully entrenched legal justifications like property rights and freedom of commerce. Those hurdles suggest why so few cases arguing discrimination were brought to court before the early twentieth century.[4]

This chapter will explore the emotions of discrimination by focusing on two different situations: race-based denial of service and hostility towards members of a minority religion. While the cases that follow were all individual actions for damages, the subjective feelings of the individual plaintiffs were both supported and shaped by collective political responses looking to effect social change. Such cases were on the boundary between individual prejudice and collective, politicized civil rights, and in them the emotional and the political mingled in interesting ways. They thus shed light on a different aspect of the early history of civil rights in Quebec than has been hitherto explored, on its personal rather than systemic aspects.[5] We will begin with one of the first reported cases of racial discrimination to appear before the Quebec courts in our period, in which a Black man hoping to impress a date was confronted with segregated seating in a Montreal theatre.[6]

No Blacks Allowed in the Orchestra Chairs: *Johnson v. Sparrow*

It started with a gratuity for a hard-working bellhop.[7] At the Queen's Hotel in Montreal, on Friday, 11 March 1898, a Mr. Swizzel gave two theatre passes to Fred W. Johnson, a twenty-one-year old Black man, in thanks for his service.[8] Swizzel was one of the managers of the New York theatre company in town to put on that week's performances of *A Stranger in New York* at the Academy of Music, considered Montreal's finest theatre. The Academy's co-owner, John Sparrow, was a local entertainment power player, whose close ties to Broadway interests regularly brought hit New York shows north.[9] *A Stranger in New York* was one such production, advertised as a "sumptuously staged" and "beautifully costumed" farce, featuring "dialogue original and witty" and "pretty girls."[10] Among the cast was a white actor playing Handel Grubb, "a colored waiter."[11] Such racist humour was a staple of the theatre of the time, and indeed the next show at the Academy was to be the ever-popular Al Field's Big White Minstrel Company, promising "lots of mirth."[12]

Johnson planned to take a date to the show, and so early Friday afternoon he went to the box office and exchanged his passes for two tickets in the orchestra chairs for Saturday evening's performance. He was hoping to impress his companion. As he later said, "When I am by myself I am not particular where I go, but when I buy tickets for a certain place, and have a lady with me, I like to give her the best I can get."[13] He had been to the Academy several times before and, he later testified, had on occasion sat in the orchestra chairs. The tickets for that particular evening gave the seat numbers and the date, and enjoined the bearer to "RETAIN THIS CHECK."[14] They did not, however, include any of the "management reserves the right …" disclaimers often found on theatre tickets. On Saturday evening the weather was bad, and according to the surviving box office record, the theatre's 1800-plus seats were far from full.[15] Arriving with his date, a Black woman visiting from Quebec City who was never named in the case file, Johnson presented his tickets, and then, he said, began to get the runaround.[16] After the doorman let him pass, the usher refused to take him to his seats, claiming that the seats were already occupied. He was then led out to the lobby to speak with Edwin Varney, the acting manager, who first claimed the tickets were for the matinee, not the evening performance, then that they were for the balcony only, and finally he refused outright to admit the couple. In court, the theatre presented a different story: that Johnson had simply been told all along that he had the wrong tickets. The lawyers for the defence also tried to get their own witnesses to say that Johnson had been rude or disruptive, without success. The usher in question testified that Johnson had been gentlemanly throughout, and that there had been no

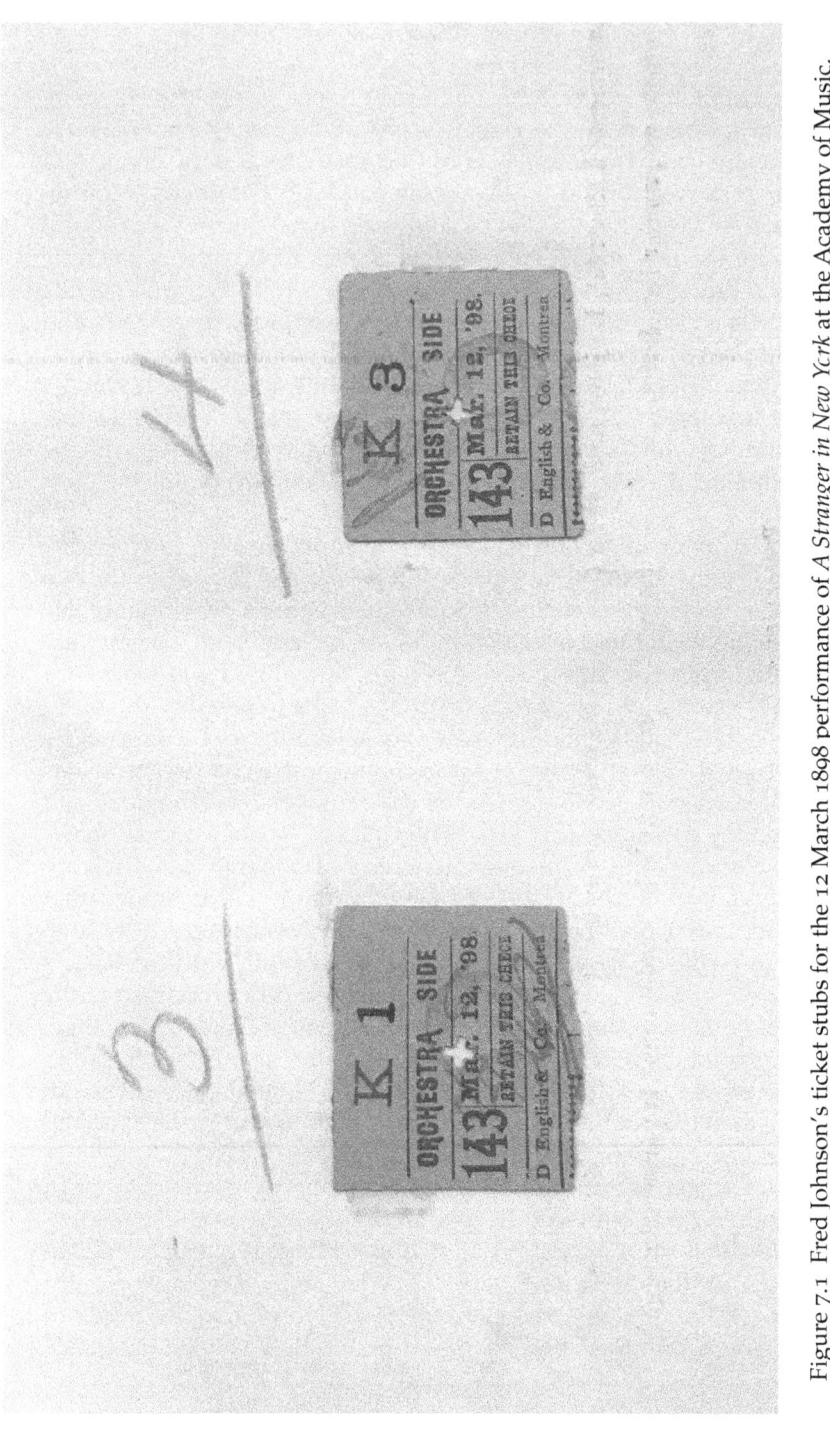

Figure 7.1 Fred Johnson's ticket stubs for the 12 March 1898 performance of *A Stranger in New York* at the Academy of Music, Montreal. BAnQ-VM, *Johnson v. Sparrow*, Superior Court case file, Plaintiff's Exhibits 1 and 2. Photograph by the author. Reproduced with permission of Bibliothèque et Archives nationales du Québec.

"loud talk or any scandal."[17] Some of the other defence witnesses gave a different picture: Varney, who had dealt with Johnson subsequently, testified that Johnson had snatched the tickets from his hand and said loudly that "he would have those or none."[18] After being barred from the Academy, Johnson tried to salvage the evening and paid fifty cents for a cab ride with his date to the Théâtre Français, a cheaper and less grand venue, where they saw a play called *Friends* and "the marvelous juggler O.K. Sato" instead. They watched that performance from the orchestra chairs.[19]

On Monday Johnson went directly to a lawyer, and three weeks later, he began proceedings against the owners of the Academy, alleging that they had had no right to exclude him, and that he had been "profoundly humiliated and insulted" by having been refused admission when he had a right to enter. Moreover, he claimed, his exclusion had attracted the notice of a large number of people at the theatre, and word of it had got back to Johnson's friends and acquaintances. The result was that Johnson "suffered damage to his reputation, his honour, and his feelings" in the amount of $500, plus a few dollars for the unused tickets and the cab ride.[20] Interestingly, Johnson's declaration did not mention that he was Black; that fact first came into the case in the defendant's plea. It was a clever strategic choice, since it allowed Johnson to focus on the unreasonableness of refusing someone holding valid tickets, while it forced the defendant to raise the issue of their segregation policy and to try to defend that as reasonable, which they did by arguing that it was necessary because of (white) public sentiment concerning a high-class theatre like the Academy.[21] That had the effect of downplaying the racial issue, and as in all such denial of service cases, the lawyers' wrangling focused mainly on contractual issues and the scope of the respective rights of ticket holders and business owners.[22] The theatre in its defence stressed how Johnson had got his tickets, alleging that he had misrepresented himself as picking up tickets for someone else. The defendants argued that a clear policy against Blacks sitting in the orchestra level was in place, that Johnson had been "well aware" of the rule, and that if he had said the tickets were for his own use he would never have been able to exchange the passes at all. Any unwanted attention was his own fault for arguing the point and refusing quietly to accept the alternative seats he had been offered.[23]

Johnson's action against the Academy of Music seems to have been spontaneous, a reaction to his anger and (perhaps) shame at the treatment he received in front of his date and other onlookers. Or was it? The defence clearly suspected it was a cooked-up affair and asked several of the plaintiff's witnesses whether they were in any way involved in bringing the case forward (which all denied).[24] When Johnson himself was asked in cross-examination to specify where in the orchestra he had sat on previous occasions, he could not say, answering, "I never dreamt of any such thing coming up as this case, and that I would have to prove that I had been there."[25] On its face, his answer suggests he had not been carefully planning a challenge to the theatre's discriminatory policy. It could, however, be strategic forgetfulness to avoid giving the impression that his alleged injury was the result of his own calculated actions. The theatre certainly argued that Johnson must have been aware of its seating policies and had deliberately defied them. Another possibility is that Johnson knew of the policies and was attempting what had worked for other Blacks before – trying to "pass" at the box office.

Test case or not, Johnson's challenge to the theatre's policy quickly drew in Montreal's Black community, and more particularly the Black railway porters who lived in the neighbourhood of Windsor Station. A social club for porters, the Recreation Key Club, mobilized in his support, and several of the club's officers and members testified at trial. Clubs like this were both somewhat controversial for moral reasons within the Black community, and a source of racist mirth to whites. An 1898 article described the Recreation Key Club as a place "where all types of Blacks gather to enjoy themselves. It is decorated in country style, people smoke Turkish pipes, they scrape around on the banjo, and they loaf about. There are also a number of billiard tables that offer not a little amusement for this exotic phalanstery." The article went on to report an incident in which a visiting American pulled a gun on another patron over a bet on a billiards shot.[26] The clubs were also early sites of community consciousness among Blacks that would drive future legal and political action. Johnson's lawyer brought in several of the club's members to establish that Black men and women had indeed sat in the Academy's orchestra chairs on numerous occasions. In cross-examining each of the witnesses, the defence carefully tried to dissect the visual politics of skin colour, to distinguish degrees of darkness and establish percentages of mixed blood, all in an attempt to show that light-skinned Blacks might easily pass unnoticed at a busy box office, or that they were admitted only for certain kinds of show (minstrels particularly). The following shockingly racist exchange between the theatre's lawyer and the Recreation Key Club's secretary George Wilson illustrates the typical flavour of the questioning:

> Q: What race do you belong to?
> A: The negro race.
> Q: Are you a full blooded negro?
> A: Well, they count me that.
> Q: I want to know as a matter of fact? Was your father a negro?
> A: Yes.
> Q: Was your mother a negress?
> A: Partly.
> Q: What proportion?
> A: On her father's side.
> Q: Her mother was a white woman?
> A: Yes.
> Q: You say your father is a negro?
> A: Yes.
> Q: Was he a full-blooded negro?
> A: No sir.
> Q: What proportion did he have of negro blood?
> A: Between a Mexican and a negro, but lighter than Mr. Johnson and darker than Mr. Renfrew [another witness].
> Q: You yourself are very fair in complexion?
> A: Yes.
> Q: And almost a white man?
> A: But I do not get there.
> Q: Were those ladies you took with you somewhat of the same complexion as yourself?
> A: No sir, the two young ladies I had taken there before March were a little darker; one of them I would say was lighter than Mr. Johnson, a kind of Indian colour.
> Q: About the shade of Mr Renfrew?
> A: No sir.
> Q: Between Mr. Renfrew's shade and Mr. Johnson's?
> A: Yes, but not nearly as fair as Mr. Renfrew.
> Q: You are even fairer than Mr. Renfrew?
> A: Yes, but he has got straight hair.
> Q: You keep yours pretty short?
> A: I have to sometimes.

Q: So on both sides of your family, both on your mother's and father's there is white blood?
A: Yes.
Q: Did you take your hat off when you bought your tickets?
A: No sir.[27]

Such questioning must hardly have surprised the Black witnesses, and its absurdity was evident not just to the witnesses. At one point the plaintiff's lawyer, in cross-examining the manager of the Academy, asked whether the theatre kept colour tint cards in the box office to compare complexions. The witness denied this, but affirmed that their rule was "the colour has to be strong," no doubt a practical precaution to avoid mistakenly challenging the race of a white patron.[28] The legal import of introducing testimony on skin colour was not to establish discrimination. Rather, it was to determine whether the theatre had in the past knowingly sold tickets to Blacks and seated them on the main floor, which would have made their refusal to seat Johnson in those same seats unreasonable.

Alongside the technical points arose some broader issues that suggested the culture of discrimination in Montreal at the time. Clearly the segregated seating policy at the Academy had not been cooked up on the spot that evening to deny Fred Johnson and his date their seats, and the theatre never suggested as much. The defence argued that the differential treatment based on skin colour was not motivated by malice on their part, but rather came from their white clientele and the needs of commerce. They argued that "the Academy of Music is a Theatre of high class order and in fact the best in the City of Montreal and is attended by the best class of people and leading citizens of the City and in order to comply with the demands of public sentiment colored persons are not admitted to that part of the Theatre known as the Dress Circle or Gallery – all of which is a reasonable rule or regulation and was well known to Plaintiff."[29] The theatre manager testified that he personally would have admitted many of the plaintiff's witnesses: he suggested that to avoid potentially giving offence to "white" people with darkish complexions, he would err on the side of permissiveness, which could mean that some "coloured" people might slip through the net. He went further still: when asked if coloured patrons were "well dressed, and polite," he responded that they were "very nice people as far as I know; I would just as soon have them as anybody else, and never had any reason to complain of them.… I never had any better people in the house."[30] In news coverage of the hearing, he was reported as spelling things out clearly: "I have nothing against the negro, but I don't want him in the orchestra of the Academy of Music. I can't afford to displease hundreds of my patrons for the sake of allowing one negro to establish his right to sit where he pleases in my theatre."[31] The operative assumption of the staff, as the Academy's assistant treasurer testified, was that any Blacks coming to ask for orchestra tickets were servants.[32]

Johnson's lawyers countered all that by stressing malice as the only explanation: since he had a right to a seat, refusing him entry was done specifically to humiliate him.[33] As usual, there was no direct testimony by Johnson or any other witness on how policies such as the Academy's affected them, aside from Johnson's assertion that he had been humiliated. But Johnson's testimony included a few subtle hints at his emotional reactions to his treatment, hints that help flesh out the meaning of humiliation in this case. He was clearly wary of the defence counsel during cross-examination, for instance. At one point he made a defensive answer when asked about his previous visits to the Academy of Music, when he claimed to have sat in the orchestra chairs: "Q. You do not pretend to remember those tickets[?] A. I secured them honestly."[34] By turning a question about his recollection into a challenge to his integrity (which it may well have been), Johnson was pushing back against the implication that he was not worthy to attend that theatre or sit in its best seats. Later, he voiced a sense of mild bewilderment about the discrimination. He asserted that he had been unaware of any policy regarding Black people at any theatre in Montreal. On questioning, he admitted that the Academy of Music claimed to be the best theatre in town, and when asked whether it might have had policies that the other theatres did not, his response was telling: "Why did they impose it on me?"[35] Though he did not make the point explicitly, he was hinting at his common humanity, citizenship, and rights, the denial of which was the source of his humiliation.

Unusually, newspapers covered the hearing of the case, and they picked up on these broader issues. In headlines and commentary, they made clear that the case was really about rights, and they vaunted the Canadian commitment to the ideals of British justice and its supposed egalitarian values, congratulating white Canadians while noting that those ideals did not always accord with social or commercial practices.[36] *La Presse* published a long editorial that ascribed the segregation at the Academy to a pandering to "Yankee" sentiments brought north by American clientele, "because Canadians hold no prejudice against

Blacks, no aversion!" Citing the bravery of Black regiments in the recent Spanish-American War, the editorialist reminded his readers of the relevant ideals:

> It is strange to note that among a people endowed with the most liberal institutions and going off to war to liberate oppressed peoples, a citizen of colour cannot sit next to a white on a bus or in a theatre, even though that white might be the worst of hooligans and the Black one of the heroes of San Juan....
>
> A Negro who knows how to conduct himself is ten times more agreeable as a neighbour than a white who behaves badly. A sober Negro is preferable to a white who stinks of gin and tobacco.[37]

A Quebec City newspaper voiced similar sentiments: "Under British law, all men, no matter what may be their color, are supposed to enjoy equal rights. Of course, everyone knows that in practice this is not precisely the case, but we have the theory at all events."[38]

Justice John Sprott Archibald's judgment was both typical and striking for its time. Archibald's career suggests he might have been unusually receptive to the issues at play in the case of the young Black man before him. Before being named to the bench, he employed as a stenographer at his law firm Sui Sin Far, the Chinese-British author born Edith Maude Eaton, and supported her first efforts at writing and publishing, albeit in a rather patronizing way that reflected her gender more than her ethnicity.[39] At some point he delivered a lecture entitled "Relations of the Two Races in Lower Canada," though details on what he said are lacking.[40] Archibald's formal ruling in *Johnson* was solidly within the expected boundaries of the law. Whatever regulation the theatre may have adopted, he found that it had not been made public and so had been unknown to Johnson. He found that the theatre's exclusion of Johnson and his companion was a breach of contract that "involved some expense and much humiliation," and he awarded Johnson $50 and costs. The judge went beyond breach of contract, however, and suggested in his holding that the case was also about rights: "Considering that defendants had no right to make any regulation excluding negroes from their theatre or from any part of it, and that any such regulation was and is unreasonable and illegal."[41] In his discursive reasons, however, read out in court, included in the reported judgment, and covered in the newspapers, he went further still, in a remark with significantly wider implications: "I should certainly hold any regulation which deprived negroes as a class of privileges which all other members of the community had a right to demand, was not only unreasonable but entirely incompatible with our free democratic institutions."[42] The Montreal *Gazette*, however, was less taken with these sentiments and noted that although "it is not a creditable prejudice" that leads white patrons to refuse to sit next to Blacks, "it is a prejudice that amusement caterers have to take sharp recognition of, at the risk of losing patronage."[43]

Justice Archibald's remarks were not without precedent. Barrington Walker has shown that Ontario judges at this time employed tropes of British justice and equality of citizenship in criminal cases involving Black defendants, both to demonstrate paternalistic mercy and to justify pitiless rigour, depending on the circumstances in different cases. Black defendants themselves at times couched their own entreaties in terms of their common humanity, whether while on trial in court or when faced by angry mobs threatening to lynch them for a suspected crime.[44] As Lyndsay Campbell shows for English Canada, however, that rhetoric was fading, particularly as the Supreme Court and the Privy Council were sending strong signals that racial equality could be ignored.[45] In the Quebec civil courts, judges of the time were more reluctant to read citizenship rights broadly, as the Court of Queen's Bench demonstrated when the theatre's appeal came before it. The newspapers continued to present the case as about citizenship and rights.[46] But in court, the appeal allowed both sides to sharpen their rhetoric and focus on presenting issues in ways more likely to appeal to an appellate bench. The appellants explained that their policy was "a reasonable one," given that theirs "was the leading theatre in this city and catered to the best class of theatre-goers," people who demanded racially exclusive seating.[47] In response to the plaintiff's many Black witnesses who at trial had testified to having sat in the orchestra chairs at the Academy, the theatre assured the judges that the reason was that "a number of them had but very slight traces of being coloured, and that, as a fact, some had but a small percentage of negro blood in their veins." Any others were surely in the habit of buying their tickets just before curtain time, when the box office was busiest and employees most distracted.[48] Further, the only time Blacks were allowed to sit in the orchestra chairs was during minstrel shows, when rules were relaxed because "a different class of people visited the theatre on such occasions."[49] They were careful not to reject Justice Archibald's expansive rhetoric about British freedoms, but they argued it did not apply to this case: "If all men are free under the British flag, all men are not equal, nor do all men possess equal rights and privileges.... The respondent is a free man, but his freedom does not deprive Appellants of their rights to conduct their business in their own way. If Respondent does not like that way he can avail himself of his freedom and stay at home."[50] In sum, the theatre had "a perfect right to adopt the regulations in question," while a ticket holder had "no absolute right which he can enforce."[51]

Johnson's team carefully played to their audience of conservative appellate justices. In their written submission they ignored the toehold Justice Archibald had offered them. However tempting a rights-based argument might have been, they conceded that there were no basic rights that could not be surrendered by consent or nullified by a contract of adhesion. Once that concession had been made, the only way to proceed was via the technical point of the terms of the contract: an officer of the theatrical company putting on the play had given Johnson a valid pass, and that officer had the right to bestow that pass on whomever he chose. The tickets issued to Johnson included no disclaimer, and no seating policy was posted at the theatre.[52]

The justices dismissed the appeal, but they explicitly rejected the trial judge's rhetoric on racial equality.[53] They also rejected Johnson's evidence that other Blacks had sat in the orchestra chairs before: those examples were all, Justice Joseph-Guillaume Bossé found, "mulattoes, quadroons and even octoroons, and these last especially are easily confused with whites."[54] The justices refused to go beyond holding that the theatre had never announced its claimed policy to the public, and that a contract had been made between the parties, which the theatre had violated without valid reason.

Johnson, for his part, vowed never to return to the Academy of Music.[55] His case had some impact, both in Quebec and beyond, a testament to its novelty and to the prevalence of racial discrimination throughout Canadian society. Justice Archibald's judgment, while hardly a full-blown call for civil liberties, went further in recognizing discrimination for what it was than most other judges would for decades. His remarks in *Johnson* were singled out for mention both when he was rumoured to be in the running for chief justice in 1914 (he was named associate chief justice instead) and when he died in 1932.[56] Despite that praise for the white judge's decision, however, future Black plaintiffs found the case to be a shaky foundation on which to build their own challenges to segregation.

Refusal of Service Cases: Successes at Trial, Reversals on Appeal

Fred Johnson's success in court – tempered, but success nonetheless – was followed by a few similar challenges to racial discrimination in Quebec over the following decades.[57] Like *Johnson*, all involved Black plaintiffs who had been refused service in cinemas or taverns where discriminatory policies either excluded Black patrons altogether or segregated them once inside. Discrimination was likely practised against other groups and in other contexts such as public transit, but those seem not to have been brought to court in Quebec in this period, at least from the evidence of reported cases. The post-*Johnson* refusal of service cases present a disappointing story of legal doors opened slightly by trial judges, only to be forced shut by higher courts, most notoriously by the Supreme Court of Canada in *Christie v. York Corporation*, its 1939 decision that locked the door on racial discrimination actions in Quebec (and indeed elsewhere) for decades after.[58] Like *Johnson*, its successors mixed individual moral injury with individual and collective pressure for legal and social change. Separating those threads is difficult, and probably counterproductive. The personal and the political mingled, and individuals' emotional and other responses to racism resonated with other Black Montrealers to create community consciousness that spurred political action.[59] Also as in *Johnson*, plaintiffs encountered powerful legal and social arguments against their claims. Defence arguments about contract and property rights invited judges to brush aside arguments about discrimination and its effects in favour of a technical reading of formal legal principles, while social views of the self-evident naturalness of hierarchy, racial and otherwise, would have made it difficult to challenge differential treatment based on what later came to be called discrimination.[60]

The first reported case after *Johnson* came up in 1913, when a Black man, John Delmour Curl, was refused admission to the new Imperial Theatre in Montreal.[61] On 10 July, Curl was out with his wife for an evening of music, ready to enjoy the performances of Rae Eleanor Ball, billed as "The World's Greatest Lady Violinist," and the tenor "Signor Manetta."[62] After buying two orchestra-level tickets at the box office, the couple were refused admission at the door, without explanation. Curl, a former resident of Halifax where such segregation was common, no doubt understood why.[63] The theatre offered him a refund, which he refused, and the couple left. The following January Curl sued the owners of the theatre for $1000 damages, alleging that he had been "grossly insulted" by the treatment he and his wife had received at the door. For reasons today obscure, after the unusually long delay in launching the action, the case dragged on quietly for the next couple of years, finally coming to life and to resolution in early 1917.[64] Eventually, on the day before the trial was to be heard, the defendant offered to settle the case for $50, which Justice Charles Archer dismissed for technical reasons.[65] The case went to trial, and after hearing Curl, his wife, and one other witness, the judge found for Curl and awarded him $50 damages, the nature of which he left unspecified. As for the basis of the decision, it was strictly breach of contract: Justice Archer found no valid reason for the refusal to honour the tickets. The defendant's explanation – that they suspected Curl had been with a woman who was not his wife (more about this shortly) – failed to impress the judge.

What did Curl feel about all this? The case file does not survive, so we must rely even more than usually on reasonable inferences drawn from the few surviving clues about the situation at the theatre. Most significant was a fact unmentioned in the judgment and in the news coverage that followed it. In an earlier article at the time of the institution of proceedings (a stage that warranted coverage only for the largest cases or those with a human-interest angle), the reporter in *Le Devoir* noted that Curl's wife "is white, not just in parentheses, but really."[66] In other words, she was a white woman, and not a light-skinned Black who might "pass" as white at the box office. As a Black man, Curl's having a white wife was, in the eyes of many at the time, clearly transgressive, even if it was not illegal, though the Black witnesses in *Johnson* made it clear that in the 1890s at least there was considerable dating between Black men and white women.[67] The marriage itself was noteworthy: Eunice (Truman) Curl was the daughter of a white fisherman from Hackett's Cove, a small town just west of Halifax.[68] How she ended up marrying a Black railway porter is unknown. The theatre employees' assumption that Curl's companion was not his wife doubtless rested on the racist understanding that a Black man could not have a white wife. The bogus matrimonial standard applied to Curl's companion seems clearly to have been an attempt to shift the employees' response from race towards morality, though the latter itself rested on racist fears of miscegenation. Furthermore, Curl's (or his lawyer's) characterization of the action – that he had been "grossly insulted" – offers further hints about the emotional side of the case. On the one hand, as with Fred Johnson fifteen years earlier, for Curl to be treated as he was in front of

Indignation, Anger, Fear 273

Figure 7.2 Imperial Theatre, Montreal, under construction, 8 February 1913, photographed by "W.W.K." McCord Museum, MP-1977.140.18.1. Reproduced with permission.

his wife – rejected both as unworthy to enter the theatre but even more so dismissed as a possible mate for a white woman – would have been humiliating, demeaning, and angering. On the other hand, Curl seems to have raised a broader point in his case as well, which suggested different aspects of the gross insult he suffered. As the same *Le Devoir* reporter put it, "John Delmour Curl is black. As black as he is, he is just as much a British subject as it is possible to be. That is why he claims he should be treated with all the respect ordinarily given to people of that kind."[69] That argument, suggesting fundamental rights of citizenship and hinting also at the broader idea of common humanity, rested on the guarantee in article 18 CCLC: "Every British subject is, as regards the enjoyment of civil rights in Lower Canada, on the same footing as those born therein, saving the special rules relating to domicile." We saw similar points voiced during the *Johnson* case by the editorialist at *La Presse*, among others. And just as the higher court in *Johnson* balked at such a broad reading of the issues, in *Curl* too, the final judgment remained entirely silent on the rights of citizenship.

As far as we know, Curl's challenge to segregation at the Imperial Theatre was his own, motivated by his personal reaction to the treatment he and his wife had received. The sketchy details in the press contain no hint that he had any connections with or support from Montreal's Black community in pursuing his case, though of course that cannot be ruled out. The long delay in instituting proceedings might itself suggest that influence (and funding) from others eventually pushed Curl to take the matter to court. Similarly, his refusal of the offered refund might simply have been a reflection of his indignation, or it could have been a sign that he was planning legal action and was both making a point not to acquiesce in the terms set by the theatre and looking towards the public airing of the issues in court. Still, the late 1910s were years of growing organization and activism within North American Black communities, and Montreal was no exception.[70] The year 1917, when Curl's judgment was handed down, was crucial for Black activism in Montreal. That fall and in the months following, three political associations began operations in the city: the Colored Political and Protective Association, the Association of Universal Loyal Negroes (predecessor of the National Association for the Advancement of Colored People), and Marcus Garvey's Universal Negro Improvement Association. Though they were ostensibly rivals for members and influence, and they drew on different parts of the Black community (long-time Canadians, recent American immigrants, and West Indians respectively), the three associations did cooperate at times. One example was a series of actions in 1918 targeting the racially segregated seating policy at Loew's Theatre in downtown Montreal.[71] A letter to the editor of *The Gazette* in September 1918, written by a member of the Colored Political and Protective Association, called attention to discriminatory seating and differential prices at Loew's and other theatres in Montreal. The writer noted that Montreal's coloured citizens were solidly behind the war effort, and so they could not "remain passive" before "this Prussian-like spirit."[72] Two separate instances of exclusion, similar in general terms to *Johnson* and *Curl*, were brought before the courts that year, and those cases illustrate still more clearly how personal emotional injury and collective political action intersected in the issue of discrimination.

The first incident took place on 26 January 1918 and was explicitly a test case against Loew's by the Colored Political and Protective Association.[73] A pamphlet produced by the association at the time to drum up support for the case appealed to readers: "You offered your life in the Great War because Democracy and Justice were the watch-words. Will you not join hands with hundreds of your own Race to secure redress for wrongs done to us?"[74] Solomon "Sol" Reynolds, the Black assistant manager of the Standard Club for Canadian Pacific Railway porters, was sent to the theatre to be refused entry. He was accompanied by two white men, his landlord Albert Lachaine and L.R. Sénécal, who were there both as witnesses and to establish differential treatment by afterwards counting empty seats in the orchestra level.[75] Reynolds purchased an orchestra-level ticket; he was careful to request and pay for his ticket himself.[76] Inside the theatre, he was told by the "blonde girl" taking tickets, "We are not allowing colored people to sit downstairs," even though many hundreds of downstairs seats were empty in the cavernous hall.[77] Reynolds refused to sit upstairs and declined a refund of his ticket price; he then left the theatre while his companions stayed behind counting seats.[78] Two weeks later he sued Loew's for $500 for having been "grossly and publicly insulted and humiliated" by his treatment, which resulted in "serious injury to his feelings and reputation."[79]

The second incident followed on 19 November later that year.[80] Norris Dodson, a Black chemist who had studied at the University of Michigan and was at the time working in Montreal in the defence industry, was out to Loew's with his wife and four friends, all Black. Dodson and most of the others had passed the ticket taker when the darkest member of the party was pulled aside and told to wait. Dodson turned back to object and got into an argument with the ticket taker, whereupon he was taken outside, either "like a lamb" (the theatre's version) or "in a very rough way" by grabbing his neck and arm and shoving him (his side's version).[81] He sued the theatre for $1000 for "the great humiliation, loss, damage and injury" he had suffered, "aggravated in consideration of Plaintiff's high standing and position."[82] Dodson's was less clearly a test case, but some witnesses testified that everyone in the party was aware of Loew's segregation policy and the other cases (meaning *Reynolds*) that had recently begun challenging it.[83] Immediately after the ejection, William Gates, who testified that he had himself never been refused admission because of his light skin colour, went into the theatre to count empty seats in the orchestra level. That prompted a sceptical grilling from the defence lawyer: "So within one or two minutes of the incident occurring you were preparing for the future event of investigating conditions, without the issue being raised?" Gates's answer was evasive, though he repeated several times: "We saw what we were up against."[84] The party also made a point of not asking for a refund, to forestall the anticipated argument that they had consented to the exclusion. Whether that was a spur-of-the-moment strategy to help Dodson or a planned way to set the groundwork for a test case, their actions show growing consciousness within Montreal's Black community about strategies for challenging discrimination and what sort of evidence would be needed.

Both Sol Reynolds and Norris Dodson framed their complaints in similar terms, specifically that they had been humiliated before an audience of onlookers. Both cases also hinted in revealing ways at how legal and political points mixed with personal reactions to the discrimination. Reynolds was most explicit. Asked on discovery (by the defence) why he set his demand at $500, he responded, "I don't know. I think it is worth $500.00 to have my feelings hurt in this way, in this free country, – not only myself, but the whole population of Montreal." In court, he backed off from that expansive claim somewhat, but still noted (this time in response to a question by his own lawyer) that the injury of discrimination transcended the individual: "I figure my feelings were hurt to that extent, and the feelings of my friends."[85] The similarity in the two answers likely indicates that he was coached on this point, but even so, his answers suggest how his personal emotional reaction would have resonated with a broader community used to similar treatment. To be denied what a "free country" granted to others was humiliating; the dollar amount was an estimation of just how humiliating. But the planned nature of the case created problems that the defence exploited. Why would he deliberately return to a theatre that had on past occasions hurt his feelings? His answer, "To make a case against the theatre," was frank, but left unexplained the emotional issue the question brought up.[86] Would it not make more sense for a victim of insult to avoid a situation he knew would multiply the insult and the feelings it provoked? One of Norris Dodson's witnesses voiced the same issue in the other case, when asked whether she knew that Loew's had a discriminatory admissions policy: "I heard some were getting by and I certainly would not have gone there had I known I was going to be refused."[87]

Norris Dodson testified more briefly than Reynolds and was not asked at all about his injury. Still, the situation as narrated in the testimony of various witnesses points to why he responded as indignantly as he did. His reaction to the refusal to admit his friend was, according to the ticket taker, put in terms of rights: "That man is a friend of mine; he is with me. He has just as much right in the theatre as I have."[88] The manager was summoned, and the ticket taker explained the situation: "Look who he has with him," pointing at Roderick Wiseman, a young Black medical student and by far the darkest of the party.[89] Dodson's reaction to that dismissive characterization of his friend was predictable, but resulted in his own removal – whether gentle or not, it was physical – from the premises after he had already passed through. The defence witnesses all testified that Dodson was talking in a loud voice, was "very much excited," and "would not listen to anything." All the white witnesses dismissed Dodson's reaction as unreasonable.[90] The ticket taker testified that "if he had walked in and gone to his seat like a gentleman there would be nothing done to him."[91] The manager raised a similar point: "He just kept on arguing.... I told him to go in about his business and we would take care of Wiseman ourselves. He seemed to be interfering with the management of the theatre."[92] All missed or ignored the reasons for Dodson's angry and indignant reaction (though as hostile witnesses one would hardly expect otherwise): the insult to his friend in front of a large number of onlookers, and the implied insult to his own respectability as an educated and upstanding citizen. The Black witnesses understood the incident differently, of course. Aside from Dodson's indignation, his friend William Gates stressed the peremptory and physical way in which the theatre handled the incident: "If my party had been asked in a courteous way to leave they would have left."[93]

Against this, the theatre's argument in both cases was that they had a clear right to determine seating within the hall at their discretion, and that the ticket was a contract that allowed entry only, not a specific seat. The losses in *Johnson* and *Curl* were lessons learned for Montreal's segregators, and the theatre carefully refined its position in response. The president of the theatre made clear that the policy was strictly about business: "It does not apply to colored people necessarily, because we have no feeling in the matter of the colored question. It is purely a matter of satisfying the majority of our patrons." He himself, he testified, actually preferred sitting in the mezzanine, suggesting an odd "separate but superior" interpretation of segregated seating. Segregating on the basis of skin colour, he argued, was really no different from excluding smelly labourers coming to see the show right after work.[94] The focus on breach of contract kept the emphasis on the factual situation, rather than looking at equality or the meaning of discrimination. Equal rights were mentioned in the press, and apparently in the courtroom hearings as well, but the legal wrangling was mostly about rights of a different and more limited kind: the rights of a business to set its own policy, and the much more limited contractual rights of a patron to service. The lengthy examinations of witnesses in both cases about whether the plaintiffs were causing a disturbance (an invitation to judges to consider norms of propriety) or were blocking the entrance (an opening to think about norms of safety) focused debate squarely on whether management had reasonable grounds to exclude. Whether plaintiffs had reason to be upset was beside the point. One suspects that exploiting the emotions involved was a deliberate house strategy for enforcing discrimination and segregation. The theatre would make an unreasonable request – telling Sol Reynolds to go to different seats than ticketed because of his skin colour, or ordering the darkest member of Norris Dodson's party to stand aside to await management's pleasure – and then expel anyone who questioned or resisted or refused to leave.

The two cases were heard the same week by Justice Thomas Fortin and were joined for deliberation.[95] He found in Sol Reynolds's favour, since nowhere in the theatre or on the ticket had the defendant announced a restricted seating policy, nor had Reynolds been warned personally about any such policy. The ticket for an unreserved seat gave Reynolds the choice of sitting in either the orchestra or the mezzanine, and skin colour was no justification for forcing him to sit in the latter. He awarded Reynolds $10 "nominal" damages, not for any humiliation or other injury he might have suffered personally, but because the theatre's policy was "illegal" and for the symbolic reason that "in this country the colored or white people are governed by the same laws and enjoy the same rights, without any discrimination whatever."[96] Despite equal rights, only nominal damages were warranted because, the judge wrote, Reynolds knew going in that he would not be allowed to sit in the orchestra level, but persisted nonetheless.[97] Though Reynolds's behaviour made sense within a community strategy to challenge unjust and humiliating policies, to a judge it smacked of consenting to be humiliated, something that clearly undermined a claim for moral damages.

Norris Dodson had not even symbolic success. Justice Fortin found insufficient proof that the reason for the expulsion was that Dodson and his wife were Black; rather, the defendant's version of events and explanations of motivation were "more in accordance with the real facts and more credible and ought to prevail."[98] As in *Reynolds*, credibility and reasonability went hand in hand, and both were defined by a white man's idea of how one might react in such a situation. The judge seems to have had a hard time understanding why Dodson would have been upset that his darker companion was denied entry, when he himself had already been able to pass. Dodson's own argument showed frustration – anger, really – at the unjustified exclusion of his party. The cause of his reaction was not his own expulsion from the theatre – that occurred only after he got angry – but the exclusion of a member of his party on racial grounds. The theatre's characterization of the incident as involving a disruptive patron who was blocking a narrow hallway and causing a fuss was an invitation to Justice Fortin to sidestep the race issue and the emotional injuries it would be reasonable to assume it caused, an invitation the judge readily accepted in dismissing the action.

Both cases were appealed, and both received support from organizations within the Black community in Montreal and further afield. The Colored Political and Protective Association made a call for contributions in the *Canadian Observer*, a Toronto newspaper with wide circulation among Canada's Black communities, urging all to "show that the Negroes in Canada are entrenched, and willing to fight and kill the monster discrimination, which is threatening not one but all the Negroes throughout the Dominion." The editors agreed, decrying that there were "too many pious people among us, who take insults and slams as a mere instant." Action was needed, and "the time has come when we must stand for our rights, and the fair-minded people of Canada are willing to give us our rights, if we have the courage and the conviction to make a stand for them." The target was to raise $1000 to fund both appeals.[99]

Before the Court of King's Bench, the breach of contract arguments were front and centre, but the racial issue was raised as well. Dodson was represented by Robert Stanley Weir, English lyricist of "O Canada," while Reynolds was represented by Laflamme, Mitchell, and Callaghan. The two appeals bore some general similarities in argument, suggesting that the lawyers consulted each other but worked largely independently. Reynolds led with breach of contract, but added the argument that in cases of "oppression" like this, damages were not strictly compensatory and may "impose a punishment on the Defendant as an example to the community."[100] Dodson, for his part (or his lawyer's), similarly devoted most of the space in his factum to breach of contract, labelling the racial issue a "subsidiary" point. But his argument too ended with the question of damages, and an interesting appeal to the justices "to assess the damages as a jury would," by which he presumably meant focusing on humanity rather than strict legality. The theatre's race-based exclusion, he argued, was "most reprehensible, humiliating and public. Their present defense is disingenuous, an attempt to conceal their policy of discrimination against coloured people." Exemplary damages, he submitted, were necessary to "emphasize the principle of equality before the law."[101]

In separate judgments handed down on the same day, two slightly different configurations of the Court of King's Bench each found in Loew's favour.[102] The justices made a point of putting both Black men in their place. Chief Justice Gustave Lamothe blamed Dodson for "his own obstinance," informing him that he "had no right to rise up against the established order." Dodson's reaction allowed all the justices to assert that the case was not about race at all, but rather was an unreasonable personal reaction to a clear policy. It mattered not, Justice John Edward Martin said, whether Dodson was "white, black or yellow," though as Justice Louis-Philippe Pelletier helpfully pointed out, he was "a Black – or rather a mulatto." None addressed the question of injury, though Justice Robert Greenshields commented, "If he suffered any damage, I fancy he should know where to place the blame. If he repeats his performance, he probably will meet with the same treatment, and the same result will follow."[103] In *Reynolds* too, even more so than in *Dodson* because it was a test case, the justices chastised the plaintiff for bringing it all on himself. The management, Justice Pelletier asserted, could make whatever seating rules it liked, and given the proof that the presence of Blacks kept whites away, the defendant was hardly obliged to lose revenue in the name of idealism. Justice Martin rejected any idea that discrimination might cause harm: theatre policy must conform to "public policy or good morals," and segregated seating clearly conformed. Justice Henry George Carroll was the lone dissenter in *Reynolds* (*Dodson* was unanimous), on the grounds that the theatre had violated a firm contract. He did, however, acknowledge that whites and Blacks had the same rights and obligations in Quebec, and that the way Reynolds, "a man of good education," had been treated had seriously injured his feelings.[104]

Following the defeat in the two appeals, a mass meeting of Montreal's Black community was held in January 1920, at which it was decided to raise funds to take the matter to the Privy Council. The cost proved prohibitive, however, and the judgments stood; vague plans to launch further test cases seem to have come to nothing.[105]

After the discouraging results of the *Reynolds* and *Dodson* appeals, court challenges – at least reported ones – stopped until the famous *Christie* case twenty years later. In 1932 newspapers reported an intriguing criminal assault case involving a white racehorse owner visiting from Kentucky who struck a Black stable-hand across the face with a horsewhip, claiming the youngster had used for his own entertainment some money the man had loaned him to help his ailing mother. The judge, in fining the American $20, stressed to him that whatever the customs in Kentucky, in Canada "the law protected all, irrespective of colour." The press agreed, lauding Canadian justice in terms reminiscent of the editorial in *La Presse* about the *Johnson* case. As a Windsor, Ontario, paper put it, "The Montreal judge's attitude will have the hearty backing of the Canadian public.... There is no sympathy in this land for a social system which reduces one section of the human population to the status of mere animals."[106] With the courts effectively shut to denial of service cases, the Montreal Black community looked to other avenues to push for reform – particularly politics, under the influence of the more radical organizations like Marcus Garvey's Universal Negro Improvement Association that became active in Montreal in the years immediately following the *Reynolds* and *Dodson* cases.[107]

Given this history, when denial of service was next challenged in the Quebec courts in the unsuccessful *Christie* case, the outcome would have been disappointing, but hardly surprising. In July 1936, Black chauffeur Fred Christie and two friends, one Black and the other white, were refused service at the York Tavern in the Montreal Forum for the explicit reason of skin colour.[108] The two Black men, Christie and Emile King, sued the owners of the tavern for $200 for the humiliation they had suffered in being refused in front of other patrons. Christie won at trial: Justice Louis-Philippe Demers found that hotels and restaurants "have no right to discriminate between their guests" since they provided a public service, and Christie "has been humiliated by this refusal." He awarded Christie $25 and costs. (King's action was dismissed without costs, because unlike Christie he had not actually offered to pay for any beer.[109]) The judges at the Court of King's Bench were once again less receptive. The majority of four all agreed that, as Justice Gregor Barclay put it, any humiliation Christie suffered was "not actionable, because it is committed in the exercise of a right" on the part of the tavern, namely its freedom of commerce. Christie moreover had brought the humiliation on himself, since "he was told politely that he could not be served, and it was upon his own insistence only that the reason was divulged and it was owing to his own actions that the reason obtained any publicity."[110] Justice William Bond went so far as to assert that he was "not called upon to express any opinion upon the abstract philosophical concept that all men are born equal."[111] Justice Antonin Galipeault dissented, finding that in the face of a humiliating refusal, Christie had comported himself "as a gentleman," and that as a respectable British subject, he had as much right as anyone else to pay his money and receive his beer.[112]

The Supreme Court of Canada, in one of its least shining moments, dismissed the appeal, largely adopting the same reasoning as the Court of King's Bench. Even the lone dissenter, Justice Henry Davis, would have allowed the appeal not on substantive grounds, but only because the operative licensing legislation in Quebec was insufficiently specific to allow a licence holder to refuse service on racial grounds. After *Christie*, refusal of service was a dead issue in the Quebec civil courts, as the weight of the Supreme Court's ruling would have discouraged plaintiffs from bringing cases of discrimination forward, at least in the absence of significant changes to the legislative landscape, which Quebec was slow to undertake.[113]

The denial of services cases reveal a complex intermingling of emotions, politics, racial attitudes, norms of comportment, and formal legal rules. That so few of the judges ruling on the cases – even most of those who referenced the equality ideals of British citizenship – were prepared to recognize that discrimination might cause humiliation or other moral injury is in striking contrast to most of the other cases we have examined. In other kinds of cases, judges embraced self-evident moral injury with little or no evidence beyond their intuitive empathy for certain plaintiffs who were similar to them. In cases of race-based injury, however, situations that Black plaintiffs and Black witnesses saw as unmistakably humiliating were beyond the experience of white judges. The Black plaintiffs alleged the moral injury of humiliation that arose from their having been treated as lesser human beings. Judges, or some of them anyway, could see the injustice of treating Black patrons differently, and might even (like Justice Fortin in *Reynolds*) assess nominal damages as a (rather mild) punishment. They could not, however, understand or articulate the injury in those cases.

Most of the judges did not even go that far. Judges in the upper courts almost unanimously reached for ready rationalizations that allowed them to deny any racism, while at the same time uphold the discriminatory policies of business owners. Their rationalizations provided both a plausibly formalist basis on which to the dismiss the cases, and an apparently neutral way to deny the plaintiffs' affective concerns like humiliation or indignation. In *Reynolds*, for example, politics made it easier on the judges: they could implicitly invoke a form of *volenti non fit iniuria* (no injury to the willing) to argue that if one went looking for trouble, one should not be surprised to find it. In *Dodson*, the rationalization was different: the justices found that Norris Dodson's reaction to his treatment – to get a bit heated and raise his voice in indignation – disqualified him from any recompense. Those were feeble rationalizations, when we consider that they allowed judges to dismiss genuine emotional responses that, had the plaintiffs been white, would undoubtedly have been accepted without question. Sol Reynolds's reaction was unjustified because it was just a political stunt; Norris Dodson's and Fred Christie's responses were likewise to be rejected because, well, they responded – Dodson by making clear his indignation, Christie by politely inquiring as to the reason for his exclusion. Euphemia Tudor, by contrast, who voiced her own indignation in strong terms, saw her claim unquestioningly upheld by a judge who accepted it as the justified reaction of an upper-class white lady in the face of questionable treatment by a social inferior. The difference was that in cases that brought up values like honour and propriety more clearly linked to the white social world, judges could understand the injury on a personal level, even if there were class or gender differences they had to negotiate. The harms of race-based discrimination, however, were something with which white judges had little experience, whether personal or legal.

Even if the emotions failed to sway most of the judges, however, they did serve a crucial role in mobilizing collective action against discrimination, and this points to a different role emotions played in this socio-legal world. Though the cases were about the alleged humiliation of Black individuals like Sol Reynolds or Norris Dodson, other Black men and women could identify emotionally because they too had been victims of similar treatment. The feelings raised by exclusion – the tense uncertainty about whether one was light enough to "pass" in the eyes of white observers, the discomfort of being singled out in front of onlookers, the frustration of being denied entry to the best part of the theatre – were emotional responses that all Blacks shared as part of an emotional community.

While the racial discrimination Fred Johnson and the others experienced provoked feelings of indignation and anger, other situations of discrimination were designed to elicit other reactions, notably fear. To be in a minority was to feel vulnerable – always, but particularly within an actively hostile majority, and more especially when that majority was supported by a state that did not just look the other way, but that actively condoned the majority's hostility and reinforced it legislatively and administratively. Such was the situation of various minority groups within Quebec. Communists, Jews, trade unionists, pacifists, and Jehovah's Witnesses were all subject to harassment by the state and its agents and by private citizens alike.[114] For the Witnesses in particular, the sense of vulnerability would have been especially strong, since they went door-to-door in pairs, often within small communities where they tried to convince members of other faiths of the error of their ways, employing pointed and frequently offensive language to do so. Threats of mob violence were ever present. A photograph from September 1945 shows Witnesses Frank Roncarelli and his son being driven from Châteauguay, south of Montreal, by an advancing mob, with two menacing-looking police officers at its head. Frank, who a few months later would famously challenge Premier Duplessis over the cancellation of the liquor permit for his popular Montreal restaurant, holds up a hand as if to try to halt the advance, while his son looks over his shoulder nervously.[115] Another physical instance of mob intimidation against Witnesses occurred in Joliette in December 1949.

Get Out of Town: *Lundell v. Masse*

Maurice Duplessis declared a *guerre sans merci* (war without mercy) against the Jehovah's Witnesses in 1946, which brought the full weight of the premier's considerable power to bear against the group's members through a campaign of harassment and arrests calculated to drive them from Quebec entirely.[116] Police, liquor authorities, and local mayors and councillors were among the state agents charged with pursuing the campaign against the Witnesses' supposed subversion, blasphemy, and sedition. The foot soldiers of the war, however, were local citizens who objected to the Witnesses' door-to-door proselytizing and their often stridently critical views of secular government and organized religion, Roman Catholicism in particular. Citizens were stirred up in these views by newspaper and radio coverage of the activities of the Witnesses, coverage that depicted their views in the most negative light possible, tracked their movements, and eagerly reported on the arrests and prosecutions of individual members. Lines were deliberately blurred: the Witnesses' proselytizing was characterized in exaggerated terms as full-blown sedition, and their theological ideas were seen as both an anarchistic threat to social order and a diabolical imperilling of the souls of good Catholics.[117]

Joliette, a small city about sixty-five kilometres northeast of Montreal, was one location where battle was engaged. A local weekly, the clerically associated *L'Action populaire*, provided its readers with a short history of the Witnesses and a summary of their supposed beliefs, published in December 1946, a couple of weeks after Roncarelli's liquor licence was cancelled in Montreal. The article, under the pseudonym "La Frontière," included statements such as "For them, all the world's religions are the work of the devil. They alone have truth in all its purity. They especially have it in for the Catholic Church. For them, the pope is just about the most diabolical thing after Satan himself." If they found themselves persecuted, the article went on, the Witnesses would have only themselves to blame, and should not be surprised if the government they condemn as diabolical should send the police to "restore them to reason." The author closed on what was undoubtedly supposed to be a tolerant note: "Let's endure these people with whatever patience we are able, but let's not allow them to pervert our youth. With God's grace, Canada has always remained true to the faith of its ancestors."[118]

By 1949, matters in Joliette had reached the boiling point. Sometime during the spring, two Witnesses, thirty-two-year-old Olive Lundell of Maidstone, Saskatchewan, and twenty-three-year-old Winnifred Parsons of Sarnia, Ontario, moved into town to pursue their evangelical mission. Described by locals as strangers who nevertheless spoke passable French, the two self-described "Ministers and Evangelist Missionaries" went door-to-door, passing out leaflets, playing recorded speeches on a portable gramophone, and asking to teach the Bible to residents.[119] They preferred speaking to women, and eventually always turned the discussion towards the errors of the Catholic Church. When engaged in debate, according to one hostile observer, they shrugged their shoulders and claimed their French was not up to understanding the question. Citizens began complaining to police, inspired by the message coming from Quebec City that linked the teachings of the missionaries to sedition. The local press took up the complaints and amplified them, warning readers about "this infernal plague" that legal means seemed incapable of combatting.[120] In August, two female "propagandists" – unnamed but likely Lundell and Parsons – were arrested on the complaint of several residents "tired of their solicitations." The women were quickly released, but residents noted that the two returned immediately to their work.[121] Possibly connected to the events that followed, on Sunday, 11 December, at a meeting of the members of Joliette Local 32 of the artisans' union, the "very thorny" question of the two Witnesses was discussed "at length." Members described themselves as fed up with the women's questionable theology. Ominously, after debating the matter in open session with journalists in attendance, the reporters were asked to leave and the discussion continued behind closed doors.[122]

A few days later, on Wednesday evening, 14 December, some male citizens of the city took the *guerre sans merci* into their own hands.[123] A group of around twenty young men surrounded the women while they were on their rounds and forced them to the city's bus station. When the mob discovered that the Montreal–bound bus had already left, they pushed the women into Fortunat Masse's taxi, five other men piled in after, and they drove Lundell and Parsons out of town, towards Montreal.

The menace of the event would have been palpable, though the two women were familiar with those sorts of tactics, albeit in milder form. Word had been going around Joliette that something was planned, and Lundell and Parsons had been warned by several of the people

14   TORONTO DAILY STAR: Thurs., Dec. 15, 1949

TORONTO, SARNIA GIRLS RUN OUT OF JOLIETTE BY MOB

(Continued from Page One)

per cent Roman Catholic here, and it was like putting dynamite in the place. For myself, I felt they should be free to carry on, and resisted efforts of some to have the girls sent away."

Warned for Some Time

Winifred Parsons in Montreal said there had been warnings to leave town for some time. "Police Chief La Pierre himself told us to get out, and I know nothing of reports that he has invited us back under police protection.

"Last night we received a call from a lady interested in our teachings. We made a call first at another home, and noticed a car draw up behind us. Then as we walked through town we saw about 15 men walking in pairs on the sidewalk. But we expected nothing, and were leaving the lady's house when these men suddenly appeared below the veranda.

"They asked us to leave in 24 hours. We refused. They then gave us until 6 the next morning, and we again refused.

"We were then told that if we remained more than five hours, we would be taken 50 miles farther out of town for every succeeding hour."

Witnesses said the girls showed no alarm, and agreed to walk to their apartments with the men. They were taken instead through back streets to the outskirts.

Discussed Getting Possessions

"They hollered 'Jehovah' behind us, and though we walked fast, they kept shouting to us to go faster. Finally we stopped and there was a discussion about getting our possessions," said Miss Parsons. "Then a taxi drove up and six of the men bundled us in with them."

It was then very dark and cold. "The man sitting beside the driver started a prayer," said Miss Parsons. "The others chanted it with him. The language later grew foul, and when we reached Montreal we were taken first to Fullum St. women's jail, then to No. 13 police station and finally to Ontario St. where we were turned out."

WINIFRED PARSONS
Possessions Abandoned

OLIVE LUNDELL
... As Two Kidnapped

Figure 7.3 Winifred Parsons and Olive Lundell. *Toronto Daily Star* (15 December 1949), 14. Reproduced with permission of the Toronto Reference Library.

whose homes they had visited.[124] They were seasoned missionaries and no strangers to Maurice Duplessis's war. Both had been arrested several times in Montreal in late 1946 during the crackdowns on pamphlet distribution that ultimately led to the *Roncarelli* case: Lundell three times for peddling without a licence, Parsons twice for the same offence and once for soliciting without a licence.[125] More recently, in February 1949 both had undergone a similar forced expulsion from Edmundston, New Brunswick, when they and two other Witnesses had been surrounded by a mob, marched to the train station, and deposited on the Quebec City–bound train. Since the four had little money, the mob generously took up a collection to pay their way, then surrounded the station until the train had departed, to the light of a bonfire of Witnesses pamphlets.[126] The physicality of the Joliette kidnapping was new, however, and far more ominous. Bystanders reported that the women showed no signs of alarm as they were marched towards the taxi, with the crowd shouting "Jehovah" at their heels and pushing them to walk faster.[127] But fear would certainly have been a natural reaction once they were confined in a car with six strange men, being driven they knew not where. The men debated throwing them in a lake – it was December, recall – but rejected that in favour of driving them to Montreal and demanding their incarceration. The discussion in the car went in an even more sinister direction, if the Witnesses' highly polemical newspaper *Awake!* is to be believed: "Uproarious, devilish laughter greeted the suggestion by the driver that these two Christian lady evangelists be forcibly violated by the Catholic, prayer-reciting criminals who had abducted them. The automobile was then stopped in the darkness and the prisoners ordered to get out. A hurried conference was held which evidently changed the wicked and warped minds of their captors, and the two missionaries were ordered back into the taxi without being molested."[128] The judge later made veiled reference to those plans ("words that it would not be suitable to repeat here"), suggesting that it had indeed been discussed.[129] When they were not debating their captives' fate, the men filled the time en route by chanting liturgy and praying for the souls of their involuntary guests. Taxi driver Masse at one point asked about his fare; one of the others paid him $10, enough for expenses, but not the regular cost of the trip. Masse continued on his way.

In Montreal, the taxi called first at the Fullum Street women's prison, in the east end of the city, where the men were told that walk-in clientele were not accepted. Around the corner at Police Station 13, they again demanded the incarceration of their captives. The officer on duty, Hilaire Anctil, no doubt bemused by the request, claimed the municipal police had no jurisdiction to lock up "the undesirables of other municipalities."[130] Anctil's response says much about the recent history of the Witnesses in Montreal: while he did say the posse might consider releasing their captives, he also suggested they could ask the provincial police about other options. The taxi proceeded onwards. When the men failed to locate the provincial police outpost, they simply left the two women on the street in Montreal and sped off into the night, back to Joliette.

Lundell and Parsons returned to Joliette the next day, determined to defy the mob. "'With Witnesses encountering persecution and difficulties everywhere,' they said, 'we are willing to accept the risks here.'"[131] They brought with them Paul Couture, one of the leaders of the Witnesses in Quebec, and Toronto lawyer Glen How, who was making a name for himself as the Witnesses' chief counsel challenging Duplessis's *guerre sans merci* in the courts. Couture and How approached the Joliette chief of police, Valmore Lapierre, about the incident. Lapierre's response was less than enthusiastic: "The people of Joliette are aroused … These Witnesses are persistent.… If they file a complaint against the people who want to get rid of them and have some peace, I fear the mob's reaction. Unfortunate things might happen, like during our last strike."[132] He offered to help Lundell and Parsons gather their things so they could leave town for good, but beyond that he could not guarantee their safety.[133]

The following week, at a meeting of the municipal council on Monday, 19 December, the question of the Witnesses in Joliette dominated the agenda. The local Knights of Columbus, supported by notary Jean Fontaine, presented council with a draft resolution and a petition signed by more than two hundred residents, demanding the immediate expulsion of Lundell and Parsons from the city and a complete bar on further activities by any Witnesses.[134] The propaganda of the Witnesses, Fontaine argued, was a first step towards Communism and must be stopped. After brief discussion, with frequent chants and catcalls from the overflow crowd, the councillors unanimously passed the resolution. At that point – the theatricality was deliberate – Glen How rose and began speaking (in English), but was ruled out of order. One of the councillors instructed the police chief to remove How and Couture from the chamber, but the two left willingly. Outside, locals – around five hundred, reported Canadian Press – made sure How and Couture got into their car, which was escorted on its way back to Montreal by a phalanx of other cars packed with locals. Lundell and Parsons, afraid the mob might burn their rooming house, left town as well, under police escort.[135] A reporter and photographer for the *Toronto Star* were themselves forced into a car and driven out of the city.[136] The excitement over for the evening, the council moved on to the more mundane question of whether to require that all taxis be insured.

Lundell and Parsons launched various legal actions, especially once it became clear that criminal kidnapping charges were not forthcoming.[137] In response to the resolution of Joliette city council, they brought actions in defamation against the city of Joliette, notary Jean Fontaine and twelve other members of the Knights of Columbus, and the two weekly newspapers (*L'Action populaire* and *L'Etoile du Nord*) that had covered the affair in particularly hostile terms.[138] All four actions were dismissed two years later, with Justice Joseph Jean finding that nothing had been said that was directly defamatory towards the two plaintiffs, only to the Jehovah's Witnesses generally.[139] Our focus here is two further actions that resulted more directly from their enforced trip to Montreal, in which Lundell and Parsons each sued three of their captors jointly for $8000 damages resulting from their treatment.[140] There had been six in the car, but the women could not identify the others. Moreover, the ringleader of the whole scheme had apparently slipped away into the crowd before the cab started on its way, and the defendants were not volunteering his identity.

The three defendants were hardly thrill-seeking teenagers.[141] Labourer Roch Rouleau was the youngest at around twenty-three. Gédéon Dion was thirty-seven and a prominent Joliette merchant, while taxi driver Fortunat Masse had owned his cab since the 1930s and was likely in his forties. Only Masse appeared in court, filing a separate defence that argued he was just a simple cabbie trying to make a living. The other two were deposed out of court and retained separate representation from Masse. The plaintiffs, for their part, were represented by the Montreal firm of Albert Louis Stein and Samuel Stein, which handled many of the Duplessis-era civil liberties cases, assisted by Glen How, the regular counsel of the Jehovah's Witnesses in Canada. The rapid involvement of the Steins and How was a testament to the organization of the Witnesses during that period of suspicion and persecution.[142] It also brought the case within the broader political and legal strategy of the Witnesses in Quebec. A.L. Stein immediately sent a telegram to

Premier Duplessis, demanding investigation into the "brutality toward two girls 20 years old [sic]" and into the violation of their "freedom to think and express the opinion of their choice."[143]

In April 1953, Justice André Demers upheld the women's actions.[144] He rejected Masse's simple cab driver defence outright: he found that Masse had held the door for the women, negotiated his payment, and in general could not have failed to see that a criminal act was taking place. As for the other two, it was their deliberate and calculated insults to the women that struck the judge. Dion, when asked why they had decided to drop the women at the police station, replied, "That was a place where women of no fixed address were kept." Such an obvious attempt to connect Lundell and Parsons with streetwalkers was not lost on the judge, who saw it as having "grossly insulted" the women. Rouleau went even further by suggesting the sexual assault. The judge saw all three men as effectively traitors to the proud history of "three hundred years of liberty" by "those who came to clear and colonize our great land and who even spilled their blood to build it." Though none of the three was the ringleader – they were, the judge said, just "pale stooges" – their eager participation in the shocking events of that evening made their liability incontestable.[145] Though Justice Demers was clearly scandalized by the defendants' conduct, he nevertheless sharply discounted the plaintiffs' damages claims and rejected any pecuniary loss, since the women's missionary work was unremunerated. He awarded Lundell and Parsons only $300 each against the three defendants jointly. He also added, no doubt upon the specific demand of the plaintiffs' lawyers, a prohibition on the defendants from any further interference with the plaintiffs' lawful activities in Joliette. The defendants did not appeal.

Beyond the specifics of this case, matters continued as before for the Witnesses in Quebec. A year before judgment was rendered, Olive Lundell and an unnamed colleague were surrounded by more than 150 bicyclists in Arthabaska while the women were going door-to-door. They demanded police protection, which the chief eventually granted, sending a patrol car to make sure nothing untoward happened.[146] A few weeks after Justice Demers's decision, Cardinal Paul-Émile Léger, archbishop of Montreal, denounced the Witnesses to a meeting of the Catholic social action group Action catholique, calling them "fanatics" and "fierce adversaries of the Church."[147] And ten years after the kidnapping of Lundell and Parsons, when word of the Supreme Court of

Canada's decision in *Roncarelli v. Duplessis* reached Joliette, local mayors emptied their own pockets to help the premier, sending him $525, which they hoped he would put towards the expense of appealing the decision to the Privy Council.[148]

What of the emotions in the case? In the absence of the case file we do not have even the cryptic hints afforded in other cases. The coverage in the *Toronto Star*, which interviewed Parsons at length in the days following the incident, noted only that the women seemed unfazed while being pursued by the mob that evening, but that upon their return to Joliette in the days following, they feared physical violence and so thought it prudent to leave town. We are thus in the realm of inference and reasonable interpretation of responses to situations, common terrain for the historian of emotions. Various factors would have shaped Lundell and Parsons's reactions to their ordeal. On the one hand, they had experienced similar mistreatment, albeit in milder versions, and their millenarian theology, which taught them to be prepared for imminent salvation, would certainly have offered them a degree of solace and courage.[149] On the other hand, the attack would have underscored in stark terms the vulnerability to which they were constantly exposed in their missionary work. As a religious minority within a predominantly Catholic city, and particularly as women on their own, their safety and their reputation alike depended on the unreliable tolerance of a largely hostile community. In his judgment, Justice Demers focused mainly on "the insults and outrages" committed against the two women, both the physical deprivation of "that which they held most dear: the right of each individual to the liberty of the person," and the situational slander of treating two virtuous young women as prostitutes.[150] The damage was purely moral, but moral damage always had an emotional side. The legal characterization as insult and outrage captured only some of the injury suffered: fear engendered by vulnerability was part of it, but fear and vulnerability were hard to put into legal terms, since they spoke to potential rather than actual damage. But it is certainly not going too far to suggest that two women forcibly detained in a car by six men openly debating whether to throw them into a frozen lake or to sexually assault them would be frightened.

Justice Demers's decision illustrates a move away from the language of sentiment and feeling, a shift in terminology that was becoming increasingly evident in cases like this around the middle of the twentieth century. His judgment rested on the traditional and well-established basis of insult and outrage, but at the same time also on a newer idea of the violation of individual civil liberties. The latter was the core of the plaintiffs' position, presented to the court by A.L. Stein and Glen How, both of whom were central figures in the growing post-war attention to civil liberties.[151] The links being made in the case between liberty of the person and insult provided a way to characterize the situation that avoided the fluid subjectivity of sentiment in favour of the language of rights. That same language of civil liberties was argued in the other Jehovah's Witness cases from Quebec, though the reception by the Quebec judiciary was cool in most of the cases.[152] Lundell and Parsons succeeded where most of the Jehovah's Witnesses cases failed (at least until they reached Supreme Court of Canada), because the allegations were so egregious that it was virtually impossible to rule any other way. The existence of the rights being invoked – more security of the person than freedom of worship or conscience – were relatively uncontested even at the time, so it was hardly a stretch for a judge, even a conservative francophone Catholic, to agree that they existed and needed protecting.

The kidnapping of Olive Lundell and Winnifred Parsons came as a shift was occurring in the legal analysis of moral injury. The sentiments, feelings, and emotions that had been the focus in moral injury cases were beginning to be supplemented with an emphasis on rights and freedoms. In large part that was due to a more explicit articulation of developments that had been evident for most of our period. As we saw in chapter 1, the language of "right" and "no right" as applied to defendants was a common shorthand for fault, with the "no right" formulation being particularly prominent. By the middle of the twentieth century, the argument had shifted in cases such as *Lundell* from what the defendant did not have to what the plaintiff did have: interests that were often referred to as rights. Alongside that continuity, however, were signs of something new in the mid-twentieth century: a movement of the language of rights and freedoms from public into private law. An editorial about the Lundell and Parsons affair from the Toronto *Telegram*, reprinted in the *Sherbrooke Daily Record*, made that connection explicitly: "Canadians who respect rights of free speech, free assembly and worship cannot look with complacency or disinterest upon recent events in Joliette, Que." It went on to link what had had happened to the two women to the constitutional cases involving Jehovah's Witnesses that were making their way through the courts at the time, and in particular to Justice Ivan Rand's remarks about "the unchallengeable rights of Canadians" in the Supreme Court of Canada's recent decision in the sedition trial of Aimé Boucher.[153] We will take up this issue in the concluding chapter; here it is enough to stress that while the language of fault and injury was changing, emotions continued to shape proceedings through the reading of situations and the mostly unstated application of self-evident social norms.

8

Conclusion: From Wounded Feelings to Violated Rights

Lurking around the edges of the stories of wounded feelings, moral injury, and *injure* throughout this book were rights. Sometimes they were expressed, as in the "right" to determine where to bury a loved one's body that we examined in chapter 6, but more often they were implicit, a logical but unstated counterpart to the much more common "no right" formulation discussed in chapter 1. If the defendant had a right, the plaintiff was out of luck and had "no right" to do or demand (or feel?) whatever he or she was claiming. In those rare cases when the discussion turned to what the plaintiff had, judges tended to articulate it in terms of intangible *biens* like reputation or family honour or virtue, not as some kind of right that had been violated. One can point to exceptions, of course, and we will look at some below, but it was mostly in the mid-twentieth century, the end of our period, that the idea of private-law subjective rights began to take shape in Quebec and to change the way that moral injury was analysed. This concluding chapter will continue the analysis begun in chapter 1 of how moral injury was discussed in legal terms by sketching the broad outlines of the history of personality rights in Quebec law.

We might begin in the middle of the story, with an 1898 case in which Justice Michel Mathieu developed a distinctive perspective on the nature of rights and their place within the law of civil liability and damages. Mathieu was a particularly academically minded judge, more likely than most of his contemporaries to bring a degree of doctrinal

Figure 8.1 Justice Michel Mathieu of the Superior Court of Montreal, c. 1900. BAnQ, P1000, S4, D83, PM60. Reproduced with permission of Bibliothèque et Archives nationales du Québec.

Conclusion: From Wounded Feelings to Violated Rights   297

sophistication to his rulings. His résumé attests to a prodigious work ethic. Alongside his judicial duties on the Superior Court, he taught civil law at the Université Laval in Montreal; he continued as editor of the *Revue légale*, a periodical he had helped found in 1869; he worked on the *Rapports judiciaires révisés de la province de Québec* from 1891 to 1905; he published a number of treatises and editions of Quebec's various codes; and he reportedly began work (never completed) on a local edition with commentary of François Dareau's classic treatise on *injure*.[1] In the case in question, *McCuaig v. Cité de Montréal*, the owners of a private hospital sued the city for refusing to transport a patient with smallpox to the city hospital, with resultant damage (they claimed) to their health and their business.[2] The plaintiffs moved for a jury trial, for which they argued they were eligible because their action involved "*torts personnels* / personal wrongs."[3] In parsing those problematic terms (which we introduced in chapter 1), Justice Mathieu discussed the nature of wrongs in a striking passage, worth quoting at some length:

> Since wrongs are simply an infraction or violation of rights, it follows that the negative system of wrongs ought to correspond and fit with the positive system of rights. As all rights are divided into rights of persons and rights over things, wrongs should likewise generally be divided into those that affect the rights of persons and those that affect property rights. The rights of persons are divided into absolute rights and relative rights. Absolute rights belong to men in particular, considered simply as individuals, in isolation. Relative rights are those with which men are endowed as members of a society, and as linked to others by different ties or relationships. The absolute rights of each individual are the right to personal security, the right to personal liberty, and the right to personal property. In consequence, the wrongs or *injures* that harm those rights ought to be of a corresponding nature.
>
> The wrongs or *injures* against the personal security of individuals attack either their life or their body or their body parts; their health; or their reputation.[4]

He was evidently taken with his reasoning, since he repeated it word-for-word three days later in his judgment in a case about coercive imprisonment (*contrainte par corps*). This was an issue that depended on the similar terminology of "*injures personnels* / personal wrongs." He repeated it subsequently at least one more time in another *contrainte* case.[5] Mathieu was clearly grappling with the question of rights within private law in the passage, an issue he had raised in different terms in an 1887 judgment, *Brissette v. Boucher*, about defamation via false arrest. In that earlier case, he had written "That, if being subject to damages requires having committed a harmful act, which does not derive from positive law, in the same way, in order to be able to claim reparation, one must have been injured in an acquired right, either personal or real. *Personal* rights cover any attack on liberty, reputation, and honour, while real rights cover attacks on property."[6]

By linking wrongs and rights in that way, as two sides of a liability equation, Mathieu moved beyond the limits of the "no right" conceptualization of liability, language he himself had employed in some earlier decisions.[7] Whereas "no right" left the nature of the plaintiff's injury unspecified and focused instead on the question of the defendant's fault, Mathieu complemented the negative idea of a wrong with the positive idea of a right, the latter being something the plaintiff held whose violation supported the injury caused by the fault. In that way, he related the violation of health in the hospital case and the violation of liberty in the false arrest case to the plaintiffs' absolute right to personal security, a capacious right that for Mathieu comprised life, body, health, and reputation – most of what the old idea of *injure* covered.

Where those "absolute rights" (*droits acquis personnels* in the earlier formulation) came from Mathieu did not say – he was writing a judgment, after all, not a treatise on natural rights. But he was clearly drawing on European theory, and in particular on the French jurist Auguste Sourdat, from whose important treatise on civil liability he borrowed mostly word-for-word the passage from *Brissette* quoted above. For Sourdat, basing damage on a violated right separated it from "simple proprieties, unrealized hopes, in a word expectations." The law attached no consequences to the violation of such vague interests, since "the damage would not be appreciable."[8] Other European authors – such as William Belime and Émile Beaussire in France, Ernest Roguin in Switzerland, and Heinrich Ahrens in Germany – expressed similar ideas over the course of the nineteenth century, drawing on natural-law traditions to articulate within private law the existence of fundamental rights.[9] Roguin, for example, categorized the "legal relations that bear on the personality of the active subject" into rights to moral integrity, moral activity, physical activity, and bodily integrity. Those rights "have the distinctive character that their material object is the individuality itself of the active subject, and they are moreover classed as absolute rights, since all legal subjects form the passive subject, because a certain forbearance imposed on them constitutes the juridical object of the right."[10] The rights these authors were discussing were conceptually related to the *biens innés* we introduced in chapter 1, but were reconceived as rights that were attached to the legal subject and that juridicized aspects of the individual's personality.

Building on those antecedents, the French jurist Édouard Perreau first set out the idea of personality rights in an influential 1909 article.[11] Drawing also on the sort of cases we examined in this book – mostly moral injury of various kinds – Perreau enumerated a list of personality rights that the French courts had protected. They included rights of the individual as individual, such as rights to liberty and honour; rights of the individual as member of a family, such as rights to paternal authority, to a name, and to a coat of arms; and rights of the individual as member of society, such as rights to a nationality and to vote. The crucial elements, he argued, were that personality rights were opposable to all (they were *erga omnes*) and could not be evaluated in monetary terms (they were extrapatrimonial).

Perreau's reconceptualization of aspects of the personality like name, reputation, and bodily integrity as a new kind of subjective right analogous to others like the right of ownership was criticized by various authors who saw it as doctrinally incoherent. Though arcane in its details, the debate was important for our purposes in one key respect. Roger Nerson, most prominent among the critics, drew on Friedrich Carl von Savigny to argue that the aspects of the human personality that Perreau termed "rights" were in fact simply interests that the law protected. Far from being absolute or natural rights, those protected interests solidified only following a judgment, at which point a right to recover damages appeared.[12] Rather than carving the personality into fundamental rights, Nerson argued, what we had were specific factual situations, which should be treated as such and not generalized into vague and indefinable rights.[13] Applying the "rights" label to such situations might provide rhetorical power to the claims being argued, but it ignored a fundamental contradiction. Unlike property rights, which acted on things in the outside word, the subject of so-called personality rights (the rights holder) and their object (the personality of that rights holder) were one and the same.[14] As Paul Roubier put it later, "A person has no right to life; there is just – what is very different – a duty for all other persons not to violate unjustly the life of another, and that duty is sanctioned by an action in liability."[15]

Whatever the merit of such criticisms, Quebec ultimately adopted the idea of extrapatrimonial personality rights, first in the *Charter of Human Rights and Freedoms* of 1975 and later in article 3 of the *Civil Code of Québec* in 1991.[16] Both came out of the work of the Civil Code Revision Office, which was guided, as its president Paul-André Crépeau put it, by "a desire to place the human person, with its rights and its duties, in the place of honour it deserves, by making it the cornerstone of all legal relations in private law."[17] We are getting ahead of the story, however, and need to return to pick up the history of rights in Quebec in the later nineteenth century.

While personality rights were being articulated in Europe, Michel Mathieu was alone, for the most part, among Quebec jurists in presenting a rights-based understanding of civil liability, with fault being the defendant's absence of right and damage flowing from the violation of the plaintiff's right. Rights talk was not new with him, of course. We saw in chapter 1 that Maximilien Bibaud, writing in 1861, described *injure* as "injury to another or wilful violation of another's right," but Bibaud's influence was minimal.[18] Nineteenth-century discussions of rights in Quebec, as in the different legal system in Ontario, centred mainly on their public aspects: citizenship values and fundamental liberties within the British constitutional system.[19] In 1851, for example, lawyer and literary figure Antoine Gérin-Lajoie noted in his *Catéchisme politique*, "The inhabitants of Canada individually enjoy certain rights guaranteed to them either by treaties, by explicit laws, by their status as English subjects, or finally by public law and natural law." Gérin-Lajoie saw certain rights as inherent, such as the rights to life, to seek happiness, and to adore the supreme being.[20] In 1867, to cite just one more example, Joseph Roy linked fundamental rights to individual liberty in his commentary on the CCLC, bringing rights within private law: "These can be reduced to three principal rights, namely: security of the person, personal liberty, and the right to private property. To violate one or the other of these rights is to strip man of his liberty."[21] Both of these brief discussions located rights in the grey area between what later would be called constitutional rights and subjective rights, the former looking towards public law, the latter towards private law.

Later in the nineteenth century, the rights of the individual began to appear in the litigation of certain issues that straddled public and private law. Religious liberty was an early and important example, and those debating the Jewish schools question and religious burial rights (the latter especially in the Guibord affair of 1869–74) used rights as a way to strengthen legal positions.[22] Another area was libel involving the press, in which defendants asserted constitutional ideas of public interest and press freedom.[23] Elsbeth Heaman has argued that those threads of rights history represented anti-liberal views about the Canadian polity and its legal basis, stressing conservative collective British liberties over individual rights.[24] That was certainly part of it, but within Quebec private law the adoption of public-law values was also a means of reorienting onto a liberal, individualist footing areas of law like family matters and civil liability that had previously been discussed differently.

That last point came out most clearly in the long debate over *contrainte par corps*.[25] As in France, the debate in Quebec touched issues of fundamental liberty and the morality of allowing a plaintiff to demand the imprisonment of an unsuccessful defendant.[26] It also raised the question of the nature of civil liability. In Quebec, the controverted wording "*injures personnels* / personal wrongs" in the threshold requirement for *contrainte* led some judges, most notably Michel Mathieu and Siméon Pagnuelo, to think about the nature and scope of personal interests in private law.[27] By the first decades of the twentieth century the different threads – *injure*, aspects of the personality, and rights – were coming together in some of the *contrainte* cases. The most interesting example is a 1924 appeal before the Court of King's Bench. The main import of the decision was to broaden the meaning of the phrase "*injures personnelles*" beyond moral injury only (to which Mathieu had argued it should be limited) to include physical and material damage as well. Chief Justice Pierre-Eugène Lafontaine went further and used the occasion to elaborate on certain "rights of the person" to honour and respect. Honour was not part of the patrimony, he explained, because "even though its value is beyond price, ... it is not, according to the accepted expression, 'in commerce,' and because it is not appreciable in money and it is inherent to the person." Violation of honour "is called an *injure personnelle* or a *tort personnel* because it consists of 'a violation of the dignity of another's person by an act that good morals condemn.'"[28] The chief justice continued with rights to physical integrity and the material damage that interference with those rights entailed. The key point, however, is that in viewing honour as an extrapatrimonial right inherent in the person, Lafontaine was echoing Perreau's personality rights exactly, just without using the term of art.

Outside the courts too, commentators were by the end of the nineteenth century beginning to address the existence and role of rights within Quebec private law, though their interventions were less interesting and less perceptive than the judges'. Pierre-Basile Mignault, writing in 1895 in the first volume of his *Le droit civil canadien*, distinguished the different kinds of rights but said little more.[29] On the one hand were rights he called "civil" (such as the right to property, to paternal authority, and to successions) and "political" (such as the right to vote and otherwise participate in government). On the other hand were a more amorphous group that some called "public rights," which depended neither on one's relations with others (like civil rights) nor on public participation (like political rights). Public rights included various liberties, of the press, of the individual, of conscience, and were held (if not exercised) by every individual, regardless of age, sex, or nationality. Mignault's rights taxonomy drew implicitly on the earlier discussions of absolute rights mentioned above, but it contained not a whiff of the personality rights that were developing at the time. His view of fault too stayed close to the old "no right" idea: "*the regular exercise of a right is not a fault.*"[30] A few years later, in 1905, François Langelier included at the beginning of his *Cours de droit civil* a section of basic preliminary ideas, including different senses of the word *right*. Alongside "acquired rights" (*droits acquis*), that is the familiar personal (contractual) and real (property) rights, were "innate rights" (*droits innés*), which he defined as a kind of individual power guaranteed by civil society. Innate rights were possessed by everyone "by the fact that one is human, and which one holds from birth." He gave just one example, "the mastery of one's own person," and like Mignault developed the idea no further.[31] For Langelier too, fault was the absence of a right: "there is never fault in the exercise of a right."[32]

Throughout this book, but mostly in cases from the early twentieth century, we have seen some examples of rights language entering into the argument and adjudication of moral injury cases, such as the right of survivors to determine where a relative's body was to be buried, the rights of the family to refuse an autopsy of a deceased relative, the hints of a right to bodily integrity in the face of compulsory medical exams, and the suggestions of a right to equal treatment in the refusal of service cases. Development of rights language was slow, however, and even at the end of our period around 1950 older ways of analysing cases of wounded feelings continued. Cases in which sentiments were foregrounded, like actions in alienation of affection or breach of promise, continued to focus on factual, situational reasoning. Those cases were harder to fit into rights language, which in its early days at

Conclusion: From Wounded Feelings to Violated Rights   303

least was closely connected to traditional legal values like liberty and citizenship. Defamation cases too continued to use the older conceptualization of aspects of the personality as *biens*, such as a 1931 case involving the break-up of a business, where one partner called the other a thief. Justice Wilfrid Mercier described the reputation as "among the most important of assets," awarding the plaintiff $300, a "very minimal compensation if one considers that reputation and honour cannot be bought like some vulgar piece of merchandise."[33]

The language of "no right" also continued. The defendant's right was not the automatic bar to fault it had been earlier, since it had by the turn of the century been limited by new ideas like abuse of right. But in certain areas, defamation in particular, the focus remained on whether or not the defendant had a right rather than on a violated interest of the plaintiff. One example among many is a 1944 case in which an anti-conscription activist sued a newspaper for questioning his bravery and accusing him of subversion. The court rejected the newspaper's fair comment defence, finding that it "had gone beyond its rights in its commentary."[34]

Alongside this continuity was evidence of change, and the 1940s in particular were a key period in the development of rights language in both Canadian public law and Quebec private law. On the public side, scholars and activists in the late 1940s were calling for a national bill of rights to address issues like discrimination, abuses of due process and natural justice, and suppression of labour organization.[35] In Quebec, the Duplessis cases involving Jehovah's Witnesses and communists, which raised rights-based questions in the grey area straddling public and private law, were particularly important in bringing a civil liberties approach into Quebec courtrooms. *Roncarelli v. Duplessis*, for example, was ostensibly a damages action under article 1053 CCLC, but by the time it reached the Supreme Court of Canada it had picked up the issue of fundamental liberties as well.[36]

Lawyers and judges working on private-law cases also drew on the language of constitutional rights and fundamental liberties to reshape how fault was talked about. We saw this in the *Lundell* case in chapter 7, which, along with others, pushed the idea of civil rights beyond citizenship to embrace newer ideas like anti-discrimination, bodily integrity, and privacy. Fault in those cases was moving from simply looking to the absence of right in the defendant's actions to focus on the plaintiff's violated right. That transition took place mainly in the courts, as judges were prompted by civil liberties lawyers like Frank Scott, Glen How, and Albert Stein to make connections between the expansive language of fundamental rights in public-law cases and questions of relations between individuals.

The transition was subtle, and older and newer language mingled in the cases. Privacy in particular was an early site for rights language, such as two harassment cases in the 1950s in which the plaintiffs were besieged with telephone calls at home, one by television viewers who were encouraged to "cheer him up" when his letter of complaint was read on air, another by a creditor over an unpaid bill.[37] In each case, the court saw the damage as self-evident: such harassment was an egregious breach of norms of propriety, which the defendants had "no right" to do. But the judges also based their decisions on the invasion of the plaintiffs' solitude, suggesting (if not stating) that a right to privacy had been violated.

The earliest clear expression of rights of personality in Quebec, one that influenced the privacy cases just mentioned, came from an unlikely source: conservative Supreme Court of Canada Justice Robert Taschereau in *Chaput v. Romain*, one of the Duplessis cases involving Jehovah's Witnesses.[38] The facts of the case were similar in many ways to the liquor raid on the Polish christening in *Rinkuk* thirty years earlier. In 1949 on Allumette Island in Chapeau, Quebec (west of Ottawa), Esymier Chaput, a Jehovah's Witness minister, held in his home a Bible study and prayer meeting with around thirty fellow Witnesses. The meeting was broken up by provincial police officers who had been alerted by a Roman Catholic clergyman. The police entered the home without a warrant, dispersed the meeting, escorted some of the guests to the ferry to Ontario, and seized Bibles and other literature. Chaput sued for the violation of his home and for having been humiliated and insulted in front of his guests. The Quebec courts found that the case presented "no particular difficulty," whether on the level of fact or law, and dismissed the case.[39] At the hearing before the Supreme Court, Glen How urged the justices to hold the province and its agents to respect for "the liberty of a subject and his liberty to exercise his rights," protected by federal law to which provincial law should bend. Justice Roy Kellock asked How whether he was arguing that "any breach of any such right carries a remedy and it does not matter what the Quebec government might legislate?" How answered, "Yes."[40]

The Supreme Court unanimously overturned the lower courts and awarded Chaput $2000 in damages. In his decision, with which two colleagues concurred, Justice Taschereau supplied the link between the

Conclusion: From Wounded Feelings to Violated Rights

defendant's act and the plaintiff's injury, identifying the connection as the infringement of extrapatrimonial rights held by the plaintiff: "[Moral damages] certainly include the prejudice suffered in the present case. In effect, they extend to any violation of extrapatrimonial rights, such as the right to liberty, to honour, to one's name, to freedom of conscience or of speech. The courts cannot refuse to award them in cases in which, for example, *religious or patriotic sentiments have been wounded.*"[41] The other justices followed substantially similar reasoning, though they translated Taschereau's *dommage moral* and *droits extrapatrimoniaux* into terms more congenial to common lawyers: "general damages" and "the ordinary rights of a citizen" for Justice Roy Kellock, and "absolute and very precious rights," according to Justice Charles Locke.[42]

The language of rights gave discussions about moral injury a more abstractly legalistic tone, different from how such cases had been discussed earlier. This masked (though did not entirely remove) the emotions behind the rights violations, and it limited the need for fine-grained, detailed narration of the situations that provoked and shaped those emotional responses. Plaintiffs succeeded because defendants had violated their right (and it helped when, like in Esymier Chaput's case, the violation was so egregious and obvious that even a judicial conservative like Robert Taschereau agreed). Rights became an intensifier, a way to put a case about feelings onto footing similar to property or contract claims. They also sharpened the analysis of fault: instead of defendants having free rein as long as they could plausibly point to a right of some kind, plaintiffs were now armed with a range of personal interests protected by rights, whose violation could ground a damages claim whether or not the defendant had a right.

What was lost? Nothing in the sense that plaintiffs could still make their case, and still won or lost depending on how well they did so. But "my right was violated" substituted objective legalistic precision for the subjective power of "I was humiliated." If witnesses in the cases we examined in this book were seldom asked directly how they felt, and plaintiffs' emotions were reduced to semi-formulaic complaints that they were injured "in their honour, in their feelings, and in their *biens*," stories of wounded feelings were nevertheless central to the inquiry. Plaintiffs had to narrate compelling situations of betrayal, dishonour, justified anger, or insupportable bodily intrusion. Judges, while they sometimes dismissed emotional injury as "mere feelings," and often complained of the difficulty in accurately assessing something as fleeting and personal as emotion, still had to place themselves within those situations with empathy and an understanding of the individuals standing in front of them. A legal history of emotions allows us to focus on that powerfully human element in legal storytelling. It shows that for all its rationality and objectivity, law was, indeed remains, also a world of emotion and feeling.

Abbreviations

AM	Archives de Montréal
BAnQ-Q	Bibliothèque et Archives nationales du Québec, Quebec City
BAnQ-TR	Bibliothèque et Archives nationales du Québec, Trois-Rivières
BAnQ-VM	Bibliothèque et Archives nationales du Québec, Vieux-Montréal
CCLC	*Civil Code of Lower Canada* (as periodically amended)
CCP	*Code of Civil Procedure* (Quebec) (as periodically amended and re-enacted)
CHR	*Canadian Historical Review*
Circ. Ct.	Circuit Court
DCB	*Dictionary of Canadian Biography*, accessed via http://www.biographi.ca
J.C.P.C.	Judicial Committee of the Privy Council
K.B.	Court of King's Bench
Lovell Directory	Annuaires *Lovell* de Montréal et sa banlieue (various titles) (Montreal, 1842–1992), online: http://bibnum2.banq.qc.ca/bna/lovell/
Q.B.	Court of Queen's Bench
RHAF	*Revue d'histoire de l'Amérique française*
S.C.C.	Supreme Court of Canada
Sup. Ct.	Superior Court
Sup. Ct. Rev.	Superior Court in Review

Case Citations

Archival case citations, abbreviated in the notes, are listed in full below. For consistency, I have styled all the cases by original plaintiff v. original defendant, even for appeals that were usually reported with the appellant listed first.

Agnew et uxor v. Gober et vir (Montreal, Sup. Ct. and Sup. Ct. Rev., no. 801)
  Case file: BAnQ-VM, TP11, S2, SS2, SSS42, cont. 1987-05-007/430
Agnew et uxor v. Gober et vir (Montreal, K.B., no. 77)
  Case file: BAnQ-VM, TP9, S2, SS5, SSS1, cont. 2002-09-001/862
Barrette v. Bourbonnière (Montreal, Sup. Ct., no. 1049)
  Case file: BAnQ-VM, TP11, S2, SS2, SSS1, cont. 1987-05-007/2896
Belair v. Chaussé (Montreal, Sup. Ct., no. 1354)
  Case file: BAnQ-VM, TP11, S2, SS2, SSS1, cont. 1987-05-007/2979
Breux v. City of Montreal (Montreal, Sup. Ct., no. 169)
  Case file: BAnQ-VM, TP11, S2, SS2, SSS1, cont. 1987-05-007/2630
Brouillette v. Religieuses de l'Hôtel-Dieu (Montreal, Sup. Ct., no. 188,353)
  Case file missing
  Plumitif: BAnQ-VM, TP11, S2, SS2, SSS7, cont. 1992-07-002/568 (1939–40, vol. 13)
Brouillette v. Religieuses de l'Hôtel-Dieu (Montreal, K.B., no. 2148)
  Case file: BAnQ-VM, TP9, S2, SS6, SSS1, cont. 2002-09-001/108
  Plumitif: BAnQ-VM, TP9, S2, SS6, SSS7, cont. 2002-09-001/504
Chiniquy v. Bégin (Montreal, Sup. Ct. and Sup. Ct. Rev., no. 2881)
  Case file: BAnQ-VM, TP11, S2, SS2, SSS42, cont. 1987-10-014/4579

Chiniquy v. Bégin (Montreal, K.B., no. 359)
　Case file: BAnQ-VM, TP9, S2, SS5, SSS1, cont. 2002-09-001/901
Collin v. Gilot (Montreal, Sup. Ct., no. 65,359)
　Case file missing
　Plumitif: BAnQ-VM, TP11, S2, SS2, SSS7, cont. 1987-10-014/2956 (1930, vol. 66)
　Register: BAnQ-VM, TP11, S2, SS2, SSS4, cont. 1987-10-014/3390 (1930, vol. 4)
Collin v. Gilot (Montreal, K.B., no. 259)
　Case file: BAnQ-VM, TP9, S2, SS6, SSS1, cont. 2002-09-001/39
Corbeil v. Dominion Park Co. (Montreal, Sup. Ct. and Sup. Ct. Rev., no. 1006)
　Case file: BAnQ-VM, TP11, S2, SS2, SSS1, cont. 1987-05-007/2019
Couillard v. Jeannotte (Montreal, Sup. Ct., no. 1912)
　Case files: BAnQ-VM, TP11, S2, SS2, SSS42, cont. 1897-05-007/165 (vs. defendant Jeannotte) and BAnQ-M, TP11, S2, SS2, SSS1, cont. 1987-05-007/2301 (vs. defendant Devins)
Couillard v. Jeannotte (Montreal, K.B., no. 492)
　Case file: BAnQ-VM, TP9, S2, SS5, SSS1, cont. 2002-09-001/759
　Register: BAnQ-VM, TP9, S2, SS5, SSS4, cont. 2002-09-001/992
Curl v. Quebec Amusement Co. (Montreal, Sup. Ct., no. 2775)
　Case file missing
　Plumitif: BAnQ-VM, TP11, S2, SS2, SSS7, cont. 1987-10-014/2733 (1914, vol. 7); … cont. 1987-10-014/2728 (1915, vol. 7); … cont. 1987-10-014/2792 (1916, vol. 7); … cont. 1987-10-014/2787 (1917, vol. 7)
D. v. City of Montreal (Montreal, Sup. Ct., no. 239,930)
　Case file missing
　Plumitif: BAnQ-VM, TP11, S2, SS2, SSS7, cont. 1993-11-005/174 (1945, vol. 70)
Decelles v. International Shows Ltd. (Montreal, Sup. Ct., no. 1297)
　Case file missing
　Plumitif: BAnQ-VM, TP11, S2, SS2, SSS7, cont. 1987-10-014/2838 (1920, vol. 3)
Delisle v. Boisvert (Montreal, Sup. Ct., no. 80)
　Case file: BAnQ-VM, TP11, S2, SS2, SSS1, cont. 1987-05-007/2595
Demers v. Hébert (Montreal, Sup. Ct., no. 2046)
　Case file: BAnQ-VM, TP11, S2, SS2, SSS1, cont. 1987-05-007/3094
Dodson v. Loew's Montreal Theatres Ltd. (Montreal, Sup. Ct., no. 165)
　Case file: BAnQ-VM, TP11, S2, SS2, SSS42, cont. 1987-10-014/1992
Dodson v. Loew's Montreal Theatres Ltd. (Montreal, K.B., no. 318)
　Case file: BAnQ-VM, TP9, S2, SS5, SSS1, cont. 2002-09-001/922
Dorion v. Hogan (Montreal, Q.B., no. 294)
　Case file: BAnQ-VM, TP9, S2, SS5, SSS1, cont. 2009-02-001/145
Driscoll v. Wray (Montreal, Sup. Ct. and Sup. Ct. Rev., no. 212)
　Case file: BAnQ-VM, TP11, S2, SS2, SSS1, cont. 1987-10-014/3956

Driscoll v. Wray (Montreal, Sup. Ct., no. 755)
　Case file: BAnQ-VM, TP11, S2, SS2, SSS1, cont. 1987-10-014/656
Duquette v. Pesant dit Sans-Cartier (Montreal, Sup. Ct. and Sup. Ct. Rev., no. 2191)
　Case file: BAnQ-VM, TP11, S2, SS2, SSS1, cont. 1987-05-007/2387
Duquette v. Sans-Cartier (Montreal, Sup. Ct., no. 2636)
　Case file: BAnQ-VM, TP11, S2, SS2, SSS1, cont. 1987-05-007/2532
Duquette v. Turcot (Montreal, Sup. Ct. and Sup. Ct. Rev., no. 495)
　Case file: BAnQ-VM, TP11, S2, SS2, SSS1, cont. 1987-05-007/2733
Germain v. Ryan (Quebec City, Sup. Ct., no. 66)
　Case file: BAnQ-Q, TP11, S1, SS2, SSS1, cont. 1960-01-353/148
　Register: BAnQ-Q, TP11, S1, SS2, SSS4, cont. 1980-09-026/4119 (1918, vol. 1)
Gober v. Agnew et al. (Montreal, Sup. Ct., no. 932)
　Case file: BAnQ-VM, TP11, S2, SS2, SSS42, cont. 1987-05-007/469
　Plumitif: BAnQ-VM, TP11, S2, SS2, SSS7, cont. 1987-05-007/5661 (1907, vol. 3); ... cont. 1987-10-014/2723 (1908, vol. 3); ... cont. 1987-10-014/2718 (1909, vol. 3); ... cont. 1987-10-014/2707 (1910, vol. 3); ... cont. 1987-10-014/2696 (1911, vol. 3)
　Register: BAnQ-VM, TP11, S2, SS2, SSS4, cont. 1987-05-007/6015 (1907, vol. 3)
Gober v. Agnew (Montreal, Sup. Ct., no. 4047)
　Case file: BAnQ-VM, TP11, S2, SS2, SSS1, cont. 1987-10-014/619
　Plumitif: BAnQ-VM, TP11, S2, SS2, SSS7, cont. 1987-10-014/2704 (1909, vol. 9)
Grothé v. North American Life Assurance Co. (Montreal, Sup. Ct., no. 344)
　Case file: BAnQ-VM, TP11, S2, SS2, SSS1, cont. 1987-05-007/1892
Huberman v. Jacobson (Montreal, Sup. Ct., no. 4789)
　Case file: BAnQ-VM, TP11, S2, SS2, SSS1, cont. 1987-10-014/3725
Huot v. Noiseux (St. Hyacinthe, Sup. Ct., no. 349)
　Case file missing
　Register: BAnQ-VM, TP11, S21, SS2, SSS4, cont. 1995-09-001/27 (1889–92, vol. 8)
Huot v. Noiseux (Montreal, Q.B., no. 320, appeal of Huot)
　Case file: BAnQ-VM, TP9, S2, SS5, SSS1, cont. 2002-09-001/749
　Register: BAnQ-VM, TP9, S2, SS5, SSS5, cont. 2002-09-001/990
Huot v. Noiseux (Montreal, Q.B., no. 324, appeal of Noiseux)
　Case file: BAnQ-VM, TP9, S2, SS5, SSS1, cont. 2002-09-001/750
　Register: BAnQ-VM, TP9, S2, SS5, SSS5, cont. 2002-09-001/990
In re C.O. Grothé and North American Life Assurance Co. v. Children of C.O. Grothé (Montreal, Sup. Ct., no. 553)
　Case file missing
　Plumitif: BAnQ-VM, TP11, S2, SS12, SSS7, cont. 1987-05-007/6165 (1903–5, vol. 17)

Jeannotte v. Citizen Printing & Publishing Co. (Montreal, Sup. Ct., no. 1855)
  Case file: BAnQ-VM, TP11, S2, SS2, SSS1, cont. 1987-05-07/2280
Jinchereau v. Roy (Quebec City, Sup. Ct., no. 1613)
  Case file: BAnQ-Q, TP11, S1, SS2, SSS1, cont. 1960-01-353/978
Jinchereau v. Roy (Quebec City, Sup. Ct. and Sup. Ct. Rev., no. 2057)
  Case file: BAnQ-Q, TP11, S1, SS2, SSS1, cont. 1960-01-353/1149
Johnson v. Sparrow (Montreal, Sup. Ct., no. 659)
  Case file: BAnQ-VM, TP11, S2, SS2, SSS42, cont. 1987-05-007/308
  Plumitif: BAnQ-VM, TP11, S2, SS2, SSS7, cont. 1987-05-007/5549 (1898, vol. 2);
    … cont. 1987-05-007/5654 (1899, vol. 2)
Johnson v. Sparrow (Montreal, Q.B., no. 6)
  Case file: BAnQ-VM, TP9, S2, SS5, SSS1, cont. 2002-09-001/805
  Register: BAnQ-VM, TP9, S2, SS5, SSS5, cont. 2002-09-001/997
Labarre v. Morin (Trois-Rivières, Sup. Ct., no. 158)
  Case file: BAnQ-TR, TP11, S2, SS2, SSS1, cont. 1983-11-001/88
Lebeau v. Plouffe (Montreal, Sup. Ct. and Sup. Ct. Rev., no. 2401)
  Case file: BAnQ-VM, TP11, S2, SS2, SSS42, cont. 1987-05-007/207
  Plumitif: BAnQ-VM, TP11, S2, SS2, SSS7, cont. 1987-05-007/5583 (1892, vol. 9);
    … cont. 1987-05-007/5566 (1893, vol. 9); … cont. 1987-05-007/5573 (1894, vol. 7)
Leblanc v. Lebeau (Montreal, Sup. Ct., no. 1430)
  Case file: BAnQ-M, TP11, S2, SS2, SSS1, cont. 1987-05-007/2995
  Plumitif: BAnQ-VM, TP11, S2, SS2, SSS7, cont. 1987-05-007/5579 (1892, vol. 5); … cont. 1987-05-007/5588 (1893, vol. 5); … cont. 1987-05-007/5570 (1894, vol. 4); … cont. 1987-05-007/5553 (1895, vol. 4); … cont. 1987-05-007/5560 (1896, vol. 4); … cont. 1987-05-007/5544 (1897, vol. 4)
Lortie v. Claude (Montreal, Sup. Ct., no. 2571)
  Case file: BAnQ-VM, TP11, S2, SS2, SSS1, cont. 1987-05-007/2509
Lundell v. Masse et al.; Parsons v. Masse et al. (Joliette, Sup. Ct., nos. 9521–2)
  Case files missing
  Plumitif: BAnQ-VM, TP11, S16, SS2, SSS7, cont. 1986-11-051/1623 (1948–50, vol. 32)
Maheu v. Cloutier (Quebec City, Q.B., no. 440)
  Case file: BAnQ-Q, TP11, S1, SS2, SSS1, cont. 1960-01-353/369
Malboeuf v. Montreal General Hospital (Montreal, Sup. Ct., no. 77,994)
  Case file missing
  Plumitif: BAnQ-VM, TP11, S2, SS2, SSS7, cont. 1987-10-014/2952 (1930, vol. 78)
  Register: BAnQ-VM, TP11, S2, SS2, SSS4, cont. 1987-10-014/3419 (1931, vol. 23)
Marchand v. Chartrand (Montreal, Sup. Ct., no. 3840)
  Case file: BAnQ-VM, TP11, S2, SS2, SSS1, cont. 1987-10-014/535

Marchand v. Royal Victoria Hospital (Montreal, Sup. Ct., no. 122,068)
  Case file missing
  Plumitif: BAnQ-VM, TP11, S2, SS2, SSS7, cont. 1992-07-002/504 (1933 vol. 133)
Parnell v. Springle (Montreal, Sup. Ct., no. 378)
  Case file: BANQ-VM, TP11, S2, SS2, SSS1, cont. 1987-05-007/2694
Parsons v. Action Populaire Ltd. and City of Joliette et al.; Lundell v. Action Populaire Ltd. and City of Joliette et al. (Joliette, Sup. Ct., nos. 9539-42)
  Case file (*Parsons v. Action Populaire Ltd.*, no. 9540): BAnQ-VM, TP11, S16, SS2, SSS1, cont. 1986-11-051/110; other case files missing
  Plumitif: BAnQ-VM, TP11, S16, SS2, SSS7, cont. 1986-11-051/1623 (1948–50, vol. 32)
Phillips v. Montreal General Hospital (Montreal, Sup. Ct., no. 1608)
  Case file missing
  Plumitif: BAnQ-VM, TP11, S2, SS2, SSS7, cont. 1987-05-007/5662 (1907, vol. 4); ... cont. 1987-10-014/2711 (1908, vol. 4)
R. v. Mathurin (Montreal, Ct. of Sessions of the Peace, no. 1152)
  Case file missing
  Plumitif: BAnQ-VM, TP12, S2, SS29, SSS7, cont. 2003-06-001/846 (1920, vol. 6)
Ravary v. Grand Trunk Railway (Montreal, Q.B., no. 20)
  Case file: BAnQ-VM, TP9, S2, SS5, SSS1, cont. 2009-02-001/102
Reynolds v. Loew's Montreal Theatres Ltd. (Montreal, Sup. Ct., no. 162)
  Case file: BAnQ-VM, TP11, S2, SS2, SSS42, cont. 1987-10-014/1992
Reynolds v. Loew's Montreal Theatres Ltd. (Montreal, K.B., no. 316)
  Case file: BAnQ-VM, TP9, S2, SS5, SSS1, cont. 2002-09-001/922
Rinkuk v. Ville St-Pierre (Montreal, Sup. Ct. and Sup. Ct. Rev., no. 5165)
  Case file: BAnQ-VM, TP11, S2, SS2, SSS42, cont. 1987-10-014/4884
Roncarelli v. Duplessis (Montreal, Sup. Ct., no. 253,124)
  Case file: BAnQ-VM, TP11, S2, SS2, SSS2, D253124, cont. 1971-00-000/13192
Roy v. Turgeon (Quebec City, Sup. Ct., no. 376)
  Case file: BAnQ-Q, TP11, S1, SS2, SSS1, cont. 1960-01-353/332
Tudor v. Quebec & Lake St. John Railway (Quebec City, Sup. Ct., no. 1330)
  Case file: BAnQ-Q, TP11, S1, SS2, SSS1 cont. 1960-01-353/845
  Register: BAnQ-Q, TP11, S1, SS2, SSS4, cont. 1980-09-026/4073 (1911, vol. 5)
Weingart v. Jacobson (Montreal, Sup. Ct. and Sup. Ct. Rev., no. 1501)
  Case file: BAnQ-VM, TP11, S2, SS2, SSS42, cont. 1987-10-014/4846
Weingart v. Jacobson (Montreal, Sup. Ct. and Sup. Ct. Rev., no. 4847)
  Case file: BAnQ-VM, TP11, S2, SS2, SSS42, cont. 1987-10-014/4880

Notes

Introduction

1 The jury trial on the merits was extensively covered in newspapers locally and beyond: "Breach of Promise of Marriage," *Montreal Herald* (10 September 1869), 1–2; "Breach of Promise of Marriage," *Montreal Herald* (11 September 1869), 2; "Grange vs Benning," *La Minerve* (13 September 1869), 2; "Breach of Promise of Marriage," *Montreal Witness* (15 September 1869), 1–2. (The articles from the *Herald* are the source of the quotations from the trial in what follows.) The defendant's challenge to the jury's verdict (a motion for judgment *non obstante veredicto*) was dismissed in *Grange v. Benning* (1869), 13 L.C.J. 290 (Sup. Ct., Mackay J.), affirmed on appeal in *Grange v. Benning* (1870), 14 L.C.J. 284 (Q.B.).
2 *An Act for the relief of James Benning*, S.P.C. 1865, c. 175. Until the 1960s, divorce in Quebec was available only through a private act of Parliament. See James G. Snell, *In the Shadow of the Law: Divorce in Canada, 1900–1939* (Toronto: University of Toronto Press, 1991), 48–51.
3 Grange retained Bernard Devlin (later Liberal M.P.) and J.J.C. Abbott, Q.C. (later prime minister of Canada), while Benning had the services of Désiré Girouard (matrimonial law expert and later a Supreme Court of Canada justice), W.H. Kerr, Q.C., and A.-A. Dorion (Liberal M.P.). Grange was an "orphan" in the nineteenth-century sense of having lost her father. According to records in ancestry.ca, following her father's death, her

mother married Sophia's uncle Thomas Grange, who brought his brother's children into his household.
4 The declaration was quoted in *Grange v. Benning* (Sup. Ct.), 291. She claimed nothing for material damage, since Benning had agreed to reimburse any out-of-pocket expenses she had incurred. During the trial, the lawyers presented her with agreed-upon questions (*faits et articles*, a means of streamlining procedure), which limited her to "direct ..., categorical and precise" answers: art. 228 CCP (1867 ed.); see art. 251 CCP for the bar on testifying on one's own behalf (that bar was removed in 1897: *An Act to amend the Code of Civil Procedure*, S.Q. 1897 (60 Vic.), c. 54, s. 1).
5 "Grange vs Benning," *La Minerve* (13 September 1869), 2.
6 Hermione, "Chronique," *Le Constitutionnel (Trois-Rivières)* (13 September 1869, édition semi-quotidienne), 2: "quand le cœur s'attache à un homme qui vaut $100,000, il est aisé de comprendre qu'une rupture doit causer un chagrin profond et bien amer."
7 *Grange v. Benning* (Q.B.), 287.
8 René Demogue, *De la réparation civile des délits (étude de droit et de législation)* (Paris, 1898), 51; François Givord, *La réparation du préjudice moral* (Paris: Dalloz, 1938), 11–17.
9 Ian McKay, "The Liberal Order Framework: A Prospectus for a Reconnaissance of Canadian History," *CHR* 81 (2000): 633–34; Jean-François Constant and Michel Ducharme, eds., *Liberalism and Hegemony: Debating the Canadian Liberal Revolution* (Toronto: University of Toronto Press, 2009); Fernande Roy, *Progrès, harmonie, liberté: le libéralisme des milieux d'affaires francophones de Montréal au tournant du siècle* (Montreal: Boréal, 1988), 151–91; Sylvio Normand, "Les juristes et le libéralisme au tournant du XXe siècle," in *Combats libéraux au tournant du XXe siècle*, ed. Yvan Lamonde, 213–29 ([Saint-Laurent, QC]: Fides, 1995). More generally, see especially Susanna L. Blumenthal, *Law and the Modern Mind: Consciousness and Responsibility in American Legal Culture* (Cambridge, MA: Harvard University Press, 2016).
10 On common sense in law, see James W. St.G. Walker, *"Race," Rights and the Law in the Supreme Court of Canada: Historical Case Studies* (Waterloo, ON: Osgoode Society for Canadian Legal History and Wilfrid Laurier University Press, 1997), 12–23; Patricia Cochran, *Common Sense and Legal Judgment: Community Knowledge, Political Power, and Rhetorical Practice* (Montreal and Kingston: McGill-Queen's University Press, 2017).
11 François Rigaux, "L'évaluation communautaire du seuil de tolérance aux atteintes à un bien de la personnalité," in *La douleur et le droit*, ed.

Bernard Durand, Jean Poirier, and Jean-Pierre Royer, 479–88 (Paris: Presses universitaires français, 1997).
12 Paul Gewirtz, "Narrative and Rhetoric in the Law," in *Law's Stories: Narrative and Rhetoric in the Law*, ed. Peter Brooks and Paul Gewirtz (New Haven, CT: Yale University Press, 1996), 5. See also Greig Henderson, *Creating Legal Worlds: Story and Style in a Culture of Argument* (Toronto: University of Toronto Press, 2015).
13 And of course from a jury, if there was one. Aside from *Grange v. Benning* and some of the fatal accident cases in chapter 6, however, few of the cases we will consider in this book were tried before a jury. We will discuss one reason for this in chapter 1.
14 The best overview is Giorgio Resta, "Personnalité, Persönlichkeit, Personality," in *Les intraduisibles en droit civil*, ed. Alexandra Popovici, Lionel Smith, and Régine Tremblay, 185–215 (Montreal: Thémis, 2014). Key early contributions were E.H. Perreau, "Des droits de la personnalité," *Revue trimestrielle de droit civil* 8 (1909): 501–36; and Roger Nerson, *Les droits extrapatrimoniaux* (Lyons: Bosc Frères, M. & L. Riou, 1939). On the roots of personality rights, see especially Manfred Herrmann, *Der Schutz der Persönlichkeit in der Rechtslehre des 16.-18. Jahrhunderts* (Stuttgart: W. Kohlhammer, 1968); Hans-Joachim Vergau, *Der Ersatz immateriellen Schadens in der Rechtsprechung des 19. Jahrhunderts zum französischen und zum deutschen Deliktsrecht* (Potsdam: Universitätsverlag Potsdam, 2006); Olivier Descamps, *Les origines de la responsabilité pour faute personnelle dans le Code civil de 1804* (Paris: L.G.D.J., 2005), 298–303.
15 Eric M. Adams, "Building a Law of Human Rights: *Roncarelli v. Duplessis* in Canadian Constitutional Culture," *McGill Law Journal* 55 (2010): 442–51.
16 R.W. Sandwell, "The Limits of Liberalism: The Liberal Reconnaissance and the History of the Family in Canada," *CHR* 84 (2003): 423–50; Sandwell, "Missing Canadians: Reclaiming the A-Liberal Past," in *Liberalism and Hegemony: Debating the Canadian Liberal Revolution*, ed. Jean-François Constant and Michel Ducharme, 246–73 (Toronto: University of Toronto Press, 2009). See also Nancie Christie, "A 'Painful Dependence': Female Begging Letters and the Familial Economy of Obligation," in *Mapping the Margins: The Family and Social Discipline in Canada, 1700–1975*, ed. Nancy Christie and Michael Gauvreau (Montreal and Kingston: McGill-Queen's University Press, 2004), 91–2.
17 Excellent orientations in the field include Nicole Eustace, Eugenia Lean, Julie Livingston, Jan Plamper, William M. Reddy, and Barbara H. Rosenwein, "*AHR* Conversation: The Historical Study of Emotions," *American Historical Review* 117 (2012): 1487–531; and Susan J. Matt and Peter N. Stearns, eds.,

Doing Emotions History (Urbana: University of Illinois Press, 2014). Some defining works, in chronological order, are: Lucien Febvre, "La sensibilité et l'histoire: comment reconstituer la vie affective d'autrefois?" *Annales d'histoire sociale* 3 (1941): 5–20, translated as "Sensibility and History: How to Reconstitute the Emotional Life of the Past," trans. K. Folca, in *A New Kind of History: From the Writings of Febvre*, ed. Peter Burke, 12–26 (New York: Harper & Row, 1973); Peter N. Stearns and Carol Z. Stearns, "Emotionology: Clarifying the History of Emotions and Emotional Standards," *American Historical Review* 90 (1985): 813–36; William M. Reddy, *The Navigation of Feeling: A Framework for the History of Emotions* (Cambridge: Cambridge University Press, 2001); Thomas Dixon, *From Passions to Emotions: The Creation of a Secular Psychological Category* (Cambridge: Cambridge University Press, 2003); Barbara H. Rosenwein, *Emotional Communities in the Early Middle Ages* (Ithaca, NY: Cornell University Press, 2006).

18 The recent *Oxford Handbook of Legal History*, ed. Markus D. Dubber and Christopher Tomlins (Oxford: Oxford University Press, 2018), does not cover the emotions in legal history. See Natalie Zemon Davis, *Fiction in the Archives: Pardon Tales and Their Tellers in Sixteenth-Century France* (Stanford: Stanford University Press, 1987); William M. Reddy, *The Invisible Code: Honor and Sentiment in Postrevolutionary France* (Berkeley: University of California Press, 1997); Daniel Lord Smail, *The Consumption of Justice: Emotions, Publicity, and Legal Culture in Marseille, 1264–1423* (Ithaca, NY: Cornell University Press, 2003). Other model examples of the emerging field, from different disciplinary and methodological perspectives, include Laura Hanft Korobkin, *Criminal Conversations: Sentimentality and Nineteenth-Century Legal Stories of Adultery* (New York: Columbia University Press, 1998); Jennifer Travis, *Wounded Hearts: Masculinity, Law, and Literature in American Culture* (Chapel Hill: University of North Carolina Press, 2005); Alecia Simmonds, "'She Felt Strongly the Injury to Her Affections': Breach of Promise of Marriage and the Medicalization of Heartbreak in Early Twentieth-Century Australia," *Journal of Legal History* 38 (2017): 179–202. For a recent overview, see Laura Kounine, "Emotions, Mind, and Body on Trial: A Cross-Cultural Perspective," *Journal of Social History* 51 (2017): 219–30.

19 For overviews, see Susan A. Bandes, ed., *The Passions of Law* (New York: New York University Press, 1999); Richard L. Wiener, Brian H. Bornstein, and Amy Voss, "Emotion and the Law: A Framework for Inquiry," *Law and Human Behavior* 30 (2006): 231–48; Terry A. Maroney, "Law and Emotion: A Proposed Taxonomy of an Emerging Field," *Law and Human Behavior* 30 (2006): 119–42; Susan A. Bandes and Jeremy A. Blumenthal, "Emotion and the Law," *Annual Review of Law and Social Science* 8 (2012): 161–81.

20 Jeffrey L. McNairn, "'The Common Sympathies of Our Nature': Moral Sentiments, Emotional Economies, and Imprisonment for Debt in Upper Canada," *Histoire sociale/Social History* 49 (2016): 49–71; Gian Marco Vidor, "The Press, the Audience, and Emotions in Italian Courtrooms (1860s–1910s)," *Journal of Social History* 51 (2017): 231–54; Jürgen Martschukat, "A Horrifying Experience? Public Executions and the Emotional Spectator in the New Republic," in *Emotions in American History: An International Assessment*, ed. Jessica Geinow-Hecht, 181–200 (New York: Berghahn Books, 2010); Amy Milka and David Lemmings, "Narratives of Feeling and Majesty: Mediated Emotions in the Eighteenth-Century Criminal Courtroom," *Journal of Legal History* 38 (2017): 155–78.
21 Richard Weisman, *Showing Remorse: Law and the Social Control of Emotion* (Farnham: Ashgate, 2014). Another example is the ingratitude that could nullify a donation in Quebec, which we will consider in chapter 5.
22 Sandra Schnädelbach, "The Jurist as Manager of Emotions: German Debates on 'Rechtsgefühl' in the Late 19th and Early 20th Cenury as Sites of Negotiating the Juristic Treatment of Emotions," *InterDisciplines* 6, no. 2 (2015): 47–74; James M. Donovan, "Culture and the Courts in France: The *Plaidoirie Sentimentale* in the Nineteenth and Early Twentieth Centuries," *Law and History Review* 35 (2017): 789–828; Pavel Vasilyev, "Beyond Dispassion: Emotions and Judicial Decision-Making in Modern Europe," *Rechtsgeschichte/Legal History* 25 (2017): 277–85.
23 Ute Frevert, *Emotions in History: Lost and Found* (Budapest: Central European University Press, 2011); Frevert, "Defining Emotions: Concepts and Debates over Three Centuries," in *Emotional Lexicons: Continuity and Change in the Vocabulary of Feeling 1700–2000*, ed. Ute Frevert, Christian Bailey, Pascal Eitler, Benno Gammerl, Bettina Hitzer, Margrit Pernau, Monique Scheer, Anne Schmidt, and Nina Verheyen, 1–31 (Oxford: Oxford University Press, 2014).
24 Robert A. Nye, *Masculinity and Male Codes of Honor in Modern France* (New York: Oxford University Press, 1993); Courtney Erin Thomas, *If I Lose Mine Honour I Lose Myself: Honour among the Early Modern English Elite* (Toronto: University of Toronto Press, 2017).
25 William Ian Miller, *Humiliation and Other Essays on Honor, Social Discomfort, and Violence* (Ithaca, NY: Cornell University Press, 1993), 93.
26 Reddy, *Navigation of Feeling*, 105.
27 William M. Reddy, "Against Constructionism: The Historical Anthropology of Emotions," *Current Anthropology* 38 (1997): 336–8; Reddy, *Invisible Code*; Reddy, *Navigation of Feeling*, 257–314.
28 Barbara H. Rosenwein, *Generations of Feeling: A History of Emotions 600–1700* (Cambridge: Cambridge University Press, 2016), 3.

29 Rosenwein, *Generations of Feeling*, 842. On putting the idea of emotional communities to use, see also Barbara H. Rosenwein, "Problems and Methods in the History of Emotions," *Passions in Context* 1 (2010): 1–32.
30 Monique Scheer, "Are Emotions a Kind of Practice (and Is That What Makes Them Have a History)? A Bourdieuian Approach to Understanding Emotions," *History and Theory* 51 (2012): 193–220.
31 Scheer, "Are Emotions a Kind of Practice," 207, 214–15.
32 Scheer, "Are Emotions a Kind of Practice," 218.
33 Rosenwein, *Generations of Feeling*, 6; Rosenwein, "Problems and Methods," 21.
34 Travis, *Wounded Hearts*, 43.
35 Davis, *Fiction in the Archives*, 3.
36 Franca Iacovetta and Wendy Mitchinson, eds., *On the Case: Explorations in Social History* (Toronto: University of Toronto Press, 1998); Mariana Valverde, J.R. Miller, Doug Owram, Shirley Tillotson, Bryan D. Palmer, Franca Iacovetta, and Wendy Mitchinson, "On the Case: Explorations in Social History: A Roundtable Discussion," *CHR* 81 (2000): 266–92.
37 See, e.g., arts. 312–54 CCP (1903 ed.).
38 *Goyer v. Duquette* (1937), R.J.Q. 61 B.R. 503 at 505: "dans son honneur, dans sa personne et dans ses biens, des dommages incalculables."
39 *Goyer v. Duquette*, 510–11 (quoting the testimony): "D. Dans votre personne, votre honneur doit résider dans votre personne? R. Si vous le dites. D. Vous êtes témoin, je vous le demande? R. Je n'ai pas de réponse à vous faire là-dessus. D. Pourquoi demandez-vous des dommages dans votre personne, et à part cela, pourquoi faites-vous une distinction entre votre personne et votre honneur, vous dites cela dans votre déclaration, c'est vous qui le dites? R. Vous feriez mieux d'argumenter cela avec M. Lanctot, c'est lui qui a rédigé cela. ... D. Je veux avoir une réponse de vous. Pourquoi avez-vous demandé des dommages dans votre personne? R. Je n'ai rien demandé comme cela, j'ai demandé $999 de dommages exemplaires, qui comprennent toutes ces choses-là."
40 *Marchand v. Chartrand*, Bref et déclaration (produced 6 November 1912), 2: "a souffert et souffre et souffrira à jamais dans le plus intime de son être, qu'il a été blessé dans son honneur, sa sensibilité, dans sa personne, dans son cœur, dans sa famille, et dans son avenir."
41 A.W.B. Simpson, *Leading Cases in the Common Law* (Oxford: Clarendon, 1995), 11.
42 Miller, *Humiliation*, 101.
43 Frédéric Chauvaud, "La parole captive: l'interrogatoire judiciaire au XIXe siècle," *Histoire et archives* 1 (1997): 33–60.

44 Reddy, *Invisible Code*, 4.
45 Davis, *Fiction in the Archives*, 20–1.
46 Notable exceptions include Thierry Nootens, *Fous, prodigues et ivrognes: familles et déviance à Montréal au XIXème siècle* (Montreal and Kingston: McGill-Queen's University Press, 2007); *Genre, patrimoine et droit civil: les femmes mariées de la bourgeoisie québécoise en procès, 1900–1930* (Montreal and Kingston: McGill-Queen's University Press, 2018); and Sylvio Normand, "L'affaire *Plamondon*: un cas d'antisémitisme à Québec au début du XXe siècle," *Cahiers de droit* 48 (2007): 477–504. On legal archaeology, coined and most famously practised by Brian Simpson in *Leading Cases*, 12, see Debora L. Threedy, "Legal Archaeology: Excavating Cases, Reconstructing Context," *Tulane Law Review* 80 (2006): 1197–238; and William Twining, "What Is the Point of Legal Archaeology?" *Transnational Legal Theory* 3 (2012): 166–72.
47 On the focus on individual cases, cf. Walker, "Race," *Rights and the Law*, 322–3; Constance Backhouse, *Colour-Coded: A Legal History of Racism in Canada, 1900–1950* (Toronto: University of Toronto Press for Osgoode Society for Canadian Legal History, 1999), 15–16.
48 Darrin M. McMahon, "Finding Joy in the History of Emotions," in *Doing Emotions History*, ed. Susan J. Matt and Peter N. Stearns (Urbana: University of Illinois Press, 2014), 104–7. Carolyn Strange too has noted an "attachment to negative emotions" in the history of emotions: "Reconsidering the 'Tragic' Scott Expedition: Cheerful Masculine Homemaking in Antarctica, 1910–1913," *Journal of Social History* 46 (2012): 69–70, 80 (quotation).

1. Feelings and the Law in Nineteenth-Century Quebec

1 On the structure of the civil law and the law of persons within it, see especially Anne Lefebvre-Teillard, *Introduction historique au droit des personnes et de la famille* (Paris: Presses Universitaires de France, 1996); Donald R. Kelley, "Gaius Noster: Substructures of Western Social Thought," *American Historical Review* 84 (1979): 619–48; André-Jean Arnaud, *Les origines doctrinales du Code civil français* (Paris: L.G.D.J., 1969); Arnaud, *Essai d'analyse structurale du Code civil français: la règle du jeu dans la paix bourgeoise* (Paris: L.G.D.J., 1973); Eric Descheemaeker, *The Division of Wrongs: A Historical Comparative Study* (Oxford: Oxford University Press, 2009).
2 On France: Arnaud, *Les origines doctrinales*; Nader Hakim, *L'autorité de la doctrine civiliste française au XIXe siècle* (Paris: L.G.D.J., 2002). On the

common-law world: A.W.B. Simpson, "The Rise and Fall of the Legal Treatise: Legal Principles and the Form of Legal Literature," *University of Chicago Law Review* 48 (1981): 632–79; Michael H. Hoeflich, *Legal Publishing in Antebellum America* (New York: Cambridge University Press, 2010); Angela Fernandez and Markus D. Dubber, eds., *Law Books in Action: Essays on the Anglo-American Legal Treatise* (Oxford: Hart, 2012). On Quebec: Sylvio Normand, "Une analyse quantitative de la doctrine en droit civil québécois," *Cahiers de droit* 23 (1982): 1009–28; Pierre-Gabriel Jobin, "L'influence de la doctrine française sur le droit civil québécois: le rapprochement et l'éloignement de deux continents," *Revue internationale de droit comparé* 44 (1992): 381–408; Sylvie Parent, *La doctrine et l'interprétation du Code civil* (Montreal: Thémis, 1997).

3 See especially W. Wesley Pue, *Lawyers' Empire: Legal Professions and Cultural Authority, 1780–1950* (Vancouver: UBC Press, 2016); Michael H. Hoeflich, "*Plus ça change, plus c'est la même chose*: The Integration of Theory and Practice in Legal Education," *Temple Law Review* 66 (1993): 123–41; Sylvio Normand, *Le droit comme discipline universitaire: une histoire de la Faculté de droit de l'Université Laval* (Sainte-Foy, QC: Presses de l'Université Laval, 2005); Christine Veilleux, *Aux origines du Barreau québécois, 1779–1849* (Sillery, QC: Septentrion, 1997); G.-Édouard Rinfret, *Histoire du Barreau de Montréal*, 2nd ed. (Cowansville, QC: Yvon Blais, 1999); Gilles Gallichan, "La Bibliothèque du Barreau de Québec: l'émergence d'une institution," *Cahiers de droit* 34 (1993): 125–52.

4 See generally Hoeflich, *Legal Publishing*.

5 See Ludger Pichet, "Grandeurs et misères de nos ouvrages de droit," *Revue du Barreau* 5 (1945): 294–6; Sylvio Normand, "Profil des périodiques juridiques québécois au XIXe siècle," *Cahiers de droit* 34 (1993): 153–82; Martha L. Foote, *Law Reporting and Legal Publishing in Canada: A History* (Kingston, ON: Canadian Association of Law Libraries, 1997); Sylvio Normand, "Les débuts de la littérature juridique québécoise, 1767–1840," in *Essays in the History of Canadian Law: Volume XI – Quebec and the Canadas*, ed. G. Blaine Baker and Donald Fyson, 96–130 (Toronto: University of Toronto Press for Osgoode Society for Canadian Legal History, 2013).

6 Eric H. Reiter, "Imported Books, Imported Ideas: Reading European Jurisprudence in Mid-Nineteenth-Century Quebec," *Law and History Review* 22 (2004): 445–92.

7 See esp. David Howes, "From Polyjurality to Monojurality: The Transformation of Quebec Law, 1875–1929," *McGill Law Journal* 32 (1987): 523–58; Howes, "La domestication de la pensée juridique québécoise," *Anthropologie et sociétés* 13 (1989): 103–25; Robert Yalden, "Unité et

Différence: The Structure of Legal Thought in Late-Nineteenth-Century Quebec," *University of Toronto Faculty of Law Review* 46 (1988): 365–89; André Morel, "L'émergence du nouvel ordre juridique instauré par le Code civil du Bas Canada (1866–1890)," in *Le nouvel Code civil: interprétation et application. Les Journées Maximilien-Caron 1992*, 49–63 (Montreal: Thémis, 1993); Michel Morin, "La perception de l'ancien droit et du nouveau droit français au Bas-Canada, 1774–1866," in *Droit québécois et droit français: communauté, autonomie, concordance*, ed. H.P. Glenn, 1–41 (Cowansville, QC: Yvon Blais, 1993); Brian Young, *The Politics of Codification: The Lower Canadian Civil Code of 1866* (Montreal and Kingston: McGill-Queen's University Press for Osgoode Society for Canadian Legal History, 1994); F. Murray Greenwood, "Lower Canada (Quebec): Transformation of Civil Law, from Higher Morality to Autonomous Will, 1774–1866," *Manitoba Law Journal* 23 (1996): 132–82; H. Patrick Glenn, "Quebec: Mixité and Monism," in *Studies in Legal Systems: Mixed and Mixing*, ed. Esin Örücü, Elspeth Attwooll, and Sean Coyle, 1–15 (The Hague: Kluwer Law International, 1996); Sylvio Normand, "Une culture en redéfinition: la culture juridique québécoise durant la seconde moitié du XIXe siècle," in *Transformation de la culture juridique québécoise*, ed. Bjarne Melkevik, 221–35 (Sainte-Foy, QC: Presses de l'Université Laval, 1998); Michel Morin, "Des jurists sédentaires? L'influence du droit anglais et du droit français sur interprétation du *Code civil du Bas Canada*," *Revue du Barreau* 60 (2000): 247–386; Morin, "Blackstone and the Birth of Quebec's Legal Culture, 1765–1867," in *Re-Interpreting Blackstone's Commentaries: A Seminal Text in National and International Contexts*, ed. Wilfrid Prest, 105–24 (Oxford: Hart, 2014).

8 Bruce W. Frier, *A Casebook on the Roman Law of Delict* (Atlanta: Scholars' Press, 1989), 2.
9 Frier, *Casebook*, 1; Alan Watson, *The Law of the Ancient Romans* (Dallas: Southern Methodist University Press, 1970), 76.
10 See Descamps, *Les origines*; Thomas Moosheimer, *Die actio iniuriarum aestimatoria im 18. und 19. Jahrhundert: Eine Untersuchung zu den Gründen ihrer Abschaffung* (Tübingen: Mohr Siebeck, 1997). In the common-law tradition, see Eric Descheemaeker and Helen Scott, eds., *Iniuria and the Common Law* (Oxford: Hart, 2014).
11 Sylvio Normand, "Mathieu, Michel," *DCB* vol. 14. No notes from the project seem to have survived.
12 François Dareau, *Traité des injures dans l'ordre judiciaire: Ouvrage qui renferme particulièrement la Jurisprudence du Petit-Criminel* (Paris, 1775), 2: "ce qui se dit, ce qui s'écrit, ce qui se fait, & même ce qui s'omet à dessein d'offenser

quelqu'un dans son honneur, dans sa personne ou dans ses biens." Cf. Jean Domat, "Supplément du titre III du Droit public," in *Les loix civiles dans leur ordre naturel; le droit public, et legum delectus*, nouvelle édition, 2 vols. (Paris, 1777), 2:311; Jean-Baptiste Denisart, *Collection de décisions nouvelles et de notions relatives à la jurisprudence actuelle*, 3 vols. (Paris, 1763–4), 2:369.

13 Dareau, *Traité des injures*, 139–388, chapter entitled "Des Injures entre Particuliers, par la qualité des personnes entr'elles."

14 See Charles Walton, *Policing Public Opinion in the French Revolution: The Culture of Calumny and the Problem of Free Speech* (Oxford: Oxford University Press, 2009), 45, who notes (following Dareau) that *injure* in the ancien régime centred on status rather than truth.

15 A good overview of the French situation, dependent on French legislation, is Maurice Boulanger, *De la diffamation et de l'injure envers les particuliers* (Rennes, 1882). See also Descamps, *Les origines*, 303–7.

16 See, e.g., *An Abstract of the Criminal Laws That Were in Force in the Province of Quebec in the Time of the French Government, Drawn up by a Select Committee of Canadian Gentlemen, Well Skilled in the Laws of France, and of That Province, by the Desire of the Honourable Guy Carleton, Esquire, Captain-General, and Governour in Chief, of the Said Province* (London, 1773), 170; Joseph-François Perrault, *Formules des ordres que l'on délivre le plus communément pour les termes inférieurs de la Cour du banc du roi, en tournée* (n.p., [1812?]), 21 (Perrault included forms for an action in damages and a demand for a *réparation d'honneur*); Perrault, *Questions et réponses sur le droit criminel du Bas-Canada: dédiées aux étudiants en droit* (Quebec City, 1814), 252–5, 367; Henry Des Rivières Beaubien, *Traité sur les lois civiles du Bas-Canada*, 3 vols. (Montreal, 1832–3), 1:172–4, 2:103. Surprisingly little has been written on the culture of insult in Quebec; see André Lachance, "Une étude de mentalité: les injures verbales au Canada au XVIIIe siècle (1712–1748)," *RHAF* 31 (1977): 229–38.

17 Churchwarden: *Ex parte Dumouchel; Ex parte Dalton* (1853), 3 L.C. Rep. 493 (Sup. Ct.) (the trial decision was, however, overturned by Justice Charles Day, a Protestant who characteristically rejected the idea that "the person of a churchwarden is invested with a particular sanctity," at 495). Marriage: *Larocque v. Michon* (1858), 8 L.C. Rep. 222, 2 L.C.J. 267 (Q.B.), reversing (1857) 1 L.C.J. 187 (Sup. Ct.), discussed in detail in Eric H. Reiter, "From Shaved Horses to Aggressive Churchwardens: Social and Legal Aspects of Moral Injury in Lower Canada," in *Essays in the History of Canadian Law: Volume XI – Quebec and the Canadas*, ed. G. Blaine Baker and Donald Fyson, 460–502 (Toronto: University of Toronto Press for Osgoode Society for

Canadian Legal History, 2013). Communion: *Angé v. Curé de la Pointe-aux-Trembles* (1821), 2 R. de L. 63 (K.B.), details below, note 24.

18 François-Maximilien Bibaud, *Commentaires sur les lois du Bas-Canada, ou Conférences de l'école de droit liée au collège des RR. PP. Jésuites, suivis d'une notice historique*, 2 vols. (Montreal, 1859–61), 2:557: "la lésion d'autrui ou la violation volontaire du droit d'autrui. Nous disons volontaire, selon l'acception morale du mot injure; cependant, le droit social, qui n'est pas toujours juge de l'intention, donne souvent le nom d'injure au tort purement matériel, c'est-à-dire causé sans intention de nuire." On Bibaud, see André Morel and Yvan Lamonde, "Bibaud, François-Maximilien," in *DCB*, vol. 11.

19 [Pierre Cocatrix], *La science du confesseur, ou conférences ecclésiastiques sur le sacrement de pénitence par une société de prêtres réfugiés en Allemagne*, 5 vols. (Lille, 1830), 4:44: "L'obligation de réparer suppose une injure, c'est-à-dire, une violation volontaire du droit d'autrui."

20 S.M. Waddams, *Sexual Slander in Nineteenth-Century England: Defamation in the Ecclesiastical Courts, 1815–1855* (Toronto: University of Toronto Press, 2000).

21 Walton, *Policing Public Opinion*, 40.

22 Brian Young, *Patrician Families and the Making of Quebec: The Taschereaus and McCords* (Montreal and Kingston: McGill-Queen's University Press, 2014).

23 Bibaud, *Commentaires*, 2:557: "tout ce qui compose les facultés de l'homme."

24 E.g., *Angé v. Curé de la Pointe-aux-Trembles* (1821), 2 R. de L.63 (K.B.), in which the *capitaine de la côte* sued the curé for failing to serve him the eucharist directly after the seigneur. The court dismissed the action, finding that the captain's right applied only when he was seated in the *banc d'honneur*; the churchwardens were not required to search the church for him.

25 John Fabian Witt, "The Political Economy of Pain," in *Making Legal History: Essays in Honor of William E. Nelson*, ed. Daniel J. Hulsebosch and R.B. Bernstein (New York: New York University Press, 2013), 244–5.

26 I leave aside more focused uses of *injure*, such as in art. 2262 CCLC, where actions for "*injures verbales ou écrites* / slander or libel" and "*injures corporelles* / bodily injuries" are subject to prescription of one year. See the historical overview in *Notre-Dame Hospital v. Patry*, [1975] 2 S.C.R. 388.

27 Art. 189 CCLC. Marie-Aimée Cliche, "Les séparations de corps dans le district judiciaire de Montréal de 1900 à 1930," *Canadian Journal of Law and Society* 12, no. 1 (1997): 88–90.

28 Art. 813 no. 2 CCLC. See below, chapter 5.
29 Art. 893 no. 1 CCLC. See below, chapter 8.
30 Art. 2272 no. 4 CCLC. This was repealed in 1896–7 (60 Vic., c. 50, s. 38), but moved in almost identical terms to art. 833 CCP (the new provision limited imprisonment to judgments awarding damages of $50 or more).
31 Arts. 348–9 CCP (1867 ed.).
32 E.g., *Durocher v. Meunier* (1857), 1 L.C.J. 290 (Sup. Ct.).
33 *Morrisson v. Mullins* (1888), 16 R.L. 114 (Sup. Ct.). Mathieu (the editor of the reporter) added a lengthy footnote under the case summarizing the relevant jurisprudence, but despite his efforts his position would be overruled by the Court of King's Bench in the early twentieth century. We will return to this issue in chapter 8.
34 Reddy, *Invisible Code*, 70–2.
35 *Dasylva v. Plante* (1882), 8 Q.L.R. 349 at 349 (Sup. Ct.): "se rend coupable de masturbation, sa passion étant pour des personnes de son sexe."
36 Charles Demolombe, *Cours de code civil*, 31 vols. (Paris, 1845–82), 4:484–5: "outrageantes par lesquels l'un des époux attente à l'honneur et à la considération de l'autre, et témoigne pour lui des sentiments de haine, d'aversion ou de mépris."
37 *Dasylva v. Plante*, 350: "passion honteuse"; "ne peut attaquer que son honneur à lui, et ne détruire et n'atteindre que la considération dont il peut jouir"; "cette insulte révoltante à sa pudeur et à ses mœurs serait une injure grave qui témoignerait de ses sentiments de mépris pour sa femme."
38 *Hibbard v. Cullen* (1893), R.J.Q. 4 C.S. 369 at 373 (Sup. Ct. Rev.): "Toutes nos actions se résument à la poursuite criminelle pour libelle écrit et à l'action en dommages intérêts. Cette dernière n'est régie que par les règles du droit commun." Criminal libel remained an offence in Canada and was codified with the rest of the criminal law in 1892: *Criminal Code* (1892 ed.), ss. 285–302.
39 *Jasmin v. Sauriol (Clermont v. Sauriol)* (12 April 1900, Sup. Ct.), reversed (27 December 1900), R.J.Q. 10 B.R. 294 (Q.B.).
40 *Jasmin v. Sauriol*, 297: "une espèce d'amende infligée au coupable pour le punir, et donnée à la victime de l'injure comme une espèce de *solatium*."
41 *McFarran et vir v. Montreal Park & Island Railway Co.* (1900), 30 S.C.R. 410.
42 François Langelier, *Cours de droit civil de la province de Québec*, 6 vols. (Montreal: Wilson & Lafleur, 1905–11), 1:viii.
43 Langelier, *Cours*, 3:471–2.
44 Langelier's only convert seems to have been Laval doctoral student Ferdinand Roy, *Des restrictions au droit de plaider en matière civile* (Quebec

City: Darveau, Jos. Beauchamp, Successeur, 1902), 272–3. As dean of the faculty, Langelier reviewed and approved the thesis (see p. 273).
45 Fernandez and Dubber, *Law Books in Action*; G. Edward White, "The Emergence and Doctrinal Development of Tort Law, 1870–1930," *University of St. Thomas Law Journal* 11 (2014): 463–527.
46 See above, note 1.
47 David Deroussin, "Personnalité et 'biens innés' chez Aubry et Rau: entre nature et abstraction," in *Aubry et Rau: leurs œuvres, leurs enseignements*, ed. Jean-Michel Poughon, 91–110 (Strasbourg: Presses universitaires de Strasbourg, 2006); Alain Sériaux, "Heurs et malheurs de l'esprit de système: la théorie du patrimoine d'Aubry et Rau," in *Aubry et Rau: leurs œuvres, leurs enseignements*, ed. Jean-Michel Poughon, 79–89 (Strasbourg: Presses universitaires de Strasbourg, 2006); François Rigaux, *La protection de la vie privée et des autres biens de la personnalité* (Paris: L.G.D.J., 1990); Nicholas Kasirer, "Translating Part of France's Legal Heritage: Aubry and Rau on the Patrimoine," *Revue générale de droit* 38 (2008): 453–93; Anne-Marie Patault, *Introduction historique au droit des biens* (Paris: Presses universitaires de France, 1989), 100–2; Madeleine Cantin Cumyn and Michelle Cumyn, "La notion de biens," in *Mélanges offerts au professeur François Frenette: études portant sur le droit patrimonial*, ed. Sylvio Normand, 127–50 (Sainte-Foy, QC: Presses de l'Université Laval, 2006).
48 K.-S. Zachariæ, *Le droit civil français, traduit de l'allemand sur la cinquième édition, annoté et rétabli suivant l'ordre du Code Napoléon*, trans. G. Massé and Ch. Vergé, 5 vols. (Paris, 1854–60), esp. 2:38–48, translated from Karl Salomo Zachariä, *Handbuch des französischen Civilrechts*, 5th ed. by August Anschütz, 4 vols. (Heidelberg, 1853). The titles of the successive editions of Aubry and Rau's work reveal the weakening of the debt to Zachariä: *Cours de droit civil français, traduit de l'allemand de M. C.S. Zachariæ, professeur à l'Université de Heidelberg; revu et augmenté, avec l'agrément de l'auteur*, 5 vols. (Strasbourg, 1839–46); *Cours de droit civil français, traduit de l'allemand de M. C.S. Zachariæ*, 2nd ed., 5 vols. (Strasbourg, 1843–4); *Cours de droit civil français d'après l'ouvrage allemand de C.-S. Zachariæ*, 3rd ed., 6 vols. (Paris, 1856); *Cours de droit civil français d'après la méthode de Zachariæ*, 4th ed., 8 vols. (Paris, 1869–79).
49 Alain Sériaux, "La notion juridique de patrimoine: brèves notations civilistes sur le verbe avoir," *Revue trimestrielle de droit civil* (1994): 801–13.
50 Aubry and Rau, *Cours* (1st ed.), 4:100; see also Deroussin, "Personnalité," 104.
51 E.g., Demolombe, *Cours de code civil*, 9:6. Charles Toullier's terminology was slightly different. For him, one of the earliest commentators on the

French code, *choses* meant all things that could be of utility, even if one did not possess them and they were not part of one's patrimony, while *biens* were those things that one possessed and that were part of one's patrimony. C.-B.-M. Toullier, *Le droit civil français, suivant l'ordre du Code Napoléon, ouvrage dans lequel on a tâché de réunir la théorie à la pratique*, 8 vols. (Rennes, 1811–18), 3:6–7.

52 Aubry and Rau, *Cours* (1st ed.), 1:332n5 (emphasis in original): "plus large que celui de *prix* ou de *valeur vénale*; il comprend tout ce qui peut contribuer au bien-être moral ou matériel de l'homme, et par conséquent, des avantages non appréciables en argent."

53 Aubry and Rau, *Cours* (1st ed.), 1:331 and n2: "qui se confond avec l'existence de la personne qui a des droits à exercer sur eux."

54 Aubry and Rau, *Cours* (1st ed.), 4:99.

55 E.g., Demolombe, *Cours de code civil*, 9:6–10. See also G. Vacher-Lapouge, *Théorie du patrimoine* (Paris, 1879), 17–20 (rejecting as part of the patrimony both *biens innés* and moral utility).

56 Aubry and Rau, *Cours* (3rd ed.), 5:2.

57 Aubry and Rau, *Cours* (4th ed.), 6:230–1.

58 Laurent Bouchel, *La bibliothèque ou trésor du droit français* (Paris, [1615] 1671), 2:541, under "Libelles diffamatoires," cited in Walton, *Policing Public Opinion*, 40, 249n6.

59 Kasirer, "Translating Part of France's Legal Heritage," 464.

60 Bibaud, *Commentaires*, 2:306–7: "Tout ce qui nous apporte quelque utilité ou quelque plaisir est donc à bon droit appelé bien." This echoes Claude-Joseph de Ferrière, *Dictionnaire de droit et de pratique*, nouvelle édition by M. ***, 2 vols. (Paris, 1769), 1:185, which in turn quotes *Digest* 50.16.49.

61 August Finger, "Rechtsgut oder rechtlich geschütztes Interesse: Zur Lehre vom Objecte des Verbrechens," *Der Gerichtssaal* 40 (1888): 139–57; Markus Dirk Dubber, "Comparative Criminal Law," in *The Oxford Handbook of Comparative Law*, ed. Mathias Reimann and Reinhard Zimmerman (Oxford: Oxford University Press, 2008), n103.

62 Bibaud, *Commentaires*, 2:557–60.

63 See, among many other examples, [François Genet], *Théologie morale, ou resolution des cas de conscience selon l'Ecriture-Sainte, les Canons, & les Saints Pères* (Paris, 1703), 7:328; Christian Wolff, *Institutions du droit de la nature et des gens* (Leiden, 1772), 1:199; Henri Storch, *Cours d'économie politique, ou exposition des principes qui déterminent la prospérité des nations* (Paris, 1823), 1:91–2; G.-F. Monnier, *Le grand don de Dieu à la terre: cours complet de religion comprenant le dogme, la morale, les sacrements et la liturgie* (Lyons, 1861), 2:278–9.

64 Greenwood, "Lower Canada (Quebec)."
65 François-Maximilien Bibaud, "Développement de deux points des Observations sur le projet de code canadien," in *Exégèse de jurisprudence* (n.p., [1861?]), 16.
66 Édouard Lefebvre de Bellefeuille, "Code civil du Bas-Canada: législation sur le mariage," *Revue canadienne* 1 (1864): 602–19, 654–72, 731–48, and 2 (1865): 30–44; Lefebvre de Bellefeuille, "Une question de mariage," *Revue canadienne* 4 (1867): 838–49. In the 1920s, Pelland used his editorship of the *Revue du droit* to produce frequent opinion pieces against divorce and adoption, with evocative titles such as "À bas le divorce!" *Revue du droit* 5 (1926–7): 449–60.
67 *Chef dit Vadeboncoeur v. Léonard et vir* (1862), 6 L.C.J. 305 at 307, 13 L.C. Rep. 74 (Sup. Ct.): "tellement attachée à [la] personne." In the twentieth century the courts reversed this position, except for defamation damages: Pierre Beullac, *La responsabilité civile dans le droit de la Province de Québec* (Montreal: Wilson & Lafleur, 1948), 728–9.
68 *Chamberland v. Parent* (1882), 8 Q.L.R. 299 (Sup. Ct.): "ce qu'elle a perdu ou manqué d'avoir n'étant pas dans le commerce, et échappant à toute évaluation."
69 E.g., in his judgment in *Jasmin v. Sauriol (Clermont v. Sauriol)* (1900), R.J.Q. 10 B.R. 294 at 298 (Sup. Ct.).
70 John Corrigan, *Business of the Heart: Religion and Emotion in the Nineteenth Century* (Berkeley: University of California Press, 2002), 163–85 (quotation at 163).
71 For American theorist Wesley Hohfeld, a "no-right" was the jural opposite of a "right," both used in the technical senses that he elaborated. As will be made clear shortly, "no right" in these Quebec cases was a more vernacular and less technical usage. See Wesley N. Hohfeld, *Fundamental Legal Conceptions as Applied in Judicial Reasoning*, ed. Walter Wheeler Cook (New Haven, CT: Yale University Press, 1920), reprinting earlier articles.
72 *Hart v. Therien* (1879), 5 Q.L.R. 267 at 268, 9 R.L. 579 (Q.B.): "une Blennorrhée, vulgairement appelée 'chaude pisse.'" The Court of Queen's Bench, reversing the 1878 decision of the Superior Court, awarded the patient $10 damages plus costs.
73 *Hart v. Therien* (Q.L.R.), 268: "n'avait aucun droit de formuler son compte en y indiquant le nom d'une maladie honteuse."
74 *Hart v. Therien* (Q.L.R.), 273: "un médecin n'a pas le droit de publier dans un compte pour services professionnels la nature de la maladie pour laquelle il réclame le prix de ses services, lorsque telle publication est de nature à blesser ou injurier son débiteur."

75 It should be noted that this absence of "right" was not necessarily characteristic of other areas of law or other types of action. In actions in recovery of debt, for example, plaintiffs asserted a "right" of recovery. Such procedural rights were different from the substantive rights we are considering here.
76 Auguste Sourdat, *Traité général de la responsabilité ou de l'action en dommages-intérêts en dehors des contrats*, 3rd ed., 2 vols. (Paris, 1876), 1:462; Henri Fromageot, *De la faute comme source de la responsabilité en droit privé* (Paris, 1891), 74–9; Demogue, *De la réparation civile des délits*, 36–7. Quebec authors adopted the French viewpoint: Pierre-Basile Mignault, *Le droit civil canadien basé sur les "Répétitions écrites sur le code civil" de Frédéric Mourlon avec revue de la jurisprudence de nos tribunaux*, 9 vols. (Montreal, 1895–1916), 5:333; Langelier, *Cours*, 3:463.
77 Louis Josserand, *De l'abus des droits* (Paris: Arthur Rousseau, 1905).
78 E.g., *Poulin v. Vigeant* (1890), 20 R.L. 567 (Q.B.).
79 See chapter 7.
80 Alphonse Boistel, *Cours de philosophie du droit*, 2 vols. (Paris, 1899), 1:189–98; Heinrich Ahrens, *Cours de droit naturel ou de philosophie du droit, fait après l'état actuel de cette science en Allemagne* (Paris, 1838), 96: "On appelle encore ces droits, droits *innés* et *absolus*, et on compte parmi eux, le droit de chaque homme à sa vie, à la liberté, à la dignité, à l'honneur, etc."
81 Richard Risk and Robert C. Vipond, "Rights Talk in Canada in the Late Nineteenth Century: 'The Good Sense and Right Feeling of the People,'" *Law and History Review* 14 (1996): 1–32. We will discuss this issue more fully in chapter 8.
82 *Dorion v. Hogan* (1882), 2 Déc. C.A. 238 (Q.B.): "humiliation déshonorante." The case file fills out the sketchy published report.
83 Édouard Fuzier-Herman, ed., *Répertoire général alphabétique du droit français*, 37 vols. (Paris, 1886–1906), 18:194; Vergau, *Der Ersatz immateriellen Schadens*.
84 Jean-Pierre Royer, "La traduction de la douleur en 'espèces sonnantes et trébuchantes': origines historiques, méthodes, statistiques, doctrine et jurisprudence, ancienne et contemporaine, judiciaire et administrative," in *La douleur et le droit*, ed. Bernard Durand, Jean Poirier, and Jean-Pierre Royer, 439–50 (Paris: Presses universitaires français, 1997).
85 Simmonds, "She Felt Strongly the Injury to Her Affections."
86 Witt, "Political Economy of Pain," 241–2.
87 *Delisle v. Boisvert*, case file, Bref et déclaration (produced 19 September 1904), 3: "Le demandeur, de ces attaques à l'innocence et à la fidélité de sa fiancée, souffre dans sa sensibilité, son honneur et sa personne et ses biens des dommages qu'aucune compensation pécuniaire ne pourrait égaler et que pour éviter à frais il veut bien réduire à la somme de deux cents dollars."

88 France: Demogue, *De la réparation civile des délits*; Armand Dorville, "La réparation pécuniaire du dommage moral," *Canadian Bar Review* 6 (1928): 670–8; Givord, *La réparation du préjudice moral*. England: John D. Mayne, *A Treatise on the Law of Damages: Comprising Their Measure, the Mode in Which They Are Assessed and Reviewed, the Practice of Granting New Trials, and the Law of Set-Off*, 2nd ed. by Lumley Smith (London, 1872), 25; Frederick Pollock, *The Law of Torts: A Treatise on the Principles of Obligations Arising from Civil Wrongs in the Common Law*, 2nd ed. (London, 1890), 169–70.

89 *Angers v. Pacaud* (1896), R.Q.J. 5 B.R. 17 at 19: "Ce dommage, qu'on l'appelle 'réel' ou 'exemplaire,' 'général' ou 'spécial,' 'vindictif,' 'pénalité' ou 'amende,' 'punition' ou 'châtiment,' doit toujours représenter la réparation du tort causé à autrui."

90 John E.C. Brierley and Roderick A. Macdonald, eds., *Quebec Civil Law: An Introduction to Quebec Private Law* (Toronto: Emond Montgomery, 1993), 471.

91 E.g., "penal and exemplary damage" (*dommage pénal et exemplaire*) in *Pope v. Post Printing and Publishing Co.* (1887), 32 L.C.J. 50 at 51 (Sup. Ct., Papineau J.), affirmed without reasons by the Court of Review.

92 *Chalin v. Gagnon* (1899), 5 R. de J. 320 at 320 (Circ. Ct., Sorel).

93 *Antille v. Marcotte* (1888), 11 L.N. 339 at 340 (Circ. Ct., Hull).

94 *Charest v. Hurtubise* (1893), R.J.Q. 4 C.S. 93.

95 *Chiniquy et vir v. Bégin* (1915), R.J.Q. 24 B.R. 294: "une punition suffisante de la faute commise par l'intimé" (the quotation is not in the reported judgment, but appears in the judgment in the case file).

96 *Talbot v. Duhaime* (1937), R.J.Q. 64 B.R. 386 at 392 (Rivard J.).

97 *Levi v. Reed* (1881), 6 S.C.R. 482 at 489–90.

98 *Levi v. Reed*, 491.

99 *Levi v. Reed*, 489.

100 *Levi v. Reed*, 496: "autant de têtes, autant d'opinion."

101 *Hétu v. French* (1908), R.J.Q. 17 B.R. 429 at 433: "La mesure de ces dommages n'est pas et ne peut être fixe: elle doit varier suivant la fortune et la position des parties, suivant leur rang, ou leur influence sociale, et aussi, il faut bien le dire, suivant la balance dans laquelle un chacun de nous pèse et apprécie la compensation à accorder, suivant son mode, la mesure, en l'appliquant aux circonstances."

102 Thomas McCord, *Synopsis of the Changes in the Law Effected by the Civil Code of Lower Canada* (Ottawa, 1866), 4–5.

103 Along similar lines, see Philip Girard's distinction between "facilitative liberalism" and "embedded liberalism": Philip Girard, "Land Law, Liberalism, and the Agrarian Ideal: British North America, 1750–1920," in *Despotic Dominion: Property Rights in British Settler Societies*, ed. John McLaren, A.R. Buck, and Nancy E. Wright (Vancouver: UBC Press, 2005), 122.

2. Shame, Mortification, Disgrace, Dishonour

1 E.g., Dareau, *Traité des injures*, vii: "De tous les biens, le plus précieux à soigner"; Boistel, *Cours*, 1:243: "un bien très précieux"; François Laurent, *Principes de droit civil*, 4th ed. (Brussels, 1887), 20:415: "l'essence de notre être."
2 On these intersections between honour and other factors, see Cecilia Morgan, "'In Search of the Phantom Misnamed Honour': Duelling in Upper Canada," *CHR* 76 (1995): 529–62; Frank Henderson Stewart, *Honor* (Chicago: University of Chicago Press, 1994), 9–29.
3 Édouard-Zotique Massicotte, "Brève histoire du Parc Sohmer," *Cahiers des dix* 11 (1946): 97–117; Yvan Lamonde and Raymond Montpetit, *Le Parc Sohmer de Montréal, 1889–1919: un lieu populaire de culture urbaine* (Quebec City: Institut québécois de recherche sur la culture, 1986).
4 On Dominion Park, see "Parc Dominion Park Recreation Grounds (1906–1929–1938?)," Closed Canadian Parks, http://cec.chebucto.org/ClosPark/Dominion.html. Incubator exhibits, containing real babies and staffed by medical professionals, were a common feature at the era's amusement parks: William A. Silverman, "Incubator-Baby Side Shows," *Pediatrics* 64 (1979): 127–41.
5 Kathy Peiss, *Cheap Amusements: Working Women and Leisure in Turn-of-the-Century New York* (Philadelphia: Temple University Press, 1986), 62–7, 115–38, quotation at 62; Peter Bailey, *Popular Culture and Performance in the Victorian City* (Cambridge: Cambridge University Press, 2003), 13–29; Michèle Dagenais, *Faire et fuir la ville: espaces publics de culture et de loisirs à Montréal et Toronto, XIXe et XXe siècles* (Sainte-Foy, QC: Presses de l'Université Laval, 2006).
6 On walking and riding as social and performative activities, see Laurent Turcot, "L'émergence d'un loisir: les particularités de la promenade en carrosse au Canada au XVIIIe siècle," *RHAF* 64 (2010): 31–70; Laurent Turcot and Christophe Loir, "La promenade: un objet de recherche en plein essor," in *La promenade au tournant des XVIIIe et XIXe siècles (Belgique-France-Angleterre)*, ed. Laurent Turcot and Christophe Loir, 7–20 (Brussels: Université de Bruxelles, 2011).
7 "Le Parc Dominion," *La Patrie* (4 June 1906), 3.
8 "Deux accidents 18 victimes," *La Presse* (12 March 1906), 1; "The Civil Courts," *The Gazette* (20 January 1909), 8.
9 "J.P. Henderson, of St. Lambert, Falls from Car on Dominion Park Scenic Railway," *The Gazette* (16 August 1906), 3; "Scenic Railway Action," *The Gazette* (11 May 1907), 5; "Dominion Park Loses Suit," *The Gazette* (14 May 1907), 9.

10 "Dominion Park Swept by Fire," *(Quebec City) Daily Telegraph* (7 November 1907), 1; "Seven Killed in Blaze at Dominion Park," *The Gazette* (11 August 1919), 1.
11 "Alleged Pickpocket Arrested," *The Gazette* (11 September 1906), 3.
12 *Corbeil v. Dominion Park Co.* (1907), 13 R.L. (n.s.) 432 (Sup. Ct. Rev.), affirming the 1906 judgment of the Superior Court. On ridership, see *Corbeil v. Dominion Park* (case file), deposition of Lee Seymour for defendant (19 October 1906), 3. See also Eric H. Reiter, "Translating the Untranslatable: Historical Aspects of the Protection of Honour and Other Extrapatrimonial Interests in Quebec Civil Law," in *Les intraduisibles en droit civil*, ed. Alexandra Popovici, Lionel Smith, and Régine Tremblay, 157–84 (Montreal: Thémis, 2014).
13 Corbeil first appears in the 1871 census for Sault-au-Récollet, north of Montreal, the third of at least ten children of joiner (*menuisier*) Roch and Eléanor Corbeil. Later he had moved to Montreal and worked as a retail grocer (1891 census), a saloon keeper (1893 Lovell Directory), and a businessman of some kind earning $700 yearly (1901 census, occupation illegible). By 1904 he owned a restaurant near the Montreal courthouse, ads for which appeared frequently in the gossip column "Couacs" in *Le Canard*, e.g. (22 October 1904), 8, and others. By the time of the incident at the park he had bought the Grand Hotel nearby, which he kept until 1908. By 1909, when he testified before the Cannon Commission on illegal liquor sales in Montreal's hotels and restaurants, he had sold the hotel and was living back in Sault-au-Récollet with his father and an unmarried sister (*Témoignages de la Commission Royale 1909*, vol. 2, AM P39-2-1_2, 10 May 1909; 1911 census). By the 1921 census, he appears to have married Bernardette Aubé and was living with her and her two brothers in Ahuntsic, near his childhood home and down the street from one of his brothers. On the hotel, see "St. Gabriel Hotel: Historic Structure to Be Razed to Make Way for Law Centre," *The Gazette* (16 March 1963), 15. Couture would later buy into the hotel as Corbeil's partner: "Une grave accusation," *La Presse* (23 January 1908), 4 (they are listed as co-owners in this story of an alleged arson attack on the hotel).
14 "Police Court News," *The Gazette* (18 April 1894), 3; "The Criminal Courts," *The Gazette* (18 June 1894), 3; "Three Saloon-Keepers May Lose Licenses," *The Gazette* (31 December 1904), 5.
15 *Corbeil v. Dominion Park* (case file), deposition of Lee Seymour for defendant (19 October 1906), 3–4.
16 *Corbeil v. Dominion Park* (case file), depositions of Marie Falardeau for plaintiff (19 October 1906), 6; Theodore Lauezzari for defendant (19 October 1906), 5; Wilfrid Corbeil on his own behalf (19 October 1906), 12.

17 *Corbeil v. Dominion Park* (case file), deposition of Theodore Lauezzari for defendant (19 October 1906), 5.
18 *Corbeil v. Dominion Park* (case file), deposition of Theodore Lauezzari for defendant (19 October 1906), 12–14. The defence witnesses all denied the blow on the head.
19 The park's owner and chief constable both testified to this effect, and that Corbeil said nothing about himself. *Corbeil v. Dominion Park* (case file), depositions of Harry A. Dorsey for defendant (22 October 1906), 2–3; Lee Seymour for defendant (19 October 1906), 5.
20 *Corbeil v. Dominion Park* (case file), Bref et déclaration (produced 16 July 1906), 1: "humiliation profonde"; "un honnête et paisible citoyen"; "l'intention malicieuse de nuire à la réputation du demandeur et de lui faire du tort et le disgracier comme un criminel aux yeux de ses concitoyens."
21 *Corbeil v. Dominion Park* (case file), Bref et déclaration (produced 16 July 1906), 1: "dans son honneur, dans sa personne, dans ses biens et sa sensibilité."
22 *Corbeil v. Dominion Park* (case file), Bref et déclaration (produced 16 July 1906), 1–2: "un carotteur, un voleur et un exploiteur qui se permettait d'assister à des spectacles sans payer le prix d'entrée."
23 *Corbeil v. Dominion Park* (case file), deposition of Wilfrid Corbeil on his own behalf (19 October 1906), 6: "je connaissais Monsieur Lamoureux un peu, c'est un marchand tailleur et sa dame et ses deux filles étaient là; c'était une insulte."
24 *Corbeil v. Dominion Park* (case file), deposition of Wilfrid Corbeil on his own behalf (19 October 1906), 7: "tout le monde me regardait naturellement, tout le monde n'était pas supposé si j'avais raison ou tort; c'était une grande insulte."
25 *Corbeil v. Dominion Park* (case file), deposition of Marie Falardeau for plaintiff (19 October 1906), 6: "Vous voyez vous deux, vous êtes témoins que la police m'a touché, enfin c'est une insulte."
26 *Corbeil v. Dominion Park* (case file), Factum du demandeur (dated 6 March 1907), 2: "qu'il est très humiliant pour un respectable citoyen de se faire bousculer par un constable devant une grande foule.… Il n'y a pas de prix qui puisse indemniser d'un tel affront."
27 *Corbeil v. Dominion Park* (case file), deposition of Pierre Carignan for plaintiff (19 October 1906).
28 *Corbeil v. Dominion Park* (case file), deposition of Marie Falardeau for plaintiff (19 October 1906), 7: "Cela a attiré l'attention sur Monsieur Corbeil et sur nous-autres. Quand on va à une place comme cela et qu'on est insulté de même, vous comprenez que les yeux se jettent sur nous."

29 *Corbeil v. Dominion Park* (case file), deposition of Sarah Caveny for defendant (19 October 1906), 4.
30 *Corbeil v. Dominion Park* (case file), depositions of Charles-Édouard Lamoureux for plainitff (19 October 1906), 6; Wilfrid Corbeil on his own behalf (19 October 1906), 11–12.
31 *Corbeil v. Dominion Park* (case file), deposition of Léon Couture for plaintiff (19 October 1906), 4.
32 *Corbeil v. Dominion Park* (case file), depositions of Marie Falardeau for plaintiff (19 October 1906), 3, 8; Cecile Lamoureux for plaintiff (19 October 1906), 2.
33 On links between honour and masculinity, see especially Nye, *Masculinity*.
34 *Corbeil v. Dominion Park* (case file), deposition of Léon Couture for plaintiiff (19 October 1906), 9: "laissez-moi faire, parce que je peux en manger deux ou trois comme cela."
35 *Corbeil v. Dominion Park* (case file), deposition of F. Lorne McAllen for defendant (19 October 1906), 2–3, 4.
36 *Corbeil v. Dominion Park* (case file), deposition of Sarah Caveny for defendant (19 October 1906), 10.
37 *Corbeil v. Dominion Park* (case file), deposition of Theodore Lauezzari for defendant (19 October 1906), 12–13.
38 *Corbeil v. Dominion Park* (case file), deposition of Marie Falardeau for plaintiff (19 October 1906), 10: "Pour moi, j'aimerais autant avoir des coups de poings que d'être poussée comme cela."
39 *Corbeil v. Dominion Park* (case file), Plea (produced 10 September 1906), 1.
40 *Corbeil v. Dominion Park* (case file), depositions of Theodore Lauezzari for defendant (19 October 1906), 6; Sarah Caveny for defendant (19 October 1906), 3.
41 *Corbeil v. Dominion Park* (case file), deposition of Theodore Lauezzari for defendant (19 October 1906), 3.
42 *Corbeil v. Dominion Park* (case file), deposition of Sarah Caveny for defendant (19 October 1906), 3–4, 14–15 (quotation).
43 *Corbeil v. Dominion Park* (case file), deposition of Charles-Édouard Lamoureux for plaintiff (19 October 1906), 3.
44 *Corbeil* (R.L.), 433–5.
45 *Corbeil v. Dominion Park* (case file), Defendant's Factum in Review (dated 22 April 1907), 1–2.
46 *Corbeil v. Dominion Park* (case file), Factum du demandeur (dated 6 March 1907), 8–9: "N'était-ce pas humiliant au suprême degré pour le demandeur de se faire trainer ainsi alors qu'il n'avait absolument rien fait de dérogatoire à l'ordre ou aux bonnes mœurs? De quel droit un constable peut-il trainer ainsi, sans le mettre sous arrêt un citoyen paisible?"

47 *Corbeil v. Dominion Park* (case file), Factum du demandeur (dated 6 March 1907), 11: "un ancien soldat anglais habitué à une discipline très rigide.... Il est chatouilleux et par trop susceptible. Il est orgueilleux."
48 *Corbeil v. Dominion Park* (case file), Factum du demandeur (dated 6 March 1907), 13–16.
49 Some details of the review judgment not in *Corbeil* (R.L.), including this quotation, are in "The Civil Courts," *The Gazette* (6 July 1907), 13.
50 Peter Berger, "On the Obsolescence of the Concept of Honor," *Archives européennes de sociologie* 11 (1970): 339–47; Alison Lever, "Honour as a Red Herring," *Critique of Anthropology* 6, no. 3 (1986): 83–106. In addition to works cited elsewhere in this chapter, I have drawn particularly on the following: Miller, *Humiliation*; Martin Ingram, "Law, Litigants, and the Construction of 'Honour': Slander Suits in Early Modern England," in *The Moral World of the Law*, ed. Peter Coss, 134–60 (Cambridge: Cambridge University Press, 2000); Nicholas Kasirer, "Honour Bound," *McGill Law Journal* 47 (2002): 237–59; Joel F. Harrington, *The Faithful Executioner: Life and Death, Honor and Shame in the Turbulent Sixteenth Century* (New York: Picador, 2014); Carolyn Strange, Robert Cribb, and Christopher E. Forth, eds., *Honour, Violence and Emotions in History* (London: Bloomsbury Academic, 2014).
51 Though art. 1056 para. 2 CCLC explicitly addressed deaths by duelling, I have found no evidence of civil cases involving duelling in our period, nor any reports of Quebec duels in the newspapers. Ægidius Fauteux, *Le duel au Canada* (Montreal: Éditions du Zodiaque, 1934) gives Quebec examples from the pre-Confederation period only.
52 Nye, *Masculinity*, 15–30; Reddy, *Invisible Code*, 8–14; Thomas, *If I Lose Mine Honour*.
53 Colombine [Éva Circé-Côté], *Bleu, blanc, rouge: poésies, paysages, causeries* (Montreal: Deom frères, 1903), 186: "Qu'adviendra-t-il de notre race, si nous laissons le sentiment de l'honneur s'atrophier chez la jeune génération? Malheur! si le feu sacré vient à s'éteindre. Vestales préposées à sa garde, nous serons enterrées toutes vivantes dans ce flot d'égoïsme qui monte, qui monte toujours, et menace de nous envahir."
54 On the social dimensions of honour, see especially (albeit on an earlier period) Thomas, *If I Lose Mine Honour*.
55 *Poitevin v. Morgan* (1866), 10 L.C.J. 93 at 97–8 (Sup. Ct.).
56 This mixing is evident throughout Pierre Beullac's discussion of defamation and libel: *La responsabilité civile*, 104–73.
57 See Joseph Kary, "The Constitutionalization of Quebec Libel Law, 1848–2004," *Osgoode Hall Law Journal* 42 (2004): 229–70.

58 See, e.g., the remarks by Justice François Langelier in *Marcotte v. Bolduc* (1906), R.J.Q. 30 C.S. 222 at 224.
59 *Poulin v. Vigeant* (1890), 20 R.L. 567 (Q.B.), overturning the Superior Court judgment of 13 June 1889.
60 *Angers v. Pacaud* (1894), R.J.Q. 5 C.S. 339, affirmed (1896) R.J.Q. 5 B.R. 17.
61 *Dorion v. Hogan* (case file), deposition of Henry Hogan for plaintiff (7 October 1880), 11.
62 *Dorion v. Hogan* (1882), 2 Déc. C.A. 238 at 239–40 (Q.B.): "souffert moralement"; "les procédés ignominieux."
63 *Gauthier v. Jeannotte* (1897), R.J.Q. 6 B.R. 520 at 527. The trial decision was reversed on appeal, a decision confirmed by the Supreme Court of Canada: (1898) 28 S.C.R. 590.
64 *Ouimet v. Compagnie d'imprimerie et de publication du Canada* (1887), 17 R.L. 242 (Sup. Ct.). The Court of Queen's Bench agreed: (1889) M.L.R. 6 Q.B. 36.
65 *Compagnie de publication du Canada Revue v. Fabre* (1895), R.J.Q. 8 C.S. 195 at 272 (Sup. Ct. Rev.): "La presse est une immense armée qui a déjà conquis le monde ... elle a ses bataillons réguliers, commandés par des officiers d'élite; mais elle a aussi ses hordes indisciplinées, qui n'ont pour chefs trop souvent que des bandits, et pour soldats que des barbares. Gare aux flèches empoisonnées de ceux-ci! L'état est trop souvent incapable d'empêcher les excès de ces soldats d'aventure."
66 *Beaubien v. Verner* (1899), 6 R. de J. 409 at 417 (Q.B.). Once again, Justice Henri-Thomas Taschereau, writing for the majority, took the contrary view and dismissed the point about press freedom (at 418).
67 *Auburn v. Berthiaume* (1903), R.J.Q. 23 C.S. 476 at 481.
68 Discussed in Stewart, *Honour*, 15, citing Moritz Liepmann, *Die Beleidigung* (Berlin: Puttkammer & Mühlbrecht, 1909), 14. On the French terminology, see Bernard Beignier, *L'honneur et le droit* (Paris: L.G.D.J., 1995), 153–4. Jean-Jacques Rousseau, *Discours sur l'origine et les fondemens de l'inégalité parmi les hommes* (Amsterdam, 1755), 252–3, quoted in Hervé Mauroy, "L'amour-propre: une analyse théorique et historique," *Revue européenne des sciences sociales* 52, no. 2 (2014): 73–104.
69 *Guay v. Meunier* (1874), 6 R.L. 174 at 177–8 (Circ. Ct.): "sa sensibilité froissée."
70 For a discussion of this case, see Nootens, *Genre, patrimoine et droit civil*, 166–80.
71 *Stevenson v. Baldwin* (1919), 26 R.L. (n.s.) 298 at 299–300 (K.B., Martin J.).
72 *Stevenson v. Baldwin* (1920), R.J.Q. 34 B.R. 41 at 42 (K.B., Carroll J.): "Il faut, en ces matières, considérer la position sociale des parties, leur âge, leurs habitudes, toutes choses qui influent sur le plus ou moins de gravité des

faits invoqués. En effet, il est probable qu'un mot grossier ne sera pas injurieux si les parties manquent d'instruction ou d'éducation."
73 *Tudor et vir v. Quebec & Lake St. John Railway Co.* (1911), R.J.Q. 41 C.S. 19. The reported judgment differs significantly in wording and details from the copy in the archival register of judgments. Citations below will indicate the source.
74 On the celebrations, see Ronald Rudin, *Founding Fathers: The Celebration of Champlain and Laval in the Streets of Quebec, 1878–1908* (Toronto: University of Toronto Press, 2003), 163–7.
75 "Workman's Death Not Due to Work," *The Gazette* (30 January 1919), 5. Her appeal to the Court of Review failed: "The Civil Courts," *The Gazette* (8 December 1919), 19.
76 *An Act for the relief of Euphemia Tudor Slade*, S.C. 1925 (15–16 Geo. V), c. 191; "Quebec Social Notes," *The Gazette* (16 August 1927), 8 (on her literary work); Euphemia Tudor, "Some Difficulties of the Canadian Writer," *The Gazette* (2 November 1929), 20.
77 *Tudor v. Quebec & Lake St. John Railway* (case file), deposition of James Sunderland for defendant (2 November 1910), 3, 5–6.
78 *Tudor v. Quebec & Lake St. John Railway* (case file), deposition of Antoine Cantin for defendant (2 November 1910), 10.
79 *Tudor v. Quebec & Lake St. John Railway* (case file), deposition of Euphemia Tudor on her own behalf (2 November 1910), 6.
80 *Tudor v. Quebec & Lake St. John Railway* (case file), deposition of Antoine Cantin for defendant (2 November 1910), 13–14.
81 *Tudor v. Quebec & Lake St. John Railway* (case file), Writ of Summons and Declaration (entered 21 October 1908), 1–2.
82 *Tudor v. Quebec & Lake St. John Railway* (case file), deposition of Euphemia Tudor on her own behalf (2 November 1910), 14.
83 *Tudor v. Quebec & Lake St. John Railway* (case file), deposition of Antoine Cantin for defendant (2 November 1910), 14.
84 *Tudor v. Quebec & Lake St. John Railway* (case file), deposition of Euphemia Tudor on her own behalf in rebuttal (2 November 1910), 1.
85 *Tudor v. Quebec & Lake St. John Railway* (case file), deposition of Margaret Slade for plaintiff (2 November 1910), 2.
86 *Tudor v. Quebec & Lake St. John Railway* (case file), deposition of Euphemia Tudor on her own behalf (2 November 1910), 16–17.
87 *Tudor v. Quebec & Lake St. John Railway* (case file), deposition of Victor Hamel for defendant (2 November 1910), 3: "paraissait de mauvaise humeur."

88 *Tudor v. Quebec & Lake St. John Railway* (case file), deposition of Euphemia Tudor on her own behalf (2 November 1910), 5, 12.
89 *Tudor v. Quebec & Lake St. John Railway* (case file), Plaidoyer (filed 18 January 1909), 1: "avec beaucoup de courtoisie et de délicatesse"; "avec impolitesse"; "n'a qu'à s'en prendre à elle-même, si elle a souffert des ennuis en cette occasion."
90 *Tudor v. Quebec & Lake St. John Railway* (case file), deposition of James Sunderland for defendant (2 November 1910), 6.
91 *Tudor v. Quebec & Lake St. John Railway* (case file), deposition of Joseph E. Breton for defendant (2 November 1910), 1: "s'était oubliée, c'est-à-dire qu'elle allait trop loin, elle n'était pas polie pour le conducteur."
92 "Il obtient des dommages," *Le Soleil (Quebec City)* (7 February 1911), 3; "Judgment for Damages," *Quebec (City) Chronicle* (7 February 1911), 10.
93 *Tudor* (R.J.Q.), 28.
94 *Tudor* (R.J.Q.), 30.
95 *Tudor* (R.J.Q.), 30.
96 *Tudor* (R.J.Q.), 29.
97 *Tudor* (R.J.Q.), 32.
98 Craig Heron, *Booze: A Distilled History* (Toronto: Between the Lines, 2003), 169–85.
99 *Premier Congrès de Tempérance de Montréal (partie ouest) tenu à Ville St-Pierre le 25 octobre 1909: procès-verbal et travaux* (Montreal: Imprimerie des sourds-muets, 1909). Desrosiers contributed a speech, "Le prêtre dans la lutte contre l'alcool," 51–68.
100 "Against the Barroom," *The Gazette* (16 January 1911), 7; "Blue Bonnets Votes 'Dry,'" *The Gazette* (24 January 1911), 3. Blue Bonnets was the area's former name, ironically named after a racetrack that had itself been named after a local tavern: Al Palmer, "Blue Bonnets 1830 Had Horsy Set Too," *The Gazette* (9 April 1964), 3; John Fraser, *Canadian Pen and Ink Sketches* (Montreal, 1890), 197–9.
101 "Lachine Closes 'Dry' Campaign," *The Gazette* (12 October 1915), 4; "Lachine to Have Total Prohibition," *The Gazette* (20 October 1915), 4.
102 "Lachine in Midst of Big Campaign," *The Gazette* (30 December 1916), 6.
103 The humour newspaper *Le Canard* (2 July 1916), 7, mentioned an upcoming plebiscite on liquor scheduled for 10 July 1916, but I have found no coverage of the result in the Montreal papers. See also the discussion of the town's liquor control regime in a later liquor transport and sale case, *Ville St-Pierre v. Zeppieri* (1924), 32 R. de J. 67 at 68–9 (Recorder's Ct., Ville St-Pierre).

104 Vadim Kukushkin, *From Peasants to Labourers: Ukrainian and Belarusan Immigration from the Russian Empire to Canada* (Montreal and Kingston: McGill-Queen's University Press, 2007), 110–14.
105 Kukushkin, *From Peasants to Labourers*, 120.
106 *Rinkuk v. Ville St-Pierre* (1918), R.J.Q. 56 C.S. 43 (Sup. Ct. Rev.). The haphazard spelling of Slavic names at the time makes locating any of the people involved in the case in other documents difficult. For example, one of the witnesses, Rinkuk's neighbour named "Hrecza," seems to be the "Reskuk" in the 1916–17 Lovell Directory (p. 2105), living at 154 St. Jacques St., next door to number 152 where the Rinkuks lived (though the latter are not listed). "Rinkuk" (which is given as "Renkuk" or "Rinsuk" in some of the news coverage) might be a phonetic attempt at "Hrynchuk" or something similar. The case took place between the 1911 and 1921 censuses, and so even if the orthographical difficulties could be overcome, the immigrant population was mobile enough to make it extremely difficult to locate these individuals.
107 *Rinkuk v. Ville St-Pierre* (case file), deposition of Peter Rinkuk on his own behalf (23 January 1917), 3–4.
108 On community bonds among Polish immigrants, see Joshua C. Blank, "Pitching, Pies and Piety: Early Twentieth Century St. Hedwig's Parish Picnics," *CCHA Historical Studies* 76 (2010): 61–85.
109 *Rinkuk v. Ville St-Pierre* (case file), depositions of Peter Rinkuk on his own behalf (23 January 1917), 4; Katrina Hrecza for plaintiff (23 January 1917), 4; Rigarie Pisodashneag for plaintiff (23 January 1917), 4–5.
110 "Bloody Fights at Christenings: Well Wishers of the Newcomers in the Polish Colony Finish in Town Court," *Bridgeport (Connecticut) Herald* (7 November 1909), 6. See, along similar lines, "Polish Warriors," *Meriden (Connecticut) Record* (5 June 1905), 6; "Liquor Breaks Up Christening Party," *Ottawa Citizen* (15 August 1916), 3; "Christening Started It," *(Toronto) Globe* (2 October 1925), 12.
111 *Rinkuk v. Ville St-Pierre* (case file), deposition of Katrina Hrecza for plaintiff (23 January 1917), 3–4.
112 *Rinkuk v. Ville St-Pierre* (case file), deposition of Peter Rinkuk on his own behalf (23 January 1917), 2. Polish priests were themselves often opposed to alcohol, or at least its excessive consumption: William Galush, "The Unremembered Movement: Abstinence among Polish Americans," *Polish American Studies* 63, no. 2 (2006): 13–22.
113 *Leguerrier v. Ville St-Pierre* (1919), 25 R. de J. 437 (Sup. Ct.).
114 *Rinkuk v. Ville St-Pierre* (case file), depositions of Peter Rinkuk on his own behalf in rebuttal (23 January 1917), 2; Emilien Leguerrier for defendant (23 January 1917), 6: "était furieuse, elle était pareille comme un tigre."

115 *Rinkuk v. Ville St-Pierre* (case file), deposition of Adrien Richer for defendant (23 January 1917), 4.
116 *Rinkuk v. Ville St-Pierre* (case file), Bref de sommation (reportable 1 September 1916) and Judgment of Recorder's Court (Recorder J.O. Lacroix, Ville St-Pierre, 2 October 1916).
117 *Rinkuk v. Ville St-Pierre* (case file), Plaintiff's Declaration (dated 2 November 1916), 1.
118 Though at one point the stenographer mistakenly identified Isidore Popliger as "K.C.," he was just three years out of law school (though he would in fact later be named K.C.). See "Three Young Jewish Men Pass the Bar Examination," *Canadian Jewish Times* (11 July 1913), 13; Vladimir F. Wertsman, *Salute to the Romanian Jews in America and Canada, 1850–2010: History, Achievements, and Biographies* (n.p.: Xlibris, 2010), 213–14. Around this time, Popliger was mentioned in the newspapers in frequent legal notices for actions in which he represented Jewish wives seeking separation as to property from their husbands: e.g. *Le Devoir* (8 September 1917), 8; *Le Devoir* (3 November 1917), 10; *Le Devoir* (19 December 1917), 5.
119 Lovell Directory (1917–18), 2112.
120 *Rinkuk v. Ville St-Pierre* (case file), deposition of Adrien Richer for defendant (23 January 1917), 6–7.
121 *Rinkuk v. Ville St-Pierre* (case file), deposition of Emilien Leguerrier for defendant (23 January 1917), 12.
122 *Rinkuk v. Ville St-Pierre* (case file), deposition of Emilien Leguerrier for defendant (23 January 1917), 9–10: "après qu'ils sont saoûls, ils donnent leur argent."
123 *Rinkuk v. Ville St-Pierre* (case file), deposition of Peter Rinkuk on his own behalf (23 January 1917), 8–9.
124 *Rinkuk v. Ville St-Pierre* (case file), deposition of Peter Rinkuk on his own behalf (23 January 1917), 11–12.
125 *Rinkuk v. Ville St-Pierre* (case file), deposition of Rigarie Pisodashneag for plaintiff (23 January 1917), 3–4. Elsewhere in the file, it is clear the witness's given name is Gregory or Grigory. The surname is spelled this way throughout the file.
126 *Rinkuk v. Ville St-Pierre* (case file), deposition of Rigarie Pisodashneag for plaintiff (23 January 1917), 5.
127 *Rinkuk v. Ville St-Pierre* (case file), deposition of Emilien Leguerrier for defendant (23 January 1917), 7–8: "Naturellement quand on arrive dans un troupeau, surtout de ces gens-là qui sont de quarante à cinquante et qui ont de la bière à profusion, bien souvent il y a des orgies-là que j'ai saisi la bière, il y avait déjà trop de barils, j'ai fait trois prisonniers, ils étaient saoûls tous les trois, c'était pour prévenir les orgies que j'ai saisi la bière."

128 *Rinkuk v. Ville St-Pierre* (case file), deposition of Katrina Hrecza for plaintiff (23 January 1917), 1–2.
129 *Rinkuk v. Ville St-Pierre* (case file), Judgment (19 February 1917, Sup. Ct., Weir J.), 4 (the reported judgment gives excerpts only; the complete reasons are in the case file).
130 E.g., *Hart v. Shorey* (1897), R.J.Q. 12 C.S. 84 at 86: enticing plaintiff's wife to leave him and move with defendant to the United States brought "disgrace and humiliation" on him.
131 *Rinkuk v. Ville St-Pierre* (case file), Factum de la défenderesse intimée (produced 5 November 1918), 4: "Faut-il trop blâmer Le Guerrier d'avoir voulu empêcher une orgie, alors que la loi permettait d'interner les Autrichiens dans les camps de concentration?"
132 *Rinkuk v. Ville St-Pierre* (case file), Factum of Plainitff in Review (produced 1 October 1918), 2–3.
133 *Rinkuk v. Ville St-Pierre* (case file), Factum of Plaintiff in Review (produced 1 October 1918), 6.
134 *Rinkuk v. Ville St-Pierre* (1918), R.J.Q. 56 C.S. 43 (Sup. Ct. Rev.).
135 "La police s'est fourvoyée," *Le Devoir* (23 January 1917), 6: "Les Polonais ont la réputation d'être de bons buveurs et cette réputation n'est pas surfaite si l'on en juge par des faits particuliers. Ce qui n'est pour des Polonais qu'un simple apéritif peut souvent paraître à d'autres personnes une quantité suffisante pour étourdir la population de tout un bourg." See also "Tout est relatif…," *Le Devoir* (20 February 1917), 2. The other papers adopted a similar tone: "Police Mistook Baptism for Revel," *The Gazette* (20 February 1917), 5; "L'intervention de la police n'avait pas de raison d'être," *Le Canada* (20 February 1917), 8; "La bière leur était indispensable," *La Patrie* (20 February 1917), 7; "Awarded Damages for False Arrest," *Montreal Daily Mail* (20 February 1917), 3; "La police n'aurait pas dû intervenir dans cette réunion," *La Presse* (20 February 1917), 13.
136 On charivari in Quebec, see especially René Hardy, *Charivari et justice populaire au Québec* (Quebec City: Septentrion, 2015), which is based on criminal prosecutions. See also Édouard-Zotique Massicotte, "Le charivari au Canada," *Bulletin des recherches historiques* 32 (1926): 712–25; Stephen Kenny, "'Cahots' and Catcalls: An Episode of Popular Resistance in Lower Canada at the Outset of the Union," *CHR* 65 (1984): 184–208; René Hardy, "Le charivari dans la sociabilité rurale québécoise au XIXe siècle," in *De la sociabilité: spécificité et mutations*, ed. Roger Levasseur, 59–72 (Montreal: Boréal, 1990); Allan Greer, "From Folklore

to Revolution: Charivaris and the Lower Canadian Rebellion of 1837," *Social History* 15 (1990): 25–43; René Hardy, "Le charivari: divulguer et sanctionner la vie privée?" in *Discours et pratiques de l'intime*, ed. Manon Brunet and Serge Gagnon, 50–69 (Quebec City: Institut québécois de recherche sur la culture, 1993); Wendie Nelson, "'Rage against the Dying of the Light': Interpreting the Guerre des Éteignoirs," *CHR* 81 (2000): 551–89. For Canada and elsewhere, see Bryan D. Palmer, "Discordant Music: Charivaris and Whitecapping in Nineteenth-Century North America," *Labour/Le Travail* 3 (1978): 5–62; E.P. Thompson, "Rough Music Reconsidered," *Folklore* 103 (1992): 3–26; Pauline Greenhill, *Make the Night Hideous: Four English-Canadian Charivaris, 1881–1940* (Toronto: University of Toronto Press, 2010).

137 On political charivaris, see Reiter, "From Shaved Horses to Aggressive Churchwardens," 461–3; Hardy, *Charivari*, 188–222.

138 *Lortie v. Claude* (1892), R.J.Q. 2 C.S. 369. The case file (no. 2571) includes depositions from two separate actions, by father and daughter (nos. 2569 and 2571). Various other actions involving these same parties are listed on an undated typed sheet in the case file (added later by an anonymous researcher). One such case is a nuisance action involving the said stream, *Weir v. Claude* (1888), M.L.R. 4 Q.B. 197.

139 John J. Bigsby, *The Shoe and Canoe, or Pictures of Travels in the Canadas* (London, 1850), 1:34, quoted in Michael S. Cross, "The Laws Are Like Cobwebs: Popular Resistance to Authority in Mid-Nineteenth-Century British North America," *Dalhousie Law Journal* 8 (1984): 109.

140 *Duquette v. Pesant dit Sans-Cartier* (1892), R.J.Q. 1 C.S. 465. The charivari gave rise to several actions by the same plaintiff: the reported case, *Duquette v. Pesant dit Sans-Cartier* (no. 2191); an action against the same defendants alleging facts arising after the main action, *Duquette v. Sans-Cartier* (no. 2636); and *Duquette v. Turcot* (no. 495). All three actions went as far as the Court of Review.

141 In the 1881 census he was listed (as "Davilla," occupation "commis" or assistant) in the St. Eustache household of his father (a saddler). In 1891, he was listed as thirty-two years old and himself a saddler in St. Léonard with his wife Delphine (thirty-nine years old) and her father and sister, Antoine and Eliza Paquette. One witness testified that he was unsure whether Duquette had been living in St. Léonard as long as ten years: *Duquette v. Turcot* (case file), deposition of Louis Sicard for defendants (13 May 1892), 2. I have not been able to establish from the census whether or not his wife was from the St. Léonard area.

142 E.g., *Duquette v. Turcot* (case file), depositions of Gédéon Limoges for defendants (13 May 1892), 4; Anthine Desautels for defendants (13 May 1892), 3.

143 *Duquette v. Turcot* (case file), deposition of Louis Sicard for defendants (13 May 1892), 2.

144 *Duquette v. Turcot* (case file), deposition of Louis Turcot for plaintiff (27 May 1892), 1–2, quotation at 2: "Je n'ai pas voulu aller au bout avec lui."

145 *Duquette v. Pesant dit Sans-Cartier* (case file), deposition of Alfred Deschamps for plaintiff (7 April 1892), 2. This was also alluded to briefly in *Duquette v. Turcot* (case file), deposition of Anastasie Brochu for plaintiff (13 May 1892), 1r.

146 *Duquette v. Turcot* (case file), deposition of Joseph Martineau for plaintiff (27 May 1892), 1.

147 *Duquette v. Turcot* (case file), deposition of Catherine Martineau for defendants (27 May 1892).

148 *Duquette v. Turcot* (case file), deposition of Joseph Filiatrault for defendants (27 May 1892), 4: "pour l'amour des patates."

149 *Duquette v. Turcot* (case file), deposition of Bazile Collerette for defendants (27 May 1892), 1: "des bonnes patates nouvelles."

150 *Lortie v. Claude* (case file), deposition of Philomène Lortie for plaintiffs (3 February 1892), 1–2 (other witnesses confirmed this).

151 *Duquette v. Pesant dit Sans-Cartier* (case file), deposition of Joseph Collerette dit Bourguignon for plaintiff (26 November 1891), 1–2. Sinaï Martineau himself denied doing this, but he denied virtually everything: *Duquette v. Pesant dit Sans-Cartier* (case file), deposition of Sinaï Martineau for defendant (11 April 1892). Jean-Baptiste Duquette, the plaintiff's father, said that Sinaï entered the house without permission: *Duquette v. Pesant dit Sans-Cartier* (case file), deposition of Jean-Baptiste Duquette for plaintiff (7 April 1892), 1r.

152 *Duquette v. Pesant dit Sans-Cartier* (case file), deposition of Alfred Deschamps for plaintiff (7 April 1892), 5: "Lorsqu'on ne veut pas se mêler à quelque chose, on ne remarque rien. Lorsque quelqu'un disait: 'ils font du bruit,' je restais dans ma maison tranquille."

153 *Duquette v. Pesant dit Sans-Cartier* (case file), deposition of Jean-Baptiste Duquette for plaintiff (25 November 1891), 6–7; *Duquette v. Turcot* (case file), deposition of Jean-Baptiste Duquette for plaintiff (13 May 1892), 3r.

154 *Duquette v. Pesant dit Sans-Cartier* (case file), deposition of Bazile Collerette dit Bourguignon for plaintiff (30 November 1891), 1r.

155 *Duquette v. Turcot* (case file), depositions of Emélie David for plaintiff (13 May 1892), 1r; Frédéric Martineau for plaintiff (13 May 1892), 6–7. The

Notes to pages 93–4   345

various phases of the trials were covered in several Montreal papers, but I have found no coverage at the time of the charivari itself.

156 On money payments, see, e.g., Massicotte, "Le charivari au Canada," 715–16; Greer, "From Folklore to Revolution," 31–2, 39, 78–80; Hardy, *Charivari*, 130 (on "cruel" charivaris), 139–41.

157 *Duquette v. Pesant dit Sans-Cartier* (case file), deposition of Léocadie Paquette for plaintiff (30 November 1891), 2r–v; *Duquette v. Turcot* (case file), deposition of Jean-Baptiste Duquette for plaintiff (13 May 1892), 4r–v.

158 *Duquette v. Pesant dit Sans-Cartier* (case file), deposition of Ovila Desautels for plaintiff (7 April 1892), 3.

159 "Arrestation d'un voleur," *La Patrie* (11 August 1891), 4; "Arrestation," *L'Étendard* (11 August 1891), 4. A copy of the complaint is in *Duquette v. Turcot* (case file).

160 A record of the police court proceedings was filed as *Duquette v. Turcot* (case file), Plaintiff's Exhibit N. The newspapers did not cover the trial, likely because an acquittal was of less interest to readers than a conviction.

161 The action against Desautels was discontinued, since he was being sued for the acts of his supposedly minor son who in fact had been of full age at the time. The action against Martineau, again for the acts of his two minor sons, was separated from the main action and ultimately dismissed after separate proof. Sans-Cartier and Pesant dit Sans-Cartier were the same man. The two actions in which he was defendant differed only in the amount of damages claimed and the presence of other defendants in the second action; the facts and allegations were substantially identical.

162 *Duquette v. Sans-Cartier* (case file), Bref et déclaration (dated 6 August 1891), 1: "calomnies répandues à profusion"; "dans le but de l'humilier, de le blesser dans son honneur, sa sensibilité et ses biens." The accusation of "calomnies" appears in the declarations of all three actions.

163 *Duquette v. Turcot* (case file), Bref et déclaration (dated 6 August 1891), 1: "dans le but de ruiner le Demandeur"; cf. *Duquette v. Pesant dit Sans-Cartier* (case file), Bref et déclaration (dated 5 September 1891), 1r.

164 *Duquette v. Pesant dit Sans-Cartier* (case file), deposition of Ovila Duquette on his own behalf (7 April 1892); *Duquette v. Turcot* (case file), deposition of Ovila Duquette for defendants (13 May 1892).

165 *Duquette v. Turcot* (case file), deposition of Jean-Baptiste Duquette for plaintiff (13 May 1892), 4r–v.

166 *Duquette v. Turcot* (case file), deposition of Frédéric Martineau for plaintiff (13 May 1892), 8: "envers moi il a toujours été honnêtement [*sic*]."

167 *Duquette v. Pesant dit Sans-Cartier* (case file), deposition of Ovila Desautels for plaintiff (7 April 1892), 3.
168 *Duquette v. Turcot* (case file), deposition of Delphine Constantineau for plaintiff (27 May 1892), 1.
169 *Duquette v. Turcot* (case file), depositions of Eliza Paquette for plaintiff in rebuttal (13 May 1892), 1r–v: "Je n'ai jamais entendu parler qu'il avait rien fait à personne"; Emélie David for plaintiff in rebuttal (13 May 1892), 1r.
170 *Duquette v. Turcot* (case file), deposition of Louis Sicard for defendants (13 May 1892), 1: "l'homme est connu du public comme étant un homme qui est aussi souvent sur le chemin la nuit que le jour, un homme dangereux."
171 *Duquette v. Turcot* (case file), depositions of Gédéon Limoges for defendants (13 May 1892), 2; Anthime Desautels for defendants (13 May 1892), 1.
172 *Duquette v. Turcot* (case file), deposition of Bazile Collerette for defendants (13 May 1892), 1r: "je n'ai rien vu; on entend dire bien des choses; mais on ne peut pas juger une personne sans voir."
173 *Duquette v. Pesant* (case file), Bref et déclaration (undated copy of lost original, produced by consent of the parties), 1v; *Duquette v. Turcot* (case file), Bref et déclaration (produced 21 August 1891), 1; *Duquette v. Sans-Cartier* (case file), Bref et déclaration (produced 22 August 1891), 2: "mon petit Duquette tu es un voleur; un voleur de patates; tu as besoin de quelque piastres pour bâtir ta petite cabane, tu peux aller les demander à Vervais l'hôtelier."
174 *Duquette v. Pesant dit Sans-Cartier* (case file), deposition of Jean-Baptiste Duquette for plaintiff (25 November 1891), 3: "Va mon petit Duquette, va voler des patates chez monsieur Louis Turcot pour faire manger à ton petit père et tu en vendras un peu pour lui acheter du whisky."
175 E.g., *Lemire v. Duclos* (1898), R.J.Q. 13 C.S. 82; *Laplante v. Parenteau* (1889), 33 L.C.J. 124 (Sup. Ct. Rev.).
176 *Duquette v. Turcot* (case file), Réponses du défendeur sur faits et articles (produced 12 February 1892), 1–2; *Duquette v. Pesant dit Sans-Cartier* (case file), depositions of Maxime Jarry for plaintiff (25 November 1891), 3–4; Frédéric Martineau for plaintiff (25 November 1891), 2r; *Duquette v. Turcot* (case file), depositions of Frédéric Martineau for plaintiff (13 May 1892), 6–7; Maxime Jarry for plaintiff (13 May 1892), 10.
177 *Duquette v. Pesant dit Sans-Cartier* (case file), deposition of Jean-Baptiste Duquette for plaintiff (25 November 1891), 3
178 *Duquette v. Pesant* (case file), Judgment against Pesant dit Sans-Cartier et al. (15 January 1892).
179 *Duquette v. Sans-Cartier* (case file), Judgment (17 May 1892).

180 *Duquette v. Pesant* (case file), Judgment against Corbeil (15 January 1892).
181 Duquette discontinued his action against the defendant Desautels, as noted above. The action against Martineau was dismissed, *Duquette v. Pesant* (case file), Judgment against Martineau (23 June 1892, Pagnuelo J.), as was the action against Turcot, *Duquette v. Turcot* (case file), Judgment (27 May 1892, Mathieu J.).
182 *Duquette v. Pesant* (case file), Judgment against Corbeil (Sup. Ct. Rev.). The judgments dismissing the actions against Martineau and Turcot were both affirmed: *Duquette v. Turcot* (case file), Judgment (Sup. Ct. Rev.); *Duquette v. Pesant* (case file), Judgment against Martineau (Sup. Ct. Rev.). *Duquette v. Sans-Cartier* was not appealed. See also "Le charivari de St Léonard," *La Presse* (31 May 1892), 4; "Legal Intelligence," *The Gazette* (1 June 1892), 7; "Legal Intelligence," *The Gazette* (1 December 1892), 7; "Charivari de St Léonard," *La Presse* (28 February 1893), 6.
183 "Charivaris," *Montreal Daily Witness* (16 January 1892), 4. This point was not made directly in any of the witnesses' transcribed depositions.
184 *Duquette* (R.J.Q.), Judgment against defendant Corbeil (15 January 1892), 466n: "cet usage suranné des charivaris ainsi que l'encouragement que leur donnent les gens, par une curiosité malsaine doivent être réprimés."
185 "Pour un charivari," *La Patrie* (15 January 1892), 4; "A propos d'un charivari," *La Presse* (15 January 1892), 4; "Charivaris," *Montreal Daily Witness* (16 January 1892), 4; "A Charivari," *The Gazette* (16 January 1892), 7.
186 *Duquette* (R.J.Q.), Judgment against defendant Pesant dit Sans-Cartier (15 January 1892), 466–7: "d'attirer le mépris public sur le demandeur, de l'humilier, lui et sa famille, et de lui causer des dommages dans ses biens, en lui faisant perdre une partie du patronage dont il jouissait auparavant dans l'exercice de son métier."
187 See, e.g., Ferrière, *Dictionnaire*, 1:261, under "Charivari."

3. Family Dishonour

1 On individual and collective legal conceptions of the family in the common law and civil law traditions, see Philip Girard, "Why Canada Has No Family Policy: Lessons from France and Italy," *Osgoode Hall Law Journal* 32 (1994): 579–611.
2 Reddy, *Invisible Code*, 72. See also Thomas, *If I Lose Mine Honour*, 160–205; Arlette Farge, "The Honor and Secrecy of Families," in *Passions of the Renaissance*, ed. Roger Chartier, trans. Arthur Goldhammer, vol. 3 of *A History of Private Life*, ed. Philippe Ariès and Georges Duby, 571–607 (Cambridge, MA: Belknap Press of Harvard University Press, 1989).

3 Nootens, *Fous, prodigues et ivrognes*; Jean-Maurice Brisson and Nicholas Kasirer, "The Married Woman in Ascendance, the Mother Country in Retreat: From Legal Colonialism to Legal Nationalism in Quebec Matrimonial Law Reform, 1866–1991," *Manitoba Law Journal* 23 (1996): 406–49.
4 Beignier, *L'honneur et le droit*, 433, 488.
5 "Mort de la veuve de l'abbé Chiniquy," *La Patrie* (3 November 1911), 8; "Mrs. Charles Chiniquy," *The Gazette* (3 November 1911), 6; "La femme de Chiniquy meurt à Worcester," *Le Devoir* (3 November 1911), 2; "La veuve de Chiniquy," *La Presse* (3 November 1911), 2.
6 Yves Roby, "Chiniquy, Charles," in *DCB* vol. 12; Richard Lougheed, *The Controversial Conversion of Charles Chiniquy* (Toronto: Clements Academic, 2008); Marcel Trudel, *Chiniquy*, 2nd ed. (Trois-Rivières: Éditions du Bien Public, 1955).
7 E.g., Charles Chiniquy, *L'Eglise de Rome est l'ennemie de la Sainte-Vierge et de Jésus-Christ* (Montreal, 1891).
8 "Mort de la veuve de l'abbé Chiniquy," *La Patrie* (3 November 1911), 8: "veuve de feu l'abbé Charles Chiniquy."
9 "A propos de Chiniquy," *La Vérité* (11 November 1911), 131: "l'ex-abbé Chiniquy"; "chez nous cet apostat est connu sous le nom tout court de *Chiniquy*."
10 Pierre Bayard, "On appelle un chat, un chat, et Chiniquy un apostat," *La Croix* (18 November 1911), 1. At least one other Catholic newspaper repeated the story word-for-word: "A propos de Chiniquy," *La Vérité* (25 November 1911), 7.
11 Bayard, "On appelle": "l'apostat Chiniquy avait pris pour compagne et décoré du titre d'épouse."
12 Bayard, "On appelle": "la malheureuse personne qu'il a voulu associer à son apostasie, il faut le faire de façon à ne pas donner à entendre qu'elle était sa femme. Chiniquy apostat ne pouvait pas plus contracter un mariage que n'importe quel prêtre ou religieux lié par les vœux solennels. Par conséquent, Euphémie Allard n'était pour Chiniquy qu'une concubine."
13 *Chiniquy et vir v. Bégin* (1912), R.J.Q. 42 C.S. 261, affirmed (but damages reduced) (1915) R.J.Q. 24 B.R. 294. The Superior Court case file includes documents prepared for both the trial and the Court of Review. The King's Bench case file includes the plaintiff's and defendant's witnesses' depositions as appendices to the respective factums. The main factums were produced for a first King's Bench hearing, on permission to appeal what both parties thought was an interlocutory decision by the Court of

Review, that Chiniquy had not been duly authorized by her husband and so the case should be sent back to the Superior Court for a new trial. The Court of King's Bench decided (unreported; 21 January 1915) that this had in fact been a final judgment, and ordered the case to be reheard before it and not sent back to the Superior Court. Each party produced additional factums at that point. The Court of King's Bench rendered its final decision in April 1915. Like most publishers of the time, Bégin was no stranger to libel actions. In 1907 he was indicted on three counts of criminal libel following complaints by Joseph Tarte, publisher of *La Patrie*: see "True Bills Found," *The Gazette* (2 March 1907), 11. See also below, note 44.

14 *Chiniquy v. Bégin* (case file), Bref et déclaration (produced 15 December 1911). See also "Libel Suit over Priest's Marriage," *The Gazette* (11 June 1912), 7; "Cette réclamation de la fille de Chs. Chiniquy," *La Presse* (11 June 1912), 5; "Ten-Thousand Dollar Action at Montreal," *(Toronto) Globe* (11 June 1912), 4; "Dragging Name of Dead Through Mire," *(Toronto) Globe* (12 June 1912), 7; "Chiniquy Judgment Held Till To-Morrow," *(Toronto) Globe* (20 June 1912), 7.

15 *Chiniquy v. Bégin* (case file), Bref et déclaration, 2–3: "dans le but d'insulter et de fait insulte à la mémoire du père et de la mère de la demanderesse"; "de nature à vouer la demanderesse à l'exécration et à la vindicte des habitants de cette province"; "est de nature à causer et cause à la demanderesse un tort considérable en la blessant dans son honneur, ainsi que dans l'honneur de ses père et mère, dans sa sensibilité et dans ses biens."

16 *Chiniquy v. Bégin* (case file), Plaidoyer (produced 10 January 1912).

17 See Charles Augustine, *A Commentary on the New Code of Canon Law* (St. Louis, MO: B. Herder, 1918), 2:195 (commentary on canon 213§2 of the 1917 Code).

18 *Chiniquy v. Bégin* (case file), Plaidoyer (produced 10 January 1912), 2: "avait droit de critiquer l'homme même, sa conduite et ses idées."

19 See *Chiniquy v. Bégin* (case file), depositions of David Latour for defendant (20 June 1912); Maria Morais for plaintiff (20 June 1912); "La preuve qu'on voudrait faire," *La Presse* (20 June 1912), 22; "Morin vs. 'La Croix'," *Le Devoir* (20 June 1912), 8; "Sensation in Chiniquy Case," *The Gazette* (21 June 1912), 18; "Chiniquy vs Bégin," *La Croix* (22 June 1912), 1; "One More Delay in Chiniquy Case," *(Toronto) Globe* (21 June 1912), 1, 11.

20 *Chiniquy v. Bégin* (case file), Factum du défendeur-intimé sur appel d'un jugement interlocutoire (28 October 1914), 34: "c'est du pharisaïsme que de s'indigner et de prétendre que l'on attaque une femme."

21 *Chiniquy v. Bégin* (case file), Factum du défendeur-intimé sur appel d'un jugement interlocutoire (28 October 1914), 39–42.

22 In 1913, he sued the Catholic *L'Action Sociale* for $25,000 over an article that suggested he was a Freemason: see "Une erreur de MM. Lanson et Faguet," *L'Action Sociale* (2 August 1913), 6, with the paper's retraction (18 September 1913), 1. The action was not contested, and judgment was rendered *ex parte* for $250, later confirmed by the Court of Review: Desaulniers v. L'Action Sociale (1914), R.J.Q. 46 C.S. 161 (Sup. Ct. Rev.). In 1923 Desaulniers was named to the Superior Court.
23 *Chiniquy v. Bégin* (case file), deposition of Rebecca Chiniquy on her own behalf (10 June 1912), 5: "Il m'a beaucoup blessé, monsieur."
24 *Chiniquy v. Bégin* (case file), deposition of Rebecca Chiniquy for defendant (11 June 1912), 4 (re-examination by defendant's lawyer).
25 R.-P. Duclos, *Histoire du protestantisme français au Canada et aux États-Unis*, 2 vols. (Lausanne: Georges Bridel; Paris: Fischbacher, [1913]), 1:37–8.
26 *Chiniquy v. Bégin* (case file), deposition of Joseph E. Morin for plaintiff (10 June 1912), 11: "Très gravement, et je ne sais pas si j'ai raison de rapporter ce que je dis, mais ma femme n'a jamais reçu d'injures comme celle-là, affectant toute la famille"; "mais quant au reste de la famille je ne crois pas que jamais on ne l'ait attaquée et je ne crois pas que la question de son mariage ait été mis en question"; "très humiliant ... ma femme a été très profondément blessée de voir une accusation comme celle-là attachée à notre famille."
27 *Chiniquy* (Sup. Ct.), 268.
28 "Dragging Name of Dead through Mire," *(Toronto) Globe* (12 June 1912), 7.
29 *Chiniquy* (Sup. Ct.), 271.
30 *Chiniquy* (Sup. Ct.), 273.
31 *Chiniquy* (Sup. Ct.), 274.
32 *Chiniquy* (Sup. Ct.), 275. "La Cour condamne M. J. Bégin à $3,000 de dommages-intérêts," *La Presse* (21 June 1912), 8; "M. Bégin est condamné à payer $3,000," *Le Devoir* (21 June 1912), 6; "Judgment in Chiniquy Case," *Sherbrooke Daily Record* (21 June 1912), 8; "Defendant Scored in Chiniquy Case," *The Gazette* (22 June 1912), 9; "Mde Morin vs La 'Croix'," *Le Pays* (29 June 1912), 8.
33 "Dismisses Action on Legal Omission," *The Gazette* (13 June 1914), 6.
34 *Chiniquy* (K.B.), 295.
35 "Le journal la 'Croix' condamné en Cour d'appel," *La Presse* (26 April 1915), 5; "Chiniquy vs la 'Croix,'" *Le Devoir* (26 April 1915), 2; "Chiniquy vs. Bégin," *La Croix* (1 May 1915), 1.
36 *Chiniquy* (K.B.), 305: "Sa douleur a dû être immense ... sa mère, qui venait d'être enlevée à son affection, et dont les cendres n'étaient pas encore refroidies. Existe-t-il au monde une mémoire plus sacrée que celle de la

femme qui nous a donné la vie, qui a bercé notre enfance dans ses bras, et qui a pris la part la plus large à nos joies et à nos douleurs?"
37 *Chiniquy* (K.B.), 306.
38 *Chiniquy* (K.B.), 310.
39 *Chiniquy* (K.B.), 311. Justice Trenholme's reasons are not recorded in the case file.
40 See, e.g., "L'affaire Chiniquy-Bégin," *La Croix* (20 July 1912), 1. Bégin's commentary continued through the summer of 1912, and picked up again around the time of the Court of Review and King's Bench judgments.
41 See, e.g., "Libel Suits against Catholic Papers," *Catholic Fortnightly Review* 19 (1912): 423.
42 M.T., "Il faut les vaincre," *La Croix* (8 May 1915), 1: "la secte chiniquiste."
43 "L'affaire Chiniquy," *La Croix* (8 May 1915), 1–2 and (15 May 1915), 2.
44 *Bouchard v. Bégin* (1921), 27 R.L. (n.s.) 341 (Sup. Ct. Rev.). A first trial had also awarded $100, but was overturned on review and sent back for retrial: *Bouchard v. Bégin* (1919), R.J.Q. 57 C.S. 9 (Sup. Ct. Rev.).
45 Henry Coleman Folkard, *Folkard's Starkie on Slander and Libel*, 4th ed. (New York, 1877), 837; W. Blake Odgers, *The Law of Libel and Slander and of Actions on the Case for Words Causing Damage*, 5th ed., Canadian notes by W.J. Tremeear (Toronto: Canada Law Book, 1912), 456.
46 Dareau, *Traité des injures*, 304; Joseph-Nicolas Guyot, *Répertoire universel et raisonné de jurisprudence civile, criminelle, canonique et bénéficiale* (Paris, 1784), 9:230; Beignier, *L'honneur et le droit*, 39.
47 Joseph-Pierre Chassan, *Traité des délits et contraventions de la parole, de l'écriture et de la presse* (Paris, 1837), 1:352: "est-il vrai que la loi n'a point voulu couvrir de sa protection la froide poussière du tombeau? le nom que nous laissons après nous et que nous léguons à nos enfans, à nos proches, à nos amis, pourra-t-il être impunément outragé? N'y a-t-il pas là aussi des intérêts à garantir, des espérances à protéger, une communauté de souvenirs, véritable propriété de famille, qu'il faut défendre contre les atteintes de la méchanceté?" See also P. Grand, *Diffamation envers les morts* (Paris, 1860), 7–15.
48 Chassan, *Traité des délits*, 1:353: "dans une autre patrie, où sont heureusement inconnus tous les sentimens de colère et de vengeance, qui nous transportent et nous possèdent ici bas."
49 Chassan, *Traité des délits*, 1:356: "Le trait lancé contre le père, en frappant la pierre du tombeau, peut réagir contre les enfants, et, en blessant leur propre réputation, atteindre ainsi leurs intérêts."
50 E.g., Dareau, *Traité des injures*, 322; Théodore Grellet-Dumazeau, *Traité de la diffamation, de l'injure et de l'outrage* (Riom, 1847), 1:39–47; Auguste Sourdat,

Traité général de la responsabilité ou de l'action en dommages-intérêts en dehors des contrats, 2 vols. (Paris, 1852), 1:38–51.
51 E.g., F. Arthur Müllereisert, *Die Ehre im deutschen Privatrecht* (Berlin: C. Heymann, 1931), 69.
52 Perreau, "Des droits de la personnalité," 530.
53 *Leclerc v. Bizier* (1874), 6 R.L. 269 at 270 (Q.B.): "une *certaine personne* que l'Intimé a souvent désignée" (appellant's factum; emphasis in original).
54 *Leclerc v. Bizier*, 270: "[P]eu soucieux de l'honneur de sa famille," Bizier "s'est fait de sa langue une *épée à deux tranchants*, car du même coup qui blesse la réputation de l'Appelant, il détruit l'honneur de sa fille et flétrit celui de sa propre famille" (emphasis in original).
55 *Joyal v. Lafontaine* (1926), 33 R. de J. 514 at 518 (Sup. Ct.): "d'empêcher que cette famille et madame Joyal soient déshonorées par cette alliance avec le demandeur."
56 *Chénier v. Martin* (1904), R.J.Q. 25 C.S. 324 at 324: "le demandeur aurait insulté et défié le fils majeur du défendeur, le défendeur lui-même et toute sa famille; et c'est à la suite de ces provocations que la bagarre commença." The reported decision is on an interlocutory issue; a decision on the merits is not reported.
57 "Les trois condamnés se sont dirigés vers le gibet avec sang-froid et résignation," *La Patrie* (23 January 1920), 1. See Jeffrey Pfeifer and Ken Leyton-Brown, *Death by Rope: An Anthology of Canadian Executions* (Regina: Vanity, 2007), 1:214–15.
58 "Seized Wax Image in Eden Museum," *The Gazette* (31 March 1920), 4: "Aujourd'hui, les trois pendus." On the museum, see Tracy S. Ludington, "Old Montreal Waxwork Museum to Close after Half a Century," *The Gazette* (10 June 1940), 10; Hervé Lepine, "Qui se souvient de Marie Scapulaire?" *La Patrie* (1 April 1965), 5; Hervé Gagnon, "Divertissement et patriotisme: la genèse des musées d'histoire à Montréal au XIXe siècle," *RHAF* 48 (1995): 321–32. On New York's Eden Musée, the model for the one in Montreal, see Andrea Stulman Dennett, *Weird and Wonderful: The Dime Museum in America* (New York: New York University Press, 1997), 115–17.
59 "Wax Figures of Hanged Men to Be Concealed," *Montreal Herald* (31 March 1920), 2.
60 *Eden Musée, Montreal, Galeries historiques, Catalogue, 10 cents, Musée Eden, Montréal* ([Montreal], n.d.), digitized at LAC (amicus 13876021). Several brochures survive, of which this is the only one with the museum's owner given as International Shows, Ltd.
61 *Eden Musée, Montreal*, 2.

62 Details from "La gérant Mathurin, du Musée Eden, devra subir son procès, aux Assizes," *La Presse* (31 March 1920), 15; "Seized Wax Image in Eden Museum," *The Gazette* (31 March 1920), 4; "Cette statue servira de témoin muet," *La Patrie* (31 March 1920), 3; "Weird Procession When Wax Figure Hauled to Court," *Montreal Daily Star* (31 March 1920), 3; "Wax Figures of Hanged Men to Be Concealed," *Montreal Herald* (31 March 1920), 2; "Est-ce un libelle?" *Le Devoir* (31 March 1920), 3; Jean Tillemont, "Une exploitation criminelle," *Le Nationaliste* (4 April 1920), 1.

63 "Wax Figures of Hanged Men to Be Concealed," *Montreal Herald* (31 March 1920), 2; see also "Le père de Roméo Lacoste poursuit pour libelle le gérant du Musée Eden," *La Presse* (23 March 1920), 11. The case file does not survive; details of the proceedings come from the newspapers and *R. v. Mathurin* (plumitif).

64 "Wax Figures of Hanged Men to Be Concealed," *Montreal Herald* (31 March 1920), 2 (quotation); "Est-ce un libelle?" *Le Devoir* (31 March 1920), 3 (other families).

65 "Weird Procession When Wax Figure Hauled to Court," *Montreal Daily Star* (31 March 1920), 3.

66 "Museum Manager Held For Trial," *The Gazette* (1 April 1920), 4; "Defamed in Wax," *The Gazette* (21 October 1920), 5.

67 "Enquete Held in Wax Figure Case," *Gazette* (14 April 1920), 7.

68 The quotations that follow are from "Argued Libel Was Not Committed," *The Gazette* (13 May 1920), 6. See also "La défense nie qu'il y ait eu un libelle," *La Patrie* (14 May 1920), 14; "Serait-ce un libelle?" *Le Devoir* (14 May 1920), 8; "Des points de droit soumis, à l'enquête," *La Presse* (14 May 1920), 32.

69 "Méli-mélo," *Le Canard* (9 May 1920), 11; Jean Tillemot, "Une exploitation criminelle," *Le Nationaliste* (4 April 1920), 1: "badauderie." The famous play *Aurore l'enfant martyre* was first produced early in 1921: Peter Gossage, "*La marâtre*: Marie-Anne Houde and the Myth of the Wicked Stepmother in Quebec," *CHR* 76 (1995): 579–80.

70 *Decelles v. International Shows Ltd.* (1920), R.J.Q. 59 C.S. 374; further information from *Decelles v. International Shows* (plumitif). Coverage of the judgment is in "Defamed in Wax," *The Gazette* (21 October 1920), 5; "Au sujet d'icones en cire," *La Patrie* (21 October 1920), 2; "Chronique judiciaire," *Le Canada* (21 October 1920), 5; "Pay Damages for Waxwork Figure," *Montreal Daily Star* (21 October 1920), 9; "Un tableau diffamatoire," *Le Devoir* (21 October 1920), 7; "Le 'Musée Eden' est condamné," *La Presse* (21 October 1920), 9; "Holds Display of Wax Figure Libel Incurring Damages," *Ottawa Citizen* (21 October 1920), 2; "Hanged,

Displayed Exhibitor Fined," *Border Cities Star (Windsor, ON)* (21 October 1920), 1.
71 *Decelles*, 375: "privilège que la loi accorde, sous certaines conditions, à l'historien, au critique, etc."
72 *Eden Musée, Montreal*, 2.
73 *Decelles*, 375: "ladite exposition constitue une diffamation illégale de la mémoire du condamné, qu'elle est de nature à légitimement humilier le demandeur et son épouse lorsqu'ils apprennent que dans le cercle des connaissances qu'ils sont dans l'occasion de voir fréquemment, il en est qui, au fait de la parenté qui les unit au nommé Delorme, viennent récemment de visiter cette exposition."
74 Conrad Poirier Collection, BAnQ-VM, P48, S1, P5192 and P5216.
75 *Wilhelmy v. Brisebois* (1883), 12 R.L. 424 at 426, 27 L.C.J. 175, 6 L.N. 276 (Circ. Ct.): "l'insulte ... rejaillit sur toute la famille." Justice Michel Mathieu also found that the required notice for actions against public officials had not been given, and that the churchwarden had been in the exercise of his functions.
76 *Labarre v. Morin* (case file), Déclaration et bref (returned 6 August 1885), 1: "humilier et jeter le déshonneur sur le Demandeur, son épouse et sa famille."
77 *Antille v. Marcotte* (1888), 11 L.N. 339 at 340 (Circ. Ct.). This collective view of family honour was a change from some earlier Quebec decisions, which rejected similar actions by fathers: e.g., *Neill v. Taylor* (1865), 13 Q.L.R. 195 (Q.B.).
78 *Barrette v. Bourbonnière* (1896), R.J.Q. 12 C.S. 271 (Archibald J.): "va donc te faire caresser par ton cavalier dans les escaliers."
79 Art. 176 CCLC.
80 *Frigon v. Massicotte* (1912), R.J.Q. 42 C.S. 445 at 445: "blessé dans ses sentiments d'époux."
81 *Frigon*, 446: "pour venger lui-même l'honneur de sa mère outragée par cette lettre."
82 *Frigon*, 447: "s'il est vrai que l'estime et la considération est le patrimoine commun de la famille, on ne saurait admettre que le déshonneur de l'un des membres rejaillisse sur les autres."
83 *Frigon*, 447: "La considération et l'honneur est un bien exclusif qu'un chacun a à défendre, dont il est le seul juge et a la responsabilité."
84 *Frigon*, 445 n. 1: "Dès lors, n'y aurait-il pas à se demander si l'injure à un père ou à une mère, même vivants, ne peut pas faire autant de mal, blesser aussi vivement les sentiments, appeler tout autant une réparation, un soulagement, un apaisement, une vindicte, que celle faite à des grands

parents, ou à des aïeux, disparus depuis un demi-siècle et plus, que l'on a peut-être jamais vus, ni connus?" The note is unsigned, but the Trois-Rivières reporter is listed as Philippe Bigué, K.C.
85 *Ortenberg v. Plamondon* (1914), R.J.Q. 24 B.R. 69 and 385. For details, see Normand, "L'affaire *Plamondon*"; Constance Backhouse, "Anti-Semitism and the Law in Québec City: The *Plamondon* Case, 1910–15," in *Transformations in American Legal History: Essays in Honor of Professor Morton J. Horwitz*, ed. Daniel W. Hamilton and Alfred L. Brophy, 2:303–25 (Cambridge, MA: Harvard University Press for Harvard Law School, 2009); David Fraser, "The Blood Libel in North America: Jews, Law, and Citizenship in the Early 20th Century," *Law and Literature* 28 (2016): 33–85.
86 *Raymond v. Abel*, [1946] C.S. 251 at 251–2: "courailleux de femmes, une potée et une gang de c[ochons] et salauds"; "que l'injure était adressée à tous les Raymond."
87 *Cloutier v. Roy* (1930), R.J.Q. 49 B.R. 313 at 316: "une vraie putain."
88 See generally Daniel Sperling, *Posthumous Interests: Legal and Ethical Perspectives* (Cambridge: Cambridge University Press, 2008).
89 Art. 893 CCLC. The codifiers based this provision on similar wording in article 1047 of the French civil code. Pothier, a source of the French code, expressed it more emphatically (and restrictively): it had to be "quelque injure sanglante à sa mémoire." See Charles-C. de Lorimier and Charles A. Vilbon, *La bibliothèque du Code civil de la Province de Québec (ci-devant Bas-Canada)*, 21 vols. (Montreal, 1871–90), 7:165–71 (quotation from Pothier at 169).
90 *Roy v. Turgeon* (1886), 12 Q.L.R. 186 (Sup. Ct.).
91 *Roy v. Turgeon* (case file), Bref et déclaration (dated 18 August 1885), 2: "de ne pas seulement flétrir la mémoire du dit Pierre Roy mais de porter atteinte à l'honneur de la famille à laquelle appartient le Demandeur et de faire rejaillir sur ce dernier ... la honte imprimée au caractère de son père."
92 *Roy v. Turgeon* (case file), deposition of Théophile Morency for plaintiff (13 February 1886), 3r (during this witness's testimony, the defence lawyers signed a formal admission of Pierre Roy's good reputation).
93 *Roy v. Turgeon* (case file), deposition of Pierre Antoine Roy for plaintiff (13 February 1886), 3r–v: "Monsieur Turgeon avait tort de reveiller les morts comme cela."
94 *Roy v. Turgeon* (case file), deposition of Damase Roy for defendant (13 February 1886), 1v: "C'est en commun, en famille."
95 *Roy v. Turgeon* (Q.L.R.), 187.
96 *Roy v. Turgeon* (Q.L.R.), 187: "ces sortes d'actions ne doivent pas être encouragées."

97 *Huot v. Noiseux* (1890), 18 R.L. 705 (Sup. Ct., St. Hyacinthe). Both parties appealed. Huot's appeal was allowed in part: *Huot v. Noiseux* (1892), R.J.Q. 2 B.R. 521 (no. 320), while Noiseux's appeal (no. 324) was dismissed. I have not located the trial file, but the appeal files contain the depositions as well as the parties' factums.

98 *Huot v. Noiseux* (case file no. 320), Factum de l'appelant, 4: "j'ai entendu dire que le père Prudent Huot avait été voté à St-Paul au nom de son fils Prudent et qu'il avait été pris sous serment et qu'il aurait fait serment." (The verb tenses in the testimony are non-standard.)

99 *Huot v. Noiseux* (case file no. 320), Factum de l'intimé, appendix B, exhibit A (letter of Fontaine & St-Jacques to Clovis Noiseux, dated 9 October 1886).

100 *Huot v. Noiseux* (case file no. 320), deposition of Clovis Noiseux for plaintiff (5 June 1888), 5.

101 *Huot* (R.L.), 706: "dans l'intention de causer de la peine et du chagrin au demandeur, et à toute sa famille, et de lui causer du tort et du dommage dans ses biens, son crédit et sa réputation."

102 *Huot* (R.L.), 709–10: "le seul intérêt de défendre la mémoire outragée de son défunt père ne suffit pas pour lui donner droit d'action contre le défendeur."

103 *Huot v. Noiseux* (case file no. 320), deposition of Prudent Huot for defendant (2 April 1889), 21: "C'est parce que, quand j'ai vu que j'avais le même droit de poursuivre pour mon père, j'ai poursuivi pour mon père. C'est ce que j'ai fait. Je trouvais que ce n'était pas bien généreux d'attaquer ma famille et puis mon père qui était mort il y avait quinze ans."

104 *Huot v. Noiseux* (case file no. 320), deposition of Philippe Dupuis for plaintiff (5 June 1888), 40–1: "Non, monsieur, pour aucune somme; je tiens trop à l'honneur pour cela"; "Ah! bien, je vais vous dire, c'est une question difficile à répondre; suivant moi, le même tort que ça pourrait faire à toute personne qui aurait un père qui aurait été faussaire"; "Je ne pourrais pas jurer qu'il en a éprouvé ni qu'il n'en a pas éprouvé, je ne connais pas cela du tout."

105 See, e.g., *Belleau v. Mercier* (1882), 8 Q.L.R. 312 at 315 (Sup. Ct.).

106 *Huot v. Noiseux* (case file no. 320), deposition of Prudent Huot for defendant (2 April 1889), 22: "Je ne suis pas capable de dire sur mon serment que ça a fait dommage, mais ça attire de mauvais doutes."

107 *Huot v. Noiseux* (case file no. 320), deposition of Octave Sénécal for defendant (7 May 1889), 37: "mais ça doit lui avoir fait mal au cœur, parce

qu'on n'aime pas à se faire mépriser, ni faire mépriser ses proches, non plus."
108 E.g. *Huot v. Noiseux* (case file no. 320), deposition of Célestin Blain for defendant (7 May 1889), 46.
109 E.g. *Huot v. Noiseux* (case file no. 320), depositions of Janvier Alix for defendant (7 May 1889), 40 and 42; Philippe Dupuis for plaintiff (5 June 1888), 40–1.
110 *Huot v. Noiseux* (case file no. 320), deposition of Nazaire Meunier for plaintiff (8 March 1889), 54: "Si mon père avait fait un faux serment, je serais peut-être bien autant respectable que je suis; mais pour passer parmi les autres je serais peut-être bien pas autant regardé. Ça arrive qu'un bon enfant naisse de parents malhonnêtes. Le crédit, l'honneur et la réputation du demandeur n'ont pas été diminués par les dires du défendeur parce que l'affaire est en marche, mais s'il avait laissé l'affaire de même, ça lui aurait fait quelque chose."
111 *Huot v. Noiseux* (case file no. 320), deposition of Fortunat Huot for defendant (2 April 1889), 12
112 *Huot v. Noiseux* (case file no. 320), deposition of Prudent Huot for defendant (2 April 1889), 23: "tous les cœurs ne sont pas pareils, il y en a qui sont plus sensibles que d'autres. Il y en a qui sont capables d'endurer des injures et d'autres qui ne sont pas capables."
113 *Huot* (R.L.), 714.
114 *Huot* (R.L.), 713: "formant une des parties les plus importantes du patrimoine de ses enfants."
115 *Huot* (R.L.), 714: "Considérant que toute attaque à la réputation d'un défunt affecte plus ou moins les enfants."
116 *Huot v. Noiseux* (case file no. 324), Factum de l'appelant, 16–17.
117 *Huot v. Noiseux* (case file no. 324), Factum de l'appelant, 13.
118 *Huot v. Noiseux* (case file no. 324), Factum de l'appelant, 16: "dans un but louable."
119 *Huot v. Noiseux* (case file no. 320), Factum de l'appelant, XI–XII: "Le chagrin de l'Appelant est amplement prouvé, et se comprend parfaitement, du reste.... Au point de vue moral, le préjudice causé, – déshonneur de toute une famille, – aurait dû provoquer une condamnation exemplaire."
120 Both judgments are reported in *Huot v. Noiseux* (1892), R.J.Q. 2 B.R. 521.
121 Nootens, *Fous, prodigues et ivrognes*, 37. On contests over legal status and family boundaries beyond Quebec, see Matthew Gerber, "On the Contested Margins of the Family: Bastardy and Legitimation by Royal Rescript in Eighteenth-Century France," in *Family, Gender, and Law in*

Early Modern France, ed. Suzanne Desan and Jeffrey Merrick, 223–64 (University Park: Pennsylvania State University Press, 2009); Rachel G. Fuchs, *Contested Paternity: Constructing Families in Modern France* (Baltimore: Johns Hopkins University Press, 2008).

122 This subject has been little explored in Quebec, though see especially Nootens, *Fous, prodigues et ivrognes*, 35–8; and, for New France, André Lachance and Sylvie Savoie, "Violence, Marriage, and Family Honour: Aspects of the Legal Regulation of Marriage in New France," in *Essays in the History of Canadian Law: Volume V – Crime and Criminal Justice*, ed. Jim Phillips, Tina Loo, and Susan Lewthwaite, 143–73 (Toronto: University of Toronto Press for Osgoode Society for Canadian Legal History, 1994). Scholars of colonial Latin America have explored these issues extensively: see Patricia Seed, *To Love, Honor, and Obey in Colonial Mexico: Conflicts over Marriage Choice, 1574–1821* (Stanford: Stanford University Press, 1988); Susan M. Socolow, "Acceptable Partners: Marriage Choice in Colonial Argentina, 1778–1810," in *Sexuality and Marriage in Colonial Latin America*, ed. Asunción Lavrin, 209–51 (Lincoln: University of Nebraska Press, 1989); Kathryn A. Sloan, *Runaway Daughters: Seduction, Elopement, and Honor in Nineteenth-Century Mexico* (Albuquerque: University of New Mexico Press, 2008).
123 Seed, *To Love, Honor, and Obey*, 240.
124 Mignault, *Le droit civil canadien*, 2:141: "l'élément moralisateur de la famille."
125 Art. 137 CCLC.
126 Art. 242 CCLC.
127 E.g., *Hagen v. Stewart* (1913), R.J.Q. 44 C.S. 121. See also the discussion of *Agnew v. Gober* below.
128 See, generally, Alexandre Vantroys, *Étude historique et juridique sur le consentement des parents au mariage de leurs enfants* (Paris, 1889); Jean Desmet, *Du consentement des parents en matière de mariage* (Lille, 1892); Albert Dumont, *Étude sur le consentement des parents au mariage de leurs enfants* (Paris: A. Chevalier-Maresq, 1903).
129 T.J.J. Loranger, *Commentaire sur le Code civil du Bas-Canada*, 2 vols. (Montreal, 1873–9), 2:266: "une procédure d'une haute utilité ... elle sauvegarde l'honneur menacé des familles et protège la bonne foi des époux eux-mêmes."
130 Desmet, *Du consentement des parents*, 16: "Ce n'est donc pas empiéter sur la liberté des époux que de les protéger contre leurs entraînements; c'est bien plutôt leur donner des armes contre leur faiblesse."
131 Mignault, *Le droit civil canadien*, 1:349.

132 François Laurent, *Principes de droit civil français*, 5th ed. (Brussels, 1893), 2:582, citing Portalis. See also the Quebec case *Larocque v. Michon*, discussed in Reiter, "From Shaved Horses to Aggressive Churchwardens," 463–4, 477–80.
133 Charles Demolombe, *Cours de Code Napoléon*, vol. 3, *Traité du mariage et de la séparation de corps* (Paris, 1874), 1:56.
134 Frédéric Mourlon, *Répétitions écrites sur le premier examen de Code Napoléon*, 8th ed. by Charles Demangeat (Paris, 1869), 1:339: "a pour base l'honneur de la famille à sauvegarder; c'est afin qu'ils puissent y maintenir le bon ordre et l'élever par ses bonnes mœurs, qu'on leur permet d'agir."
135 *Leveillé v. Leveillé* (1895), 1 R. de J. 443 (Sup. Ct.): "pure malice et caprice."
136 *Leveillé*, 444.
137 See generally André Morel, "L'enfant sans famille: de l'ancien droit au nouveau *Code civil*," in *Entre surveillance et compassion: l'évolution de la protection de l'enfance au Québec, des origines à nos jours*, ed. Renée Joyal, 7–34 (Sainte-Foy, QC: Presses de l'Université du Québec, 2000); Marie Pratte, "L'évolution du statut juridique de l'enfant naturel en droit civil québécois" (LL.M. thesis, University of Ottawa, 1981).
138 *McAulay v. McLennan* (1902), R.J.Q. 23 C.S. 419 at 421–2: "produit de rapports illégitimes et désordonnés"; "n'a pas voulu infliger un châtiment à toute une famille, qui n'est pas responsable de la faute du père."
139 See, generally, Andrée Lévesque, *La norme et les déviantes: des femmes au Québec pendant l'entre-deux-guerres* (Montreal: Les éditions du Remue-ménage, 1989), esp. 48–50, 121–38; Marie-Aimée Cliche, "Morale chrétienne et 'double standard sexuel': les filles-mères à l'hôpital de la Miséricorde à Québec, 1874–1972," *Histoire sociale/Social History* 24, no. 47 (1991): 85–125.
140 See Nootens, *Fous, prodigues et ivrognes*.
141 Arts. 326 and 349 CCLC.
142 *An Act to provide for the Interdiction and Cure of Habitual Drunkards*, S.Q. 1870 (33 Vic.), c. 26, s. 1; *An Act to amend the Civil Code, with respect to persons who make use of opium or other narcotics*, S.Q. 1895 (59 Vic.), c. 40, s. 1. These were added to the CCLC as arts. 336a–336q (drunkards) and 336r–336s (narcotic users).
143 *An Act to provide for the Interdiction and Cure of Habitual Drunkards*, s. 12 (art. 336c CCLC).
144 Quoted in Nootens, *Fous, prodigues et ivrognes*, 24: "s'enivre d'une manière dégradante & demie vêtue parcourt dans cet état les rues de la dite Cité de Montréal ... elle est par sa conduite une occasion de scandale pour le public & de honte & de disgrâce pour sa famille."

145 *Archambault v. Camirand* (1905), R.J.Q. 27 C.S. 30 at 31: "de mettre sa famille dans le trouble ou la gêne, et de conduire ses affaires au préjudice de sa famille ou de ses créanciers et surtout de l'empêcher de ruiner sa santé et d'abréger ses jours."

146 Nootens, *Fous, prodigues et ivrognes*, 78.

147 The Agnew-Gober affair spawned at least four separate actions and numerous appeals. The cases will be cited by their numbers: *Agnew et uxor v. Gober et vir and Holton* (no. 2122); *Agnew et uxor v. Gober et vir* (no. 801); *Gober v. Agnew et al.* (no. 932); *Gober v. Agnew* (no. 4047). Most of the information that follows comes from the case files, supplemented by the extensive news coverage of the case across Canada and in the United States.

148 Emma Waterous testified that she heard the news from a family friend, a "Mrs. Dr. Reddy," on 22 February: *Agnew v. Gober* (case file no. 801), deposition of Emma Johnson Waterous on her own behalf (25 January 1909), 2. In a letter to May, however, dated 20 February and filed as *Agnew v. Gober* (case file no. 801), Exhibit A of defendant at enquête, Augustus mentioned that he had just written to his sister, telling her to break the news to his mother.

149 "R.M.C. Cadet Married," *(Toronto) Globe* (23 February 1905), 1. An identical article appeared the same day under the headline "Stir at Kingston" in *Toronto Daily Star* (23 February 1905), 4. Another cadet testified that he found out about the marriage only just before Augustus left Kingston that February: *Agnew v. Gober* (case file no. 801), deposition of Douglas Gooderham Ross for plaintiffs (23 January 1906), 4–5.

150 In the court filings Gober (or her lawyers) alleged the story was a pretence: *Gober v. Agnew* (case file no. 932), Declaration (dated 20 February 1907), 2. Earlier, however, she seems to have believed it to be true: *Agnew v. Gober* (case file no. 801), deposition of Mary Gober on her own behalf on Commission in Marietta, Georgia (28 October 1905), 2. Augustus himself testified that his mother was ill: *Agnew v. Gober* (case file no. 801), deposition of Augustus Waterous Agnew for defendant (23 January 1906), 23–4.

151 *Agnew v. Gober* (case file no. 801), deposition of Emma Waterous Agnew on her own behalf (25 January 1909), 2. See also *Agnew v. Gober* (case file no. 801), deposition of Augustus Waterous Agnew for defendant (23 January 1906), 21. Augustus's studies are detailed in an anonymous memorial/obituary, "Augustus Waterous Agnew, Assoc. M. Am. Soc. C.E.," *Transactions of the American Society of Civil Engineers* 81 (1917): 1792–3.

152 *Agnew v. Gober* (case file no. 801), deposition of Augustus Waterous Agnew for defendant (23 January 1906), 10, 15. See (from an earlier period) *General Regulations Royal Military College of Canada, Kingston, Ont., February, 1888* (Ottawa, 1888), 6 (no. 12). The newspapers incorrectly reported that Augustus had been expelled: e.g. "R.M.C. Cadet Married," *(Toronto) Globe* (23 February 1905), 1.

153 "R.M.C. Cadet Married," *(Toronto) Globe* (23 February 1905), 1. The Agnews' religion was recorded in the 1901 census; on the Gobers, see the biography of her father in *Memoirs of Georgia Containing Historical Accounts of the State's Civil, Military, Industrial and Professional Interests, and Personal Sketches of Many of Its People* (Atlanta, 1895), 1:788–9.

154 "Big Sensation Society's Hit," *(Ottawa) Evening Citizen* (20 February 1907), 3.

155 See, e.g., the frequent references to his activities in *Canadian Dry Goods Review* 4 (1894). He was not, however, prominent enough to be profiled in William Cochrane and J. Castell Hopkins, *The Canadian Album: Men of Canada*, 5 vols. (Brantford, ON, 1891–6); or Henry J. Morgan, *The Canadian Men and Women of the Time: A Handbook of Canadian Biography* (Toronto, 1898).

156 See *Gober v. Agnew* (case file no. 932), Particulars and Notice (produced 11 June 1907), 2.

157 A photo of the Gober family gravestone in Citizens Cemetery, Marietta, Georgia, records her dates as 8 February 1875 to 3 July 1953, making her just under thirty years old at the time of the marriage: see http://www.goberfamily.org/Gober/gober-0/p189.htm. The marriage certificate (Ontario, Frontenac County, no. 008672, 14 December 1904) lists their ages as twenty and twenty-six. "Suit over Boy Husband," *(New York) Sun* (21 February 1907), 12, reports Agnew as "a boy of less than 18" and Gober as "a woman of 35." This story went out on the wires and was picked up across the United States.

158 *Memoirs of Georgia*, 1:788–9; "Dr. Newton Gober Dies in Hospital," *Atlanta Constitution* (26 May 1912), 14; "Newton N. Gober, M.D.," *Journal of the American Medical Association* 59 (1912): 48.

159 *Calendar of Queen's (College and) University, Kingston, Canada, for the Year 1898–99* (Kingston, 1898), 130, 180, where she was listed as from Atlanta and educated at Harwood Seminary. She appeared associated with the Kingston Ladies' College beginning in *Foster's Kingston Directory, from July, 1900, to July, 1901* (Toronto: J.G. Foster, [1900]), 7:111.

160 *Gober v. Agnew* (case file no. 932), deposition of Mary Gober on her own behalf (23 March 1907), 7, 14.

161 May Gober Agnew, "Calculated Calls: How the Cadets Got Even with Ivay," *Canadian Magazine of Politics, Science, Art and Literature* 28 (1907): 90–2.
162 *Calendar*, 177–85.
163 "Dr. Newton Gober Dies in Hospital," *Atlanta Constitution* (26 May 1912), 14. The obituary suggests he was in Montreal soon after the turn of the century but gives no further details. I have not been able to find evidence of his presence in Montreal.
164 *Gober v. Agnew* (case file no. 932), deposition of Mary Gober for defendants (20 March 1907), 6–7. This was one of the questions to be submitted to her father in case no. 932, on *commission rogatoire* to get his testimony, but the commission was never executed. *Gober v. Agnew* (case file no. 932), Interrogatories and Notice (produced 28 June 1907).
165 *Gober v. Agnew* (case file no. 932), Plaintiff's Answer to Plea of Defendant William Agnew (produced 9 September 1907), 2.
166 "Gober-Agneau," *Atlanta Constitution* (3 March 1905), 8, in the "Society" column. The story was widely reported across the United States in February and March 1905.
167 May alleged her father's illness in her motion for a *commission rogatoire* to examine him in Washington, D.C. She alleges that he was "in a precarious condition of health and is seriously ill," and that it was doubtful he would live to the trial. *Gober v. Agnew* (case file no. 932), Motion, Affidavit and Notice (dated 22 June 1907). In fact, he lived until 1912. May's sister seems to have sent the couple wedding presents, so she at least knew of the marriage: *Gober v. Agnew* (case file no. 932), deposition of Mary Gober on her own behalf (23 March 1907), 7.
168 *Agnew v. Gober* (case file no. 801), deposition of Jessie McCann for defendant on Commission Rogatoire in Kingston (18 December 1905), 4.
169 *Agnew v. Gober* (case file no. 801), deposition of Douglas Gooderham Ross for plaintiffs (23 January 1906), 2–3.
170 On consummation, see *Agnew v. Gober* (case file no. 801), deposition of Augustus Waterous Agnew for defendant (23 January 1906), 8–10. There was no hint of a pregnancy in *Agnew v. Gober* (case file no. 801), but Gober alleged the miscarriage in a later action: *Gober v. Agnew* (case file no. 932), Plaintiff's Declaration (dated 20 February 1907), 6. Virtually nothing further was said about the pregnancy in that file, and nothing at all in any of the testimony.
171 *Agnew v. Gober* (case file no. 801), Exhibit A of defendant at enquête (letter from Augustus Agnew to Mary Gober, dated 20 February 1905).

172 *Agnew v. Gober* (case file no. 801), deposition of Jessie McCann for defendant on Commission Rogatoire in Kingston (18 December 1905), 5.
173 *Agnew v. Gober* (case file no. 801), Exhibit D of defendant at enquête (letter from Augustus Agnew to P.A. Peterson, dated 20 February 1905).
174 This first action, no. 2122, was styled *Agnew et uxor v. Gober et vir and Holton*. Its principal documents were filed as exhibits in the subsequent action, no. 801. The third defendant, Edward Holton, was a lawyer who had been appointed curator to the absent Augustus.
175 Both are profiled in David Ricardo Williams, *Just Lawyers: Seven Portraits* (Toronto: Osgoode Society for Canadian Legal History, 1995), 18–55, 90–123, though the Agnew-Gober affair is not mentioned.
176 The eight reported decisions in the various actions – four in a practice-oriented reporter – trace the legal conclusions of the courts. *Agnew et uxor v. Gober et vir* (no. 801) (1906), 8 R.P.Q. 198 (Sup. Ct.) (Augustus's domicile before going to Kingston was Montreal, and there was no proof he had changed it subsequently; Quebec courts have jurisdiction); *Agnew et uxor v. Gober et vir* (no. 801) (1906), 8 R.P.Q. 198 (K.B.) (permission to appeal interlocutory decision should be granted, since question of jurisdiction was central to the action); *Agnew et uxor v. Gober et vir* (no. 801) (1907), R.P.Q. 217 (Sup. Ct.) (exception regarding *lis pendens* of case no. 2122 dismissed); *Gober v. Agnew et al.* (no. 932) (1907), 8 R.P.Q. 255 (Sup. Ct.) (Gober need not provide security for costs to all three defendants, since she had established residence in Quebec); *Agnew et uxor v. Gober et vir* (no. 801) (1907), R.J.Q. 32 C.S. 266 (defendant's demurrer allowed and action dismissed – age of majority ended paternal authority and extinguished parents' action in nullity); *Agnew et uxor v. Gober et vir* (no. 801) (1908), R.J.Q. 17 B.R. 508, 15 R.L. (n.s.) 93 (appeal of preceding allowed – parents continued to have action in nullity even after the child's majority); *Agnew et uxor v. Gober et vir* (no. 801) (1909), R.J.Q. 38 C.S. 313 (Sup. Ct.) (requirement of parental consent relates to capacity not form, so Augustus could not contract a valid marriage under Quebec law; marriage annulled); *Agnew et uxor v. Gober et vir* (no. 801) (1910), R.J.Q. 38 C.S. 313 (Sup. Ct. Rev.) (the Court of Review affirmed the preceding).
177 *Agnew v. Gober* (case file no. 801), Declaration and Writ of Summons (produced 12 June 1905).
178 *Agnew v. Gober* (case file no. 801), Motion, Affidavit and Notice (produced 26 September 1905), asking for a *commission rogatoire* to have Gober examined at Barnesville, Georgia, by local lawyer Alexander Stephens Clay (who also happened to be a sitting United States senator from Georgia). See also *Gober v. Agnew* (case file no. 932), deposition of Mary

Gober on her own behalf (20 March 1907), 3–5. According to a Kingston barrister who knew Augustus well, Gober had been trying to sell her house since even before the marriage; it sold in early 1905. *Gober v. Agnew* (case file no. 932), deposition of Arthur B. Cunningham for defendants (23 January 1906), 4. There is no indication what happened to Gober's school, which appeared in Foster's Kingston Directory for 1904–5, but not for 1905–6. *Foster's Kingston Directory from July, 1904, to July, 1905*, 11th ed. (Toronto: J.G. Foster, 1904), 203; *Foster's Kingston Directory from July, 1905, to July, 1906*, 12th ed. (Toronto: J.G. Foster, 1905), 204.

179 *Agnew v. Gober* (case file no. 801), Motion to Call in Defendant (produced 12 June 1905). Copies of the newspapers are in the file as Exhibits P3 to P6. See, e.g., *La Presse* (14–15 June 1905), 9.

180 *Agnew v. Gober* (case file no. 801), Inscription in Law and Plea of the Defendant (produced 19 February 1907). The arguments were elaborated in *Agnew v. Gober* (case file no. 801), Propositions and Authorities of the Defendant (dated 18 March 1907).

181 *Agnew et uxor v. Gober et vir* (1907), R.J.Q. 32 C.S. 266. See also "Marriage Stands," *The Gazette* (1 July 1907), 3; "Mariage maintenu," *La Presse* (1 July 1907), 12; "This Marriage Valid," *(Toronto) Globe* (1 July 1907), 1; "Cadet's Marriage Valid," *Victoria Daily Times* (8 July 1907), 10.

182 *Agnew v. Gober* (Sup. Ct., no. 801), 273.

183 *Agnew v. Gober* (Sup. Ct., no. 801), 274.

184 *Agnew et uxor v. Gober et vir* (1908), R.J.Q. 17 B.R. 508, 15 R.L. (n.s.) 93. Some of the newspapers covering the case mistakenly reported that the court had annulled the marriage; the decision on the merits was still to come. "Marriage Is Voided," *Toronto Daily Star* (22 May 1908) 6; "Marriage Annulled," *(Toronto) Globe* (23 May 1908), 1.

185 *Agnew v. Gober* (K.B.), 530.

186 *Agnew v. Gober* (K.B.), 511–12: "l'honneur même de toute la famille."

187 *Agnew v. Gober* (K.B.), 512–13: "tout intérêt, tant personnellement que pour la famille elle-même, à ce que le mariage irrégulier de son fils mineur soit annulé."

188 *Agnew v. Gober* (case file no. 801), Inscription in Law and Plea of the Defendant (produced 19 February 1907).

189 *Agnew et uxor v. Gober et vir* (1909), R.J.Q. 38 C.S. 313. See also "Le mariage Agnew-Gober," *La Presse* (23 February 1909), 14; "Agnew Wedding Has Been Annulled," *Toronto Daily Star* (23 February 1909), 1; "Cadet Agnew's Marriage," *(Toronto) Globe* (24 February 1909), 1.

190 *Agnew et uxor v. Gober et vir* (1910), R.J.Q. 38 C.S. 313. See also "Jugement maintenu," *La Presse* (22 April 1910), 16; "Mariage annulé," *Le Devoir* (23

April 1910), 1; "Quebec Cancels Marriages Here," *Toronto Daily Star* (23 April 1910), 5; "The Civil Courts," *The Gazette* (28 April 1910), 7.
191 Order of the Privy Council (dated 8 August 1911), modifying Order of the Privy Council (dated 2 August 1910), both in *Agnew v. Gober* (case file no. 801). Art. 69 CCP gave a right to appeal directly to the Judicial Committee of the Privy Council from the Court of Review if no appeal lay to the Court of King's Bench; in this case art. 43 CCP excluded the local appeal. An application to proceed *in forma pauperis* required affidavits of restricted means, supported by counsel's certificate that there were good grounds for appealing; the application was generally granted if those were in order. See (on an earlier period) P.A. Howell, *The Judicial Committee of the Privy Council 1833–1876: Its Origins, Structure and Development* (Cambridge: Cambridge University Press, 1979), 98. See also "Agnew-Gober Wedding," *(Toronto) Globe* (26 July 1910), 1.
192 Bonny Ibhawoh, *Imperial Justice: Africans in Empire's Court* (Oxford: Oxford University Press, 2013), 47 (on expense).
193 *Gober v. Agnew* (case file no. 932), deposition of Mary Gober for defendants (20 March 1907), quotation at 2.
194 *Gober v. Agnew* (case file no. 932), deposition of Thomas C. Wright for defendants (23 March 1907), 2.
195 *Gober v. Agnew* (case file no. 4047).
196 *Gober v. Agnew et al.* (case file no. 932).
197 "Big Sensation Society's Hit," *(Ottawa) Evening Citizen* (20 February 1907), 3; "Alienated Love of Her Husband," *Toronto Daily Star* (20 February 1907), 1; "Agnew vs. Agnew," *(Toronto) Globe* (21 February 1907), 10; "Montreal Excited over a Sensational Legal Suit," *(Saint John, N.B.) Sun* (21 February 1907), 6; "Suit over Boy Husband," *(New York) Sun* (21 February 1907), 12; "Action en dommages," *La Presse* (23 February 1907), 31.
198 *Gober v. Agnew* (case file no. 932), Plaintiff's Declaration (dated 20 February 1907).
199 *Gober v. Agnew* (case file no. 932), Particulars and Notice (produced 11 June 1907), 1–2.
200 All three defendants filed essentially identical pleas on 8 June 1907, all in *Gober v. Agnew* (case file no. 932): Plea of Defendant William Agnew; Plea of Defendant Dame Emma Johnson Waterous; Plea of Defendant Miss Kathleen Agnew.
201 The motions were dismissed by Archibald J. on 10 April 1907.
202 *Gober v. Agnew* (case file no. 932), Re-Inscription for Proof and Hearing (produced 9 June 1910). The 1911 plumitif contains only the note that the case was struck, and the case is not in 1912 plumitif.

203 *Agnew v. Gober* (case file no. 801), deposition of Emma Johnson Waterous on her own behalf (25 January 1909), 3.
204 *Agnew v. Gober* (case file no. 801), deposition of Mary Gober on her own behalf on commission in Marietta, Georgia (28 October 1905), 2.
205 *Agnew v. Gober* (case file no. 801), deposition of William Agnew for defendant (23 January 1906), 1–2.
206 *Gober v. Agnew* (case file no. 932), Plea of Defendant Miss Kathleen Agnew (produced 8 June 1907), 2. The other two defendants submitted substantially similar pleas on the same day.
207 *Gober v. Agnew* (case file no. 932), Plea of Defendant Miss Kathleen Agnew (produced 8 June 1907), 3.
208 *Gober v. Agnew* (case file no. 932), Particulars Furnished by Defendant Dame Emma Johnson Waterous (produced 4 July 1907), 1. The other two defendants submitted identical documents on the same day.
209 "Big Sensation Society's Hit," *(Ottawa) Evening Citizen* (20 February 1907), 3.
210 "Marriage Stands," *Gazette* (1 July 1907), 3; "The Agnew Marriage Case," letter to the editor signed Geoffrion, Geoffrion & Cusson, *The Gazette* (4 July 1907), 8.
211 *Agnew v. Gober* (case file no. 801), deposition of Augustus Waterous Agnew for defendant (23 January 1906), 10.
212 Factum des appelants (K.B. no. 77) (produced 4 November 1907), 8.
213 *Agnew v. Gober* (case file no. 801), Answer to Plaintiffs' Authorities (dated 20 March 1907), 1.
214 Notice in the "Social and Personal" column, *The Gazette* (8 October 1912), 2.
215 "Augustus Waterous Agnew." Emma Waterous died in 1917, William Agnew in 1922. Kathleen Agnew, who never married, continued to live in the family house in Victoria until her death in 1967; she was a noted philanthropist and patron of the arts. See http://www.victoriaheritagefoundation.ca/HReg/Rockland/Rockland1322.html.
216 E.g., *Atlanta Constitution* (7 July 1912), 8; *Atlanta Constitution* (28 July 1912), 8.
217 The record, dated July 1921 and available on www.ancestry.ca, listed her address as care of another in Cairo, Georgia, near the Florida border.
218 Information from the genealogy site http://www.goberfamily.org/Gober/gober-i/p189.htm.

4. Bodily Intrusion

1 *Bérubé v. Carsley* (1890), 20 R.L. 97 (Sup. Ct.).
2 The case file does not survive. What follows is based mainly on the case report, *D. v. City of Montreal*, [1947] R.L. 257 (Sup. Ct.), supplemented by

the plumitif and the following news coverage of the civil action: "Une jeune bourgeoise qui aurait été battue et mise en cellules!" *Le Canada* (14 May 1947), 3; "On conseille à la ville de régler," *Le Devoir* (14 May 1947), 12; "Judge Hints Justice Miscarriage in Woman's Suit for False Arrest," *The Gazette* (14 May 1947), 11; "City Must Pay Police Error," *Montreal Daily Star* (18 June 1947), 21; "Dommages pour une arrestation illégale," *La Presse* (18 June 1947), 10; "Respectable Woman Wins Suit on False Streetwalking Charge," *The Gazette* (19 June 1947), 13; "Mlle Gabrielle [D] a gain de cause en Cour supérieure!" *Le Canada* (19 June 1947), 7 (surname omitted from this headline); "On l'arrête mais Concordia paiera," *La Patrie* (19 June 1947), 6. Though the news coverage referred to the plaintiff by her full name, as in the headline in *Le Canada* above, I have followed the formal case report in omitting her surname, since the purpose of her action was to reassert her anonymity (see below). On the decision to name or not in legal historical writing, see Constance Backhouse, *Carnal Crimes: Sexual Assault Law in Canada, 1900–1975* (Toronto: Irwin Law for Osgoode Society for Canadian Legal History, 2008), 4–5.

3 Both events were advertised on the same page in *La Presse* (11 May 1945), 9: "la fascinante danseuse blonde."

4 On the early history, see Andrée Lévesque, "Éteindre le Red Light: les réformateurs et la prostitution à Montréal entre 1865 et 1925," *Urban History Review* 17 (1989): 191–201. For an early contemporary critic, see E.I. Hart, *Wake Up! Montreal! Commercialized Vice and Its Contributories* (Montreal: Witness, 1919).

5 Mathieu Lapointe, *Nettoyer Montréal: les campagnes de moralité publique 1940–1954* (Montreal: Septentrion, 2014), 41–98; Daniel Proulx, *Le Red Light de Montréal* (Montreal: VLB, 1997), 37–46.

6 The Archives de Montréal has put rich documentation of this campaign online: see https://archivesdemontreal.ica-atom.org/maladies-veneriennes-1942-1952 (AM, P43-4-2-D02).

7 Bureau de la moralité, Rapport de l'année 1945, unpaginated, AM, P43-4-2-D04, P43-4-2_4-1_1945op.

8 "Judge Hints Justice Miscarriage in Woman's Suit for False Arrest," *The Gazette* (14 May 1947), 11.

9 In Toronto, "I was coming home from a dance" was a typical prostitute's explanation: Amanda Glasbeek, *Feminized Justice: The Toronto Women's Court, 1913–34* (Vancouver: UBC Press, 2009), 158.

10 Bureau de la moralité, Rapport de l'année 1945, unpaginated; AM, P43-4-2-D04, P43-4-2_4-1_1945op: "flâner la nuit et vagabondage." The day before, there had been three arrests at the same intersection.

11 *D. v. City of Montreal*, 260: "le nom du premier homme qui t'a débauchée."

12 *Venereal Diseases Prevention Act*, S.Q. 1941 (5 Geo. VI), c. 55, s. 6, consolidated as R.S.Q. 1941, c. 186.
13 E.g., *An Act to establish the Provincial Bureau of Health and to amend the Revised Statutes, 1909, accordingly*, S.Q. 1922 (12 Geo. V), c. 29, ss. 89–90, consolidated as R.S.Q. 1925, c. 186, s. 91, cited in Andrée Lévesque, "Le bordel: milieu de travail contrôlé," *Labour/Le Travail* 20 (1987): 16.
14 Constance Backhouse, "Nineteenth-Century Canadian Prostitution Law: Reflection of a Discriminatory Society," *Histoire sociale/Social History* 18 (1985): 387–423; Ruth Roach Pierson, *"They're Still Women after All": The Second World War and Canadian Womanhood* (Toronto: McClelland and Stewart, 1986); Jay Cassel, *The Secret Plague: Venereal Disease in Canada 1838–1939* (Toronto: University of Toronto Press, 1987); Joan Sangster, *Regulating Girls and Women: Sexuality, Family, and the Law in Ontario, 1920–1960* (Don Mills, ON: Oxford University Press, 2001), esp. 88–9; Philippa Levine, *Prostitution, Race, and Politics: Policing Venereal Disease in the British Empire* (New York: Routledge, 2003).
15 *Débats de l'Assemblée législative*, 21st Legislature, 2nd Session, vol. 1, ed. Daniel Machabée and Martin Pelletier (Quebec City: Section de l'indexation et de l'édition des débats reconstitués, Bibliothèque de l'Assemblée nationale, 2012), 232–3 (second reading, 4 March 1941): "des pouvoirs dictatoriaux."
16 *D. v. City of Montreal*, 265.
17 Antonio Lamer to Fernand Dufresne (11 January 1944), AM, P43-4-2_2-10p.
18 "Mlle Gabrielle [D] a gain de cause en Cour supérieure!" *Le Canada* (19 June 1947), 7.
19 Montreal By-Law 333 (19 June 1905), as amended by By-Law 372 (23 December 1907), s. 2b.
20 For reasons now unclear (which the judge does not mention), the case stalled for fifteen months between 22 January 1946, when the plaintiff's reply to the defence was filed, and 22 April 1947, when the notice of hearing was filed. See *D. v. City of Montreal* (plumitif).
21 *D. v. City of Montreal*, 265–6; *Identification of Criminals Act*, R.S.C. 1927, c. 38, s. 2.
22 "On conseille à la ville de régler," *Le Devoir* (14 May 1947), 12; "Judge Hints Justice Miscarriage in Woman's Suit for False Arrest," *The Gazette* (14 May 1947), 11.
23 *D. v. City of Montreal*, 259 (the report is in English).
24 *D. v. City of Montreal*, 266.
25 "Respectable Woman Wins Suit on False Streetwalking Charge," *The Gazette* (19 June 1947), 13.

26 *D. v. City of Montreal*, 261.
27 *D. v. City of Montreal*, 261.
28 *D. v. City of Montreal*, 261.
29 Backhouse, *Carnal Crimes*.
30 Quoted in "Judge Hints Justice Miscarriage in Woman's Suit for False Arrest," *The Gazette* (14 May 1947), 11.
31 Richard J. Needham, "One Man's Opinion," *Calgary Herald* (26 June 1947), 4.
32 Michaela Freund, "The Politics of Naming: Constructing Prostitutes and Regulating Women in Vancouver, 1939–45," in *Regulating Lives: Historical Essays on the State, Society, the Individual, and the Law*, ed. John McLaren, Robert Menzies, and Dorothy E. Chunn, 231–58 (Vancouver: UBC Press, 2002).
33 Limitations of space prevent a full discussion of the thorny issue of vaccination and quarantine. Unlike in the United States, where mandatory vaccination statutes were challenged in various ways, the Quebec courts seem to have heard no such cases, despite the presence of a vigorous anti-vaccination movement. See M. Farley, Peter Keating, and Othmar Keel, "La vaccination à Montréal dans la seconde moitié du 19e siècle: pratiques, obstacles et résistances," in *Sciences et médecine au Québec: perspectives sociohistoriques*, ed. Marcel Fournier, Y. Gingras, and Othmar Keel, 87–127 (Quebec City: Institut québécois de recherche sur la culture, 1987). On compulsory vaccination elsewhere, see Lynne Curry, ed., *The Human Body on Trial: A Sourcebook with Cases, Laws, and Documents* (Indianapolis: Hackett, 2002), 51–7; Nadja Durbach, *Bodily Matters: The Anti-Vaccination Movement in England, 1853–1907* (Durham, NC: Duke University Press, 2005); Stanley Williamson, *The Vaccination Controversy: The Rise, Reign, and Fall of Compulsory Vaccination for Smallpox* (Liverpool: Liverpool University Press, 2007); Deborah Brunton, *The Politics of Vaccination: Practice and Policy in England, Wales, Ireland and Scotland, 1800–1874* (Rochester, NY: University of Rochester Press, 2008); Ubaka Ogbogu, "Vaccination and the Law in Ontario and Nova Scotia (1800–1924)" (S.J.D. thesis, University of Toronto, 2014).
34 The standoff was extensively covered in the *Montreal Daily Witness*, *The Gazette*, *La Minerve*, *La Patrie*, *La Presse*, *L'Étendard*, and other papers. Gagnon was eventually removed from the apartment, along with his fourteen-year-old son (who had briefly continued the resistance after his father was disarmed), and both were arrested. The papers quickly lost interest in the Gagnons themselves, as the incident became a proxy to either attack or defend the mayor, whom many blamed for ordering the assault on the family's home. See, generally, Michael Bliss, *Plague: A*

Story of Smallpox in Montreal (Toronto: HarperCollins, 1991), 234–41 on the Gagnon affair.

35 James C. Oldham, "On Pleading the Belly: A History of the Jury of Matrons," *Criminal Justice History* 6 (1985): 1–64; Thomas R. Forbes, "A Jury of Matrons," *Medical History* 32 (1988): 23–33; F. Murray Greenwood and Beverley Boissery, *Uncertain Justice: Canadian Women and Capital Punishment, 1754–1953* (Toronto: Dundurn for Osgoode Society for Canadian Legal History, 2000), 17. See Canada, *Criminal Code* (1892 ed.), s. 730.

36 Tamara Myers, "The Voluntary Delinquent: Parents, Daughters, and the Montreal Juvenile Delinquents' Court in 1918," *CHR* 80 (1999): 256.

37 Serge Gagnon, *Mariage et famille au temps de Papineau* (Sainte-Foy, QC: Presses de l'Université Laval, 1993), 254–64.

38 *Dorion v. Laurent* (1843), 17 L.C.J. 324 (Provincial Court of Appeal). The notice appeared in *La Minerve* (20 April 1843), 4, and again a week later.

39 *Belair v. Chaussé* (case file), Exhibit A1 de demandeur à l'enquête (produced 25 January 1899), letter from L.J.O. Cléroux, M.D.: "elle paraît être vierge."

40 See, generally, Gilles Trimaille, "L'expertise médico-légale: confiscation et traduction de la douleur," in *La douleur et le droit*, ed. Bernard Durand, Jean Poirier, and Jean-Pierre Royer, 489–500 (Paris: Presses universitaires français, 1997).

41 *Baxter v. Davis* (1894), 4 R.P.Q. 153 (Sup. Ct., Doherty J.); *Filion v. Dawes* (1897), R.J.Q. 12 C.S. 494 (Archibald J.); *Jasmin v. Bain* (1898), 5 R.L. (n.s.) 20 (Sup. Ct., Tait A.C.J.). None of these motions seem to have been contested.

42 *Manseau v. City of Montreal* (1899), 7 R. de J. 399 (Sup. Ct.); *Mousseau v. City of Montreal* (1899), 4 R.P.Q. 38 (Sup. Ct.).

43 *Bélair v. Tougas* (1901), 7 R. de J. 573 (Sup. Ct., Mathieu J.); *Dinowitzer v. Canadian Pacific Railway Co.* (1910), 11 R.P.Q. 396 (Sup. Ct., Davidson J.).

44 *An Act respecting the responsibility for accidents suffered by workmen in the course of their work, and the compensation for injuries resulting therefrom*, S.Q. 1909 (9 Edw. VII), c. 66, s. 18.

45 *Hunt v. D. Donnelly Ltd.* (1916), 17 R.P.Q. 341 (Sup. Ct.).

46 Art. 541 CCP.

47 *Hunt v. D. Donnelly Ltd.*, 342–3, quoting *Union Pacific Railway v. Botsford*, 141 U.S. 251 (1891).

48 "La personne est sacrée," *Le Devoir* (2 February 1916), 2. Other papers took a more neutral tone: "Sa demande est rejetée par la cour," *La Presse* (2 February 1916), 3.

49 *Hunt v. D. Donnelly Ltd.*, 343.

50 See, generally, Jacques Saint-Pierre and Martin Petitclerc, *Histoire de l'assurance de personnes: des sociétés de secours mutuels aux grandes institutions d'assurance* (Quebec City: Presses de l'Université Laval, 2015).

51 Art. 286b CCP, added by *An Act to amend the Code of Civil Procedure respecting examinations on discovery*, S.Q. 1930–1 (21 Geo. V), c. 110 (royal assent 11 March 1931). The bill (178 of 1930) passed without debate.
52 *Fortier v. Lamontagne* (1936), 40 R.P.Q. 66 at 67–8 (Sup. Ct., Langlais J.): "Ces examens ne constituent pas à mon sens des opérations; ce sont simplement des constatations à la suite de piqûres qui n'offrent aucun danger, qu'on rend faciles à supporter et qui sont nécessaires pour les conclusions de la science médicale moderne."
53 *Lorquet et uxor v. Sun Life Assurance Co.* (1937), R.J.Q. 64 B.R. 137 at 143–4 (Létourneau J.): "très douleureux."
54 *Lefebvre v. Mutual Life Insurance Co. of New York* (1941), [1942] B.R. 266 at 269 (St-Jacques J.): "une véritable contrainte à la liberté humaine." Further details were reported in Paul Sauriol, "Gazette des tribunaux," *Le Devoir* (16 May 1942), 2.
55 *Bélair v. Tougas*, 574.
56 On the contemporary history of medical malpractice in Canada, see R. Blake Brown, "Canada's First Malpractice Crisis: Medical Negligence in the Late Nineteenth Century," *Osgoode Hall Law Journal* 54 (2017): 777–803.
57 There is little literature on the development of the idea of informed consent in Quebec. An overview of the cases can be found in Beullac, *La responsabilité civile*, 191–9. The general literature on the history of informed consent focuses on whether or not cases employed that specific wording, and so tends to see the idea as much more recent than it was: see, e.g., Tom L. Beauchamp, "Informed Consent: Its History, Meaning, and Present Challenges," *Cambridge Quarterly of Healthcare Ethics* 20 (2011): 515–23.
58 *Parnell v. Springle* (1899), 5 R. de J. 74 (Sup. Ct.). The case file survives but contains no depositions.
59 *Parnell v. Springle* (case file), Bref et déclaration de la demanderesse (dated 30 August 1898), 1.
60 *Parnell v. Springle* (case file), Defence (dated 14 September 1898), 1.
61 *Parnell v. Springle* (case file), Bref et déclaration (dated 30 August 1898), 2.
62 *Parnell v. Springle* (case file), Defence (dated 14 September 1898), 2.
63 A.G. Brooke Claxton, "The Discretionary Powers of a Surgeon," *Montreal Medical Journal* 28 (1899): 188. See also "Legal Intelligence," *The Gazette* (23 January 1899), 2.
64 *Parnell v. Springle* (Sup. Ct.), 76.
65 Claxton, "Discretionary Powers," 186, 191–2.
66 *Beatty v. Cullingworth* (Q.B.D., 1896, Hawkins J.), reported in *British Medical Journal* (21 November 1896), 1546–8. In the same issue was an anonymous outraged commentary, "Beatty v. Cullingworth," *British Medical Journal* (21 November 1896), 1525–6. In *Beatty*, unlike *Parnell*, one of the ovaries

was much more seriously diseased than the other, but both were removed anyway.

67 See Paul Brouardel, *L'exercice de la médecine et le charlatanisme*, Cours de médecine légale de la faculté de médecine de Paris (Paris, 1899), 363, who cited approvingly the result in *Beatty*.

68 *Caron v. Gagnon* (1930), R.J.Q. 68 C.S. 155.

69 *Caron v. Gagnon*, 155: "d'avoir des enfants et d'élever une famille, tant pour leur consolation que pour satisfaire leur besoin d'affection."

70 *Caron v. Gagnon*, 164: "Ce serait téméraire de la part d'un tribunal d'interposer une opinion contraire à celle du médecin quant à l'opération, à l'urgence et à la nécessité de l'opération."

71 *Caron v. Gagnon*, 165–6: "il vaut mieux quelquefois, ne pas exposer ou étaler les causes devant le public."

72 *E. v. M.* (1939), R.J.Q. 77 C.S. 298.

73 *Mlle Bordier v. S.* (1934), R.J.Q. 72 C.S. 316: "un aspect fort disgracieux." The court awarded $450, almost half of the $971 demanded. See also "Un médecin condamné à $450 de dommages," *La Presse* (17 July 1934), 24. In a later case from beyond our period, *Dame Dufresne v. X* (1960), [1961] C.S. 119, a woman was awarded $3310 damages (out of $6950 claimed) after a dentist extracted three more teeth than agreed upon. Distinguishing *Parnell*, the court found that the situation was not a threat to the patient's life or health, and so consent could and should have been obtained before proceeding.

74 Added as art. 19 CCLC; Albert Mayrand, *L'inviolabilité de la personne humaine* (Montreal: Wilson & Lafleur, 1975).

75 See Heather Conway, *The Law and the Dead* (London: Routledge, 2016), 79–86; Remigius N. Nwabueze, *Biotechnology and the Challenge of Property: Property Rights in Dead Bodies, Body Parts, and Genetic Information* (London: Routledge, 2007), 44–53; Alison Dundes Renteln, *The Cultural Defense* (New York: Oxford University Press, 2004), 160–71.

76 See, generally, Peter N. Stearns, *Revolutions in Sorrow: The American Experience of Death in Global Perspective* (Boulder, CO: Paradigm, 2007).

77 *An Act respecting Coroners' Inquests*, S.Q. 1880 (43–4 Vic.), c. 10, s. 1, consolidated as R.S.Q. 1888, art. 2687. Alongside this discretionary provision, an inquest could also be held if the coroner believed that the death was the result of crime, violence, or "unfair means."

78 *An Act to amend the law respecting Anatomy*, S.Q. 1898 (61 Vic.), c. 29, s. 1; *An Act to consolidate the charter of Notre Dame Hospital, Montreal, and its amendments*, S.Q. 1898 (61 Vic.), c. 82, s. 20.

79 *An Act to amend the act to consolidate the charter of the Notre-Dame Hospital, Montreal, and its amendments*, S.Q. 1923–4 (14 Geo. V), c. 117, s. 15.

80 *An Act respecting the practice of Physic and Surgery, and the Study of Anatomy*, Consolidated Statutes of Canada 1859, c. 76, ss. 1 and 3, eventually included in R.S.Q. 1888, art. 3960.
81 "An Unauthorized Autopsy," *Montreal Daily Witness* (25 April 1890), 4.
82 On cremation, see below, note 113.
83 *Débats de l'Assemblée législative*, 18th Legislature, 4th Session, vol. 3, ed. Donald Chouinard (Quebec City: Section de l'indexation et de l'édition des débats reconstitués, Bibliothèque de l'Assemblée nationale, 2010), 894 (1 May 1935, second reading, committee of the whole): "Parce qu'il s'agit de pauvres, on les envoie à l'abattoir, pour les débiter au service de la science. C'est cruel. C'est déjà assez dur d'être sur l'assistance publique, sans aller à l'abattoir après sa mort."
84 *Débats de l'Assemblée législative* (1935), 883, 893–5, 1046–8, 1097. See also "To Authorize Autopsy," *The Gazette* (2 May 1935), 7; "Bill de l'anatomie," *La Patrie* (2 May 1935), 20.
85 An earlier Ontario case from 1899 touched similar issues, and was cited as an analogy in some of the Quebec cases. In *Davidson v. Garrett* (1899), 30 O.R. 653 (Div. Ct.), physicians performed an autopsy on the body of the plaintiff's wife without his consent. The action in damages was dismissed (on appeal) because the defendants had been acting on the coroner's orders.
86 His death made the front page of *La Patrie*, with a photograph: "Mort de M. Colbert Grothé," *La Patrie* (9 January 1905), 1.
87 "A la demande de l'American Life," *La Patrie* (23 February 1905), 14; "To Examine Body," *The Gazette* (23 February 1905), 5; "Feu M. C.O. Grothé," *La Presse* (23 February 1905), 3.
88 Requête pour rescinder ordonnance (dated 23 February 1905): "une violation des droits de la famille." The case file for this action does not survive, but a copy was filed in *Grothé v. North American Life* (case file), Exhibit P-3.
89 *In re C.O. Grothé and North American Life Assurance Co. v. Children of C.O. Grothé* (1905), 7 R.P.Q. 111 (Sup. Ct.). "Une pénible affaire," *La Patrie* (24 February 1905), 1, 6; "Orders Body Returned," *The Gazette* (24 February 1905), 4; "L'exhumation de M. Colbert Grothé," *La Presse* (24 February 1905), 10.
90 *Lamothe v. North American Life Assurance Co.* (1906), R.J.Q. 16 B.R. 178 (Sup. Ct.), affirmed (1907) (K.B.). This proceeding united the action of the policy's beneficiary, J.-C. Lamothe, and the company's action to cancel the policy. "Other Actions Follow," *The Gazette* (25 February 1905), 4; "De nouvelles procédures," *La Patrie* (27 February 1905), 12; "L'affaire Grothé," *La Presse* (27 February 1905), 1; "La police de M. Grothé," *La Patrie*

(28 February 1905), 1; "Mr. Lamothe Explains," *The Gazette* (28 February 1905), 8. The coverage of Lamothe's actions continued.

91 *Grothé v. North American Life Assurance Co.*, unreported. "Profanation de sépulture," *La Presse* (25 March 1905), 2; "Autumn Court Term," *The Gazette* (1 September 1906), 6; "L'inviolabilité des cimetières," *La Presse* (27 September 1906), 16.

92 *Grothé v. North American Life* (case file), Bref et déclaration (produced 6 April 1905), 2, 3–4: "de profaner une tombe pour une misérable question financière"; "dans un état de nudité le cadavre fut étendu en forme de demi cercle sur le plancher, autour d'une fournaise, pour être dégelé"; "profanation de la tombe du dit Colbert O. Grothé et l'indignité offerte à ses restes mortels"; "dans leur affection pour la mémoire de leur défunt père, dans leur respect pour ses restes mortels, dans leur sensibilité d'enfants pour un père dont le repos mortel est troublé si indignement et dans leur honneur outragé."

93 *Grothé v. North American Life* (case file), Bref et déclaration (produced 6 April 1905), 4: "choses sacrées de leur nature"; "Une pénible affaire," *La Patrie* (24 February 1904), 6: "le droit que la famille avait à l'inviolabilité du cadavre d'un des siens, qui avait droit qu'on respecte son repos."

94 *Grothé v. North American Life* (case file), Judgment Putting the Parties *hors de Cour* (9 October 1906). Details on the amount were reported in "Poursuite réglée," *La Patrie* (9 October 1906), 1; "Grothé Case Settled," *The Gazette* (10 October 1906), 8. As *La Patrie* mentioned, Justice Curran found *La Presse* in contempt of court for having included in an earlier article (likely the 27 September piece cited above) information that could prejudice the jurors who were to hear the case.

95 See, generally, the discussion of family honour in chapter 3 above. On the legal status of cadavers, see Raphaël Dierkins, *Les droits sur le corps et le cadavre de l'homme* (Paris: Masson, 1966); Xavier Labbée, *Condition juridique du corps humain avant la naissance et après la mort* (Lille: Presses universitaires de Lille, 1990), 167–244; Jean-Pierre Baud, *L'affaire de la main volée: une histoire juridique du corps* (Paris: Seuil, 1993), 30–47; Hélène Popu, *La dépouille mortelle, chose sacrée: à la redécouverte d'une catégorie juridique oubliée* (Paris: L'Harmattan, 2009). For the United States, see the cases reviewed in Berto Rogers, "Recovery for Mental Anguish Resulting from the Mutilation of a Corpse," *Law Notes* 33 (1930): 225–30; and Percival E. Jackson, *The Law of Cadavers and of Burial and Burial Places* (New York: Prentice-Hall, 1936).

96 *Phillips v. Montreal General Hospital* (1908), R.J.Q. 33 C.S. 483, 14 R.L. (n.s.) 159, 14 R. de J. 230 at 236–7.

97 See, generally, Nwabueze, *Biotechnology and the Challenge of Property*, 44–53.
98 *Phillips v. Montreal General Hospital*; the case file does not survive. See also "Makes a Curious Claim," *The Gazette* (24 September 1907), 3; "Poursuite," *Le Canada* (24 September 1907), 5; "Singulière poursuite," *La Patrie* (24 September 1907), 1; "La propriété d'un cadavre," *La Patrie* (24 February 1908), 14; "Unauthorized Autopsy a Trespass on Personal Rights," *The Gazette* (25 February 1908), 8; "L'Hôpital général condamné," *Le Canada* (25 February 1908), 2.
99 *Phillips v. Montreal General Hospital* (R.J.Q.), 483: "une dépression morale qui empoisonne son existence."
100 *Phillips v. Montreal General Hospital* (R.L.), 160. The procedure for a motion to dismiss (an inscription in law or demurrer) was to consider the legal basis of the action if all alleged facts were true.
101 *Phillips v. Montreal General Hospital* (R.J.Q.), 485.
102 *Phillips v. Montreal General Hospital* (R.J.Q.), 486.
103 *Phillips v. Montreal General Hospital* (R.J.Q.), 487.
104 *Phillips v. Montreal General Hospital* (R.J.Q.), 490. The remark about "normal relations of marriage" suggests he may have had in mind the Grothé case from three years earlier, though he did not cite it.
105 "L'Hôpital général condamné," *Le Canada* (25 February 1908), 2: "un acte d'injure aux restes du défunt."
106 The last entry in the plumitif, dated 7 March 1908, is the defendant's submission of a statement of particulars regarding the hospital's actions following the death, its findings on the cause of death, and its evidence for Phillips's alleged consent to the autopsy.
107 "Action rejetée," *Le Devoir* (22 December 1919), 4; "Dismisses Claim against Hospital," *The Gazette* (22 December 1919), 7. The judge mistook the law here, since moral damages were excluded only in fatal accident cases, as we will see in chapter 6, while in this case the plaintiff's daughter died of tuberculosis.
108 *Ducharme v. Hôpital Notre-Dame* (1933), R.J.Q. 71 C.S. 377 at 377–8, 39 R.L. (n.s.) 327: "Il n'y a aucun doute que le cadavre d'une personne demeure la propriété du conjoint et de la famille du défunt." See also "L'autopsie n'aurait pas été permise par la veuve," *La Presse* (21 March 1933), 11.
109 *Ducharme v. Hôpital Notre-Dame*, 381. See also "Autopsy 'without Consent' Is Issue," *The Gazette* (11 May 1933), 4; "Une autopsie qui cause un procès," *Le Canada* (11 May 1933), 8.
110 *Malboeuf v. Montreal General Hospital*, as described in "Une autopsie illégale?" *Le Devoir* (24 February 1931), 3; "Un hôpital est poursuivi pour une forte

somme," *La Presse* (24 February 1931), 3; "Woman Brings Suit against Hospital," *Saskatoon Star-Phoenix* (25 February 1931), 8. The settlement (terms undisclosed) was noted in *Malboeuf v. Montreal General Hospital* (plumitif). See also *Marchand v. Royal Victoria Hospital*, described in "Hôpital qui est actionné en dommages," *La Presse* (15 July 1933), 19; that case too settled out of court, according to *Marchand v. Royal Victoria Hospital* (plumitif).

111 "Un hôpital est poursuivi pour une forte somme," *La Presse* (24 February 1931), 3: "Elle allègue qu'ils avaient coupé le cuir chevelu d'une tempe à l'autre et qu'on avait de plus enlevé la cervelle, en sciant le dessus du crâne. Lors de l'examen par les médecins experts, le crâne aurait glissé comme un 'couvert de marmite.' Les organes intérieurs avaient été également enlevés et remplacés par du bran de scie.… L'embaumement fut par la suite rendu impossible et il fallut inhumer le défunt aussitôt."

112 *Brouillette v. Religieuses de l'Hôtel-Dieu* (1941), 47 R.L. (n.s.) 408 (Sup. Ct.), reversed [1943] B.R. 441, [1943] R.L. (n.s.) 83. The Superior Court file does not survive. The King's Bench file does not contain the full depositions, but some quotations appear in the factums.

113 *An Act to amend the act 19–20 Victoria, chapter 128, intituled "An Act to amend and consolidate the several acts incorporating the Mount Royal Cemetery Company,"* S.Q. 1901 (1 Edw. VII), c. 92, s. 9. See also Brian Young, *Respectable Burial: Montreal's Mount Royal Cemetery* (Montreal and Kingston: McGill-Queen's University Press, 2003), 125–39; Martin Robert, "Disposer de son cadavre: la naissance de la crémation au Québec (1874–1914)" (M.A. thesis, Université du Québec à Montréal, 2015).

114 "Hotel Dieu Bill Passes," *The Gazette* (24 March 1937), 10; *An Act to amend the charter of Les Religieuses Sœurs Hospitalières de Saint-Joseph de l'Hôtel-Dieu de Montréal*, S.Q. 1937 (1 Geo. VI), c. 136, s. 1d.

115 *Brouillette v. Religieuses de l'Hôtel-Dieu* (K.B.) (R.J.Q.), 452: "Maintenant, cette personne-là, on ne sait pas ce qui a pu arriver, il n'y avait pas toujours quelqu'un de l'hôpital dans la chambre, sa femme a été là"; "constituent pour nous une certaine impression d'étrangeté."

116 "Une veuve s'objecte résolument à l'autopsie du cadavre de son mari," *Le Petit journal* (13 August 1939), 3 (a headline for the story also appears above the masthead on page 1).

117 Factum de l'intimée (filed 4 March 1942), 33 (quoting para. 19 of the declaration): "dans sa personne, ses biens, pour frais médicaux, sa santé." See also "Une autopsie donne lieu à une action," *La Presse* (6 February 1940), 7.

118 *Brouillette v. Religieuses de l'Hôtel-Dieu* (Sup. Ct.). See also "L'épouse n'avait pas consenti à l'autopsie," *La Presse* (13 June 1941), 3.

119 *Brouillette v. Religieuses de l'Hôtel-Dieu* (Sup. Ct.) (R.L.), 419–20: "est une usurpation de droits personnels de nature à humilier, outrager et déterminer des souffrances constituant les éléments essentiels à une réparation civile"; "n'avaient pas le droit"; "la liberté illimitée à toute personne de décider et d'ordonner la crémation ou non de son corps après sa mort"; "le droit de la famille qui donne à la mémoire de ses morts toute la vénération que conserve une personne à l'égard d'un être qui lui est cher"; "indéniable"; "peut être rattaché directement aux émotions et à l'obsession dont elle a été assiégée depuis la mutilation du cadavre de son mari." See also "Woman Wins Case against Hospital," *The Gazette* (22 July 1941), 11; "Hôpital condamné à la suite d'une autopsie," *Le Canada* (22 July 1941), 7.

120 *Brouillette v. Religieuses de l'Hôtel-Dieu* (K.B.). See also "Judgment Reversed," *Montreal Daily Star* (29 December 1942), 3; "Où il est question d'autopsie," *Le Canada* (30 December 1942), 9; "Judgment Upset in Autopsy Suit," *The Gazette* (30 December 1942), 16.

121 *Brouillette v. Religieuses de l'Hôtel-Dieu* (K.B.) (R.J.Q.), 445.

122 *Brouillette v. Religieuses de l'Hôtel-Dieu* (K.B.) (R.J.Q.), 455: "incontestablement son droit"; "la sensibilité, les sentiments, la douleur des membres vivants de la famille d'un défunt ayant la garde, l'administration et même la propriété de son corps. C'est à eux qu'il appartient de décider si le cadavre doit conserver son intégrité ou s'il doit être mutilé."

123 *Brouillette v. Religieuses de l'Hôtel-Dieu* (K.B.) (R.J.Q.), 458.

5. Betrayal

1 See Patrick Brode, *Courted and Abandoned: Seduction in Canadian Law* (Toronto: University of Toronto Press for Osgoode Society for Canadian Legal History, 2002), as well as the review by Lyndsay Campbell, *Canadian Journal of Women and the Law* 15 (2003): 383–91. See also Rachel F. Moran, "Law and Emotion, Love and Hate," *Journal of Contemporary Legal Issues* 11 (2001): 772–83.

2 Weingart's names are spelled variously as Annie, Ennie, Hannah, Waingard, Weingert, and others. I have used Annie Weingart, which is the form used most often. The synagogue, located on Cadieux St., had been incorporated only in 1914, reflecting the rapid immigration of European Jews to that area of Montreal: *An Act to incorporate The Congregation Shemerin Labeker*, S.Q. 1914 (4 Geo. V), c. 159.

3 The marriage record filed as evidence in one of the actions gives their origins, and lists both as widowed: *Weingart v. Silverstine* (case file no. 4275). Jacobson appears in Montreal city directories first in 1892 (as "musician"); Weingart's date of arrival in Montreal is not clear.
4 *Weingart v. Jacobson* (case file no. 1501), deposition of Louis Huberman for plaintiff Weingart (15 February 1917), 10; *Jacobson v. Weingart* (case file no. 4847), deposition of Adolph Solomon for defendant Jacobson (22 February 1917), 2. On the religious rules, see M. Mielziner, *The Jewish Law of Marriage and Divorce in Ancient and Modern Times* (Cincinnati, 1884), 63.
5 *Jacobson v. Weingart* (case file no. 4847), deposition of Joseph Jacobson on his own behalf (22 February 1917), 2. His physician, Joseph Simon Budyk, guessed he was around forty: *Weingart v. Jacobson* (case file no. 1501), deposition of Joseph Simon Budyk for plaintiff Jacobson (15 February 1917), 3.
6 *Weingart v. Jacobson* (case file no. 1501), deposition of Annie Weingart on her own behalf in rebuttal (27 February 1917), 5.
7 Peter Gossage, "Tangled Webs: Remarriage and Family Conflict in Nineteenth-Century Quebec," in *Family Matters: Papers in Post-Confederation Canadian Family History*, ed. Lori Chambers and Edgar-André Montigny, 355–76 (Toronto: Canadian Scholars, 1998).
8 A copy of the contract was filed in *Weingart v. Silverstine* (case file no. 4275), Plaintiff's Exhibit P-1 (dated 7 April 1916).
9 On Montreal's Jewish community at this time, see Gerald Tulchinsky, *Taking Root: The Origins of the Canadian Jewish Community* (Hanover, NH: University Press of New England for Brandeis University Press, 1993); Rebecca Margolis, *Jewish Roots, Canadian Soil: Yiddish Culture in Montreal, 1905–1945* (Montreal and Kingston: McGill-Queen's University Press, 2011), esp. 22–9; Roderick MacLeod and Mary Anne Poutanen, "Little Fists for Social Justice: Anti-Semitism, Community, and Montréal's Aberdeen School Strike, 1913," *Labour/Le Travail* 70 (2012): 67–74.
10 *Weingart v. Jacobson* (case file no. 1501), Petition for authorization to *ester en justice* (dated 17 August 1916); *Weingart v. Jacobson* (case file no. 1501), Plaintiff's Declaration (dated 1 September 1916).
11 *Jacobson v. Weingart and Dominion Bank* (case file no. 4847), Plaintiff's Declaration (dated 6 September 1916).
12 *Huberman v. Jacobson* (case file no. 4789), Declaration (produced 29 September 1916).
13 In addition to motions within the main cases, at least two further actions were undertaken to enforce the main judgment: *Weingart v. Stober* (no. 4226) on Annie's claim for $420 interest due on an asset from the marriage

contract, and *Weingart v. Silverstine* (nos. 2901 and 4275), in which Annie sought revendication of a piano.

14 *Weingart v. Jacobson* (case file no. 1501), Exhibit D-1 (translation filed with Yiddish original).
15 *Weingart v. Jacobson* (case file no. 1501), Exhibit D-2 (translation filed with Yiddish original).
16 Art. 314 CCP (1903 ed.). Aside from matters relating to the administration of property belonging to the other spouse, a husband and wife could not testify against each other. They could testify on their own behalf, as here, but cross-examination would be limited strictly to matters arising from their own examination-in-chief.
17 *Jacobson v. Weingart* (case file no. 4847), deposition of Joseph Jacobson on his own behalf (22 February 1917), 52.
18 *Jacobson v. Weingart* (case file no. 4847), deposition of Joseph Jacobson on his own behalf (22 February 1917), 19.
19 *Jacobson v. Weingart* (case file no. 4847), deposition of Joseph Jacobson on his own behalf (22 February 1917), 3.
20 *Weingart v. Jacobson* (case file no. 1501), depositions of Louis Citrin for plaintiff Weingart (15 February 1917), 12; Louis Huberman for plaintiff Weingart (15 February 1917), 13.
21 *Weingart v. Jacobson* (case file no. 1501), deposition of Joseph Simon Budyk for plaintiff Jacobson (15 February 1917), 2–3.
22 *Jacobson v. Weingart* (case file no. 4847), deposition of Kolman Citrin for defendant Jacobson (27 February 1917), 2–4.
23 *Jacobson v. Weingart* (case file no. 4847), deposition of Agnes Hextes for defendant Jacobson (20 February 1917), 6–7, 20.
24 Quotations from *Huberman v. Jacobson* (case file no. 4789), deposition of Louis Huberman on his own behalf (27 December 1916), 2. There was no cross-examination, so the allegations were uncontested. The judgment (unreported, 5 January 1917) is in the case file.
25 *Jacobson v. Weingart* (case file no. 4847), deposition of Annie Stober for defendant Jacobson (20 February 1917), 8, further discussion of the kimono at 13. The kimono entered women's fashion as part of the later nineteenth-century Japan craze: see Rebecca A.T. Stevens, "Introduction," in *The Kimono Inspiration: Art and Art-to-Wear in America*, ed. Rebecca A.T. Stevens and Yoshiko Iwamoto Wada (Rohnert Park, CA: Pomegranate Artbooks for the Textile Museum, 1996), 17. See generally Barbara A. Schreier, *Becoming American Women: Clothing and the Jewish Immigrant Experience, 1880–1920* (Chicago: Chicago Historical Society, 1994).

26 *Jacobson v. Weingart* (case file no. 4847), deposition of Samuel Freifeld for defendant Jacobson (20 February 1917), 4.
27 *Jacobson v. Weingart* (case file no. 4847), deposition of Philip Rothstein for defendant Jacobson (20 February 1917), 4, further discussion at 5–7. The witness first said Huberman "had his pants on, but without shirt," but later said he was dressed in "just his underwear," 6–7.
28 *Weingart v. Jacobson* (case file no. 1501), deposition of Louis Huberman for plaintiff Weingart in rebuttal (27 February 1917), 5.
29 *Jacobson v. Weingart* (case file no. 4847), deposition of Joseph Jacobson on his own behalf (22 February 1917), 5.
30 *Jacobson v. Weingart* (case file no. 4847), deposition of Joseph Jacobson on his own behalf (22 February 1917), 9.
31 *Jacobson v. Weingart* (case file no. 4847), deposition of Joseph Jacobson on his own behalf (22 February 1917), 10–11.
32 *Jacobson v. Weingart* (case file no. 4847), deposition of Joseph Jacobson on his own behalf (22 February 1917), 22, cf. 23–4.
33 *Jacobson v. Weingart* (case file no. 4847), deposition of Joseph Jacobson on his own behalf (22 February 1917), 39.
34 *Jacobson v. Weingart* (case file no. 4847), deposition of Joseph Jacobson on his own behalf (22 February 1917), 40.
35 *Jacobson v. Weingart* (case file no. 4847), deposition of Joseph Jacobson on his own behalf (27 February 1917), 9.
36 *Jacobson v. Weingart* (case file no. 4847), deposition of Joseph Jacobson on his own behalf (22 February 1917), 49.
37 *Jacobson v. Weingart* (case file no. 4847), deposition of Annie Weingart for defendant Jacobson (20 February 1917), 2–3.
38 Her deposition makes no mention of an interpreter, though another witness, a bank manager, mentioned that Annie spoke only broken English, so likely an interpreter was being used for her testimony: *Weingart v. Jacobson* (case file no. 1501), deposition of John Snow for defendant Weingart (15 February 1917), 4.
39 *Weingart v. Jacobson* (case file no. 1501), deposition of Annie Weingart on her own behalf in rebuttal (27 February 1917), 9.
40 *Weingart v. Jacobson* (case file no. 1501), deposition of Annie Weingart on her own behalf in rebuttal (27 February 1917), 13.
41 *Jacobson v. Weingart* (case file no. 4847), Plea (produced 2 November 1916), 2–3.
42 *Weingart v. Jacobson* (case file no. 1501), deposition of Israel Lake for defendant Weingart (15 February 1917), 11–12.

Notes to pages 181–3   381

43 *Weingart v. Jacobson* (case file no. 1501), deposition of Israel Lake for defendant Weingart (15 February 1917), 11 and 13.
44 *Jacobson v. Weingart* (case file no. 4847), deposition of Philip Rothstein for defendant Jacobson (20 February 1917), 8–9. This answer was struck from the record as not alleged.
45 *Weingart v. Jacobson* (case file no. 1501), deposition of Louis Citrin for plaintiff Weingart (15 February 1917), 9.
46 *Weingart v. Jacobson* (case file no. 1501), depositions of Samuel Weingart for plaintiff Weingart (15 February 1917), 2; Louis Huberman for plaintiff Weingart (15 February 1917), 3–4, 5; *Jacobson v. Weingart* (case file no. 4847), deposition of Joseph Jacobson on his own behalf (22 February 1917), 47–8.
47 *Weingart v. Jacobson* (case file no. 1501), deposition of Louis Huberman for plaintiff Weingart (15 February 1917), 3.
48 *Jacobson v. Weingart* (case file no. 4847), depositions of Adolph Solomon for defendant Jacobson (22 February 1917), 4; Minnie Walker for defendant Jacobson (20 Februxary 1917), 13. The latter testimony was particularly problematic, as there were credible allegations that Joseph was living with Walker after the split, and that he had given her property worth $10,000.
49 *Weingart v. Jacobson* (case file no. 1501), deposition of Louis Huberman for plaintiff Weingart (15 February 1917), 23.
50 *Jacobson v. Weingart* (case file no. 4847), deposition of Samuel Freifeld for defendant Jacobson (20 February 1917), 6.
51 *Jacobson v. Weingart* (case file no. 4847), deposition of Max Crystal for defendant Jacobson (27 February 1917), 3, 6.
52 *Weingart v. Jacobson* (case file no. 1501), Judgment (20 March 1917), unreported. "Friend Husband Fails in His Plea," *The Gazette* (21 March 1917), 12; "La femme a gain de cause," *Le Devoir* (21 March 1917), 4.
53 *Jacobson v. Weingart* (case file no. 4847), Judgment (20 March 1917), unreported.
54 *Jacobson v. Weingart* (case file no. 4847), Motion of respondent (filed 22 May 1917).
55 *Jacobson v. Weingart* (case file no. 4847), Factum of Plaintiff-Appellant (dated 24 October 1917), quotations at 8 and 16.
56 *Weingart v. Jacobson* (case file no. 1501), Plaintiff Respondent's Factum (dated 21 September 1917), 10–11. Annie also submitted a brief factum in no. 4847: *Jacobson v. Weingart* (case file no. 4847), Respondent's Factum (dated 21 September 1917).
57 The two actions (nos. 1501 and 4847) were joined at the Court of Review, which rendered its judgment on 30 May 1918. The published report,

Weingart v. Jacobson (1919), R.J.Q. 57 C.S. 321 (Sup. Ct. Rev.), prints the full judgment but gives the wrong date and incorrectly styles the case "Weingart v. Stober." The judgment is reported in "Decides Point in Commercial Law," *The Gazette* (31 May 1918), 15.

58 *Weingart v. Jacobson* (Sup. Ct. Rev.), 324–6.
59 *Weingart v. Jacobson* (Sup. Ct. Rev.), 328 and 332: "l'excitabilité avec laquelle les immigrés du nord de l'Europe rendent leur témoignage"; "Il n'est pas bon que certaines femmes vivent dans l'oisiveté."
60 *Weingart v. Jacobson* (*sub nomine Weingart v. Stober, Jacobson*) (1919), R.J.Q. 57 C.S. 321n1. See *Supreme Court Act*, R.S.C. 1906, c. 139, s. 40, which allowed an appeal directly to the Supreme Court in Quebec cases in which the ruling of the Court of Review was not appealable to the Court of King's Bench. Joseph's lawyer would seem to have been relying on art. 43(3) CCP (1903 ed.), which excluded an appeal to the Court of King's Bench in matters decided by the Court of Review involving less than $200, but that clearly did not apply in this case, where the claim was for over $2000.
61 *Weingart v. Silverstine* (case file no. 4275), Judgment (5 November 1917), in which Maclennan J. found that Joseph had conspired with the defendant to keep a piano out of Annie's hands.
62 E.g., *Weingart v. Silverstine* (no 2901), Petition and affidavit (dated 28 August 1917), filed in *Weingart v. Silverstine* (case file no. 4275). The petition was granted.
63 *Huberman v. Jacobson* (case file no. 4789), Opposition (produced 18 July 1917). Walker desisted from the opposition on 23 April 1918 after her husband testified that he had never authorized her to act.
64 *Huberman v. Jacobson* (case file no. 4789), Fiat for re-issue of writ of execution (produced 7 June 1918).
65 "Police Society Recovers Loan," *The Gazette* (29 April 1921), 14.
66 *Ex parte Weingart v. Jacobson* (1921), 24 R.P.Q. 125 (Sup. Ct.); A.A. Bruneau, *Question de droit: du mariage* (Montreal: G. Ducharme, 1921).
67 The 1921 census for Laurier Ward lists "Annie Rosen," age twenty-seven, living with Jesie (?), age nine, and Harry, age eight. She is listed as having immigrated in 1911 and was naturalized in 1915. The boys were born in Canada.
68 "Les tribulations d'un professeur," *Le Devoir* (30 October 1926), 3: "ils m'ont volé sur l'Ancien Testament"; "Si vous êtes aussi grand musicien qu'orateur, vous devez être un artiste incomparable." See also "Un truc qui conduit devant le tribunal," *La Presse* (16 February 1927), 9; "Notre chef de police aime la musique," *Le Devoir* (16 February 1927), 4.

69 E.g., notices of defendants to appear, in *Le Devoir* (19 April 1928), 2; *Le Devoir* (24 February 1930), 4.
70 For the legal framework, see Constance Backhouse, "The Tort of Seduction: Fathers and Daughters in Nineteenth Century Canada," *Canadian Journal of Family Law* 10 (1991): 45–80; Martha J. Bailey, "Servant Girls and Masters: The Tort of Seduction and the Support of Bastards," *Canadian Journal of Family Law* 11 (1991): 137–62; Karen Dubinsky, "'Maidenly Girls' or 'Designing Women'? The Crime of Seduction in Turn-of-the-Century Ontario," in *Gender Conflicts: New Essays in Women's History*, ed. Franca Iacovetta and Mariana Valverde, 27–66 (Toronto: University of Toronto Press, 1992); Brode, *Courted and Abandoned*. There is little on these issues in Quebec during our period, but for earlier periods see Serge Gagnon, *Plaisir d'amour et crainte de Dieu: Sexualité et confession au Bas-Canada* (Sainte-Foy, QC: Presses de l'Université Laval, 1990); Gagnon, *Mariage et famille*.
71 *Demers v. Hébert* (1884), 13 R.L. 466 (Sup. Ct.).
72 *Demers v. Hébert* (case file), Exception péremptoire et défense (dated 29 September 1883), 1r.
73 *Demers v. Hébert* (case file), deposition of Clément Prosper Germain for defendant (9 November 1883), 2v: "selon l'expression ordinaire dont on se sert en campagne, – il passait pour riche."
74 *Demers v. Hébert* (case file), deposition of Rose de Lima Demers for defendant (20 November 1883), 2r–v.
75 *Demers v. Hébert* (case file), deposition of Clément Prosper Germain for defendant (9 November 1883), 2r. The marriage contract was filed as plaintiff's Exhibit 1 (filed 17 September 1883).
76 *Demers v. Hébert* (case file), deposition of Clément Prosper Germain for defendant (9 November 1883), 2v and 9r: "ce n'est pas généreux, c'est criant, ce n'est pas juste, ce n'est pas joli."
77 *Demers v. Hébert* (case file), deposition of Clément Prosper Germain for defendant (9 November 1883), 8v.
78 Bettina Bradbury, *Wife to Widow: Lives, Laws, and Politics in Nineteenth-Century Montreal* (Vancouver: UBC Press, 2011), 144–51, quotation at 149. I thank Peter Gossage for his thoughts here as well.
79 *Demers v. Hébert* (case file), depositions of Pierre Lefebvre for defendant (14 November 1883), 3v; Antoine Tollard for defendant (20 November 1883), 2r.
80 For the eighteenth century (and families of more elevated social standing), see Young, *Patrician Families*, 47–50. Bradbury notes that excluding dower could give rise to quid pro quo discussions: Bradbury, *Wife to Widow*, 144–51.

81 *Demers v. Hébert* (case file), deposition of Clément Prosper Germain for defendant (9 November 1883), 4v and 14v.
82 *Demers v. Hébert* (case file), deposition of Rev. George Laporte for defendant (14 November 1883), 1v.
83 The general timeline of what follows is based on *Demers v. Hébert* (case file), Exception péremptoire et défense (produced 25 October 1883); Articulation de faits du défendeur (produced 30 October 1883); and Réponse de la demandersse à l'exception du défendeur (produced 7 November 1883). Details come from the depositions, as indicated below.
84 *Demers v. Hébert* (case file), deposition of F.X. Hébert for plaintiff (9 November 1883), 2r–v.
85 *Demers v. Hébert* (case file), Réponse de la demanderesse à l'exception du défendeur (produced 7 November 1883), 3: "brusquement, sans saluer personne"; *Demers v. Hébert* (case file), deposition of Pierre Demers for plaintiff (5 November 1883), 10r–v.
86 *Demers v. Hébert* (case file), depositions of Rose de Lima Demers for defendant (20 November 1883), 2r; F.X. Hébert for plaintiff (9 November 1883), 8r.
87 *Demers v. Hébert* (case file), Exhibit A^C of defendant at Enquête – Lettre de MM. Robidoux & Fortin avocats à F.X. Hébert en date du 21 juin 1883 (produced 28 January 1884).
88 The parties each described the encounter: *Demers v. Hébert* (case file), depositions of F.X. Hébert for plaintiff (9 November 1883), 4r; Rose de Lima Demers for defendant (20 November 1883), 1r–v.
89 *Demers v. Hébert* (case file), deposition of Rose de Lima Demers for defendant (20 November 1883), 5r.
90 *Demers v. Hébert* (case file), deposition of Rose de Lima Demers for defendant (20 November 1883), 5v: "Bien, réfléchissez, peut être que dans sept ou huit jours vous reviendrez à d'autres sentiments et que nous pourrons nous entendre."
91 *Demers v. Hébert* (case file), deposition of Clément Prosper Germain for defendant (9 November 1883), 5r–6r.
92 *Demers v. Hébert* (case file), Bref et déclaration (dated 31 August 1883).
93 *Demers v. Hébert* (case file), deposition of Joseph E. Robidoux for defendant (28 January 1884), 5.
94 Brode, *Courted and Abandoned*, 105–6.
95 "$500 de dommages," *Le Temps* (3 September 1883), 3, filed as *Demers v. Hébert* (case file), Exhibit A^B of defendant at Enquête (produced 28 June 1884).

96 Brode, *Courted and Abandoned*, 100–20; Rosemary J. Coombe, "'The Most Disgusting, Disgraceful and Inequitous Proceeding in Our Law': The Action for Breach of Promise of Marriage in Nineteenth-Century Ontario," *University of Toronto Law Journal* 38 (1988): 64–108. For earlier Quebec examples, see *Asselin v. Belleau* (1844), 1 R. de L. 46 (Q.B.); *McElwee v. Darling* (1853), Mont. Cond. Rep. 10 (Sup. Ct.); *Barrette v. Poissant* (1862), 15 L.C. Rep. 51 (Sup. Ct.), damages reduced (1864) 15 L.C. Rep. 51 (Q.B.); *Bonneau v. Coupal* (1863), 10 L.C.J. 177 (Sup. Ct.), damages reduced (1865) 1 L.C.L.J. 33, 10 L.C.J. 177 (Q.B.); *Desormeaux v. Cadotte* (1868), 13 L.C.J. 211 (Circ. Ct.); and *Grange v. Benning* discussed in the Introduction.

97 On emotions in Australian breach of promise cases, see Alecia Simmonds, "'Promises and Pie-Crusts Were Made to Be Broke': Breach of Promise of Marriage and the Regulation of Courtship in Early Colonial Australia," *Australian Feminist Law Journal* 23 (2005): 99–120.

98 For the following, see generally Charles Demolombe, *Cours de code civil*, 3:41–8; Ambroise Colin, *Des fiançailles: histoire du droit et droit français des fiançailles et des promesses de mariage* (Paris, 1887), 179–87; Lefebvre-Teillard, *Introduction historique*.

99 Coombe, "'Most Disgusting, Disgraceful and Inequitous Proceeding,'" 68–70.

100 *Chamberland v. Parent* (1882), 8 Q.L.R. 299 at 303 (Sup. Ct.): "C'est l'union de deux âmes rapprochées par ce sentiment intime, spontané et si puissant que l'on nomme l'amour, ou par un autre mobile plus modeste, plus calme, et non moins respectable, la sympathie, qui plus tard produira l'amour."

101 *Grange v. Benning* (1868), 13 L.C.J. 126 (Sup. Ct. Rev.), Mondelet J.

102 Loranger, *Commentaire sur le Code civil du Bas-Canada*, 2:432: "fausse de tous points et contraire aux principes fondamentaux de la société religieuse et civile. Autant vaudrait dire que le mariage lui-même est un acte illicite et immoral, puisqu'il comprime bien davantage que la promesse, la liberté d'en contracter un autre pendant la vie des époux."

103 Brode, *Courted and Abandoned*, 100–20, esp. 118–19.

104 *Moreau v. Pelletier* (1873), 6 R.L. 720 (Sup. Ct., Kamouraska): "Il y a en effet de la bassesse pour un jeune homme à traîner devant les tribunaux celle qu'il prétendait aimer assez pour en faire sa compagne pour le reste de ses jours. Celui qui pour quelques piastres se rend si méprisable, démontre bien à celle qu'il courtisait, combien elle doit être heureuse et se réjouir d'avoir rompu avec lui."

105 *St-Jean v. Gaumont* (1889), 17 R.L. 594 at 599 (Sup. Ct., St. Hyacinthe).

106 *Chamberland v. Parent* (1882), 8 Q.L.R. 299 at 306 (Sup. Ct.): "Je suis forcé de lui répondre que ce qu'elle a perdu ou manqué d'avoir n'étant pas dans le commerce, et échappant à toute évaluation, que de plus la convention qu'elle invoque étant contraire à la liberté des mariages, et conséquemment à l'ordre public, et nulle comme telle."
107 *Demers v. Hébert* (case file), Bref et déclaration (dated 31 August 1883), 3: "ont blessé la demanderesse dans ses sentiments et son affection, l'ont exposée au ridicule et à la risée publique, et lui ont causé un préjudice moral."
108 *Demers v. Hébert* (case file), Exception péremptoire et défense (dated 29 September 1883), 2r: "blessantes et même injurieuses"; "fit naître dans l'esprit du Défendeur que sa fille n'avait [pas] pour lui beaucoup d'affection et qu'elle ne voulait probablement le marier que par intérêt."
109 *Demers v. Hébert* (case file), deposition of F.X. Hébert for plaintiff (9 November 1883), 3r–v: "elle aimait à faire de l'argent."
110 *Demers v. Hébert* (case file), deposition of F.X. Hébert for plaintiff (9 November 1883), 8v–9r: "Q. Est-ce que cela a paru lui faire de la peine quand vous lui avez dit que vous n'étiez pas pour vous marier? R. Oui, monsieur. Q. Est-ce qu'elle a pleuré? R. Non, monsieur, elle n'a pas pleuré. Q. Est-ce qu'elle vous a dit que vous seriez la cause qu'elle serait malheureuse? R. Oui, monsieur, elle m'a dit cela. Q. Est-ce qu'elle vous a parlé comme une personne qui vous aimait? R. Oui, monsieur. A cette occasion-là, elle m'a parlé comme une personne qui m'aimait."
111 *Demers v. Hébert* (case file), deposition of F.X. Hébert for plaintiff (9 November 1883), 5r: "Elle a dit que je lui en avais trop fait."
112 *Demers v. Hébert* (case file), deposition of Rose de Lima Demers for defendant (20 November 1883), 7v–8r.
113 *Demers v. Hébert* (case file), deposition of Rose de Lima Demers for defendant (20 November 1883), 8r.
114 *Demers v. Hébert* (case file), deposition of Rose de Lima Demers for defendant (20 November 1883), 1v–2r: "Je crois bien qu'il devait être un peu gêné après ce qu'il avait fait."
115 *Demers v. Hébert* (case file), deposition of Clément Prosper Germain for defendant (9 November 1883), 5v.
116 *Demers v. Hébert* (case file), deposition of Rose de Lima Demers for defendant (20 November 1883), 1v: "On n'a pas parlé d'affaire sur la rue."
117 *Demers v. Hébert* (case file), deposition of Rose de Lima Demers for defendant (20 November 1883), 1v: "le monde aurait jasé si j'avais été là; le monde aurait dit que j'allais là pour le voir, et je ne voulais pas cela."

118 *Demers v. Hébert* (case file), deposition of Rose de Lima Demers for defendant (20 November 1883), 5v–6r: "J'ai dit que oui, que je l'aimais bien; mais qu'après m'avoir fait autant d'injustices qu'il m'en avait faites, m'avoir causé autant de peine pendant tout ce temps-là; que je n'étais pas décidée de me marier dans le moment"; "après tout ce qu'il avait fait, après m'avoir fait des insultes."
119 *Demers v. Hébert* (case file), deposition of Clément Prosper Germain for defendant (9 November 1883), 7v: "Elle ne paraissait pas le regretter. J'ai cru qu'elle voulait faire de l'argent; ça été mon impression."
120 *Demers v. Hébert* (case file), deposition of Rev. George Laporte for defendant (14 November 1883), 2r: "un homme qui prendrait plaisir à faire de la peine à un autre sans raison, sans motif."
121 *Demers v. Hébert* (case file), deposition of Pierre Demers for plaintiff (5 November 1883), 2v–3r: "une bien grosse peine."
122 *Demers v. Hébert* (case file), deposition of Alexi Moquin for plaintiff (5 November 1883), 2r–v: "La rumeur qu'on était pour se marier et qu'on est laissé par son fiancé, cela empêche toujours les autres d'y aller.... Cela est de nature à faire beaucoup de dommage à une jeune fille. Cela nuit à la réputation."
123 *Demers v. Hébert* (case file), deposition of Paul Boucher for plaintiff (5 November 1883), 2v.
124 *Demers v. Hébert* (case file), deposition of Alexis Sers dit St. Jean for defendant (20 November 1883), 1v: "Un de perdu, dix de trouvés."
125 *Demers v. Hébert* (case file), deposition of Alexis Sers dit St. Jean for defendant (20 November 1883), 3r–4r: "elle était indépendante, vous savez."
126 *Demers v. Hébert* (case file), deposition of Antoine Tollard for defendant (20 November 1883), 1r–2r.
127 *Demers v. Hébert* (case file), deposition of Clément Prosper Germain for defendant (9 November 1883), 13v.
128 *Demers v. Hébert* (case file), deposition of David Desnoyers for defendant (14 November 1883), 1v: "une fille d'honneur."
129 *Demers v. Hébert* (case file), depositions of Alfred Bachand for defendant (20 November 1883), 3r; Alexis Sers dit St. Jean for defendant (20 November 1883), 2v.
130 *Demers v. Hébert* (case file), deposition of Alexis Sers dit St. Jean for defendant (20 November 1883), 2r: "Ça a passé comme une feuille au vent."
131 *Demers v. Hébert* (Sup. Ct.), 471.
132 *Demers v. Hébert* (Sup. Ct.), 470: "un dommage très réel."

133 *Demers v. Hébet* (Sup. Ct.), 469.
134 *Demers v. Hébert* (case file), Exception péremptoire et défense B (dated 29 September 1883), 3r: "dans l'intérêt des familles et de la société."
135 *Demers v. Hébert* (Sup. Ct.), 470–1.
136 "For Breach of Promise," *Montreal Daily Witness* (19 May 1884), 8; "Une leçon," *La Patrie* (20 May 1884), 3; "Dommages," *L'Étendard* (20 May 1884), 3; "Bon à méditer," *L'Électeur (Quebec City)* (23 May 1884), 3. *Le Temps* had folded by this time, or it might have weighed in as well.
137 In the 1891 census Xavier's wife is listed as "Marie R."; in 1901, she is "Rose Delima."
138 *Courteau v. Skelly* (1901), 7 R. de J. 519, R.J.Q. 20 C.S. 216 at 218.
139 "Police Matters," *The Gazette* (25 April 1884), 3.
140 *Lebeau v. Plouffe* (1893), R.J.Q. 5 C.S. 59, details from the case file. The most detailed description of Justine is in *Lebeau v. Plouffe* (case file), deposition of Pierre Soette for plaintiff (14 September 1893), 27–8.
141 On the second hotel, see below, note 200.
142 *Lebeau v. Plouffe* (case file), depositions of Jules Leblanc for plaintiff (15 September 1893), 4–5; Napoléon Taillefer for defendant (15 September 1893), 5.
143 *Lebeau v. Plouffe* (case file), deposition of Aurélie Raymond for plaintiff (13 September 1893), 9, 12, 20.
144 *Lebeau v. Plouffe* (case file), depositions of Aurélie Raymond for plaintiff (13 September 1893), 13: "la figure rouge comme une flambe"; Rose Emma Raymond for plaintiff (14–15 September 1893), 56: "l'air tout curieux."
145 *Lebeau v. Plouffe* (case file), deposition of Aurélie Raymond for plaintiff (13 September 1893), 56: "Voilà Auguste, une chance du bon Dieu, qu'il ne soit pas arrivé plus vite, il nous surprenait [sic] en haut tous les deux." See also *Lebeau v. Plouffe* (case file), deposition of Rose Emma Raymond for plaintiff (14–15 September 1893), 6–8, 46–60.
146 *Lebeau v. Plouffe* (case file), deposition of Rose Emma Raymond for plaintiff (14–15 September 1893), 15.
147 *Lebeau v. Plouffe* (case file), depositions of Aurélie Raymond for plaintiff (13 September 1893), 14–15; Rose Emma Raymond for plaintiff (14–15 September 1893), 15–16; Auguste Lebeau for defendant (18 September 1893), 2–3.
148 *Leblanc v. Lebeau* (case file).
149 "En dommages," *La Presse* (19 September 1892), 4.
150 "Amour perfide," *La Minerve* (27 December 1893), 1: "c'est dire qu'il appréciait hautement l'amour de sa femme."

151 The declaration is missing from the case file, but its essential passages were reproduced in Plouffe's factum for the Court of Review: *Lebeau v. Plouffe* (case file), Factum de l'appelant (produced 26 September 1894), 1: "par d'inconvenantes tentations et d'indiscrètes convoitises ... réussit à se faire aimer de l'épouse du Demandeur"; "Que par ses coupables assiduités et ses perverses familiarités le défendeur a réussi à séduire l'épouse du demandeur, la dite Justine Leblanc"; "la femme du demandeur aurait déclaré que maintenant elle aimait le défendeur et que personne ne lui ferait oublier."

152 Jean-François Fournel, *Traité de l'adultère, considéré dans l'ordre judiciaire* (Paris, 1778), 11: "inspecteur né des mœurs de sa femme, auxquelles il est le plus intéressé."

153 Sourdat, *Traité général de la responsabilité* (1852 ed.), 1:23: "en argent faute de pouvoir faire mieux." In this first edition, Sourdat did not mention a husband's action for seduction of his wife, but by the third edition he had added that example: Sourdat, *Traité général de la responsabilité* (1876 ed.), 1:26.

154 See Adrian Popovici, "De l'aliénation d'affection: essai critique et comparatif," *Canadian Bar Review* 48 (1970): 240.

155 Fuzier-Herman ed., *Répertoire général*, 2:632, under "Adultère."

156 Fournel, *Traité de l'adultère*, 276–7: "devient esclave de l'un & le tyran de l'autre. De là l'insubordination de la femme, son indocilité, sa résistance aux projets de son mari, sa fermeté à les combattre. Or dans cette situation peut-on dire que le mari possède véritablement sa femme? Non, sans doute. Posséder une femme, ce n'est pas seulement être en droit de disposer de sa personne ..., c'est occuper son cœur, être l'objet de ses attentions, de ses craintes, de ses alarmes; c'est diriger ses idées, gouverner son esprit, maîtriser ses volontés: voilà la véritable jouissance d'un mari, & c'est précisément celle que l'Adultère lui enlève."

157 Fournel, *Traité de l'adultère*, 14: "seroit fournir aux femmes le prétexte d'une multitude de réclamations scandaleuses."

158 Fournel, *Traité de l'adultère*, 12–14.

159 For historical overviews, see Popovici, "De l'aliénation d'affection"; Richard G. Zeiger, "Alienation of Affection and Defamation: Similar Interests – Dissimilar Treatment," *Cleveland State Law Review* 30 (1981): 331–66; Brode, *Courted and Abandoned*, 121–32. See also Susan Staves, "Money for Honor: Damages for Criminal Conversation," *Studies in Eighteenth-Century Culture* 11 (1982): 279–97; J.M. Bumsted and Wendy J. Owen, "A Note on the Nineteenth Century Law of Seduction," *Dalhousie Law Journal* 19 (1996): 411–16; Lea VanderVelde, "The Legal Ways of

Seduction," *Stanford Law Review* 48 (1996): 817–901; Korobkin, *Criminal Conversations*; Stephen Robertson, "Seduction, Sexual Violence, and Marriage in New York City, 1886–1955," *Law and History Review* 24 (2006): 331–73.

160 Zeiger, "Alienation of Affection," 333.
161 One of the earliest such cases to refer specifically to alienation of affections was *Winsmore v. Greenbank* (1745), Willes 577, 125 Eng. Rep. 1330 (U.K., Common Pleas). In the United States, an early case recognizing purely moral injury from the seduction of a married woman was *Heermance v. James* (1867), 47 Barb. 120 (N.Y. Sup. Ct.). Both are cited in Zeiger, "Alienation of Affection," 334–6.
162 See especially Susanna L. Blumenthal, "The Default Legal Person," *UCLA Law Review* 54 (2007): 1135–1265; Blumenthal, *Law and the Modern Mind*.
163 See e.g. Brode, *Courted and Abandoned*; Angus McLaren, *Sexual Blackmail: A Modern History* (Cambridge, MA: Harvard University Press, 2002).
164 *Laferrière v. Ribardy* (1874), 5 R.L. 742 (Sup. Ct.). For an earlier example, see *Maheu v. Cloutier* (case file), Declaration (dated 30 August 1849), in which the plaintiff alleged (among other things) that by the defendant's harbouring of his wife, the plaintiff "se trouve privé de l'affection & consolation & des secours qu'un époux a droit d'attendre de son épouse." This case came up in the sample made by the project "Familles, droit et justice au Québec, 1840–1920," of which I am part.
165 *Laferrière v. Ribardy*, 742.
166 *Laferrière v. Ribardy*, 743.
167 *Laferrière v. Ribardy*, 742: "Quel plus grand dommage peut on causer à un homme que de ruiner son bonheur domestique, et lui enlever toutes les jouissances de la vie conjugale et de la famille?"
168 *Laferrière v. Ribardy*, 744: "malheureusement ou plutôt heureusement pour le demandeur, puisque la perte de son procès lui rend l'honneur qu'il croyait avoir perdu."
169 E.g. *St. Laurent v. Hamel* (1891), R.J.Q. 1 B.R. 438, in which the Court of Queen's Bench reversed the Court of Review, which would have dismissed the action for want of proof, and reaffirmed the trial judge's award of damages based on presumptions.
170 *Rochon v. Verret* (1922), R.J.Q. 61 C.S. 276 at 277 (Lemieux C.J.): "véritable intérêt de la société de faciliter la reconciliation des époux et d'éviter un scandale public."
171 *Hart v. Shorey* (1897), R.J.Q. 12 C.S. 84 at 85, Archibald J. The plaintiff had sought $50,000 in damages, and was awarded $5000.

172 *Caron v. Guay* (30 September 1889), 18 R.L. 685 at 687 (Sup. Ct. Rev.): "afficher le déshonneur de cette dernière pour se procurer de l'argent."
173 *Harbec v. Lebrun* (1948), reported in *Cahiers de droit* 10 (1969): 554–5.
174 *Lebeau v. Plouffe* (case file), deposition of Pierre Soette for plaintiff (14 September 1893), 23.
175 *Lebeau v. Plouffe* (case file), deposition of Auguste Lebeau for defendant (18 September 1893), 4: "parce que je ne voulais pas faire de scandale."
176 *Lebeau v. Plouffe* (case file), deposition of Auguste Lebeau for defendant (18 September 1893), 5: "c'est impossible pour moi, cela."
177 Spouses were incompetent witnesses against one another: art. 252 CCP (1891, ed. Mignault).
178 *Lebeau v. Plouffe* (case file), depositions of Rose Emma Raymond for plaintiff (14–15 September 1893), 21, 75; Aurélie Raymond for plaintiff (13 September 1893), 4–5, 28; Pierre Soette for plaintiff (14 September 1893), 8.
179 *Lebeau v. Plouffe* (case file), depositions of Rose Emma Raymond for plaintiff (14–15 September 1893), 16, 71; Pierre Soette for plaintiff (14 September 1893), 5, 21.
180 *Lebeau v. Plouffe* (case file), deposition of Rose Emma Raymond for plaintiff (14–15 September 1893), 15–16: "qu'il parte donc!"
181 *Lebeau v. Plouffe* (case file), deposition of Aurélie Raymond for plaintiff (13 September 1893), 22.
182 *Lebeau v. Plouffe* (case file), deposition of Rose Emma Raymond for plaintiff (14–15 September 1893), 80: "son mari la retenait trop."
183 *Lebeau v. Plouffe* (case file), Plaidoyer du défendeur (produced 20 October 1892).
184 *Lebeau v. Plouffe* (case file), Plaidoyer du défendeur (produced 20 October 1892), 3: "à son propre foyer tout le bonheur domestique qu'il désire et qu'il n'a jamais eu besoin d'avoir recours à l'épouse du Demandeur."
185 *Lebeau v. Plouffe* (case file), deposition of Aurélie Raymond for plaintiff (13 September 1893), 2–3.
186 *Lebeau v. Plouffe* (case file), deposition of Rose Emma Raymond for plaintiff (14–15 September 1893), 2–4: "à se plaire ensemble"; "avaient l'air à l'aimer tous les deux."
187 *Lebeau v. Plouffe* (case file), deposition of Auguste Lebeau for defendant (18 September 1893), 5.
188 *Lebeau v. Plouffe* (case file), deposition of Rose Emma Raymond for plaintiff (14–15 September 1893), 21: "Lorsqu'ils se trouvaient ensemble, ils avaient bien du plaisir, et faisaient toutes sortes d'histoires; ils riaient souvent et on voyait qu'ils s'aimaient."

189 *Lebeau v. Plouffe* (case file), deposition of Pierre Soette for plaintiff (14 September 1893), 13, cf. 19–20: "Je n'aimais pas à voir ces choses-là. Si je l'avais su d'avance, je n'y serais pas passé."
190 *Lebeau v. Plouffe* (case file), deposition of Rose Emma Raymond for plaintiff (14–15 September 1893), 73.
191 *Lebeau v. Plouffe* (case file), depositions of Jules Leblanc for plaintiff (15 September 1893), 4–5; Pierre Soette for plaintiff (14 September 1893), 10; Napoléon Taillefer for defendant (15 September 1893), 3.
192 *Lebeau v. Plouffe* (case file), deposition of Napoléon Taillefer for defendant (15 September 1893), 6: "je trouverais cela dur, cela ne donne pas un bon nom." Cf. *Lebeau v. Plouffe* (case file), deposition of Thomas Hazelwood for plaintiff (15 September 1893), 3.
193 *Lebeau v. Plouffe* (case file), deposition of Jules Leblanc for plaintiff (15 September 1893), 4: "une situation misérable et insultante"; "de nature à lui faire de la peine et à lui faire du dommage à sa réputation et à son honneur."
194 *Leblanc v. Lebeau* (case file), deposition of Pierre Goyette for defendant (2 June 1893), 2–3: "Q. Vous savez qu'il a considéré cela comme un affront bien grave, n'est-ce pas? R. Oui, pas mal, comme tout homme doit le faire."
195 *Leblanc v. Lebeau* (case file), deposition of Edward O'Neil for defendant (8 June 1893), 3.
196 "Amour perfide," *La Minerve* (27 December 1893), 1: "il était imprudent d'entretenir dans son cœur un amour perfide." The judgment was also covered briefly in "L'affection d'une femme," *La Patrie* (26 December 1893), 4 and "L'affection d'une femme évaluée à $500," *L'Électeur (Quebec City)* (27 December 1893), 4.
197 *Lebeau v. Plouffe* (1893), R.J.Q. 5 C.S. 59.
198 *Lebeau v. Plouffe* (R.J.Q.), 60. On class in actions like this, see Popovici, "De l'aliénation d'affection," 243, and, for the common law, Staves, "Money for Honor."
199 *Lebeau v. Plouffe* (case file), Judgment (Sup. Ct. Rev., 22 December 1894), unreported.
200 Legal notices appeared in *Le Prix courant* (21 July 1893), 9; *La Presse* (25 July 1893), 5; *La Presse* (21 August 1893), 4; *La Presse* (11 September 1893), 4.
201 *Leblanc v. Lebeau* (case file), Judgment (1 October 1895, Davidson J.), quotations at 3–4.
202 The census records Germaine Lebeau as Auguste's daughter, but the record of her birth (Parish of St. Brigide, Montreal, 11 February 1897) makes clear that her father was Auguste's brother Edmond.

203 The supplement is labelled "Additions from Closed House Cards – Transfers from Absentee Family Cards."
204 Sherry Olson and Patricia Thornton, *Peopling the North American City: Montreal 1840–1900* (Montreal and Kingston: McGill-Queen's University Press, 2011), 87–8.
205 Gérard Bouchard, Jeannette Larouche, and Lise Bergeron, "Donation entre vifs et inégalités sociales au Saguenay: sur la reproduction familiale en contexte de saturation de l'espace agraire," *RHAF* 46 (1993): 443–61; Liette Côté, "La vieillesse au Québec au XIXe siècle: le cas de Saint-Hyacinthe, 1861–1891" (M.A. thesis, Université de Sherbrooke, 1998).
206 *Rousseau v. Majeur* (1900), R.J.Q. 18 C.S. 447 at 448: "de le loger, sa vie durante, avec lui dans un appartement convenable de la dite maison, avec droit d'aller et venir partout dans la dite maison et sur la dite propriété, de le chauffer, nourrir à la table commune de la famille, coucher dans une chambre et lit convenable à son état et ses moyens, blanchir et raccommoder et entretenir son linge proprement, et enfin d'en avoir bien soin et de lui procurer tous les égards que requéraient son âge, ses moyens et son état; et à son décès, de le faire inhumer dans le cimetière de la paroisse de St-Denis, avec un service de $10."
207 Ferrière, *Dictionnaire*, 1:481, under "Donation entre conjoints": "il ne seroit pas convenable que l'affection conjugale, qui doit mutuellement unir les cœurs du mari & de la femme, fût pour ainsi dire venale, & se pût acquérir ou conserver par des présens." Cited in Serge Courville, *Quebec: A Historical Geography*, trans. Richard Howard (Vancouver: UBC Press, 2008), 64. See art. 1265 CCLC, which included this bar as well, though its stated reason was to ensure that marriage contracts once made could not be altered by gifts between the spouses.
208 Art. 893 no. 1 CCLC. See the discussion of *injure* in chapter 1.
209 Art. 813 CCLC. The French "*injures graves*" was clearer in legal terms than the vague "grievous injuries" of the English, which suggested physical rather than moral injuries. See Louis-Amable Jetté, "Cours Jetté," *Revue du droit* 15 (1936–37): 477 (part of a reprinting of Jetté's lectures dating from the 1890s). Revocation for ingratitude went back to Roman law; for its general history, see Susan Scott, "Revocation of Gifts on the Ground of Ingratitude: From Justinian to LAWSA," *Journal of South African Law* (2011): 361–72.
210 *Drew v. Dean* (1887), 32 L.C.J. 310 at 311 (Sup. Ct.): "la plus noire ingratitude." Affirmed (1888), *ibid.* (Q.B.).
211 *Cournoyer et uxor v. Cournoyer* (1894), R.J.Q. 5 C.S. 312 at 313: "oublieux de l'honneur et du respect qu'en loi il doit à ses père et mère"; "des blasphèmes honteux."

212 *Roy v. Houle* (1927), 34 R.L. (n.s.) 448, quotation at 449 (Sup. Ct.): "comme un bon fils doit le faire."
213 *Roireau v. Roireau* (1936), R.J.Q. 74 C.S. 221, 42 R. de J. 319: "les soins et égards qu'il a eus de ses père et mère dans le passée"; "un forçat." A motion to dismiss (inscription in law) succeeded, since the action in revocation was open only to the donor (that is the mother) and not to a third-party beneficiary (the brother).
214 Bradbury, *Wife to Widow*, 363–75.
215 *Farand dit Viveret v. Paulos alias Paul* (1905), R.J.Q. 28 C.S. 200 at 201: "comme doit le faire un bon enfant envers sa propre mère qu'il aime et respect."
216 *Beaulieu v. Frank* (1913), 20 R. de J. 26 (Sup. Ct.).
217 *Loughrin v. Burke* (1918), R.J.Q. 55 C.S. 431, quotations at 432–3: "Le passé de cette femme est déplorable. C'est une dypsomane, qui depuis longtemps s'est adonnée au commerce illicite et clandestin des boissons enivrantes"; "des visites douteuses."
218 *Farand dit Viveret v. Paulos alias Paul* (1905), R.J.Q. 28 C.S. 200 at 204: "étant données les circonstances et la condition des parties"; "d'un caractère acariâtre et capricieuse."
219 *Nolin v. Hardy* (1932), R.J.Q. 53 B.R. 359 at 362: "la position sociale, des habitudes, de l'éducation et de facteurs qui peuvent échapper à une enquête judiciaire." The appeals court reversed the trial decision that nullified the gift.
220 *Collin v. Gilot* (1930), R.J.Q. 48 B.R. 464, reversing the trial decision of 12 June 1929. The Superior Court case file does not survive, but the King's Bench file includes copies of the depositions and principal procedural documents.
221 The Gilots were European, likely Belgians: *Collin v. Gilot* (case file), deposition of Dame Jean Gilot for defendant (6 June 1929), 44.
222 *Collin v. Gilot* (case file), Acte de donation (dated 25 July 1927), printed in the case submitted to the Court of King's Bench, pp. 54–5.
223 *Collin v. Gilot* (case file), deposition of Elzéar Collin on his own behalf (6 June 1929), 7: "n'étaient pas capables de me garder." I have not been able to make certain identifications of Collin in census or other records, and the case file provides few details on his family.
224 *Collin v. Gilot* (case file), deposition of Elzéar Collin *fils* for defendant (6 June 1929), 29. Léonie Steile mentioned the marriage, and testified that she bought Collin a suit for his son's wedding: *Collin v. Gilot* (case file), deposition of Dame Jean Gilot for defendant (6 June 1929), 43.

225 *Collin v. Gilot* (case file), deposition of Elzéar Collin on his own behalf (6 June 1929), 19.
226 *Collin v. Gilot* (case file), deposition of Elzéar Collin on his own behalf (6 June 1929), 8: "quand je reste quelque part, j'aime à payer, je paye, et je m'en vais quand cela ne fait pas mon affaire."
227 *Collin v. Gilot* (case file), deposition of Elzéar Collin on his own behalf (6 June 1929), 18: "Une pension au lait, du lait et un petit morceau de pain et un petit peu de soupane, le matin, c'était ma pension."
228 *Collin v. Gilot* (case file), deposition of Eva Beauregard for defendant (6 June 1929), 39 and 41: "et même mieux qu'on devait lui faire"; "Je n'en veux pas, il est depuis longtemps pardonné."
229 *Collin v. Gilot* (case file), deposition of Elzéar Collin on his own behalf (6 June 1929), 19: "que je serais bien comme je ne l'avais jamais été de ma vie."
230 *Collin v. Gilot* (case file), Déclaration (dated 29 March 1929), 1; *Collin v. Gilot* (case file), depositions of Dame Jean Gilot for defendant (6 June 1929), 45; Elzéar Collin on his own behalf in rebuttal (6 June 1929), 50.
231 "Terrible aventure," *La Presse* (11 April 1928), 29. Photos of Gilot, Steile, and Collin appeared the following day: *La Presse* (12 April 1928), 3.
232 *Collin v. Gilot* (case file), deposition of Elzéar Collin on his own behalf (6 June 1929), 16: "ce n'était pas joli, les jeunes filles allaient s'asseoir de même sur les garçons et elles les poignaient par le cou. J'ai dit à la plus grande: 'Quand même vous seriez dans la vie, ce n'est pas joli devant le monde.'" I am grateful to Thierry Nootens and Peter Gossage for help with Collin's obscure synatax in this passage.
233 The allegations are detailed in *Collin v. Gilot* (case file), Déclaration (dated 29 March 1929), 2–3.
234 *Collin v. Gilot* (case file), deposition of Jean Gilot on his own behalf (6 June 1929), 22–3: "comme le vrai père de la maison."
235 *Collin v. Gilot* (case file), deposition of Dame Jean Gilot for defendant (6 June 1929), 42: "M. Collin a été chez moi traité comme le père. Tous les soirs, tout le personnel, je leur disais: 'Traitez-le comme un père.'"
236 *Collin v. Gilot* (case file), Déclaration (dated 29 March 1929), 2: "ses secrets de l'avenir"; "dol et artifices."
237 *Collin v. Gilot* (case file), Plaidoyer (dated 22 April 1929), 4–5.
238 *Collin v. Gilot* (K.B.), 468–9: "aucune personne honnête n'aurait consenti à habiter dans la maison du défendeur, sachant ce qui s'y passait."
239 *Collin v. Gilot* (K.B.), 473: "Le fait pour un citoyen respectable et de l'âge du demandeur, d'être forcé de vivre dans un milieu où il est constamment

témoin d'actes révoltants et scandaleux ne constitue-t-il pas une injure grave, un outrage à sa personne et une marque de mépris."

240 *Collin v. Gilot* (K.B.), 474: "dans un antre de vice et de corruption où il lui répugne de vivre."

241 On proceedings *in forma pauperis*, see arts. 89–93 CCP (1903 ed.).

242 The case file for this action (no. 65,359) does not survive, so the details are drawn primarily from the plumitif.

243 Notices appeared in *La Presse*: (16 September 1931), 15; (10 March 1932), 21; (19 November 1932), 52. Collin disappeared from the record, but Gilot continued to figure in the news periodically. In 1935, someone was arrested while attempting to steal Gilot's pigeons from behind his home in Sault-au-Récollet: "Found in Pigeon Loft," *The Gazette* (26 August 1935), 6. In 1945 Gilot and Steile were again involved in a car crash, in which Steile suffered injuries: "Woman Hurt in Crash," *The Gazette* (29 June 1945), 17.

244 Bradbury, *Wife to Widow*, 363–75.

6. Grief and Mourning

1 Bradbury, *Wife to Widow*; Julie-Marie Strange, *Death, Grief and Poverty in Britain, 1870–1914* (Cambridge: Cambridge University Press, 2005); Stearns, *Revolutions in Sorrow*; Pat Jalland, *Death in the Victorian Family* (Oxford: Oxford University Press, 1996); Lou Taylor, *Mourning Dress: A Costume and Social History* (1983; repr., London: Routledge, 2009).

2 Bradbury, *Wife to Widow*; Nan Goodman, *Shifting the Blame: Literature, Law, and the Theory of Accidents in Nineteenth-Century America* (Princeton: Princeton University Press, 1998); John Fabian Witt, *The Accidental Republic: Crippled Workingmen, Destitute Widows, and the Remaking of American Law* (Cambridge, MA: Harvard University Press, 2004); Julie-Marie Strange, "'She Cried a Very Little': Death, Grief and Mourning in Working-Class Culture, 1880–1914," *Social History* 27 (2002): 143–61. On an earlier period in Quebec, see Jacques Légaré and Jean-François Naud, "The Dynamics of Household Structure in the Event of the Father's Death: Québec City in the 18th Century," *History of the Family* 6 (2001): 519–29.

3 Child: *Poitras v. Quebec Railway, Light & Power Co.* (1904), R.J.Q. 14 B.R. 429; husband: *Robinson v. Canadian Pacific Railway Co.* (1887), 14 S.C.R. 105.

4 *Couillard v. Jeannotte* (1894), R.J.Q. 3 B.R. 461. Details from the case files.

5 Jeannotte graduated in medicine from McGill in 1874: "College of Physicians and Surgeons of Lower Canada," *Canada Medical and Surgical Journal* 2 (1874): 576. A large number of the main figures in the Montreal

medical community attended his funeral in 1914: "Les obsèques du Dr Jeannotte," *Le Canada* (4 March 1914), 3.
6 *Couillard v. Jeannotte* (Sup. Ct. case file), deposition of Herménégilde Jeannotte for plaintiff re Jeannotte (12 June 1890), 1r–v.
7 "Death from Morphine: Two Girls Given That Drug Instead of Quinine – Fatal Results," *Sarnia (Ontario) Observer* (7 October 1887), 2; "Sad Case of Poisoning: Morphine Mistaken for Quinine," *Meriden (Connecticut) Daily Republican* (5 September 1876), 3. That this was a common error was noted in "Mistakes in Medicine: Careless Physicians Who Make Grave Errors in Their Prescriptions," *Eugene (Oregon) City Guard* (17 April 1886), 6.
8 Various experts produced copious testimony on the production and properties of these compounds of morphine. See *Couillard v. Jeannotte* (Sup. Ct. case file), depositions of Jean-Baptiste Adolphe Lamarche for plaintiff re Jeannotte (13 June 1890); Norbert Fafard for plaintiff re Jeannotte (13 June 1890); Salluste Duval for plaintiff re Jeannotte (16 June 1890); John D.L. Ambrosse for plaintiff re Jeannotte (16 June 1890).
9 *Couillard v. Jeannotte* (Sup. Ct. case file), deposition of Henriette Lafrance for plaintiff re Jeannotte (13 June 1890), 1v.
10 *Couillard v. Jeannotte* (Sup. Ct. case file), deposition of Henriette Lafrance for plaintiff re Jeannotte (13 June 1890), 2v.
11 *Couillard v. Jeannotte* (Sup. Ct. case file), deposition of Henriette Lafrance for plaintiff re Jeannotte (13 June 1890), 3r: "Ces remèdes-là vont faire mourir ton enfant."
12 There was some question whether two additional doses were administered, and Charles testified as well that two doses were given to the other child when the quinine pills ran out; the older boy slept unusually deeply, but there were no further effects. *Couillard v. Jeannotte* (Sup. Ct. case file), deposition of Thomas Charles Couillard for defendant Jeannotte (18 June 1890), 8r–10r.
13 *Couillard v. Jeannotte* (Sup. Ct. case file), depositions of Charles Beausoleil for plaintiff re Jeannotte (12 June 1890), 3v, 4v; Henriette Lafrance for plaintiff re Jeannotte (13 June 1890), 4v; Louisa Demers for plaintiff re Jeannotte (13 June 1890), 1v, 2v.
14 *Couillard v. Jeannotte* (Sup. Ct. case file), deposition of Herménégilde Jeannotte for plaintiff re Jeannotte (12 June 1890), 3v–4r: "J'ai répondu que non, que je n'avais pas de dommages à lui payer pour cela, de me poursuivre, que je n'étais pas responsable de cet accident-là"; "je serais heureux d'être poursuivi dans cette cause-là pour faire un test-case, pour savoir qui serait responsable dans ce cas-là."

15 *Couillard v. Jeannotte* (Sup. Ct. case file), deposition of Herménégilde Jeannotte for plaintiff re Jeannotte (12 June 1890), 3v–4r: "Elle vous a félicté, je suppose?"
16 "A Doctor's Fatal Mistake," *Ottawa Daily Citizen* (9 August 1889), 1. See also "City and Suburban," *Montreal Herald and Daily Commercial Gazette* (16 August 1889), 6; "Action en dommage," *La Presse* (17 August 1889), 3. The libel action was discontinued without hearing on 2 December 1889: *Jeannotte v. Citizen Printing & Publishing Co.* (case file). The newspaper published a retraction (which nevertheless repeated the libellous allegations twice more): "The Montreal Poisoning Case," *Ottawa Daily Citizen* (29 November 1889), 1.
17 *Couillard v. Jeannotte* (Sup. Ct. case file), Bref et déclaration (returned 20 September 1889), 4–5: "dommages tant réels qu'exemplaires." For comparisons, see *Lord v. Cie du chemin de fer du nord* (1885), 14 R.L. 297 (action for $6000 for death of child; dismissed at Sup. Ct., affirmed by Q.B.); *Vanasse v. Cité de Montréal* (1888), 16 R.L. 386 (action for $5000 for death of elderly woman; Sup. Ct. awarded $1000). See also Peter Gossage, "On Dads and Damages: Looking for the 'Priceless Child' and the 'Manly Modern' in Quebec's Civil Courts, 1921–1960," *Histoire sociale/Social History* 49 (2016): 603–23.
18 "Action en dommages," *La Patrie* (6 September 1889), 4; "Cause importante," *La Presse* (6 September 1889), 4; "The Child Poisoning Case," *Ottawa Daily Citizen* (7 September 1889), 1. For developments at this time outside Quebec, see Brown, "Canada's First Malpractice Crisis."
19 *Couillard v. Jeannotte* (R.J.Q.), 467: "une erreur grossière."
20 On the history of *solatium doloris*, see Michel Morin, "Une analyse historique et comparative de l'indemnisation du *solatium doloris* au Québec," in *Mélanges Claude Masse: en quête de justice et d'équité*, ed. Pierre-Claude Lafond (Cowansville, QC: Yvon Blais, 2003), 347–86; Jean-Sébastien Poirier, "Autopsie d'une disposition disparue: l'article 1056 du Code civil du Bas Canada et le *solatium doloris*," *Revue juridique Thémis* 29 (1995): 657–703.
21 This brought up various related issues, which I will not discuss in any detail here, such as the extent to which Supreme Court precedents were seen as binding in Quebec and whether provisions of the CCLC should be interpreted in the same way or differently from ordinary statutes.
22 E.g., Mignault, *Le droit civil canadien*, 5:340.
23 In their original forms, the French and English versions of the article differed, the former reading "ses père, mère et enfants," the latter "his ascendant and descendant relations." By S.Q. 1930 (20 Geo. V), c. 98, the

French version was modified to "ses ascendants et ses descendants," in keeping with the English wording. See Poirier, "Autopsie d'une disposition disparue," 666.
24 This is not to say the Quebec code was a slavish copy of the French: see Young, *Politics of Codification*; Greenwood, "Lower Canada (Quebec)."
25 Aix, 6 May 1872, quoted in François Laurent, *Principes de droit civil*, 4th ed. (Brussels, 1887), 20:569 (no. 525): "Après tout, on ne peut payer la vie d'un père ou d'un époux, et sa mort ne doit point devenir le sujet d'une spéculation qui enrichirait sa famille."
26 Pollock, *Law of Torts*, 54.
27 See Peter Handford, "Lord Campbell and the Fatal Accidents Act," *Law Quarterly Review* 129 (2013): 420–49; Morin, "Une analyse historique," 358–62; John Fabian Witt, "From Loss of Services to Loss of Support: The Wrongful Death Statutes, the Origins of Modern Tort Law, and the Making of the Nineteenth-Century Family," *Law and Social Inquiry* 25 (2000): 731.
28 Handford, "Lord Campbell," 420.
29 9 & 10 Vic. (1846), c. 93 (U.K.) [*Fatal Accidents Act* (U.K.)].
30 *Fatal Accidents Act* (U.K.), s. II.
31 *Blake v. Midland Railway Co.* (1852), 18 Q.B. Rep. 93 (U.K.).
32 *Blake v. Midland Railway Co.*, 109.
33 *Blake v. Midland Railway Co.*, 111.
34 *An Act for compensating the Families of Persons killed by Accident, and for other purposes therein mentioned*, S.P.C. 1847 (10 & 11 Vic.), c. 6 (P.C.), quotation from s. II.
35 *Ravary v. Grand Trunk Railway*. The decision of the Superior Court in Review (with overview of the jury verdict) is (1857) 1 L.C.J. 280 (Sup. Ct. Rev.); the appeal is (1860) 6 L.C.J. 49 (Q.B.). The Superior Court case file is missing, but the appeal file survives (minus the depositions, however): *Ravary v. Grand Trunk Railway* (Q.B. case file). On the background and course of the case, see Reiter, "From Shaved Horses to Aggressive Churchwardens," 466–7, 482–5.
36 *Ravary v. Grand Trunk Railway* (Sup. Ct. Rev.), 282–3.
37 *Ravary v. Grand Trunk Railway* (Sup. Ct. Rev.), 282.
38 *Ravary v. Grand Trunk Railway* (Q.B.), 59 (the bilingual wording is in the original). By "common law" here the court was referring to the *droit commun* of Quebec (still at that time uncodified), not to the English common law.
39 *Ravary v. Grand Trunk Railway* (Q.B.), 52.
40 *Ravary v. Grand Trunk Railway* (Q.B.), 57.
41 *Ravary v. Grand Trunk Railway* (Q.B.), 59.

42 The Grand Trunk contemplated taking the case to the Privy Council and filed security for the appeal, but the Committee never heard the case (I have not been able to determine whether because the Committee refused permission to appeal or because the railway decided not to pursue the matter).
43 The main apparent outlier was *Provost v. Jackson* (1869), 13 L.C.J. 170 (Q.B.), in which the plaintiff's son drowned when his canoe was overturned by the defendant's steamship. Though occasionally cited later as rejecting *solatium doloris*, the case was actually decided on other grounds. The trial, held in 1860 before the decision of the Court of Queen's Bench in *Ravary* was handed down, went forward on the 1847 statute. The jury awarded £1000, but the presiding judge allowed the defendants' motion for nonsuit, since the statute (as interpreted by the Superior Court in *Ravary*) required proof of special damages, which had not been alleged. On appeal, the Court of Queen's Bench upheld that ruling, on the narrow and formalistic basis that although the statute gave a right of action to parents, the plaintiffs had not provided proof that the victim was their son. See also "Law Intelligence," *Montreal Herald and Daily Commercial Gazette* (21 January 1860), 2 and (23 January 1860), 2 (covering the trial); and "Law Intelligence," *Montreal Herald and Daily Commercial Gazette* (3 June 1869), 1 (on the appeal).
44 *Vanasse v. Cité de Montréal et Gagnon* (1888), 16 R.L. 386 at 396 (Sup. Ct.)
45 *Cadoret v. Cité de Montréal et Gagnon* (1888), 16 R.L. 386 at 397n (Sup. Ct.): "l'affection naturelle"; "puisque dans notre système légal, on doit une réparation pour tout préjudice que l'on cause."
46 The main reported judgments in the case are: (1886) M.L.R. 2 Q.B. 25, 4 Déc. C.A. 297; (1887) 14 S.C.R. 105; (1889) M.L.R. 5 SC. 225, 33 L.C.J. 145 (Sup. Ct. Rev.); (1890) M.L.R. 6 Q.B. 118, 19 R.L. 485; (1891) 19 S.C.R. 292; [1892] A.C. 491 (J.C.P.C.).
47 *Robinson v. Canadian Pacific Railway* (Q.B. 1886), 33, Ramsay J.
48 *Robinson v. Canadian Pacific Railway* (S.C.C. 1887), 110.
49 *Robinson v. Canadian Pacific Railway* (S.C.C. 1887), 123 and 128–9.
50 On juries, see R. Blake Brown, *A Trying Question: The Jury in Nineteenth-Century Canada* (Toronto: University of Toronto Press for Osgoode Society for Canadian Legal History, 2009).
51 *Robinson v. Canadian Pacific Railway* (S.C.C. 1891), 307, 309 (Strong J. on judicial notice and excessive damages).
52 *Robinson v. Canadian Pacific Railway* (J.C.P.C.), 490.
53 *Robinson v. Canadian Pacific Railway* (J.C.P.C.), 487. The latter reference is to *An Act respecting compensation to the Families of Persons killed by Accident, and in duels*, C.S.C. 1859, c. 78 (United Canadas).

54 "A Defence in Law," *The Gazette* (13 November 1889), 5.
55 The hearing was extensively covered in the Montreal press: "The Wrong Drug," *Montreal Daily Witness* (12 June 1890), 6; "Analysing the Drug," *Montreal Daily Witness* (14 June 1890), 1; "L'affaire Couillard," *La Presse* (16 June 1890), 1.
56 *Couillard v. Jeannotte* (Sup. Ct. case file), deposition of Thomas Charles Couillard for defendant Jeannotte (18 June 1890). Charles also testified on his own behalf, under objection by the defence and with the permission of the judge, since principals were at this time generally prohibited from testifying in support of their own case. The case file is somewhat ambiguous about whether Aline testified. In *Couillard v. Jeannotte* (Sup. Ct. case file), Procès-verbal des procédés à l'enquête & mérite (produced 31 October 1890), a transcript of the process by which the testimony was taken, she was listed as having been sworn and examined for the plaintiff on 6 October 1890 (and taxed at $1.00). That entry appears just after the note that the defendant Devins had declared his evidence closed. No deposition by Aline appears in the trial court files or in the printed case submitted to the Court of Queen's Bench, and no other reference to her testimony appears in any of the surviving documentation from the case.
57 *Couillard v. Jeannotte* (1891), R.J.Q. 3 B.R. 461 at 462–77 (Sup. Ct.), quotation at 471–2: "Si quelqu'un assassine votre vieux père, que vous êtes obligé de faire vivre, non seulement vous n'avez pas de dommages, mais vous lui devez de la reconnaissance, de ce qu'il vous a débarrassé de cette charge; voilà la conséquence de la doctrine de la cour suprême."
58 *Couillard v. Jeannotte* (R.J.Q.), 472: "un principe barbare qui n'est pas admissible"; "la véritable doctrine."
59 *Couillard v. Jeannotte* (R.J.Q.), 474.
60 *Couillard v. Jeannotte* (R.J.Q.), 477: "à titre de dommages exemplaires et de peine imposée aux défendeurs."
61 "Death of Mr. R.J. Devins," *The Gazette* (22 February 1892), 5.
62 "A Mistake Case in Court," *Druggists' Circular and Chemical Gazette* 35, no. 11 (November 1891): 241. See also "Shirking Responsibility," *Druggists' Circular and Chemical Gazette* 38, no. 6 (June 1894): 122: "So ends a case remarkable for persistent effort to legally impose upon the pharmacist all responsibility for the error of the physician."
63 *Couillard v. Jeannotte* (1894), R.J.Q. 3 B.R. 461. See, on the hearing, "Legal Intelligence," *The Gazette* (17 January 1894), 2 and, on the decision, "Legal Intelligence," *The Gazette* (30 March 1894), 6; "Revue judiciaire," *La Minerve* (30 March 1894), 1.
64 *Couillard v. Jeannotte* (R.J.Q.), 496.
65 *Couillard v. Jeannotte* (R.J.Q.), 498.

66 His opinion is not in the case file and is summarized in the report. A slightly more detailed summary is in "Legal Intelligence," *The Gazette* (30 March 1894), 6.
67 Couillard cross-appealed, but not to get more damages. Though he felt the amounts awarded were minimal, he argued only that the Superior Court's award should be affirmed. *Couillard v. Jeannotte* (Q.B. case file), Factum de l'intimé, 25.
68 *Couillard v. Jeannotte* (Q.B. case file), Factum de l'intimé, "Du dommage matériel," 15–16.
69 *Couillard v. Jeannotte* (Q.B. case file), Factum de l'intimé, "Du dommage moral," 16–23: "le sentiment, étant le plus grand et le plus noble mobile des actions humaines, n'avait pas besoin d'un long espace de temps pour déterminer celui qui souffre de la mort de son père, ou de son enfant, à poursuivre l'auteur du délit"; "Vous admettez donc que vous me causez du tort en me privant de ce bonheur qui devait augmenter à mesure que mon enfant aurait avancé en âge. Pourquoi me priverez-vous de ce bonheur sans que je reçoive compensation?"; "d'une manière aussi cruelle"; "mais, sa douleur, comment la paiera-t-il?"; "sans cesse le souvenir de sa mort viendra briser son cœur"; "sachent que si la terre recèle quelquefois leurs fautes, du moins lorsqu'elles sont connues, elles sont sévèrement punies par la loi."
70 *Couillard v. Jeannotte* (Sup. Ct. case file), depositions of François-Xavier Beausoleil for plaintiff re Jeannotte (12 June 1890), 2r; Jean-Baptiste Adolphe Lamarche for plaintiff re Jeannotte (13 June 1890), 8; Louis Bédard for plaintiff re Jeannotte (13 June 1890), 3; Norbert Fafard for plaintiff re Jeannotte (13 and 16 June 1890), 3r.
71 *Couillard v. Jeannotte* (Sup. Ct. case file), deposition of Norbert Fafard for plaintiff re Jeannotte (13 and 16 June 1890), 3r.
72 *Couillard v. Jeannotte* (Sup. Ct. case file), deposition of Clara Côté for plaintiff re Jeannotte (18 June 1890), 6r: "ça n'est pas grand chose"; "C'est une grosse perte, parce qu'on a toujours espérance sur l'enfant."
73 Viviana A. Zelizer, *Pricing the Priceless Child: The Changing Social Value of Children* (New York: Basic Books, 1985); see also Gossage, "On Dads and Damages."
74 *Couillard v. Jeannotte* (Sup. Ct. case file), deposition of Jean-Baptiste Adolphe Lamarche for plaintiff re Jeannotte (13 June 1890), 8–9: "il en avait des masses, dix, douze"; "la valeur serait moindre, ... il n'y a pas de doute que ça soulage la famille quand il en part deux ou trois. Quand un homme gagne cinquante piastres par mois et qu'il a huit enfants à élever s'il en perd trois ou quatre, il me semble qu'il ne fait pas une grosse

perte, au moins pécuniairement parlant; ça peut saigner le cœur du père et de la mère, mais il me semble que financièrement il ne perd pas grand chose"; "Sur cette évaluation-là je demanderais à la cour de ne pas trop me prendre au sérieux; je fais cela bien à peu près, et je n'ai pas l'habitude de faire ces calculs-là."

75 *Couillard v. Jeannotte* (Q.B. case file), Factum de l'intimé, 21–2: "moi, pauvre, mon bonheur c'est l'amour de mes enfants, mon épouse, mon père, ma mère"; "loin de me reconnaître le droit d'avoir une réparation, vous me répondez: 'Votre enfant était à votre charge, votre bien-être augmentera donc d'autant.' N'est-ce pas profondément immoral?"

76 "Les parents des victimes du 'Laurier Palace' sont-ils protégés?" *Le Devoir* (10 February 1927), 1–2 (quotation at 2): "ne peuvent compter sur des dommages bien élevés"; "ils n'ont pas droit au solatium doloris, à une compensation pour la peine morale."

77 I will address the post-*Robinson* situation in a later project. The clearest example of both critique and camouflage is the judgment of the Court of King's Bench in *Hunter v. Gingras* (1921), R.J.Q. 33 B.R. 403, in which the plaintiff's nine-year-old daughter was killed by the defendant speeding in a car. Chief Justice Gustave Lamothe, writing for the majority, made clear his disagreement with the Supreme Court's denial of moral damages in fatal accident cases (at 409–10): "Cela révolte le sens commun. C'est un point de vue trop réaliste. Autant vaudrait dire que l'auteur de la mort d'un enfant de deux ans aurait conféré un bénéfice au père de cet enfant en le relevant, par-là, de l'obligation de le nourrir ... Toute cette argumentation révolte, – ce qui démontre la fausseté de la base que l'on voudrait adopter pour la mesure des dommages." The trial judgment, (1921) R.J.Q. 60 C.S. 182, had awarded just $136 in material damages; the appeals court increased that by $500, ostensibly for lost expectations, but no doubt also as a move towards compensating the family's grief. See also Gossage, "On Dads and Damages," 608.

78 E.g., Pierre-Basile Mignault, "L'avenir de notre droit civil," *Revue du droit* 1 (1922): 56–65, 104–16. See generally Sylvio Normand, "Un thème dominant de la pensée juridique traditionnelle au Québec: la sauvegarde de l'intégrité du droit civil," *McGill Law Journal* 32 (1987): 559–601.

79 *Augustus v. Gosset*, [1996] 3 S.C.R. 269; Louise Langevin, "L'œuvre de Claire L'Heureux-Dubé: une lecture féministe de l'arrêt *Augustus c. Gosset*," *Canadian Journal of Women and the Law* 15 (2003): 122–37. The case involved the damages claim of the mother of a young Black man wrongfully killed by a Montreal police officer.

80 See Bradbury, *Wife to Widow*, 206–14; Taylor, *Mourning Dress*.

81 Denisart, *Collection de décisions nouvelles*, 1:724–7, under "Deuil."
82 E.g., Nootens, *Genre, patrimoine et droit civil*, 187–91.
83 E.g., *Bradley v. Ménard* (1900), R.J.Q. 18 C.S. 382. This reflected long tradition in French law, which entered Quebec via the Custom of Paris. See Bradbury, *Wife to Widow*, 214, and the literature cited there.
84 *Mailloux v. Paquette* (1908), R.J.Q. 35 C.S. 166 at 172–3: "dans cette province."
85 Bradbury, *Wife to Widow*, 233–4.
86 Bradbury, *Wife to Widow*, 213–14, citing *Larue v. Desautels* (30 December 1872) from Mackay's bench books in the McGill University Archives.
87 E.g., *L'Heureux v. Carmel*, in *Le Canada* (26 September 1936), 10.
88 *Fairgreave v. Gray* (1932), R.J.Q. 71 C.S. 73 at 75–6 (quotations at 75).
89 *Jodoin v. Larivière* (1894), R.J.Q. 6 C.S. 345 (Sup. Ct. Rev.), reversing (1893) R.J.Q. 5 C.S. 39 (Sup. Ct.). See also *O'Brien v. Bahen* (1936), R.J.Q. 75 C.S. 55 at 62; damages reduced (1938), R.J.Q. 65 B.R. 64.
90 *Lague v. Archambault* (1929), R.J.Q. 68 C.S. 102, quotation at 104: "absolument extravagante."
91 *L'Heureux v. Carmel*, in *Le Canada* (26 September 1936), 10. L'Heureux was, however, beneficiary of a $6000 life insurance policy.
92 *Mailloux v. Paquette* (1908), R.J.Q. 35 C.S. 166 at 172: "La demanderesse avait un petit pécule qu'elle avait amassé, par son travail avant le mariage. Elle avait donc, personnellement les moyens de s'acheter un joli deuil; elle me paraît en avoir profité pour renouveler sa garde-robe"; "très libérale."
93 Gossage, "Tangled Webs."
94 Judges applied a similar calculus in cases in which the suitability of amounts spent on funeral services were challenged, usually by the deceased's creditors. See, e.g., *Beaudry v. Desjardins* (1870), 4 R.L. 555 (Sup. Ct.), affirmed by the Court of Review; *Barrette et uxor v. Lallier et uxor* (1893), R.J.Q. 3 C.S. 541.
95 For an analysis of this issue in the present, see Heather Conway, "Dead, but Not Buried: Bodies, Burial and Family Conflicts," *Legal Studies* 23 (2003): 423–52.
96 E.g., *An Act for the better regulation of Interments and Disinterments*, S.Q. 1888 (51–2 Vic.), c. 48, and especially R.S.Q. 1888, arts. 3458 ff. (chapter "Interments and Disinterments").
97 Fuzier-Herman ed., *Répertoire général*, 24:231–64, under "Inhumation et sépulture."
98 E.g., *Ex parte Wurtele* (1851), 1 L.C. Rep. 414 (Sup. Ct. in chambers); *Les curé et marguilliers de l'œuvre et fabrique de la paroisse de St-Hyacinthe v. Renaud* (1878), 9 R.L. 417 (Circ. Ct.). On the Guibord Affair, see Adrien Thério,

Joseph Guibord, victime expiatoire de l'évêque Bourget: l'Institut canadien et l'affaire Guibord revisités (Montreal: XYZ, 2000).
99 *The Holy Bible Translated from the Latin Vulgate* (New York: P.J. Kennedy & Sons, 1914), Gen. 2:24, echoed in Matt. 19:5, Eph. 5:31.
100 Augustine, *Commentary on the New Code of Canon Law*, 6:126 (canon 1223 on choice) and 133 (canon 1229 on family tombs).
101 "Ordre d'exhumer," *La Presse* (24 July 1890), 4; "A Delicate Point," *The Gazette* (24 July 1890), 5 (quotation), reprinted in *(Quebec City) Saturday Budget* (2 August 1890), 1; R.S.Q. 1888, art. 3485.
102 *Driscoll v. Wray* (1914), 23 R. de J. 561 (Sup. Ct. Rev.), reversing Superior Court judgment of 10 May 1912. The main action was *Driscoll v. Wray* (no. 212). Separate earlier actions granting the sisters permission to dispose of the body and to exhume the corpse were *Driscoll v. Wray* (no. 755).
103 *Driscoll v. Wray* (case file no. 212), Petition, Affidavit and Notice (filed 1 December 1911), 2–3.
104 "Fin d'une cause très contestée," *La Presse* (25 March 1914), 11. Justice Robert Greenshields dissented, but his reasons are not recorded.
105 Legal notice in *Le Devoir* (29 August 1914), 3. Art. 89 CCP (1910 ed.) exempted losing litigants *in forma pauperis* from their lawyers' fees, but not from an award of costs.
106 *Flaherty v. Montreal Tramways* (1931), R.J.Q. 69 C.S. 515 at 516; "Immigrant irlandais tué par un tramway," *La Presse* (26 June 1929), 25; "Mort accidentelle," *La Presse* (27 June 1929), 1; "Le demandeur n'aurait pas le droit d'action," *La Presse* (19 November 1931), 3; "Right to Sue for Damages Denied," *The Gazette* (30 November 1931), 4.
107 *Flaherty v. Montreal Tramways*, 517–18.
108 Stearns, *Revolutions in Sorrow*, 31–2.
109 *Jinchereau v. Roy* (1914), 20 R. de J. 422 (Sup. Ct.). The decision of the Court of Review was not reported but was mentioned in the anonymous commentary on the case, "À qui appartient le choix du lieu de sépulture, au conjoint survivant ou aux héritiers," *Revue du notariat* 17 (1914): 109–17. The case comprised several distinct actions at the Superior Court: an *ex parte* motion by Roy et al. for exhumation (no. 84 of 1913; I have not seen this file, though details are in the following); the main action by Jinchereau (no. 2057, including the trial, an appeal to the Court of Review, and a subsequent *ex parte* motion by Jinchereau for exhumation); and a motion for injunction by Jinchereau (no. 1613).
110 *L'Action sociale (Quebec City)* (12 March 1913), 8; *Quebec (City) Chronicle* (12 March 1913), 5 (brief notice) and (13 March 1913), 5 (details about interment); "Funérailles de M. Alphonse Roy," *Le Soleil (Quebec City)* (14

March 1913), 10 (coverage of the funeral). Despite her testimony that the notices stated the burial would be at St-Charles cemetery, in fact they indicated Belmont cemetery. Cf. *Jinchereau v. Roy* (case file no. 2057), deposition of Belzémire Jinchereau on her own behalf (26 January 1914), 5.

111 Serge Gagnon, *Mourir hier et aujourd'hui: de la mort chrétienne dans la campagne québécoise au XIXe siècle à la mort technicisée dans la cité sans Dieu* (Quebec City: Presses de l'Université Laval, 1987), 75–8; Young, *Respectable Burial*, 32 and 102; Bradbury, *Wife to Widow*, 219.

112 *Jinchereau v. Roy* (case file no. 2057), deposition of Belzémire Jinchereau on her own behalf (26 January 1914), 6.

113 *Jinchereau v. Roy* (case file no. 2057), deposition of Octave Mercier for defendant (26 January 1914), 6–7.

114 *Jinchereau v. Roy* (case file no. 2057), depositions of Joseph Damase Beaudoin for plaintiff (26 January 1914), 1; Belzémire Jinchereau on her own behalf (26 January 1914), 2.

115 *Jinchereau v. Roy* (case file no. 2057), deposition of Belzémire Jinchereau on her own behalf (26 January 1914), 3 (quotation) and 6: "presque sans connaissance."

116 *Jinchereau v. Roy* (case file no. 2057), Bref d'assignation et déclaration (dated 21 October 1913). The reason for the relatively long delay in instituting the action is not clear from the file.

117 In the 1911 census, their respective dates of birth were given as 1851 and 1868. In the 1881 and 1891 censuses, Alphonse was listed as single; Belzémire was listed as single in 1881 (as Ginchereau), but I have not found her in 1891. That could indicate that she was married and listed in her husband's household, though other explanations are of course possible. I have found no previous marriage records for either.

118 *Cherrier's Quebec City Directory ... for the Year Ending May 3, 1882*, 23rd ed. (Quebec City, 1881), and following years.

119 *Jinchereau v. Roy* (case file no. 2057), depositions of Henriette Jinchereau for plaintiff (26 January 1914), 4; Octave Mercier for defendant (26 January 1914), 2.

120 Arts. 606, 632, and 636 CCLC, amended by *An Act to amend the Civil Code respecting successions*, S.Q. 1915 (5 Geo. V), c. 74. See Nicole Roy, "La lutte des femmes pour la réforme du droit de la famille 1900–1955," in *Du Code civil du Québec: contribution à l'histoire immédiate d'une recodification réussie*, ed. Serge Lortie, Nicholas Kasirer, and Jean-Guy Belley (Montreal: Thémis, 2007), 496–7.

121 *Jinchereau v. Roy* (case file no. 2057), deposition of F.-X. Couillard for defendant (26 January 1914), 3. Since the case was not directly about the succession, the file contains few details.

Notes to pages 248–50   407

122 *Jinchereau v. Roy* (case file no. 2057), deposition of F.-X. Couillard for defendant (26 January 1914), 7: "On vous accordera tout ce que vous demandez." Cf. *Jinchereau v. Roy* (case file no. 2057), deposition of Belzémire Jinchereau on her own behalf (26 January 1914), 11. Alfred Roy did not testify.

123 *Jinchereau v. Roy* (case file no. 2057), depositions of Belzémire Jinchereau on her own behalf (26 January 1914), 13; Octave Mercier for defendant (26 January 1914), 2–3; F.-X. Couillard for defendant (26 January 1914), 4.

124 *Jinchereau v. Roy* (case file no. 2057), deposition of Belzémire Jinchereau on her own behalf (26 January 1914), 10 and 16: "en faisant leurs empereurs"; "C'est à nous autres la maison."

125 *Jinchereau v. Roy* (case file no. 2057), deposition of F.-X. Couillard for defendant (26 January 1914), 3.

126 *Jinchereau v. Roy* (case file no. 2057), deposition of Belzémire Jinchereau on her own behalf (26 January 1914), 12: "Laissez ça là!"

127 *Jinchereau v. Roy* (case file no. 2057), deposition of F.-X. Couillard for defendant (26 January 1914), 5–6: "je n'ai jamais vu une femme aussi violente comme celle-là … c'est parce qu'elle me paraissait être en boisson."

128 *Jinchereau v. Roy* (case file no. 2057), deposition of Édouard Foley for defendant (26 January 1914); Foley was the clerk of the Recorder's Court. See also *Jinchereau v. Roy* (case file no. 2057), depositions of Henriette Jinchereau for defendant (26 January 1914); Belzémire Jinchereau on her own behalf in rebuttal (26 January 1914). This last and the Foley transcript were dated February, but it is clear from the procès-verbaux of the proceedings that all testimony was heard on 26 January.

129 *Jinchereau v. Roy* (case file no. 2057), deposition of Belzémire Jinchereau on her own behalf (26 January 1914), 10: "Quand ils sont polis, je les reçois bien, et quand ils sont grossiers, je les reçois en conséquence."

130 *Jinchereau v. Roy* (case file no. 2057), deposition of Belzémire Jinchereau on her own behalf (26 January 1914), 8.

131 *Jinchereau v. Roy* (case file no. 2057), deposition of F.-X. Couillard for defendant (26 January 1914), 6.

132 Bradbury, *Wife to Widow*, 323–55.

133 *Jinchereau v. Roy* (case file no. 2057), deposition of Belzémire Jinchereau on her own behalf (26 January 1914), 2.

134 *Jinchereau v. Roy* (case file no. 2057), depositions of Belzémire Jinchereau on her own behalf (26 January 1914), 14–15 (cross-examination); Octave Mercier for defendant (26 January 1914), 2, 8; F.-X. Couillard for defendant (26 January 1914), 3–4.

135 *Jinchereau v. Roy* (case file no. 2057), deposition of Belzémire Jinchereau on her own behalf (26 January 1914), 14: "R. … je devais aimer mon mari,

puisque je l'ai marié. Q. Vous l'avez toujours aimé? R. Certainement. Q. Vous n'avez jamais eu de chicane ensemble? R. Comme tous les autres, des petits mots passagers, mais pas pour se battre."

136 *Jinchereau v. Roy* (case file no. 2057), deposition of Octave Mercier for defendant (26 January 1914), 5: "On n'a pas eu rien."

137 *Jinchereau v. Roy* (case file no. 2057), deposition of F.-X. Couillard for defendant (26 January 1914), 4.

138 *Jinchereau v. Roy* (case file no. 2057), deposition of Octave Mercier for defendant (26 January 1914), 6.

139 *Jinchereau v. Roy* (case file no. 2057), depositions of Octave Mercier for defendant (26 January 1914), 2; F.-X. Couillard for defendant (26 January 1914), 3.

140 R.S.Q. 1909, art. 4442.

141 *Jinchereau v. Roy* (case file no. 2057), deposition of F.-X. Couillard for defendant (26 January 1914), 3-4.

142 A copy of the judgment is in *Jinchereau v. Roy* (case file no. 2057). The plaintiff asked that the original motion be produced at trial, but it never was.

143 *Jinchereau v. Roy* (case file no. 2057), deposition of Octave Mercier for defendant (26 January 1914), 7: "Q. Vous n'avez pas pensé que ça serait au moins décent de lui faire savoir? R. Si ça avait été obligatoire, c'est correct, mais ce n'était pas obligatoire."

144 *Jinchereau v. Roy* (case file no. 2057), deposition of F.-X. Couillard for defendant (26 January 1914), 8: "je n'ai pas cru devoir le faire."

145 *Jinchereau v. Roy* (case file no. 2057), deposition of F.-X. Couillard for defendant (26 January 1914), 8: "exposé les faits honnêtement."

146 *Jinchereau v. Roy* (case file no. 2057), deposition of Octave Mercier for defendant (26 January 1914), 9: "Si elle avait eu droit, on ne pouvait pas l'empêcher." This hypothetical question was allowed by the judge after objection by the defence.

147 *Jinchereau v. Roy* (case file no. 2057), Bref d'assignation et déclaration (dated 21 October 1913, writ returned 28 October 1913), 2: "de blesser la demanderesse en ses sentiments les plus chers et les plus intimes."

148 *Jinchereau v. Roy* (case file no. 2057), Bref d'assignation et déclaration (dated 21 October 1913, writ returned 28 October 1913), 3: "de la consolation de pouvoir facilement se rendre à la tombe de son mari et de l'entourer de ses soins que l'on s'honore d'avoir pour les morts qui nous sont chers."

149 *Jinchereau v. Roy* (case file no. 2057), deposition of Belzémire Jinchereau on her own behalf (16 January 1914), 6-7: "Q. Est-ce que les souffrances que vous avez subies, valent au moins $400.00? R. Certainement et ça

m'a coûté beaucoup d'argent. Q. Je parle de vos souffrances, la peine que vous avez eue? R. Oui, et ensuite de ça, ma santé s'épuise."
150 *Jinchereau v. Roy* (case file no. 2057), deposition of Belzémire Jinchereau on her own behalf (26 January 1914), 14.
151 *Jinchereau v. Roy* (case file no. 2057), deposition of Octave Mercier for defendant (26 January 1914), 7: "Non, je n'ai pensé que ça lui en ferait beaucoup."
152 *Jinchereau v. Roy* (case file no. 2057), deposition of F.-X. Couillard for defendant (26 January 1914), 6: "bien poliment, bien doucement."
153 *Jinchereau v. Roy* (case file no. 2057), Factum des défendeurs appelants (filed 25 April 1914), 2 and 6: "inabordable"; "intraitable."
154 *Jinchereau v. Roy* (case file no. 2057), deposition of Henriette Jinchereau for plaintiff (26 January 1914), 3; cf. *Jinchereau v. Roy* (case file no. 2057), deposition of Belzémire Jinchereau on her own behalf (26 January 1914), 2. In what follows, I am presenting the parties' claims, rather than trying to determine precisely who was buried in which plot in the various cemeteries, since the depositions are contradictory.
155 *Jinchereau v. Roy* (case file no. 2057), depositions of Octave Mercier for defendant (26 January 1914), 2; F.-X. Couillard for defendant (26 January 1914), 4. Henriette Jinchereau confirmed that the Roy parents were buried in Mercier's plot but testified that the Roy sister was buried elsewhere in the same cemetery; *Jinchereau v. Roy* (case file no. 2057), deposition of Henriette Jinchereau for plaintiff (26 January 1914), 5.
156 This was the case, for example, in the Mauricie in a later period: Jean-François Martel, "Les pratiques funéraires en usage dans les milieux populaires ruraux et urbains de la Mauricie entre 1945 et 1998" (M.A. thesis, Université du Québec à Trois-Rivières, 2001), 102.
157 *Jinchereau v. Roy* (case file no. 2057), deposition of Henriette Jinchereau for plaintiff (26 January 1914), 4: "ce n'est pas un lot de famille."
158 *Jinchereau v. Roy* (case file no. 2057), Factum de la demanderesse intimée (filed 22 April 1914), 13.
159 See generally Gagnon, *Mourir hier et aujourd'hui*, 82–3; Marie-Aimée Cliche, "L'évolution des clauses religieuses traditionnelles dans les testaments de la région de Québec au XIXe siècle," in *Religion populaire, religion de clercs?*, ed. Benoît Lacroix and Jean Simard (Quebec City: Institut québécois de recherche sur la culture, 1985), 374–6.
160 *Jinchereau v. Roy* (case file no. 2057), deposition of Octave Mercier for defendant (26 January 1914), 3–4.
161 *Jinchereau v. Roy* (case file no. 2057), deposition of Octave Mercier for defendant (26 January 1914), 2.

162 Fuzier-Herman ed., *Répertoire général*, 24:241 (no. 81), and 242 (nos. 98–102), under "Inhumation et sépulture."
163 *Jinchereau v. Roy* (case file no. 2057), Factum des défendeurs appelants (filed 25 April 1914), 6–7, quotation at 7: "la preuve établit que la demanderesse est dépourvue de ce sens intime que nous révèlent notre conscience et notre nature, puisqu'elle fait preuve d'une conduite indigne, tant au point de vue de la morale, qu'au point de vue de la mémoire et des attentions pieuses qu'elle devait à son mari."
164 *Jinchereau v. Roy* (case file no. 2057), Factum de la demanderesse intimée (filed 22 April 1914), 14–15: "Si les défendeurs n'ont pas agi avec malice, … ils ont, en toute certitude, agit avec un manque de discernement et un mépris des convenances et des bienséances les plus élémentaires qui certainement équivalent à malice."
165 *Jinchereau v. Roy* (case file no. 2057), deposition of Belzémire Jinchereau on her own behalf (26 January 1914), 3: "ne devait pas s'en occuper; j'étais sa femme, il me semble que mon mari devait m'appartenir."
166 Similar property-based language arose in the context of autopsies, as we saw in chapter 4. For discussion based on United States cases, see W.F.C., "The Property Right in a Corpse," *Albany Law Review* 2 (1933): 122–6.
167 *Jinchereau v. Roy* (case file no. 2057), deposition of Octave Mercier for defendant (26 January 1914), 7: "moi, je ne veux pas faire aucun train dans cette affaire, je veux que ce soit une affaire nette, qu'on ait le plein droit de faire ça"; "On a le plein droit, du moment que Monseigneur signe avec un juge, et c'est vous autres qui payez."
168 *Jinchereau v. Roy* (case file no. 2057), Bref d'assignation et déclaration (dated 21 October 1913), 2: "droit souverain … de disposer du corps de son conjoint et de choisir le lieu de sa sépulture."
169 *Jinchereau v. Roy* (case file no. 2057), Bref d'assignation et déclaration (dated 21 October 1913), 3.
170 *Jinchereau v. Roy* (case file no. 2057), Plaidoyer (filed 3 November 1913), 3 (no. 28).
171 *Jinchereau v. Roy* (case file no. 2057), Factum des défendeurs appelants (filed 25 April 1914), 6–7.
172 Josserand, *De l'abus des droits*.
173 *Jinchereau v. Roy* (case file no. 2057), Réponse au plaidoyer (filed 19 December 1913), 1–2: "ont usé de ce droit d'une façon abusive de manière à préjudicier au droit supérieur de la demanderesse."
174 *Jinchereau v. Roy* (case file no. 2057), Factum de la demanderesse intimée (filed 22 April 1914), 1: "de disposer du corps de son défunt mari et de choisir l'endroit de sa sépulture, à l'exclusion de toute autre personne."

175 *Jinchereau v. Roy* (case file no. 2057), Factum de la demanderesse intimée (filed 22 April 1914), 13: "C'est là un sentiment fort respectable et absolument universel qui veut que l'union des époux se marque jusque dans une sépulture commune et c'est une consolation pour le survivant de savoir qu'il ira, lorsque l'appel viendra, dormir lui aussi l'éternel sommeil près de l'époux enlevé à son affection."
176 R.S.Q. 1909, art. 4442; Pierre-Basile Mignault, *Le droit paroissial* (Montreal, 1893), 556.
177 *Jinchereau v. Roy* (Sup. Ct.), 436–7: "droit primitif ... sanctionné par cette Cour." See also "On se bat pour la possession d'un cadavre," *Le Soleil (Quebec City)* (26 January 1914), 10; "The Burial of a Husband," *The Gazette* (3 March 1914), 4.
178 *Jinchereau v. Roy* (Sup. Ct.), 427: "d'un ordre d'idée plus élevé, qui s'inspire des relations intimes que créent la nature, la religion et la loi entre l'homme et la femme unis par les liens du mariage."
179 *Jinchereau v. Roy* (Sup. Ct.), 434: "Il répugne à notre sens intime et à nos mœurs chrétiennes, de déclarer qu'aucun lien ne rattache plus après la mort ceux qui ont ainsi confondu leur existence terrestre, qu'ils seront désormais étrangers l'un à l'autre et rendus à leurs familles respectives."
180 *Jinchereau v. Roy* (Sup. Ct.), 434: "pays où domine le sentiment religieux, et où on peut faire entendre la note chrétienne."
181 *Jinchereau v. Roy* (Sup. Ct.), 431–2. See above, note 99.
182 E.g., Fuzier-Herman ed., *Répertoire général*, 24:241–2 (nos. 80–105).
183 *Jinchereau v. Roy* (Sup. Ct.), 435: "sentiments de famille, considération d'intim[it]é et d'affection, questions de mœurs et d'usage."
184 *Jinchereau v. Roy* (Sup. Ct.), 436.
185 "Pour un cadavre," *Le Soleil (Quebec City)* (29 April 1914), 5.
186 The original letter with its envelope is in *Jinchereau v. Roy* (case file no. 1613): "Madame: L'on m'a chargé de vous dire que le service anniversaire de feu M. Alphonse Roy, votre mari, aura lieu ..."
187 *Jinchereau v. Roy* (case file no. 1613), Requête pour injonction (filed March 25, 1914): "aucun préjudice réel ou moral." The judgment was written on the back of the motion.

7. Indignation, Anger, Fear

1 Ritu Gill and Kimberly Matheson, "Responses to Discrimination: The Role of Emotion and Expectations for Emotional Regulation," *Personality and Social Psychology Bulletin* 32 (2006): 149–61; Robert T. Carter and Jessica Forsyth, "Reactions to Racial Discrimination: Emotional Stress and

Help-Seeking Behaviors," *Psychological Trauma* 2 (2010): 183–91; Jennifer Wang, Janxin Leu, and Yuichi Shoda, "When the Seemingly Innocuous 'Stings': Racial Microaggressions and Their Emotional Consequences," *Personality and Social Psychology Bulletin* 37 (2011): 1666–78; Shawn C.T. Jones, Daniel B. Lee, Ashly L. Gaskin, and Enrique W. Neblett, Jr., "Emotional Response Profiles to Racial Discrimination: Does Racial Identity Predict Affective Patterns?" *Journal of Black Psychology* 40 (2014): 334–58.

2 See especially Kathryn Abrams, "Emotions in the Mobilization of Rights," *Harvard Civil Rights – Civil Liberties Law Review* 46 (2011): 551–89; Gill and Matheson, "Responses to Discrimination"; Ron Eyerman, "How Social Movements Move: Emotions and Social Movements," in *Emotions and Social Movements*, ed. Helena Flam and Debra King, 41–56 (London: Routledge, 2005).

3 As suggested in Bob Tarantino, "'Free to Deal as He May Choose': The Displacement of 'Freedom of Commerce' as a Necessary Condition to the Creation of Canadian Multiculturalism," *Common Law World Review* 39 (2010): 14.

4 One nineteenth-century issue that touched discrimination and was at times debated in the language of equality rights was the question of access to schools by religious minorities. The litigation it provoked, however, was systemic challenges focusing on citizenship, rather than individuals suing over the personal effects of exclusion. See David Fraser, *"Honorary Protestants": The Jewish School Question in Montreal, 1867–1997* (Toronto: University of Toronto Press for Osgoode Society for Canadian Legal History, 2015); Janet Epp Buckingham, *Fighting over God: A Legal and Political History of Religious Freedom in Canada* (Montreal and Kingston: McGill-Queen's University Press, 2014), 32–48.

5 See, generally, Christopher MacLennan, *Toward the Charter: Canadians and the Demand for a National Bill of Rights, 1929–1960* (Montreal and Kingston: McGill-Queen's University Press, 2003); George Egerton, "Entering the Age of Human Rights: Religion, Politics, and Canadian Liberalism, 1945–50," *CHR* 85 (2004): 451–79; Ross Lambertson, *Repression and Resistance: Canadian Human Rights Activists, 1930–1960* (Toronto: University of Toronto Press, 2005); Eric M. Adams, "The Idea of Constitutional Rights and the Transformation of Canadian Constitutional Law, 1930–1960" (S.J.D. thesis, University of Toronto, 2009).

6 For earlier evidence of Blacks using the courts to assert private and community interests, see Donald Fyson, "Minority Groups and the Law in Quebec, 1760–1867," in *Essays in the History of Canadian Law: Volume*

XI – Quebec and the Canadas, ed. G. Blaine Baker and Donald Fyson (Toronto: University of Toronto Press for Osgoode Society for Canadian Legal History, 2013), 290–8 and the literature cited there.
7 *Johnson v. Sparrow* (1899), R.J.Q. 15 C.S. 104, affirmed (1899) R.J.Q. 8 B.R. 379.
8 I have found no information about Fred Johnson outside of this case.
9 Mireille Barrière, "Sparrow, John Bolingbroke," *DCB* vol. 14. The Academy was described as "the best house in Montreal" in S.E. Dawson, *Hand-Book for the City of Montreal and Its Environs* (Montreal, 1888), 85.
10 Advertisement in *The Gazette* (5 March 1898), 4; "Charles H. Hoyt's New Farce," *New York Times* (16 February 1897), 7.
11 *Johnson v. Sparrow* (Sup. Ct. case file), Inventaire des productions de demandeur à l'enquête, which includes the original program.
12 "Al Field's Minstrel Company," *The Gazette* (11 March 1898), 3.
13 *Johnson v. Sparrow* (Sup. Ct. case file), deposition of Fred W. Johnson on his own behalf (14 November 1898), 5.
14 *Johnson v. Sparrow* (Sup. Ct. case file), Exhibits (including the original stubs).
15 The records survive at the Houghton Library at Harvard University. That evening, the weather was listed as "bad," and 828 tickets were sold at various price levels, as well as four exchanges at the highest price (two of those were presumably Fred Johnson's). I am grateful to Patricia Marsden of the Houghton Library for sending me a scan of that evening's entries. On the theatre's layout and capacity, see Maurice Lemire and Denis Saint-Jacques, eds., *La vie littéraire au Québec* (Sainte-Foy, QC: Presses de l'Université Laval, 2005), 5:166.
16 What follows is based on *Johnson v. Sparrow* (Sup. Ct. case file), deposition of Fred W. Johnson, recalled on his own behalf (14 November 1898).
17 *Johnson v. Sparrow* (Sup. Ct. case file), deposition of Fred Boyden for defendant (14 November 1898), 12–17.
18 *Johnson v. Sparrow* (Sup. Ct. case file), deposition of Edwin W. Varney for defendant (14 November 1898), 19.
19 *Johnson v. Sparrow* (Sup. Ct. case file), Bref et déclaration (filed 29 March 1898). The show at the Théâtre Français was advertised in *La Patrie* (11 March 1898), 7: "le merveilleux jongleur O.K. Sato." On their seats, see *Johnson v. Sparrow* (Sup. Ct. case file), deposition of Fred W. Johnson on his own behalf (14 November 1898), 4.
20 *Johnson v. Sparrow* (Sup. Ct. case file), Bref et déclaration (filed 29 March 1898), 2: "profondément humilié et injurié"; "a souffert des dommages dans sa réputation, son honneur et sa sensibilité."

21 *Johnson v. Sparrow* (Sup. Ct. case file), Plea (dated 7 May 1898), 2.
22 For a somewhat later survey of the law, focusing on the United States but including reference to Canadian cases (including this one), see Louis D. Frohlich and Charles Schwartz, *The Law of Motion Pictures* (New York: Baker, Voorhis, 1918), 291–9.
23 *Johnson v. Sparrow* (Sup. Ct. case file), Plea (dated 7 May 1898), 2–3.
24 *Johnson v. Sparrow* (Sup. Ct. case file), depositions of William H. Bell for plaintiff (14 November 1898), 19; Edward Durrent for plaintiff (14 November 1898), 28.
25 *Johnson v. Sparrow* (Sup. Ct. case file), deposition of Fred W. Johnson on his own behalf (14 November 1898), 5.
26 "Entre nègres," *Le Courrier de St-Hyacinthe* (27 January 1898), 3: "où se réunissent pour s'amuser toutes les variétés de noirs. On se donne l'illusion du pays, on fume le chibouque, on râcle le banjo, et l'on bat de la semelle. Il y a aussi plusieurs billards qui ne sont pas le moindre amusement de ce phalanstère exotique."
27 *Johnson v. Sparrow* (Sup. Ct. case file), deposition of George Wilson for plaintiff (14 November 1898), 17–18, on cross-examination. See also the cross-examinations in *Johnson v. Sparrow* (Sup. Ct. case file), depositions of William H. Renfrew for plaintiff (14 November 1898), 14; Harry Brown for plaintiff (14 November 1898), 23; Edward Durrent for plaintiff (14 November 1898), 25–6.
28 *Johnson v. Sparrow* (Sup. Ct. case file), deposition of William A. Edwards for defendant (14 November 1898), 8.
29 *Johnson v. Sparrow* (Sup. Ct. case file), Plea (filed 20 May 1898), 2. In its previous point, the theatre had just argued that Johnson had been offered tickets in the Dress Circle instead of the Orchestra, which would appear to be inconsistent with the argument made here.
30 *Johnson v. Sparrow* (Sup. Ct. case file), deposition of William A. Edwards for defendant (14 November 1898), 3, 5.
31 "The Color Line," *The Gazette* (19 November 1898), 9.
32 *Johnson v. Sparrow* (Sup. Ct. case file), deposition of Joseph E. Wall for defendant (7 December 1898), 48.
33 *Johnson v. Sparrow* (Sup. Ct. case file), Réponse (filed 4 June 1898), 1.
34 *Johnson v. Sparrow* (Sup. Ct. case file), deposition of Fred W. Johnson on his own behalf (14 November 1898), 5.
35 *Johnson v. Sparrow* (Sup. Ct. case file), deposition of Fred W. Johnson on his own behalf (14 November 1898), 6.
36 On British justice, see especially Lyndsay Campbell, "Race, Upper Canadian Constitutionalism and 'British Justice,'" *Law and History Review*

33 (2015): 41–91; Barrington Walker, *Race on Trial: Black Defendants in Ontario's Criminal Courts, 1858–1958* (Toronto: University of Toronto Press for Osgoode Society for Canadian Legal History, 2010), 20–1.
37 "Question de couleur," *La Presse* (15 November 1898), 4: "car les Canadiens, n'ont, eux, contre les noirs aucun préjugé, aucune aversion!"; "Il est étrange de constater chez un peuple doté des institutions les plus libérales et partant en guerre pour affranchir les peuples opprimés, qu'un citoyen de couleur ne peut s'asseoir à côté d'un blanc dans un omnibus ou un théâtre, quand même ce blanc serait le pire des voyoux et le noir un des héros de San-Juan ... Un nègre qui sait se conduire est un voisin dix fois plus agréable qu'un blanc qui se tient mal. Un nègre sobre est préférable à un blanc qui empeste le gin et le tabac."
38 "The Color Line," *Saturday Budget (Quebec City)* (19 November 1898), 2. See also "The Color Line," *The Gazette* (19 November 1898), 9; "Color Line in Montreal," *(Toronto) Globe* (15 November 1898), 4.
39 Annette White Parks, "Sui San Far: Writer on the Chinese-Anglo Borders of North America, 1885–1914" (Ph.D. thesis: Washington State University, 1991), 44 and n68.
40 The lecture (sometimes called an essay) was mentioned widely in contemporary biographical material on Archibald, but I find no evidence that it was ever published. It is also unclear whether the title referred to skin colour or French and English, though references to it suggest the former. See Morgan, *Canadian Men and Women of the Time*, 27.
41 *Johnson v. Sparrow* (Sup. Ct. case file), Judgment (5 January 1899), 3–4. This is from the official reasons for judgment, for the register of the Superior Court.
42 *Johnson v. Sparrow* (Sup. Ct.), 108. These reasons were printed in full in "Legal Intelligence," *The Gazette* (6 January 1899), 5.
43 Editorial, *The Gazette* (6 January 1899), 5.
44 Walker, *Race on Trial*, 116–40, esp. 124 and 127–8.
45 Campbell, "Race, Upper Canadian Constitutionalism and 'British Justice,'" 85–90.
46 "Les droits des personnes de couleur," *La Patrie* (24 June 1899), 16; "Rights of Colored Persons," *The Gazette* (24 June 1899), 7.
47 *Johnson v. Sparrow* (Q.B. case file), Appellant's Case (filed 6 May 1899), iii–iv.
48 *Johnson v. Sparrow* (Q.B. case file), Appellant's Case (filed 6 May 1899), v.
49 *Johnson v. Sparrow* (Q.B. case file), Appellant's Case (filed 6 May 1899), v.
50 *Johnson v. Sparrow* (Q.B. case file), Appellant's Case (filed 6 May 1899), vii.
51 *Johnson v. Sparrow* (Q.B. case file), Appellant's Case (filed 6 May 1899), ix–x.

52 *Johnson v. Sparrow* (Q.B. case file), Factum de l'intimé (produced 28 April 1899), 8.
53 *Johnson v. Sparrow* (Q.B.), 383.
54 *Johnson v. Sparrow* (Q.B.), 381: "des mulâtres, des quarterons et même des octorons, et, pour ces derniers surtout, ils ont pu facilement être confondus avec les blancs."
55 *Johnson v. Sparrow* (Sup. Ct. case file), deposition of Fred W. Johnson on his own behalf (14 November 1898), 5.
56 "Dame rumeur au Palais," *Le Devoir* (28 October 1914), 7 (describing the case as one "de très haute importance"); "Ex-Chief Justice John S. Archibald Dies in 89th Year," *The Gazette* (18 January 1932), 8 (describing the case as "notable …, which attracted international attention and comment").
57 See generally Walker, *"Race," Rights and the Law*, 122–81; Dorothy W. Williams, *The Road to Now: A History of Blacks in Montreal* (Montreal: Véhicule, 1997), 39–40; Backhouse, *Colour-Coded*, 252–60; Robin W. Winks, *The Blacks in Canada: A History*, 2nd ed. (Montreal and Kingston: McGill-Queen's University Press, 2000), 430–4; Daniel Gay, *Les noirs du Québec 1629–1900* (Sillery, QC: Septentrion, 2004), 162–5; Sarah-Jane Mathieu, *North of the Color Line: Migration and Black Resistance in Canada, 1870–1955* (Chapel Hill: University of North Carolina Press, 2010), 169–70.
58 *Christie v. York Corporation* (1937), R.J.Q. 75 C.S. 136, reversed (1938) R.J.Q. 65 B.R. 104, latter judgment affirmed (1939) [1940] S.C.R. 139. On the case, see Walker, *"Race," Rights and the Law*, 122–81; Eric M. Adams, "Errors of Fact and Law: Race, Space, and Hockey in *Christie v. York*," *University of Toronto Law Journal* 62 (2012): 463–97.
59 This phenomenon is described and analysed, for the recent and contemporary United States, in Abrams, "Emotions."
60 I thank Lyndsay Campbell for suggesting the latter point. On legal aspects of denial of service, see Ian A. Hunter, "Civil Actions for Discrimination," *Canadian Bar Review* 55 (1977): 108–11; Hunter, "Human Rights Legislation in Canada: Its Origin, Development and Interpretation," *University of Western Ontario Law Review* 15 (1976): 21–4; Béatrice Vizkelety, "Discrimination, the Right to Seek Redress and the Common Law: A Century-Old Debate," *Dalhousie Law Journal* 15 (1992): 304–35; Tarantino, "'Free to Deal as He May Choose.'"
61 *Curl v. Quebec Amusement Co.* (1917), 23 R.L. (n.s.) 345 (Sup. Ct.); "Un nègre poursuit un théâtre," *La Patrie* (20 January 1914), 12; "Noir comme Benito et comme lui maltraité," *Le Devoir* (20 January 1914), 6; "Un noir intente une action en dommages à la direction d'un théâtre," *Le Canada* (21 January 1914), 3 (virtually identical to the preceding article); "Barred

at Theatre, Gets $50 Damages," *The Gazette* (31 January 1917), 6; "Un noir à qui on avait refusé l'entrée de ce théâtre est indemnisé," *La Presse* (31 January 1917), 13; "L'admission des nègres au théâtre," *La Patrie* (31 January 1917), 5; "Les billets de théâtre," *Le Devoir* (31 January 1917), 2; "Damages for Negro," *Daily Province (Vancouver)* (31 January 1917), 4; "Les billets de théâtre," *Le Canada* (1 February 1917), 4 (a translation of the article in *The Gazette*); "Darkies Can See Movies," *Manitoba Free Press (Winnipeg)* (1 February 1917), 12.

62 Advertised in *The Gazette* (10 July 1913), 7. The Imperial was an early movie house, but filled its bill with music and vaudeville performances.

63 John Delmour Curl married Emily Ford in 1903 in Halifax. Whether this was the same man as John Curl, born 3 December 1872 to a single mother in Poor's Asylum in Halifax, is uncertain. What happened to Emily Ford after the marriage is also unknown, as by the time of the incident in Montreal, Curl was married to Eunice Truman, a native of Hackett's Cove, Nova Scotia. The marriage and birth information comes from www.novascotiagenealogy.com. At some point following the incident described here, Curl moved with Eunice and their four children to the United States. See the obituary of John Delmour Curl, Jr., in the *(Sumter, S.C.) Item* (8 July 1995), 9A.

64 Almost nothing proceeded in 1915 or 1916: *Curl v. Quebec Amusement* (plumitif).

65 The settlement, technically a demand for confession of judgment under art. 527 CCP, was rejected because it had been signed by the theatre manager, without supporting documentation that he had been authorized by the defendant company to make the offer.

66 "Noir comme Benito et comme lui maltraité," *Le Devoir* (20 January 1914), 6: "est blanche, non seulement, entre parenthèses, mais réellement." The reference in the headline to "Benito" seems confused; Herman Melville's novel *Benito Cereno* is about a slave revolt, but the title character is the white captain of a slave ship. See also "Un nègre poursuit un théâtre," *La Patrie* (20 January 1914), 12.

67 On intermarriage and attitudes towards it, see Winks, *The Blacks in Canada*, 495–6; Walker, *"Race," Rights and the Law*, 82–3; Backhouse, *Colour-Coded*, 234; Judith Fingard, "Race and Respectability in Victorian Halifax," *Journal of Imperial and Commonwealth History* 20 (1992): 178–9.

68 She appears in the 1891 and 1901 censuses but was no longer living with the family in 1911.

69 "Noir comme Benito et comme lui maltraité," *Le Devoir* (20 January 1914), 6: "John Delmour Curl est noir. Tout noir qu'il est il n'en reste pas moins

aussi sujet britannique que possible. Voilà pourquoi il prétend être traité avec tous les égards que l'on a ordinairement pour les gens de cette sorte."
70 See especially the details in Wilfred Emmerson Israel, "The Montreal Negro Community" (M.A. thesis, McGill University, 1928), 111–12, 183–6. See also Leo W. Bertley, "The Universal Negro Improvement Association of Montreal, 1917–1979" (Ph.D. thesis, Concordia University, 1979); Winks, *Blacks in Canada*, 414–18; Williams, *Road to Now*.
71 The cooperation surrounding the Loew's cases was noted in Israel, *Montreal Negro Community*, 102 and 110.
72 "Drawing the Color Line," *The Gazette* (18 September 1918), 13. The letter is signed "R.D. Saunders," and the address given is that of the Colored Political and Protective Association at 243 St. Antoine Street.
73 *Reynolds v. Loew's Montreal Theatres Ltd.* (1919), R.J.Q. 30 B.R. 459, reversing the unreported decision of the Sup. Ct. (4 March 1919, Fortin J.).
74 Quoted in Rosanne Waters, "African Canadian Anti-Discrimination Activism and the Transnational Civil Rights Movement, 1945–1965," *Journal of the Canadian Historical Association* 24 (2013): 396n55 (a copy of the pamphlet is among the NAACP files at the Library of Congress). The participation of the association is nowhere mentioned in the case file but is confirmed in Israel, *Montreal Negro Community*, 108–10. See also Walker, "*Race," Rights and the Law*, 147–9.
75 *Reynolds v. Loew's Montreal Theatres* (Sup. Ct. case file), deposition of Albert Lachaine for plainitff (11 February 1919), 3–5. Sénécal did not testify.
76 *Reynolds v. Loew's Montreal Theatres* (Sup. Ct. case file), deposition on discovery of Sol Reynolds for defendant (5 February 1919), 2.
77 *Reynolds v. Loew's Montreal Theatres* (Sup. Ct. case file), deposition on discovery of Sol Reynolds for defendant (5 February 1919), quotations at 4; deposition of Sol Reynolds on his own behalf (11 February 1919).
78 *Reynolds v. Loew's Montreal Theatres* (Sup. Ct. case file), deposition of Albert Lachaine for plaintiff (11 February 1919).
79 *Reynolds v. Loew's Montreal Theatres* (Sup. Ct. case file), Plaintiff's Declaration (dated 8 February 1918), 2. "On exclut un noir de ce cinéma," *La Presse* (11 February 1919), 11; "Le juge émet son opinion," *Le Devoir* (11 February 1919), 3; "Un nègre amateur de Vaudeville intente un procès," *La Patrie* (11 February 1919), 3; "Is Issue of Ticket a Legal Contract?" *The Gazette* (12 February 1919), 4.
80 *Dodson v. Loew's Montreal Theatres Ltd.* (4 March 1919, Sup. Ct., Fortin J.), affirmed (29 December 1919, K.B.). The judgments are in the case files; neither was reported.

81 *Dodson v. Loew's Montreal Theatres* (Sup. Ct. case file), depositions of Edmond Pomanville for defendant (13 February 1919), 11; Norris A. Dodson on his own behalf (13 February 1919), 5; William Gates for plaintiff (13 February 1919), 10–11.
82 *Dodson v. Loew's Montreal Theatres* (Sup. Ct. case file), Plaintiff's Declaration (dated 25 September 1918), 2. "Une autre cause à propos de nègres," *La Presse* (13 February 1919), 7; "On lui refuse l'entrée," *Le Devoir* (14 February 1919), 7; "Sues Theatre for $1,000 for Ejection," *The Gazette* (14 February 1919), 11.
83 Dodson's witnesses were cagey on the point, no doubt coached that any hint of concerted action could be damaging to his case. On cross-examination, several admitted that they had heard of others being refused admission: *Dodson v. Loew's Montreal Theatres* (Sup. Ct. case file), depositions of Roderick Wiseman for plainitff (13 February 1919), 32–3; Minnie Sides for plaintiff (13 February 1919), 24.
84 *Dodson v. Loew's Montreal Theatres* (Sup. Ct. case file), deposition of William Gates, recalled for plaintiff in rebuttal (13 February 1919), 8–10.
85 *Reynolds v. Loew's Montreal Theatres* (Sup. Ct. case file), deposition on discovery of Sol Reynolds on his own behalf (5 February 1919), 6; deposition of Sol Reynolds on his own behalf (11 February 1919), 7.
86 *Reynolds v. Loew's Montreal Theatres* (Sup. Ct. case file), deposition of Sol Reynolds on his own behalf (13 February 1919), 8.
87 *Dodson v. Loew's Montreal Theatres* (Sup. Ct. case file), deposition of Minnie Sides for plaintiff (13 February 1919), 24.
88 *Dodson v. Loew's Montreal Theatres* (Sup. Ct. case file), deposition of Edmond Pomanville for defendant (13 February 1919), 6.
89 *Dodson v. Loew's Montreal Theatres* (Sup. Ct. case file), depositions of Norris A. Dodson on his own behalf (13 February 1919), 5; Roderick Wiseman for plaintiff (13 February 1919), 29–30.
90 *Dodson v. Loew's Montreal Theatres* (Sup. Ct. case file), depositions of Edward Ferry for defendant (13 February 1919), 16 (loud); Nina Forest for defendant (13 February 1919), 39 (excited); Ethan A. Lake for defendant (13 Feburary 1919), 22 (would not listen).
91 *Dodson v. Loew's Montreal Theatres* (Sup. Ct. case file), deposition of Edmond Pomanville for defendant (13 February 1919), 10.
92 *Dodson v. Loew's Montreal Theatres* (Sup. Ct. case file), deposition of Ethan A. Lake for defendant (13 February 1919), 23.
93 *Dodson v. Loew's Montreal Theatres* (Sup. Ct. case file), deposition of William Gates for plaintiff (13 February 1919), 12.

94 *Reynolds v. Loew's Montreal Theatres* (Sup. Ct. case file), deposition of Thomas P. Birchall for defendant (11 February 1919), 8–9.
95 "Court Says Color Line Is Illegal; All Equal in Law," *The Gazette* (5 March 1919), 4; "Le Loew est condamné," *Le Devoir* (5 March 1919), 4; "Un théâtre ne peut refuser l'entrée à un client parce qu'il est nègre. Jugement," *La Patrie* (5 March 1919), 5; "Blancs et noirs sont des égaux," *La Presse* (5 March 1919), 19; "White and Colored Have Equal Rights," *Montreal Daily Star* (5 March 1919), 23; "Les nègres, nos égaux," *Le Soleil (Quebec City)* (5 March 1919), 12; "Un noir vaut un blanc," *La Tribune (Sherbrooke)* (7 March 1919), 7; "Tous égaux," *La Vérité* (15 March 1919), 3.
96 *Reynolds v. Loew's Montreal Theatres* (Sup. Ct. case file), Judgment (4 March 1919), 2.
97 *Reynolds v. Loew's Montreal Theatres* (Sup. Ct. case file), Judgment (4 March 1919), 3.
98 *Dodson v. Loew's Montreal Theatres* (Sup. Ct. case file), Judgment (4 March 1919), 4.
99 "Help to Fight Discrimination against the Race," *Canadian Observer (Toronto)* (24 May 1919), 1, 3; Editorial, "The Unfairness of Loew's," *Canadian Observer (Toronto)* (24 May 1919), 4.
100 *Reynolds v. Loew's Montreal Theatres* (K.B. case file), Respondent's Factum (produced 10 November 1919), 5. "Can Theatre Draw the Color Line?" *The Gazette* (25 November 1919), 11; "Les nègres ont-ils les privilèges des sièges d'orchestre?" *La Presse* (25 November 1919), 21; "L'admission d'un nègre au théâtre," *La Patrie* (25 November 1919), 2; "La question de couleur," *Le Devoir* (25 November 1919), 4; "La Cour d'appel entend une autre affaire de nègres," *La Presse* (26 November 1919), 3; "Another Phase of the Color Line," *The Gazette* (26 November 1919), 14.
101 *Dodson v. Loew's Montreal Theatres* (K.B. case file), Appellant's Factum (produced 10 November 1919), 5.
102 *Reynolds v. Loew's Montreal Theatres Ltd.* (1919), R.J.Q. 30 B.R. 459; *Dodson* is unreported. The substitution on the bench was not explained. "Theatre May Draw the Color Line," *The Gazette* (30 December 1919), 6; "La compagnie est maîtresse de ce théâtre," *La Presse* (30 December 1919), 19; "Ce théâtre était dans son droit," *La Patrie* (30 December 1919), 2; "Theatre Manager Master of House," *Montreal Daily Star* (30 December 1919), 20; "Le théâtre Loew's a gain de cause," *Le Canada* (30 December 1919), 5; "Over the Footlights," *Vancouver Daily World* (10 January 1920), 8.
103 *Dodson* (K.B.), "sa propre obstination"; "n'avait aucun droit de s'insurger contre l'ordre établi"; "un Noir – ou plutôt un mulâtre."
104 *Reynolds* (K.B.), 462–3: "un homme de bonne éducation."

105 "Les nègres iront porter leur cause au Conseil privé," *La Presse* (7 January 1920), 18; "May Take Case Further," *The Gazette* (7 January 1920), 9.
106 "No Color Line in Canadian Justice," *The Gazette* (1 July 1932), 4. The story was picked up in "No Color Line," *Border Cities Star (Windsor, ON)* (4 July 1932), 4 (the story is substantially similar to the one in *The Gazette*, but with the further editorial commentary added).
107 See generally Bertley, "The Universal Negro Improvement Association of Montreal"; James W. St.G. Walker, "African Canadians," in *Encyclopedia of Canada's Peoples*, ed. Paul Robert Magocsi (Toronto: University of Toronto Press, 1999), 155.
108 See note 58 above.
109 "Ruling on Negroes Fought by Tavern," *The Gazette* (12 April 1938), 1.
110 *Christie v. York Corporation* (K.B.), 124.
111 *Christie v. York Corporation* (K.B.), 112.
112 *Christie v. York Corporation* (K.B.), 137–8: "comme un gentil-homme."
113 The subsequent history of discrimination in Quebec is beyond our scope, but a few words are in order. Already in the 1930s, Jewish groups took the lead in lobbying the Quebec government (unsuccessfully at first) for protection against defamatory libels and organized boycotts of Jewish businesses: Walker, *"Race," Rights and the Law*, 192–5. On Black activism in mid-century, see Winks, *Blacks in Canada*, 413–69. By the 1960s, some Quebec judges were distancing themselves from the reasoning in *Christie* and its implications. In *Gooding v. Edlow Investment Corp.* (1965), [1966] C.S. 436, an apartment rental company refused to rent to a Black woman, leading Justice André Nadeau to assert that "toute discrimination raciale est illégale parce que contraire à l'ordre public et aux bonnes mœurs." See also "Dommages de $525 pour discrimination raciale," *La Presse* (20 October 1965), 22. One contemporary commentator argued that *Gooding*, despite being only a trial-level decision, in effect overruled *Christie*: Laurence Murray Tanny, "Ethnocentric Discrimination and Freedom of Contract in a Changing Social Climate," *McGill Law Journal* 13 (1967): 189–90.
114 In addition to the literature on Jehovah's Witnesses cited below, see MacLennan, *Toward the Charter*; Lambertson, *Repression and Resistance*; Dominique Clément, *Canada's Rights Revolution: Social Movements and Social Change, 1937–82* (Vancouver: UBC Press, 2008); Brock Millman, *Polarity, Patriotism, and Dissent in Great War Canada, 1914–1919* (Toronto: University of Toronto Press, 2016); Dennis G. Molinaro, *An Exceptional Law: Section 98 and the Emergency State, 1919–1936* (Toronto: University of Toronto Press for Osgoode Society for Canadian Legal History, 2017).

115 The photo was originally published in *Maclean's Magazine* (1 March 1947), 9; it was reproduced in Michel Sarra-Bournet, *L'affaire Roncarelli: Duplessis contre les Témoins de Jéhovah* (Quebec City: Institut québécois de recherche sur la culture, 1986), 38, and accompanying "Duplessis contre Jéhovah," *La Presse* (14 August 1994), A6. On the riot, see "Witnesses of Jehovah Are Mobbed, Arrested at Chateauguay Meeting," *The Gazette* (10 September 1945), 13.

116 Sarra-Bournet, *L'affaire Roncarelli*, 36–51; William Kaplan, *State and Salvation: The Jehovah's Witnesses and Their Fight for Civil Rights* (Toronto: University of Toronto Press, 1989), 230–53; Gary Botting, *Fundamental Freedoms and Jehovah's Witnesses* (Calgary: University of Calgary Press, 1993), 35–64.

117 E.g., Léo Forest, "Les Témoins de Jéhovah viennent sonder le terrain à Joliette," *L'Action populaire (Joliette)* (16 June 1949), 7.

118 La Frontière, "Les Témoins de Jéhovah," *L'Action populaire (Joliette)* (19 December 1946), 1, 4: "pour eux, toutes les religions qui existent sur la terre sont l'œuvre du diable. Eux seuls ont la vérité toute pure. Ils en veulent surtout à l'Église catholique. Pour eux, le Pape est à peu près ce qu'il y a de plus diabolique en dehors de Satan lui-même"; "les remettre à la raison"; "Supportons ces gens avec la patience que nous pouvons, mais ne les laissons pas pervertir notre jeunesse. Grâce à Dieu, le Canada est toujours resté fidèle à la foi de ses ancêtres." The pseudonym is not identified in Bernard Vinet, *Pseudonymes québécois* (Quebec City: Garneau, 1974), but likely refers to Léo Forest, who wrote other opinion pieces in the paper.

119 Description from Léo Forest, "Les Témoins de Jéhovah viennent sonder le terrain à Joliette," *L'Action populaire (Joliette)* (16 June 1949), 7. See also L.F., "Les Témoins de Jéhovah de nouveau à Joliette," *L'Action populaire (Joliette)* (11 August 1949), 1.

120 "Les Témoins de Jéhovah," *L'Action populaire (Joliette)* (18 August 1949), 1: "cette peste infernale."

121 "Arrestation de propagandistes des 'Témoins,'" *L'Étoile du Nord (Joliette)* (18 August 1949), 1: "propagandistes"; "ennuyés par leurs sollicitations."

122 "Chez les Artisans: Locale 32 Joliette," *L'Action populaire (Joliette)* (15 December 1949), 3: "très épineuse"; "longuement."

123 What follows is drawn from the case report of Olive Lundell's action, *Lundell v. Masse*, [1954] C.S. 59, as well as the extensive news coverage of the event. The case file does not survive, and Stein & Stein of Montreal, the plaintiffs' lawyers, confirm that they kept no records of the case in their own archives. The best news coverage was ironically not in the

Quebec papers but in the *Toronto Daily Star*, which had a reporter in Joliette the next day. See especially "Mob Witness Girls in Quebec," *Toronto Daily Star* (15 December 1949), 1, 14; "Girl Witnesses Back to Resume Joliette Work," *Toronto Daily Star* (17 December 1949), 3; Charles Coady, "'Treatment Planned' Will Keep Witnesses Out, Joliette Threat," *Toronto Daily Star* (19 December 1949), 25; Charles Coady, "'Kidnapped' in Joliette by Foes of Witnesses Given Ride Like Girls," *Toronto Daily Star* (20 December 1949), 1–2. Extensive coverage also appeared in *La Presse, The Gazette, La Patrie*, and *Le Devoir* for 15 December 1949 and after. See also, from the Witnesses' perspective, "Burning Hate Flares in Joliette," *Awake! (Brooklyn, NY)* (8 April 1950), 9–14.

124 "Mob Witness Girls in Quebec," *Toronto Daily Star* (15 December 1949), 1, 14.
125 Relevé alphabétique des causes pendantes des Témoins de Jéhovah devant la Cour du Recorder de Montréal du 29 mai 1944 au 26 septembre 1947, filed as evidence in *Roncarelli v. Duplessis* (case file).
126 "Jehovah Members Attacked by Mob," *The Gazette* (14 February 1949), 9; "Jehovah Witnesses Driven out of Maritime Centre," *Lethbridge Herald* (14 February 1949), 2; "The Shame of Edmundston," *Awake! (Brooklyn, NY)* (8 May 1949), 8–11.
127 "Mob Witness Girls in Quebec," *Toronto Daily Star* (15 December 1949), 14.
128 "Burning Hate Flares in Joliette," *Awake! (Brooklyn, NY)* (8 April 1950), 10.
129 *Lundell v. Masse*, 61: "des paroles qu'il ne serait pas convenable de répéter ici."
130 "2 témoins de Jéhovah expulsés de Joliette," *La Presse* (15 December 1949), 56: "les indésirables des autres municipalités."
131 "Girl Witnesses Back to Resume Joliette Work," *Toronto Daily Star* (17 December 1949), 3.
132 "Le chef de police de Joliette 'endoctriné,'" *La Presse* (16 December 1949), 47: "La population de Joliette est soulevée…. Les témoins sont persistants…. S'ils déposent une plainte contre ceux qui veulent se débarrasser d'eux et avoir la paix, je crains la réaction de la foule. Des choses regrettables peuvent se passer, comme lors de notre dernière grève."
133 "Retour des Témoins dans la ville de Joliette" and "Les Témoins de Jéhovah mécontents," *Le Devoir* (17 December 1949), 8.
134 In addition to the coverage in the Montreal papers, details of the meeting are in "Les étrangers fauteurs de séditions sont déclarés indésirables à Joliette," *L'Action populaire (Joliette)* (22 December 1949), 1, 4; "Les témoins de Jéhovah expulsés de Joliette," *L'Étoile du Nord (Joliette)* (22 December

1949), 1, 4. See also *Parsons v. L'Action Populaire* (case file), Notes & autorités de la défenderesse (produced 9 October 1952).
135 "Witnesses Threatened at Joliette," *Sherbrooke Daily Record* (20 December 1949), 1.
136 Charles Coady, "'Kidnapped' in Joliette by Foes of Witnesses Given Ride Like Girls," *Toronto Daily Star* (20 December 1949), 1–2.
137 The only case file that survives is *Parsons v. L'Action Populaire* (case file), but it includes some copies of material from the identical action *Lundell v. L'Action Populaire*. See "Plainte d'enlèvement portée par les Témoins de Jéhovah," *La Patrie* (19 December 1949), 20; "Will Demand Action by Duplessis," *(Ottawa) Evening Citizen* (21 December 1949), 4 (Glen How seeking intervention of Duplessis, who was attorney general as well as premier); "Ask Duplessis to Investigate," *(Ottawa) Evening Citizen* (21 December 1949), 18 (Association for Civil Liberties also demanding Duplessis's involvement).
138 "Witnesses File Damage Actions," *Sherbrooke Daily Record* (22 March 1950), 1, 5; Omer Valois, "A propos d'un article de Joliette Journal," *L'Action populaire (Joliette)* (13 April 1950), 7; "La ville de Joliette poursuivie par les Témoins de Jéhovah," *La Presse* (4 April 1952), 16.
139 *Parsons v. L'Action Populaire* (case file), Judgment (4 March 1953). See "'Les Témoins de Jéhovah' perdent leur procès," *L'Etoile du Nord (Joliette)* (25 March 1953), 1; "L'Action Populaire Ltée gagne son procès," *L'Action populaire (Joliette)* (26 March 1953), 1; "Le privilège de critique," *La Presse* (7 April 1953), 18.
140 "$16,000 réclamés à 3 Joliettains par des 'missionnaires,'" *La Presse* (8 March 1950), 8; "Les échos de la Cour," *L'Étoile du Nord (Joliette)* (9 March 1950), 1, 6. Neither the news coverage nor the judgment went into detail about the specifics of the damages claim.
141 The information about the defendants comes from records on ancestry.ca, as well as contemporary references in the Joliette papers to Dion and Masse.
142 Kaplan, *State and Salvation*, 57–60, 230–53.
143 Quoted in "Kidnapping Count to Be Laid by Sect," *The Gazette* (19 December 1949), 7. Lundell and Parsons were both in their thirties, but the coverage consistently depicted them as "young girls" in their twenties.
144 "Bagarre à Joliette," *La Presse* (30 April 1953), 3, 9; "Il leur en coûte $300 pour avoir expulsé ces témoins de Jéhovah," *La Patrie* (30 April 1953), 4; "Condamnés à l'amende pour avoir expulsé des témoins de Jéhovah," *Le Devoir* (1 May 1953), 3; "Driven Out of Joliette, 'Witnesses' Get $600," *The Gazette* (1 May 1953), 4.

145 *Lundell v. Masse*, 63–4: "c'était une place où on logeait des femmes sans adresse"; "grossièrement insulté"; "trois cents ans de liberté"; "ceux qui sont venus défricher et coloniser notre grand pays et qui ont même versé leur sang pour l'édifier"; "pâles comparses."
146 "Deux Témoins de Jéhovah demandent la protection de la police," *L'Union des Cantons de l'Est (Arthabaska)* (29 May 1952), 4.
147 "Les Témoins de Jéhovah dénoncés par le cardinal," *La Presse* (19 May 1953), 13: "fanatiques"; "adversaires acharnés de l'Eglise."
148 "La corporation municipale du comté de Joliette," *L'Action populaire (Joliette)* (18 February 1959), 2. Since *Roncarelli* had been launched before the abolition of Privy Council appeals in 1949, it was still eligible to be heard by the Judicial Committee. Duplessis's death in September 1959 ended any such plans.
149 On the Witnesses' millenarianism, see M. James Penton, *Apocalypse Delayed: The Story of Jehovah's Witnesses*, 2nd ed. (Toronto: University of Toronto Press, 1997), 3–9.
150 *Lundell v. Masse*, 63: "les insultes et les outrages"; "ce qu'elles ont de plus cher: le droit de chaque individu à la liberté de sa personne."
151 W. Glen How, "The Case for a Canadian Bill of Rights," *Canadian Bar Review* 26 (1948): 759–96.
152 The main cases were *R. v. Boucher*, [1951] S.C.R. 265; *Saumur v. City of Quebec*, [1953] 2 S.C.R. 299; *Chaput v. Romain*, [1955] S.C.R. 834; *Lamb v. Benoit*, [1959] S.C.R. 321; *Roncarelli v. Duplessis*, [1959] S.C.R. 121. See generally Kaplan, *State and Salvation*, 230–53.
153 "Reprehensible Mob Action in a Quebec Town," *Sherbrooke Daily Record* (28 December 1949), 4; *R. v. Boucher*, [1951] S.C.R. 265. *Boucher* was first heard in 1949, then reheard at the Supreme Court the following year in lieu of a new trial. Justice Rand, whose quoted words appear at p. 285 of the final judgment, repeated his reasons from the first hearing.

8. Conclusion: From Wounded Feelings to Violated Rights

1 Sylvio Normand, "Mathieu, Michel," *DCB* vol. 14.
2 *McCuaig v. Cité de Montréal* (1898), 4 R.L. (n.s.) 368, R.J.Q. 14 C.S. 175, 1 R.P.Q. 258.
3 Art. 421 CCP (1903 ed.).
4 *McCuaig v. Cité de Montréal* (R.L.), 369–70:

> Les torts ne sont qu'une infraction ou violation des droits, il s'ensuit que le système négatif des torts doit correspondre et cadrer avec le système positif des droits. Comme on divise tous les droits en droits des personnes et droits

sur les choses, on doit diviser de même généralement les torts en ceux qui affectent les droits des personnes et ceux qui affectent les droits de propriété. Les droits des personnes sont divisés en droits absolus et droits relatifs. Les droits absolus appartiennent et sont propres aux hommes en particulier, considérés simplement comme individus, comme isolés. Les droits relatifs sont ceux dont les hommes sont investis, comme membres d'une société, et comme liés, les uns aux autres par différents nœuds ou rapports. Les droits absolus de chaque individu consistent en le droit de la sûreté personnelle, le droit de la liberté personnelle et le droit de la propriété personnelle. Par conséquent, les torts ou injures qui nuisent à ces droits doivent être d'une nature correspondante;

Les torts ou injures contre la sûreté personnelle des individus attaquent ou leur vie ou leur corps ou leurs membres, ou leur santé, ou leur réputation.

5 Art. 833(4) CCP (1903 ed.). *Peltier v. Martin* (1898), R.J.Q. 13 C.S. 223 at 228–9, 4 R.L. (n.s.) 373; *Chouinard v. Raymond* (1900), R.J.Q. 18 C.S. 319 at 323.
6 *Brissette v. Boucher* (1887), 31 L.C.J. 104 at 110 (Circ. Ct.): "Que, si pour être passible de dommages-intérêts, il faut avoir commis une action nuisible, qui ne dérive pas d'un droit positif, de même, il faut, pour pouvoir réclamer cette réparation, que l'on ait été lésé dans un droit acquis, personnel ou réel, *personnel* comprenant tout attentat à la liberté, à la réputation et à l'honneur, et réel, comprenant les attentats à la propriété" (emphasis in original).
7 E.g., *Duquette v. Major* (1889), M.L.R. 5 S.C. 134 at 135; *Cusson v. Bédard* (Sup. Ct., 1890), reported with the appeal judgment in R.J.Q. 1 B.R. 105 at 112–13.
8 Sourdat, *Traité général de la responsabilité* (1876 ed.), 1:495: "de simples convenances, des espérances non réalisées, des attentes, en un mot"; "Le dommage ne serait pas appréciable."
9 William Belime, *Philosophie du droit, ou Cours d'introduction à la science du droit*, 2 vols. (Paris, 1844–8), 2:13–20; Émile Beaussire, *Les principes du droit* (Paris, 1888), 51–2; Ahrens, *Cours de droit naturel ou de philosophie du droit*, 84, 96 (Ahrens was a German who taught at Göttingen, Brussels, and Graz).
10 Ernest Roguin, *La règle de droit: analyse générale, spécialités, souveraineté des états, assiette de l'impôt, théorie des statuts, système des rapports de droit privé, précédé d'une introduction sur la classification des disciplines* (Lausanne, 1889), 256: "les relations juridiques portant sur la personnalité même du sujet actif"; "ont le caractère particulier que l'objet matériel en est l'individualité même du sujet actif, et se rangent d'ailleurs dans les droits absolus,

puisque tous les justiciables forment le sujet passif, et qu'une certaine abstention à eux imposée constitue l'objet juridique du droit."
11 Perreau, "Des droits de la personnalité."
12 Nerson, *Les droits extrapatrimoniaux*, 320–44. Nerson's ideas were amplified later by Paul Roubier, *Droits subjectifs et situations juridiques* (1963; repr., Paris: Dalloz, 2005), 77, 364.
13 Nerson, *Les droits extrapatrimoniaux*, 340.
14 Nerson, *Les droits extrapatrimoniaux*, 356–9.
15 Roubier, *Droits subjectifs*, 50 (quotation), 77: "Il n'existe pas de droit pour une personne à la vie; il existe – ce qui est très différent – un devoir pour toutes les autres personnes de ne pas porter injustement atteinte à la vie d'autrui, et ce devoir est sanctionné par une action en responsabilité."
16 *Charter of Human Rights and Freedoms*, preamble: "Whereas every human being possesses intrinsic rights and freedoms designed to ensure his protection and development"; *Civil Code of Québec*, article 3: "Every person is the holder of personality rights, such as the right to life, the right to the inviolability and integrity of his person, and the right to the respect of his name, reputation and privacy." See also Madeleine Caron, "Le Code civil québécois, instrument de protection des droits et libertés de la personne," *Canadian Bar Review* 56 (1978): 197–232.
17 Paul-André Crépeau, *La réforme du droit civil canadien: une certaine conception de la recodification, 1965–1977* (Montreal: Thémis, 2003), 41: "une volonté de placer la personne humaine, avec ses droits et ses devoirs, à la place d'honneur qui lui revient, en faisant d'elle la pierre d'angle de l'ensemble des relations juridiques de droit privé."
18 Bibaud, *Commentaires*, 2:557: "la lésion d'autrui ou la violation volontaire du droit d'autrui."
19 Risk and Vipond, "Rights Talk," esp. 29–30; Campbell, "Race, Upper Canadian Constitutionalism and 'British Justice.'"
20 Antoine Gérin-Lajoie, *Catéchisme politique; ou élémens du droit public et constitutionnel du Canada* (Montreal, 1851), 11: "Les habitans du Canada jouissent individuellement de certains droits qui leur sont garantis, soit par des traités, soit par des lois expresses, soit par leur qualité de sujets anglais, soit enfin par le droit public et le droit naturel."
21 Joseph Roy, *Explication du Code civil du Bas-Canada* (Montreal, 1867), 1:28: "ces droits peuvent se réduire à trois principaux, savoir: celui de la sûreté des personnes, celui de la liberté personnelle, et le droit de propriété privée. Enfreindre l'un ou l'autre de ces droits, c'est dépouiller l'homme de sa liberté."
22 Fraser, "*Honorary Protestants.*" A contemporary view of rights in the Guibord affair (from the liberal side) is Désiré Girouard, "Church and

State," *Revue critique de législation et de jurisprudence du Canada* 1 (1871): 431–56, 2 (1872): 1–32, 113–46 (see esp. 2:130–1).
23 Kary, "Constitutionalization of Quebec Libel Law."
24 E.A. Heaman, "Rights Talk and the Liberal Order Framework," in *Liberalism and Hegemony: Debating the Canadian Liberal Revolution*, ed. Jean-François Constant and Michel Ducharme, 147–75 (Toronto: University of Toronto Press, 2009).
25 Evelyn Kolish, "Imprisonment for Debt in Lower Canada, 1791–1840," *McGill Law Journal* 32 (1987): 602–35; Jeffrey L. McNairn, "'A Just and Obvious Distinction': The Meaning of Imprisonment for Debt and the Criminal Law in Upper Canada's Age of Reform," in *Essays in the History of Canadian Law: Volume XI – Quebec and the Canadas*, ed. G. Blaine Baker and Donald Fyson, 187–234 (Toronto: University of Toronto Press for Osgoode Society for Canadian Legal History, 2013); McNairn, "'Common Sympathies of Our Nature.'"
26 See, e.g., J.-L. Crivelli, *De la contrainte par corps, considérée sous les rapports de la morale, de la religion, du droit naturel et du droit civil, et dans l'intérêt de l'humanité en général* (Paris, 1830); Jules Levieil de la Marsonnière, *Histoire de la contrainte par corps* (Paris, 1843); M. Lassime, *Traité de la contrainte par corps* (Paris, 1863); Jules Leveillé, "De l'abolition de la contrainte par corps," *Revue pratique de droit français* 22 (1866): 305–32; Henri Hardouin, *Essai sur l'abolition de la contrainte par corps* (Paris, 1874).
27 Coercive imprisonment (with the wording in question) was codified as art. 2272(4) CCLC, then moved in 1897 to art. 833(4) CCP by *An Act to amend the Civil Code*, S.Q. 1897 (60 Vic.), c. 50, s. 38. It was abolished by the 1965 revision of the CCP, S.Q. 1965, c. 80, s. 1.
28 *Boucher v. Armstrong* (1924), R.J.Q. 37 B.R. 194 at 203: "droits de la personne"; "bien que d'une valeur sans prix,… il n'est pas, suivant l'expression consacrée 'dans le commerce' et est inappréciable en argent et inhérent à la personne"; "est appelé injure personnelle ou tort personnel parce qu'il consiste dans une 'atteinte portée à la dignité de la personne d'autrui par un fait que les bonnes mœurs réprouvent.'" The source of the embedded quotation at the end is not indicated in the report.
29 Mignault, *Le droit civil canadien*, 1:131.
30 Mignault, *Le droit civil canadien*, 5:333: "*l'exercice régulier d'un droit* n'est pas une *faute*" (emphasis in original); this volume was published in 1901. The word *régulier* here hints at the new idea of abuse of right, which Mignault himself would later accept (though warily) in Pierre-Basile Mignault, "The Modern Conception of Civil Responsibility: A Study of Comparative Law," *Journal of the Society for Comparative Legislation and International Law* (n.s.) 11

(1910): 102–13; Mignault, "The Modern Evolution of Civil Responsibility," *Canadian Bar Review* 5 (1927): 10–14.
31 Langelier, *Cours*, 1:3: "par cela qu'on est homme, et qu'on apporte avec soi en naissant"; "la maîtrise de sa propre personne."
32 Langelier, *Cours*, 3:463 (this volume appeared in 1907): "il n'y a jamais de faute dans l'exercise d'un droit."
33 *Pilon v. Demers* (1931), 37 R. de J. 364 at 373–4 (Sup. Ct.): "un capital des plus important"; "compensation bien minime si l'on considère que la réputation et l'honneur ne s'achètent pas comme un vulgaire article de commerce."
34 *Chaloult v. Chronicle Telegraph Publishing Co. Ltd.*, [1944] R.L. 1 at 10 (Sup. Ct.): "a outre-passé ses droits dans son commentaire."
35 Arthur R.M. Lower, "Some Reflections on a Bill of Rights," *Fortnightly Law Journal* 16 (1947): 216–18, 234–7; H. McD. Clokie, "The Preservation of Civil Liberties," *Canadian Journal of Economics and Political Science* 13 (1947): 208–32; How, "Case for a Canadian Bill of Rights"; F.R. Scott, "Dominion Jurisdiction over Human Rights and Fundamental Freedoms," *Canadian Bar Review* 27 (1949): 497–536; MacLennan, *Toward the Charter*; Lambertson, *Repression and Resistance*; Adams, "Idea of Constitutional Rights."
36 Claude-Armand Sheppard, "Roncarelli v. Duplessis: Art. 1053 C.C. Revolutionized," *McGill Law Journal* 6 (1960): 75–97; Roderick A. Macdonald, "Was Duplessis Right?" *McGill Law Journal* 55 (2010): 401–36; Adams, "Building a Law of Human Rights."
37 *Robbins v. Canadian Broadcasting Corporation* (1957), [1958] C.S. 152; *Cooperberg v. Buckman* (1957), [1958] C.S. 427. See H. Patrick Glenn, "Le secret de la vie privée en droit québécois," *Revue générale de droit* 5 (1974): 24–42.
38 *Chaput v. Romain*, [1955] S.C.R. 834. The Supreme Court hearing and decision were extensively covered in the press. See esp. Frank Swanson, "Witness Appeal Goes to Supreme Court Canada," *Ottawa Citizen* (22 September 1954), 20; J.A. Hume, "Quebec's Jehovah's Witnesses in Court," *Ottawa Citizen* (23 April 1955), 21; Hume, "Unlawful Police Action Charged in Chapeau Case," *Ottawa Citizen* (5 May 1955), 3; "Policemen Compared to Burglars, Killers," *The Gazette* (5 May 1955), 2; J.A. Hume, "Against Law to Read the Bible?" *Ottawa Citizen* (6 May 1955), 12; Hume, "Says 'Witnesses' May Suffer Lack of Freedom of Worship for Years," *Ottawa Citizen* (7 May 1955), 2; Bernard Dufresne, "'Witness' Meet Breakup by Police Ruled Illegal," *The Gazette* (16 November 1955), 1.
39 *Chaput v. Romain*, [1954] B.R. 794 at 794: "aucune difficulté particulière" (Bissonnette J. for the unanimous court). The Court of Queen's Bench

upheld the Superior Court judgment (unreported, 10 June 1952), which had dismissed the action.
40 J.A. Hume, "Unlawful Police Action Charged in Chapeau Case," *Ottawa Citizen* (5 May 1955), 3.
41 *Chaput v. Romain* (S.C.C.), 841: "[Le dommage moral] comprend certainement le préjudice souffert dans la présente cause. Il s'entend en effet de toute atteinte aux droits extrapatrimoniaux, comme le droit à la liberté, à l'honneur, au nom, à la liberté de conscience ou de parole. Les tribunaux ne peuvent refuser de l'accorder, comme par exemple, si les *sentiments religieux ou patriotiques ont été blessés*" (emphasis in original, a reference to Dalloz, *Nouveau Répertoire*). Chief Justice Patrick Kerwin and Justice James Wilfred Estey concurred.
42 *Chaput v. Romain* (S.C.C.), 858 and 860 (Kellock J., with Rand J. concurring), 864 (Locke J.).

Bibliography

Archival Sources

Archives de Montréal
    P39 – Fonds Commission royale d'enquête sur l'administration des affaires de la cité de Montréal
        P39-2-1-2 (Témoignages de la Commission Royale 1909, vol. 2), online: https://archivesdemontreal.ica-atom.org/p39-2-1-2
    P43 – Fonds Commission d'enquête présidée par le juge François Caron
        P43-4-2-D02 (Maladies vénériennes), online: https://archivesdemontreal.ica-atom.org/maladies-veneriennes-1942-1952
            P43-4-2-2-10p (Letter, Antonio Lamer to Fernand Dufresne, 11 January 1944)
        P43-4-2-D04, P43-4-2-4-1-1945op (Bureau de la moralité, Rapport de l'année 1945), online: https://archivesdemontreal.ica-atom.org/bureau-de-la-moralite-1945-1948
Bibliothèque et Archives nationales du Québec, Vieux-Montréal
    P48, S1 – Conrad Poirier Collection (Photographs)
    TP9 – Fonds Cour du banc du Roi/de la Reine
    TP10 – Fonds Cour de circuit
    TP11 – Fonds Cour supérieure
Bibliothèque et Archives nationales du Québec, Quebec City
    TP9 – Fonds Cour du banc du Roi/de la Reine
    TP11 – Fonds Cour supérieure

Bibliothèque et Archives nationales du Québec, Trois-Rivières
TP11 – Fonds Cour supérieure
Harvard University, Houghton Library
Theater Collection – TS 1701.211, Academy of Music, Box Office Statement (21 September 1896 to 12 March 1898)

Legislation

(Quebec unless otherwise noted)

An Act for compensating the Families of Persons killed by Accidents, 9–10 Vic. (1846), c. 93 (United Kingdom).

An Act for compensating the Families of Persons killed by Accident, and for other purposes therein mentioned, S.P.C. 1847 (10–11 Vic.), c. 6 (United Canadas).

An Act for the better regulation of Interments and Disinterments, S.Q. 1888 (51–52 Vic.), c. 48.

An Act for the relief of Euphemia Tudor Slade, S.C. 1925 (15–16 Geo. V), c. 191 (Canada).

An Act for the relief of James Benning, S.P.C. 1865 (29 Vic.), c. 175 (United Canadas).

An Act respecting compensation to the Families of Persons killed by Accident, and in duels, C.S.C. 1859, c. 78 (United Canadas).

An Act respecting Coroners' Inquests, S.Q. 1880 (43–4 Vic.), c. 10.

An Act respecting the practice of Physic and Surgery, and the Study of Anatomy, C.S.C. 1859, c. 76 (United Canadas).

An Act respecting the responsibility for accidents suffered by workmen in the course of their work, and the compensation for injuries resulting therefrom, S.Q. 1909 (9 Edw. VII), c. 66.

An Act to amend the act 19–20 Victoria, chapter 128, intituled "An Act to amend and consolidate the several acts incorporating the Mount Royal Cemetery Company," S.Q. 1901 (1 Edw. VII), c. 92.

An Act to amend the act to consolidate the charter of the Notre-Dame Hospital, Montreal, and its amendments, S.Q. 1924 (14 Geo. V), c. 117.

An Act to amend the charter of Les Religieuses Sœurs Hospitalières de Saint-Joseph de l'Hôtel-Dieu de Montréal, S.Q. 1937 (1 Geo. VI), c. 136.

An Act to amend the Civil Code respecting successions, S.Q. 1915 (5 Geo. V), c. 74.

An Act to amend the Civil Code, with respect to persons who make use of opium or other narcotics, S.Q. 1895 (59 Vic.), c. 40.

An Act to amend the Code of Civil Procedure, S.Q. 1897 (60 Vic.), c. 54.

An Act to amend the law respecting Anatomy, S.Q. 1898 (61 Vic.), c. 29.

Bibliography   433

An Act to consolidate the charter of Notre Dame Hospital, Montreal, and its amendments, S.Q. 1898 (61 Vic.), c. 82.
An Act to establish the Provincial Bureau of Health and to amend the Revised Statutes, 1909, accordingly, S.Q. 1922 (12 Geo. V), c. 29.
An Act to incorporate The Congregation Shemerin Labeker, S.Q. 1914 (4 Geo. V), c. 159.
An Act to provide for the Interdiction and Cure of Habitual Drunkards, S.Q. 1870 (33 Vic.), c. 26.
Charter of Human Rights and Freedoms (as periodically amended).
Civil Code of Lower Canada (as periodically amended).
Civil Code of Québec (as periodically amended).
Code civil des français: édition originale et seule officielle. Paris, 1804 (France).
Code of Civil Procedure (as periodically amended).
The Consolidated Statutes for Lower Canada. Quebec City, 1861.
Criminal Code, S.C. 1892 (55–6 Vic.), c. 29 (Canada).
Identification of Criminals Act, R.S.C. 1927, c. 38 (Canada).
The Revised Statutes of the Province of Quebec, 2 vols. Quebec City, 1888.
The Revised Statutes of the Province of Quebec 1909, 4 vols. Quebec City: Charles Pageau, 1909.
The Revised Statutes of the Province of Quebec 1925, 5 vols. Quebec City: Ls. A. Proulx, 1925.
Revised Statutes of the Province of Quebec, 1941, 5 vols. Quebec City: Rédempti Paradis, 1941.
Supreme Court Act, R.S.C. 1906, c. 139 (Canada).
Venereal Diseases Prevention Act, S.Q. 1941 (5 Geo. VI), c. 55.

Published Case Reports

Agnew et uxor v. Gober et vir (1906), 8 R.P.Q. 198 (K.B.).
Agnew et uxor v. Gober et vir (1907), R.J.Q. 32 C.S. 266.
Agnew et uxor v. Gober et vir (1907), R.P.Q. 217 (Sup. Ct.).
Agnew et uxor v. Gober et vir (1908), R.J.Q. 17 B.R. 508, 15 R.L. (n.s.) 93.
Agnew et uxor v. Gober et vir (1909), R.J.Q. 38 C.S. 313 (Sup. Ct. Rev.).
Angers v. Pacaud (1894), R.J.Q. 5 C.S. 339.
Angers v. Pacaud (1896), R.J.Q. 5 B.R. 17.
Angé v. Curé de la Pointe-aux-Trembles (1821), 2 R. de L. 63 (K.B.).
Antille v. Marcotte (1888), 11 L.N. 339 (Circ. Ct.).
Archambault v. Camirand (1905), R.J.Q. 27 C.S. 30.
Asselin v. Belleau (1844), 1 R. de L. 46 (Q.B.).

Auburn v. Berthiaume (1903), R.J.Q. 23 C.S. 476.
Augustus v. Gosset, [1996] 3 S.C.R. 269 (S.C.C.).
Barrette et uxor v. Lallier et uxor (1893), R.J.Q. 3 C.S. 541.
Barrette v. Bourbonnière (1896), R.J.Q. 12 C.S. 271.
Barrette v. Poissant (1864), 15 L.C. Rep. 51 (Q.B.).
Baxter v. Davis (1894), 4 R.P.Q. 153 (Sup. Ct.).
Beatty v. Cullingworth (Q.B.D., 1896), reported in *British Medical Journal* (21 November 1896), 1546–8 (U.K.).
Beaubien v. Verner (1899), 6 R. de J. 409 (Q.B.).
Beaudry v. Desjardins (1870), 4 R.L. 555 (Sup. Ct. Rev.).
Beaulieu v. Frank (1913), 20 R. de J. 26 (Sup. Ct.).
Bélair v. Tougas (1901), 7 R. de J. 573 (Sup. Ct.).
Belleau v. Mercier (1882), 8 Q.L.R. 312 (Sup. Ct.).
Bérubé v. Carsley (1890), 20 R.L. 97 (Sup. Ct.).
Blake v. Midland Railway Co. (1852), 18 Q.B. Rep. 93 (U.K.).
Bonneau v. Coupal (1865), 1 L.C.L.J. 33, 10 L.C.J. 177 (Q.B.).
Bouchard v. Bégin (1919), R.J.Q. 57 C.S. 9 (Sup. Ct. Rev.).
Bouchard v. Bégin (1921), 27 R.L. (n.s.) 341 (Sup. Ct. Rev.).
Boucher v. Armstrong (1924), R.J.Q. 37 B.R. 194.
Bradley v. Ménard (1900), R.J.Q. 18 C.S. 382.
Brissette v. Boucher (1887), 31 L.C.J. 104 (Circ. Ct.).
Brouillette v. Religieuses de l'Hôtel-Dieu (1941), 47 R.L. (n.s.) 408 (Sup. Ct.).
Brouillette v. Religieuses de l'Hôtel-Dieu, [1943] B.R. 441, [1943] R.L. (n.s.) 83.
Cadoret v. Cité de Montréal et Gagnon (1888), 16 R.L. 386 (Sup. Ct.).
Caron v. Gagnon (1930), R.J.Q. 68 C.S. 155.
Caron v. Guay (1889), 18 R.L. 685 (Sup. Ct. Rev.).
Chalin v. Gagnon (1899), 5 R. de J. 320 (Circ. Ct.).
Chaloult v. Chronicle Telegraph Publishing Co. Ltd., [1944] R.L. 1 (Sup. Ct.).
Chamberland v. Parent (1882), 8 Q.L.R. 299 (Sup. Ct.).
Chaput v. Romain, [1954] B.R. 794.
Chaput v. Romain, [1955] S.C.R. 834 (S.C.C.).
Charest v. Hurtubise (1893), R.J.Q. 4 C.S. 93.
Chef dit Vadeboncoeur v. Léonard et vir (1862), 6 L.C.J. 305, 13 L.C. Rep 74 (Sup. Ct.).
Chénier v. Martin (1904), R.J.Q. 25 C.S. 324.
Chiniquy et vir v. Bégin (1912), R.J.Q. 42 C.S. 261.
Chiniquy et vir v. Bégin (1915), R.J.Q. 24 B.R. 294.
Chouinard v. Raymond (1900), R.J.Q. 18 C.S. 319.
Christie v. York Corporation (1937), R.J.Q. 75 C.S. 136.
Christie v. York Corporation (1938), R.J.Q. 65 B.R. 104.

Christie v. York Corporation (1939), [1940] S.C.R. 139 (S.C.C.).
Clermont v. Sauriol (1900), R.J.Q. 10 B.R. 294 (Sup. Ct.).
Cloutier v. Roy (1930), R.J.Q. 49 B.R. 313.
Collin v. Gilot (1930), R.J.Q. 48 B.R. 464.
Compagnie de publication du Canada Revue v. Fabre (1895), R.J.Q. 8 C.S. 195 (Sup. Ct. Rev.).
Cooperberg v. Buckman (1957), [1958] C.S. 427.
Corbeil v. Dominion Park Co. (1907), 13 R.L. (n.s.) 432 (Sup. Ct. Rev.).
Couillard v. Jeannotte (1894), R.J.Q. 3 B.R. 461.
Cournoyer et uxor v. Cournoyer (1894), R.J.Q. 5 C.S. 312.
Courteau v. Skelly (1901), 7 R. de J. 519, R.J.Q. 20 C.S. 216.
Curl v. Quebec Amusement Co. (1917), 23 R.L. (n.s.) 345 (Sup. Ct.).
Cusson v. Bédard (1892), R.J.Q. 1 B.R. 105.
D. v. City of Montreal, [1947] R.L. 257 (Sup. Ct.).
Dame Dufresne v. X (1960), [1961] C.S. 119.
Dasylva v. Plante (1882), 8 Q.L.R. 349 (Sup. Ct.).
Davidson v. Garrett (1899), 30 O.R. 653 (Ontario, Div. Ct.).
Decelles v. International Shows Ltd. (1920), R.J.Q. 59 C.S. 374.
Demers v. Hébert (1884), 13 R.L. 466 (Sup. Ct.).
Desaulniers v. L'Action Sociale (1914), R.J.Q. 46 C.S. 161 (Sup. Ct. Rev.).
Desormeaux v. Cadotte (1868), 13 L.C.J. 211 (Circ. Ct.).
Dinowitzer v. Canadian Pacific Railway Co. (1910), 11 R.P.Q. 396 (Sup. Ct.).
Dorion v. Hogan (1882), 2 Déc. C.A. 238 (Q.B.).
Dorion v. Laurent (1843), 17 L.C.J. 324 (Provincial Court of Appeal).
Drew v. Dean (1888), 32 L.C.J. 310 (Q.B.).
Driscoll v. Wray (1914), 23 R. de J. 561 (Sup. Ct. Rev.).
Ducharme v. Hôpital Notre-Dame (1933), R.J.Q. 71 C.S. 377, 39 R.L. (n.s.) 327.
Duquette v. Major (1889), M.L.R. 5 S.C. 134.
Duquette v. Pesant dit Sans-Cartier (1892), R.J.Q. 1 C.S. 465.
Durocher v. Meunier (1857), 1 L.C.J. 290 (Sup. Ct.).
E. v. M. (1939), R.J.Q. 77 C.S. 298.
Ex parte Dumouchel; Ex parte Dalton (1853), 3 L.C. Rep. 493 (Sup. Ct.).
Ex parte Weingart v. Jacobson (1921), 24 R.P.Q. 125 (Sup. Ct.).
Ex parte Wurtele (1851), 1 L.C. Rep. 414 (Sup. Ct.).
Fairgreave v. Gray (1932), R.J.Q. 71 C.S. 73.
Farand dit Viveret v. Paulos alias Paul (1905), R.J.Q. 28 C.S. 200.
Filion v. Dawes (1897), R.J.Q. 12 C.S. 494.
Flaherty v. Montreal Tramways (1931), R.J.Q. 69 C.S. 515.
Fortier v. Lamontagne (1936), 40 R.P.Q. 66 (Sup. Ct.).
Frigon v. Massicotte (1912), R.J.Q. 42 C.S. 445.

Gauthier v. Jeannotte (1897), R.J.Q. 6 B.R. 520.
Gauthier v. Jeannotte (1898), 28 S.C.R. 590 (S.C.C.).
Gober v. Agnew et al. (1907), 8 R.P.Q. 255 (Sup. Ct.).
Gooding v. Edlow Investment Corp. (1965), [1966] C.S. 436.
Goyer v. Duquette (1937), R.J.Q. 61 B.R. 503.
Grange v. Benning (1868), 13 L.C.J. 126 (Sup. Ct. Rev.).
Grange v. Benning (1868), 13 L.C.J. 153 (Q.B.).
Grange v. Benning (1869), 13 L.C.J. 290 (Sup. Ct.).
Grange v. Benning (1870), 14 L.C.J. 284 (Q.B.).
Guay v. Meunier (1874), 6 R.L. 174 (Circ. Ct.).
Hagen v. Stewart (1913), R.J.Q. 44 C.S. 121.
Harbec v. Lebrun (1948), reported in *Cahiers de droit* 10 (1969): 554–5.
Hart v. Shorey (1897), R.J.Q. 12 C.S. 84.
Hart v. Therien (1879), 5 Q.L.R. 267, 9 R.L. 579 (Q.B.).
Heermance v. James (1867), 47 Barb. 120 (N.Y. Sup. Ct.).
Hétu v. French (1908), R.J.Q. 17 B.R. 429.
Hibbard v. Cullen (1893), R.J.Q. 4 C.S. 369 (Sup. Ct. Rev.).
Hunt v. D. Donnelly Ltd. (1916), 17 R.P.Q. 341 (Sup. Ct.).
Hunter v. Gingras (1921), R.J.Q. 60 C.S. 182.
Hunter v. Gingras (1921), R.J.Q. 33 B.R. 403.
Huot v. Noiseux (1890), 18 R.L. 705 (Sup. Ct.).
Huot v. Noiseux (1892), R.J.Q. 2 B.R. 521.
In re C.O. Grothé and North American Life Assurance Co. v. Children of C.O. Grothé (1905), 7 R.P.Q. 111 (Sup. Ct.).
Jasmin v. Bain (1898), 5 R.L. (n.s.) 20 (Sup. Ct.).
Jasmin v. Sauriol (Clermont v. Sauriol) (1900), R.J.Q. 10 B.R. 294.
Jinchereau v. Roy (1914), 20 R. de J. 422 (Sup. Ct.).
Jodoin v. Larivière (1893), R.J.Q. 5 C.S. 39 (Sup. Ct.).
Jodoin v. Larivière (1894), R.J.Q. 6 C.S. 345 (Sup. Ct. Rev.).
Johnson v. Sparrow (1899), R.J.Q. 15 C.S. 104.
Johnson v. Sparrow (1899), R.J.Q. 8 B.R. 379.
Joyal v. Lafontaine (1926), 33 R. de J. 514 (Sup. Ct.).
Laferrière v. Ribardy (1874), 5 R.L. 742 (Sup. Ct.).
Lague v. Archambault (1929), R.J.Q. 68 C.S. 102.
Lamb v. Benoit, [1959] S.C.R. 321 (S.C.C.).
Lamothe v. North American Life Assurance Co. (1907), R.J.Q. 16 B.R. 178.
Laplante v. Parenteau (1889), 33 L.C.J. 124 (Sup. Ct. Rev.).
Larocque v. Michon (1857), 1 L.C.J. 187 (Sup. Ct.).
Larocque v. Michon (1858), 8 L.C. Rep. 222, 2 L.C.J. 267 (Q.B.).
Lebeau v. Plouffe (1893), R.J.Q. 5 C.S. 59.

Leclerc v. Bizier (1874), 6 R.L. 269 (Q.B.).
Lefebvre v. Mutual Life Insurance Co. of New York (1941), [1942] B.R. 266.
Leguerrier v. Ville St-Pierre (1919), 25 R. de J. 437 (Sup. Ct.).
Lemire v. Duclos (1898), R.J.Q. 13 C.S. 82.
Les curé et marguilliers de l'œuvre et fabrique de la paroisse de St-Hyacinthe v. Renaud (1878), 9 R.L. 417 (Circ. Ct.).
Leveillé v. Leveillé (1895), 1 R. de J. 443 (Sup. Ct.).
Levi v. Reed (1881), 6 S.C.R. 482 (S.C.C.).
Lord v. Cie du chemin de fer du nord (1886), 14 R.L. 297 (Q.B.).
Lorquet et uxor v. Sun Life Assurance Co. (1937), R.J.Q. 64 B.R. 137.
Lortie v. Claude (1892), R.J.Q. 2 C.S. 369.
Loughrin v. Burke (1918), R.J.Q. 55 C.S. 431.
Lundell v. Masse, [1954] C.S. 59.
Mailloux v. Paquette (1908), R.J.Q. 35 C.S. 166.
Manseau v. City of Montreal (1899), 7 R. de J. 399 (Sup. Ct.).
Marcotte v. Bolduc (1906), R.J.Q. 30 C.S. 222.
McAulay v. McLennan (1902), R.J.Q. 23 C.S. 419.
McCuaig v. Cité de Montréal (1898), 4 R.L. (n.s.) 368, R.J.Q. 14 C.S. 175, 1 R.P.Q. 258.
McElwee v. Darling (1853), Mont. Cond. Rep. 10 (Sup. Ct.).
McFarran et vir v. Montreal Park & Island Railway Co. (1900), 30 S.C.R. 410 (S.C.C.).
Mlle Bordier v. S. (1934), R.J.Q. 72 C.S. 316.
Moreau v. Pelletier (1873), 6 R.L. 720 (Sup. Ct.).
Morrisson v. Mullins (1888), 16 R.L. 114 (Sup. Ct.).
Mousseau v. City of Montreal (1899), 4 R.P.Q. 38 (Sup. Ct.).
Neill v. Taylor (1865), 13 Q.L.R. 195 (Q.B.).
Nolin v. Hardy (1932), R.J.Q. 53 B.R. 359.
Notre-Dame Hospital v. Patry, [1975] 2 S.C.R. 388 (S.C.C.).
O'Brien v. Bahen (1936), R.J.Q. 75 C.S. 55.
O'Brien v. Bahen (1938), R.J.Q. 65 B.R. 64.
Ortenberg v. Plamondon (1914), R.J.Q. 24 B.R. 69 and 385.
Ouimet v. Compagnie d'imprimerie et de publication du Canada (1887), 17 R.L. 242 (Sup. Ct.).
Ouimet v. Compagnie d'imprimerie et de publication du Canada (1889), M.L.R. 6 Q.B. 36, 17 R.L. 242.
Parnell v. Springle (1899), 5 R. de J. 74 (Sup. Ct.).
Peltier v. Martin (1898), R.J.Q. 13 C.S. 223, 4 R.L. (n.s.) 373.
Phillips v. Montreal General Hospital (1908), R.J.Q. 33 C.S. 483, 14 R.L. (n.s.) 159, 14 R. de J. 230.
Pilon v. Demers (1931), 37 R. de J. 364 (Sup. Ct.).

Poitevin v. Morgan (1866), 10 L.C.J. 93 (Sup. Ct.).
Poitras v. Quebec Railway, Light & Power Co. (1904), R.J.Q. 14 B.R. 429.
Pope v. Post Printing and Publishing Co. (1887), 32 L.C.J. 50 (Sup. Ct. Rev.).
Poulin v. Vigeant (1890), 20 R.L. 567 (Q.B.).
Provost v. Jackson (1869), 13 L.C.J. 170 (Q.B.).
R. v. Boucher, [1951] S.C.R. 265 (S.C.C.).
Ravary v. Grand Trunk Railway (1857), 1 L.C.J. 280 (Sup. Ct. Rev.).
Ravary v. Grand Trunk Railway (1860), 6 L.C.J. 49 (Q.B.).
Raymond v. Abel, [1946] C.S. 251.
Reynolds v. Loew's Montreal Theatres Ltd. (1919), R.J.Q. 30 B.R. 459.
Rinkuk v. Ville St-Pierre (1918), R.J.Q. 56 C.S. 43 (Sup. Ct. Rev.).
Robinson v. Canadian Pacific Railway Co. (1886), M.L.R. 2 Q.B. 25, 4 Déc. C.A. 297.
Robinson v. Canadian Pacific Railway Co. (1887), 14 S.C.R. 105 (S.C.C.).
Robinson v. Canadian Pacific Railway Co. (1889), M.L.R. 5 S.C. 225, 33 L.C.J. 145 (Sup. Ct. Rev.).
Robinson v. Canadian Pacific Railway Co. (1890), M.L.R. 6 Q.B. 118, 19 R.L. 485.
Robinson v. Canadian Pacific Railway Co. (1891), 19 S.C.R. 292 (S.C.C.).
Robinson v. Canadian Pacific Railway Co., [1892] A.C. 491 (J.C.P.C.).
Robbins v. Canadian Broadcasting Corporation (1957), [1958] C.S. 152.
Rochon v. Verret (1922), R.J.Q. 61 C.S. 276.
Roireau v. Roireau (1936), R.J.Q. 74 C.S. 221, 42 R. de J. 319.
Roncarelli v. Duplessis, [1959] S.C.R. 121 (S.C.C.).
Rousseau v. Majeur (1900), R.J.Q. 18 C.S. 447.
Roy v. Houle (1927), 34 R.L. (n.s.) 448 (Sup. Ct.).
Roy v. Turgeon (1886), 12 Q.L.R. 186 (Sup. Ct.).
Saumur v. City of Quebec, [1953] 2 S.C.R. 299 (S.C.C.).
St. Laurent v. Hamel (1891), R.J.Q. 1 B.R. 438.
St-Jean v. Gaumont (1889), 17 R.L. 594 (Sup. Ct.).
Stevenson v. Baldwin (1919), 26 R.L. (n.s.) 298 (K.B.).
Stevenson v. Baldwin (1920), R.J.Q. 34 B.R. 41 (K.B.).
Talbot v. Duhaime (1937), R.J.Q. 64 B.R. 386.
Tudor et vir v. Quebec & Lake St. John Railway Co. (1911), R.J.Q. 41 C.S. 19.
Union Pacific Railway v. Botsford, 141 U.S. 251 (1891) (U.S. Supreme Ct.).
Vanasse v. Cité de Montréal et Gagnon (1888), 16 R.L. 386 (Sup. Ct.).
Ville St-Pierre v. Zeppieri (1924), 32 R. de J. 67 (Recorder's Ct., Ville St-Pierre).
Weingart v. Jacobson (1919), R.J.Q. 57 C.S. 321 (Sup. Ct. Rev.).
Weir v. Claude (1888), M.L.R. 4 Q.B. 197.
Wilhelmy v. Brisebois (1883), 12 R.L. 424, 27 L.C.J. 175, 6 L.N. 276 (Circ. Ct.).
Winsmore v. Greenbank (1745), Willes 577, 125 Eng. Rep. 1330 (U.K., Common Pleas).

Newspapers and Magazines

(Published in Montreal unless otherwise noted)
L'Action populaire (Joliette)
L'Action sociale (Quebec City)
Atlanta Constitution (Atlanta, GA)
Awake! (Brooklyn, NY)
Border Cities Star (Windsor, ON)
Bridgeport Herald (Bridgeport, CT)
Calgary Herald (Calgary, AB)
Le Canada
Canadian Jewish Times
Le Canard
Le Constitutionnel (Trois-Rivières)
Le Courrier de St-Hyacinthe (St-Hyacinthe)
La Croix
Daily Province (Vancouver, BC)
Daily Telegraph (Quebec City)
Le Devoir
Druggists' Circular and Chemical Gazette (New York, NY)
L'Électeur (Quebec City)
L'Étendard
L'Étoile du Nord (Joliette)
Eugene City Guard (Eugene, OR)
The Gazette
The Globe (Toronto, ON)
The Item (Sumter, SC)
Lethbridge Herald (Lethbridge, AB)
Maclean's Magazine (Toronto, ON)
Manitoba Free Press (Winnipeg, MB)
Meriden Daily Republican (Meriden, CT)
Meriden Record (Meriden, CT)
La Minerve
Le Monde illustré
Montreal Daily Mail
Montreal Daily Star
Montreal Herald; Montreal Herald and Daily Commercial Gazette
Montreal Witness; Montreal Daily Witness
Le Nationaliste
New York Times (New York, NY)

Ottawa Citizen; Ottawa Daily Citizen; Ottawa Evening Citizen (Ottawa, ON)
Quebec Chronicle (Quebec City)
La Patrie
Le Petit journal
La Presse
Le Prix courant
Sarnia Observer (Sarnia, ON)
Saskatoon Star-Phoenix (Saskatoon, SK)
Saturday Budget (Quebec City)
Sherbrooke Daily Record (Sherbrooke)
Le Soleil (Quebec City)
The Sun (New York, NY)
The Sun (Saint John, NB)
Le Temps
Toronto Daily Star (Toronto, ON)
La Tribune (Sherbrooke)
L'Union des Cantons de l'Est (Arthabaska)
Vancouver Daily World (Vancouver, BC)
La Vérité
Victoria Daily Times (Victoria, BC)

Printed Sources

Abrams, Kathryn. "Emotions in the Mobilization of Rights." *Harvard Civil Rights – Civil Liberties Law Review* 46 (2011): 551–89.

An Abstract of the Criminal Laws That Were in Force in the Province of Quebec in the Time of the French Government, Drawn up by a Select Committee of Canadian Gentlemen, Well Skilled in the Laws of France, and of That Province, by the Desire of the Honourable Guy Carleton, Esquire, Captain-General, and Governour in Chief, of the Said Province. London, 1773.

Adams, Eric M. "Building a Law of Human Rights: *Roncarelli v. Duplessis* in Canadian Constitutional Culture." *McGill Law Journal* 55 (2010): 437–60.

Adams, Eric M. "Errors of Fact and Law: Race, Space, and Hockey in *Christie v. York*." *University of Toronto Law Journal* 62 (2012): 463–97.

Adams, Eric M. "The Idea of Constitutional Rights and the Transformation of Canadian Constitutional Law, 1930–1960." S.J.D. thesis, University of Toronto, 2009.

Ahrens, Heinrich. *Cours de droit naturel ou de philosophie du droit, fait après l'état actuel de cette science en Allemagne.* Paris, 1838.

Annuaire *Lovell* de Montréal et sa banlieu (various titles). Montreal, 1842–1992. http://bibnum2.banq.qc.ca/bna/lovell/.

"À qui appartient le choix du lieu de sépulture, au conjoint survivant ou aux héritiers." *Revue du notariat* 17 (1914): 109–17.

Arnaud, André-Jean. *Essai d'analyse structurale du Code civil français: la règle du jeu dans la paix bourgeoise.* Paris: L.G.D.J., 1973.

Arnaud, André-Jean. *Les origines doctrinales du Code civil français.* Paris: L.G.D.J., 1969.

Aubry, Charles, and Charles Rau. *Cours de droit civil français, traduit de l'allemand de M. C.S. Zachariæ, professeur à l'Université de Heidelberg; revu et augmenté, avec l'agrément de l'auteur.* 5 vols. Strasbourg, 1839–46.

Aubry, Charles, and Charles Rau. *Cours de droit civil français, traduit de l'allemand de M. C.S. Zachariæ.* 2nd ed. 5 vols. Strasbourg, 1843–4.

Aubry, Charles, and Charles Rau. *Cours de droit civil français d'après l'ouvrage allemand de C.-S. Zachariæ.* 3rd ed. 6 vols. Paris, 1856.

Aubry, Charles, and Charles Rau. *Cours de droit civil français d'après la méthode de Zachariæ.* 4th ed. 8 vols. Paris, 1869–79.

Augustine, Charles. *A Commentary on the New Code of Canon Law.* 8 vols. St. Louis, MO: B. Herder, 1918–28.

"Augustus Waterous Agnew, Assoc. M. Am. Soc. C.E." *Transactions of the American Society of Civil Engineers* 81 (1917): 1792–3.

Backhouse, Constance. "Anti-Semitism and the Law in Québec City: The Plamondon Case, 1910–15." In *Transformations in American Legal History: Essays in Honor of Professor Morton J. Horwitz*, vol. 2, edited by Daniel W. Hamilton and Alfred L. Brophy, 303–25. Cambridge, MA: Harvard University Press for Harvard Law School, 2009.

Backhouse, Constance. *Carnal Crimes: Sexual Assault Law in Canada, 1900–1975.* Toronto: Irwin Law for Osgoode Society for Canadian Legal History, 2008.

Backhouse, Constance. *Colour-Coded: A Legal History of Racism in Canada, 1900–1950.* Toronto: University of Toronto Press for Osgoode Society for Canadian Legal History, 1999.

Backhouse, Constance. "Nineteenth-Century Canadian Prostitution Law: Reflection of a Discriminatory Society." *Histoire sociale/Social History* 18 (1985): 387–423.

Backhouse, Constance. "The Tort of Seduction: Fathers and Daughters in Nineteenth Century Canada." *Canadian Journal of Family Law* 10 (1991): 45–80.

Bailey, Martha J. "Servant Girls and Masters: The Tort of Seduction and the Support of Bastards." *Canadian Journal of Family Law* 11 (1991): 137–62.

Bailey, Peter. *Popular Culture and Performance in the Victorian City*. Cambridge: Cambridge University Press, 2003.
Bandes, Susan A., ed. *The Passions of Law*. New York: New York University Press, 1999.
Bandes, Susan A., and Jeremy A. Blumenthal. "Emotion and the Law." *Annual Review of Law and Social Science* 8 (2012): 161–81.
Baud, Jean-Pierre. *L'affaire de la main volée: une histoire juridique du corps*. Paris: Seuil, 1993.
"Beatty v. Cullingworth." *British Medical Journal* (21 November 1896): 1525–6.
Beauchamp, Tom L. "Informed Consent: Its History, Meaning, and Present Challenges." *Cambridge Quarterly of Healthcare Ethics* 20 (2011): 515–23.
Beaussire, Émile. *Les principes du droit*. Paris, 1888.
Beignier, Bernard. *L'honneur et le droit*. Paris: L.G.D.J., 1995.
Belime, William. *Philosophie du droit, ou Cours d'introduction à la science du droit*. 2 vols. Paris, 1844–8.
Berger, Peter. "On the Obsolescence of the Concept of Honor." *Archives européennes de sociologie* 11 (1970): 339–47.
Bertley, Leo W. "The Universal Negro Improvement Association of Montreal, 1917–1979." Ph.D. thesis, Concordia University, 1979.
Beullac, Pierre. *La responsabilité civile dans le droit de la Province de Québec*. Montreal: Wilson & Lafleur, 1948.
Bibaud, François-Maximilien. *Commentaires sur les lois du Bas-Canada, ou Conférences de l'école de droit liée au collège des RR. PP. Jésuites, suivis d'une notice historique*. 2 vols. Montreal, 1859–61.
Bibaud, François-Maximilien. *Exégèse de jurisprudence*. N.p., [1861?].
Bigsby, John J. *The Shoe and Canoe, or Pictures of Travels in the Canadas*. 2 vols. London, 1850.
Blank, Joshua C. "Pitching, Pies and Piety: Early Twentieth Century St. Hedwig's Parish Picnics." *CCHA Historical Studies* 76 (2010): 61–85.
Bliss, Michael. *Plague: A Story of Smallpox in Montreal*. Toronto: HarperCollins, 1991.
Blumenthal, Susanna L. "The Default Legal Person." *UCLA Law Review* 54 (2007): 1135–265.
Blumenthal, Susanna L. *Law and the Modern Mind: Consciousness and Responsibility in American Legal Culture*. Cambridge, MA: Harvard University Press, 2016.
Boistel, Alphonse. *Cours de philosophie du droit*. 2 vols. Paris, 1899.
Botting, Gary. *Fundamental Freedoms and Jehovah's Witnesses*. Calgary: University of Calgary Press, 1993.

Bouchard, Gérard, Jeannette Larouche, and Lise Bergeron. "Donation entre vifs et inégalités sociales au Saguenay: sur la reproduction familiale en contexte de saturation de l'espace agraire." *Revue d'histoire de l'Amérique française* 46 (1993): 443–61.

Bouchel, Laurent. *La bibliothèque ou trésor du droit français*. 1615; Paris, 1671.

Boulanger, Maurice. *De la diffamation et de l'injure envers les particuliers*. Rennes, 1882.

Bradbury, Bettina. *Wife to Widow: Lives, Laws, and Politics in Nineteenth-Century Montreal*. Vancouver: UBC Press, 2011.

Brierley, John E.C., and Roderick A. Macdonald, eds. *Quebec Civil Law: An Introduction to Quebec Private Law*. Toronto: Emond Montgomery, 1993.

Brisson, Jean-Maurice, and Nicholas Kasirer. "The Married Woman in Ascendance, the Mother Country in Retreat: From Legal Colonialism to Legal Nationalism in Quebec Matrimonial Law Reform, 1866–1991." *Manitoba Law Journal* 23 (1996): 406–49.

Brode, Patrick. *Courted and Abandoned: Seduction in Canadian Law*. Toronto: University of Toronto Press for Osgoode Society for Canadian Legal History, 2002.

Brouardel, Paul. *L'exercice de la médecine et le charlatanisme*, Cours de médecine légale de la faculté de médecine de Paris. Paris, 1899.

Brown, R. Blake. "Canada's First Malpractice Crisis: Medical Negligence in the Late Nineteenth Century." *Osgoode Hall Law Journal* 54 (2017): 777–803.

Brown, R. Blake. *A Trying Question: The Jury in Nineteenth-Century Canada*. Toronto: University of Toronto Press for Osgoode Society for Canadian Legal History, 2009.

Bruneau, A.A. *Question de droit: du mariage*. Montreal: G. Ducharme, 1921.

Brunton, Deborah. *The Politics of Vaccination: Practice and Policy in England, Wales, Ireland and Scotland, 1800–1874*. Rochester, NY: University of Rochester Press, 2008.

Buckingham, Janet Epp. *Fighting over God: A Legal and Political History of Religious Freedom in Canada*. Montreal and Kingston: McGill-Queen's University Press, 2014.

Bumsted, J.M., and Wendy J. Owen. "A Note on the Nineteenth Century Law of Seduction." *Dalhousie Law Journal* 19 (1996): 411–16.

C., W.F. "The Property Right in a Corpse." *Albany Law Review* 2 (1933): 122–6.

Calendar of Queen's (College and) University, Kingston, Canada, for the Year 1898–99. Kingston, 1898.

Campbell, Lyndsay. "Race, Upper Canadian Constitutionalism and 'British Justice.'" *Law and History Review* 33 (2015): 41–91.

Campbell, Lyndsay. Review of *Courted and Abandoned*, by Patrick Brode. *Canadian Journal of Women and the Law* 15 (2003): 383–91.

Cantin Cumyn, Madeleine, and Michelle Cumyn, "La notion de biens." In *Mélanges offerts au professeur François Frenette: études portant sur le droit patrimonial*, edited by Sylvio Normand, 127–50. Sainte-Foy, QC: Presses de l'Université Laval, 2006.

Caron, Madeleine. "Le Code civil québécois, instrument de protection des droits et libertés de la personne." *Canadian Bar Review* 56 (1978): 197–232.

Carter, Robert T., and Jessica Forsyth. "Reactions to Racial Discrimination: Emotional Stress and Help-Seeking Behaviors." *Psychological Trauma* 2 (2010): 183–91.

Cassel, Jay. *The Secret Plague: Venereal Disease in Canada 1838–1939*. Toronto: University of Toronto Press, 1987.

Chassan, Joseph-Pierre. *Traité des délits et contraventions de la parole, de l'écriture et de la presse*. 3 vols. Paris, 1837–9.

Chauvaud, Frédéric. "La parole captive: l'interrogatoire judiciaire au XIXe siècle." *Histoire et archives* 1 (1997): 33–60.

Cherrier's Quebec City Directory ... for the Year Ending May 3, 1882, 23rd ed. Quebec City, 1881.

Chiniquy, Charles. *L'Église de Rome est l'ennemie de la Sainte-Vierge et de Jésus-Christ*. Montreal, 1891.

Christie, Nancie. "A 'Painful Dependence': Female Begging Letters and the Familial Economy of Obligation." In *Mapping the Margins: The Family and Social Discipline in Canada, 1700–1975*, edited by Nancy Christie and Michael Gauvreau, 69–102. Montreal and Kingston: McGill-Queen's University Press, 2004.

Claxton, A.G. Brooke. "The Discretionary Powers of a Surgeon." *Montreal Medical Journal* 28 (1899): 184–92.

Clément, Dominique. *Canada's Rights Revolution: Social Movements and Social Change, 1937–82*. Vancouver: UBC Press, 2008.

Cliche, Marie-Aimée. "L'évolution des clauses religieuses traditionnelles dans les testaments de la région de Québec au XIXe siècle." In *Religion populaire, religion de clercs?*, edited by Benoît Lacroix and Jean Simard, 365–90. Quebec City: Institut québécois de recherche sur la culture, 1985.

Cliche, Marie-Aimée. "Morale chrétienne et 'double standard sexuel': les filles-mères à l'hôpital de la Miséricorde à Québec, 1874–1972." *Histoire sociale/Social History* 24, no. 47 (1991): 85–125.

Cliche, Marie-Aimée. "Les séparations de corps dans le district judiciaire de Montréal de 1900 à 1930." *Canadian Journal of Law and Society* 12, no. 1 (1997): 71–100.

Clokie, H. McD. "The Preservation of Civil Liberties." *Canadian Journal of Economics and Political Science* 13 (1947): 208–32.

[Cocatrix, Pierre.] *La science du confesseur, ou conférences ecclésiastiques sur le sacrement de pénitence par une société de prêtres réfugiés en Allemagne.* 5 vols. Lille, 1830.

Cochran, Patricia. *Common Sense and Legal Judgment: Community Knowledge, Political Power, and Rhetorical Practice.* Montreal and Kingston: McGill-Queen's University Press, 2017.

Cochrane, William, and J. Castell Hopkins. *The Canadian Album: Men of Canada.* 5 vols. Brantford, ON, and Toronto, 1891–5.

Colin, Ambroise. *Des fiançailles: histoire du droit et droit français des fiançailles et des promesses de mariage.* Paris, 1887.

"College of Physicians and Surgeons of Lower Canada." *Canada Medical and Surgical Journal* 2 (1874): 575–6.

Colombine [Éva Circé-Côté]. *Bleu, blanc, rouge: poésies, paysages, causeries.* Montreal: Deom frères, 1903.

Constant, Jean-François, and Michel Ducharme, eds. *Liberalism and Hegemony: Debating the Canadian Liberal Revolution.* Toronto: University of Toronto Press, 2009.

Conway, Heather. "Dead, but Not Buried: Bodies, Burial and Family Conflicts." *Legal Studies* 23 (2003): 423–52.

Conway, Heather. *The Law and the Dead.* London: Routledge, 2016.

Coombe, Rosemary J. "'The Most Disgusting, Disgraceful and Inequitous Proceeding in Our Law': The Action for Breach of Promise of Marriage in Nineteenth-Century Ontario." *University of Toronto Law Journal* 38 (1988): 64–108.

Corrigan, John. *Business of the Heart: Religion and Emotion in the Nineteenth Century.* Berkeley: University of California Press, 2002.

Côté, Liette. "La vieillesse au Québec au XIXe siècle: le cas de Saint-Hyacinthe, 1861–1891." M.A. thesis, Université de Sherbrooke, 1998.

Courville, Serge. *Quebec: A Historical Geography.* Translated by Richard Howard. Vancouver: UBC Press, 2008.

Crépeau, Paul-André. *La réforme du droit civil canadien: une certaine conception de la recodification, 1965–1977.* Montreal: Thémis, 2003.

Crivelli, J.-L. *De la contrainte par corps, considérée sous les rapports de la morale, de la religion, du droit naturel et du droit civil, et dans l'intérêt de l'humanité en général.* Paris, 1830.

Cross, Michael S. "The Laws Are Like Cobwebs: Popular Resistance to Authority in Mid-Nineteenth-Century British North America." *Dalhousie Law Journal* 8 (1984): 103–23.

Curry, Lynne, ed. *The Human Body on Trial: A Sourcebook with Cases, Laws, and Documents*. Indianapolis: Hackett, 2002.

Dagenais, Michèle. *Faire et fuir la ville: espaces publics de culture et de loisirs à Montréal et Toronto, XIXe et XXe siècles*. Sainte-Foy, QC: Presses de l'Université Laval, 2006.

Dareau, François. *Traité des injures dans l'ordre judiciaire: Ouvrage qui renferme particulièrement la Jurisprudence du Petit-Criminel*. Paris, 1775.

Davis, Natalie Zemon. *Fiction in the Archives: Pardon Tales and Their Tellers in Sixteenth Century France*. Stanford: Stanford University Press, 1987.

Dawson, S.E. *Hand-Book for the City of Montreal and Its Environs*. Montreal, 1888.

Débats de l'Assemblée législative, 18th Legislature, 4th Session, vol. 3 (1935), edited by Donald Chouinard. Quebec City: Section de l'indexation et de l'édition des débats reconstitués, Bibliothèque de l'Assemblée nationale, 2010.

Débats de l'Assemblée législative, 21st Legislature, 2nd Session, vol. 1 (1941), edited by Daniel Machabée and Martin Pelletier. Quebec City: Section de l'indexation et de l'édition des débats reconstitués, Bibliothèque de l'Assemblée nationale, 2012.

de Lorimier, Charles-C., and Charles A. Vilbon. *La bibliothèque du Code civil de la Province de Québec (ci-devant Bas-Canada)*. 21 vols. Montreal, 1871–90.

Demogue, René. *De la réparation civile des délits (étude de droit et de législation)*. Paris, 1898.

Demolombe, Charles. *Cours de code civil*. 31 vols. Paris, 1845–82.

Demolombe, Charles. *Cours de Code Napoléon*. Vol. 3, *Traité du mariage et de la séparation de corps*, t. 1. Paris, 1874.

Denisart, Jean-Baptiste. *Collection de décisions nouvelles et de notions relatives à la jurisprudence actuelle*. 3 vols. Paris, 1763–4.

Dennett, Andrea Stulman. *Weird and Wonderful: The Dime Museum in America*. New York: New York University Press, 1997.

Deroussin, David. "Personnalité et 'biens innés' chez Aubry et Rau: entre nature et abstraction." In *Aubry et Rau: leurs œuvres, leurs enseignements*, edited by Jean-Michel Poughon, 91–110. Strasbourg: Presses universitaires de Strasbourg, 2006.

Descamps, Olivier. *Les origines de la responsabilité pour faute personnelle dans le Code civil de 1804*. Paris: L.G.D.J., 2005.

Descheemaeker, Eric. *The Division of Wrongs: A Historical Comparative Study*. Oxford: Oxford University Press, 2009.

Descheemaeker, Eric, and Helen Scott, eds. *Iniuria and the Common Law*. Oxford: Hart, 2014.

Desmet, Jean. *Du consentement des parents en matière de mariage*. Lille, 1892.

Des Rivières Beaubien, Henry. *Traité sur les lois civiles du Bas-Canada*. 3 vols. Montreal, 1832–3.
Dictionary of Canadian Biography, edited by G.W. Brown et al. Toronto: University of Toronto Press, 1966–. http://www.biographi.ca.
Dierkins, Raphaël. *Les droits sur le corps et le cadavre de l'homme*. Paris: Masson, 1966.
Dixon, Thomas. *From Passions to Emotions: The Creation of a Secular Psychological Category*. Cambridge: Cambridge University Press, 2003.
Domat, Jean. *Les loix civiles dans leur ordre naturel; le droit public, et legum delectus*. Nouvelle édition, 2 vols. Paris, 1777.
Donovan, James M. "Culture and the Courts in France: The *Plaidoirie Sentimentale* in the Nineteenth and Early Twentieth Centuries." *Law and History Review* 35 (2017): 789–828.
Dorville, Armand. "La réparation pécuniaire du dommage moral." *Canadian Bar Review* 6 (1928): 670–8.
Dubber, Markus Dirk. "Comparative Criminal Law." In *The Oxford Handbook of Comparative Law*, edited by Mathias Reimann and Reinhard Zimmerman, 1327–62. Oxford: Oxford University Press, 2008.
Dubinsky, Karen. "'Maidenly Girls' or 'Designing Women'? The Crime of Seduction in Turn-of-the-Century Ontario." In *Gender Conflicts: New Essays in Women's History*, edited by Franca Iacovetta and Mariana Valverde, 27–66. Toronto: University of Toronto Press, 1992.
Duclos, R.-P. *Histoire du protestantisme français au Canada et aux États-Unis*. 2 vols. Lausanne: Georges Bridel; Paris: Fischbacher, [1913].
Dumont, Albert. *Étude sur le consentement des parents au mariage de leurs enfants*. Paris: A. Chevalier-Maresq, 1903.
Durbach, Nadja. *Bodily Matters: The Anti-Vaccination Movement in England, 1853–1907*. Durham, NC: Duke University Press, 2005.
Eden Musée, Montreal, Galeries historiques, Catalogue, 10 cents, Musée Eden, Montréal. [Montreal], n.d.
Egerton, George. "Entering the Age of Human Rights: Religion, Politics, and Canadian Liberalism, 1945–50." *Canadian Historical Review* 85 (2004): 451–79.
Eustace, Nicole, Eugenia Lean, Julie Livingston, Jan Plamper, William M. Reddy, and Barbara H. Rosenwein. "*AHR* Conversation: The Historical Study of Emotions." *American Historical Review* 117 (2012): 1487–531.
Eyerman, Ron. "How Social Movements Move: Emotions and Social Movements." In *Emotions and Social Movements*, edited by Helena Flam and Debra King, 41–56. London: Routledge, 2005.
Farge, Arlette. "The Honor and Secrecy of Families." In *Passions of the Renaissance*, translated by Arthur Goldhammer, edited by Roger Chartier.

Vol. 3 of *A History of Private Life*, edited by Philippe Ariès and Georges Duby, 571–607. Cambridge, MA: Belknap Press of Harvard University Press, 1989.

Farley, M., Peter Keating, and Othmar Keel. "La vaccination à Montréal dans la seconde moitié du 19e siècle: pratiques, obstacles et résistances." In *Sciences et médecine au Québec: perspectives sociohistoriques*, edited by Marcel Fournier, Y. Gingras, and Othmar Keel, 87–127. Quebec City: Institut québécois de recherche sur la culture, 1987.

Fauteux, Ægidius. *Le duel au Canada*. Montreal: Éditions du Zodiaque, 1934.

Febvre, Lucien. "La sensibilité et l'histoire: comment reconstituer la vie affective d'autrefois?" *Annales d'histoire sociale* 3 (1941): 5–20.

Febvre, Lucien. "Sensibility and History: How to Reconstitute the Emotional Life of the Past." Translated by K. Folca. In *A New Kind of History: From the Writings of Febvre*, edited by Peter Burke, 12–26. New York: Harper & Row, 1973.

Fernandez, Angela, and Markus D. Dubber, eds. *Law Books in Action: Essays on the Anglo-American Legal Treatise*. Oxford: Hart, 2012.

Ferrière, Claude-Joseph de. *Dictionnaire de droit et de pratique*. Nouvelle édition by M. ***. 2 vols. Paris, 1769.

Fingard, Judith. "Race and Respectability in Victorian Halifax." *Journal of Imperial and Commonwealth History* 20 (1992): 169–95.

Finger, August. "Rechtsgut oder rechtlich geschütztes Interesse: Zur Lehre vom Objecte des Verbrechens." *Der Gerichtssaal* 40 (1888): 139–57.

Folkard, Henry Coleman. *Folkard's Starkie on Slander and Libel*. 4th ed. New York, 1877.

Foote, Martha L. *Law Reporting and Legal Publishing in Canada: A History*. Kingston, ON: Canadian Association of Law Libraries, 1997.

Forbes, Thomas R. "A Jury of Matrons." *Medical History* 32 (1988): 23–33.

Foster's Kingston Directory, from July, 1900, to July, 1901. Vol. 7. Toronto: J.G. Foster, [1900].

Foster's Kingston Directory from July, 1904, to July, 1905. 11th ed. Toronto: J.G. Foster, 1904.

Foster's Kingston Directory from July, 1905, to July, 1906. 12th ed. Toronto: J.G. Foster, 1905.

Fournel, Jean-François. *Traité de l'adultère, considéré dans l'ordre judiciaire*. Paris, 1778.

Fraser, David. "The Blood Libel in North America: Jews, Law, and Citizenship in the Early 20th Century." *Law and Literature* 28 (2016): 33–85.

Fraser, David. *"Honorary Protestants": The Jewish School Question in Montreal, 1867–1997*. Toronto: University of Toronto Press for Osgoode Society for Canadian Legal History, 2015.

Fraser, John. *Canadian Pen and Ink Sketches*. Montreal, 1890.
Freund, Michaela. "The Politics of Naming: Constructing Prostitutes and Regulating Women in Vancouver, 1939–45." In *Regulating Lives: Historical Essays on the State, Society, the Individual, and the Law*, edited by John McLaren, Robert Menzies, and Dorothy E. Chunn, 231–58. Vancouver: UBC Press, 2002.
Frevert, Ute. "Defining Emotions: Concepts and Debates over Three Centuries." In *Emotional Lexicons: Continuity and Change in the Vocabulary of Feeling 1700–2000*, edited by Ute Frevert, Christian Bailey, Pascal Eitler, Benno Gammerl, Bettina Hitzer, Margrit Pernau, Monique Scheer, Anne Schmidt, and Nina Verheyen, 1–31. Oxford: Oxford University Press, 2014.
Frevert, Ute. *Emotions in History: Lost and Found*. Budapest: Central European University Press, 2011.
Frier, Bruce W. *A Casebook on the Roman Law of Delict*. Atlanta: Scholars' Press, 1989.
Frohlich, Louis D., and Charles Schwartz. *The Law of Motion Pictures*. New York: Baker, Voorhis, 1918.
Fromageot, Henri. *De la faute comme source de la responsabilité en droit privé*. Paris, 1891.
Fuchs, Rachel G. *Contested Paternity: Constructing Families in Modern France*. Baltimore: Johns Hopkins University Press, 2008.
Fuzier-Herman, Édouard, ed. *Répertoire général alphabétique du droit français*. 37 vols. Paris, 1886–1906.
Fyson, Donald. "Minority Groups and the Law in Quebec, 1760–1867." In *Essays in the History of Canadian Law: Volume XI – Quebec and the Canadas*, edited by G. Blaine Baker and Donald Fyson, 278–329. Toronto: University of Toronto Press for Osgoode Society for Canadian Legal History, 2013.
Gagnon, Hervé. "Divertissement et patriotisme: la genèse des musées d'histoire à Montréal au XIXe siècle." *Revue d'histoire de l'Amérique française* 48 (1995): 321–32.
Gagnon, Serge. *Mariage et famille au temps de Papineau*. Sainte-Foy, QC: Presses de l'Université Laval, 1993.
Gagnon, Serge. *Mourir hier et aujourd'hui: de la mort chrétienne dans la campagne québécoise au XIXe siècle à la mort technicisée dans la cité sans Dieu*. Quebec City: Presses de l'Université Laval, 1987.
Gagnon, Serge. *Plaisir d'amour et crainte de Dieu: Sexualité et confession au Bas-Canada*. Sainte-Foy, QC: Presses de l'Université Laval, 1990.
Gallichan, Gilles. "La Bibliothèque du Barreau de Québec: l'émergence d'une institution." *Cahiers de droit* 34 (1993): 125–52.
Galush, William. "The Unremembered Movement: Abstinence among Polish Americans." *Polish American Studies* 63, no. 2 (2006): 13–22.

Gay, Daniel. *Les noirs du Québec 1629–1900*. Sillery, QC: Septentrion, 2004.
General Regulations Royal Military College of Canada, Kingston, Ont., February, 1888. Ottawa, 1888.
[Genet, François.] *Théologie morale, ou résolution des cas de conscience selon l'Écriture-Sainte, les Canons, & les Saints Pères*. Nouvelle édition, 7 vols. Paris, 1703.
Gerber, Matthew. "On the Contested Margins of the Family: Bastardy and Legitimation by Royal Rescript in Eighteenth-Century France." In *Family, Gender, and Law in Early Modern France*, edited by Suzanne Desan and Jeffrey Merrick, 223–64. University Park: Pennsylvania State University Press, 2009.
Gérin-Lajoie, Antoine. *Catéchisme politique; ou éléments du droit public et constitutionnel du Canada*. Montreal, 1851.
Gewirtz, Paul. "Narrative and Rhetoric in the Law." In *Law's Stories: Narrative and Rhetoric in the Law*, edited by Peter Brooks and Paul Gewirtz, 2–13. New Haven, CT: Yale University Press, 1996.
Gill, Ritu, and Kimberly Matheson. "Responses to Discrimination: The Role of Emotion and Expectations for Emotional Regulation." *Personality and Social Psychology Bulletin* 32 (2006): 149–61.
Girard, Philip. "Land Law, Liberalism, and the Agrarian Ideal: British North America, 1750–1920." In *Despotic Dominion: Property Rights in British Settler Societies*, edited by John McLaren, A.R. Buck, and Nancy E. Wright, 120–43. Vancouver: UBC Press, 2005.
Girard, Philip. "Why Canada Has No Family Policy: Lessons from France and Italy." *Osgoode Hall Law Journal* 32 (1994): 579–611.
Girouard, Désiré. "Church and State." *Revue critique de législation et de jurisprudence du Canada* 1 (1871): 431–56; and 2 (1872): 1–32, 113–46.
Givord, François. *La réparation du préjudice moral*. Paris: Dalloz, 1938.
Glasbeek, Amanda. *Feminized Justice: The Toronto Women's Court, 1913–34*. Vancouver: UBC Press, 2009.
Glenn, H. Patrick. "Quebec: Mixité and Monism." In *Studies in Legal Systems: Mixed and Mixing*, edited by Esin Örücü, Elspeth Attwooll, and Sean Coyle, 1–15. The Hague: Kluwer Law International, 1996.
Glenn, H. Patrick. "Le secret de la vie privée en droit québécois." *Revue générale de droit* 5 (1974): 24–42.
Gober Agnew, May. "Calculated Calls: How the Cadets Got Even with Ivay." *Canadian Magazine of Politics, Science, Art and Literature* 28 (1907): 90–2.
Goodman, Nan. *Shifting the Blame: Literature, Law, and the Theory of Accidents in Nineteenth-Century America*. Princeton: Princeton University Press, 1998.

Gossage, Peter. "*La marâtre*: Marie-Anne Houde and the Myth of the Wicked Stepmother in Quebec." *Canadian Historical Review* 76 (1995): 563–97.
Gossage, Peter. "On Dads and Damages: Looking for the 'Priceless Child' and the 'Manly Modern' in Quebec's Civil Courts, 1921–1960." *Histoire sociale/ Social History* 49 (2016): 603–23.
Gossage, Peter. "Tangled Webs: Remarriage and Family Conflict in Nineteenth-Century Quebec." In *Family Matters: Papers in Post-Confederation Canadian Family History*, edited by Lori Chambers and Edgar-André Montigny, 355–76. Toronto: Canadian Scholars, 1998.
Grand, P. *Diffamation envers les morts*. Paris, 1860.
Greenhill, Pauline. *Make the Night Hideous: Four English-Canadian Charivaris, 1881–1940*. Toronto: University of Toronto Press, 2010.
Greenwood, F. Murray. "Lower Canada (Quebec): Transformation of Civil Law, from Higher Morality to Autonomous Will, 1774–1866." *Manitoba Law Journal* 23 (1996): 132–82.
Greenwood, F. Murray, and Beverley Boissery. *Uncertain Justice: Canadian Women and Capital Punishment, 1754–1953*. Toronto: Dundurn for Osgoode Society for Canadian Legal History, 2000.
Greer, Allan. "From Folklore to Revolution: Charivaris and the Lower Canadian Rebellion of 1837." *Social History* 15 (1990): 25–43.
Grellet-Dumazeau, Théodore. *Traité de la diffamation, de l'injure et de l'outrage*. 2 vols. Riom, 1847.
Guyot, Joseph-Nicolas. *Répertoire universel et raisonné de jurisprudence civile, criminelle, canonique et bénéficiale*. 17 vols. Paris, 1784–5.
Hakim, Nader. *L'autorité de la doctrine civiliste française au XIXe siècle*. Paris: L.G.D.J., 2002.
Handford, Peter. "Lord Campbell and the Fatal Accidents Act." *Law Quarterly Review* 129 (2013): 420–49.
Hardouin, Henri. *Essai sur l'abolition de la contrainte par corps*. Paris, 1874.
Hardy, René. "Le charivari dans la sociabilité rurale québécoise au XIXe siècle." In *De la sociabilité: spécificité et mutations*, edited by Roger Levasseur, 59–72. Montreal: Boréal, 1990.
Hardy, René. "Le charivari: divulguer et sanctionner la vie privée?" In *Discours et pratiques de l'intime*, edited by Manon Brunet and Serge Gagnon, 50–69. Quebec City: Institut québécois de recherche sur la culture, 1993.
Hardy, René. *Charivari et justice populaire au Québec*. Quebec City: Septentrion, 2015.
Harrington, Joel F. *The Faithful Executioner: Life and Death, Honor and Shame in the Turbulent Sixteenth Century*. New York: Picador, 2014.

Hart, E.I. *Wake Up! Montreal! Commercialized Vice and Its Contributories.* Montreal: Witness, 1919.
Heaman, E.A. "Rights Talk and the Liberal Order Framework." In *Liberalism and Hegemony: Debating the Canadian Liberal Revolution*, edited by Jean-François Constant and Michel Ducharme, 147–75. Toronto: University of Toronto Press, 2009.
Henderson, Greig. *Creating Legal Worlds: Story and Style in a Culture of Argument.* Toronto: University of Toronto Press, 2015.
Heron, Craig. *Booze: A Distilled History.* Toronto: Between the Lines, 2003.
Herrmann, Manfred. *Der Schutz der Persönlichkeit in der Rechtslehre des 16.–18. Jahrhunderts.* Stuttgart: W. Kohlhammer, 1968.
Hoeflich, Michael H. *Legal Publishing in Antebellum America.* New York: Cambridge University Press, 2010.
Hoeflich, Michael H. "*Plus ça change, plus c'est la même chose*: The Integration of Theory and Practice in Legal Education." *Temple Law Review* 66 (1993): 123–41.
Hohfeld, Wesley N. *Fundamental Legal Conceptions as Applied in Judicial Reasoning*, edited by Walter Wheeler Cook. New Haven, CT: Yale University Press, 1920.
The Holy Bible Translated from the Latin Vulgate. New York: P.J. Kennedy & Sons, 1914.
How, W. Glen. "The Case for a Canadian Bill of Rights." *Canadian Bar Review* 26 (1948): 759–96.
Howell, P.A. *The Judicial Committee of the Privy Council 1833–1876: Its Origins, Structure and Development.* Cambridge: Cambridge University Press, 1979.
Howes, David. "La domestication de la pensée juridique québécoise." *Anthropologie et sociétés* 13 (1989): 103–25.
Howes, David. "From Polyjurality to Monojurality: The Transformation of Quebec Law, 1875–1929." *McGill Law Journal* 32 (1987): 523–58.
Hunter, Ian A. "Civil Actions for Discrimination." *Canadian Bar Review* 55 (1977): 106–30.
Hunter, Ian A. "Human Rights Legislation in Canada: Its Origin, Development and Interpretation." *University of Western Ontario Law Review* 15 (1976): 21–58.
Iacovetta, Franca, and Wendy Mitchinson, eds. *On the Case: Explorations in Social History.* Toronto: University of Toronto Press, 1998.
Ibhawoh, Bonny. *Imperial Justice: Africans in Empire's Court.* Oxford: Oxford University Press, 2013.
Ingram, Martin. "Law, Litigants, and the Construction of 'Honour': Slander Suits in Early Modern England." In *The Moral World of the Law*, edited by Peter Coss, 134–60. Cambridge: Cambridge University Press, 2000.

Israel, Wilfred Emmerson. "The Montreal Negro Community." M.A. thesis, McGill University, 1928.
Jackson, Percival E. *The Law of Cadavers and of Burial and Burial Places*. New York: Prentice-Hall, 1936.
Jalland, Pat. *Death in the Victorian Family*. Oxford: Oxford University Press, 1996.
Jetté, Louis-Amable. "Cours Jetté." *Revue du droit* 1–17 (1922–39): passim.
Jobin, Pierre-Gabriel. "L'influence de la doctrine française sur le droit civil québécois: le rapprochement et l'éloignement de deux continents." *Revue internationale de droit comparé* 44 (1992): 381–408.
Jones, Shawn C.T., Daniel B. Lee, Ashly L. Gaskin, and Enrique W. Neblett, Jr. "Emotional Response Profiles to Racial Discrimination: Does Racial Identity Predict Affective Patterns?" *Journal of Black Psychology* 40 (2014): 334–58.
Josserand, Louis. *De l'abus des droits*. Paris: Arthur Rousseau, 1905.
Kaplan, William. *State and Salvation: The Jehovah's Witnesses and Their Fight for Civil Rights*. Toronto: University of Toronto Press, 1989.
Kary, Joseph. "The Constitutionalization of Quebec Libel Law, 1848–2004." *Osgoode Hall Law Journal* 42 (2004): 229–70.
Kasirer, Nicholas. "Honour Bound." *McGill Law Journal* 47 (2002): 237–59.
Kasirer, Nicholas. "Translating Part of France's Legal Heritage: Aubry and Rau on the Patrimoine." *Revue générale de droit* 38 (2008): 453–93.
Kelley, Donald R. "Gaius Noster: Substructures of Western Social Thought." *American Historical Review* 84 (1979): 619–48.
Kenny, Stephen. "'Cahots' and Catcalls: An Episode of Popular Resistance in Lower Canada at the Outset of the Union." *Canadian Historical Review* 65 (1984): 184–208.
Kolish, Evelyn. "Imprisonment for Debt in Lower Canada, 1791–1840." *McGill Law Journal* 32 (1987): 602–35.
Korobkin, Laura Hanft. *Criminal Conversations: Sentimentality and Nineteenth-Century Legal Stories of Adultery*. New York: Columbia University Press, 1998.
Kounine, Laura. "Emotions, Mind, and Body on Trial: A Cross-Cultural Perspective." *Journal of Social History* 51 (2017): 219–30.
Kukushkin, Vadim. *From Peasants to Labourers: Ukrainian and Belarusan Immigration from the Russian Empire to Canada*. Montreal and Kingston: McGill-Queen's University Press, 2007.
Labbée, Xavier. *Condition juridique du corps humain avant la naissance et après la mort*. Lille: Presses universitaires de Lille, 1990.
Lachance, André. "Une étude de mentalité: les injures verbales au Canada au XVIIIe siècle (1712–1748)." *Revue d'histoire de l'Amérique française* 31 (1977): 229–38.

Lachance, André, and Sylvie Savoie. "Violence, Marriage, and Family Honour: Aspects of the Legal Regulation of Marriage in New France." In *Essays in the History of Canadian Law: Volume V – Crime and Criminal Justice*, edited by Jim Phillips, Tina Loo, and Susan Lewthwaite, 143–73. Toronto: University of Toronto Press for Osgoode Society for Canadian Legal History, 1994.

Lambertson, Ross. *Repression and Resistance: Canadian Human Rights Activists, 1930–1960*. Toronto: University of Toronto Press, 2005.

Lamonde, Yvan, and Raymond Montpetit. *Le Parc Sohmer de Montréal, 1889–1919: un lieu populaire de culture urbaine*. Quebec City: Institut québécois de recherche sur la culture, 1986.

Langelier, François. *Cours de droit civil de la province de Québec*. 6 vols. Montreal: Wilson & Lafleur, 1905–11.

Langevin, Louise. "L'œuvre de Claire L'Heureux-Dubé: une lecture féministe de l'arrêt *Augustus* c. *Gosset*." *Canadian Journal of Women and the Law* 15 (2003): 122–37.

Lapointe, Mathieu. *Nettoyer Montréal: les campagnes de moralité publique 1940–1954*. Montreal: Septentrion, 2014.

Lassime, M. *Traité de la contrainte par corps*. Paris, 1863.

Laurent, François. *Principes de droit civil*. 4th ed., 33 vols. Brussels, 1887.

Laurent, François. *Principes de droit civil français*. 5th ed., 33 vols. Brussels, 1893.

Lefebvre de Bellefeuille, Édouard. "Code civil du Bas-Canada: législation sur le mariage." *Revue canadienne* 1 (1864): 602–19, 654–72, 731–48; and 2 (1865): 30–44.

Lefebvre de Bellefeuille, Édouard. "Une question de mariage." *Revue canadienne* 4 (1867): 838–49.

Lefebvre-Teillard, Anne. *Introduction historique au droit des personnes et de la famille*. Paris: Presses Universitaires de France, 1996.

Légaré, Jacques, and Jean-François Naud. "The Dynamics of Household Structure in the Event of the Father's Death: Québec City in the 18th Century." *History of the Family* 6 (2001): 519–29.

Lemire, Maurice, and Denis Saint-Jacques, eds. *La vie littéraire au Québec*. Vol. 5. Sainte-Foy, QC: Presses de l'Université Laval, 2005.

Leveillé, Jules. "De l'abolition de la contrainte par corps." *Revue pratique de droit français* 22 (1866): 305–32.

Lever, Alison. "Honour as a Red Herring." *Critique of Anthropology* 6, no. 3 (1986): 83–106.

Lévesque, Andrée. "Le bordel: milieu de travail contrôlé." *Labour/Le Travail* 20 (1987): 13–32.

Lévesque, Andrée. "Éteindre le Red Light: les réformateurs et la prostitution à Montréal entre 1865 et 1925." *Urban History Review* 17 (1989): 191–201.
Lévesque, Andrée. *La norme et les déviantes: des femmes au Québec pendant l'entre-deux-guerres.* Montreal: Les éditions du remue-ménage, 1989.
Levieil de la Marsonnière, Jules. *Histoire de la contrainte par corps.* Paris, 1843.
Levine, Philippa. *Prostitution, Race, and Politics: Policing Venereal Disease in the British Empire.* New York: Routledge, 2003.
"Libel Suits against Catholic Papers." *Catholic Fortnightly Review* 19 (1912): 423.
Loranger, T.J.J. *Commentaire sur le Code civil du Bas-Canada.* 2 vols. Montreal, 1873–9.
Lougheed, Richard. *The Controversial Conversion of Charles Chiniquy.* Toronto: Clements Academic, 2008.
Lower, Arthur R.M. "Some Reflections on a Bill of Rights." *Fortnightly Law Journal* 16 (1947): 216–18, 234–7.
Macdonald, Roderick A. "Was Duplessis Right?" *McGill Law Journal* 55 (2010): 401–36.
MacLennan, Christopher. *Toward the Charter: Canadians and the Demand for a National Bill of Rights, 1929–1960.* Montreal and Kingston: McGill-Queen's University Press, 2003.
MacLeod, Roderick, and Mary Anne Poutanen. "Little Fists for Social Justice: Anti-Semitism, Community, and Montréal's Aberdeen School Strike, 1913." *Labour/Le Travail* 70 (2012): 61–99.
Margolis, Rebecca. *Jewish Roots, Canadian Soil: Yiddish Culture in Montreal, 1905–1945.* Montreal and Kingston: McGill-Queen's University Press, 2011.
Maroney, Terry A. "Law and Emotion: A Proposed Taxonomy of an Emerging Field." *Law and Human Behavior* 30 (2006): 119–42.
Martel, Jean-François. "Les pratiques funéraires en usage dans les milieux populaires ruraux et urbains de la Mauricie entre 1945 et 1998." M.A. thesis, Université du Québec à Trois-Rivières, 2001.
Martschukat, Jürgen. "A Horrifying Experience? Public Executions and the Emotional Spectator in the New Republic." In *Emotions in American History: An International Assessment*, edited by Jessica Geinow-Hecht, 181–200. New York: Berghahn Books, 2010.
Massicotte, Édouard-Zotique. "Brève histoire du Parc Sohmer." *Cahiers des dix* 11 (1946): 97–117.
Massicotte, Édouard-Zotique. "Le charivari au Canada." *Bulletin des recherches historiques* 32 (1926): 712–25.
Mathieu, Sarah-Jane. *North of the Color Line: Migration and Black Resistance in Canada, 1870–1955.* Chapel Hill: University of North Carolina Press, 2010.

Matt, Susan J., and Peter N. Stearns, eds. *Doing Emotions History*. Urbana: University of Illinois Press, 2014.

Mauroy, Hervé. "L'amour-propre: une analyse théorique et historique." *Revue européenne des sciences sociales* 52, no. 2 (2014): 73–104.

Mayne, John D. *A Treatise on the Law of Damages: Comprising Their Measure, the Mode in Which They Are Assessed and Reviewed, the Practice of Granting New Trials, and the Law of Set-Off*. 2nd ed. by Lumley Smith. London, 1872.

Mayrand, Albert. *L'inviolabilité de la personne humaine*. Montreal: Wilson & Lafleur, 1975.

McCord, Thomas. *Synopsis of the Changes in the Law Effected by the Civil Code of Lower Canada*. Ottawa, 1866.

McKay, Ian. "The Liberal Order Framework: A Prospectus for a Reconnaissance of Canadian History." *Canadian Historical Review* 81 (2000): 617–45.

McLaren, Angus. *Sexual Blackmail: A Modern History*. Cambridge, MA: Harvard University Press, 2002.

McMahon, Darrin M. "Finding Joy in the History of Emotions." In *Doing Emotions History*, edited by Susan J. Matt and Peter N. Stearns, 103–19. Urbana: University of Illinois Press, 2014.

McNairn, Jeffrey L. "'The Common Sympathies of Our Nature': Moral Sentiments, Emotional Economies, and Imprisonment for Debt in Upper Canada." *Histoire sociale/Social History* 49 (2016): 49–71.

McNairn, Jeffrey L. "'A Just and Obvious Distinction': The Meaning of Imprisonment for Debt and the Criminal Law in Upper Canada's Age of Reform." In *Essays in the History of Canadian Law: Volume XI – Quebec and the Canadas*, edited by G. Blaine Baker and Donald Fyson, 187–234. Toronto: University of Toronto Press for Osgoode Society for Canadian Legal History, 2013.

Memoirs of Georgia Containing Historical Accounts of the State's Civil, Military, Industrial and Professional Interests, and Personal Sketches of Many of Its People. 2 vols. Atlanta, 1895.

Mielziner, M. *The Jewish Law of Marriage and Divorce in Ancient and Modern Times*. Cincinnati, 1884.

Mignault, Pierre-Basile. "L'avenir de notre droit civil." *Revue du droit* 1 (1922): 56–65, 104–16.

Mignault, Pierre-Basile. *Le droit civil canadien basé sur les "Répétitions écrites sur le code civil" de Frédéric Mourlon avec revue de la jurisprudence de nos tribunaux*. 9 vols. Montreal, 1895–1916.

Mignault, Pierre-Basile. *Le droit paroissial*. Montreal, 1893.

Mignault, Pierre-Basile. "The Modern Conception of Civil Responsibility: A Study of Comparative Law." *Journal of the Society for Comparative Legislation and International Law* n.s. 11 (1910): 102–13.
Mignault, Pierre-Basile. "The Modern Evolution of Civil Responsibility." *Canadian Bar Review* 5 (1927): 1–18.
Milka, Amy, and David Lemmings. "Narratives of Feeling and Majesty: Mediated Emotions in the Eighteenth-Century Criminal Courtroom." *Journal of Legal History* 38 (2017): 155–78.
Miller, William Ian. *Humiliation and Other Essays on Honor, Social Discomfort, and Violence*. Ithaca, NY: Cornell University Press, 1993.
Millman, Brock. *Polarity, Patriotism, and Dissent in Great War Canada, 1914–1919*. Toronto: University of Toronto Press, 2016.
"A Mistake Case in Court." *Druggists' Circular and Chemical Gazette* 35, no. 11 (November 1891): 241.
Molinario, Dennis G. *An Exceptional Law: Section 98 and the Emergency State, 1919–1936*. Toronto: University of Toronto Press for Osgoode Society for Canadian Legal History, 2017.
Monnier, G.-F. *Le grand don de Dieu à la terre: cours complet de religion comprenant le dogme, la morale, les sacrements et la liturgie*. 3 vols. Lyons, 1861.
Moosheimer, Thomas. *Die actio iniuriarum aestimatoria im 18. und 19. Jahrhundert: Eine Untersuchung zu den Gründen ihrer Abschaffung*. Tübingen: Mohr Siebeck, 1997.
Moran, Rachel F. "Law and Emotion, Love and Hate." *Journal of Contemporary Legal Issues* 11 (2001): 747–84.
Morel, André. "L'émergence du nouvel ordre juridique instauré par le Code civil du Bas Canada (1866–1890)." In *Le nouvel Code civil: interprétation et application. Les Journées Maximilien-Caron 1992*, 49–63. Montreal: Thémis, 1993.
Morel, André. "L'enfant sans famille: de l'ancien droit au nouveau *Code civil*." In *Entre surveillance et compassion: l'évolution de la protection de l'enfance au Québec, des origines à nos jours*, edited by Renée Joyal, 7–34. Sainte-Foy: Presses de l'Université du Québec, 2000.
Morgan, Cecilia. "'In Search of the Phantom Misnamed Honour': Duelling in Upper Canada." *Canadian Historical Review* 76 (1995): 529–62.
Morgan, Henry J. *The Canadian Men and Women of the Time: A Handbook of Canadian Biography*. Toronto, 1898.
Morin, Michel. "Une analyse historique et comparative de l'indemnisation du *solatium doloris* au Québec." In *Mélanges Claude Masse: en quête de justice et d'équité*, edited by Pierre-Claude Lafond, 347–86. Cowansville, QC: Yvon Blais, 2003.

Morin, Michel. "Blackstone and the Birth of Quebec's Legal Culture, 1765–1867."
In *Re-Interpreting Blackstone's Commentaries: A Seminal Text in National and International Contexts*, edited by Wilfrid Prest, 105–24. Oxford: Hart, 2014.

Morin, Michel. "Des jurists sédentaires? L'influence du droit anglais et du droit français sur interprétation du *Code civil du Bas Canada*." *Revue du Barreau* 60 (2000): 247–386.

Morin, Michel. "La perception de l'ancien droit et du nouveau droit français au Bas-Canada, 1774–1866." In *Droit québécois et droit français: communauté, autonomie, concordance*, edited by H.P. Glenn, 1–41. Cowansville, QC: Yvon Blais, 1993.

Mourlon, Frédéric. *Répétitions écrites sur le premier examen de Code Napoléon*. 8th ed. by Charles Demangeat. 3 vols. Paris, 1869–70.

Müllereisert, F. Arthur. *Die Ehre im deutschen Privatrecht*. Berlin: C. Heymann, 1931.

Myers, Tamara. "The Voluntary Delinquent: Parents, Daughters, and the Montreal Juvenile Delinquents' Court in 1918." *Canadian Historical Review* 80 (1999): 242–68.

Nelson, Wendie. "'Rage against the Dying of the Light': Interpreting the Guerre des Éteignoirs." *Canadian Historical Review* 81 (2000): 551–89.

Nerson, Roger. *Les droits extrapatrimoniaux*. Lyons: Bosc Frères, M. & L. Riou, 1939.

"Newton N. Gober, M.D." *Journal of the American Medical Association* 59 (1912): 48.

Nootens, Thierry. *Fous, prodigues et ivrognes: familles et déviance à Montréal au XIXème siècle*. Montreal and Kingston: McGill-Queen's University Press, 2007.

Nootens, Thierry. *Genre, patrimoine et droit civil: les femmes mariées de la bourgeoisie québécoise en procès, 1900–1930*. Montreal and Kingston: McGill-Queen's University Press, 2018.

Normand, Sylvio. "L'affaire *Plamondon*: un cas d'antisémitisme à Québec au début du XXe siècle." *Cahiers de droit* 48 (2007): 477–504.

Normand, Sylvio. "Une analyse quantitative de la doctrine en droit civil québécois." *Cahiers de droit* 23 (1982): 1009–28.

Normand, Sylvio. "Une culture en redéfinition: la culture juridique québécoise durant la seconde moitié du XIXe siècle." In *Transformation de la culture juridique québécoise*, edited by Bjarne Melkevik, 221–35. Sainte-Foy, QC: Presses de l'Université Laval, 1998.

Normand, Sylvio. *Le droit comme discipline universitaire: une histoire de la Faculté de droit de l'Université Laval*. Sainte-Foy, QC: Presses de l'Université Laval, 2005.

Normand, Sylvio. "Les débuts de la littérature juridique québécoise, 1767–1840." In *Essays in the History of Canadian Law: Volume XI – Quebec and the Canadas*, edited by G. Blaine Baker and Donald Fyson, 96–130. Toronto: University of Toronto Press for Osgoode Society for Canadian Legal History, 2013.

Normand, Sylvio. "Les juristes et le libéralisme au tournant du XXe siècle." In *Combats libéraux au tournant du XXe siècle*, edited by Yvan Lamonde, 213–29 [Saint-Laurent, QC]: Fides, 1995.

Normand, Sylvio. "Profil des périodiques juridiques québécois au XIXe siècle." *Cahiers de droit* 34 (1993): 153–82.

Normand, Sylvio. "Un thème dominant de la pensée juridique traditionnelle au Québec: la sauvegarde de l'intégrité du droit civil." *McGill Law Journal* 32 (1987): 559–601.

Nwabueze, Remigius N. *Biotechnology and the Challenge of Property: Property Rights in Dead Bodies, Body Parts, and Genetic Information*. London: Routledge, 2007.

Nye, Robert A. *Masculinity and Male Codes of Honor in Modern France*. New York: Oxford University Press, 1993.

Odgers, W. Blake. *The Law of Libel and Slander and of Actions on the Case for Words Causing Damage*. 5th ed., Canadian notes by W.J. Tremeear. Toronto: Canada Law Book, 1912.

Ogbogu, Ubaka. "Vaccination and the Law in Ontario and Nova Scotia (1800–1924)." S.J.D. thesis, University of Toronto, 2014.

Oldham, James C. "On Pleading the Belly: A History of the Jury of Matrons." *Criminal Justice History* 6 (1985): 1–64.

Olson, Sherry, and Patricia Thornton. *Peopling the North American City: Montreal 1840–1900*. Montreal and Kingston: McGill-Queen's University Press, 2011.

The Oxford Handbook of Legal History, edited by Markus D. Dubber and Christopher Tomlins. Oxford: Oxford University Press, 2018.

Palmer, Bryan D. "Discordant Music: Charivaris and Whitecapping in Nineteenth-Century North America." *Labour/Le Travail* 3 (1978): 5–62.

Parent, Sylvie. *La doctrine et l'interprétation du Code civil*. Montreal: Thémis, 1997.

Parks, Annette White. "Sui San Far: Writer on the Chinese-Anglo Borders of North America, 1885–1914." Ph.D. thesis: Washington State University, 1991.

Patault, Anne-Marie. *Introduction historique au droit des biens*. Paris: Presses universitaires de France, 1989.

Peiss, Kathy. *Cheap Amusements: Working Women and Leisure in Turn-of-the-Century New York*. Philadelphia: Temple University Press, 1986.

Pelland, Léo. "À bas le divorce!" *Revue du droit* 5 (1926–7): 449–60.

Penton, M. James. *Apocalypse Delayed: The Story of Jehovah's Witnesses*. 2nd ed. Toronto: University of Toronto Press, 1997.

Perrault, Joseph-François. *Formules des ordres que l'on délivre le plus communément pour les termes inférieurs de la Cour du banc du roi, en tournée*. N.p., [1812?].

Perrault, Joseph-François. *Questions et réponses sur le droit criminel du Bas-Canada: dédiées aux étudiants en droit*. Quebec City, 1814.

Perreau, E.H. "Des droits de la personnalité." *Revue trimestrielle de droit civil* 8 (1909): 501–36.

Pfeifer, Jeffrey, and Ken Leyton-Brown. *Death by Rope: An Anthology of Canadian Executions*. Vol. 1, *1867–1923*. Regina: Vanity, 2007.

Pichet, Ludger. "Grandeurs et misères de nos ouvrages de droit." *Revue du Barreau* 5 (1945): 294–6.

Pierson, Ruth Roach. *"They're Still Women after All": The Second World War and Canadian Womanhood*. Toronto: McClelland and Stewart, 1986.

Poirier, Jean-Sébastien. "Autopsie d'une disposition disparue: l'article 1056 du Code civil du Bas Canada et le *solatium doloris*." *Revue juridique Thémis* 29 (1995): 657–703.

Pollock, Frederick. *The Law of Torts: A Treatise on the Principles of Obligations Arising from Civil Wrongs in the Common Law*. 2nd ed. London, 1890.

Popovici, Adrian. "De l'aliénation d'affection: essai critique et comparatif." *Canadian Bar Review* 48 (1970): 236–69.

Popu, Hélène. *La dépouille mortelle, chose sacrée: à la redécouverte d'une catégorie juridique oubliée*. Paris: L'Harmattan, 2009.

Pratte, Marie. "L'évolution du statut juridique de l'enfant naturel en droit civil québécois." LL.M. thesis, University of Ottawa, 1981.

Premier Congrès de Tempérance de Montréal (partie ouest) tenu à Ville St-Pierre le 25 octobre 1909: procès-verbal et travaux. Montreal: Imprimerie des sourds-muets, 1909.

Proulx, Daniel. *Le Red Light de Montréal*. Montreal: VLB, 1997.

Pue, W. Wesley. *Lawyers' Empire: Legal Professionals and Cultural Authority, 1780–1950*. Vancouver: UBC Press, 2016.

Reddy, William M. "Against Constructionism: The Historical Anthropology of Emotions." *Current Anthropology* 38 (1997): 327–40.

Reddy, William M. *The Invisible Code: Honor and Sentiment in Postrevolutionary France*. Berkeley: University of California Press, 1997.

Reddy, William M. *The Navigation of Feeling: A Framework for the History of Emotions*. Cambridge: Cambridge University Press, 2001.

Reiter, Eric H. "From Shaved Horses to Aggressive Churchwardens: Social and Legal Aspects of Moral Injury in Lower Canada." In *Essays in the History of Canadian Law: Volume XI – Quebec and the Canadas*, edited by G. Blaine Baker and Donald Fyson, 460–502. Toronto: University of Toronto Press for Osgoode Society for Canadian Legal History, 2013.

Reiter, Eric H. "Imported Books, Imported Ideas: Reading European Jurisprudence in Mid-Nineteenth-Century Quebec." *Law and History Review* 22 (2004): 445–92.

Reiter, Eric H. "Translating the Untranslatable: Historical Aspects of the Protection of Honour and Other Extrapatrimonial Interests in Quebec Civil Law." In *Les intraduisibles en droit civil*, edited by Alexandra Popovici, Lionel Smith, and Régine Tremblay, 157–84. Montreal: Thémis, 2014.

Renteln, Alison Dundes. *The Cultural Defense*. New York: Oxford University Press, 2004.

Resta, Giorgio. "Personnalité, Persönlichkeit, Personality." In *Les intraduisibles en droit civil*, edited by Alexandra Popovici, Lionel Smith, and Régine Tremblay, 185–215. Montreal: Thémis, 2014.

Rigaux, François. *La protection de la vie privée et des autres biens de la personnalité*. Paris: L.G.D.J., 1990.

Rigaux, François. "L'évaluation communautaire du seuil de tolérance aux atteintes à un bien de la personnalité." In *La douleur et le droit*, edited by Bernard Durand, Jean Poirier, and Jean-Pierre Royer, 479–88. Paris: Presses universitaires français, 1997.

Rinfret, G.-Édouard. *Histoire du Barreau de Montréal*. 2nd ed. Cowansville, QC: Yvon Blais, 1999.

Risk, Richard, and Robert C. Vipond. "Rights Talk in Canada in the Late Nineteenth Century: 'The Good Sense and Right Feeling of the People.'" *Law and History Review* 14 (1996): 1–32.

Robert, Martin. "Disposer de son cadavre: la naissance de la crémation au Québec (1874–1914)." M.A. thesis, Université du Québec à Montréal, 2015.

Robertson, Stephen. "Seduction, Sexual Violence, and Marriage in New York City, 1886–1955." *Law and History Review* 24 (2006): 331–73.

Rogers, Berto. "Recovery for Mental Anguish Resulting from the Mutilation of a Corpse." *Law Notes* 33 (1930): 225–30.

Roguin, Ernest. *La règle de droit: analyse générale, spécialités, souveraineté des états, assiette de l'impôt, théorie des statuts, système des rapports de droit privé, précédé d'une introduction sur la classification des disciplines*. Lausanne, 1889.

Rosenwein, Barbara H. *Emotional Communities in the Early Middle Ages*. Ithaca, NY: Cornell University Press, 2006.

Rosenwein, Barbara H. *Generations of Feeling: A History of Emotions 600–1700*. Cambridge: Cambridge University Press, 2016.

Rosenwein, Barbara H. "Problems and Methods in the History of Emotions." *Passions in Context: Journal of the History and Philosophy of the Emotions* 1 (2010): 1–32.

Roubier, Paul. *Droits subjectifs et situations juridiques*. 1963. Reprint, Paris: Dalloz, 2005.

Rousseau, Jean-Jacques. *Discours sur l'origine et les fondemens de l'inégalité parmi les hommes*. Amsterdam, 1755.

Roy, Ferdinand. *Des restrictions au droit de plaider en matière civile*. Quebec City: Darveau, Jos. Beauchamp, Successeur, 1902.

Roy, Fernande. *Progrès, harmonie, liberté: le libéralisme des milieux d'affaires francophones de Montréal au tournant du siècle*. Montreal: Boréal, 1988.

Roy, Joseph. *Explication du Code civil du Bas-Canada*. Vol. 1. Montreal, 1867.

Roy, Nicole. "La lutte des femmes pour la réforme du droit de la famille 1900–1955." In *Du Code civil du Québec: contribution à l'histoire immédiate d'une recodification réussie*, edited by Serge Lortie, Nicholas Kasirer, and Jean-Guy Belley, 477–618. Montreal: Thémis, 2007.

Royer, Jean-Pierre. "La traduction de la douleur en 'espèces sonnantes et trébuchantes': origines historiques, méthodes, statistiques, doctrine et jurisprudence, ancienne et contemporaine, judiciaire et administrative." In *La douleur et le droit*, edited by Bernard Durand, Jean Poirier, and Jean-Pierre Royer, 439–50. Paris: Presses universitaires français, 1997.

Rudin, Ronald. *Founding Fathers: The Celebration of Champlain and Laval in the Streets of Quebec, 1878–1908*. Toronto: University of Toronto Press, 2003.

Saint-Pierre, Jacques, and Martin Petitclerc. *Histoire de l'assurance de personnes: des sociétés de secours mutuels aux grandes institutions d'assurance*. Quebec City: Presses de l'Université Laval, 2015.

Sandwell, R.W. "The Limits of Liberalism: The Liberal Reconnaissance and the History of the Family in Canada." *Canadian Historical Review* 84 (2003): 423–50.

Sandwell, R.W. "Missing Canadians: Reclaiming the A-Liberal Past." In *Liberalism and Hegemony: Debating the Canadian Liberal Revolution*, edited by Jean-François Constant and Michel Ducharme, 246–73. Toronto: University of Toronto Press, 2009.

Sangster, Joan. *Regulating Girls and Women: Sexuality, Family, and the Law in Ontario, 1920–1960*. Don Mills, ON: Oxford University Press, 2001.

Sarra-Bournet, Michel. *L'affaire Roncarelli: Duplessis contre les Témoins de Jéhovah*. Quebec City: Institut québécois de recherche sur la culture, 1986.

Schnädelbach, Sandra. "The Jurist as Manager of Emotions: German Debates on 'Rechtsgefühl' in the Late 19th and Early 20th Century as Sites of Negotiating the Juristic Treatment of Emotions." *InterDisciplines* 6, no. 2 (2015): 47–74.

Scheer, Monique. "Are Emotions a Kind of Practice (and Is That What Makes Them Have a History)? A Bourdieuian Approach to Understanding Emotions." *History and Theory* 51 (2012): 193–220.

Schreier, Barbara A. *Becoming American Women: Clothing and the Jewish Immigrant Experience, 1880–1920*. Chicago: Chicago Historical Society, 1994.

Scott, F.R. "Dominion Jurisdiction over Human Rights and Fundamental Freedoms." *Canadian Bar Review* 27 (1949): 497–536.

Scott, Susan. "Revocation of Gifts on the Ground of Ingratitude: From Justinian to LAWSA." *Journal of South African Law* (2011): 361–72.

Seed, Patricia. *To Love, Honor, and Obey in Colonial Mexico: Conflicts over Marriage Choice, 1574–1821*. Stanford: Stanford University Press, 1988.

Sériaux, Alain. "Heurs et malheurs de l'esprit de système: la théorie du patrimoine d'Aubry et Rau." In *Aubry et Rau: leurs œuvres, leurs enseignements*, edited by Jean-Michel Poughon, 79–89. Strasbourg: Presses universitaires de Strasbourg, 2006.

Sériaux, Alain. "La notion juridique de patrimoine: brèves notations civilistes sur le verbe avoir." *Revue trimestrielle de droit civil* (1994): 801–13.

Sheppard, Claude-Armand. "Roncarelli v. Duplessis: Art. 1053 C.C. Revolutionized." *McGill Law Journal* 6 (1960): 75–97.

"Shirking Responsibility." *Druggists' Circular and Chemical Gazette* 38, no. 6 (June 1894): 122.

Silverman, William A. "Incubator-Baby Side Shows." *Pediatrics* 64 (1979): 127–41.

Simmonds, Alecia. "'Promises and Pie-Crusts Were Made to Be Broke': Breach of Promise of Marriage and the Regulation of Courtship in Early Colonial Australia." *Australian Feminist Law Journal* 23 (2005): 99–120.

Simmonds, Alecia. "'She Felt Strongly the Injury to Her Affections': Breach of Promise of Marriage and the Medicalization of Heartbreak in Early Twentieth-Century Australia." *Journal of Legal History* 38 (2017): 179–202.

Simpson, A.W.B. *Leading Cases in the Common Law*. Oxford: Clarendon, 1995.

Simpson, A.W.B. "The Rise and Fall of the Legal Treatise: Legal Principles and the Form of Legal Literature." *University of Chicago Law Review* 48 (1981): 632–79.

Sloan, Kathryn A. *Runaway Daughters: Seduction, Elopement, and Honor in Nineteenth-Century Mexico*. Albuquerque: University of New Mexico Press, 2008.

Smail, Daniel Lord. *The Consumption of Justice: Emotions, Publicity, and Legal Culture in Marseille, 1264–1423*. Ithaca, NY: Cornell University Press, 2003.

Snell, James G. *In the Shadow of the Law: Divorce in Canada, 1900–1939*. Toronto: University of Toronto Press, 1991.

Socolow, Susan M. "Acceptable Partners: Marriage Choice in Colonial Argentina, 1778–1810." In *Sexuality and Marriage in Colonial Latin America*, edited by Asunción Lavrin, 209–51. Lincoln: University of Nebraska Press, 1989.

Sourdat, Auguste. *Traité général de la responsabilité ou de l'action en dommages-intérêts en dehors des contrats*. 2 vols. Paris, 1852.

Sourdat, Auguste. *Traité général de la responsabilité ou de l'action en dommages-intérêts en dehors des contrats*. 3rd ed., 2 vols. Paris, 1876.

Sperling, Daniel. *Posthumous Interests: Legal and Ethical Perspectives*. Cambridge: Cambridge University Press, 2008.

Staves, Susan. "Money for Honor: Damages for Criminal Conversation." *Studies in Eighteenth-Century Culture* 11 (1982): 279–97.

Stearns, Peter N. *Revolutions in Sorrow: The American Experience of Death in Global Perspective*. Boulder, CO: Paradigm, 2007.

Stearns, Peter N., and Carol Z. Stearns. "Emotionology: Clarifying the History of Emotions and Emotional Standards." *American Historical Review* 90 (1985): 813–36.

Stevens, Rebecca A.T., and Yoshiko Iwamoto Wada, eds. *The Kimono Inspiration: Art and Art-to-Wear in America*. Rohnert Park, CA: Pomegranate Artbooks for the Textile Museum, 1996.

Stewart, Frank Henderson. *Honor*. Chicago: University of Chicago Press, 1994.

Storch, Henri. *Cours d'économie politique, ou exposition des principes qui déterminent la prospérité des nations*. 4 vols. Paris, 1823.

Strange, Carolyn. "Reconsidering the 'Tragic' Scott Expedition: Cheerful Masculine Home-making in Antarctica, 1910–1913." *Journal of Social History* 46 (2012): 66–88.

Strange, Carolyn, Robert Cribb, and Christopher E. Forth, eds. *Honour, Violence and Emotions in History*. London: Bloomsbury Academic, 2014.

Strange, Julie-Marie. *Death, Grief and Poverty in Britain, 1870–1914*. Cambridge: Cambridge University Press, 2005.

Strange, Julie-Marie. "'She Cried a Very Little': Death, Grief and Mourning in Working-Class Culture, 1880–1914." *Social History* 27 (2002): 143–61.

Tanny, Laurence Murray. "Ethnocentric Discrimination and Freedom of Contract in a Changing Social Climate." *McGill Law Journal* 13 (1967): 186–91.

Tarantino, Bob. "'Free to Deal as He May Choose': The Displacement of 'Freedom of Commerce' as a Necessary Condition to the Creation of Canadian Multiculturalism." *Common Law World Review* 39 (2010): 7–26.

Taylor, Lou. *Mourning Dress: A Costume and Social History*. 1983. Reprint, London: Routledge, 2009.

Thério, Adrien. *Joseph Guibord, victime expiatoire de l'évêque Bourget: l'Institut canadien et l'affaire Guibord revisités*. Montreal: XYZ, 2000.

Thomas, Courtney Erin. *If I Lose Mine Honour I Lose Myself: Honour among the Early Modern English Elite*. Toronto: University of Toronto Press, 2017.

Thompson, E.P. "Rough Music Reconsidered." *Folklore* 103 (1992): 3–26.

Threedy, Debora L. "Legal Archaeology: Excavating Cases, Reconstructing Context." *Tulane Law Review* 80 (2006): 1197–238.

Toullier, C.-B.-M. *Le droit civil français, suivant l'ordre du Code Napoléon, ouvrage dans lequel on a tâché de réunir la théorie à la pratique*. 8 vols. Rennes, 1811–18.

Travis, Jennifer. *Wounded Hearts: Masculinity, Law, and Literature in American Culture*. Chapel Hill: University of North Carolina Press, 2005.

Trimaille, Gilles. "L'expertise médico-légale: confiscation et traduction de la douleur." In *La douleur et le droit*, edited by Bernard Durand, Jean Poirier, and Jean-Pierre Royer, 489–500. Paris: Presses universitaires français, 1997.

Trudel, Marcel. *Chiniquy*. 2nd ed. Trois-Rivières: Éditions du Bien Public, 1955.

Tulchinsky, Gerald. *Taking Root: The Origins of the Canadian Jewish Community*. Hanover, NH: University Press of New England for Brandeis University Press, 1993.

Turcot, Laurent. "L'émergence d'un loisir: les particularités de la promenade en carrosse au Canada au XVIIIe siècle." *Revue d'histoire de l'Amérique française* 64 (2010): 31–70.

Turcot, Laurent, and Christophe Loir. "La promenade: un objet de recherche en plein essor." In *La promenade au tournant des XVIIIe et XIXe siècles (Belgique-France-Angleterre)*, edited by Laurent Turcot and Christophe Loir, 7–20. Brussels: Université de Bruxelles, 2011.

Twining, William. "What Is the Point of Legal Archaeology?" *Transnational Legal Theory* 3 (2012): 166–72.

Vacher-Lapouge, G. *Théorie du patrimoine*. Paris, 1879.

Valverde, Mariana, J.R. Miller, Doug Owram, Shirley Tillotson, Bryan D. Palmer, Franca Iacovetta, and Wendy Mitchinson. "On the Case: Explorations in Social History: A Roundtable Discussion." *Canadian Historical Review* 81 (2000): 266–92.

VanderVelde, Lea. "The Legal Ways of Seduction." *Stanford Law Review* 48 (1996): 817–901.

Vantroys, Alexandre. *Étude historique et juridique sur le consentement des parents au mariage de leurs enfants*. Paris, 1889.

Vasilyev, Pavel. "Beyond Dispassion: Emotions and Judicial Decision-Making in Modern Europe." *Rechtsgeschichte/Legal History* 25 (2017): 277–85.
Veilleux, Christine. *Aux origines du Barreau québécois, 1779–1849*. Sillery, QC: Septentrion, 1997.
Vergau, Hans-Joachim. *Der Ersatz immateriellen Schadens in der Rechtsprechung des 19. Jahrhunderts zum französischen und zum deutschen Deliktsrecht.* Potsdam: Universitätsverlag Potsdam, 2006.
Vidor, Gian Marco. "The Press, the Audience, and Emotions in Italian Courtrooms (1860s–1910s)." *Journal of Social History* 51 (2017): 231–54.
Vinet, Bernard. *Pseudonymes québécois*. Quebec City: Garneau, 1974.
Vizkelety, Béatrice. "Discrimination, the Right to Seek Redress and the Common Law: A Century-Old Debate." *Dalhousie Law Journal* 15 (1992): 304–35.
Waddams, S.M. *Sexual Slander in Nineteenth-Century England: Defamation in the Ecclesiastical Courts, 1815–1855.* Toronto: University of Toronto Press, 2000.
Walker, Barrington. *Race on Trial: Black Defendants in Ontario's Criminal Courts, 1858–1958.* Toronto: University of Toronto Press for Osgoode Society for Canadian Legal History, 2010.
Walker, James W. St.G. "African Canadians." In *Encyclopedia of Canada's Peoples*, edited by Paul Robert Magocsi, 139–76. Toronto: University of Toronto Press, 1999.
Walker, James W. St.G. *"Race," Rights and the Law in the Supreme Court of Canada: Historical Case Studies*. Waterloo, ON: Osgoode Society for Canadian Legal History and Wilfrid Laurier University Press, 1997.
Walton, Charles. *Policing Public Opinion in the French Revolution: The Culture of Calumny and the Problem of Free Speech.* Oxford: Oxford University Press, 2009.
Wang, Jennifer, Janxin Leu, and Yuichi Shoda. "When the Seemingly Innocuous 'Stings': Racial Microaggressions and Their Emotional Consequences." *Personality and Social Psychology Bulletin* 37 (2011): 1666–78.
Waters, Rosanne. "African Canadian Anti-Discrimination Activism and the Transnational Civil Rights Movement, 1945–1965." *Journal of the Canadian Historical Association* 24 (2013): 386–424.
Watson, Alan. *The Law of the Ancient Romans*. Dallas: Southern Methodist University Press, 1970.
Weisman, Richard. *Showing Remorse: Law and the Social Control of Emotion*. Farnham: Ashgate, 2014.
Wertsman, Vladimir F. *Salute to the Romanian Jews in America and Canada, 1850–2010: History, Achievements, and Biographies*. N.p.: Xlibris, 2010.
White, G. Edward. "The Emergence and Doctrinal Development of Tort Law, 1870–1930." *University of St. Thomas Law Journal* 11 (2014): 463–527.

Wiener, Richard L., Brian H. Bornstein, and Amy Voss. "Emotion and the Law: A Framework for Inquiry." *Law and Human Behavior* 30 (2006): 231–48.
Williams, David Ricardo. *Just Lawyers: Seven Portraits*. Toronto: Osgoode Society for Canadian Legal History, 1995.
Williams, Dorothy W. *The Road to Now: A History of Blacks in Montreal*. Montreal: Véhicule, 1997.
Williamson, Stanley. *The Vaccination Controversy: The Rise, Reign, and Fall of Compulsory Vaccination for Smallpox*. Liverpool: Liverpool University Press, 2007.
Winks, Robin W. *The Blacks in Canada: A History*. 2nd ed. Montreal and Kingston: McGill-Queen's University Press, 2000.
Witt, John Fabian. *The Accidental Republic: Crippled Workingmen, Destitute Widows, and the Remaking of American Law*. Cambridge, MA: Harvard University Press, 2004.
Witt, John Fabian. "From Loss of Services to Loss of Support: The Wrongful Death Statutes, the Origins of Modern Tort Law, and the Making of the Nineteenth-Century Family." *Law and Social Inquiry* 25 (2000): 717–55.
Witt, John Fabian. "The Political Economy of Pain." In *Making Legal History: Essays in Honor of William E. Nelson*, edited by Daniel J. Hulsebosch and R.B. Bernstein, 235–63. New York: New York University Press, 2013.
Wolff, Christian. *Institutions du droit de la nature et des gens*. 6 vols. Leiden, 1772.
Yalden, Robert. "Unité et Différence: The Structure of Legal Thought in Late-Nineteenth-Century Quebec." *University of Toronto Faculty of Law Review* 46 (1988): 365–89.
Young, Brian. *Patrician Families and the Making of Quebec: The Taschereaus and McCords*. Montreal and Kingston: McGill-Queen's University Press, 2014.
Young, Brian. *The Politics of Codification: The Lower Canadian Civil Code of 1866*. Montreal and Kingston: McGill-Queen's University Press for Osgoode Society for Canadian Legal History, 1994.
Young, Brian. *Respectable Burial: Montreal's Mount Royal Cemetery*. Montreal and Kingston: McGill-Queen's University Press, 2003.
Zachariä, Karl Salomo. *Handbuch des französischen Civilrechts*. 5th ed. by August Anschütz. 4 vols. Heidelberg, 1853.
Zachariä, Karl Salomo. *Le droit civil français, traduit de l'allemand sur la cinquième édition, annoté et rétabli suivant l'ordre du Code Napoléon*, translated by G. Massé and Ch. Vergé. 5 vols. Paris, 1854–60.
Zeiger, Richard G. "Alienation of Affection and Defamation: Similar Interests – Dissimilar Treatment." *Cleveland State Law Review* 30 (1981): 331–66.
Zelizer, Viviana A. *Pricing the Priceless Child: The Changing Social Value of Children*. New York: Basic Books, 1985.

Index

Note: Page numbers in *italics* refer to illustrations.

Abbott, J.J.C., 317n3
abuse of right, 46, 255, 303, 428n30
Academy of Music, 261–70, *262*, 413n15
adultery, 32, 109–10, 201–3; as bar to mourning allowance, 240, 243; as grounds for separation or divorce, 72, 175, 200
affection, 6, 26–7, 173–4; for children, 160; and damages, 201–2, 204, 236–7; for friends, 194; and gifts, 211–12; for parents, 106, 164, 231; for spouse, 139, 142, 175, 198, 204–7, 210–11, 255–6. *See also* alienation of affection; love
Agnew, Augustus Waterous, 130–43, *134–5*, 360n148
Agnew, Kathleen, 130–3, 136–43, 366n215
Agnew, William, 130–3, 136–43, 366n215
Ahrens, Heinrich, 47, 298
alienation of affection, 138–41, 198–210, 302, 390n164; criticism of, 174, 202, 204; difficulty assessing damages for, 26; and disgrace, 86–7; and emotional language, 19–21
Allard, Euphémie, 100–6
Allard, Victor, 218–19
Anctil, Hilaire, 289
Andrews, Frederick, 121
anger, 12–13, 61, 76, 161, 178, 200, 205, 305; and autopsy, 171; and discrimination, 27, 259–60, 263, 274, 275–9, 284; and grief, 239, 251
Angers, Auguste-Réal, 66
anguish, 105, 228, 251
Archambault, Horace, 106
Archambault, Joseph, 168
Archer, Charles, 272
Archibald, John Sprott, 61, 154, 183, 198, 268–70, 415n40
Arthabaska, Quebec, 118, 291
Association of Loyal Negroes, 274
Atlanta, Georgia, 131–2, 143, 361n159
Aubry, Charles, and Charles Rau, 29, 40–2, 116, 237
autopsy, 26, 145, 162–72, 239, 302, 373n85
Aylwin, Thomas, 230

Badgley, William, 7, 65, 230
Baldwin, Maurice Day, 70
Barclay, Gregor, 171, 282
Beauce, Quebec, 118–19
Beaudoin, Joseph-Damase, 247
Beaugrand, Honoré, 151
Beaumont, Quebec, 120–1
Beauregard, Eva, 215, 217
Beaussire, Émile, 298
Bégin, Joseph, 101–7, 349n13, 351n40
Beignier, Bernard, 99
Belime, William, 298
Belleau, Isidore, 256–7
Belmont cemetery, 247, 250, 406n110
Benning, James, 3–8, 5
Bernard, Lucien, 222
Bertrand, Pierre, 163
betrayal, 7, 26, 173–219, 305
Bibaud, Maximilien, 43; and *biens*, 42–4, 237; and *injure*, 34, 40, 300
biens, 31–2, 34, 40–5, 68, 295; *biens innés*, 41, 52, 237, 299; distinguished from property, 10, 23, 167; happiness as, 237–8; honour as, 53, 64, 101, 117, 125, 303; and patrimony, 39–41
Bizier, Gaspard, 109
body, 297–8, 369n33; as *bien*, 41, 44; mutilation of corpse, 162–71; non-consensual interference, 25, 145–61
Boistel, Alphonse, 47
Bond, William, 282
books and publishing, 30
Bossé, Joseph-Guillaume, 51–2, 235, 270
Boucher, Aimé, 294
Bradbury, Bettina, 187, 219, 241
breach of promise to marry, 3–7, 35, 173–4, 186–98, 302; and affection, 204; criticism of, 26, 191–2; difficulty assessing damages for, 45, 48

British justice, 47, 300–1; and juries, 232; and race, 267–70, 274, 281–2
Brode, Patrick, 191
Brouillette, Sarah, 169–71
Bruneau, Arthur-Aimé, 184, 241–2
Bruneau, Jean-Casimir, 230
burial, 169, 243–57; as clause in gifts, 210–15; and grief, 221; and rights, 167, 295, 300, 302

Cairns, James, 166
Campbell, Lyndsay, 269
Canadian Pacific Railway, 232–3, 275
canon law. *See* religion
Cantin, Antoine, 72–9
Caron, Louis-Bonaventure, 45, 191–3
Carroll, Henry George, 106, 281
categorization in law, 29–31, 40, 52, 65; and attributes of the person, 42, 298; difficulties regarding emotions, 7–8, 14, 20, 22–3
Caveny, Sarah, 56, 60–1
Chagnon, Hubert-Wilfrid, 69
Chambly, Quebec, 222, 224
Chapeau, Quebec, 304
Chaput, Esymier, 304–5
charivari, 63, 88–90, 107, 191; in Côte-des-Neiges, 89–90, 92, 96; in Richelieu, 97; in St Léonard, 25, 54, 90–9
Chassan, Joseph-Pierre, 108, 121
Châteauguay, Quebec, 284
Chiniquy, Charles, 100–2, 104–6, 110
Chiniquy, Rebecca. *See* Morin
Christie, Fred, 281–3
Circé-Côté, Eva, 64
citizenship rights. *See* rights
Citrin, Kolman, 178
Citrin, Louis, 177, 181, 183

Index   471

Civil Code of Lower Canada, art. 18, 274; art. 19, 161; art. 119, 127; art. 137, 127; art. 163, 138; art. 176, 116; art. 189, 35; art. 242, 64, 127; art. 324, 137; art. 326, 129; arts. 336*a–s*, 129; art. 349, 129; art. 606, 248; art. 632, 248; art. 636, 248; art. 813, 35, 209, 218; art. 893, 35, 120, 211, 355n89; art. 1053, 30, 37, 39, 46, 49, 226, 231, 303; art. 1056, 226–7, 230–4, 236, 246, 336n51, 398–9n23; art. 1073, 49; art. 1265, 393n207; art. 1368, 240, 241, 243; art. 2002, 240, 241; art. 2262, 325n26; art. 2272, 35, 301; art. 2613, 39
Civil Code Revision Office, 300
civil law tradition, 22, 29, 40, 227, 239; and family honour, 102; and injury, 8, 26, 31, 108 174; and revocation of gifts, 211; and rights, 10. *See also* French law
civil liberties, 300–1; and defamation, 65, 67–8; and discrimination, 270; and Jehovah's Witnesses, 290, 293, 303
civil rights. *See* rights
class, 12, 61, 69–79, 95, 140; attitudes of judges towards, 8–9, 174, 183, 208, 214, 234, 242–3, 283; and hierarchy, 32, 35, 52, 260, 271; and honour, 63–4, 126–7; and liberalism, 52; and race, 269; and social norms, 24, 32, 240–3, 253–4
Claxton, A.G. Brooke, 159
Cléroux, L.J.O., *153*
Cocatrix, Pierre, 34
Code of Canon Law, 244
Code of Civil Procedure, and appeals (art. 43), 138, 365n191, 382n60; and bar on spousal testimony (arts. 252, 314), 177, 205, 379n16, 391n177; and bar on testifying on one's own behalf (art. 251), 6, 316n4; and *contrainte par corps* (art. 833), 35, 297, 301, 326n30, 428n27; and evidence (art. 289), 154–5; and execution of judgments (art. 541), 154; and *in forma pauperis* proceedings (arts. 89–93), 246, 396n241, 405n105; and jury trials (arts. 348–9, 421), 35, 297; and medical exams (art. 286*b*), 155, 371n51; and Privy Council appeals (art. 69), 138, 365n191; and settlements (art. 527), 272, 417n65; and testimony by *faits et articles* (art. 228), 6, 316n4; and testimony under objection (arts. 312–54), 18
codification, 30, 52, 226, 230
Coleridge, John Taylor, 228
Collège Mont-St-Louis, 145
Collerette, Joseph, 92
Collerette dit Bourguignon, Bazile, 92–3, 95
Collin, Elzéar (father), 214–19, *216*
Collin, Elzéar (son), 215
Colored Political and Protective Association, 274–5, 279–80, 418n72
Colton, Jacob, 174
common law tradition, 22, 29, 40, 201–2, 227–8, 235; and corpses, 166–7; and damages, 50, 305; and emotional injury, 26, 35, 174, 192, 207, 238–9; and family honour, 102; and rights, 155. *See also* English law
consent, 25–6; and autopsy, 162–72; and discrimination, 270, 276, 279; informed consent, 144, 158, 160, 371n57; and marriage, 192; and medical procedures, 150–2, 157–61;

parental consent, 34, 127–8, 133, 136–7, 142–3
consideration, 38, 63, 68–9, 77, 211
Constantineau, Delphine, 94
contempt, 104, 113, 173, 219, 254; and charivari, 97; and separation from bed and board, 37
contract, 45, 302, 305; and liberalism, 44, 52, 212; and promise to marry, 3, 191–2; and refusal of service, 263–81. *See also* marriage contract
contrainte par corps, 35–6, 297, 301, 428n27
Corbeil, Joseph, 93, 96
Corbeil, Wilfrid, 55–62, 68, 70, 144, 333n13
Corrigan, John, 45
Côté, Clara, 237
Coteau-du-Lac, Quebec, 229
Côte-des-Neiges, Quebec, 89–90, 92, 96
Couillard, Alexandre, 221–2, 224–5
Couillard, Aline, 221–2, 224, 234, 401n56
Couillard, Charles, 221–2, 224–5, 234–6, 401n56
Couillard, François-Xavier, 248–54
Couillard, Thomas, 221, 224, 397n12
Couture, Léon, 55–6, 59–60, 333n13
Couture, Paul, 289–90
cremation, 163, 167, 169–70
Crépeau, Paul-André, 300
criminal law, 42, 50, 118–19, 228, 232, 269, 281, 290–1; and adultery, 201; criminal libel, 34, 37, 107, 113–14; and *injure*, 31–4, 37, 49
Cross, Alexander, 106
Crystal, Max, 182
Curl, Eunice, 272, 417n63, 417n68
Curl, John Delmore, 271–2, 274, 417n63

Curran, John Joseph, 66, 158–9, 166, 374n94
Custom of Paris, 30, 42, 211, 241

D., Gabrielle, 145–51, 161, 367n2
damages, 24, 26, 44–5, 48–52, 299; and alienation of affection, 191–3, 201; compensatory damages, 8–9, 29, 38, 49, 148–9, 161, 201, 280; exemplary damages, 19, 50, 94, 125, 168, 225, 235, 280; general damages, 24, 48–9, 125, 161, 168, 234, 305; and *injure*, 32, 35–9, 89, 108; and interference with a corpse, 166–7; material (real) damages, 26, 39, 48, 50, 94, 193, 225, 237, 239; moral damages, 39, 48, 50–2, 149, 186, 193, 226–33, 236–9, 251, 255, 279, 305; nominal damages, 119, 166, 246, 278–9, 283; punitive damages, 38, 50, 106, 108, 280, 283; special damages, 24, 50–1; vindictive damages, 8, 50–1, 229–30
Dareau, François, 31–4, *33*, 36, 38, 42, 237, 297
Davidson, Charles, 136–7, 167, 172, 209
Davis, Henry, 282
Davis, Natalie Zemon, 11, 17, 21
Day, Charles Dewey, 229
Decelles, Henri, 114–15, 126
defamation, 8, 53–4, 64–8, 101–5, 139, 421n113; and damages, 50–2; of the dead, 119, 121–3; and family honour, 101–5, 109–19, 126; in French law, 37; group libel, 117–18, 290; and honour, 89–90; and *injure*, 23–5, 31–5, 94; and the press, 67–8; and reputation, 74; and rights, 47, 65, 303; sources of Quebec law of, 64–5, 107, 227; and virtue, 292

de Lorimier, Charles Chamilly, 128–9
Demers, André, 291–2
Demers, Joseph, 219
Demers, Louis-Philippe, 282
Demers, Pierre, 186–90, 196, 198
Demers, Rose de Lima, 186–98, *188*
Demolombe, Charles, 36–7
Denis, Jean-Joseph, 160
Denisart, Jean-Baptiste, 30
Desaulniers, Gonzalve, 102, 104, 106, 350n22
Desautels, Amable, 93, 345n161
Desautels, Ovila, 94
Deschamps, Alfred, 92
Desnoyers, David, 197
Desrosiers, Joseph-Placide, 80
Devins, Richard J., 222, 225, 235
Devlin, Bernard, 6, 315n3
dignity, 9, 28, 31, 47, 209, 260, 301
Dion, Gédéon, 290–1
discrimination, 303, 421n113; against Blacks, 260–84; emotions of, 27, 259–60; against immigrants, 79, 88; against religious minorities, 284–94; as violated right, 10
disgrace, 24–5, 53, 58, 63, 66, 190, 204; and culture, 79, 86–8; and family honour, 113, 124, 130
dishonour, 7–8, 16, 25, 62–4, 305; and audience, 59; and charivari, 88–9, 97; and culture, 88; and family, 109–10, 116–17, 125, 130; and *injure*, 31–2, 47; judges and, 58, 68–9, 204, 208; and masculinity, 60, 79; physical aspects of, 144; and rights, 10
Dodson, Norris, 275–81, 283–4
Doherty, Charles, 68, 208–9
Domat, Jean, 30, 31
Dominion Park, 54–62, 57
Dorion, Antoine-Aimé, 315n3

Dorion, Charles-Édouard, 251
Driscoll, Frances, 246
Driscoll, John, 245
droit commun, 37, 154, 227, 230, 399n38
Duclos, Charles-Albert, 147–9
duelling, 63, 89, 226–7, 231, 336n51
Duplessis, Maurice, 146, 284–5, 288, 291–2, 425n148
Dupuis, Philippe, 122
Duquette, Ovila, 90–8, 343n141
Duval, Jean-François-Joseph, 230

Eaton, Edith Maude (Sui Sin Far), 268
Eden Musée, 111–19, *112*
Edmundston, New Brunswick, 288
embarrassment, 13, 53, 63, 149, 152
emotional communities, 14–17, 69, 74, 78, 284
emotional regimes, 13–16
emotives, 13–14, 16, 20
empathy, 9, 10, 283, 306
English law, 159, 167, 239; and damages, 50; and defamation, 34, 64–5, 116; and family honour, 102, 107–9, 121; and *solatium doloris*, 226–34. See also common law tradition
exhumation, 164–6, 245, 247, 250–1, 256–7
extrapatrimonial rights. See rights

Fabre, Édouard-Charles, 67, 231
Fafard, Norbert, 237
Fairgreave, Helen, 241
Falardeau, Marie, 56, 59–60
family, 173–4, 299; and autopsy, 162–72; as *bien*, 41, 45; blended families, 175, 221, 242; conflict, 177, 180, 240–5, 247–57; and damages, 230, 237; as economic support,

210–13; and honour, 25–6, 99–143;
  and liberalism, 10, 44, 104–5, 107;
  and marriage, 189, 195
fault, 30, 49, 225; and damages, 106,
  193; and rights, 10, 24, 28, 46–7,
  255, 293–4, 298–305
fear, 12, 16, 27; of physical injury, 157;
  of reputational injury, 129, 141, 190,
  205; vulnerability and, 145, 149,
  213, 215, 249, 260, 284–92
femininity, 24, 54, 71–8, 243; judges'
  dismissing of, 8, 26, 69, 243. *See also*
  gender
Ferrière, Claude-Joseph de, 30, 42, 211
Fontaine, Jean, 289–90
Forest, Alfred, 170, 172
formulas, legal, 6, 17–20, 32, 49, 58,
  68, 89, 104, 106, 210, 305
Fortin, Thomas, 168, 278–9, 283
Fournel, Jean-François, 201–2
Fournier, Télesphore, 51
freedom. *See* liberty
Freifeld, Samuel, 178–9, 182
French law, 30–1, 49–50, 121, 239; and
  adultery, 201–2; and *biens*, 40–2;
  and burial, 244, 254, 256; and defamation, 107–9, 116; and honour,
  68, 99; and injury, 8, 23, 31–9, 64–5;
  and marriage, 127; and mourning clothes, 240–2; and promise of
  marriage, 191–2; and rights, 46–7,
  298–9; and *solatium doloris*, 226–34.
  See also civil law tradition
Frevert, Ute, 12
frustration, 78–9, 160–1, 174, 213; and
  discrimination, 259, 279, 284

Gagnon, Aurore, 113–14
Gagnon, Elie, 151, 369n34
Galipeault, Antonin, 171, 282
Garvey, Marcus, 274, 281

Gates, William, 276–7
Gauthier, Louis-Joseph, 80
Gayety Theatre, 145
gender, 8–9, 12, 24–6, 150, 254, 260;
  and breach of promise, 192–3, 195,
  197; double standards, 152, 202; and
  honour, 53–4, 63, 70–1; and judges,
  67, 157, 283; and propriety, 71–9. *See
  also* femininity; masculinity
Geoffrion, Aimé, 133
Gérin-Lajoie, Antoine, 300
Germain, Clément Prosper, 186–7,
  189–91, 195–7
Gewirtz, Paul, 9
gifts, 175, 188–9, 190–1, 205, 210–13;
  revocation, 35, 173, 210–14, 218
Giguère, Elisée, 215
Gill, Charles-Ignace, 96–7
Gilot, Jean, 214–19, *216*, 396n243
Girouard, Désiré, 6, 315n3
Gober, Mary, 130–43, *134–5*,
  361n157
Gober, Napoleon, 131–2
Gossage, Peter, 175
Goyette, Pierre, 207
Grand Hotel, 55
Grand Trunk Railway, 143, 229–30
Grange, Mary Sophia, 3–8, *4*
Greenshields, Robert, 105, 246, 280
Greenwood, F. Murray, 44
Grellet-Dumazeau, Théodore, 121
grief, 26–7, 220–1, 245–6, 251–2; and
  damages, 48–9, 225–39; and propriety, 162, 171, 243; social codes
  of, 241
Grothé, Colbert O., 163–6, *165*
group libel, 117–18
Guelph and Goderich Railway, 132–3,
  134–5
Guibord affair, 244, 300
Guyot, Joseph-Nicholas, 108, 121

Hall, Robert, 235
hatred, 37, 113, 141
Heaman, Elsbeth, 301
Hébert, François-Xavier, 186–98, *188*
Hextes, Agnes, 178
Hilliard, Francis, 121
Hohfeld, Wesley, 329n71
honour, 8–12, 24–5, 28, 52, 53–4, 62–71; and alienation of affection, 201–5, 207–9; as *bien*, 42–4, 53, 64, 295; changing meanings of, 12; and community, 89–98; and damages, 49; and discrimination, 263; and family, 99–130, 136–7, 166, 212; and gender, 12; and *injure*, 31–7; judges and, 66, 68, 148, 283; in legal formulas, 18–20, 58; and rights, 46–7, 298–305; social views of, 67–9, 87–9; and status, 63–4, 238
Hopmeyer, Harry, 82–3
horror, 53, 145, 162
Hôtel-Dieu Hospital, 169–71
How, W. Glen, 289–90, 293, 303–4
Hrecza, Katrina, 85–6
Huberman, Louis, 175–84
Hull, Quebec, 116
humiliation, 8, 16, 25, 62–4, 305; and alienation of affection, 202–4; and audiences, 58–62, 87; and autopsy, 170; and breach of promise, 193; and charivari, 90–7; and culture, 83–8; and damages, 161, 168; and discrimination, 259–60, 263–84, 304–5; and family, 104–5, 114–16; and *injure*, 31, 47; judges and, 67–8; and masculinity, 79; and physical affronts, 144, 147–50; and social norms, 49, 52
Huot, Fortunat, 124
Huot, Prudent (father), 121–5
Huot, Prudent (son), 121–5, 126

illegitimacy, 101–2, 104–5, 129
immigrants, 54, 79; Blacks, 274; Jews, 82–3, 174–85; Poles, 24, 80–8, 340n106; Romanians, 82–3
Imperial Theatre, 271, 273, 274
imprisonment. *See contrainte par corps*
indignation, 27, 78, 102; and discrimination, 259–60, 274, 277, 283–4
indignity, 8, 155, 164, 169
ingratitude, 159, 173; of gift recipient, 26, 35, 186, 210–19
injure, 23, 31–40, 49, 52, 108; and autopsy, 167–8; and charivari, 89–90, 94; and damages, 44–5; and defamation, 106; emotions and, 68–9; and family honour, 115, 128; and reputation, 53; and revocation of bequests and gifts, 120, 212; and rights, 47, 295–301; sources of Quebec law of, 64–5
innate rights. *See* rights
insult, 8, 24, 74–7; and alienation of affection, 207–9; of ancestors, 121, 124; and audiences, 78, 304; and breach of promise, 193–4, 196; and charivari, 89, 92; and class, 69–70; and culture, 84–5; and discrimination, 259–60, 263, 272–9; of family, 101, 104–5, 108–10, 116–18; and *injure*, 23, 35–7; physical affronts, 58–61, 144, 291–3; and revocation of gifts, 212, 214, 217; and separation from bed and board, 173, 175–82
insurance, 25, 187, 210, 214, 221, 227; companies, and autopsies, 162–8; companies, and medical exams, 155–7
interdiction, 38, 99, 126, 129–30
intrusion, 25–6, 144–62, 171; and rights, 10, 305
irritation, 75, 170, 259

Jacobson, Joseph, 174–86, 210, 381n48
Jean, Joseph, 290
Jeannotte, Herménégilde, 222–5, 223, 235–6
Jehovah's Witnesses, 27, 284–93, 303–4
Jetté, Louis-Amable, 225, 234–5, 238
Jinchereau, Belzémire, 247–57, 406n117
Jinchereau, Henriette, 253
Jodoin, Elodie, 242
Johnson, Fred W., 261–71, 262, 284
Joliette, Quebec, 27, 176, 178–81, 183, 185, 284–92
Judicial Committee of the Privy Council, 138, 239, 292, 365n191, 400n42, 425n148; and race, 269, 281; and *solatium doloris*, 232–3
jury, 6–7, 164, 280, 317n13, 374n94; choice of parties for, 35, 140, 297; of matrons, 152; and *solatium doloris*, 228–34, 400n43

Kamouraska, Quebec, 213
Kasirer, Nicholas, 42
Kellock, Roy, 304–5
Kerr, W.H., 315n3
King, Emile, 282
Kingston, Ontario, 130–2, 136, 139, 141–2
Knights of Columbus, 289–90

Lachaine, Albert, 275
Lachine, Quebec, 80
Lacoste, Ferdinand, 113, 126
Lacroix, J.O., 82
Laflamme, N.K., 113
Lafleur, Eugène, 133
Lafontaine, Louis-Hippolyte, 230
Lafontaine, Pierre-Eugène, 301
Lafontaine, Victor, 110

Lafrance, Henriette, 224
Lake, Israel, 181, 183
Lake St Joseph, Quebec, 71–2, 73
Lamarche, Jean-Baptiste Adolphe, 237–8
Lamer, Antonio, 147
Lamothe, Gustave, 280, 403n77
Lamoureux, Charles-Édouard, 56, 58–61
Langelier, François, 29, 45, 67–8; and *injure*, 37–40, 326n44; and rights, 302
language difference, 286; conflict over, 59–60, 72, 74, 79; in the courtroom, 82–3, 180, 380n38
Lapierre, Valmore, 289
Laporte, George, 189, 196
Laprairie, Quebec, 190, 198
L'Assomption, Quebec, 66, 115
Lauezzari, Theodore, 56, 58–61
Laurent, François, 53, 116
Laurier Palace cinema fire, 238–9
Lebeau, Auguste, 198–210
Leblanc, Jules, 207
Leblanc, Justine, 199–210
Leclerc, Théophile, 109–10
Leet, Seth, 113–14
Lefebvre de Bellefeuille, Édouard, 44
Léger, Paul-Émile, 291
Leguerrier, Emilien, 81–7
Lemieux, François-Xavier, 129, 130, 160, 257
Levi, Reuben, 51
Lévis, Quebec, 247, 250, 253, 257
L'Heureux, Rosa, 242
libel. *See* defamation
liberalism, 52, 64, 100, 118, 301; Catholic resistance to, 44, 102; and law, 8, 10, 25, 119, 212; and pre-liberal values, 10, 41, 99, 104–5, 107

liberty, 80, 170, 182, 215; as *bien*, 41; and consent, 156; as freedom, 268–70, 276, 291–2; freedom of commerce, 260, 282; and liberalism, 52; and marriage, 128, 192–3, 197–8; as right, 9–10, 47, 297–305
Liepmann, Moritz, 68
Locke, Charles, 305
Loew's Theatre, 275–81
Longueuil, Quebec, 114
Loranger, Thomas-Jean-Jacques, 127–8, 192
Lord Campbell's Act, 228–9, 231–3
love, 3, 26, 243; and alienation of affection, 139–41, 200, 204–5, 208; and breach of promise, 194–7; judges and, 192; between parents and children, 213, 225, 236, 238; and separation from bed and board, 198; between spouses, 173, 175–6, 206–7, 210, 250, 252. *See also* affection
Lundell, Olive, 286–93, *287*

Mackay, Robert, 241
Maclennan, Farquhar, 155, 182
Marietta, Georgia, 131
marriage, breach of promise of. *See* breach of promise to marry
marriage, parental opposition to, 34, 126–43
marriage contract, 175, 182–5, 188, 196–7, 210, 248; negotiations, 186–9
Martin, Dean, 145
Martin, John Edward, 280–1
Martineau, Catherine, 91–2
Martineau, Frédéric, 94
Martineau, Jean-Baptiste, 93, 345n161
Martineau, Paul-Gédéon, 114–15, 138, 184, 218

Martineau, Sinaï, 92
masculinity, 24, 54, 86–7; and breach of promise, 192–3; and emotion, 17; and honour, 60, 71, 79, 208–9. *See also* gender
Masse, Fortunat, 286, 288, 290–1
Mathieu, Michel, 96, 124–5, 197–8, 231, 296; on *injure*, 31, 36; on rights, 295–301
Mathurin, Édouard, 113
McAllen, Lorne, 60
McCann, Jessie, 132–3
McCord, Thomas, 52
McCorkill, Charles Joseph, 78
McDougall, Errol, 170–1
McGill University, 51, 82, 104, 222
McMahan, Darrin, 24
medical procedures, 25–6, 144–5, 146, 148–9, 151–61, 372n73
memory, 25, 236; as *bien*, 44; of relatives and ancestors, 99, 101–9, 115, 119–25, 164–6, 170, 241, 254, 257; and revocation of bequests, 35, 211, 355n89
Mercier, Octave, 247–54
Mercier, Wilfrid, 242, 303
Meunier, Nazaire, 124
Midway Cinema, 182
Mignault, Pierre-Basile, 127–8, 302, 428n30
Miller, William Ian, 12, 20
minstrels, 261, 264, 269
Mondelet, Charles, 229
Montreal, 23, 93, 288–9; Abattoirs de l'est, 198–9, 209; anti-vaccination resistance in, 151; Bonsecours Market, 93; cases set in, 3, 47, 54–62, 100–7, 111–15, 116, 128–9, 130–43, 145–50, 152, 158–9, 163–71, 174–85, 198–210, 221–6, 231, 232–3,

234–9, 245–6, 260–82; docks, 190; Jewish neighbourhood, 174–85; Outremont, 185; Red Light, 145; Westmount, 246
Montreal General Hospital, 166–7, 245
Montreal Medico-Chirurgical Society, 159
Moquin, Alexi, 196
morality, 64, 85, 116, 217–18, 272, 301; and culture, 184–5; and damages, 238–9; judges' views of, 64, 67, 204; and law, 9, 44, 255–6, 301
Morin, Joseph, 104
Morin, Rebecca Chiniquy, 101–7, *103*, 110–11, 117, 119, 126
mortification, 20, 24–5, 31, 49, 53, 63, 68, 74–9, 114–15, 148
Mount Royal Cemetery, 169
mourning clothes, 27, 221, 240–3, 248
Myers, Tamara, 152

Nadeau, André, 421n113
Nerson, Roger, 299
Noiseux, Clovis, 121–5
Nootens, Thierry, 126, 129
Notman, William, 3

Odgers, W. Blake, 108, 121
outrage, 8, 26, 49, 53, 116, 218, 239; and autopsy, 162, 166, 168, 170–1; and bodily intrusion, 145, 149, 292; and discrimination, 259; and *injure*, 31, 35–6; and memory of the dead, 108, 122; of spouses, 182, 208

Pagnuelo, Siméon, 37, 62, 301
Paquette, Eliza, 94
Parc Sohmer, 54
Parnell, Madge, 158–9

Parsons, Winnifred, 286–93, *287*
paternal authority, 99, 127–8, 130, 136–7, 299, 302
patrimony, 29, 39, 40–1, 44–5, 52, 237; honour as, 45, 99, 117, 125, 301
Peiss, Kathy, 55
Pelland, Léo, 44, 329n66
Pelletier, Louis-Philippe, 280
performance, and body language, 75; emotions as, 15–17; and honour, 61, 87, 126; and respectability, 54–5, 59, 77
Perreau, Édouard, 299, 301
personality rights. *See* rights
personhood, 9–10, 29, 39, 44; and patrimony, 41–2; and rights, 27–8, 299–300
Pesant dit Sans-Cartier, Joseph, 92–3, 96, 345n161
Phillips, Charlotte, 166
Piché, Alphonse, 221
Pilotte, Édouard, 195
Plouffe, Joseph, 199–200, 205–6, 208–9
Pollock, Frederick, 228
Popliger, Isidore, 82, 85, 87, 341n118
Pothier, Robert, 355n89
privacy, 10, 28, 46, 303–4; private life, 65, 105, 110, 125, 201
property, 297–302; and *biens*, 10, 23, 42; corpses as, 166–8; and discrimination, 47, 260, 271; emotions as, 45; honour as, 64, 108, 124–5; and patrimony, 38–9; wife as husband's, 202–3
propriety, 8–9, 24, 28, 53–4, 63; and alienation of affection, 201; and audiences, 195; and autopsy, 163, 171; and burial, 246, 251–6; and charivari, 89; and defamation, 67–8; and

family, 110, 116; and gender, 71–9, 119; judges and, 174, 278, 283; and medical exams, 152; and privacy, 304; and social norms, 61, 79, 122, 189, 212, 239–44
puissance paternelle. *See* paternal authority

quarantine, 369n33
Quebec & Lake St John Railway, 71–2, 74–9
Quebec City, 23, 71–9, 117–18, 247–57
Queen's Hotel, 260
Queen's University, 131–2

race and racism, 8, 27, 32, 54, 259–84
Ramaeckers, Auguste, 169
Rand, Ivan, 293
Ravary, Elizabeth, 229–30
Raymond, Adélard, 118
Raymond, Alcide, 118
Raymond, Aurélie, 199–200, 206
Raymond, Charles-Édouard, 118
Raymond, Rose, 199, 205–7, 209
Recreation Key Club, 264–6
Reddy, William M., 11, 13–16, 20, 36, 99
Reed, James, 51
religion, 34, 82–3, 220, 256–7, 285–6; canon law, 102, 142, 244, 250–1, 253; Jewish law, 174, 184; marriage, theology, 127, 191; Roman Catholic influence on law, 44, 169
reputation, 63, 68–70, 107–11; and alienation of affection, 205, 207; of ancestors, 120–5; and audiences, 79, 82–6, 90, 94–8; as *bien*, 44, 53, 101, 295, 303; and discrimination, 263, 275; of family, 25, 99, 102–5, 115–16, 126–30; and gender, 143,

147–50, 196–7; and *injure*, 36, 39, 53–4; in legal formulas, 18; and rights, 297–9
respectability, 63, 206, 218; as performance, 55, 79; and reputation, 124, 126; as self-image, 24–5, 47, 58–9, 66, 77–9, 149, 277, 282; as standard of behaviour, 61, 214; and virtue, 70–1
revulsion, 37, 162, 218
Reynolds, Solomon "Sol," 275–81, 283–4
Richelieu, Quebec, 97
rights, 27–8, 45–8, 260–84, 293, 295–306, 330n75; to bury the dead, 244–6, 251, 254–7; citizenship rights, 10, 52, 267, 269, 274, 283, 300, 303–5, 412n4; civil rights, 137, 182, 260, 274, 302, 303; to corpses, 166–72; extrapatrimonial rights, 28, 39, 42, 299–301, 305; innate rights, 47, 302; to mourning clothes, 240–3; no right, 24, 45–8, 293; personality rights, 9–10, 28, 31, 42, 295, 299–302; property rights, 260, 271; subjective rights, 9–10, 27–8, 31, 47, 295, 299–300
Rinkuk, Petro, 81–8
Risk, Richard, 47
Ritchie, William Johnstone, 51, 232
Robinson, Agnes, 232–4
Roguin, Ernest, 298–9
Roman law, 23, 30–2, 38, 40, 191, 241
Roncarelli, Frank, 284–5, 288, 292, 303, 425n148
Rosenwein, Barbara H., 14–16
Rothstein, Philip, 178–9
Roubier, Paul, 299
Rouleau, Roch, 290
Rousseau, Jean-Jacques, 68–9

Routhier, Adolphe-Basile, 203, 208
Rouville, Quebec, 121
Roy, Alfred, 248
Roy, Alphonse, 247–57, 406n117
Roy, Amaryllis, 247
Roy, Damase, 120–1
Roy, Joseph, 300
Roy, Pierre, 120
Roy, Pierre Antoine, 120
Royal Military College, 130–2, 139, 142
Royal Victoria Hospital, 168

sadness, 259
Sandwell, R.W., 10
Sault-au-Récollet, Quebec, 199, 209, 215, 217, 333n13
Savigny, Friedrich Carl von, 299
Scheer, Monique, 15–16
scorn, 104, 136, 173, 213
Scott, Frank, 303
seduction, 32, 127, 191, 200–2, 229; judges' scepticism of, 70
Seed, Patricia, 126–7
Sénécal, L.R., 275
Sénécal, Octave, 124
separation from bed and board, 70, 173, 175–85, 198, 200, 204, 209; double standard and, 202; and honour, 36; and *injure*, 35
Sériaux, Alain, 40
Sers dit St Jean, Alexis, 196–7
shame, 8, 16, 24–5, 37, 53, 63–4; and breach of promise, 196–7, 201; and culture, 79, 84–6, 88; and discrimination, 263; and family honour, 120, 128–30; and *injure*, 31–2, 52; and medical procedures, 149; and reputation, 113–15
Shemerin Labeker synagogue, 174, 377n2

Sherbrooke, Quebec, 129
Sicard, Louis, 91, 95
Simmonds, Alecia, 48
Simpson, A.W.B., 20
Slade, Edward, 72, 73
slander. *See* defamation
Smail, Daniel Lord, 11
Smith, James, 44, 229
social codes and norms, 7–17, 20–1, 24–6, 54, 61–4, 294; and burial, 244–6, 254–6; and class, 69–71, 76; and culture, 86–9; and family honour, 107–9; and grief, 220, 240–3; and *injure*, 32–5; interplay with legal rules, 67, 162, 166 192; judges' understandings of, 7–9, 69, 78, 125, 144, 171, 174, 221, 233–4; and liberalism, 8, 10, 52; and race, 271, 282–3; and testimony, 49
social standing. *See* class
Soette, Pierre, 199–200, 207
solatium doloris, 26, 168, 226–39, 246, 375n107, 400n43, 403n77
Sorel, Quebec, 50
Sourdat, Auguste, 108, 116, 121, 201, 237, 298
Sparrow, John, 261
Springle, John Anderson, 158–9
Stackhouse, Russell Thomas, 241–2
Standard Club, 275
Starkie, Thomas, 108, 125
status, 95, 105, 140, 253; and honour, 53, 127; and *injure*, 32, 35; and judges, 78, 109, 174; and law of persons, 29; and liberalism, 107; as self-evident, 260, 271. *See also* class
St Césaire, Quebec, 121–5
St-Charles cemetery, 247–8, 406n110
St-Cyr, Lili, 145
Stearns, Peter, 246

Ste Foy, Quebec, 247
Steile, Léonie, 214–19, *216*, 396n243
Stein, Albert Louis, 290, 293, 303
St Eustache, Quebec, 91, 94
Stevenson, Mary, 70
St-Jean-sur-Richelieu, Quebec, 69
St-Joseph-de-Lévis cemetery, 247–8, 253
St Laurent, Quebec, 95
St Lawrence Hall, 47
St Léonard de Port Maurice, Quebec, 90–8, 343n141
Stober, Annie, 178
St Philippe, Quebec, 186–91, 193–8
strategy, 17–18, 21, 133, 152, 246, 263, 276, 278–9, 290, 419n83; appealing to emotion, 164, 168; appealing to judges' assumptions, 58, 142–3, 270, 280; about damages, 48, 123; in face of legal uncertainty, 226, 235–6; hardball tactics, 139–40, 164; pushing legal boundaries, 104; strategic errors, 177, 184
subjective rights. *See* rights
Supreme Court of Canada, 51; appeals to, 106, 184, 291–2, 382n60; and civil liberties, 293–4, 303–5; and Quebec civil law, 38–9, 398n21; and race, 269, 271, 282; and *solatium doloris*, 226, 232–9
Supreme Court of the United States, 155

Taillefer, Napoléon, 207
Taschereau, Elzéar-Alexandre, 67, 231
Taschereau, Henri-Elzéar, 192–3, 232, 235
Taschereau, Henri-Thomas, 67, 137
Taschereau, Robert, 304–5
Tellier, Joseph-Mathias, 218

Tellier, Louis, 193
temperance, 80–1, 100, 339n103, 340n112
Terrebonne, Quebec, 245
testimony, 20–1, 49, 205; bar on spousal testimony, 18, 379n16; bar on testifying on one's own behalf, 6
Théâtre Français, 263
Thompson, E.P., 93
Toullier, Charles, 327–8n51
Tourigny, François-Siméon, 117
Travis, Jennifer, 16–17
Trenholme, Norman, 106, 137
Trois-Rivières, Quebec, 6, 116
Tudor, Euphemia, 71–9, *73*, 283
Turcot, Louis, 91–5
Turgeon, Joseph, 120

Universal Negro Improvement Association, 274, 281
Université Laval, 38–9, 297, 326–7n44

vaccination, 151, 369n33
Varney, Edwin, 261, 263
venereal disease, 25, 46, 145–8, 150–1
Vervais, Léon, 95
Victoria, British Columbia, 143
Ville St-Pierre, Quebec, 80–8
Vipond, Robert, 47
virtue, 53, 63, 90, 143, 243, 292, 295; attacks on, 32, 70, 149, 167; social codes of, 8–9, 70, 152

Walker, Barrington, 269
Walker, Minnie, 183–4, 381n48
Waterous, Emma Johnson, 130–3, 136–43, 360n148, 366n215
Weingart, Annie, 174–86, 377n2, 382n67

Weir, Robert Stanley, 280
Weir, William Alexander, 84–7
widows, 100–1, 110, 115, 130, 143; and autopsies, 168–71; conflicts with husband's family, 27, 164, 221, 239–43, 247–56; economic situation of, 187, 189, 249–52; as plaintiffs, 226, 228–33
wills and testaments, 245–6; and cremation, 167, 169; revocation of bequests, 35, 120, 211

Wilson, George, 265–6
Wilson, Thomas, 229–30
Wiseman, Roderick, 277
Worcester, Massachusetts, 100, 247
Wurtele, Jonathan, 67, 116

York Tavern, 282
Young, Brian, 34

Zachariä, Karl Salomo, 29, 40
Zelizer, Viviana, 238

PUBLICATIONS OF THE OSGOODE SOCIETY FOR CANADIAN LEGAL HISTORY

2019 Harry W. Arthurs, *Connecting the Dots: The Life of an Academic Lawyer*
      Eric H. Reiter, *Wounded Feelings: Litigating Emotions in Quebec, 1870–1950*
2018 Philip Girard, Jim Phillips, and R. Blake Brown, *A History of Law in Canada, Volume One: Beginnings to 1866*
      Suzanne Chiodo, *The Class Actions Controversy: The Origins and Development of the Ontario Class Proceedings Act*
2017 Constance Backhouse, *Claire L'Heureux-Dubé: A Life*
      Dennis G. Molinaro, *An Exceptional Law: Section 98 and the Emergency State, 1919–1936*
2016 Lori Chambers, *A Legal History of Adoption in Ontario, 1921–2015*
      Bradley Miller, *Borderline Crime: Fugitive Criminals and the Challenge of the Border, 1819–1914*
      James Muir, *Law, Debt, and Merchant Power: The Civil Courts of Eighteenth-Century Halifax*
2015 Barry Wright, Eric Tucker, and Susan Binnie, eds., *Canadian State Trials, Volume IV: Security, Dissent, and the Limits of Toleration in War and Peace, 1914–1939*
      David Fraser, *"Honorary Protestants": The Jewish School Question in Montreal, 1867–1997*
      C. Ian Kyer, *A Thirty Years War: The Failed Public/Private Partnership that Spurred the Creation of the Toronto Transit Commission, 1891–1921*
      Dale Gibson, *Law, Life, and Government at Red River: Settlement and Governance, 1812–1872*
2014 Christopher Moore, *The Court of Appeal for Ontario: Defining the Right of Appeal, 1792–2013*
      Paul Craven, *Petty Justice: Low Law and the Sessions System in Charlotte County, New Brunswick, 1785–1867*
      Thomas GW Telfer, *Ruin and Redemption: The Struggle for a Canadian Bankruptcy Law, 1867–1919*
      Dominique Clément, *Equality Deferred: Sex Discrimination and British Columbia's Human Rights State, 1953–1984*
2013 Roy McMurtry, *Memoirs and Reflections*
      Charlotte Gray, *The Massey Murder: A Maid, Her Master, and the Trial that Shocked a Nation*
      C. Ian Kyer, *Lawyers, Families, and Businesses: The Shaping of a Bay Street Law Firm, Faskens 1863–1963*
      G. Blaine Baker and Donald Fyson, eds., *Essays in the History of Canadian Law, Volume XI: Quebec and the Canadas*

2012 R. Blake Brown, *Arming and Disarming: A History of Gun Control in Canada*
Eric Tucker, James Muir, and Bruce Ziff, eds., *Property on Trial: Canadian Cases in Context*
Shelley Gavigan, *Hunger, Horses, and Government Men: Criminal Law on the Aboriginal Plains, 1870–1905*
Barrington Walker, ed., *The African Canadian Legal Odyssey: Historical Essays*

2011 Robert J. Sharpe, *The Lazier Murder: Prince Edward County, 1884*
Philip Girard, *Lawyers and Legal Culture in British North America: Beamish Murdoch of Halifax*
John McLaren, *Dewigged, Bothered, and Bewildered: British Colonial Judges on Trial, 1800–1900*
Lesley Erickson, *Westward Bound: Sex, Violence, the Law, and the Making of a Settler Society*

2010 Judy Fudge and Eric Tucker, eds., *Work on Trial: Canadian Labour Law Struggles*
Christopher Moore, *The British Columbia Court of Appeal: The First Hundred Years*
Frederick Vaughan, *Viscount Haldane: 'The Wicked Step-father of the Canadian Constitution'*
Barrington Walker, *Race on Trial: Black Defendants in Ontario's Criminal Courts, 1858–1958*

2009 William Kaplan, *Canadian Maverick: The Life and Times of Ivan C. Rand*
R. Blake Brown, *A Trying Question: The Jury in Nineteenth-Century Canada*
Barry Wright and Susan Binnie, eds., *Canadian State Trials, Volume III: Political Trials and Security Measures, 1840–1914*
Robert J. Sharpe, *The Last Day, the Last Hour: The Currie Libel Trial* (paperback edition with a new preface)

2008 Constance Backhouse, *Carnal Crimes: Sexual Assault Law in Canada, 1900–1975*
Jim Phillips, R. Roy McMurtry, and John T. Saywell, eds., *Essays in the History of Canadian Law, Volume X: A Tribute to Peter N. Oliver*
Greg Taylor, *The Law of the Land: The Advent of the Torrens System in Canada*
Hamar Foster, Benjamin Berger, and A.R. Buck, eds., *The Grand Experiment: Law and Legal Culture in British Settler Societies*

2007 Robert Sharpe and Patricia McMahon, *The Persons Case: The Origins and Legacy of the Fight for Legal Personhood*
Lori Chambers, *Misconceptions: Unmarried Motherhood and the Ontario Children of Unmarried Parents Act, 1921–1969*

	Jonathan Swainger, ed., *A History of the Supreme Court of Alberta*
	Martin Friedland, *My Life in Crime and Other Academic Adventures*
2006	Donald Fyson, *Magistrates, Police, and People: Everyday Criminal Justice in Quebec and Lower Canada, 1764–1837*
	Dale Brawn, *The Court of Queen's Bench of Manitoba, 1870–1950: A Biographical History*
	R.C.B. Risk, *A History of Canadian Legal Thought: Collected Essays*, edited and introduced by G. Blaine Baker and Jim Phillips
2005	Philip Girard, *Bora Laskin: Bringing Law to Life*
	Christopher English, ed., *Essays in the History of Canadian Law: Volume IX – Two Islands: Newfoundland and Prince Edward Island*
	Fred Kaufman, *Searching for Justice: An Autobiography*
2004	Philip Girard, Jim Phillips, and Barry Cahill, eds., *The Supreme Court of Nova Scotia, 1754–2004: From Imperial Bastion to Provincial Oracle*
	Frederick Vaughan, *Aggressive in Pursuit: The Life of Justice Emmett Hall*
	John D. Honsberger, *Osgoode Hall: An Illustrated History*
	Constance Backhouse and Nancy Backhouse, *The Heiress versus the Establishment: Mrs Campbell's Campaign for Legal Justice*
2003	Robert Sharpe and Kent Roach, *Brian Dickson: A Judge's Journey*
	Jerry Bannister, *The Rule of the Admirals: Law, Custom, and Naval Government in Newfoundland, 1699–1832*
	George Finlayson, *John J. Robinette, Peerless Mentor: An Appreciation*
	Peter Oliver, *The Conventional Man: The Diaries of Ontario Chief Justice Robert A. Harrison, 1856–1878*
2002	John T. Saywell, *The Lawmakers: Judicial Power and the Shaping of Canadian Federalism*
	Patrick Brode, *Courted and Abandoned: Seduction in Canadian Law*
	David Murray, *Colonial Justice: Justice, Morality, and Crime in the Niagara District, 1791–1849*
	F. Murray Greenwood and Barry Wright, eds., *Canadian State Trials, Volume II: Rebellion and Invasion in the Canadas, 1837–1839*
2001	Ellen Anderson, *Judging Bertha Wilson: Law as Large as Life*
	Judy Fudge and Eric Tucker, *Labour before the Law: The Regulation of Workers' Collective Action in Canada, 1900–1948*
	Laurel Sefton MacDowell, *Renegade Lawyer: The Life of J.L. Cohen*
2000	Barry Cahill, *'The Thousandth Man': A Biography of James McGregor Stewart*
	A.B. McKillop, *The Spinster and the Prophet: Florence Deeks, H.G. Wells, and the Mystery of the Purloined Past*

	Beverley Boissery and F. Murray Greenwood, *Uncertain Justice: Canadian Women and Capital Punishment*
	Bruce Ziff, *Unforeseen Legacies: Reuben Wells Leonard and the Leonard Foundation Trust*
1999	Constance Backhouse, *Colour-Coded: A Legal History of Racism in Canada, 1900–1950*
	G. Blaine Baker and Jim Phillips, eds., *Essays in the History of Canadian Law: Volume VIII – In Honour of R.C.B. Risk*
	Richard W. Pound, *Chief Justice W.R. Jackett: By the Law of the Land*
	David Vanek, *Fulfilment: Memoirs of a Criminal Court Judge*
1998	Sidney Harring, *White Man's Law: Native People in Nineteenth-Century Canadian Jurisprudence*
	Peter Oliver, *'Terror to Evil-Doers': Prisons and Punishments in Nineteenth-Century Ontario*
1997	James W.St.G. Walker, *'Race,' Rights and the Law in the Supreme Court of Canada: Historical Case Studies*
	Lori Chambers, *Married Women and Property Law in Victorian Ontario*
	Patrick Brode, *Casual Slaughters and Accidental Judgments: Canadian War Crimes and Prosecutions, 1944–1948*
	Ian Bushnell, *The Federal Court of Canada: A History, 1875–1992*
1996	Carol Wilton, ed., *Essays in the History of Canadian Law: Volume VII – Inside the Law: Canadian Law Firms in Historical Perspective*
	William Kaplan, *Bad Judgment: The Case of Mr Justice Leo A. Landreville*
	Murray Greenwood and Barry Wright, eds., *Canadian State Trials: Volume I – Law, Politics, and Security Measures, 1608–1837*
1995	David Williams, *Just Lawyers: Seven Portraits*
	Hamar Foster and John McLaren, eds., *Essays in the History of Canadian Law: Volume VI – British Columbia and the Yukon*
	W.H. Morrow, ed., *Northern Justice: The Memoirs of Mr Justice William G. Morrow*
	Beverley Boissery, *A Deep Sense of Wrong: The Treason, Trials, and Transportation to New South Wales of Lower Canadian Rebels after the 1838 Rebellion*
1994	Patrick Boyer, *A Passion for Justice: The Legacy of James Chalmers McRuer*
	Charles Pullen, *The Life and Times of Arthur Maloney: The Last of the Tribunes*
	Jim Phillips, Tina Loo, and Susan Lewthwaite, eds., *Essays in the History of Canadian Law: Volume V – Crime and Criminal Justice*
	Brian Young, *The Politics of Codification: The Lower Canadian Civil Code of 1866*

1993 Greg Marquis, *Policing Canada's Century: A History of the Canadian Association of Chiefs of Police*
Murray Greenwood, *Legacies of Fear: Law and Politics in Quebec in the Era of the French Revolution*
1992 Brendan O'Brien, *Speedy Justice: The Tragic Last Voyage of His Majesty's Vessel Speedy*
Robert Fraser, ed., *Provincial Justice: Upper Canadian Legal Portraits from the Dictionary of Canadian Biography*
1991 Constance Backhouse, *Petticoats and Prejudice: Women and Law in Nineteenth-Century Canada*
1990 Philip Girard and Jim Phillips, eds., *Essays in the History of Canadian Law: Volume III – Nova Scotia*
Carol Wilton, ed., *Essays in the History of Canadian Law: Volume IV – Beyond the Law: Lawyers and Business in Canada, 1830–1930*
1989 Desmond Brown, *The Genesis of the Canadian Criminal Code of 1892*
Patrick Brode, *The Odyssey of John Anderson*
1988 Robert Sharpe, *The Last Day, the Last Hour: The Currie Libel Trial*
John D. Arnup, *Middleton: The Beloved Judge*
1987 C. Ian Kyer and Jerome Bickenbach, *The Fiercest Debate: Cecil A. Wright, the Benchers, and Legal Education in Ontario, 1923–1957*
1986 Paul Romney, *Mr Attorney: The Attorney General for Ontario in Court, Cabinet, and Legislature, 1791–1899*
Martin Friedland, *The Case of Valentine Shortis: A True Story of Crime and Politics in Canada*
1985 James Snell and Frederick Vaughan, *The Supreme Court of Canada: History of the Institution*
1984 Patrick Brode, *Sir John Beverley Robinson: Bone and Sinew of the Compact*
David Williams, *Duff: A Life in the Law*
1983 David H. Flaherty, ed., *Essays in the History of Canadian Law: Volume II*
1982 Marion MacRae and Anthony Adamson, *Cornerstones of Order: Courthouses and Town Halls of Ontario, 1784–1914*
1981 David H. Flaherty, ed., *Essays in the History of Canadian Law: Volume I*

Lightning Source UK Ltd.
Milton Keynes UK
UKHW040431071119
353068UK00001B/295/P